The Mental Health Industry: A Cultural Phenomenon *by Peter A. Magaro,* ? '
David McDowell, and Ivan W. Miller III

Nonverbal Communication: The State of the Art *by Robert G. Harper, A*
Joseph D. Matarazzo

Alcoholism and Treatment *by David J. Armor, J. Michael Polich, and Har*

A Biodevelopmental Approach to Clinical Child Psychology: Cognitive
Control Theory *by Sebastiano Santostefano*

Handbook of Infant Development *edited by Joy D. Osofsky*

Understanding the Rape Victim: A Synthesis of Research Findings *by Sedelle Katz and*
Mary Ann Mazur

Childhood Pathology and Later Adjustment: The Question of Prediction *by Loretta K. Cass and*
Carolyn B. Thomas

Intelligent Testing with the WISC-R *by Alan S. Kaufman*

Adaptation in Schizophrenia: The Theory of Segmental Set *by David Shakow*

Psychotherapy: An Eclectic Approach *by Sol L. Garfield*

Handbook of Minimal Brain Dysfunctions *edited by Herbert E. Rie and Ellen D. Rie*

Handbook of Behavioral Interventions: A Clinical Guide *edited by Alan Goldstein and Edna B. Foa*

Art Psychotherapy *by Harriet Wadeson*

Handbook of Adolescent Psychology *edited by Joseph Adelson*

Psychotherapy Supervision: Theory, Research and Practice *edited by Allen K. Hess*

Psychology and Psychiatry in Courts and Corrections: Controversy and Change *by*
Ellsworth A. Fersch, Jr.

Restricted Environmental Stimulation: Research and Clinical Applications *by Peter Suedfeld*

Personal Construct Psychology: Psychotherapy and Personality *edited by Alvin W. Landfield and*
Larry M. Leitner

Mothers, Grandmothers, and Daughters: Personality and Child Care in Three-Generation Families
by Bertram J. Cohler and Henry U. Grunebaum

Further Explorations in Personality *edited by A.I. Rabin, Joel Aronoff, Andrew M. Barclay, and*
Robert A. Zucker

Hypnosis and Relaxation: Modern Verification of an Old Equation *by*
William E. Edmonston, Jr.

Handbook of Clinical Behavior Therapy *edited by Samuel M. Turner, Karen S. Calhoun, and*
Henry E. Adams

Handbook of Clinical Neuropsychology *edited by Susan B. Filskov and Thomas J. Boll*

The Course of Alcoholism: Four Years After Treatment *by J. Michael Polich, David J. Armor, and*
Harriet B. Braiker

Handbook of Innovative Psychotherapies *edited by Raymond J. Corsini*

The Role of the Father in Child Development (Second Edition) *edited by Michael E. Lamb*

Behavioral Medicine: Clinical Applications *by Susan S. Pinkerton, Howard Hughes, and*
W.W. Wenrich

Handbook for the Practice of Pediatric Psychology *edited by June M. Tuma*

Change Through Interaction: Social Psychological Processes of Counseling and Psychotherapy *by*
Stanley R. Strong and Charles D. Claiborn

Drugs and Behavior (Second Edition) *by Fred Leavitt*

Handbook of Research Methods in Clinical Psychology *edited by Philip C. Kendall and*
James N. Butcher

A Social Psychology of Developing Adults *by Thomas O. Blank*

Women in the Middle Years: Current Knowledge and Directions for Research and Policy *edited by*
Janet Zollinger Giele

Loneliness: A Sourcebook of Current Theory, Research and Therapy *edited by Letitia Anne Peplau*
and Daniel Perlman

(continued on back)

FROM RITUAL TO REPERTOIRE

From Ritual to Repertoire

A Cognitive-Developmental Systems Approach
with Behavior-Disordered Children

ARNOLD MILLER
EILEEN ELLER-MILLER
Language and Cognitive Development Center

WILEY

A WILEY-INTERSCIENCE PUBLICATION

JOHN WILEY & SONS

New York • Chichester • Brisbane • Toronto • Singapore

This publication is designed to provide accurate and
authoritative information in regard to the subject
matter covered. It is sold with the understanding that
the publisher is not engaged in rendering legal, accounting,
or other professional service. If legal advice or other
expert assistance is required, the services of a competent
professional person should be sought. *From a Declaration
of Principles jointly adopted by a Committee of the
American Bar Association and a Committee of Publishers.*

Library of Congress Cataloging in Publication Data:

Miller, Arnold, 1927–
    From ritual to repertoire: a cognitive-developmental systems
approach with behavior-disordered children/Arnold Miller and
Eileen Eller-Miller.
        p.   cm.—(Wiley series on personality processes)
    Bibliography: p.
    ISBN 0-471-84897-2
    1. Behavior disorders in children.   2. Constructivism (Education)
I. Eller-Miller, Eileen.   II. Title.   III. Series
RJ506.B44M55   1989
618.92'89—dc20   89-5809
                                                                     CIP

Printed in the United States of America

10 9 8 7 6 5 4 3 2 1

To
Heinz Werner
1890–1964
Teacher and Friend

"In my scholarly work," Heinz Werner once remarked,
"I choose to be like the turtle: with all four feet on the ground
yet willing to stick my neck out."

Foreword

Most clinical workers in a delimited field accept one or another theoretical formulation of development implicitly or explicitly. Within that framework, the job of a good clinician is to diagnose deviations from progress toward the ideal order and to foreground danger signals along the way: modes of response, action, conduct, or communication that are taken to be prodromal to later pathology (itself a normative concept) or to be themselves pathological. Beyond this diagnostic activity—discerning anticipated or actual disorder—the complete clinician, as *interventionist,* proposes and brings into play agencies or instrumentalities that may serve to overcome defects, remedy deficiencies, overcome obstacles to progress, and forestall incipient pathologies.

In this splendid and heartwarming book, Arnold Miller and Eileen Eller-Miller—utilizing a framework they have articulated by borrowing, reshaping, and integrating categories and concepts from such developmental theorists as Werner, Piaget, Vygotsky, and von Bertalanffy, among others—show themselves to be truly complete clinicians. *Bricoleurs,* in the best sense (as described by Levi-Strauss), they have appropriated and exploited whatever they could, both conceptually and materially, in the service of aiding disturbed children's advancement in their intellectual, emotional, and interpersonal lives.

The Millers recognize that what makes an organism act (the matter of motivation)—and action here encompasses the sounds of silence where voice is expected as well as immobility where movement is expected—is not simply dependent on the Agent (Who) but also on the Scene (Where, When), the Instrumentalities or Agencies (How), and the Purpose (Why). Thus, they have experimented with each and all of these components of situations to move disturbed children from maladaptive, rigid patterns of behavior to repertoires of contextually adaptive action and have sought to promote the integration of the divided and segregated worlds in which such children characteristically live. All this has been in service of helping these children resume their development.

To be sure, rigid patterns of action, spheres of reality unconnected or disconnected from each other, and so on, are not limited to disturbed children. They obtain for each of us throughout our lives, preventing us from expanding and integrating our normal adult realities. In this sense, this superb work by Arnold Miller and Eileen Eller-Miller should enable us, with our presumptively advanced capabilities for symbolic activity, to recognize the relevance of what they say not only for the disturbed children they treat, but for all of us.

Heinz Werner would have been proud to have this splendid book dedicated to him.

BERNARD KAPLAN

Series Preface

This series of books is addressed to behavioral scientists interested in the nature of human personality. Its scope should prove pertinent to personality theorists and researchers as well as to clinicians concerned with applying an understanding of personality processes to the amelioration of emotional difficulties in living. To this end, the series provides a scholarly integration of theoretical formulations, empirical data, and practical recommendations.

Six major aspects of studying and learning about human personality can be designated: personality theory, personality structure and dynamics, personality development, personality assessment, personality change, and personality adjustment. In exploring these aspects of personality, the books in the series discuss a number of distinct but related subject areas: the nature and implications of various theories of personality; personality characteristics that account for consistencies and variations in human behavior; the emergence of personality processes in children and adolescents; the use of interviewing and testing procedures to evaluate individual differences in personality; efforts to modify personality styles through psychotherapy, counseling, behavior therapy, and other methods of influence; and patterns of abnormal personality functioning that impair individual competence.

IRVING B. WEINER

Fairleigh Dickinson University
Rutherford, New Jersey

Preface

This book presents an integration of theory and practice that allows those concerned with the development of profoundly disordered children to systematically evaluate and intervene in ways that guide the children toward the most advanced capacities within their reach. Thus, the work is directed toward psychologists, speech and language pathologists, psychiatrists, neurologists, pediatricians, and movement, occupational, and physical therapists. Above all it is intended for special education professionals who are attempting to understand and help these children.

The general orientation of the book is best characterized as a cognitive-developmental (C-D) systems approach. As such, it owes much to the thought of Heinz Werner, Jean Piaget, and Kurt Lewin as well as to the seminal formulation of systems theory by Ludwig von Bertalanffy. Beyond the impetus provided by these thinkers, the work comes from our own efforts to understand and to help disordered children during the past 25 years, both before and after founding the Language and Cognitive Development Center (LCDC) in 1965. This book distills what we have learned in a way that speaks to issues of both theory and practice.

Cognitive-developmental systems theory and the methods that derive from it have been effectively used with autistic, schizophrenic, brain-injured, developmentally delayed, emotionally deprived, and normal preschool children. All children must pass through certain stages in order to achieve mature emotional and cognitive functioning. To the extent that cognitive-developmental systems theory and the methods that derive from it facilitate this journey, they are relevant for all children.

Our intent is to help the disordered child organize behavior in a way that systematically expands his or her reality. This emphasis on organization and reality expansion rather than on control makes "time out" and aversive procedures unnecessary for even an extremely disordered child. An important vehicle for achieving developmental goals is the systematic formation of rituals that, as they become expanded, complicated, and connected, turn into functional behavioral repertoires. We hope that readers of this book will finish it with a sense that their own realities have been expanded so that they may better understand and help behavior-disordered children.

ARNOLD MILLER
EILEEN ELLER-MILLER

Boston, Massachusetts
July 1989

Acknowledgments

We wish to acknowledge the many people who have contributed to this book. Foremost was the influence of Heinz Werner with whom one of us (AM) studied as a graduate student at Clark University; both of us had the privilege of knowing him during the last decade of his life. Also important during the period of graduate study were Bernard Kaplan and the stimulating seminars on symbol formation that he conducted at Clark.

Over the years our children, David, Ethan, and Loren, taught us much as they grew up. They also actively participated in the construction of the Sign and Spoken Language Program. Later, Loren helped edit the Sign and Spoken Language Program (Chapter 10) and the Symbol Accentuation Reading Program (Chapter 11). Wendy Pearson contributed to a manual for the Sign and Spoken Language Program, whereas Seddon Wylde helped organize the Art Program. Northeastern University's civil engineering students, coordinated by Paul Livernois under the guidance of Professors Michael Kupferman and Richard Scranton, masterfully carried out our designs for LCDC's playground (Chapter 9).

Many associates assisted in the formation of the Miller Umwelt Assessment Scale (Chapter 7) and the Support-Demand Scale (Chapter 12). Of these, most important have been Dr. Cheryl Bragg and Dr. Martin Sawzin. Lisa Bloom and Pabuli Basu contributed to the Umwelt Assessment procedures. Florence Mansbach helped with the Support-Demand Scale and in her work with Fred (Chapter 5).

Observations and notes by our exceptional teaching and clinical staff provided the basis for a number of theoretical formulations in this book. Notable among these professionals is Dagmar Kristina Chretien (referred to as "K" in Chapters 8 and 12). Dr. Elizabeth Warner, clinic director, contributed insightful comments (Chapter 8) on a schizophrenic child with whom she had worked. We recognize Lynn Bishop for her courageous and ultimately successful classroom work with Roy (Chapter 4). Also noteworthy was Becky Bradley's work in sustaining Barney within the "classroom family" described in Chapter 4. Other dedicated teachers are DeeDee Angagaw, Rick Bensusan, Lisa Born, Carolyn Chuzi, Kathy Dewalt, Annette Drucklieb, Martha Gallagher, Karen Palmer-Laine, Wendy Pearson, Terry Price, and Carol Ruano.

Important C-D Systems work has also been conducted by several gifted speech and language therapists. These include Barbara Schwinger as well as Brynna Schudrich and Mary Mele for their endeavors with Fred, and Edie Clompus in her efforts with Anna (Chapter 8). We also acknowledge movement therapist Andrea Gordon's fine work with Anna (Chapter 8).

We have drawn heavily on colleagues and friends for feedback on various portions of the book. Those who read all or major portions of the manuscript and who moved us toward greater conceptual clarity include Professor Robert W. Baker of Clark University, Dr. Cheryl Bragg, and Dr. Marian Shapiro as well as the late Eugenia Hanfmann. Other helpful readers have been Drs. William and Sue Vogel, Dr. David Trimble, Dr. Janet Brown, Professor Frieda Rebelsky, Dr. Rachel Avery, Dr. Miriam Fiedler, Professor Emeritus Sue Allen Warren, Professor Jim Paul, Professor Emeritus William Cruickshank, Professor Peter Wolff, and Temple Grandin.

We wish also to acknowledge support from the U.S. Office of Education's Bureau of Education for the Handicapped from 1979 through 1986 in funding two model demonstration programs and for pre-school to early-school age children (G007900518) and for toddlers (G008302293). Reginald Hart, the Center's development director, was instrumental in gaining foundation support for the Center's programs. A grant from the Adriana Foundation and support from Kristi Jorde and Rodrigo Rocha also helped strengthen the Center's program. We also thank Kristi and Rodrigo Rocha and Barbara and John Hiscock for sharing personal experiences about their children in a manner that has helped enrich this book.

We remember with appreciation the consistent and staunch support of our parents, Charles Eller and Edna and Meyer J. Miller. Our debt to Shakong Wang, the gifted and versatile artist whose illustrations captured the unique quality of our approach, is evident in the pages that follow.

In the preparation of this complex manuscript we have been ably assisted first by Kathy Dewalt and then by Sheila McNamara. Finally, we wish to express our appreciation to Herb Reich, Senior Editor at John Wiley & Sons, for his guidance and support during the years it took to complete this work.

A.M
E.E.-M.

Contents

Introduction

Readers of this book will note the central emphasis on the unique reality that each child possesses. This reality or *Umwelt*—to use the term and concept coined by Uexküll (1934/1957) and referred to as "life space" by Lewin (1935) and as "sphere of reality" by Werner (1948)—is important because it puts the emphasis on the child's ongoing experience where it belongs. As the following instance shows, often an analysis of the child's experience of reality can make otherwise obscure behavior readily understandable.

An autistic 6-year-old girl sitting cross-legged on a carpet—with her teacher beside her—was learning to draw a picture of water by producing wavy blue lines on her paper. The teacher was perplexed to find the child suddenly taking off her shoes and socks and placing her bare feet on the paper. This unusual behavior became intelligible only after the teacher learned that for this child "water" was not simply a term representing a particular liquid, it was part of a unique reality system that, when coupled with the experience of her water drawing, *required* her to put her bare feet in the "water" as she did at the lake each summer.

By understanding the child's need to involve words with her body actions and drawings, one gains insight into her level of functioning and is better able to help her. Such emphasis on the child's experience and method of coping with reality forms an integral part of each child's evaluation at the Language and Cognitive Development Center. To get at this experience the examiner first tries to determine what kinds of reality systems the child brings to the new situation. Does the child run furiously back and forth after colliding with a wall? Does the child sit and rock with fingers twiddling in front of his or her eyes? Second, the examiner tries to determine the permeability of these systems and their potential for expansion. For example, if one interposes a barrier for the child running back and forth, does the back-and-forth system include going around the barrier or does it shrink to include wall and barrier? Similarly, it is important to observe whether the child obsessively stacking blocks picks up only the adjacent blocks or is able to accept a block from a nearby adult. Beyond this, can the child tolerate having the adult add to the block structure?

In addition to evaluating the systems the child brings, there must be evaluation of the child's capacity to become engaged in systems (spheres) that the examiner introduces. Without an array of developmentally relevant spheres, intervention would be limited to the systems already developed by the child. If during the evaluation the child can accept a sphere of activity that involves going up steps, sitting down, and going down a slide, and can gradually "take over" the sphere, this augurs well for assimilation of other introduced spheres leading to more appropriate functioning. This determination is particularly important because the difficulties of disordered children stem from their tendency to become "stalled" at early levels of functioning as a result of failure to achieve the transition to the next more advanced level.

The more that workers can expand children's existing systems or introduce new ones via spheres that help the children achieve necessary transitions, the more their functioning improves. Typically, behavior-disordered children have deficits in social and emotional contact with others, inability to cope with physical surroundings, and inability to communicate their experience to themselves and others. When, through their work at the Center, they expand the systems they possess or assimilate new ones, children make meaningful progress in their problem areas of functioning.

Our use of systems owes something to Piaget's concept of schema and to the Lewinian notion of tension systems. Elaboration of the notion within a cognitive-developmental framework makes it possible to work with disordered children without recourse to "reinforcement" as it is currently employed by behavior modification workers. In our approach, the child's system-forming tendency—with its neurologically "wired-in" disposition to relate reflexes and stereotypies to reality—is what determines early organization of behavior, not specific reinforcements for each bit of desired behavior. Even the most disordered child is not a relatively passive organism that bonds to reality by virtue of specific rewards and punishments, but an active organism with an impressive array of genetically established "part-systems" that become complete only as they become engaged with various facets of reality.

This book is divided into two major parts. Part One describes the nature of cognitive-developmental systems theory and discusses the formation of systems in normal and abnormal development as well as the shift from *sign* to *symbolic-sign* and *symbol stages* of functioning. Part Two applies the theory to assessment and intervention with behavior-disordered children.

In Part One, to link theory more closely with practice, each chapter is designed so that the theory on the particular issue under discussion and examples of the theory's application are closely related. This organization allows the child's development to be viewed solely in terms of the particular issue being discussed.

Each of the six chapters in Part One traces the emergence of a particular capacity from early to later development. After an overview of how the systems of normal and disordered children form (Chapter 1), the development of the body schema is discussed (Chapter 2). The remaining chapters explore the way the developing child copes within an expanding reality (Chapter 3), develops social relations (Chapter 4), learns to communicate through spoken language (Chapter 5), and learns how to read and write (Chapter 6).

Part Two applies the theory to assessment and intervention with disordered children and their families. Chapter 7 deals with the assessment of child systems; Chapter 8 discusses the application of cognitive-developmental systems on an individual basis; and Chapter 9 considers its application in the classroom. The next chapters describe two major aspects of the Center's program: the Sign and Spoken Language Program (Chapter 10) and the Symbol Accentuation Reading Program (Chapter 11). Finally, because the integration of home with Center is vital for the child's ability to generalize learning, Chapter 12 is devoted to this issue as well as to the manner in which the relationships between parents and professionals contribute to the progress of behavior-disordered children.

PART ONE

Cognitive-Developmental (C-D) Systems Theory

There is an existential clash when a worker confronts a profoundly disordered child for the first time. The child is obviously human, even beautiful, but behaves as if the worker did not exist. The need is to elicit some kind of response—a fleeting glance, a smile—to deal with the child in human terms. But the child does not permit this. As one parent put it, "You knock . . . but no one answers."

Cognitive-developmental (C-D) systems theory formulates such disordered behavior as systems that, for a variety of reasons, have failed to include people or to permit normal exploration. The theory describes the dynamics that allow aberrant systems to form and maintain themselves. It also suggests the kind of interventions and remedial techniques that help behavior- disordered children relate to people and objects in their environment to achieve more normal development. Guided by this theory, we have at times been able to enter the realities of disordered children and guide them into our own. We offer this theory so that others can do the same—not from a great emotional distance—but from touching range.

CHAPTER 1

Early Reality Systems as Precursors of Ordered and Disordered Development

INTRODUCTION TO REALITY SYSTEMS

The term *reality system* derives from the Umwelt concept first developed by Uexküll (1934/1957). Each organism, Uexküll pointed out, has its own Umwelt, or world around itself, to which it relates in a unique way. This Umwelt, or sphere of reality, depends on the drive patterns in play at a particular time, the nature of the immediate environment, and the developmental stage of the organism. An organism can have a number of different Umwelten, constituting the experience of the world available to that organism. If the organism is limited in its developmental stage, each sphere of reality may be experienced as quite disparate from the others. As Werner (1948) put it, with such an organism:

> One sphere succeeds the other like scenes on a revolving stage. . . . [In] poorly differentiated organisms the single spheres are more or less strictly closed off with respect to one another. . . . Only when the spheres are not rigidly divided off from one another, but intercommunicate . . . is it possible to have an identity and constancy of things. (p. 381)

Werner's point is illustrated in the behavior of a 5-month-old infant whose intense preoccupation with drinking from a bottle suggests that at that moment his or her Umwelt, or sphere of reality, consists only of this involvement. However, a moment later, when the infant drops the bottle and becomes occupied with a rattle, the bottle ceases to exist as he or she is completely caught up with a sphere of reality related to the rattle. Only at a later age will the infant be able to drink from a bottle while playing with a rattle or to recover the bottle after dropping it, as a result of developing a continued sense of its existence even when not directly involved with it. A child who can do this demonstrates that previously disparate spheres of reality have become interconnected.

Although the concept of systems used in this book owes much to Uexküll and Werner's formulation of spheres of reality, Cognitive-developmental (C-D) systems theory extends this concept by specifying the dynamic conditions that permit children to form their first systems. It also attempts to

7

show how, by exploiting the dynamics intrinsic to such systems, disordered children can act deliberately within and represent their expanding reality systems to themselves and to others.

Reality Systems in a Normal and a Disordered Child

It is useful, in discussing reality systems, to contrast the functioning of a normal and a disordered 3-year-old, as each builds a block structure.

CHILD A

A normal 3-year-old boy, playing with a pile of assorted blocks, builds a connected structure of ramps and towers. He picks up each block, examines it, selects a place for it in the block structure and inserts it carefully. Needing a block of a particular size, the child scans the blocks and spots an appropriate one near the foot of an observing adult about 6 feet away. The child looks at the adult, points at the block, and exclaims, "Block!" Handed the block, the child smiles at the adult, adds the block to his structure, and takes another block. Next, the child, while making "rmm" car sounds, "drives" his block up the ramp and around the block towers. Finished with car–block play, he gets up and sets off for something else to do.

CHILD B

Another 3-year-old boy is also building a connected structure. But this structure consists only of a row of blocks carefully placed so that each block abuts the previous one. Curved or triangular blocks are ignored. He works with rapid intensity regularly scrambling from the end of the row of blocks only to get another block to continue extending the structure. At no time does the child acknowledge the existence of the adult seated nearby. When the adult tries to hand the child a block for his structure, the child rapidly turns his body so that his back is between the adult and the blocks. When the adult removes one block from the row, the child screams, ignores the proffered block, and frantically finds another block to close the gap in the structure. The child continues extending the row of blocks until it reaches the wall. Confronted by the wall, he makes a right angle with the next block and continues placing blocks along the wall until there are no more blocks. Then the child begins rocking back and forth while twiddling his fingers in front of his eyes. Except for the screams the child has uttered no sound.

The children in the previous vignettes, although the same chronological age, are functioning at different stages of development. Child B shows a domination by the sign or signal properties of objects (found in normal 6- to 8-month-old infants) that the theory defines as *sign stage* behavior. In his symbolic play and use of language, Child A shows age-appropriate qualities designated as *symbolic-sign stage* behavior. These stages are important because the capacities intrinsic to each stage limit the kinds of reality systems available to the child.

The nature of reality systems during the sign stage is evident in the manner in which signs or signal properties of objects restrict the "plan" of Child B, compelling him to link each block with the next. A child who is organized by reality in these terms cannot experience himself as an independent agent. Stated differently, the child's lack, at this stage, of a differentiated experience of his body in relation to objects, precludes his making choices within the system he forms. In such a reality system the child, lacking the ability to deliberately intend action, experiences the properties of the blocks and his own actions as one undifferentiated totality. This totality constitutes the child's reality system and accounts for the manner in which he deals with the blocks in a single vector—laying each block alongside the next. Once he begins the row of blocks, he must continue placing them without deviation in the same direction.

For Child B, functioning at an early *sign stage,* the observing adult does not exist except as a momentary threat (when removing a block) to the integrity of the structure being built. Only when the structure confronts the wall at right angles does the child implicitly acknowledge that the row of blocks must change direction. This change, however, comes about not through any inner plan on the child's part but because the wall requires the change. Finally, there is no decision to stop connecting blocks; the child stops when he runs out of blocks. When this occurs, the child has no means of directing himself to a new activity. Apparently, the only activity remaining to the sign stage child to fill the void left by the end of the block-connecting system is rocking and hand twiddling.

In contrast, Child A, functioning at a *symbolic-sign stage,* can represent and experience both himself and the blocks as entities with independent existences. This awareness, coupled with the child's access to other systems (play with cars) not in the immediate system but suggested by the sign properties of the blocks, allows him to exploit the blocks in varied ways. It also permits him to turn away from the blocks (to request a block from an adult) and to turn back to them without losing touch with his goal. Thus, he can develop a plan that includes a choice of alternatives within his system (i.e., which of several blocks is best) and can demonstrate the flexibility to constantly change, complicate, and expand his system.

In carrying through his plan, Child A demonstrates that he can integrate or interconnect several smaller systems. Thus, if one views the act of building towers with blocks as one subsystem; if attending to and asking the adult for a block is a second subsystem; and if using a block as a car is a third subsystem; one can see how the child, guided by his inner plan, can integrate these different subsystems in a flexible and creative manner not available to Child B.

Like Child B, many disordered children are more or less stuck at early stages of development. To help such children progress to capacities intrinsic to more advanced stages, it is important to consider the nature of three broad stages through which normal infants progress and the reality systems that characterize these stages. After relating disordered reality systems to their comparable stages in normal development, this book describes procedures that, by paralleling normal progressions, help disordered children resume their development.

Sign, Symbolic-Sign, and Symbol Stages of Development

The infant develops from a largely stimulus-dominated organism (*sign stage*) to one capable of representing reality to self and others (*symbol stage*) as the culmination of a series of liberations from the "pull" exerted by the child's immediate surroundings. The terms *sign, symbolic-sign,* and *symbol* characterize different stages of liberation not only because they capture a central determinant of the child's reality systems during each stage, but because so ordered, the stages suggest an element of continuity essential to development. The stages are qualitatively distinct—with each stage being prerequisite to the next—but the prior stages also actively contribute to the achievement of later stages. Thus, the sign stage contributes to the development of the symbolic-sign stage, just as the symbolic-sign stage contributes to the development of the symbol stage.

Sign Stage: Ages 0 to 18 Months

The term *sign* characterizes the initial stage of development because the first functional reality systems form through signs or signals. Like the traffic sign to the motorist, all signs have in common certain properties. First is their imperative nature. The mobile above the crib acts as a sign that *requires* the infant do something about it just as the sign properties of the blocks *require* the disordered child to immediately juxtapose one block next to another. Signs demand an immediate response whether the infant is reacting to the sign or producing the sign. Second, signs entail a single-track response; that is, the sign's "meaning" relates to one particular action outcome. When the nipple is the sign, the single-track response is sucking the nipple. When the nursing infant's cry of distress or groping for the nipple is the sign, the single-track response related to that sign is the mother's postural adjustment so that the nipple may more readily be taken into the mouth.

At first the child's reality systems involve only transitory impressions of objects with which he or she has direct experience. New action–object relations seem to develop "accidentally"—the infant's waving arms strike and cause movement in the mobile above the crib—and the infant seems to need to reproduce that effect. Piaget (1952a) refers to such behavior as a secondary circular reaction. This reproduction of the action to cause a particular effect constitutes a reality system. Eventually, the child applies the system formed in this way to new situations to obtain similar results. Thus, when a new mobile is placed above the crib, the baby will apply the earlier system of visually searching for it and batting it until these actions become expanded into a system that includes grasping and pulling the object.

During the first part of the *sign stage* the infant becomes responsive to and initiates an expanded range of signs. Although initially only the nipple (primary sign) is able to trigger the sucking response, subsequently, the care giver's crooning to or rocking of the infant (secondary sign), or even that person's approach to the infant, can trigger a sucking response. Therefore, the term *sign* embraces not only properties of objects and events that directly trigger a response but also those signs that develop secondarily because the child has experienced or used them as part of a system with which he or she is engaged. In using signs to communicate intention, normal infants seem to show far more two-way "communication" with their parents than do disordered children. Disordered infants are less likely to initiate the inadvertent signals that start the choreography between parent and infant and establish the framework for social contact. Similarly, they are often quite unresponsive to the presence or the initiatives of parents (Ornitz, Guthrie, & Farley, 1977).

Although the shift from *sign* to *symbolic-sign stage* functioning that occurs at about 18 months marks a dramatic change in the ability of the child to relate to surroundings in a more liberated fashion, a number of very important changes occur more gradually during the sign stage making this shift possible. One such change during the first 12 months of life is the progressive organization and awareness of the body (Chapter 2) so that directed movement involving objects with people becomes possible. As this develops, the child has repeated opportunities to discover that objects as well as people have an existence independent of his or her actions toward or with them.

After the independent identities of both body and objects have been established, the newly mobile child learns during the next 6 months to cope with an expanding reality (Chapter 3). During this latter phase of the sign stage, reality systems grow in complexity as the child explores the different properties of objects and the space within which these objects exist. The child now puts one object inside another, moves an object from one hand to the other, tries to put things together and pull them apart, and travels from one object or event to another. Also evident is the infant's new ability to *spontaneously expand* his or her relations to objects. The baby, no longer satisfied with merely dropping the spoon from the high chair and watching its descent, may now vary the hand position to observe how this shift relates to the landing site. This new flexibility goes well beyond the unrelenting disposition to repeat what the signal properties of objects seem to require. Another important change during the first 12 months of life is the progressive organization and awareness of the body (Chapter 2) so that by 9 to 10 months of age (Trevarthen & Hubley, 1978) self-directed movement coordinating objects with people becomes possible (Chapter 4). This new flexibility, coupled with the independent awareness of body and object—and the possibilities of one relating to the other—makes the advance to the next stage possible.

Symbolic-Sign Stage: Ages 18 Months to 6 Years

The *symbolic-sign stage* is marked by the achievement of naming, a capacity that for the first time gives the child a means of "carrying" various reality systems internally. The packaging of reality through names provides the major tool for extricating the child from the immediate sensory impact of the surroundings in a way that enables thinking about, instead of acting within, a variety of realities. *Because the name makes it no longer necessary to act with objects in order to apprehend their meaning, inner thought processes become increasingly available to the child.*

The term *symbolic-sign* captures the duality of experience that characterizes this stage. On the one hand, the child is now able to communicate and represent reality both internally and to others through names; on the other hand, there is still a strong sign component in the use of names that binds the child's thinking to what is perceptually given. This is particularly evident in the child's requirement that particular names relate to their objects and to no other. The sign aspect is also evident in the constant and urgent need to fix various aspects of reality that impinge. At the previous stage a sign or signal property of an object requires that the child "do something" about it physically, whereas at the symbolic-sign stage the child "does something" by finding the correct name for the particular object or event. The sign aspect of the symbolic-sign stage accounts for the driven quality of children's questioning during this phase of development.

At this stage the sign aspects are also evident in the child's literal understanding of words. For example, telling a child who has done something wrong to "take your medicine" brings distress and tears not because of fear of punishment but because the child literally anticipates having to take noxious tasting medicine.

The same literalness is apparent in the manner in which the child at this stage organizes space. As Werner (1948) pointed out, "A child may be able to orient himself perfectly well so long as he can carry out a familiar sequence of movement but be quite lost if he has to start from some new point of departure" (p. 176). He then cited an incident in which a 2-year-old child returning from a long trip could orient himself in his home only after he had entered his own room. Apparently, the room provided the "starting place" for all spatial relations in his home. To regain those relations he had to proceed in an irreversible fashion reminiscent of the disordered boy who also behaved in an irreversible manner as he fixed one block to another.

The egocentric manner in which the symbolic-sign stage child organizes space also expresses itself in relation to time. From a personal, egocentric notion of time-for-breakfast, -nap, -supper comes gradual movement toward a concept of time independent of personalized events. The child grasps the notion of time as a more general concept related to light and darkness and then to the position of the hands on the clock.

The egocentric tendency is also apparent in the symbolic-sign stage child's difficulty viewing the world from the perspective of others. Only gradually does the child learn to recognize and appreciate the viewpoint of others both perceptually and socially. Finally, the symbolic-sign stage child lives in a rather "magical" world where wishing can readily transform the meaning of one thing into another. The playful transformation of objects or the manner in which one object or event acts on and thus transmits some of its quality to the object acted upon is exemplified by the star-struck movie fan who refused to wash her hand because it had been touched by the star. In such transformations the contiguity between two events plays an important role. This mode of experience is evident in the following instance:

> A 5-year-old child, riding his bicycle just before the power failure that led to the great Northeast blackout, happened to collide with a large light pole. As the light on the pole and all the lights in the vicinity flickered and went out, the child guiltily pedaled away—absolutely certain that he had precipitated the blackout.

Symbol Stage: Ages 6 Years and Older

Perhaps the major characteristic of *symbol stage* functioning is the extent to which thought becomes liberated from action, permitting "practice action" in thought. Instead of trying to solve a problem by trial and error, the symbol stage child assesses the different aspects of the situation, mentally works out likely outcomes, and then attempts to solve the problem at one stroke. With the symbol stage, thought becomes reversible because the child understands that something that can be added can also be subtracted. By visualizing a sequence of events the child can find a missing toy without having to explore the entire house. Such a child can trace the route to school and follow it back home. Whereas children at the previous stage can count with their fingers, those at the symbol stage of development can count in their heads as well.

A child at the symbol stage can classify objects by some characteristic, such as color, shape, or size. At this stage there is recognition of hierarchies of classes, and of subclasses within large classes. Such a child can also mentally arrange objects along some quantitative dimension, such as size or weight. A child at the symbolic-sign stage puts sticks in size order by picking them up and comparing them one by one, the symbol stage child can take one look at the whole group of sticks and instantly arrange them in order.

Characteristic of the symbol stage is the child's new ability to demonstrate awareness of the arbitrary nature of symbols—that a word need not be fixed to a certain object or event but can be assigned to any referent. This insight makes it possible to achieve phonics as well as arithmetic and algebra. Along with this insight comes the understanding that people experience reality from different perspectives.

The child's gradually expanding application of his or her symbolic capacity affects every aspect of contact with reality. Such children not only experience the body in space but have developed a self-concept that builds on body experience. Because knowledge of space has changed, these children can go to a remote place and return, and can represent that experience in maps.

During this stage children achieve double-track thinking—a capacity that enables them to conserve number, substance (mass), area, weight and volume, though not all concepts are achieved at the same time. Thus, as Piaget and his collaborators have shown (1952b), if the same amount of water is placed in a tall thin glass and then is poured into a short wide glass, children at the symbolic-sign stage will always assert that the tall thin glass had more water in it. However, once they achieve symbol stage functioning, children are able to keep in mind two aspects of a situation (double-track) and can conserve the total quantity of water by relating the height of the water (one aspect) to the kind of container (second aspect) in which the water is placed. Such children understand that the size or shape of the container does not determine the amount of the item contained.

The Formation of Early Reality Systems during the Sign Stage

The neonate's capacity to form early reality systems during the sign stage depends on certain *part-systems* provided by innate biological mechanisms. Our interest in biological mechanisms was spurred when we noted that many disordered children showed unusual reflexive responses to stimuli as well as a range of rhythmic stereotypic behaviors such as arm flapping, rocking, or hand twiddling in front of the eyes. These same responses were also evident in the reflexive capacities and rhythmical behavior tendencies of normal infants. However, whereas normal infants soon expand these behaviors into deliberate, functional contact with their surroundings and the people in these surroundings, many disordered children at the Center remained fixated with these repetitive, hand-twiddling behaviors. If we could formulate the manner in which normal infants transformed such behaviors into functional reality systems, perhaps we could discern the manner in which disordered children might achieve the same transformations.

We soon began to think of reflexive responses and rhythmical stereotypies as *part-systems* waiting to form a connection with a salient object or event. Although both reflexive and rhythmical stereotypies originate in the infant's central nervous system, they differ in important respects. The reflexive responses are triggered by quite specific signals, but this is not the case, at least initially, for rhythmical stereotypies. For example, to elicit the grasping reflex it is necessary to stroke the infant's palm lightly; the optokinetic (visual-tracking) reflex is triggered by an object moving across the infant's visual field; the sucking reflex is a response to touching the infant's lips. Each reflexive capacity becomes a system, however, only when the infant's reflexive capacity becomes actively engaged with the triggering signal.

On the other hand, as Esther Thelen (1981) pointed out in an important article, rhythmical stereotypies—repetitive kicking, rocking, waving, bouncing, banging, rubbing, scratching—may be actuated by a broad range of circumstances. At different times such conditions may include insufficient stimulation (sensory deprivation) and too much arousal when the caregiver arrives (Provence & Lipton, 1962; Spitz & Wolf, 1949), as well as a specific response to a particular object or event (Piaget, 1952a). The relevance of rhythmic stereotypies was first reported by Wolff (1967, 1968, p. 479). His research with normal and abnormal infants led to the view that such stereotypies were "neurophysiological [timing] mechanisms" that formed the necessary but not sufficient substrate for later coordinated and goal-directed movement, a view later supported by Thelen's work.

Rhythmical action stereotypies become part of infant systems and provide a basis for directed action when the child, noting the impact of rhythmic action on a particular object or event, seeks to reproduce that impact (secondary circular reaction). As long as the infant's activity consists only of rhythmical action stereotypies, such as repetitive kicking, arm waving, or rocking, not entailing involvement with a particular external object or event, speaking of a system is not justified. Such behaviors do not constitute systems because they do not include a coherent relationship with some external object or event. They may, however, be thought of as *motor capacities* or *part-systems* "waiting" to relate to a salient object or event that engages them. The next section describes the manner in which reflexive responses and rhythmical stereotypies become engaged by particular objects and events to form reality systems and the unique capacities that these systems make available to the infant.

THE DYNAMICS OF REALITY SYSTEMS

The disordered child who was compelled to connect one block to another, was experiencing the properties of the blocks and his own actions as an undifferentiated totality that constituted the reality system. Such syncretic body action–object states are characteristic of early childhood, said Werner (1948, p. 361), because the reacting child is unable to distinguish where the salient properties of an object or event end and the body's response to them begins. Given the child's inability to distinguish object from body input, any secondary source of stimulation that impinges while the infant is engaged by the more salient object or event, is also experienced as part of the system. States that combine input in this way become *systems* when the child organizes and maintains the combined field of stimulation from object–body sources. The infant's disposition to maintain the body–object system permits the infant to shift from a purely reactive involvement with a stimulating object or event to self-generated behavior. This behavior provides the framework for intentional action as well as for the development of receptive and expressive language.

Reality systems and the capacities they yield develop through a series of steps that are designated as *orienting, engagement,* and *compensatory action phases*. Using this model of system formation, the disorders of small children can be categorized into problems with orienting, engagement, transition from orienting to engagement, or transition from one engagement to another. For example, autistic or autisticlike children frequently fail to orient toward even a very salient source of stimulation, such as a loud shout. On the other hand, as Goldstein (1939) has shown, many neurologically impaired children orient excessively because they are "caught" by every salient stimulus that comes into their sensory field. Both kinds of orienting difficulties interfere with their ability to become functionally engaged with objects. Alternatively, the problem for some disordered children is less one of orienting than it is of detaching from an engagement already achieved. Such children, as noted elsewhere (Miller & Miller, 1973), are so involved in their own rituals that they cannot readily detach from them and direct action or interest toward new aspects of their situation. With all such problems, the model focuses on interventions that can restore the child's ability to react to and cope with the surroundings.

Orienting, Engagement, and Compensatory Action Phases

The *orienting phase* of the system-forming process enables the child to locate a salient object or event and prepares the child for further action toward or with it. Orienting begins as the normal infant turns toward the salient property of an object or event. Early effective inducing of this "turning-to" behavior depends on stimulus novelty in the region involving and surrounding the child—a touch, the motion or quality of an object in the visual field, or a sudden sound. In general, any input that varies abruptly from the just prior level of stimulation induces orienting. Although variously termed "attending" (Pillsbury, 1908), "turning-to" (Goldstein, 1939), or an "orienting reflex" (Pavlov, 1962; Sokolov, 1963), all writers are in accord with the innate, inadvertent, body-involving, and stimulation-enhancing effect of this directed response to salient facets of the environment.

The stimulus-enhancing effect of orienting occurs because the child, while orienting, is subject to both direct stimulation from the object and indirect or reafferent stimulation from its turning-to movements, as well as from its stimulus-directed postural stance. This combined input seems to enhance the child's reactivity to a particularly stimulating circumstance. The organization of the orienting mode is governed by the finding (Sokolov, 1963) that only one facet of the stimulus field (the most salient part) can induce orienting at a particular time.

Viewed in terms of figure–ground relations as elaborated by Rubin (1921), the most salient part of the field of stimulation becomes figural and all other surrounding circumstances become a secondary ground for that figure. Thus, a nipple touching an infant's cheek elicits a reflexive orienting toward the nipple that establishes it as figural against a less distinct visual ground and consequently makes the nipple more available for sucking. Similarly, the sudden appearance of an object can trigger orienting followed immediately by a particular rhythmical stereotypy such as kicking or arm waving.

The *orienting phase* transforms into an *engagement phase* that establishes the system. The system formed from the child's engagement with a particular object or event enables the child to intimately experience, adjust to, and incorporate the unique properties of an object or event as these begin to unfold. At this time the child also incorporates within the system any secondary input that accompanies engagement with the object.

Engagement may show itself in many ways. For normal infants engagement develops when a stimulating object or event triggers a response that induces the orienting child to physically engage that object; for example, the infant, after orienting to the touch of the nipple on his or her cheek, engages it with vigorous sucking movements. This changes the figure–ground relation that the child experiences; instead of nipple as figure, *sucking the nipple* becomes figure as well as any accompanying stimulation the infant experiences while nursing. Thus, the crooning or stroking stimulation from the care giver is also experienced as part of the composite figure that has become organized into a system.

The engagement of rhythmical stereotypies occurs when, following orienting toward a particular event (such as the care giver's appearance) the infant produces a particular response such as repetitive arm waving related to the care giver. At other times random rhythmical behavior becomes a system when it produces an effect that the infant seeks to repeat. Such systems were described by Piaget (1952a) as secondary circular reactions. Piaget's daughter, after discovering that dolls hanging from her bassinet shook when she kicked her feet, consistently repeated the kicking to cause the dolls to shake on other occasions. Similarly, Piaget's son in the course of waving his arms while holding an implement, happened to hit the bassinet's wicker cover, making a distinctive sound that he subsequently tried to reproduce by waving his arms in the same manner. As with reflexive reactions, as soon as the system forms, the figural experience of the child changes. Whereas at first the sound the child made on the wicker basket was figural, as his arm waving became related to the occurrence of that sound, stimulation from arms waving *and* sound emerged as the composite figure that comprised the system.

It is evident that the infant until now has not established the separation between body and object necessary for well-defined and inner-generated action toward objects. All actions have been accidentally triggered by some external event. Consequently, it is important to consider closely the conditions that enable the child to develop self-generated action toward objects or events. Although the infant lacks body–object differentiation, one condition—*interruption* of engagement with an object or event—can nevertheless produce behavior that has some of the quality of directed action. As we shall see, it matters considerably whether the interruption of the system is complete or partial.

Complete Interruption of the System

Only during engagement, when the integrity of the new figural system is challenged by the loss or sudden unavailability of the object or event part of that figure, does the infant generate directed action. The loss or diminished impact of an object or event triggers the *compensatory phase,* during which the child feels compelled by the sudden, localized drop in stimulation to direct the body part of that figure toward the site of the missing object or event. The following observations by Piaget (1952a) of his children clearly demonstrate the action of the compensatory phase.

Discussing sucking, Piaget observed:

> Thus it seems that contact of the lips with the nipple and the thumb gives rise to *pursuit* [italics added] of these objects *once they have disappeared.* [italics added] . . . (p. 9)

Directed gazing toward a suddenly lost object was evident with Piaget's daughter, Jacqueline, aged 2 months 27 days, who

> follows her mother with her eyes, and when her mother *leaves the visual field,* [italics added] continues to look in the same direction until the picture reappears. (p. 9)

Directed listening was also evident after Piaget shook the lid of a kettle in front of his son, Laurent, aged 2 months 6 days:

> When I *interrupt* [italics added] the noise, Laurent looks at me a moment, then again looks at the kettle even though it is now silent . . . in other words, he behaves with regard to the interrupted sound as he does with regard to the visual pictures which just disappeared. (p. 10)

In a sense, the compensatorily acting child is "orienting" toward the missing object or event. However, unlike the "turning-to" behavior of the orienting phase, the body movements directed toward the missing entity during the compensatory phase are varied and depend directly on the nature of the child's prior body involvement with that entity. Later, this compensatory activity—produced in the absence of the originally stimulating object—contributes to intentional action.

Rhythmical action systems, when interrupted, also induce a compensatory response. For example, Piaget's daughter Jacqueline, at 8 months, 9 days (Piaget, 1954), expressed her engagement with the sight of a saucer passing in front of her eyes by repeatedly arching herself upward with weight on shoulder blades and feet and then letting herself drop each time the plate appeared. Then, each time the saucer became motionless (interrupted system) Jacqueline arched upward again. Piaget stated, "I then definitely pause in my game; Jacqueline nevertheless draws herself up five or six times more, while looking at the object" (p. 238). Jacqueline's repetitive drawing herself up and dropping constituted a compensatory effort to restore the moving plate part of the system with which she had first been engaged.

Over time these compensatory responses to interrupted systems come increasingly under the child's control so that the impetus for activating a particular response comes not from an external stimulus but from the child's deliberate intention.

The thesis is that compensatory action, triggered by an interrupted engagement with an object or event, plays a critical role in bringing about the differentiation between body and object essential for inner-generated action.

This differentiation occurs when the child becomes aware that compensatory actions stem from his or her own body. Such an action then changes from a reflexive or involuntary act to one that the child is able to spontaneously direct toward the original or similar objects.

The beginning awareness of body or body part in relation to the object most often happens during the compensatory phase because, no longer merged with the previously engaging object or event, the child's own movements then constitute the most salient and thus engaging source of stimulation. Consequently, the infant performing sucking movements in the absence of the nipple has opportunity to vividly experience mouth movements as separate from but related to and directed toward ingesting the nipple. Similarly, the sudden absence of the care giver permits the infant to note his or her visual tracking movements independent of their relation to the missing person. And, in the example of the moving plate, Piaget's daughter had the opportunity to note her back-arching and dropping movements as separate from but connected to the missing motion of the plate.

Through body accenting within particular systems the child becomes progressively more aware that the compensatory reactions coming from the body are responsive to his or her intentions. As this happens, rhythmical stereotypies may be transformed: waving may become directed reaching, and rhythmical kicking may change into more intentional foot movements. The child may also creatively play with body movements, as when a small infant first inspects a foot, then waves it, bangs it, mouths it, and inspects it again before repeating the process.

Awareness of body parts and the actions generated by them causes the following two developments: (a) the gradual structuring of an integrated body schema, as described in Chapter 2, and (b) an increasing ability to deliberately direct behavior not only toward the previously engaging object but toward and between other objects. This new intentional capacity leads to the functional use of hands with objects (see Chapter 3) and to the use of tools to achieve particular ends—all part of the child's increasing capacity to cope with an expanding reality.

But there is another line of development—receptive understanding—that stems from early systems that we have not yet discussed. Such understanding has its earliest sources in the *partial* interruption of systems.

Partial Interruption of the System

If the nipple is unavailable, the infant who hears crooning that has been part of the nursing situation will orient to the crooning as if it were the nipple and begin to produce sucking movements. In a partial interruption of a system the originally engaging object is unavailable, but a secondary facet of the combined figural experience that makes up the system *is* available and induces the response previously reserved for the engaging object. In similar manner, as described in Chapter 5, Pavlov's (1927, 1928, 1962) dogs, deprived of food, but presented a light or sound that had previously accompanied their ingestion of food, attempted to "lick the flashing electric bulb . . . or try to eat the sound itself; in doing this the animal licks its lips and grinds its teeth as if dealing with real food" (1962, p. 89).

The infant's sucking response to crooning and the dog's effort to "eat" the light or sound are compensatory efforts to restore interrupted contact with food by directing eating movements toward that part of the composite figural system still available. This formulation has important implications for work with disordered children because it implies that simply presenting a spoken word repetitively *while the child is actively engaged with a particular object or event* will enable the child to inadvertently incorporate the word into that system. Then, when the word is presented alone (partial interruption), it will induce the child to act in a way that previously only the object could induce. Some instances of this application appear later in this chapter and, in more detail, in Chapter 5.

A similar compensatory reaction contributes to the development of expressive language. An early phase of this achievement was evidenced by our son, David, aged 8 months, who, when rocked in his crib, would utter small grunts with slightly accented body movements in cadence with the rocking. Then, each time the rocking was interrupted, he would express his wish for it to continue by urgently grunting as he lurched forward in his crib. Subsequently, David used his "grunt-rocking" behavior as a "natural sign" to ask for rocking on a variety of occasions without requiring prior rocking stimulation. Thus, just as the child's awareness of body actions makes possible a more deliberate and varied use of such actions, so the knowledge of the use of signs enables a more deliberate and varied use of sign forms. This shows itself in the child's increasing ability to use compensatory reactions as surrogates for reality, to achieve desired ends. In the following example, the child's use of a natural sign to represent a problem provided the means for solving that problem.

Piaget (1952a) described how his 16-month-old daughter, Lucienne, solved the problem of retrieving a small chain, with which she had been engaged, from a slightly open (3-mm slit) matchbox whose opening and closing capacity she did not understand. Prior to being given the chain in the almost closed box, Lucienne had solved the problem of removing the chain when the opening was larger (10 mm). She had done this by putting her index finger into the slit until she succeeded in getting out a small fragment of the chain, which she then pulled until it was completely freed from the box. Lucienne had thus learned one aspect of the matchbox system but had not learned another—that the opening of the box could be adjusted from larger to smaller or from smaller to larger. To solve this problem she had to experience the smaller opening as a variant of the larger, and both as properties of the box.

At first, confronted with the 3-mm slit, she unsuccessfully tried the former solution (putting her index finger in the opening). She then proceeded as follows:

> She looks at the slit with great attention; then, several times in succession, she opens and shuts her mouth, at first slightly, then wider and wider! . . . Soon after this phase of plastic reflection, Lucienne unhesitatingly puts her finger in the slit, and *instead of trying as before to reach the chain* [italics added], she pulls so as to enlarge the opening. She succeeds and grasps the chain. (pp. 337–338)

Lucienne solved the matchbox problem by combining two previously unrelated aspects, its 3-mm and 10-mm openings. She did so by developing a creative, compensatory response to her interrupted access to the chain— a natural sign (opening her mouth wider) uniquely designed to represent the critical feature that prevented her from reaching into the box. This dynamic natural sign enabled her to relate the small box opening to the larger, more familiar one and thus to tell herself that the box could shift from one opening to the other. Having grasped this, she was able to enlarge the box opening and pull out the chain.

The Shift from Sign to Symbolic-Sign and Symbol Stages

Shifting from the sign to symbolic-sign stage requires the child to shift from an experience of the object based on its single most salient property to a notion of the object based on the multiple properties that distinguish one category of object from another. Only then does the child have a basis for naming objects. The matchbox example is important in this regard because it suggests how natural signs contribute to the integration of varied facets of an object so that it can be understood in different contexts or attitudes. In other words, the matchbox is not a 10-mm or 3-mm opening but an object that has the potential for opening and closing. Piaget's daughter grasped the true properties of the matchbox because she was able to integrate the disparate openings of the box by referring to the immediate, sentient experience of her body.

During the sign stage, objects are experienced by virtue of their most salient property. Shinn's description of her 6-month-old nephew (Werner, 1948, pp. 65–66) who was given a round rattle instead of his customary square-edged one demonstrates this emphasis. The child tried in vain to find and bite the "corners" of the round rattle, suggesting that the rattle was not known by its visual and tactual shape but by the way its corners invited a certain involvement. Only toward the end of the sign stage does the child, through many interrupted engagements with the same object, gradually learn, for example, that a cup has a handle, can contain things, and has the potential for being drunk from whether on its side or on a shelf. When the child has synthesized object properties with a variety of objects and has learned to reflect the properties of each object within its name, he or she makes the discovery that "each thing has its name" (Stern, 1914, p. 108; Stern & Stern, 1928) and enters the symbolic-sign stage.

The shift from sign to symbolic-sign stage is marked by an increased awareness of the utterances that designate objects. Initially, children require little awareness of signs because the signs blend so closely with their referents that reference occurs by treating a sign as if it *were* the object or event to which it relates. Thus, the child who expresses a wish to eat by placing hand to mouth treats the gesture less as a distinct symbol than as part of the global system of getting food into the mouth. However, as natural signs progress to spoken names (symbolic-signs), children's awareness of the symbol–referent relation must keep pace with the increasing disparity in form between symbol and referent. Consequently, although the earliest natural signs—such as the hand-to-mouth eating gesture or the outstretched reach to be picked up—seem to develop from compensatory efforts to restore interrupted acts (eating food, holding on to care giver), a later more conscious grasp of symbol–referent relations permits children to supplant compensatory responses first with names (symbolic-sign stage) and then with spoken or printed words (symbol stage).

Each increment in the child's awareness of the nature of symbolic forms—from sign to symbolic-sign to symbol stages—permits new capacities. As children realize the efficacy of uttering names that both designate and get them desired things and events, their investment in naming allows them to shift from natural signs to spoken language and to achieve communication quite independent of the presence of the objects or events to which gestures or words refer. They extend the meaning of names to pictures and to the forms of printed words and learn that the sound forms of words are not merely names "fixed" to certain objects or their pictures, but symbols separate from and representing these objects. With this new understanding children enter the symbol stage and become capable of discursive and reversible thought, communication, and the development of phonetic reading and writing.

REALITY SYSTEMS OF DISORDERED CHILDREN

The developmental progression described previously does not occur spontaneously with many disordered children because, for a variety of reasons, they cannot translate their early sign stage experience of objects and events into intentional action toward and with these objects and events. Failing to develop meaningful action, they have no basis for transforming action into representational gesture—natural signs—or, ultimately, into meaningful spoken or written language. The task, therefore, is to use our formulation of reality systems and stages to continue the developmental process wherever it has been arrested or distorted, so that disordered children may resume a more normal progression. But first, it is useful to consider how the concept of systems and spheres evolved from efforts to help disordered children over a number of years.

Elevated Boards, Spheres, and Ritual Systems

The utility of introducing disordered children to board structures elevated 3 to 6 feet above the ground was discovered long before the conceptualization of spheres as interventions. The idea for the structures formed after observing several autistic children at an institution that was building new facilities. As part of the construction process a large ditch had been dug and partly filled in with some large rocks. An 8-year-old autistic child, whom we had previously seen religiously rocking, stumbled across these rocks and soon began intently working his way from rock to rock across the ditch, where he would turn around and then return. The contrast between this child's encapsulated rocking and the goal-directed manner in which he crossed the ditch was striking. Experimentally, we placed a plank across the ditch and guided him gently on it; after a sharp glance at us, he walked across the plank with the same directed intensity with which he had first crossed the ditch.

On the basis of these and similar observations, we started having autistic children with whom we were working cross planks between tables. Each time an autistic child stepped on the boards there was a dramatic change in behavior. Often a child would suddenly look at us, look down at the ground, then carefully proceed across the board. This new awareness and the sudden increase in intention seemed to be the result of an "edge experience" that came about as the child on the elevated structure experienced body boundaries in sharp contrast to his or her surroundings. In an effort to exploit the child's heightened awareness, obstacles were placed on the board that the child had to climb over, step on, in, and so forth, in order to get to the other side. We also said words—and later signed as we spoke—while each child dealt with particular obstacles. When coping with these obstacles, the child often became responsive to relevant words and signs, turning expectantly toward us for the next sign-word command. This responsiveness generalized to home, and soon parents began to report that the children were showing increased awareness of them and their surroundings.

To test the relevance of the approach, elevated board–sign language procedures were applied with 19 intransigent, nonverbal, autistic children in several institutions at which we were consulting (described in Chapter 5). Children who previously could not follow spoken language directions could do so when signs were paired with spoken words, and particularly when these signs and words were taught in context of elevated board structures (Miller & Miller, 1973).

Delighted with the progress of the children and noting that they were beginning to understand concepts like up–down and in–out that they had previously been unable to learn, we developed an array of elevated structures designed to challenge the children to relate signed and spoken directions to their adaptive actions when confronting different parts of the elevated board structures.

After a time, however, certain limitations in the use of boards became apparent. They were extremely effective in teaching new concepts through directed action, sign, and word, but the range of concepts was limited to the ones elicited by the board constructions. Also, the children, after a number of repetitive sequences, seemed to turn their vital involvement into sterile, unthinking rituals very much like their meaningless rocking or twiddling rituals. True, they continued to perform the various problem tasks in response to signs and words, but they did so automatically—without the alertness apparent originally.

At first this ritualization process was combatted by constantly introducing new board sequences and structures and by systematically varying sequences in an effort to keep them "alive." Soon, however, it became apparent that it was impossible to develop board structures that penetrated every aspect of the children's lives both at school and at home. Further, even if it had been possible, functions performed on these new structures would have rapidly become ritualized. Although the strategies were important because they seemed to get the children going, there was no clear transition into normal functioning. What had been functional seemed to become absorbed within the autistic, self-encapsulating process.

Accepting, gradually, that the children were not going to be "normalized" solely through board–language procedures, we began to study more closely the ritual-forming process as it occurred on the boards. It appeared that a ritual constituted a restricted form of learning. On our most elementary device, the Primary Board, a child had to climb a set of steps, walk across

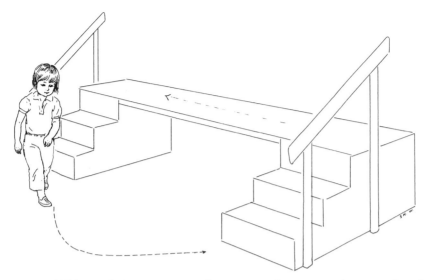

Figure 1.1. Child "needing" to cross space from one set of steps to another to continue the system.

a plank to another set of steps, walk down them, turn, and repeat the process (Figure 1.1). Typically, the child had little trouble with steps or plank; the difficulty would occur when the child stepped down on the ground, where no boards provided guidance, and had to turn and walk back to the first set of steps in order to repeat the process. At that point the child would get "lost" and wander off unless physically guided to the first set of steps. With numerous repetitions of the entire sequence, however, the child, upon reaching the bottom of a set of steps, would—even without board or physical guidance—glance expectantly toward the first steps and then, gradually, *walk unassisted to them*. This unassisted walking across the gap between the two sets of steps clearly indicated that the repetition-induced ritualization of the sequence had brought about new learning; a set of relations had become internalized enough to "pull" the child through unstructured space on the ground in order to continue the sphere.

What these observations established was that repetitive acts, guided by elevated boards, can help profoundly disordered children to achieve rituals that encompass new relations with their surroundings. This new insight about rituals and learning encouraged experimentation with the transformation of board sequences into rituals. For a time we applied repetitive, ritualizing procedures to previously developed board sequences, because of our belief that nonverbal children could only establish rituals on or with the help of elevated board structures. Eventually, rituals were introduced *without* the boards and were established successfully on the ground by pacing the activities quite rapidly, restricting alternatives, and physically guiding the child.

With this step away from the boards, it was possible to introduce new rituals, that we began to call *spheres,* in any location—at home, in the playground, in the classroom. We were no longer solely dependent on elevated board structures to form rituals on which we hoped to build subsequent development.

As we were formulating this approach, Kanner's (1943, 1971) account of Donald T., an autistic child who had achieved a positive adjustment, gave us encouragement. Kanner (1971) reported that Donald's adjustment came about, at least in part, because the couple who cared for him guided the boy in ritual fashion from his autistic preoccupations to more functional behavior. Kanner described this transformation as follows:

> They made him use his preoccupation with measurements by having him dig a well and report on its depth. When he kept collecting dead birds and bugs, they gave him a spot "for a graveyard" and had him put up markers. . . . When he kept counting rows of corn over and over, they had him count the rows while plowing them. On my visit, he plowed six long rows; it was remarkable how well he handled the horses and plow and turned the horses around. (pp. 121–122)

Kanner's case involved a child who could talk and count; consequently, his care givers could draw on this cognitive ability to guide the boy from his preoccupations. Without this capacity nonverbal children require more structured means to guide them into adaptive contact with their surroundings. Because such children had responded to the organization provided by the elevated boards, it seemed likely that boards coupled with sign and word directives would serve a similar guidance function.

After various elevated board spheres had been developed, we began to use them systematically as an Umwelt assessment (see Chapter 7) to identify the ritual- or system-forming characteristics of the children and to determine the potential usefulness of the strategies. The Anticipation Board task (part of three Primary Board Demands) from the Miller Umwelt Assessment Scale (Chapter 7) illustrates this method of evaluating a disordered child's systems. The examiner tests whether the child's systems relate only to what impinges directly on his or her body or whether it may include anticipation of a space away from the body. The child crosses a 6-foot-long board suspended between two sets of steps about 3 feet high to get to the parent who is calling and gesturing at the other end. Interfering with direct access to the parent is another board (the Anticipation Board) placed fencelike diagonally across the 6-foot board.

As Figure 1.2 shows, the diagonal board is a low barrier—easily stepped over—when it is farthest away from the parent and a higher one as it approaches the parent. The diagonal placement of the barrier results in the child's having most room to walk when farthest from the parent but progressively less room when nearing the parent. Thus, it is advantageous for the child to step over the board as early in the sequence as possible.

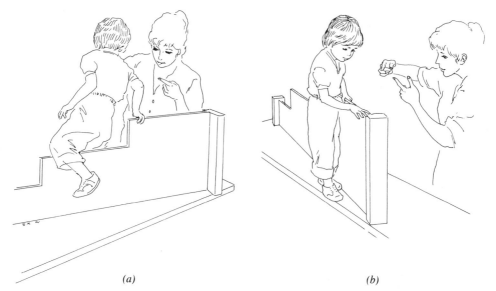

(a)   *(b)*

Figure 1.2. The Anticipation Board: Child (a) successfully crosses and (b) fails to cross over and reach the parent.

A normal 3-year-old, after glancing first at the diagonal barrier and then at the parent, swiftly steps over the barrier at the low end and walks gleefully to the parent. In contrast, an autistic child often never looks at the parent but follows the diagonal barrier until there is no further room to go without falling off the structure. Whereas the behavior of the normal 3-year-old child demonstrates the ability to interconnect two systems—board situation and relation with parent—the disordered child demonstrates how the impinging barrier dominates his or her system functioning.

Other important features of children's systems concern the ease with which they *form* and *expand* them. Both features may be evaluated on the Slide Sphere from the Miller Umwelt Assessment Scale. Here, the child must walk up steps placed at a right angle to the slide, sit down, slide to the bottom, get up, turn toward the starting position, and then repeat the sequence. The child who demonstrates the ability to integrate the components of the Slide Sphere, is given the opportunity to include different tasks within the system, such as dropping blocks down the slide, before finally going down. Because signs and spoken words accompany each component in the system, a child, when interrupted, frequently produces the relevant *down* sign with the word "down" as an expression of need to maintain the continuity of the system.

A normal 3-year-old almost immediately integrates the varied components and then begins spontaneously to expand the system by going down the slide headfirst, sideways, backward, and so forth. The child also shows no difficulty including the block and other expansions within the slide system. In contrast, a disordered 3-year-old may need guidance and support every step of the way. Reaching the bottom of the slide, the child may have to be turned toward the steps; after climbing the steps, the child must be shown how to sit down. Even after all parts of the sphere are integrated into a system, the disordered child typically has great difficulty accepting expansions within the system. Diagnostically, it is valuable to determine the number of cycles required before the child begins to put together this system as well as the extent of the child's ability to integrate expansions within the system. These issues are explored thoroughly in Chapters 7 and 8.

Another test from the Miller Umwelt Assessment Scale that sorts out important aspects of systems is the Swinging Ball task. Here, the examiner tests for three aspects of the system-forming process—*orienting, engagement,* and *compensatory reactions* to interrupted systems. *Orienting* is tested by saying, "Here it comes!" as the examiner swings the ball in the direction of the child. The child who turns toward the ball as it begins to move toward him or her demonstrates the intactness of the orienting portion of the system-forming capacity. Some children have difficulty with this first step and are unable to orient toward the ball unless their heads are turned toward it by a parent.

The *engagement* phase of the system is tested by noting whether the child begins to track the swinging ball and, as it approaches the body, lifts hands to protect the face or, at more advanced levels, pushes the ball back to the examiner. Frequently, disordered children are unable to engage the ball without support and must be assisted by having a parent place their hands on the ball and help them push it toward the examiner each time it approaches. If the child, with the parent's support, is able to engage the ball, the *compensatory phase* of the system is tested by having the parent withdraw support as the examiner momentarily interrupts the swinging motion of the ball. Should the child's hands raise in expectation of the ball resuming motion toward him or her, it provides evidence that the child has assimilated that particular system. The most advanced system is one in which the child not only anticipates the arrival of the ball but engages in the social game of pushing the ball back and forth with the examiner. However, for the many disordered children who lack the capacity to engage spontaneously in such systems, there is systematic intervention to help develop this capacity.

Expanding the Reality Systems of Disordered Children

This section describes two ways to help disordered children move beyond their restricted systems. One method entails working within these systems; the other one introduces new systems—spheres—in which the children can act deliberately within an expanded reality.

Working within a Disordered Child's Reality System

A unique aspect of this approach concerns the stereotyped, ritual behavior (e.g., rocking, twiddling, perseverative playing with objects) that disordered children frequently present (Mitchell & Etches, 1977). Unlike the rhythmical action systems of normal infants, the repetitive systems of disordered children will, without intervention, harden into bizarre, detached behaviors that persist throughout life. However, with appropriate work these nonproductive, nonfunctional ritual tendencies may become adaptive as they are systematically related to objects and events, opened up, complicated, and made available to the child for coping with reality.

For example, the ritualized block system of the disordered boy described earlier can be expanded in a variety of ways depending on short-term goals. To expand his capacity to work with his blocks in different ways, various obstacles placed in the path of the system that he is building would require him either to move the obstacles or to go around them. Obstacles can also be placed in front of or on top of the blocks he requires to complete his structure. Initially, the blocks are only partially covered, but later they are completely hidden so that he must retain the image of the desired block in its absence. As he learns to cope with a variety of challenges to the rigidity of his block system, he moves closer to being able to initiate changes on his own.

To expand this child's block system to include people, a worker attempts to take turns with him in placing blocks at the end of the row. If he accepts this maneuver the worker takes a number of the kind of blocks being used and waits near the end of the row for the child to run out of blocks. Then, as he approaches the worker to get blocks, the child must accept them from the worker's hand. At first the worker chooses a position from which the child can reach for the desired block while his row of blocks remains within his visual field. Later, the worker varies the hand position so that the child momentarily has to look away from his row in order to get the block he needs. If this is successful, the worker might then build in a greater delay by holding a block in front of his or her face so that the child has to look at the worker's face when reaching for the block. The worker can also hand him the block from different positions so that the child has to constantly adjust his reach in order to get the block.

One child, "locked" within a system that excluded people, repeatedly drove a toy car around a road drawn on a large piece of paper. The worker drew the identical pattern on a large paper adjacent to the child's. Then, with a few quick crayon marks—and with only minor distress on the child's part—the two roads were connected and the worker began to drive a car on the child's road while the child began to alternate between driving on the original road *and* the expanded road connecting his space with the worker's.

Introducing Spheric Activity

A variety of new systems can be introduced in the repetitive, ritual-forming manner most likely to engage the child. These spheres are an analogue to the rhythmical stereotypies produced by all infants during development, except that in creating these systems from spheric activity the worker deliberately includes objects with which the child becomes repetitiously engaged.

Spheres—deliberately established repetitive sequences—are effective because the worker can build such constructions into the child's functioning in a manner consistent with the child's developmental capacity. Spheres require a child to perform repetitively a particular activity while the worker uses those words that directly parallel the child's spheric activity. Chapters 3, 4, 8, and 9 describe these procedures in detail. The child's pathological rituals differ from the spheres introduced by a worker in that the latter may be more readily related to a functional, linguistic, or social activity than the child's self-produced stereotypies. Spheres may include such diverse activities as clapping hands ("clap hands"), climbing up and down steps ("up–down"), picking up blocks and dropping them into a box ("pick up–drop"), pushing over a series of objects ("push . . ."), hanging cups on a series of cup hooks ("cup on hook"), and punching holes with a hole-puncher ("punch hole").

An important aspect of intervention entails the choice of spheres for a particular child. These selections are determined by the child's developmental status and the nature of the difficulties being addressed. For example, if a child is excessively reactive to many aspects of the environment and insufficiently reactive to any one aspect, spheres are set up that emphasize greater engagement with one object or event. Alternatively, a child who is excessively reactive to only one object or event uses spheres that help establish relationships between two or more objects. For the child lacking object permanence, a sphere may be designed that incorporates the appearance and disappearance of an object; a child who does not understand the instrumental ability of his or her own hands or body may be assigned a sphere that requires repetitively pushing over objects or pounding pegs through holes in a pounding board.

Spheres are also developed to establish social interaction for children who have difficulty making contact with others (Chapter 4). The most primitive sphere level may consist of repetitive, mutual touching of the child's cheek by the worker and of the worker's cheek by the child. Later, turn-taking with objects is introduced spherically. At first, these spheres are completely controlled by the worker. Subsequently, systematic strategies enable the child to initiate and then to participate reciprocally in spheres. As spheres become internalized, they become *systems*.

Transforming Spheric into Intentional Activity

Unless the spheric activity becomes intentional, it is merely another in the list of motor sterotypies that the child performs. Consequently, careful attention is paid to transforming spheres so that they become part of the child's behavioral repertoire. In doing this the attempt is made to parallel the normal developmental response to interrupted systems. An important step in this process is interrupting the sphere. The theoretical model, buttressed by findings from a variety of developmental and experimental sources (Mandler, 1974, 1984; Piaget, 1952a, 1954; Rickers-Ovsiankina, 1976; Zeigarnik, 1927), predicts that the interruption of a sphere results in the child's compensatory tendency to continue this activity. Thus, a child repetitively hanging cups on hooks will, when momentarily prevented from continuing, typically strive to put the cup on the hook. A nonverbal child who is asked what he or she wants during such an interruption, may also indicate by a reaching or pointing gesture as well as by an occasional spoken word what is wished. Following the child's ability to "complete" the task in this way, the task is varied by using different cups, by moving the task to different parts of the room, and, most important, by involving a parent in the procedure so that the tasks may be generalized to other settings.

To transform a sphere into functional behavior, the sphere must not only be interrupted but also *expanded* and *complicated*. One kind of expansion involves simply inserting a new act within the already established sphere. Just as the normal infant inadvertently incorporates secondary stimuli into self-systems, so the disordered child can expand systems that have been introduced and accepted. For example, one child who had refused to roll a ball down a slide when the task was presented by itself could do so readily when it was presented as part of a larger sphere in which he rolled the ball down the slide just before going down himself.

Developing Representational Reality Systems

For disordered children to advance from sign stage functioning, they must develop means of representing reality to themselves and others. Because the first contact with reality entails their relationship with objects in space, they must find a way to "hold" not only their relation with a particular object but with the relations between two or more objects. Only when they achieve this capacity can they cope with sequential tasks that may require various functions with two or more objects. This work is called *lateral development* because it concerns the child's ability to relate to objects in space. Lateral development contrasts with *vertical development,* where spheres are designed to help children learn how to use gesture and words to represent objects and events to themselves and others. In these spheres the emphasis on representation furthers both thought and communication.

Lateral Development with Minispheres, Multispheres, and Integrative Spheres

One important aspect of lateral development concerns the ability to grasp the nature of an object or event in one context and generalize it to others. Although this happens spontaneously with normal children, it frequently does not occur with disordered children. To remedy this deficiency, a mini-sphere that involves repetitive engagements with a particular object, such as stacking cups, is introduced; the child then expands understanding of this sphere by stacking in different ways and in different locations. In this way the child learns that a particular sphere is operative in all situations.

Autistic children typically lack another facet of lateral development—the ability to shift from one activity to another without losing contact with the first. One autistic girl would scream piercingly when required to make such a shift. The problem was solved by setting up a *multisphere* situation that required performance of several completely unrelated tasks, such as putting peanut butter on crackers, hanging cups on hooks, and tacking bits of paper on a bulletin board. The worker was instructed to engage the child in a sphere before interrupting the activity and requiring her to move to the next sphere. At first the child was distressed when required to shift to a new sphere but soon became calmer as she began to anticipate returning to the previously interrupted task. Finally, after the worker began shifting her randomly from one sphere to another, she accepted interruption quite calmly and was able to indicate by pointing, which of the several spheres she wished to engage with next. This new capacity to shift generalized rapidly to other transitions at home and elsewhere.

Another problem that interferes with lateral development is the tendency of certain disordered children to become overly involved with one aspect of a task. For example, in putting together a house made of strips of wood with moving windows and doors and a removable roof, one child became so fascinated with the windows' ability to move up and down that she refused to deal with any other aspect of the house-assembly task. This was addressed by setting up an integrative sphere in which the parts of the house (except the frame) were distributed to different areas of the room. The child then had to go away from the house frame and come back with the necessary pieces: the roof, windows, doors, slats, and so forth. Requiring the child to detach from one aspect of the house task and, instead, to deal systematically with the task's various parts gave the child the notion of a larger entity that included several parts, of which moving windows were only one. Chapter 3 provides details of minispheres, multispheres, and integrative spheres and their role in establishing lateral development.

Vertical Development

For vertical development to occur, a child must grasp the notion that an object is categorized not only by its most salient property but by its varied properties. For example, to teach this notion to an autistic 3-year-old boy who could identify a cup only by virtue of its ability to hold a liquid, the worker established an integrative sphere designed to teach *cup* as an object with many properties. Various cup-related spheres were set up, including hanging cups on hooks, stacking cups right side up and upside down, and pouring either liquid or grain from one cup to another. In the midst of the child's engagement with a particular sphere he was interrupted and, while looking longingly at the prior activity, was brought to another station to perform a different cup-related sphere. For each subsphere the worker would say "cup" and indicate the sign for *cup* (cup to mouth as if drinking) so that the child could assimilate the various cup-related functions to the general category of cup. When such a procedure is repeated with a number of objects, children often grasp the notion that objects have certain distinguishing properties, and that the object's name captures all properties of the object.

Vertical development also entails, as described in Chapter 5, the achievement of signs and words to communicate various intentions. Sometimes children learn to use signs or words to communicate with themselves but are unable to use them to communicate with others. This was the case with one disordered boy who, as he climbed up steps, would sign *up* to himself; while walking he would sign *walk,* and so forth. However, he could not at first use his signs to tell a staff person to perform particular actions. The moment he signed *up* or *walk,* he felt compelled to produce the required action himself. His problem was solved when the syncretic merger between signing and body action was interrupted by restraining him so that he could produce the sign without the action. Then, he was free to see the effect of his sign commands on a staff person who would walk or climb stairs as the child directed. Subsequently, the boy used his entire sign vocabulary to "order" various staff members to perform various actions.

An autistic girl with verbal ability showed a somewhat similar problem. She had learned to use words to accompany her actions within a multisphere arrangement but could not detach the words from their original sources with the sphere. Thus, she could use the relevant phrases "cut the clay," "pin up paper," and "cup on hook," while performing tasks related to these words, but she could not detach the verbs so that they could be used with different nouns, for example, "cut the paper." Only by repetitively changing the relations between verbs and nouns and acting out the new meanings was she finally able to detach the words from their original spheres. Chapters 5, 8, 9, and 10 detail a range of strategies that help children differentiate their linguistic systems so that they can use signs, words, and pictures to relate to varied aspects of their world.

The fusion of words with their referents, so typical of early language development, is not merely an obstacle to the child's achievement of new capacities, particularly if they entail symbol stage functioning. Although this interpretation may be true initially, it is possible to exploit the fusion tendency to help a disordered child make the transition from symbolic-sign to symbol stage functioning, at least with regard to reading capacity. Many disordered children, when first told that printed words, such as *cup* or *hat,* signify their respective objects, refuse to accept this relation because the printed words do not resemble the objects the spoken words lead them to expect. However, animated motion picture procedures (Miller & Miller, 1968, 1971) that first show the expected object and then transform it into the representative printed word, have enabled disordered children to achieve sight reading and then phonetic reading and writing. The specific procedures are described in Chapters 6 and 11.

INTEGRATING CENTER WITH HOME

Although the strategies described clearly help disordered children make important gains, by themselves they are insufficient. For the work of the Language and Cognitive Development Center to have full impact a close alliance must exist between the child's family and the Center staff. Dramatic progress occurs most frequently when the reality systems developed at the Center can be expanded to include comparable systems at home (see Chapter 8). Then, a child has the opportunity to note that concepts developed in one place also have relevance at home and in other places.

Because the Center staff collaborate closely with parents, the child can generalize what he or she learns at the Center to the home. For example, parents learn to apply spheres developed at the Center to the various tasks that have to be done in every home, such as dealing with trash, clearing the table, placing groceries in cupboards or refrigerator, cleaning, and going to the supermarket. Workers view each task as a potential system and encourage the parents to include the child within it.

Although, typically, parents are pleased to follow through on staff suggestions, at times parents' issues get in the way. Sometimes, for example, a parent—referred to diagnostically as a High Support–Low Demand parent—assumes an extremely protective stance that precludes making appropriate demands on the child. Other times a parent—known as a High Demand–Low Support parent—denies anything is wrong with the child and assumes a very tough, uncompromising stance. Obviously, both patterns work against a child's development; the most effective pattern, which the Center encourages, is one of High Support–High Demand.

When counterproductive patterns impede work with a particular child, individual psychotherapy, group therapy, or family therapy at the Center may be recommended. In addition, there are available to parents a variety of support groups for mothers, fathers, or both parents. The Center also offers education groups on developmental or program issues, such as developing sign language skills for families of nonverbal disordered children.

With this kind of support structure and the kind of collegial relationship that the Center encourages, parents follow through on the Center's program at home and find that their child not only can perform a range of activities but can benefit in functional and social capacities from this involvement. Chapter 12 describes in some detail the range of activities that are designed to bring Center and home into close and effective working relationship. The importance of this relationship is suggested by the behavior of one child who was very responsive to and seemed to delight in being with his therapist but ignored her completely when he was with his classroom teacher or when his mother was present. Such behavior stems from the child having embedded each person in his or her respective system. Thus, except in her therapeutic context, the therapist could not exist. Obviously, progress for this child would include achieving the ability to relate to his therapist and others as people independent of their location, an outcome that requires careful planning to interconnect therapeutic, teacher, and home systems.

SUMMARY

This chapter introduces the concept of reality systems and their relation to *sign, symbolic-sign,* and *symbol stages* of development. It examines the parallels between the reality systems of normal infants and those of disordered children. It also describes the manner in which systems form from *orienting, engagement,* and *compensatory reactions* to salient stimuli. Attention is given the role of *interruption* as it triggers a compensatory reaction that possesses some of the characteristics of intentional behavior. *Complete interruption*—loss of the originally engaging object or event—relates to an enhanced experience of the body or body part in relation to a particular object or event. This experience leads, ultimately, to an integrated body schema as well as to the capacity to cope with reality. It also helps develop expressive gestures that, when paired with utterances, contribute to spoken language.

Partial interruption—occurring when the engaging object or event is absent, but secondary input is available—enables the child to respond to a secondary part of the system as if it were the originally engaging object or event. This capacity leads eventually to receptive understanding of spoken words.

Finally, the chapter demonstrates the relevance of formulations for both lateral and vertical development. By *lateral* is meant the ability to cope with objects in various sequences; *vertical* refers to the means of representing the experience of reality to oneself and to others. In this context the special system problems of disordered children are discussed as well as the manner in which the application of *minispheres, multispheres,* and *integrative spheres* may help resolve them. Thus for the overengaged child, the utility of a multisphere approach is described, whereas for the scattered child, the positive assistance of integrative spheres is outlined.

The chapter ends with a consideration of the importance of the alliance between professionals and parents to help disordered children generalize their new learning to the home and elsewhere. Both productive and counterproductive attitudes that parents have toward their children are mentioned as well as some of the structures used to foster optimal development.

CHAPTER 2

Developing the Body Schema

DEFINING THE BODY SCHEMA CONSTRUCT

When a person stubs a toe or burns a finger, attention is drawn to the injured member and is maintained in this way as long as the pain lingers. Yet, even when no such pain defines a body part, there is a continuing sense of the location and function of a hand or foot or the manner in which one side of the body differs from but is related to the other. This knowledge is indispensable whether for climbing a set of stairs or skiing down a mountainside. Most human beings also have a pretty good notion of where eyes, ears, nose, and mouth are located and the relation of each to the other—knowledge that is necessary to bring spoon to mouth or to rub an eye.

This continuing sense of the body derives from three sources: vision, balance organs (the vestibular system), and proprioception. The integration of sensory information from these sources has been termed "postural model of the body," "body image," or "body schema" by prominent neurologists such as Head (1926), Pick (1922), and Schilder (1950). They sought to account for the body distortions reported by patients who had brain lesions affecting the reception of sensory input or who had experienced amputation of a limb. Since then the terms not only have been used for the manner in which a person organizes body experience but have been broadened to include the manner in which a person acts, perceives, thinks, makes human contact, and communicates.

Up to this point the difference between awareness of the body per se and the body schema has not been defined. Although the two are clearly related, evidence indicates that the total notion of the body provided by the body schema does not necessarily conform to the sensory impressions that come from the body. For example, when a foot "falls asleep," the usual proprioceptive feedback from the foot is unavailable—almost as if it no longer existed—and it is difficult to walk without bending the ankle. Nevertheless, it is possible to do so by relying on other sources of the body schema to substitute visual impressions of the "sleeping" foot for the absent proprioception and by constantly comparing these visual impressions of motion with those of the normal foot.

The problem of moving a foot, however, is part of the larger issue of how people are able to shift from one posture to another, as in the act of walking, running, or jumping. Head (1926) sought to account for this ability by proposing:

> By means of perpetual alterations in position we are always building up a postural model of ourself which constantly changes. Every new posture . . . is recorded on this plastic schema, and the activity of the cortex brings every fresh group of sensations evoked by altered posture into relation with it (the postural model). Immediate postural recognition follows as soon as the relation is complete. (p. 605)

The postural model of the body—an aspect of the body schema—is an everchanging gestalt that provides the sense of body position from which adjustments necessary to launch new action derive. But the postural model offers more than a framework for action; it gives a sense of being alive. Schilder (1950) commented that, "Only when every sensation is brought in connection with the postural model of the body are we becoming conscious of ourselves" (p. 64). A major source of input for this experience of the body self is the proprioceptive or reafferent feedback generated by any action. The importance of this source is suggested by the case of a woman (Sacks, 1985) who, due to a "sensory neuritis, affecting the sensory roots of spinal and cranial nerves" (p. 44), lost almost all proprioception. Sacks described her situation:

> Standing was impossible—unless she looked down at her feet. She could hold nothing in her hands, and they "wandered"—unless she kept an eye on them. When she reached out for something, or tried to feed herself, her hands would miss, or overshoot wildly, as if some essential control or coordination was gone. She could scarcely even sit up—her body "gave way." Her face was oddly expressionless and slack, her jaw fell open, even her vocal posture was gone. "Something awful's happened," she mouthed, in a ghostly flat voice. "I can't feel my body. I feel weird—disembodied." (p. 44)

Ultimately, this young woman learned to walk and to carry out everyday tasks by substituting visual feedback for the lost proprioception. She succeeded only by maintaining great vigilance. If her attention was momentarily diverted she could readily lose the function with which she was engaged. However, even with this limited success, she continued to feel that her body was dead and stated: "I feel my body is blind and deaf to itself . . . it has no sense of itself" (p. 49).

We learn more about the body schema and its relative independence from the body through work done with patients who experience the illusion that limbs lost through amputation or accident continue to exist. At times this phantom limb illusion is so compelling that a patient unthinkingly begins a sequence of actions based on the presence of the missing part. Schilder (1951), in this regard, commented on an invalid "who was once sitting on a high chest and did not realize that he did not have his two legs and jumped down and hurt himself rather badly" (p. 54).

One indication that the phantom is a compensatory expression of a fully developed body schema is the finding (Kolb, 1954) that small children who have experienced amputations do not report phantoms, presumably because they have not yet built up the integrated body schema required to project a phantom. With an adult amputee the phantom appears immediately after the amputation and then gradually fades, moving closer to the site of the amputation as the person adjusts to the absence of the limb. Sometimes the phantom persists for years. Schilder (1951, p. 54) cited the case of a person who lost his hands while shooting and maintained a phantom for many years that preserved the last position of the hands prior to their loss. Sacks (1985) cited a similar case of a sailor who accidentally cut off his right index finger and was plagued for 40 years by "an intrusive phantom of the finger rigidly extended, as it was when cut off" (pp. 63–64). In general, the formation and the maintenance of such persistent phantoms signify a compensatory disposition to project the body's continuing integrity by activating, through the phantom, the original body schema.

If the phantom is a compensatory expression of an interrupted body schema (system), then the phantom response is most likely when the body schema is *suddenly* disrupted (interrupted) by loss of a body part because the schema does not have time to adjust to the new contours of the body. Support for this view derives from the finding that not all losses of a limb result in phantoms. Schilder noted (1950, p. 54) and Simmel (1956) confirmed, that the phantom limb experience only occurs when a limb is lost *suddenly,* by amputation or trauma. A person who loses a limb because of tuberculosis, diabetes, or some other chronic disease, does not have the phantom limb experience. Neither does it happen, as Kolb (1954) pointed out, if the amputated limb was not used for a long time prior to the loss. In testing the importance of sudden loss of a functioning limb, Simmel studied 18 patients suffering from leprosy who had lost body parts either abruptly through amputation or gradually through the absorption process characteristic of leprosy. She found that all patients with amputations experienced phantom parts, whereas no patients with part loss related to gradual absorption reported phantoms. These findings support the present view that the phantom is a compensatory response to the disruption—through amputation or sudden loss of a functioning body part—of the fully developed body schema.

If the body schema is formed by direct contact of body parts with reality, it seems reasonable to assume that, following amputation of a body part, the persistence of the phantom that develops should be related to the lost part's potential for sensitive contact with the immediate environment. Consistent with this view was the observation by Schilder (1950) that the phantoms lasting longest were related to parts of the body in close and varied contact with the external world, notably hands and feet. Thus, hand phantoms persisted longest because they related to the part of the arm that "comes in varied relations to objects. The other parts of the arm have comparatively little contact with the varied experience the touch of objects gives" (p. 64). In this way, Schilder accounted for the repeated finding that in a phantom of the arm, the hand came nearer to the elbow, or in the disappearance of a phantom foot the patient felt first the toes and heel with nothing in between and then experienced the heel disappearing before the toes "[because] contacts of the anterior part of the toe are more varied than the contacts of the heel" (p. 64).

Entirely consistent with Schilder's finding was the observation by Simmel (1956) that the order in which the phantoms disappear relates to their part representation in the Penfield-Boldrey homunculus projected on the sensorimotor cortex. These size representations were discovered during brain surgery by stimulating points on the sensorimotor cortex of the conscious patient and noting specific body movements and areas of reported body sensation. In relating phantom disappearance to the homunculus, Simmel stated:

> Those (body) parts which have large areas of representation on the homunculus . . . are the very same parts which have the longest phantom life. By contrast, those (body) parts which have minimal representation on the homunculus are relatively short lived phantoms. (p. 643)

Although the body schema may appear largely restricted to body boundaries, the evidence suggests that it not only can go beyond the confines of the body but can do so in a highly variable, adaptive, and idiosyncratic manner. Sacks (1985), citing Weir Mitchell, a Civil War physician, noted the necessity of such an extension beyond body boundaries if an amputee was to use a prosthesis successfully. Thus, if an amputee who was to be fitted with an artificial leg had lost his phantom, vigorous efforts would be made to bring it back by peripherally stimulating the stump. One patient had to "wake up" his phantom each morning by first flexing the thigh stump toward himself and then slapping it sharply. On the fifth or sixth slap the phantom would reappear, enabling him to put on his prosthesis and walk. Apparently, walking became possible because the phantom (body schema) had extended to include the prosthesis. Such extensions of the body schema are consistent with a view of it as a system that constantly changes while interacting with the world.

The variable nature of the body schema—and the manner in which it "takes in" and expresses the nature of subjective reality via sensory input from both the external and internal environment—has been well documented by the studies of Wapner and Werner (1965) and their associates at Clark University. For example, in one study, Wapner, McFarland, and Werner (1962) found that in open space the schema expands whereas in constricted space it contracts. In danger situations the entire body schema seems to become more defined, presumably so that functional action to protect the body is enabled. Further, during a "high" or "low" mood—as in psychologically induced success or failure (Wapner, Werner, & Krus, 1957)—the changed body schema is expressed in an upward (success) or downward (failure) experience of eye level. This effect is also evident with manic-depressive psychotics in manic or depressive phases (Rosenblatt, 1956). A related study (Miller, Werner, & Wapner, 1958) showed that changes in the body experience—feelings of rising and falling—induced by ascending and descending tones were accompanied by corresponding changes in the apparent movement of a pinpoint of light in a dark room.

Also contributing to the structuring of the body schema are pain stimuli from inside the body (hunger pains, etc.) as well as from collisions with outside objects. In addition, when planned action requires one part of the body to move in a certain way, that aspect of the body schema becomes more figurally defined while other aspects of the body schema lapse into the background. The findings of Jacobson (1931) and Shaw (1940) support this view. Shaw (1940) found that people thinking about lifting various weights produced muscle action potentials (maps) in their arms related to the anticipated heaviness of the weights. Jacobson found that merely thinking about bending an arm (but not doing so) induced maps in those arm muscles involved in actually bending the arm. Further, if the subject was requested to *visualize* bending the arm, the maps would shift from the arm to the ocular region. This shifting of maps is the physiological correlate of the shifting figural definition of the body schema. The intent to move a foot momentarily makes the foot part figural (increased maps) until a hand intends action at which point the hand part becomes figural, and so on. Various parts of the body schema are involved in constant, everchanging waves of accented peaking and shifting of maps, depending on the location of the intended movement.

Prior to developing the body schema the body can reflexively relate and adjust only to those objects, events, and people with which it is directly engaged. However, once the body schema forms, early contacts are organized, internalized within the body schema, and become "portable." They provide a framework for anticipating and relating to objects, events, and people at a distance from the body. At this point the developing body schema becomes a hierarchically organized system grounded in the body but ranging far beyond it.

The hierarchic nature of the body schema means that two kinds of systems are always in play. One is concerned with maintaining the body schema's integrity; the other draws on body–object systems acquired in earlier stages of development. Thus, the body schema is both a structural entity organized around the physical contours of the body and a process that makes earlier systems from a body repertoire of means–ends relationships available for problem solving. The activation of the body schema's problem-solving capacity depends on challenges to its organization as a system. Any system—no matter how complex—shows a tendency, when system integrity is compromised, to restore it through compensatory activity. As previously noted, the compensatory activity of the body schema may become evident through the formation of a phantom limb when the body schema is interrupted through the sudden loss of a body part (Sacks, 1985; Schilder, 1950); or it may become evident when a cognitive process is interrupted, as in an aphasic person's inability to remember a particular spoken word (Head, 1926), in which case the body schema facilitates earlier gesture meanings that aid in the word's retrieval.

This chapter and the next can be viewed as two sides of a body–world coin, with this chapter emphasizing the body schema side; whereas Chapter 3 emphasizes the world-coping side. Clearly, both the developing body schema and the expanding reality with which the child copes are concurrent, functionally inextricable events that are artificially separated only to permit focusing first on one and then on the other. This chapter follows the infant's development from a being unable to distinguish the self from the surroundings to one that can coordinate body parts with vision and hearing to act toward objects and events. Chapter 3 details the extension of the body beyond its boundaries to cope with and make sense of objects and events in different times and places.

BODY SCHEMA DEFICITS AMONG DISORDERED CHILDREN

One of the infant's central tasks during the 1st year or so of life is to discover the boundaries of the body and the means by which the various body parts work together under the guidance of vision, hearing, and touch. In the course of achieving this organization, signal-triggered reflexive responses and rhythmical stereotypies are developed into an array of body part systems that are—toward the end of the infant's 2nd year—integrated into a body schema that provides a framework for reality-oriented action. Unfortunately, many disordered children fail to achieve the integration that results in a functional body schema. By observing their responses in a variety of demand situations, it is possible to group disordered children in terms of how their body–world organization interferes with body schema development. Depending on the kind of body schema problem present, a child at the Center is referred to as having a *system-forming disorder,* a *closed-system disorder,* or a *syncretic system disorder.*

System-Forming Disorder

One group of children—often diagnosed as brain-damaged or as having seizure disorders—show scattered and disconnected behavior that seems to preclude relating their bodies in any organized way to their surroundings. On the ground these children display great difficulty forming coherent systems because they are constantly "caught" by events around them. They do much better on elevated board structures because the boards help organize them by guiding them from one part of a situation to another. However, even with the structured guidance of the boards, these children require many repetitions before they can form a behavioral system. To learn something new, a child must first build a system around an object or event and then expand the system by exploring it to discover other properties. Children with system-forming disorders have great difficulty doing this because, victimized by their reactivity, they are jerked from one salient event to another in a way that precludes their forming connected systems leading to a coherent experience of either their bodies or reality.

Such behavior has important features in common with the normal infant's "disconnected" state from 3 to 6 months of age. Piaget (1954) described how the infant of 3 to 4 months experiences reality in disconnected fashion by orienting successively toward a "mouth space," a "visual space," an "auditory space," a "tactile space," and so on. Like disordered system-forming children, at first the baby directs activities toward the "space" with the most salient stimuli, without regard to the others. The baby does not use hands to seize the bottle because the bottle belongs to the mouth space and thus is engaged only with the lips. Similarly, an object felt with the hands has only a tactile space totally separate from the visual experience of the same object. Until the different spaces become integrated, the infant may not recognize his or her own moving body parts. Piaget noted in this regard that his daughter Jacqueline at 4 months was frightened by the visual impression of her hand as it moved toward her nose and finally hit her in the eye. Obviously, when either the normal infant or the child with a system-forming disorder lacks coordination of impressions from different sensory spaces, neither the body experience nor the experience of objects can have a continuing existence because each tends to disappear and reappear as it is subject to stimulation from first one then another sense modality.

Closed-System Disorder

In contrast to the heightened and indiscriminate reactivity of children with system-forming disorders, children with closed-system disorders—frequently diagnosed as autistic—often seem quite oblivious of even intrusive stimulation. Frequently they cannot readily distinguish where their bodies end and the world begins. Consequently, such children are often as unreactive to injury as to other impinging events and seem unable to distinguish themselves from others. Perhaps because of their uncertain body boundaries, these children are readily guided into ritualized systems (usually involving objects). Often they require only a few cycles of an elevated board sequence before establishing a ritual that is readily transferred to the ground, where they can also build new rituals if properly paced. However, once such a child forms a ritualized system it tends to remain closed because the child seems unable to spontaneously vary or expand it.

Children with closed-system disorders may have a few stereotypies that they produce in many situations. Typically, other people have no special relevance for them; nor do words, gestures, or sounds from the immediate surroundings have significance. Such children may not be able to mimic actions or sounds and have no means of communicating needs except, perhaps, through tantrums or crying that can be interpreted by their parents. Although they may produce strange sounds or babbling, these sounds are internally driven and do not change in response to an outside stimulus.

More insight into the nature of closed-system disorders can be gained by noting the manner in which normal infants begin with relatively closed systems and then gradually open them. Mahler, Pine, & Bergman (1967) have observed that during the first 5 months of life "the infant behaves and functions as though he and his mother were an omnipotent dual unity within one common boundary" (p. 290). However, a mutual cuing or signaling develops within this relatively closed system—first the mother's moving of her body to adjust to the infant, then the infant's moving or grunting—a dynamic engagement in which the infant adjusts or molds body contours to closely conform with the mother's body. The adaptive aspects of such an infant–mother system are evident in the enhanced life support—feeding, warmth, nurturing, protection—that the mother provides. Equally important is the emotional bond between mother and infant forged by their fusion of boundaries.

If such systems, and the subtle interactions they entail, characterize normal development, then closed systems that preclude infant–mother interchange characterize the disordered child's aberrant form of development. These closed systems may include body parts or objects but not people. Once formed, the systems are not readily modified by external events. In spite of changing circumstances the children tend to reproduce the same unmodified behavior. Their system rigidity may stem from difficulty initiating or interrupting the engagement with an object or event in order to engage with another person, object, or event, or to relate one event to another. Instead, they become stuck in stereotyped repetitions of early systems and have to wait until more compelling circumstances drive them into another closed system. As a consequence, such children have little sense of spatial extent and readily get lost going from place to place. They react to objects and events in their surroundings—not through any purposeful act toward them—but by inadvertently colliding with them.

In general, children with closed-system disorders will, when given input, such as a new activity, object, person, resist relating to and thus incorporating it; however, they will more readily take in objects than people. The existence of closed systems is one important reason why certain children, often but not invariably those designated autistic, have difficulty learning in conventional fashion.

Syncretic System Disorder

Children with syncretic system disorders differ from those with closed-system and system-forming disorders. Children suffering from a syncretic system disorder, often diagnosed as childhood schizophrenia, tend to fuse their thoughts, dreams, or fantasies (inner systems) with what is happening in reality because of poorly defined boundaries between the self and the world. As a result, they may either experience their own feelings of anger, distress, or sadness as coming from outside or react to others' feelings as if they were their own. Although all children demonstrate a certain amount of syncretism during their early development (Werner, 1948), children with a syncretic system disorder continue this fusion tendency at older ages and have difficulty in sorting out reality from fantasy.

Children with either syncretic system disorders or closed-system disorders lack an adequate body–world organization. However, the two disorders differ in the way the organization breaks down. Children with closed-system disorders have not systematized the body parts and functions in a way that clearly distinguishes them from nonbody entities. Consequently, these children have difficulty using their bodies as the framework from which to act toward and explore objects and events in their surroundings. Children with syncretic system disorders, in contrast, present no such action–object problem but, instead, have a system breakdown at a cognitive-affective level. Because their inability to cohere and own their thoughts and feelings prevents identifying them as *self*-generated, they are unable to distinguish inner life from outer reality. The confusion that results, so evident in their thought and language, characterizes children with syncretic system disorders.

Characteristic of all system-disordered children, although for different reasons, is an impairment in the ability to react to, cope with, and influence the world. The passivity such children demonstrate toward external events suggests that they do not readily feel capable of changing or modifying their circumstances. Behind this impairment is a fundamental lack of polarity between the body and the external world. Lacking a clear sense of the body or self in relation to the world, they cannot sense that they exist as separate entities or that they can "cause things to happen" in a manner so characteristic of children with normal body schema development.

THE DEVELOPING BODY SCHEMA: OUTCOME OF EFFICACY AND DISRUPTION

Two dispositions come into play in the formation of the body schema. One, an active disposition, derives from the infant's sense of the body as a "zone of efficacious intent" (Piaget, 1954, pp. 228–229) that generates influential actions; the other, a reactive disposition, is operative when the infant—in response to disruptive stimulation such as pain—detaches the body from its surroundings. Both forces, finally, result in a human organism aware of a separate existence and able to cope with and represent the world to the self and others.

The Body as a "Zone of Efficacious Intent"

A feature that sharply distinguishes normal children from many who are disordered is the feeling of being able to cause an effect on the world. Even before achieving basic awareness of body parts and how they are responsive to intentions, the normal infant has a vague sense that certain body actions are somehow related to outcomes. However, because the infant's body is not well defined in terms of its parts or the mechanical functions of these parts, the infant has no clear understanding of the consequences of body actions. At best the infant diffusely senses that his or her action has caused something that is not quite part of the body to do something.

For example, when Piaget's daughter Jacqueline, at 8 months, drew herself up on her shoulder blades and dropped down as her father swung a saucer in front of her eyes, and then repeated this behavior five or six times more after her father interrupted his activity by holding the saucer motionless, *she behaved as if her actions were functionally engaged with the moving object, as if her repeating this action sequence would keep the object moving.* Even though she still lacked a clear sense that there had to be direct physical contact between what she did and a particular outcome, she clearly expected her action somehow to have an effect on the plate. It seems likely that the same diffuse sense of efficacy that enabled Jacqueline to relate her body actions to the moving plate was operating in the important studies by Rovee and her colleagues (Rovee & Rovee, 1969; Rovee-Collier, Morrongiello, Aron, & Kupersmidt, 1978) that showed the transformation of a repetitive stereotypy, infant kicking, into an instrumental behavior. The authors showed that 2- to 3-month-old infants who activated a mobile by kicking, using a cord tied from the leg to the mobile, showed rapid and sustained increases in kick rate in contrast to control infants exposed to mobile movement when they were not kicking. The experimental group also learned to increasingly limit their kicking to the leg tied to the mobile.

Rovee and her colleagues demonstrated the possibility of artificially structuring situations so that secondary circular reactions—expanded reality systems—develop. They showed that it is unnecessary to wait for the child to spontaneously transform a stereotypy into an expanded reality system; the likelihood of such an expansion can be facilitated, for example, by tying an infant's leg to a mobile. However, it is not the tying of leg to mobile, per se, that causes the infant to increase leg kicking, it is the child's formation of a kicking leg–mobile moving system when he or she experiences body motion as influential—as causing the mobile to move. Only when the infant experiences leg kicking as *acting upon* the mobile can the augmentation of kicking occur. The following model suggests this sequence: Infant kicks, mobile moves (a system forms); infant stops kicking momentarily, mobile slows (partial interruption); infant kicks more vigorously to compensatorily restore prior mobile movement level, and so forth.

Such compensatory activity would have the same system-maintaining purpose as that of Piaget's (1954, p. 22) 7-month-old son, Laurent, who after losing a cigarette box he had just grasped and swung to and fro, immediately looked at his empty hand for a long time with surprise and disappointment, then compensatorily swung his hand and looked at it again (apparently expecting that repeating the swinging gesture would bring with it the cigarette box). In all these examples the children behaved as if their body actions and the desired outcome (moving saucer, moving mobile, cigarette box), were part of the same totality. And, just as certain intentions to move the body result in a hand or foot moving, so other intentions to move the body cause an object or event to behave as a somewhat unreliable extension of the body (the mobile or the distant plate moves, the cigarette box reappears). Later, when these same outcomes can be produced relatively independent of an engaging stimulus (Piaget's deferred circular reaction), it is possible to infer a more differentiated relation between body and external reality because then the compensatory action has to be stored and self-initiated to bring about the desired outcome.

The early "causal" systems contribute toward this goal by (a) helping establish the body, no matter how diffusely organized, as a source of intention; and (b) providing a framework for storing compensatory dispositions to act in a certain way. The body becomes more defined as a zone for intentional activity each time the child experiences body activity as the "cause" of a particular event. However, when such a system does not work (e.g., the arching back does not move the plate; the swinging arm gesture does not reincarnate the cigarette box) the interruption triggers a series of unrequited body actions that, even after being abandoned, leave stored within the child's body a disposition to reproduce that body action. Further, each time the child fails to cause an event to happen there is increasing differentiation between those aspects of reality (the body) that directly respond to intention and those aspects (external objects) that do not.

Efficacy in the Sensory Guidance of Body Action

The same sense of efficacy that permits the infant to relate the body to various events also enables coordinating touch, vision, and hearing with body movement in order to deal in a more functional way with objects and events and to enhance understanding of body organization. Clearly, before the child can act in a deliberate and functional manner toward objects, the child must know the location of the body parts and be able to guide them toward objects through touch, vision, and hearing. The body and body parts become identified and coordinated with the senses through influential infant-generated activities. One kind of activity—apparent shortly after birth—

concerns the infant's systematic tactual-motor discovery of various body parts. In describing this tactual exploration, Twitchell (1965) referred to "instinctive grasp reactions" (p. 248), in which the infant's hand responds to slight stationary or moving contact stimuli by adopting a position of readiness for a series of slight palpating or grasping movements, followed by finally grasping the body part. Such stationary or moving contact stimuli act as signals that trigger the infant's moving hand to grasp the body part.

A study by Kravitz, Goldenberg, and Neyhus (1978) documents the order in which 12 normal infants sequentially explored with their hands the mouth, face, ears, head, nose, and eyes during the first 3 days of life. With another group these investigators found that in the course of the first 26 weeks of life, 100 normal male infants explored and tactually discovered in sequential fashion the hand (12 weeks), torso (15 weeks), knee (16 weeks), foot (19 weeks), penis (26 weeks). It is interesting to note that this body part discovery pattern conforms to the cephalo-caudal principle (Coghill, 1929) asserting that development of the head-and-trunk region precedes that of the lower part of the body.

But how, once discovered, does a body part such as the hand get individuated and guided by vision as well as touch so that it can be used in a more deliberate and functional manner? Recent evidence (Thelen, 1981) suggests that the infant's "prewired" disposition toward rhythmical stereotypic actions of various body parts may facilitate visual guidance and functional use of these parts. Evidence supporting this view comes from Thelen's finding that the rhythmical stereotypic activity of body parts by infants in her study systematically preceded their ability to use those parts in a functional manner. Thus, repetitive waving of arms and hands preceded the ability to use arms and hands in a directed manner. Similarly, rhythmical stereotypies involving kicking of legs and feet preceded the ability to stand and walk. In no case did an infant achieve functional action with a particular body part without first having gone through rhythmical stereotypic action with that part.

The emergence of functional activity—for example, directed use of the hands after rhythmical stereotypic waving of the hands—suggests that rhythmical activity, although at first intentionless, becomes intentional as it "invites" integration of vision with that activity. Infants performing rhythmical stereotypies of body parts, such as, arm–hand waving, learn to visually guide their arm–hand movements through the same sequence of orienting, engagement, and compensatory reaction first described for involvement with external objects (Chapter 1). Consistent with this view are Preyer's (1889) observations that the infant was engaged by the motion of his arms and legs just as by the flickering flame of a candle and that he looked at his grasping hand as attentively as at any foreign object.

Suppose, following our model, that the infant in the course of rhythmically waving the arms, pauses momentarily. The sudden cessation of movement stimulation causes the child to orient toward (look at) the arm that had been moving. Then, when the arm again moves as part of its prewired rhythmic stereotypic tendency, the infant becomes engaged by it (visually tracks the arm's motion). As this sequence occurs, the infant's visuo-motor engagement with his or her own arm movements becomes a system. This means that the arm-engaged infant's next pause in rhythmical arm activity will be experienced as an *interrupted* system that needs to be maintained by compensatorily jerking the arm back into the former movement pattern. While performing this motion, the child has the opportunity to note the congruity between the sudden visual displacement of the arm and the reafferent sensations that come from the arm's sudden motion. After a number of such compensatory actions, the infant has a framework for guiding the repetitive motion of the arm.

How does an infant's visually guided arm–hand system begin to include auditory input? Suppose the infant crudely moving his or her visually guided arm and hand happens to bump the hand into an object, producing a scratching sound. As Piaget found, the infant is disposed to repeat the activity, guiding the hand repeatedly toward the point of contact so that the sound can again be heard. When this occurs, the child has expanded the original visually guided arm–hand system to include sound making by *acting upon* a particular object. In this way not only the sight but the sound and feel of the object become integrated into an expanded system that began with the visually guided arm and hand. Similar integration of sound and vision into expanded systems may occur as the infant, after shaking a rattle or other noisemaking objects, finds that a particular sound occurs and that, after pausing, the sound may be reproduced by repeating the shaking movement. This leads to the following principle:

> Whenever one engaging system acts upon a new property of an object or event, for example, sound or tactual quality, that property becomes an expanded part of the original system. The infant then maintains the integrity of the newly expanded system when it is interrupted just as if it were the original system.

Thus, having expanded the arm–hand system to include the sound and feel of the object, any interruption of that scratching sound or the feel of that object triggers a compensatory waving arm action that is visually guided toward the point of contact. As this waving arm–hand system acts upon other properties of objects, these different seen, felt, and heard properties are experienced as other expansions of the system.

As the visually guided arm–hand system *acts upon* other parts of the body (e.g., one hand fingers another, hand grabs foot), the child can observe that these seen and held body parts feel different from external objects. Eventually the child learns that body parts share certain visual and sensory qualities that distinguish them from nonbody objects—for example, body parts feel different from a teething ring. Perhaps some of the more vigorous infant behaviors described by Preyer (1889) are part of the infant's effort to differentiate the body from the world. Preyer, for example, reported that infants observe and touch themselves in the bath, especially their feet (39th week), and bang their heads violently against another object (41st week).

Disruption as a Factor in Body–World Differentiation

In spite of active, influential efforts at distinguishing the body from the world, the child must still depend on reactivity to events that act on the body for adequate body–world differentiation. The substantial fusion between the infant's body action and the immediate surroundings has been noted by Mahler et al. (1967), who commented that the infant's body seems to blend into and conform with the contours of the mother. However, if the infant is to become a relatively autonomous human, the growing baby must achieve separate body boundaries while maintaining the relationship with the mother, with other persons, and with objects. Only as these body boundaries begin to exist can the infant actively explore the immediate environment.

One circumstance that seems to help body boundaries develop is periodic disruptions—interruptions—of the mother–infant system by either inner or outer events. Inner disruptive events include hunger, colic, and ear infections; whereas disruptive outer events, referred to as *collisions,* include sudden contacts, movements, or sounds that affect the infant's body. When engaged by a sudden pain (colic, earache), the infant stiffens arms and legs and arches the back away from the mother. As Mahler et al. (1967) pointed out, both the pain and the stiffening may help the infant distinguish his or her body from that of the mother. Then, as the pain ebbs, the infant may become aware of the loss of intimate contact with the mother and seek compensatorily to restore it. The infant's shifting investment in mother-molding and separation-stiffening may provide one means whereby the infant begins to experience the body as separate from but related to his or her mother's body. Ultimately, the normal infant learns to carry the mother-blending feeling internally even while moving away from the mother. It may well be that the balance between blending and apartness established at this time affects the child's later emphasis on social versus more separate ways of being.

One of the reactive factors that trigger the separation-stiffening cycle is the experience of pain. In discussing pain Uexküll (1928) suggests that it is biologically necessary for survival because it signals the existence of one's own body and serves to prevent self-mutilation. Yet, even as late as 10 months of age, according to Dix (1911–1923), the normal child does not respond to pain as one might expect, but bangs his or her head on the wall as if it were a foreign object; with others, during the first few months of life, a bleeding wound provokes no pain reaction. Such behavior occurs because the developing infant has not yet established a body schema that locates the pain in a certain part of the body. Failing to locate the pain, the infant may be unable to experience it.

Observations of pain response at the Center among severely autistic children (3 to 6 years of age) with closed-system disorders have been quite similar to Dix's for children under a year of age. On a number of occasions an autistic child has either displayed no reaction or expressed, at most, a diffuse distress after falling or being struck on the head by a block.

How serious this problem of receiving and/or interpreting input from various parts of the body is for autistic children was brought home one day when a worker was attempting unsuccessfully to engage the attention of a large, 15-year-old autistic boy who was profoundly involved with his twiddling fingers. Finally, in order to elicit a response the worker stepped on and maintained steady pressure on his shoe. After about 15 seconds the twiddling slowed; after another 15 seconds the boy slowly looked down to examine his foot's situation; after another 15 seconds one could note a slight tugging as he sought to withdraw his foot; at the end of a full minute he successfully withdrew his foot.

Fortunately, after intensive work to help the child define his or her body— as seen in the ability to correctly point to body parts on request—such a child will respond to pain or pressure on the body more appropriately and often learns to bring the hurt part to the teacher for comfort. At this point the disordered child behaves like the normal child who, after active involvement with his or her own body during the 1st and 2nd years of life, no longer needs to continue that pattern. Having visually and tactually grasped the general boundaries of the body and the location of its parts, the child need no longer investigate it in this way.

Thus, in contrast to normal development where the experience of pain may play an important role in distinguishing the body from its surroundings, the limited ability of many disordered children to experience pain or other tactual-motor feedback from their body sensations (Ornitz, 1985, 1987; Rimland, 1964) may be a factor in their delayed body–world differentiation. Obviously, the child who cannot readily discern that the body feels different from nonbody sources of stimulation, will be hampered in defining boundaries and, perhaps, in feeling alive. The tendency of some autistic children to compensate for this boundary deficit by seeking "edge experiences" has been described earlier (Miller & Miller, 1973). The article cited one 5-year-old autistic girl who frequently climbed outside her 3d-story window and hung by her fingertips until discovered and pulled to safety. Another autistic child sought curbstones and would walk with one foot on the curb and the other in the street; still another child constantly crossed the changing boundary between beach and water. A 7-year-old girl—initially quite fearless on boards elevated 3 to 6 feet above the ground—suddenly became quite tentative and fearful when, after a period of body-defining work, she became more aware of her own existence. Such repetitive emphasis on the interface between body boundaries and immediate surroundings, although quite common among autistic children, is usually a transitory phenomenon among normal children, who readily translate their collisions with reality into the distinction between what is and what is not their bodies.

When normal children experience the differentiation of the body from its surroundings, which disordered children develop only through intervention, they are able to use the body in a more deliberate and functional manner. Instead of the magical and diffuse causal extensions previously described, the child begins to store pragmatic body action dispositions. The manner in which stored action dispositions are called into play is suggested by the 13-month-old child (Werner & Kaplan, 1963) who "lifted his leg fully 3 feet before he reached the first step" (p. 93) and who, 2 months later, while looking for his sand shovel, "made shoveling movements with his right arm as he held his hand in a scooping position" (p. 93).

Here, the advance over Jacqueline's arching back and dropping behavior to get the stalled saucer to move is evident. Now, the body is sufficiently defined so that its actions are clearly understood by the child as tool functions of the body directly related to particular outcomes (climbing stairs, shoveling). Accordingly, the causality implied between body action and outcome is more pragmatic and less magical. During the next 6 months, the child learns to exploit the properties of the body as one side of the body gets integrated with the other so that objects may be passed from hand to hand, so that hands may address an object asymmetrically (as when one hand holds a jar while the other unscrews the lid). In addition, obstacles may be stepped over or detoured to get desired objects.

Gradually, through the sense that they can cause things to happen, through engagement with the motion of their body parts (with the addition of diffuse causal experiences that may or may not bring about expected outcomes), and through the reaction to disruptive influences such as collisions, pain, and "edge experiences," the child achieves awareness of and intentional control of body parts. Unfortunately, this same kind of differentiation and control of body parts does not occur spontaneously with many disordered children. Often a disordered child's functioning provides evidence that the process of body schema formation has progressed to permitting control of body parts under one condition but not under another. This was the case for Kevin, an 8-year-old autistic boy, who was being taught to swim by one of us (AM).

After much work, I had finally taught Kevin how to move his arms for the "dog paddle" in the water. He was having great difficulty, however, coordinating the leg kick with his arm movements. Each time he tried to swim he would use only his arms—allowing his extended legs to gradually settle to the bottom. To help him with this task, I had him kick to my command while lying on his back in shallow water in a way which allowed him to see and feel himself kicking. He did well with this. However, as soon as I had him turn over on his stomach and try to kick, he failed completely to move his legs. Only after

repeated experiences of my moving his legs vigorously in rhythm with "kick
. . . kick . . . kick!" commands and with the help of his looking over his
shoulder to see what his legs were doing, was he finally able to kick on command
without seeing his legs.

Clearly, Kevin had developed a partial body schema or else he could not
have deliberately moved his legs under any condition. Yet, his awareness
of leg function was largely limited to those conditions in which he could see
as well as feel his legs' actions. Moving his legs on command, when he could
not see them, required a more developed body schema than he had; it
required an internalized notion of how his arms and legs worked solely on
the basis of proprioception. Once he had incorporated kicking sensations
into his body schema he could kick in any position without having to see
his legs.

Other useful strategies that parallel the normal body–world differentiation
process and help disordered children develop more adequate body schemas
are indicated in the following section.

Establishing Body–World Differentiation among Disordered Children

Lacking the sense that they can influence the world, disordered children
appear largely dependent on forces acting on the body to bring about required
differentiation. Often, system-disordered children seem to lack any clear
awareness of where their bodies end and the external world begins. They
behave very much like infants under a year of age who inadvertently bite
their hands or bang their heads as part of discovering how their bodies differ
from nonbody objects. Typically such children seem only marginally aware
of their own and others' existence and are either totally or variably unresponsive to sounds or words. Nevertheless, such children often can respond
and adjust to certain kinds of intrusive stimulation or to collisions with their
immediate surroundings. It is as if the sudden arousal (Des Lauriers &
Carlson, 1969) occasioned by such intrusive events momentarily accents the
boundaries between their own bodies and the event. If this is correct, then
one important task of the worker is to parlay such momentary awareness
of body–world relations into a continuing sense of the body as separate from
but related to its surroundings. One way to bring this about is to regularly
introduce an array of arousal strategies.

Arousal strategies include *Rough and Tumble* play, *Body Compression,*
selective tickling, the use of elevated board structures, and guided collisions
with obstacles and people. All arousal strategies entail the formation of
systems through repetition, followed by interruptions of these systems to
stimulate compensatory body reactions.

Rough and Tumble systems are initiated by the worker, with the child
lying on the floor facing upward. The worker begins playfully to roll the
child from side to side, interrupting periodically to determine whether or not

the child will compensatorily continue the rolling. This is followed by a Body Compression procedure in which the child—with back to the worker's chest—has knees pressed against his or her own chest by the worker's encircling arms and is then abruptly released. The alternation between compression and release, like that between the normal infant's mother-molding and separation stiffening, provides a contrasting experience that seems to enhance body–world awareness. Next, if a parent is available, the child can be playfully (but carefully) tossed back and forth, thrown in the air and caught under the arms, or tossed in a blanket. Some children also respond well to being swung first while being held under the arms and later—with the help of another person—while being held by ankles and under the arms (Figure 2.1).

All such throwing or swinging activities are periodically interrupted to determine if the child seeks their resumption. Obviously, care must be taken to adjust the level of stimulation to the child's ability to accept it, and the child's safety must always be paramount. For children who are too large (or staff who are too small) or when only one person is available, some of the movement techniques introduced by Ayres (1979), such as rolling a child on a large ball or using a swing, are useful substitutes to provide adequate vestibular stimulation and arousal. Here, too, the worker should periodically interrupt the movements to determine whether the child produces compensatory reactions to continue the system.

Following general arousal activity, the worker may seek to help the child define specific body parts through a combined teasing-tickling approach. The worker slowly approaches the child in a teasing manner saying, "I'm going to tickle your . . . [pausing to build up tension] . . . foot [nose, hand, tummy, etc.]," moving unpredictably to each part before tickling or touching that part, then interrupting to watch carefully for signs that the child is attempting

Figure 2.1. Child being swung to help develop improved body awareness.

to anticipate the location of the next tickle. This procedure may be supplemented by hiding parts of the child's body—a foot, hand—under blocks or a cloth and then asking, "Where is _____ 's [child's name] foot [hand]?"

Another arousal activity entails guiding the child on a narrow (10 in. wide) board elevated about 3 feet above the ground, to help induce an edge experience. The child becomes aware of the body's position above the ground and proceeds with great care, documenting an awareness of the body in contrast to the surroundings. This response dramatizes the polarity between the child's body and the surroundings. A child with this level of response can be guided through a series of obstacles such as found in the *Template Tunnel* (Figure 2.2), requiring the child to adjust the body to different templates in order to pass through. While turning and twisting to accommodate to the different templates, the child must attend to and note the location of body boundaries—shoulders, hips, legs, and so forth.

Still another procedure designed to enhance body experience involves the *Tip Stairs* (Figure 2.3). Under careful supervision, the child, after climbing a set of stairs, moves to the edge in preparation for jumping off; the weight shift suddenly tilts the stairtop, making it necessary to jump before being ready. After a number of repetitions the child begins to realize that a subtle shift of weight on top of the stairs triggers the tilt. As a consequence the child becomes more sensitive to the impact of the body on its immediate surroundings.

Also contributing to the goal of enhanced body–world differentiation is the *Change-of-Direction* structure. This structure is built like an X (Figure 2.4), with two openings where the X crosses. One opening allows the child to continue downward (leaning backwards to avoid striking the head) until

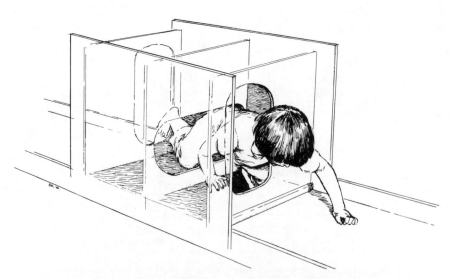

Figure 2.2. Child working her way through the Template Tunnel.

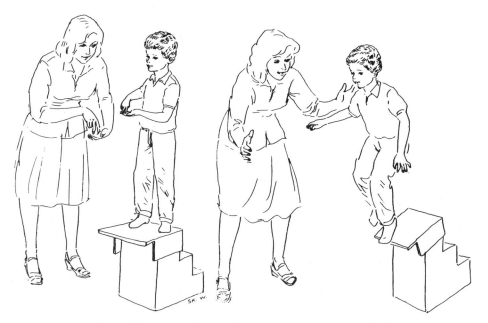

Figure 2.3. Child responding to the sign-word "Jump!" on the Tip Stairs.

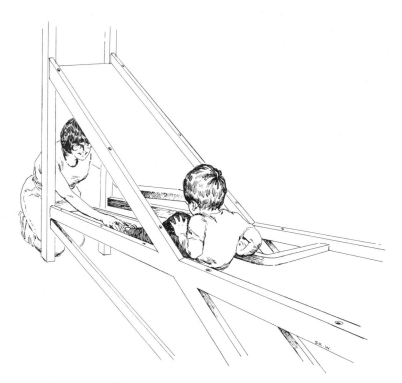

Figure 2.4. Child starting down the Change-of-Direction structure.

reaching the bottom; an adjacent opening allows the child to change direction and end up on the same side he or she started from. Children first learn to go down one leg of the X before being taught to change direction and go down the other side. Often the child offers some resistance before learning that there is an option to go one way or the other. The child's knowledge that change is possible even when caught by the downward valence of one facet of the system (midway down one part of the X), so that the reverse direction can be initiated down the other part of the X, communicates important understanding about the flexibility of the body in initiating changes.

In refusing to go down this structure, one 5-year-old autistic boy demonstrated how dependent his actions, and thus his body schema, were on visual input. Although this child went down a conventional slide without difficulty, he was panicked by the visual loss of the lower part of his body in this device (see Figure 2.4) as his legs passed through. He refused to continue through the hole until his mother peered up from the other side, touched his feet, and called him while gently pulling him through. After three or four trips down the slide, with mother calling and touching his feet, he gradually lost his fear. With the certainty that his legs continued to exist even if he momentarily could not see them, he then learned how to change direction.

In addition to achieving a more defined body–world relationship, children at the Center learn to function in a more organized and intentional manner. So that certain body parts come into focal awareness, each child's body is challenged with selected collisions through the use of *Parallel Boards, Mini-Mazes, Crawl Boards,* and *Swiss Cheese Boards.* To develop awareness of hands, the *Hand Box* is employed.

Parallel Boards situated 3 feet above the ground are used to help the child gain awareness of how one side of the body differs from the other. On this structure the child must learn to shift weight from one side of the body to the other in order to unweight one foot to move it forward on the board. A child unable to move the foot because of not having consciously distinguished one side of the body from the other is assisted by the worker, who touches the foot (Figure 2.5) to be moved or leans the child gently to one side to unweight the foot. This procedure is repeated for the other foot. As the child learns to deliberately move each side of the body on this structure, obstacles are placed so that the child must perform a different movement for each foot, such as pulling a foot back before lifting it over the obstacle on one side of the board and then merely lifting the other foot over the obstacle.

The *Mini-Maze* improves eye-hand-foot coordination by requiring the child, while situated 3 feet above the ground, to move step by step around a series of four large blocks positioned on parallel boards (Figure 2.6). In doing this the child not only learns to differentiate one side from the other, but also to coordinate hands and feet.

A somewhat similar but more demanding device is the *Crawl Board.* The task is to crawl by using the blocks placed on each side of the board for

Figure 2.5. (*a*) Parallel Boards used to help differentiate sides of the body. (*b*) Obstacles added to help accent awareness of feet.

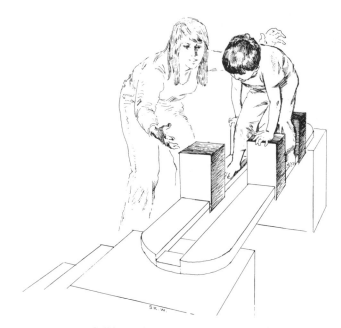

Figure 2.6. Child working her way through the Mini-Maze.

Figure 2.7. Supported child negotiating placement of hands and feet on the Crawl Board.

handholds and the spaces between the blocks for inserting the feet (Figure 2.7). To succeed, the child must first place the hands and then look backward to where the feet are located in order to guide them to spaces between the blocks. Typically, children proceed very slowly at first, requiring substantial assistance to place their hands and then to remember their feet so that they can move forward. To keep the task challenging, the positions of the blocks can be altered so that the child must keep attending to both hand and foot placement. To ensure safety in the event of a slip, the child wears a harness held by the worker.

The *Swiss Cheese Board,* elevated about 3 feet from the ground, is an important device for establishing improved awareness of eye–foot relations. This device requires the child to step around or across variously shaped holes while moving—with careful monitoring—from one end of the board to the other (Figure 2.8). As children master this device they are required to walk through it more rapidly to develop greater capacity to adjust to changing circumstances. Children who step into holes are caught but are usually startled by the sudden loss of balance; on subsequent trips it is important to determine if the child has learned from the experience and successfully avoids holes. Swiss Cheese Boards with different shapes (free form and geometric) are periodically introduced (see lower level of structure

Figure 2.8. Child on the Swiss Cheese Board responding to mother's sign-word "Come!"

on Figure 2.8) so that the child must deliberately plan a course of action and anticipate the approaching holes in order to avoid falling into them. Ultimately, the child learns to rely on the visual experience of the hole shapes to avert mishap, without the necessity of feeling each hole with an exploratory foot.

To enhance eye–hand coordination, a device called the *Hand Box* is placed on a table. This device has a transparent top and hand-size openings on four sides (Figure 2.9). The Hand Box helps children become conscious that they have two hands and that one hand differs from the other by requiring them to get various desired objects that are placed in different positions within a Plexiglas box. When objects are placed out of reach in the box, children learn that either by moving one hand to an opening on the side of the box or by moving the box, they can retrieve the desired object. Through these exercises children achieve increased awareness of the flexible manner in which hands can function.

Also contributing to eye–hand coordination as well as improved awareness of others is the *Competition-Cup* game. To play this game, children sit around a table and face a cup covering a desired object. When the teacher and assistants release the children's hands, the children go for the object. Sometimes, a child will lift the cup with one hand and pause, astonished by

Figure 2.9. Child reaching in different ways for an object in the Hand Box.

the discovery of the object, inadvertently permitting another child to swoop in and capture it. Even quite impaired children quickly learn to pick up the cup with one hand and swiftly reach for the desired object with the other hand to prevent such a disaster from recurring. The game can be modified by moving the cup closer to one child, and so forth, so that all children have a chance to develop the asymmetrical two-handed coordination with vision necessary to compete effectively.

The interventions that have been described in this section, essentially, bring disordered children to a level comparable to that of normal 12 to 14-month-old children.

BODY SCHEMA DURING SIGN, SYMBOLIC-SIGN, AND SYMBOL STAGES

This section first considers body schema characteristics of the *sign, symbolic-sign,* and *symbol stages* and then discusses interventions that have assisted disordered children in moving from one stage of body schema development to the next. The nature of the child's body organization during sign, symbolic-sign, and symbol stages of development dictates rather striking changes in the manner in which the child experiences and relates the body to reality. Thus, the infant's limited body–world organization during the latter part of the sign stage permits intentional and coordinated movement with objects and events, the ability to use natural signs, and a very limited capacity to understand and use spoken word forms. The body schema of the symbolic-sign stage, because it is significantly less bound to the immediate environment, enables the child to represent the body, objects, events, or people by naming them. Finally, because the symbol stage body schema is liberated from the demands of the immediate environment, the child is able to "look on" his or her own body or adaptively draw on particular expressions of the body schema to relate in a variety of ways to different aspects of reality.

Body–World Organization during the Late Sign Stage

During the latter part of the sign stage (12 to 18 months), normal children extend their experience of the body to include various tools to mediate the relation to objects. Most children in this range can, particularly when the act is modeled, use a string or stick to pull a desired object closer (Uzgiris & Hunt, 1975/1980). On the other hand, nonverbal autistic children 3 and 4 years of age commonly have substantial difficulty in relating a tool to its object, as evidenced in the way that one 4-year-old autistic boy first solved the use of a rake to pull a favorite toy car closer.

> Handed the rake, the child made several unsuccessful attempts to get the car by banging the rake in its general vicinity. Finally, the worker gave him the toy car. Abruptly, the child took the car, held it firmly against the inside arm of the rake, and then peered closely at car and rake for about 20 seconds. Subsequently, when the car was placed out of his arm's reach, he immediately picked up the rake, placed it in back of the car, and pulled it toward himself.

Apparently, although the child had begun to use the rake as an extension of his hand, he had not grasped, away from his body, the necessary relationship between rake arm and desired object. Only by experiencing this relationship *close* to his body, with rake arm and car juxtaposed, could he generalize the relation of rake arm to car *away* from his body.

A helpful strategy in establishing tool use with disordered children involves a pouring device (Figure 2.10) in which the child has repeated opportunities to notice how movement of each tube results in different things coming out—sand, gravel, small objects, and so forth. Such redundant tasks are effective because they provide the child with many examples of his or her ability to influence the world through specific body initiatives.

Another useful device for helping to establish the sense of efficacy so important in developing the body schema is the *Pinball Machine* (Figure 2.11). This device helps the child understand how movement of different levers can determine the movement of the ball down an inclined plane.

Among normal children the next important development within the sign stage, suggesting a further differentiation of the body–world relation, is the child's ability (Bates, Benigni, Bretherton, Camaioni, & Volterra, 1979) to point at objects away from the body and then, while continuing to point, to

Figure 2.10. Child engaged in a repetitive pouring sphere.

Figure 2.11. Child moving levers on the Pinball Machine.

shift gaze from the object to a nearby adult as if wishing to share or to comment on the object. This important capacity to deal with the "three-object problem" (child, adult, and object) is notable for its absence among autistic children (Curcio, 1978). It is discussed in Chapters 4 and 5 in terms of social and language development.

Establishing minispheres around pointing-related activities helps develop pointing ability among disordered children. One minisphere involves the

Pointing Board with a narrow channel through which the child, index finger extended, learns to push various small objects to a person opposite. This person, in turn, also with extended index finger, pushes another object back. At first the procedure is supported by a worker who helps the child alternately guide different small objects through the groove. Periodically, the sphere is interrupted to determine if the child can continue the action without support. The repeated process serves to encourage pointed finger orientation toward objects. A variation of this procedure entails using a device with doors of different colors into which various desired small objects are placed (Figure 2.12). The child must first press the different doors to discover the objects inside, and then must point—at first with assistance—at the desired door from a distance of several feet so that the adult can open the door and get the object for the child.

Disordered children also have difficulty relating one object or event to another in a way that makes it difficult for them to indicate to the adult (one object) their wish for a particular (second) object. They tend to operate in a single-track fashion so that they completely lose touch with the desired object when they shift to the adult. To help them with this and related problems requiring a sense of the relationship between two entities, the worker sets up a *multisphere* arrangement so that the child must first become involved with one task, for example, putting cups on hooks, and then must shift to an entirely different task, for example, slicing bananas. In order to help the child retain the first task, the worker interrupts it when the child is well engaged and—even as he or she tries to complete putting cups on hooks—guides the child to the slicing-bananas task. When the interruptions are done properly, the child, while becoming involved in the second task, glances repeatedly at the first task. Then, the second task is interrupted, the child is taken back to the first task, and the process is repeated. Using this

Figure 2.12. Child engaged in reaching sphere with multiple doors preparatory to pointing.

strategy, children with system-forming and closed-system disorders achieve the expanded body awareness required to maintain cognitive relations between two disparate events.

Concurrent with the development of pointing and relating one event to another is the progressive investment of meaning within the child's sound-making capacity. It is important to note that sound making, unlike body action, is not in direct contact with objects and events. Consequently, it is not surprising to find evidence suggesting that there is a transition state (Bates et al., 1979; Carter, 1974, 1975) during which body action accompanies sound making before sound making can be used autonomously to convey meanings. Once sound making develops, however, the child has increasingly at his or her disposal a flexible and less body-involved means of establishing reference. This includes the use of sound making to capture salient properties of objects both close to and remote from the body with the help of natural signs, such as the "rr-rr-rr" sound of a coffee grinder, the "ch-ch" sound of a train, and so forth. The body's increased differentiation during the latter part of the sign stage makes possible a more differentiated use of body expressions such as gesture and sound making to express salient properties of objects and events.

The importance of natural signs is that they enable the child to draw on body organization, and the implied developing body schema, to relate to surroundings at a distance from the body. That there is still a magical quality to these body expressions seems likely because children at this stage systematically use the body as a plastic means of understanding and inducing changes in their surroundings. When Piaget's (1962) child at 16 months—following his father's turning on and off the light—opened and closed his eyes and then looked first at his father and then at the switch, the child in all likelihood was trying to make sense of the change, to magically make it happen, and to signal his father through eye movements to "do it again."

These changes also imply a change in the way meaning is invested in the child's sound making. Whereas previously, feelings of efficacy could be invested in a gesture only through the body's direct involvement with an object or event, now the causal impression can be invested in a sound solely by virtue of the manner in which two external entities act upon one another (e.g., hammer hits a nail, "ping" sound emerges; person opens a bottle, "fft" sound occurs). In all such situations the causal element is remote from the body. Yet the sound that emerges from such activity is picked up by the child and is used to represent the total situation. Not only does such a capacity imply a body schema experienced as being quite separate from but related to objects and events, it implies a considerable degree of initiative. The child is now less a "victim" of intense engaging stimuli and more an active seeker of interesting objects and events so that the new "trick" of capturing the object via natural signs is increasingly brought into play. Subsequently, as described in Chapter 5, natural signs act on and blend their meanings with conventional spoken words (e.g., "ch-ch train," "rm-rm car"). The natural signs then gradually drop out, leaving the conventional word invested with natural-sign meaning.

Typically, disordered children do not spontaneously develop natural signs to capture properties of objects; consequently, integrative spheres are designed to enable them to include signs and spoken words within their action systems. For example, a child both hears the word "push" and sees the sign for *push* as he or she pushes one box next to another on the elevated board and, similarly, as the child climbs *in* and then, *pulls* another box near in order to climb *out*. Or, in another integrative sphere, the child *picks up* the cross bar on a door, *opens* it, and then goes *through* (Figure 2.13(*a-c*)). As the child does this, the worker both says the word and produces the relevant sign. On successive cycles, when the child is fully engaged in the sphere, the worker interrupts at a point of *maximal tension* so that the child needs to utter the word or produce the sign in order to continue the sphere. The importance of these procedures for body schema development is that the child begins to include signs and words as part of the body action system in a way that ultimately allows the child to be sign- or word-guided and to use these signs and words to express intentions. A number of autistic children linger in this mode and find it extraordinarily difficult to liberate their spoken words from the body actions with which they first occur. This was evident, for example, with the 4-year-old autistic girl who had learned to respond to the word "come" but only when used by her teacher. Thus, whenever the teacher's assistant signed and said, "Come," the child would respond by going to the teacher even when the latter was at right angles to the calling assistant. For this child, *come,* and the action it elicited, belonged only to her teacher. Clearly, before this child could understand and use words intentionally, she had to learn that words conveyed particular meanings independent of the person using them.

By observing children's use of both words and actions, it is possible to determine when their functioning is sign-weighted and when it has crossed the threshold to more symbol-weighted functioning. The key is the child's awareness of body action and object as separate entities. When body action and its object are merged and independent use of one without the other is not yet possible, then the child is still functioning within a sign orientation even though some degree of deliberate action is evident. Such a determination was made from observations of Patricia (aged 3 years 10 months), a developmentally delayed girl attending the Center, when she was presented a life-size picture of a chocolate chip cookie and asked to both name ("What's this?") and copy it.

Patricia first passed her hand over the cookie picture (presumably to determine whether or not it could be picked up) and then said "cookie" as she brought her hand to her mouth (demonstrating that she could designate that picture when it was part of an action–object system concerned with eating). However, when given crayon and paper and asked to copy the circular contour of the

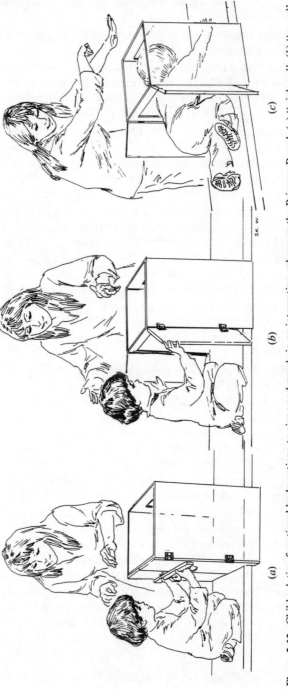

Figure 2.13. Child relating functional body actions to signs and words in an integrative sphere on the Primary Board: (*a*) "pick up"; (*b*) "open"; (*c*) "through."

picture, she made repetitive crayon marks lateral to her body but could not reproduce the circle contour of the cookie. When her teacher tried to assist her by drawing a series of circles and then pausing, Patricia responded by making dots within the circles but could not, unassisted, reproduce the circle contour. Her best effort consisted of a slight arc to her lateral motion achieved in part by bending her wrist so that it slightly approximated the arc of the circle.

The nature of Patricia's difficulty became even more evident in another copying task. In this task, the teacher facing Patricia alternately clapped her hands and paused. Patricia responded to each pause, not by copying the activity, but by repeatedly pressing her teacher's hands together in an effort to get her to resume clapping.

Patricia's behavior with both cookie and clapping situations suggested that although she could intend action, her action was rapidly captured by the object toward which it was directed. Thus, making dots inside the circle (possibly simulating chocolate chips) and pressing her teacher's hands together had more the quality of compensatory activity to continue a system than of an effort to mimic or copy it. In both instances, she seemed to lack awareness that her hand movements could initiate and mimic what she saw. Even though Patricia used a few spoken words and initiated directed activity, her use of both words and body action betrayed a sign origin. She could use words only in the context of a particular object or event and could initiate action toward or with an object or event, but never with enough detachment to permit copying or simulating a model.

Before children—whether normal or disordered—can advance to the next stage of development, they must grasp the notion that words as names can refer to objects or events without the necessity of accompanying body action toward the object. In other words, they need to learn that it is possible to refer to an object by a particular term, a name, that relates to that object independent of action or surrounding context.

To teach this concept to disordered children, workers use minispheres that include the systematic introduction of named objects in a variety of contexts. These spheres differ most sharply from normal child functioning in that the worker, not the disordered child, introduces the repetitive sphere and the various object expansions. For example, to establish the concept of a cup, various cup minispheres might entail pouring water from a cup, stacking a cup, and hanging a cup on a hook. To establish knowledge of a ball, mini-spheres may be organized around repetitively throwing, catching, bouncing, and rolling the ball to different people. These minispheres develop into systems when, following interruption, the child continues the action. True naming develops when the child can name a particular object—and others like it—in varied contexts. At that point the child has achieved the ability to use names for reference relatively independent of body involvement.

Symbolic-Sign Stage Body Schema

In addition to implying the ability to designate complex objects no matter what the context, the achievement of naming during the 2nd part of the 2nd year implies *the shifting of its inherent integrative capacity toward the body*. When this happens, the child is able to designate and experience the body not merely as a diffuse source of intention but as a coherent entity with arms, legs, hands, feet, a certain sex, and a particular name.

The basis for the child's understanding of the body as an integrated entity stems from the range of forces previously described, including the variety of interrupted engagements and the storage of compensatory body dispositions that the child has experienced during the first 18 months of life. If we agree with Schilder (1950) that each action toward an object requires awareness of the "image of the limb or part of the body which is performing the movement" (p. 4), then it follows that, as each compensatory body action to maintain an interrupted system is initiated, the child has an opportunity to experience the body part performing the action as related to *but separate from* the originally engaging object or event. For example, when the signs for eating (placing hand to mouth), ball (motion of holding or catching a ball), and knife (cutting action) have emerged from interrupted engagements, the common feature the child notes is the *hand* as an entity that can perform a variety of functions. Just as the name brings together various properties of the object into one entity, so does knowledge of the hand bring together awareness of the hand as a tool of the body's intention, capable of a multitude of actions. Then, what has happened with the hands, happens with the feet and other parts of the body, until a proprietary feeling for all body parts develops.

A humorous instance of this integration is evident in an account of a film by Kurt Lewin (1935, pp. 82–83; Werner, 1948, p. 192) that shows the difficulties experienced by a 3-year-old child trying to seat himself on a rock. The child's problem—which he finally resolves—is how to relate his bottom (which he cannot see) to the position of the rock. After several experimental attempts the child succeeds and, in so doing, develops a clearer understanding of how his invisible bottom participates in the postural model of his body.

A similar body–object planning problem can be observed in older (4 to 7 years) disordered children as they try to seat themselves in the limited space at the top of a slide. In the course of trying to arrange their legs and feet so that they can go down the slide, they frequently lose track of the limited space for sitting and will, if not caught, try to "sit on air." Only after repeated opportunities to experience the relationships among feet, legs, and required space for bottom are such children able to solve this problem.

During the period that they integrate body parts as tool functions of the body, children also become able to use tools (sticks, rakes, string) as body extensions in increasingly sophisticated ways. Elaborate detours are possible as well, because they now understand how to go around an obstacle to get a desired object—evidence of increasing awareness of the distinction be-tween body and world. The same awareness invites mimicry in many forms, both of objects and of people. This new symbolic capacity is apparent in children's drawings. These move from direct expression of body action in terms of scribbles during the sign stage to greater differentiation, organi-zation, and finally representational drawing (Kellogg, 1970; Werner, 1948, p. 74) during the symbolic-sign stage.

Citing Muchow, Werner (1948) demonstrated the close relation between felt body experience and graphic expression by noting:

Children often see pointed figures as shooting, flying, or aiming above, down-ward or sidewise in some particular direction in accordance with the shape, and they copy them on the paper by setting down sweeping, tearing lines. [In another instance] a little girl while drawing a large circle with a perpendicular line running through its center, involuntarily puffed out her cheeks. (p. 75)

Figure 2.14 (Kellogg, 1970) suggests how expressive scribbles characteristic of sign stage functioning gradually become more complex as they move toward the differentiated and representational drawings that become appar-ent around the age of 3, well after the symbolic-sign stage begins.

Among normal children the shift from drawings that are quite direct expressions of the body to those that *represent* people and things, and thus are more detached from body experience, is quite smooth. This is not the case for many disordered children who, without assistance, remain stuck at the expressive level. To assist these children, a drawing program has been developed at the Center (see Chapter 9) that, with the help of progressively expanded minispheres, guides the children from scribbles to more complex and representational drawings. For example, a child who cannot yet scribble is assisted in doing so by the worker, who guides the hand in rapid lateral scribbling movements. Abruptly, the worker halts guidance to determine if the child tries to carry on the patterned scribbling motion. When the child can do this, the worker expands the pattern by guiding the scribbling motion in a vertical direction before interrupting. Further expansions entail intro-ducing new scribble forms, such as circles, which are further complicated by introducing figures within the circle. Following this, the child has op-portunities to trace hands and feet, as well as various other objects, in the same repetitive manner until assuming command of various forms.

Workers at the Center were delighted to find one autistic 8-year-old boy who had participated in these repetitive scribble spheres achieve his first graphic representation of an event—"peeing"—by drawing an arc to reflect that familiar trajectory.

With this new capacity to represent experience graphically, there is a change in the way that the child forms and draws upon systems. Although during the sign stage the child's system forming was largely dependent on the direct impact of objects and events on the body, now, with the advent

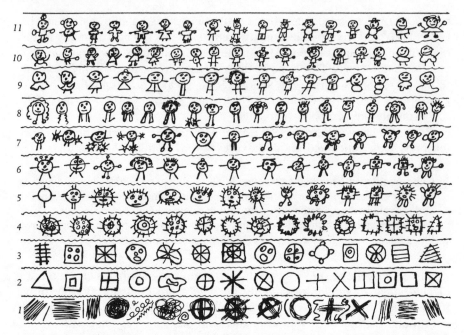

Figure 2.14. From scribbles to humans. Going from bottom to top, these Gestalts represent the probable evolution of Humans from earlier scribbling. (1) The Basic Scribbles at the bottom lead to (2) Diagrams and Combines; (3) Aggregates; (4) Suns; (5) Sun faces and figures; (6) Humans with head-top markings and with arms attached to the head; (7) Humans without head-top markings; (8) Armless humans; (9) Humans with varied torsos; (10) Humans with arms attached to the torso; (11) Relatively complete human images (author's sketches). Not all of the evolutionary steps may appear in the work of every child. Each drawing made by the child over a 3-year period would be needed to determine the point. However, the steps apply well to large quantities of work by many children. Similar steps apply to the evolution of other pictorial items. From R. Kellogg. Copyright 1970 by R. Kellogg. Used with permission of Mayfield Publishing Co.

of representational capacity, the child can initiate new systems merely by naming or drawing a particular object or event. Further, such deliberately formed objects refer to all objects with properties in common with the originally named object. For example, the child who names a table is also able to name a variety of different tables because they share the same critical properties. What has happened is that the child, who previously needed to make direct body contact with an object or event to make sense of it, can now use varied expressions of the body—signs, names, drawings—to hold these meanings and even examine relations between them. Obviously, with this vastly more efficient means of creating systems, the child's ability to order and categorize the experience of reality increases dramatically.

However, even with this new way of systematizing experience through representation, the name, sign, and drawing still show their sign origin in the child's need to fix these vehicles to the "correct" object or event. The imperative relation characteristic of the sign stage is now transmuted into the imperative relation between representational form and a particular object category. For example, just as a drawing or sign must relate to a particular object or event so must the name "hat" or "dog" designate some kind of hat or dog. It is inconceivable that the term "dog" refer to a hat and vice versa. As shown in Chapter 5, only gradually does the body–world relationship change to the point that the child understands that symbolic forms are only arbitrarily and not immutably assigned to their referents.

As a step toward detaching names from their objects—and thus freeing the body from its fixed dependence on a particular symbol–referent relation—the child learns to use names magically in a subjective transformation of reality. This is evident in the child's name-guided ability to find pigs, bears, and elephants in cloud forms or in the shapes of rocks or pieces of wood. In some contexts this capacity leads to play in which a familiar object such as a chair becomes a fire engine. These playful transformations constitute an important extension of the body schema since they develop the child's ability to assign meanings to nonpictorial forms, that is, to printed words. This capacity also clearly demonstrates how the initiative for action toward the world now depends far more on the *inner* intentions of the child than on the events or perceptual properties *acting on* the child.

The disposition of both normal and disordered children to transform reality can be exploited in developing the capacity to accept conventional printed words as meaningful symbols. Gesture signs and accentuation procedures facilitate this transfer of meaning. As explained in Chapters 6 and 11, disordered children or normal preschool children readily learn to identify printed words by first relating a relevant body action to the word; for example, they simulate putting a hat on the head while hearing the word "hat" and looking at an animated sequence of a hat that turns into the printed word *hat*. Similar procedures are used with common words such as *bird, cat, dog,* and *cup.* As children become accustomed to finding meanings in the forms of conventional printed words through such transformation procedures, they require less and less body gesture and perceptual support. Gradually they are weaned from contextual support until they can accept any printed word form as meaning a particular referent simply by pairing the printed word with its usual object and asserting that the word *means* that object.

Finally, the child learns that the relation between symbolic forms and referents is quite arbitrary—that there need be no perceptual linkage between words and their referents for the words to convey referential meaning. Efforts to teach reading provide the impetus for the child to shift from the symbolic-sign stage to the symbol stage. Reading, of course, requires the child to accept as meaningful, symbolic forms that bear no resemblance to their objects. It seems likely that, as the child repeatedly invests picture-meaning in the forms of printed words, he or she eventually discovers that words do not have to resemble their meanings. From this it is but a small step to the *fiat* insight (Chapters 5 and 6), in which children discover that they can assign any meaning they wish to particular word forms.

Symbol Stage Body Schema

Children who have achieved symbol stage functioning have two important new capacities that dramatically increase the flexibility and scope of their functioning. The first is the awareness that their bodies exist separate from the objects and events with which they engage and that the bodies of other people experience reality from a different perspective. The second is the ability to select from among an array of earlier experiences at sign and symbolic-sign stages, in order to achieve new goals. This latter capacity makes it possible for a child who cannot recall the meaning of the printed word *hat,* for example, to put hand on head and *then* be able to say "hat" in a manner often seen among aphasic people. The achievement of symbol stage body schema does not mean that earlier body action–object meanings common to the sign stage are no longer relevant. On the contrary, it means that these earlier stages may be used to serve more complex conceptual goals.

The achievement of the symbol stage also enables the child to begin to think about himself or herself and to develop a self-concept that builds on a sense of the body as well as on a more comprehensive sense of gender and its implications. Obviously, if there are deficiencies in the body schema as it develops from sign and symbolic-sign stages, these deficiencies will be reflected in a self-concept that incorporates them. Thus, a child whose limited awareness of his or her body in space precludes adequate coordination or ability to follow verbal directions must develop a self-concept reflecting these difficulties in some manner.

The self-concept of a disordered child can be improved or strengthened by establishing a more competent sense of body functioning. Consequently, the children at the Center are frequently videotaped performing various activities; then they are allowed to watch themselves in action. Often, for American children, the ability to ride a two-wheeler bike constitutes an important rite of passage, leading to acceptance in a peer group. One psychotic 9-year-old boy was persistently rejected by children near his age because he was "weird" until he learned to ride a two-wheeler. Observing him ride, several normal children pronounced him "okay" and invited him to ride and "do wheelies" with them. Following this group acceptance, there developed over the next few months a sharp diminution of bizarre behavior as well as improved social awareness and language development.

Other useful self-concept building activities that need to be part of an effective program include controlled athletic competition in which the child learns how to hop on one foot, broad jump, somersault, run, swim, hold breath, lift heavy objects, and participate in team competitions such as "tug of war." As disordered children participate in these activities, they develop the self-confidence and skill that make them increasingly able to participate with normal children.

SUMMARY

This chapter begins by defining the body schema construct both as a system with a disposition to maintain itself through compensatory reactions (such as phantom limb production) when its integrity is abruptly interrupted and as a hierarchically organized system. The latter aspect's importance is evident when the failure of more advanced cognitive goals triggers within the body schema a compensatory retrieval of earlier action–object meanings to achieve these interrupted goals. Thus, the body schema is defined as a structure closely related to the contours of the body as well as a process that facilitates adaptation to varied circumstances.

Subsequently, the chapter describes different kinds of body–world organization problems related to limited body schema development that are characteristic of many disordered children. Three kinds of system disorders are described:

System-Forming Disorders. Usually characterized by brain injury or seizure disorders, in which the child because of hyperreactivity to stimuli constantly orients toward but rarely engages relevant stimuli. Such children may fail to form coherent body schemas because they are unable to adequately integrate sensory and motor functioning.

Closed-System Disorders. Usually but not invariably diagnosed autistic, in which the children become so engaged with aspects of the environment that they cannot adequately distinguish their bodies or body parts from the objects or events with which they are engaged.

Syncretic System Disorders. Usually diagnosed childhood schizophrenia, in which the children often demonstrate adequate body coordination and ability to cope with many everyday activities. However, they tend to fuse their inner experience with outer events and vice versa in ways that indicate impaired body schema and the cognitive and interpersonal deficits that this entails.

The chapter next considers the development of the body schema among normal children. In such a child the body schema develops partially as a function of an innate sense of the body as a "zone of efficacious intent." This sense of efficacy helps coordinate the senses with body action in a way that leads to visually guided actions and the ability to integrate touch and sound sensations with action–object systems. Also contributing to the formation of the body schema are the child's reactions to disruptive influences— pain, collisions with reality—that define the body in opposition to its surroundings. Many disordered children seem to lack the sense of efficacy and, consequently, cannot draw on this important means of defining the body. They are also deprived of body-defining input because of their impaired ability to process sensory information, often not responding to pain.

The chapter then describes an array of strategies and devices to help disordered children achieve the body–world differentiation that they cannot master by themselves.

In the final section certain characteristics of the developing body schema during the sign, symbolic-sign, and symbol stages are discussed. During the symbolic-sign stage the child achieves—in various modalites such as naming, signing, play, and drawing—the ability to represent experience. There is a discussion of methods for helping disordered children achieve the differentiated body schemas that permit advanced symbolic functioning through drawing as well as reading instruction. The chapter ends with a brief discussion of the relationship of self-concept to an intact body schema.

CHAPTER 3

Coping within an Expanding Reality

Children trapped within rhythmical stereotypies or driven to react to stimuli are trying to cope with their immediate surroundings. Their limited body schema development makes it difficult for them to move from one location to another without getting lost or to make sense of objects away from their bodies. Frequently they are unable either to relate to concealed objects or to reach objects via detours. Often they lack even the simplest awareness of how things work—of basic cause and effect. Problems also include inability to grasp the concept of time: the relationship between one moment and the next as well as yesterday, today, and tomorrow. Such children do not understand the relation of pictures to objects and of signs or words to their referents in a way that permits understanding or communicating with themselves and others.

IDENTIFYING DISORDERED FUNCTIONS

To work effectively with a disordered child having these difficulties it is important to identify the most central disordered functions, relate them to normal developmental progressions, and then intervene in a developmentally relevant manner. This process is illustrated with Fred, a 26-month-old autistic child locked into closed systems, who has shown great difficulty initiating behavior toward objects or recognizing them when they are away from his body.

CASE STUDY: FRED—INTRODUCTION

Fred's initial behavior at a large hospital was described in the course of a psychological evaluation:

> Fred stood in the middle of the room staring ahead. He occasionally rolled his eyes and head backward and around. Periodically, he slapped his hands, postured, and shook his head in self-stimulating fashion. He touched a few toys, batted at some large blocks, and then sat rocking a cradle repetitively for a long time without interruption. He was inattentive to his mother or the examiner. His affect was bland and his face expressionless. . . . Although Fred was able to execute repetitive motor sequences—such as stereotypically throw-

ing any small object that came to hand—he did not initiate or play in a goal-directed manner. His eye contact was hard to attain and sustain.

Five months later, when Fred was 31 months of age, an Umwelt Assessment was conducted at the Center:

Fred's difficulty relating to objects was apparent from a number of sources: He could not at first readily track or push the swinging ball to the examiner. He could not stack blocks or cups. He could not use a string or a rake to pull a toy closer. Where spatial relations were concerned he seemed not to understand that he had to climb over the Anticipation Board that separated him from his beckoning father in order to reach him; nor did he at first understand how to avoid the holes in the Swiss Cheese Board or to go down a slide and return to the steps so that he could slide down again.

However, with repetitive, spheric presentations of the Swinging Ball, Swiss Cheese Board, and Slide Sphere tasks, Fred's performance began to improve. He began to put hands in front of his face to avoid being struck by the swinging ball and then to push it away from himself. On the Swiss Cheese Board he began to step over and around holes and on the Slide Sphere task he began, in the course of a dozen trials, to turn toward the steps in anticipation of his next slide.

Fred's manner of dealing with objects in a repetitive, cyclic manner is similar to that seen with normal infants between 3 and 8 months of age. Both share the disposition, stimulated by the sight of an intriguing object, to engage it repetitively: batting or swiping at the object by the infant; compulsive and stereotypic throwing of objects for Fred. Further, both the infant and Fred view the object as "nothing more than the material at the disposal of these actions" (Piaget, 1954, p. 24).

The difference is an experimental quality to the infant's repetitive functioning as it constantly reproduces all sorts of interesting results that is totally lacking in Fred's behavior. Nevertheless, for both normal infant and Fred, such crude, repetitive acts involving an object constitute a system that has within it the potential for more varied and intentional action toward the object. *At first the intention is limited because the child's repetitive action and the object's response are so fused within a particular action–object system that the child cannot detach the action to address the object in different ways.* In this sense both the normal infant and Fred are captives of the event that engages them. They lack the ability to spontaneously vary and expand their range of involvement with an engaging object. The capacity to spontaneously engage objects in a more varied manner, according to Piaget (1954, p. 44), appears as the normal infant 8 to 12 months of age begins to study displacements of objects—how they move, how they look as they go from one place to another—by grasping them, shaking them, swinging them, hiding and finding them, in a way that not only firmly coordinates vision with prehension, but contributes to the notion of a permanent object with an independent existence.

Fred's inability to address objects in the spontaneous, exploratory manner common to normal infants 8 to 12 months of age means that his sense of efficacy is limited to a few stereotyped body actions such as throwing objects. Consequently, he lives in an objectless world. If Fred is unable to explore and act upon the varied and unique properties of objects, he cannot develop the notion of an object that remains stable independent of his involvement with it; nor can he sense the possible relations that may exist between himself and objects. Without these relations he has no basis for eventually representing them in signs, words, or pictures. Fred's distorted relation with objects is better understood by examining the normal infant's relation with objects, as expressed in both lateral and vertical development.

LATERAL AND VERTICAL DEVELOPMENT

In this context lateral development and vertical development refer to different uses of the object. Lateral development is concerned with the real object and its relation to other objects, as in coping with detours that block access to a desired object. Vertical development concerns the object as a member of a particular category of objects, represented with signs, pictures, or words. The end product of lateral development is the ability to recognize, act toward, or integrate objects with each other; the end product of vertical development is the ability to think and communicate about objects and events.

The same process that makes it possible to grasp the unique nature of particular objects also enables the child to understand possible relations between objects. Both the formation of the unique object and the formation of relations *between* objects depend on how each system is organized in space. To correctly identify and distinguish one object from another, the child must perceptually organize the properties of each object—for example, the nipple of a bottle is in a particular spatial relation to the bottom of the bottle; the handle of the cup has a unique spatial relation with the cup's opening; the wheels of the toy car are uniquely related to the body of the car.

Similarly, to grasp the relation *between* objects, the child must perceptually organize the manner in which they relate to each other in space. Both the object and the relations between objects are spatial constructions: the child uses the same process to "find the way" from one property of an object to another property as to find the way from one object to another in space. The organization of space, therefore, involves two or more objects as a kind of "larger object" constructed by the child. Within the single object, of course, the space between varied properties is small, whereas between objects the space is larger. Nevertheless, the child who "walks," (acts upon) with mouth and fingers from the bottom of a bottle to the nipple is performing the same function as when walking in space from a chair to a door. In the case of the bottle, varied properties are integrated into an object identifiable as a bottle; in the case of the chair and door, the two objects are organized in relation to each other so that the child can move from one object to another. It follows, therefore, that a child like Fred who cannot explore or integrate the varied properties of an object is also unable to integrate the varied objects that exist in relation to each other in space.

Ultimately, normal children learn to act toward objects and identify them directly through vision and touch or, at a distance, by vision alone. A child achieving this understanding not only defines objects, but also the body relation to each object as a particular construction of spatially related properties. The object-related child comprehends the extension of space *within* the object as well as *under, between,* and *around* relevant objects. This outcome empowers the child to move freely from property to property within the object and from object to object. The child can now understand that if one path to an object is blocked, it is possible to detour the obstacle and reach it by another path. The object-related child can act upon or with other objects, first by using the body as a tool and then by using tools as body extensions to manipulate objects by varying the spatial relations between tool and object (bringing the object closer or pushing it away) or by acting on the object with implements.

In contrast, the outcome of vertical development has less to do with the object's existence in a particular space than it has to do with its function as a referent for various symbolic relations. Lateral development deals with the immediate, phenomenal object and its surroundings in the real world; vertical development deals with the abstract notion of a particular object and its possible relations as something to talk or think about. The object as a foundation for vertical development is finally grasped in terms of the unique properties that distinguish one category of object from others.

Ultimately, the task is to integrate lateral with vertical development so that the child not only can deal with objects and events in the immediate environment, but can think about and communicate their nature—even in their absence—to self and others. Disordered children like Fred have major problems with both lateral and vertical development and their necessary integration. The source of these problems can be found by examining how normal children construct the notion of an object with certain properties.

The Notion of an Object

Infants begin to develop a notion of the object and its varied properties when the course of their engagement with the object is interrupted by loss, intrusion, or collision. These events induce them to cope compensatorily with the object's most salient property. Interruption helps accent object properties when, for example, the infant engaged with a bottle suddenly loses contact with it and then makes compensatory sucking movements and sounds related to the missing nipple; intrusion helps accent the object when, as in Bühler's (1931, p. 421) experiment, placing a cloth over the infant's face, disrupts the child's equilibrium. Bühler, carefully observing infants' ability to remove the cloth at different ages, found that by 7 months of age more than half their movements were directed toward removing the cloth. Her findings demonstrated that even with very young infants the "intrusion" of the cloth triggered intentional and adaptive efforts toward the object. Similarly, Fred's response to repeated "collisions" with the holes in the Swiss Cheese Board, or with the Swinging Ball that repeatedly moved toward his face during his Umwelt Assessment, was clearly both adaptive and object defining: Fred began to avoid the holes in the Swiss Cheese Board; in response to the Swinging Ball, he learned to place his hands in front of his face and then, repetitively, to push it toward the worker.

Such collisions bring about adaptive responses to objects and events because they so disrupt (interrupt) the prior system involvement that the child makes vigorous compensatory efforts to restore it. In doing so, he or she inadvertently adjusts to the source of the intrusion (Fred pushes the swinging ball away and avoids holes in the Swiss Cheese Board). As this happens, the child expands the prior system to include the adaptive response caused by the collision. Then, for example, the Swiss Cheese Board—formerly only a surface to walk on—becomes an object with holes that must be walked around.

Closely related to intrusion and collision is the child's motor response to the signal or "thing-of-action" properties of certain objects. According to Werner (1948), certain objects have a particular valence that "pulls," or invites the child to become involved in a certain way. He cited Shinn's observation of her 6-month-old nephew who, given a round rattle instead of the customary square-edged one, tried persistently to find and bite the "corners" of the round rattle. As Werner pointed out:

> The child who relates to an object in this manner is not addressing it as a thing standing out there in contrasting relation to the subject, a thing of distinct, fixed significance, but as a "something with corners to be bitten." (p. 65)

The ability of certain objects to elicit such responses in children is supported by the finding (Iwai & Volkelt, 1932) that among children from 9 to 12 months of age those objects with strongest thing-of-action properties, that is, those most easily gripped with the hands, are most preferred.

At first the infant reacts only to the most salient, or thing-of-action, properties of the object—the nipple part of the bottle for sucking, the square edge of the rattle for biting, and so forth. However, as children repeatedly engage, interrupt, and resume engagement with salient, thing-of-action properties, they come into regular contact with more secondary aspects of the object. The infant, for example, holds the bottom of the bottle while sucking from the nipple and thus makes it part of the total sucking-from-bottle experience. Then the bottom of the bottle may act as a signal for the nipple—as when the nursling, given the bottle with bottom upward (secondary property), first sucks on it and then turns the bottle around to get at the nipple. As a number of these secondary or ground properties signal the existence of the more salient property of the object, the child begins to construct a notion of the object in which secondary properties maintain a fixed spatial relation with the thing-of-action part of the object.

Having constructed a sense of the object through direct multisensory involvement with it, the child's next task is to maintain contact with and recognize it even at a distance from the body.

The Shift to Visually Identified Objects

The shift that makes possible the visual identification of an object occurs when the child seeks to restore an interrupted multisensory engagement with that object by compensatorily relating body actions toward the object in space. Subsequently, merely the *sight* of the object is sufficient to trigger anticipatory body actions toward the object. The outstretched arms of the infant on sight of the mother, for example, document the existence of such object-oriented body actions. Then, as eye–hand coordination improves, the infant's reaching hand begins to define the object more precisely. Anticipatory adjustments by the infant toward the object are apparent as early as the 3rd month. Caplan (1973) stated:

> As the baby accumulates experience at fisted swiping (at the object), the movement will become more controlled, a slow approach of the hand to the object, sometimes accompanied by glances between hand and object and completed with a fumbling grasp. (p. 85)

Such groping implies that certain properties of the object have become sufficiently internalized to allow the infant's recognition of the object at a distance from the body.

Schilder (1950) provided a perceptive analysis of the required relation between body and object before adaptive action toward the object or object recognition is possible:

> There always must be the knowledge that I am acting with my body, that I have to start the movement with my body, that I have to use a particular part of my body. But in the plan there must also be the aim of my action. There is always an object toward which the action is directed. . . . In order to act we must know something about the object of our intention. And finally, we must also know in what way we want to approach the object. The formula obtains, therefore, the image of the limb or part of the body which is performing the movement. (p. 3)

In other words, relating one's body or body part to the object in a certain way, implicitly defines the relations between the body and the object in space and prepares the body for direct action toward or with it. The manner in which the child's body action contributes to visually locating and identifying the object in space is suggested by Senden's (1932/1960) analysis of patients who were blind from birth but later had cataracts removed, restoring their visual capacity. These studies strongly suggest that visual space and the objects within this space must be constructed through body action involving these objects. Only when direct body recognition of objects is transferred to vision can vision as an extension of the body "take in" the notion of an object moving at some distance from the body. The 8-year-old boy who had regained vision, but not visual perception of moving objects, after cataract removal clearly illustrates this point:

When he was presented with a hand [the physician's] in motion and had continually repeated (when asked what it was) his "I don't know," the test was taken a step further by saying to him, "Don't you see that it's moving?" Again the child's answer was "I don't know," in a voice of questioning ignorance. It could be seen how the child was struggling to grasp the meaning of this phrase in relation to the gesture . . . but without success. His eye failed to follow the long swinging motions of the hand. . . . Not until he was allowed to touch the moving hand while it was beginning to stir did he cry out joyfully in a voice of triumph: "It's moving." (p. 40)

It was not the visual impressions of the moving hand that were first recognized, but "rather the familiar sequence of changing tensions thereby occasioned in his arm-muscles, which was produced in him by touching the moving hand" (Senden, 1932/1960, p. 41). This "blindness" in spite of an intact visual apparatus documents the need for the body experience of object motion to be transformed into visual tracking so that object motion can be carried in purely visual terms. This need for transfer was brought home even more vividly by another of Senden's cases—a 9-year-old boy—who spent days over the distinction of shape between a cube and a sphere.

It was only after several days that he could or would tell by the eyes alone, which was the sphere and which the cube; when asked, he always, before answering, wished to take both into his hands; even when this was allowed, when immediately afterwards the objects were placed before the eyes, he was not certain of the figure. (p. 183)

An intermediate stage in this process is apparent in Piaget's (1954) observation of his daughter as she tried to identify a favorite object that was partially concealed.

At 0;8 (15) [0 years 8 months 15 days] Lucienne looks at a celluloid stork which I have just taken away from her and which I cover with a cloth. She does not attempt to raise the cloth to take the toy. But when a part of the stork appears outside the cloth, Lucienne immediately grasps this bit as though she recognized the whole animal.

[But] . . . not every partial presentation is equally propitious. The head or tail immediately gives rise to a search: Lucienne removes the cloth in order to extricate the animal. But sight of the feet alone . . . the child does not try to grasp. (p. 85)

Having absorbed the notion of an object with certain properties, the infant needs to learn how to relate one object to another. Perhaps the earliest experiences of this occur between 8 and 12 months as the infant learns with an object in each hand to bang one against the other or to observe how dropped objects relate to the ground. Once crawling and toddling begin, the infant learns to move from one object to another and, in doing so, to expand knowledge of the immediate environment. Seeing an interesting object a few feet away, the infant moves toward it, examines the object by shaking it, and then returns to the mother or other care giver. Mahler et al. (1967) has brilliantly described this process of moving out into the world, returning for "refueling" from the mother, and then venturing further. In this way the small child not only begins to map spaces between mother, self, and objects further from the body, but also achieves self-awareness in relation to the mother and to objects. This differentiation of self–other relations, coupled with the ability to refuel, provides a framework for intentional exploration of the world.

DEVELOPING A PREDICTABLE WORLD

CASE STUDY: FRED—COPING WITH OBJECTS

Children like Fred with closed-system disorders seem not to have developed an integrated sense of the object or the notion of a space that contains varied objects in relation to each other. When Fred did relate to an object, he did so only through its most salient, functional property, not in terms of its relation to other objects. Consequently, he had no basis for systematically discovering how to move purposefully in space and explore objects and their relations to each other. Thus, Fred needed intervention that could help him achieve knowledge of objects in a controlled space via the same leaving–returning process that normal infants achieve spontaneously.

A major source of Fred's difficulty stemmed from his disposition to become caught up in stereotypic systems, such as his need to throw every small object he saw. The first task at the Center was to free Fred's hands from their throwing compulsion while orienting him in space. Two tools—

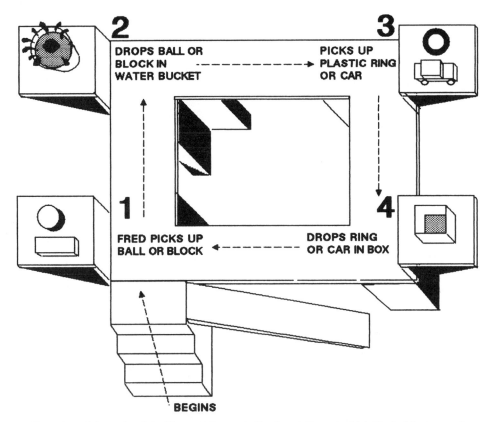

Figure 3.1. Schematic of the Elevated Square indicating stations at which Fred picked up and dropped objects.

the minisphere and the Elevated Square (Miller & Miller, 1982)—were indispensable in this effort.

The worker sought to help Fred develop more varied and intentional body action toward objects by transforming his ritualistic throwing into a deliberate picking up and dropping of objects at specific locations. This process began by teaching him to perform a minisphere that included a particular function—picking up and dropping something—in different spaces on the Elevated Square and in different ways while the signs and words relating to those functions remained constant. The design of the Elevated Square—a 6- by 4-foot structure 2.5 feet above the ground, with one station at each corner—is indicated in the schematic (Figure 3.1).

The worker, in the course of a single session, selected and spatially expanded minispheres that helped Fred not only begin to assume control of his actions but to bind previously unrelated spaces. Once particular spaces were brought into relationship with each other, they became familiar to him as spaces within which deliberate actions with objects became possible. So that Fred's actions might eventually be guided within these spaces, the worker consistently introduced signs and words related to them.

The *minispheres* were designed to substitute for the normal infant's spontaneous capacity to explore and expand the knowledge of objects and their relations in the immediate environment. The essential nature of a minisphere is the child's cyclic organization around or with a particular object or event. When minispheres are designed to establish the varied properties of an object, they may entail dealing with the same object in different ways. Thus, to establish the concept of a cup, various cup minispheres may entail pouring water from a cup, stacking cups, hanging a cup on a hook, and so forth; to establish knowledge of a ramp or a set of stairs, minispheres may be organized around going up and down a ramp or stairs in different ways. Minispheres develop when a worker repetitively introduces a single, coherent function around an object or event that can be systematically expanded. A worker tries to select as minispheres those activities within reach of the child's capacity to perform and that, when developed into systems, the child can use and recognize in the context of normal, everyday behavior.

In establishing a minisphere the worker must decide whether its main purpose is to establish the varied properties of a particular object or to assist the child in establishing the body's relation to the object in space. Once a minisphere is established—as evident in the child's ability to carry through the introduced activity with little or no support—the minisphere must be systematically expanded. Introducing a minisphere without making careful provision for its expansion in space is like building a boat without having access to water.

Fred's first minispheres on the *Elevated Square* paralleled the normal infant's tendency to chart space by defining an object at a certain point, leaving it, and then returning. A minisphere may readily be introduced on the Elevated Square simply by setting up the sphere on one or two of the four stations placed at each angle of the square. This arrangement effectively limits the child's options for movement. On the ground, left to his own devices, Fred could move in any direction and might never return to the object with which he was involved. On the square his movements were limited by the constraints of the square. He could only move to the left or right and if he continued moving he would always return to the object with which he was engaged. In addition, Fred's position above the ground helped him focus his attention on the space around his body. Further, the worker was at eye level and in a position both to assist and to interrupt the particular minisphere with which he was engaged. Finally, if the worker decided to divide a minisphere between different station locations, the linear vectors inherent in the structure (combined with the pull of sign-words) would help guide Fred to the second location of the minisphere. The following account illustrates the process:

Session 1

Minisphere. Fred was taught to pick up and drop objects on the Elevated Square.

Procedure. Fred, after climbing on the Elevated Square, was given the opportunity to walk around it a few times. He showed the usual enhanced alertness and focused manner expected in this situation. All four stations on the square were used to develop and expand one pick-up–drop minisphere. Fred was required to pick up an object (a ball or block) at Station 1 and then walk to Station 2 and drop it in the bucket of water located there. (These actions were designed to pull together that side of the square.) Next, to expand the pick-up–drop function and to define the other side of the square, Fred had to walk to Station 3, where he picked up another object (plastic ring or car) that he carried to Station 4, where he dropped it in a box (no water). During this process the worker and father uttered and signed relevant words as Fred performed various actions.

Response. After a few cycles, Fred got involved with the activity and appeared to anticipate the next step. However, he would periodically lose contact with what he was doing and go into his stereotypic movements— head rolling backward, eyes wandering without focusing. At first he required assistance to release the objects, but after a time, he released them unassisted as he connected the splash and sound that followed his release (looking at his hand and then at the bucket) with the act of opening his hand. Initially, each release was followed by the stereotypic movements.

Fred's ability, after picking up an object at one station, to anticipate dropping it at a second station—thus connecting the different stations—was encouraging, as was the beginning awareness of his hand's function in dropping things.

Following the promising transformation of throwing into dropping, the worker decided to extend it. Because throwing-dropping was a major preoccupation for Fred, during Sessions 2 through 8 he was given a variety of different objects to pick up and throw-drop (the worker and parent constrained his throwing so that it became dropping). Then he was guided into throw-dropping a variety of objects into specific containers. All such activities rapidly became part of spheres that, following interruption, Fred tended to continue.

Minispheres developed during Sessions 9 through 11, in addition to pick up-drop, included action concepts *put in, bang,* and *throw.* These terms were expanded with a broad variety of objects—blocks, cups, hammers, bottles, and so forth—that Fred put into containers, banged, and threw. As Fred became engaged with each of these spheres, the worker would interrupt the sphere just before the event was completed. Fred demonstrated that the spheres had become internalized systems by continuing them when they were interrupted and by accepting all expansions. Fred readily engaged in these activities, and when the worker introduced a new sphere, he accepted it without much difficulty. Because systematic expansion of minispheres plays a vital role in opening up a disordered child's reality, such expansions are described at some length in the following section.

Expanding Minispheres

The principle guiding all expansions of minispheres is that the major vector of the task—whether picking up and dropping, climbing up and down, stacking, or pulling—remains constant while other features—the location, position, time lag between parts, object, and person aspects of the sphere—vary. As a child learns to tolerate such expansions, he or she develops a more complex repertoire for dealing with that particular object or event as well as the space within which that object or event exists. In general, minispheres begin with *location,* followed by *position, object,* and *person* expansions.

For example, a *location* expansion for a minisphere concerned with stacking blocks or cups might consist of offering these objects in a variety of locations (above, below, and to the right or left of the child), so that the child has to orient toward the object in a different way each time before being able to grasp and stack it. A variation is to require the child to get up, fetch the needed block, and then bring it to the stack. Typically, location expansions start quite modestly—only a foot or so from the child and within the field of vision—so that the child does not have to turn away from the stack. After the child masters the more limited expansions, location expansions are attempted that require the child to completely turn away from the first part of a minisphere task.

As the child learns to cope with location expansions, important new understanding develops. The child learns, for example, that objects and events

Figure 3.2. Fred participating in the Cup-on-Hook sphere.

are not bound to a particular location; they can occur and be used in a variety of locations. Further, when a minisphere is divided into two parts separated by space, the child learns to delay a response and to internalize goals. In such a situation, as shown with Fred, the minisphere is a vehicle for bringing together or binding previously unrelated spaces. For example, a child who learns to pick up a cup at one part of a room, walk holding it to the other side, and there hang the cup on one of a series of cup hooks (see Figure 3.2) has begun to internalize one property of the cup (that it can be hung up by the handle) and can wait until the time to do this. Further, in the act of walking across the room, the child shows that he or she can traverse this space for a particular purpose. When children can independently—outside of spheres—intend such activity, they are well on their way to exploring the space in which they live and the objects and events that define space for them.

The process of connecting spaces can often be assisted by introducing part-objects on different stations. For example, after a child has learned to stack cups and place them on cup hooks, it is useful to divide a cup in such a way that it can be put together by the child with Velcro seals. Then, half the cup is placed on one station and the other half on another station; the child who picks up half a cup feels compelled to complete the object by getting the remaining half at the other station. This same procedure may be used with a broken ball, broken shoe, broken dog, and other objects, as illustrated in Figure 3.3.

Figure 3.3. Broken Objects used in minispheres or integrative spheres.

Systematic *position* expansions for disordered children are a substitute for the spontaneous exploratory behavior with objects characteristic of normal children. For example, if cups have been offered right side up, then a position expansion might entail presentation of the cup upside down or sideways so that the child has to adjust the cup in order to stack it. Too often workers feel that children demonstrate complete knowledge of the object when they can retrieve it from behind a screen, as in the Uzgiris-Hunt Scales (1975/1980). Although such awareness of the object's continuing existence is a necessary part of developing knowledge about the object, the achievement is by no means complete with this knowledge.

Even with normal infants the position expansions that contribute to full object knowledge develop gradually. This is also true for system-disordered children. For example, just as for the developing infant (Piaget, 1954; Werner, 1948) the bottle at first exists only when the nipple is oriented toward the mouth, so for some system-disordered children a cup exists only when it is standing on its bottom; upside down or on its side it can no longer be experienced as a cup. Similarly, a chair is a chair only in the upright position in which it can be sat upon. Only when children have grasped the nature of objects with all their properties in all contexts do objects exist with sufficient clarity and dimension to enable children to refer to them with sign or word. For the system-disordered child who cannot spontaneously achieve such knowledge by exploring the properties of objects, the worker's systematic introduction of position expansions provides a necessary substitute.

Object expansions of particular action functions enable disordered children to detach functions from their initial context. For example, if a child has been involved in a clay-cutting sphere, then the worker might introduce other items for cutting such as bread, soap, butter, and salami. This expansion permits the child to detach and experience actions as separate from but related to the objects acted upon. A cutting action must be performed a certain way—back and forth—modified somewhat by the different objects being cut. Similarly, a throwing action can be applied to a variety of objects but must be adapted to the characteristics (size, weight) of the object being thrown. Thus, content expansions, by dramatizing the distinction between body action and object acted upon, contribute to the definition of the body experience and the ability to act in a range of contexts.

Person expansions allow disordered children to generalize behavior to contexts involving new people. The small child may first use the toilet only for his or her parents but eventually learns that the same behavior can be performed for the teacher; ultimately the child becomes self-motivated. Similarly, if the worker has customarily been handing cups to the child for stacking, a person expansion can be achieved simply by having the parent or another worker do the same activity with the child. If the minisphere requires the child to hand an object to a person, then a person expansion would require the child to hand objects to different people.

The child who achieves person expansions learns that many actions relate to people independent of who they are. At this point it is important that the child not experience certain actions and functions as necessarily bound to certain people, that is, the child can roll a ball not only to mother and father but to brothers and sisters, and so forth. Later the child learns to discriminate between special people, with whom one relates intimately, and strangers, with whom one relates more cautiously.

Integrative Spheres

If a disordered child such as Fred is to function more normally in the everyday world, he not only must master various expansions of minispheres, but must learn to perform sequential tasks of two, three, or more steps leading to a particular outcome. The strategies that teach such functional sequencing are referred to as *integrative spheres*.

During normal development the infant, who has spontaneously learned to perform various expansions, develops an additional capacity between 8 and 10 months of age to use intervening behaviors to achieve goals. The child who pulls a cloth to one side to get a desired object or the child who pulls the hand of an adult toward an unreachable object demonstrates the capacity to use and integrate an intermediate means in the service of a desired goal. A bit later this same instrumental capacity is evident in the child's ability to use tools—a string attached to an object, or a stick—or to make a detour around an obstacle (Lockman, 1984) to reach desired objects.

This critical capacity to mediate behavior may either not occur at all among disordered children or may occur only in a limited degree. To remedy this deficiency a combination of minispheres lead the disordered child from the beginning to the end of a task. Any complex task with the goal not immediately in sight requires a degree of mediation and inner planning. A child who is planning to go down a slide must *first* grasp the notion that there are steps to be climbed before he or she can slide down. In that sense the stairs are the necessary instrument that mediates going down the slide. Before mastering this integrative sphere, the child must be able to handle the minisphere of going up and down the steps and the minisphere of going down the slide. In the context of the integrative sphere such minispheres are referred to as *components*. When the child can go up the steps in order to go down the slide and can return to the steps for another sequence, the components have combined into an integrative *system*.

Through integrative spheres the system-disordered child learns to cope with familiar sequences—such as cleaning the table, or washing and drying dishes, or putting food on shelves—that are naturally linked together in service of completing a particular task. Thus, unlike minispheres, which are organized around a unitary event, integrative spheres help the disordered child connect the minisphere components that make it possible to perform a particular task.

Disordered children more readily combine complex integrative spheres on elevated boards than on the ground because, having completed one part of a complex task at one station, they are easily guided to the next part at another station by the board vector. For example, to master a sequence that includes washing dirty cups and then putting them on hooks to dry, the child must first master a washing-cup minisphere component at one elevated board station and then integrate it with the cup-on-hook minisphere at an adjacent station. The child who can put both together in a functional manner has internalized them into an integrative system. Still another instance of an integrative sphere becoming a system is evident in the child who learns how to carry an object to a cupboard, open the door, place the object inside, close the door, and repeat the process with different objects. Before attempting this last integrative sphere, the child must solve all its components—carrying objects from one place to another, opening and closing doors, and placing objects on shelves.

Integrative sphere arrangements are set up by first establishing two and then three or four entirely disparate minispheres. The ability to continue the sphere following interruption identifies it as a *minisystem*. The number of minisystems bonded together depends on the complexity of the task performance being taught. Each minisystem is systematically followed by the next until the task is complete. The child has successfully internalized an integrative sphere when he or she can complete it without physical guidance by parent or worker.

In carrying through this procedure, most disordered children may not, at first, grasp the necessary relation between one part of the integrative system and another. Thus, at first the task may be conducted as a ritual where the means–end relation is obscure. However, as the task is repeated with appropriate expansions, disordered children begin to understand that each part of the system must occur in its proper order in order to reach the eventual end product.

CASE STUDY: FRED—INTEGRATIVE SPHERES

An integrative sphere is introduced with Fred to expand his ability to work in a sequential manner and to enhance his understanding of why, with certain tasks, things must be done in a certain order:

Session 12

Integrative Sphere. Fred picked up a pitcher, filled it with water, and poured water from it into a bucket (three stations).

Procedure. The integrative sphere of repetitively filling a pitcher with water and pouring it into a bucket was divided among three stations. At Station 1 Fred had to *pick up* an empty pitcher; he then walked to Station 2 to place it in the water and *fill it;* at Station 3 he was required to *pour* the water into a bucket and drop the pitcher; after pouring at Station 3, he had to pass Station 4 to pick up a new empty pitcher at Station 1. His father, at Station 1, called and signed, "Come!" to Fred to help him make the turn at Station 4. The sequence was repeated four or five times.

Response. Fred seemed intrigued with the task and, unassisted, after pouring and dropping the pitcher at Station 3, walked toward Station 1 (where his father was signing and calling). However, at times, after picking up a new pitcher at Station 1, he would be drawn by the more engaging water-pouring station, and instead of walking to Station 2 to fill his pitcher, he would turn around (without water in his pitcher) and start walking back to Station 3. He seemed genuinely surprised—when allowed to do this—that no water came out as he tilted the pitcher.

Fred performed the task and showed some response to his father's calling and signing. But in turning the corner at Station 3, he clearly had not yet grasped the means–end relation that requires filling up a pitcher *before* attempting to empty it. Lacking this understanding, Fred's behavior suggested that the sphere meant that one was supposed to do something with a pitcher at certain places and that somehow at one particular place tilting the pitcher meant that water would come out.

To make the means–end relation more apparent to Fred, another integrative sphere was introduced, presenting the steps in the sequence closer together both spatially and temporally:

Integrative Sphere. Fred put a doll in a car and sent the car down a ramp.

Procedure. Fred was required to pick up a wooden car with a hole in the center (for inserting a wooden doll) at Station 1 and walk to Station 2, where he was to pick up the doll placed there, put it into the car, and then send the car down the inclined plane. Following this, he was to return to Station 1 to repeat the process. This was to be done four to five times.

Response. When Fred first picked up the car at Station 1, he wanted to throw it. Deterred from doing this and guided toward Station 2, he had some initial difficulty fitting the doll into the car. However, by the third and fourth repetitions he was no longer trying to throw the car but was, without support, inserting the doll in the car and pushing the car down the ramp. Sometimes in the middle of a successful sequence he faltered as if confused. At these times he seemed, momentarily, to have lost his sense of what to do next.

Fred's occasional faltering with the car sequence seemed related to the difficulty he had internalizing steps in a sequence—picking up doll, putting it into the car, then sending it down the slide (three steps). Further data on his difficulty internalizing sequences came from another task performed the same day as the doll-in-car task. In this task he had to pick one of two pegs and place it in one of two holes in a pegboard. He did well with this. However, if the worker "happened" to leave a small peg in the larger hole for which he had a peg, he seemed unable to remove the small peg to make the bigger hole available but would try to force his big peg into the adjacent smaller hole.

The latter response, coupled with his response to the water-pouring sphere and the doll-in-car task, suggested that when he could not sustain an inner thought sequence he would become confused and falter, resort to stereotypic throwing, or shift to magical solutions. This demonstrated that his experience of object forms still lacked constancy. His incomplete understanding that each object had a fixed shape *and* his inability to mentally portray and hold a sequence of events that went from beginning to end seemed responsible for his lapses of function. To improve his sense of the object and the possible relation of one object or event to another, a different set of procedures was introduced—multispheres.

Multispheres closely simulate the structure of certain real-life situations by helping the child maintain the relation between two unrelated sources of involvement, as when a child interrupts a game to perform a chore but then resumes the game without difficulty. The capacity for such shifts between one system and another occurs quite early (around 7 months) as infants engage with an object, turn away from it, and then return to it with the expectation that it has not disappeared. As Piaget (1954) put it, "The child returns of his own accord to the position and gestures necessary for the resumption of the interrupted act and (in so doing) endows the objects thus rediscovered and recognized with a permanence" (p. 24). In contrast, for closed-system children like Fred, the movement from *first* to *second* object involvement often results in loss of contact with the first object, an "out of sight, out of mind" phenomenon. This response was evident in Fred's response to his first multisphere:

Session 14

Multisphere. Fred attempted to relate two disparate tasks.

Procedure. Fred was required to perform two *unrelated* minispheres in succession. The first entailed picking up a pitcher filled with water (Station 1) and then walking to Station 2, where it was poured over a waterwheel in a bucket. The second minisphere required Fred to walk to Station 3 to pick up a ball and continue to Station 4 where he dropped or threw the ball into a basket.

Response. As Fred picked up the pitcher of water and walked toward Station 2, he looked back at the station he had just left. Often shaking his head, he showed no expression or emotional response. He became caught by the way water coming from his pitcher caused the waterwheel to move and tended to forget the second sphere. When he was guided to the second sphere, he had difficulty dropping the ball into the basket at Station 4; he needed to throw it as soon as he picked it up at Station 3.

Fred seemed confused by the complexity of shifting from one sphere to another. However, his looking back at the station he had just left might have reflected a beginning sense of how the pitcher he picked up at Station 1 was related to pouring from it at Station 2. His fascination with the turning of the waterwheel as he poured water on it might reflect his increasing interest in the causal relations within a particular sphere. His difficulty dropping the ball in the basket in the second sphere—a task that he could perform when dropping the ball as part of a single minisphere—seemed related to the disorganizing impact of trying to cope with two disparate spheres. Once Fred became disorganized his throwing stereotypy reasserted itself.

A week later (Session 13) a somewhat modified multisphere (sending a car down a ramp instead of dropping a ball into a basket), was attempted, and Fred responded in identical fashion. This time, instead of throwing the ball, he threw the car. His behavior on both occasions clearly indicated that he was not yet able to combine two disparate spheres. The inability to relate to more than one aspect of reality at a time underlies the failure of many system-disordered children to adequately investigate and cope with surroundings, to initiate social contact, or to represent contacts with objects, events, or people, to themselves and others. It also accounts for much tantrum behavior when routines are changed without relating a disordered child to the new events.

Children readily achieve multispheres on elevated structures because the space between one sphere and another is connected by the board. Thus, a child with an intention deficit can readily be guided from one minisphere to another in a way that would not be possible on the ground. Multisphere arrangements are set up by establishing two and then three entirely disparate minispheres. Within a multisphere each minisphere is related to others by first interrupting one minisphere at the point of *maximal tension* and then proceeding to an entirely different minisphere. Once the child becomes engaged by the new sphere, that sphere is interrupted and the child is brought back to the first sphere, where the process is repeated. The difference between multi- and integrative spheres, of course, is that multispheres do not lead to a particular functional goal, such as washing dishes.

The rationale for the multisphere procedure is as follows. When the first sphere is interrupted, the child experiences, in Lewinian (1935; 1936) terms, a tension state related to the need to complete that first sphere. By maintaining that tension state while having the child become engaged with an entirely different sphere, the first sphere continues to remain "alive" in the child's psychological economy even during the engagement with the second sphere. *This duality of experience begins to make it possible for the child to relate one sphere to another.* After a number of cycles involving the two spheres, the child starts to demonstrate, by glancing at the second sphere while still engaged by the first, a sense of relation between the two spheres. This was evident in Fred's later attempt at a new multisphere arrangement on the Elevated Square:

Session 20

Multisphere. Fred had difficulty shifting from one task to another.

Procedure. At Station 1 on the square, Fred began the first minisphere by picking up a saltshaker and bringing it to Station 2; here he would shake salt into a bucket. He then began the second minisphere by walking to Station 3 to pick up a metal soap whisk that he used at Station 4 to whip up soapy water and make suds.

Response. There was excessive engagement with the Shake-Salt minisphere at Stations 1 and 2 because Fred, after shaking the salt in the bucket, became obsessed with picking up and eating the salt until he was literally pulled away from the salt station. However, he did well with the Whip-Suds minisphere on Stations 3 and 4. He picked up the whisk at Station 3, without throwing it, and walked to Station 4 where he proceeded to whip up the soapy water in a very organized manner.

Fred's ability to engage with the second minisphere, even after being forcibly detached from the first minisphere, constituted a beginning adaptation to the multisphere format. On earlier multisphere arrangements he had refused to participate in any sphere if more than one was presented. Encouraged by Fred's partial success within a multisphere, the worker decided to introduce a multisphere with emphasis on the form properties of certain objects. This task had been difficult for him previously:

Session 21

Multisphere. Fred successfully shifted from one task to another.

Procedure. In the first minisphere Fred picked up a ring at Station 1 and placed it on a pole at Station 2. The second minisphere required him to pick up a puzzle piece at Station 3 and place it in the puzzle at Station 4.

Response. The multisphere worked better on this attempt. There was more engagement with less throwing. Fred seemed to enjoy stacking rings. He looked back when he walked to Stations 2 and 4. He did better with the puzzle sphere. There was some vocalizing—more when he was engaged in the tasks. There was good eye contact. He smiled several times while stacking rings on the pole.

Because Fred had done well within a multisphere involving two minispheres, the worker now planned a multisphere that included three minispheres. Once a third minisphere is added, the worker assists the child to shift to either the first or second minisphere until the child clearly shows through behavior (usually by glancing at the other spheres) an understanding that he or she may soon be participating in one of the two other spheres.

Specific theoretical considerations are involved with multispheres of such complexity. Suppose, for example, that a child is engaged with the Cup-on-Hook minisphere and that the worker has interrupted this task just as the child is ready to place the cup on the hook. While the child is still urgently trying to place the cup on the hook, the worker firmly takes the child to the Pour-Water minisphere. Typically, the child will protest and either move toward, point, or otherwise signal the wish to continue with the first sphere until becoming engaged by the Pour-Water minisphere, at which time pointing at the previous sphere ceases. When the child is fully engaged with the Pour-Water sphere, the worker interrupts it at the point of maximal tension and moves the child back to the Cup-on-Hook sphere. As the child moves closer to and gets caught in the "gravitational field" of the second sphere, the "pull" of the previous sphere diminishes without ever quite disappearing. After a few such arbitrary shifts from one minisphere to another, the child no longer protests but merely glances at the anticipated sphere and then back at the original sphere, suggesting full awareness that there will soon be an opportunity to get back to the interrupted sphere.

At this point, a third minisphere—for example, Knives-in-Rack (Figure 3.4)—is added to the two bonded spheres. Again there is protest (although usually much less than before) when the Knives-in-Rack sphere is added to the Cup-on-Hook and Pour-Water spheres. Initially, the development of multispheres follows an A, B, C pattern, with each interrupted minisphere systematically following the adjacent sphere. However, once the child establishes chained sequencing of spheres, the pattern should be changed to

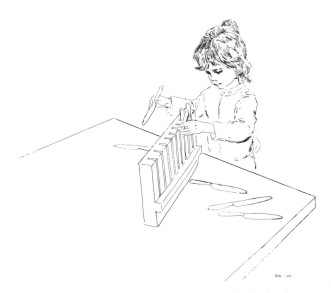

Figure 3.4. Child participating in the Knives-in-Rack sphere.

other sequences, such as A, C, B or B, A, C. Finally, after the child is comfortable moving among any of the spheres, the worker gives the child choice by asking which one he or she wishes to do next.

At first multisphere sequences should be no more than 2 or 3 feet from each other. Later, location expansions may allow placement at different parts of the room and even require a child to turn away from one minisphere in order to reach another.

The multisphere procedure effectively conveys to the child that although each minisphere is a separate entity it is possible to leave the sphere and then return to it. In this way the all-or-none relation between one aspect of reality and another begins to yield to a notion of a world populated by different objects and events that may relate to each other. The change in attitude that stems from knowledge of the possibility of relations between disparate events is indispensable for progress toward higher level functioning.

The achievement of multispheres constitutes a shift from encapsulated minispheres, during which the child's reality is limited to engagement with a particular object or event, to a broader reality defined by the new superordinate relation that embraces several disparate events. This change in the child's experience of reality parallels the developmental pattern found in normal children. For example, just as normal 2-year-olds at first require the steps in a song or story to follow rigidly the manner in which they were first introduced, so is this true with certain system-disordered children as they master multispheres. And, just as normal children learn to tolerate and then initiate changes in such sequences, so—with the help of multisphere strategies—do system-disordered children. The striking difference is that normal children achieve this understanding spontaneously, whereas system-disordered children must be led through the changes from mini- to multispheres before their new flexibility becomes apparent.

The manner in which a complex multisphere helps solve not only shifting among three different minispheres but shifting between the function and form of objects is evident in this example:

Session 21

Multisphere. Fred successfully shifted among three unrelated tasks.

Procedure. Fred began the first minisphere (picking up a ball and dropping it down a tube) at Station 1. He then proceeded to the second minisphere (picking up a ring and putting it on a pole for graduated rings) at Station 2. Finally, he performed his third minisphere (picking up a cup and placing it in a cup nest) at Station 3. He repeated this sequence four or five times.

Response. Fred's engagement in this multisphere was better*—more

---

*Undoubtedly contributing to Fred's improved multisphere performance was the placement of each minisphere—in its entirety—at each of the 3 stations, a strategy that enabled him to quickly complete each act.

focused—than in previous spheres. He had clearly improved his ability to shift from the function of objects (throwing ball) to their form requirements as evident in his discriminating between different forms (graduated rings and cup nesting). His stereotypic throwing was at a minimum, and he smiled frequently.

During this session and the four sessions that followed (Sessions 22 through 26) Fred was no longer troubled by the shift from object function to form discrimination; he shifted very well from throwing-dropping the ball down the tube (object function) to distinguishing between shapes (nesting cups, rings on pole). Notable was Fred's new ability to leave a task at one station to go to completely different tasks at other stations, not only without distress, but with a smile. During the 2-week period that spanned the next four sessions, the gains were consolidated.

In terms of lateral development Fred could now cope with the structured reality represented by the Elevated Square and the tasks that were introduced on the square. He could cope with integrative and multisphere tasks of up to three separate components—pick up doll, put in car, send car down slide—and with a variety of two-component tasks. He could now deal with the form and function of objects as well as their varied spatial relations on the Elevated Square—shifting from one task to another and then back to the first—without becoming disoriented. Further, the worker was increasingly able to guide some behavior with the signs and words that had previously accompanied Fred's actions in the spheres.

Progress was less evident in his ability to mediate experience indirectly (vertical development) through tools, signs, or words. The acceptance of multispheres *does* suggest that Fred had found a means of representing the object left when he went to a second sphere. There was also increased interest in how things worked (waterwheel) although it was too soon to tell whether this was part of his stereotypic tendency. There was also increasing indication that his movement from station to station on the Elevated Square was guided not only by the vectors of the square, but by the sign-word expressions used by the worker and father.

DEVELOPING AUTONOMOUS FUNCTIONING

Although noteworthy, Fred's achievements could be viewed as nothing more than a series of rote exercises limited to the Elevated Square. Only when Fred demonstrated use of these capacities on the ground and in all settings would he have an increased ability to cope with an expanding reality. During the 2nd year of life normal infants expand their capacity to understand signs and words independent of setting, to solve detours, to express preferences, and to respond to, show interest in, and negotiate with people. The first step in helping Fred develop the autonomy inherent in such behavior was to begin working with him on the ground.

Without the structure provided by the Elevated Square, Fred's struggle to make sense of sign-words to guide his functioning became more evident. On the square, the vectors inherent in the contours, coupled with the relevant sign-word induced him to respond. For example, with Fred standing at one angle of the square, and his father calling and gesturing, "Come!. . . Come!" from another, Fred tended to move toward the father—and nowhere else— because the board both restricted alternatives and guided him in the same direction as his father's self-orienting gestures. On the ground, however, he could only rely on gesture and word. For this exercise to succeed, the directive properties of the Elevated Square and the sign-words now had to be carried solely by the signs and words used by the people working with him.

Sometimes the influence of board-vectors on sign-words is immediately apparent in the way a child responds to a signed and spoken request on the ground. Nancy, an autistic 5-year-old girl (Miller & Miller, 1973, p. 83), had to use a wide stance as she shuffled on an elevated parallel board toward her mother in her initial response to her mother's "Come!" When the procedure was repeated on the ground (without the board), Nancy could at first respond to her mother's "Come!" only by assuming the same wide stance and shuffling foot movement that she had used on the board. Several days later, she could respond to her mother's call without using this board gait.

Sign-Word Guidance on the Ground

During the next 40 sessions Fred showed substantial ability to respond to and be guided by signs and words while on the ground. The nature of his progress is suggested by the following:

Session 27

Integrative Sphere. Fred (age: 36 months) learned to follow directions on the ground.

Procedure. Fred was required to walk over the Artificial Hill to his father (see Figure 3.5(*a*), (*b*)), who was signing and saying "Come!" When he arrived and his father signed and said "Pick up!" he was to pick up a bottle of water. Following this, when the worker on the other side of the hill signed and said "Come!" Fred was to turn around and bring the bottle to her. When Fred reached her, she signed and said, "Pour!" and pointed to the bucket at her feet, requiring Fred to pour the water into it. This procedure was repeated five to six times.

Subsequently, the procedure was expanded so that when Fred came to his father, the father directed him by sign and word in alternating fashion to *come, pick up the bottle* of water as before or a *car* placed next to the bottle. Then, directed by the worker's signs and words, Fred had to

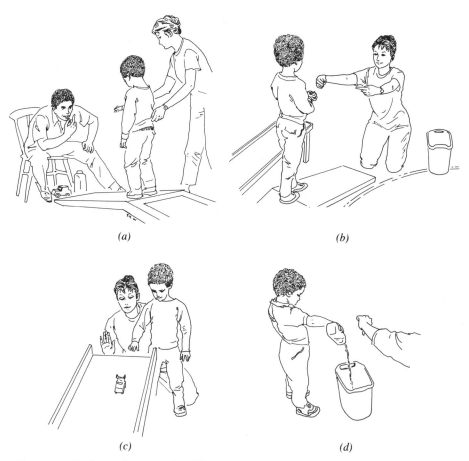

(a)   *(b)*

(c)   *(d)*

Figure 3.5. Fred choosing and using different objects after walking over the Artificial Hill: (*a*) "Come"; (*b*) "Car"; (*c*) "Down"; (*d*) "Pour."

respond either to "Pour!" by pouring the water or to "Down!" by sending the car down a slide next to the bucket (Figure 3.5(*c*), (*d*)).

Response. Fred followed directions well in the first part of the task, climbing up the Artificial Hill and then rapidly going down the other side first to his father and then to his worker. He had some difficulty with the expansion that required him to discriminate between two different objects and two different commands—showing his old disposition toward stereotypic throwing. However, with minimal physical support and with vigorous guidance through the sign-word "Stop!" to which he responded for the first time, followed by responses to "Come!" and "Down!" he was able about half the time to alternate between pouring and sending the car down.

As Fred began to follow directions on the ground, he became confused at times when the same words related to different functions toward the object. This was evident in the following sessions:

Session 28

Fred showed confusion in following directions related to the sign-words *put on* and *put in*. When *put on* related to both stacking blocks and putting rings on a pole, he faltered. Also the morphemic similarity between *put on* and *put in* might have been getting in the way.

Session 29

With distinctly different words *pick up* and *down* relating to different functions, Fred had no difficulty following relevant directions to pick up either a car or a ball and send it down an inclined plane.

In the following two sessions Fred demonstrated the ability to follow directions from longer strings of sign-words:

Session 37

Fred demonstrated ability to be guided by signs and words to perform an elaborate sequence. (He *comes* when called, *picks up* a small doll, then walks to a dollhouse, *opens* the door, *puts in* the doll, *closes* the door.)

Session 38

Fred responded to sentences of three to four sign-words to decide which of two small figures to pick up and perform an action with: "Come . . . put (animal) in the water" or "Come . . . open the door (of dollhouse) and put (the doll) in the house."

In the following session Fred showed increasing sensitivity to the sign-words guiding his behavior. He was able to consistently distinguish between different objects and their functions:

Session 58

Integrative Sphere. Fred (age: 3 years 5 months) alternated between two similar tasks.

Procedure. Three stations separated by 8–10 ft were distributed in different parts of a 12- by 14-ft room. At Station 1, on an alternating basis, Fred had to pick up a cup or a glass (both already filled with water). He was then to carry the filled vessel to Station 2 and pour the water into a bucket. At Station 3 there were two setups: one for putting cups on hooks and the other for stacking glasses. All activities were guided by the relevant sign-words, for example, "Put cup on hook." Sequences were repeated four or five times.

Response. Fred became very engaged by this sphere. Checking regularly (turning toward the worker) to get the right instructions, Fred, making cheerful sounds, put cups on hooks and stacked glasses flawlessly.

The next few sessions (59 through 61) indicate how sign-word guidance enabled Fred to master a variety of everyday living skills:

Integrative Sphere. Fred learned to wash, dry, and place dishes.

Guided by relevant sign-words, Fred was able, with minimal difficulty, to pick up either a dirty plate or cup at Station 1 and then walk to Station 2 where he put it in the water, picked up a brush, washed the dish, and put it on the towel. Then he moved to another location (Station 3) on the same table where he dried the dish or cup. Finally, he moved to Station 4 where he successfully stacked plates or put cups on hooks.

Integrative Sphere. Fred awkwardly washed his "dirty" hands.

Fred cried when his hands were soiled with mud by the worker, but he did not spontaneously go to the sink to wash them. As the worker assisted him, he began awkwardly, with poor hand manipulation, to try to get the dirt off. Because of his distress around his dirty hands, the worker chose not to carry through repeated cycles of this activity.

Integrative Sphere. Fred learned to take off his jacket.

Fred, guided by sign-words, came to the worker (situated about 8 ft from him), sat down on a chair next to her, and took off his jacket. This procedure was repeated three or four times. Through all daily living spheres, with the exception of hand washing, Fred was effectively guided by sign-words. He responded not only to the worker but to his parents both during sessions and at home.

New Initiatives on the Ground

Concurrent with the development of sign-word guidance, Fred showed increasing ability to initiate behavior independent of the spheres introduced by the worker. Examples of these initiatives follow:

Session 30

Fred, with the help of sign-word guidance, performed a detour—opening a door so that he could pull a wagon through. This achievement suggests that he was now better able to grasp means–end relations: The door (means) had to be opened first to allow the wagon (end) to go through.

Session 39

Fred, on his own initiative, walked the doll up the stairs to the dollhouse. The same sequence had been introduced 5 minutes earlier by the worker in spheric fashion.

Session 54

After the worker established a sphere in which sticks were placed in modeling clay, the task was interrupted to see how long Fred would continue with the task without any sign-word guidance. Worker reported that he continued on his own for about 2 to 3 minutes. However, after this, with no further structuring from the worker, he reverted to stereo-typic mannerisms.

Session 58

Fred demonstrated limited tool use when, after happily shaking salt from a saltshaker, he was interrupted by the worker, who took the shaker and placed it out of arm's reach but reachable with a rake placed near the shaker. Fred was able to use the rake to get the shaker but only when the rake arm was directly behind it.

Initiatives toward People

In an effort to expand Fred's awareness of the manner in which adults could assist him in various tasks, the following "stolen marker" session was set up:

Session 30

Integrative Sphere. Fred retrieved the stolen marker from different people so that he could continue drawing.

Procedure. Fred was given a marker and, with help, began to draw-scribble. When he was engaged by the task, the worker interrupted by taking the marker and giving it to a person at the other end of the room. That person then called Fred to get his marker in order to continue draw-ing. This process was repeated several times with location, person, and marker expansions.

Response. Fred seemed intrigued with the way movements of his hand with the marker produced different kinds of markings on the paper. Fol-lowing interruption of his drawing by the worker, who stole his marker and gave it to his father, he was guided by the father's "Come!" retrieved the marker, and again resumed drawing. As this sequence was repeated with other people, Fred did equally well with location (father moved to different parts of the room), person (worker took role of father and vice versa), and object (stealing different-colored markers).

The ability to detach from and return to a task that Fred demonstrated with the drawings may well have contributed to his successful achievement of one of his first detours. In order to detour an obstacle, children must, as with the drawing task, first detach their attention from the desired object, perform a mediating action that bypasses the obstacle, and then move toward the desired goal. Fred's increasing ability to detach from situations set up for him in order to initiate his *own* systems is suggested by the behavior—having some of the oppositional quality of normal 2-year-olds—shown in the following sessions:

Session 38

Fred suddenly "tuned out" after following the worker's directions quite well (responding to come, getting one of two objects and placing it in the water, then getting the other and placing it in the dollhouse) by deliberately placing a variety of objects in the water. He did this not as a repetitive compulsion but as if he were expressing a personal preference.

Session 39

Fred constantly turned toward the worker for the signs and words he needed to guide his behavior toward one of the two sets of tasks before him. (This was the same session in which he spontaneously walked the doll up the stairs.)

Over the next several months (Sessions 40 through 53), in addition to interventions concerned with sign-word guidance and problem solving, a variety of reciprocal spheres having a gamelike quality were introduced. These included alternately throwing blocks or balls in a box, as well as alternately banging on a drum and a xylophone. Combined with these were interventions where the worker would playfully tease Fred. One variant of this involved the swing.

In this sphere Fred would sit in the swing while the worker stood in front of him. Then, the worker would gently move the swing so that Fred repeatedly approached her. Each time Fred swung closer, the worker would playfully say, "I'm going to touch your foot [nose, hand, etc.]," while reaching toward and touching the designated body part. Then, varied interruptions would be used. Sometimes the worker said the words but did not use the gesture, sometimes the gesture was used but not the words, and sometimes there was a complete interruption. Fred, at different times, would respond to an interruption by cheerfully offering a foot or hand to be touched—clearly indicating that he had begun not only to better define his body but to initiate responses to others. These activities, in conjunction with the ones previously described, contributed to the outcome described in the following session:

Session 64

Fred (age: 3 years 6 months) started his own interactive game instead of following the worker's plan.

The worker had planned to have Fred open a bottle with soapy water at Station 1, walk to his father at Station 2 to get the bubble wand, and then walk to the worker at Station 3, where he was to put the wand in the bottle of water prior to bringing it to the worker's mouth for blowing. Fred, however, had other ideas. He came in unusually responsive to the worker. He smiled when he saw her in the corridor, took her hand, and pulled her toward the room in which they worked. When the worker tried to involve him in the bubble task he had always enjoyed, he began, instead, to initiate simple, teasing, chasing games with the worker. At one point, becoming excited, he started throwing things and was reprimanded by both father and the worker. At this, he began to cry bitterly. Later, as the worker attempted to resume the session, Fred would repeatedly interrupt the activity by approaching the worker and giggling. Then he would turn away while looking over his shoulder at her, waiting to be chased.

This was the first occasion at the Center in which Fred spontaneously, without prior structuring, initiated a game with the worker. Clearly, his interest in her as a source of fun, coupled with a new sense that he could initiate activities, overrode her structuring his actions through spheres. Whereas in previous sessions the interactive aspects of his relationship with his worker were secondary to his involvement with various tasks that she required, at this session his relationship with the worker became primarily important and the tasks quite secondary. With this new way of behaving, Fred showed promise, for the first time, of a whole spectrum of social development.

In reviewing the 40 sessions summarized, certain themes become apparent. One is the marked increase in Fred's responsiveness to signs and words. In fact, this dependence on the sign-word and its fixed relation to its referent seems to have become so strong that deviations in the referent caused him difficulty, as was evident in the confusion around "Put on." But, perhaps most striking were the increasing indications that Fred had a "mind of his own," whether that showed itself in bits of spontaneous play, as in the doll climbing steps, in his selective tuning out of directions when he wished to do something else, or in *his* initiating a game of "Chase Me" to supplant the worker's offering. Fred's increasing ability to make sense of and manipulate objects, events, and people in his immediate surroundings represents his lateral development.

TOWARD VERTICAL DEVELOPMENT

Perhaps Fred's most significant progress toward vertical development had to do with his new capacity to be guided by signs and words. Because signs and spoken words were initially alien to him, it is necessary to consider the conditions that made his guidance by them possible. Signs and words assumed their new power because they were introduced repeatedly in the context of Fred's ritualized actions toward or with objects. Seeing these signs and hearing the words while he was performing action–object rituals enabled Fred to incorporate them within his systems. Then, hearing and seeing them alone (partial interruption) induced him to perform the action–object part of the system in order to complete it. At first, Fred behaved as if he had no choice in the matter because both sign and word operated as powerful signals requiring that he produce the rest of the system. Later, however, he experienced a greater sense of choice as *he* began to decide whether he would respond to signs and words, do something else, or initiate a game of "Chase Me" with the worker.

Such progress toward vertical development presages other achievements such as the ability to relate pictures to their objects and, eventually, to find meaning in the arbitrary forms of printed words. For children like Fred, however, progress in this direction entails crossing various gaps between immediate and more abstract modes of coping with reality. It is, after all, one thing to recognize an object by sight and feel and quite another to recognize it in a picture that presents a visual image of the object in a two-dimensional plane. The next section considers procedures that have proven effective in helping disordered children cross such gaps in their vertical development.

Representing Space and Time with Tableau and Picture Calendars

Even after intensive work on elevated board structures, many disordered children still have difficulty in determining how one event follows another during their day. Specifically, they need to know *what, when,* and *where* with regard to key events that happen to them during the school day. To help children with *what,* the Tableau Calendar has been devised at the Center, consisting of three-dimensional tableaus of the major events that take place during the day (see Figure 9.4)—the snack period, the audio-visual period, the elevated-board room period, lunch, toileting, and dressing. For example, the tableau of the snack period shows a model of the Center's uniquely shaped table with stools in each of the bays, the A-V period is represented by stools grouped around the monitor, and toileting is represented by a toilet and washbasin.

When is communicated by constructing each tableau so that it fits into one of five or six slots. The order in which the tableaus are placed in the slots (from left to right) represents the order of events for that day. Often, a teacher gives a child a tableau to place in the calendar just prior to participating in that event. When a particular event has been completed, the teacher or worker may take the tableau out of the slot so that the child can readily focus on the next event. When the event takes place in another part of the building or outside—as with an outside picnic for lunch—the worker may have the child carry the tableau to the new site in order to include the picnic within the general notion of lunch. If the schedule requires a reorganization of events, the teacher has the children place the tableaus in the proper order. Often a child "checks" the Tableau Calendar to determine what is going to happen next.

After the children have become familiar with the function of the Tableau Calendar, a picture calendar representing exactly the same events, in the same order, is set up in back of the three-dimensional tableau. These pictures are used exactly the same way as the tableaus. The worker or teacher calls attention to the similarity between tableau and picture so that after a time the children find it possible to use the picture calendar instead of the tableau calendar. However, many disordered children cannot make the transition from three-dimensional to two-dimensional forms. For these children, there is another set of transitional strategies.

From Object to Picture—3D/2D Strategies

Normal children, during the first part of the 2nd year of life, begin to recognize pictures of familiar objects. Typically, they do not demonstrate any clear notion that the picture is a symbolic representation of the object but behave toward the picture as if it were the object. A small child often reaches toward a picture of a cookie or candy and attempts to pick it up and eat it. That is, they incorporate the picture within a system that may contain the heard word as well as action toward that object. A child who behaves in this manner has spontaneously expanded a particular action–object system to include the picture. Subsequently, the picture as well as the sign or spoken word elicits within the child a disposition to act toward or indicate desire for the object represented.

Assistance is provided by paralleling normal progress in the following way: To help a child recognize a picture of a cup, a sphere is introduced involving a cup—for instance, lifting a cup to the mouth and putting it down. The sign and spoken word are then introduced within the sphere so that the child sees the sign (simulating bringing cup to mouth) and hears the word "cup" while performing that act with a cup. Finally, part of the cup is presented on one side of a card; an exact replica of it (a picture) is on the other side. As the child becomes engaged by the partial cup on one side of the card, the worker suddenly flips the card to the other side so that the child confronts only the picture. Often the child will then try to pick up the picture of the cup in the way that normal children do. The identical procedure is performed with a hat as well as with other common forms such as bird, dog, and car (see Figure 3.6).

After children have achieved about a dozen 3D/2D transfers, they begin to look at pictures with new interest and seem able to interpret subsequent pictures in object terms without requiring additional transfers, merely by

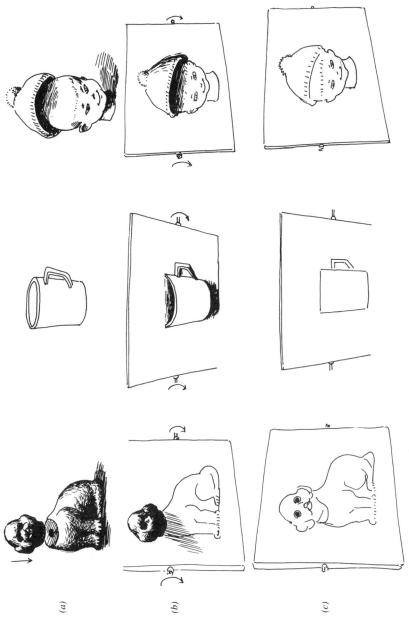

Figure 3.6. Cards showing 3D/2D setup for transfer of meaning: (*a*) Objects (dog, cup, hat); (*b*) Part objects/part pictures; (*c*) Pictures.

107

virtue of the worker's designating it by sign or word. Following this, the children often discover new pictures of familiar objects by themselves and bring them to the adult's attention for confirmation.

From Picture to Printed Word with Fusion Strategies

All children—but particularly disordered children—experience another gap after the development of spoken language (symbolic-sign stage) when they first confront the arbitrary forms of printed words and are asked by teachers and parents to attribute specific object meanings to these forms. Then, just as some children have difficulty with the shift from object to picture, so others have difficulty with the shift from picture to printed word. Assisting children with this transition is another set of strategies, as described in Chapters 6 and 11. The central notion behind these strategies is that although children may be able to designate and identify objects and pictures of objects because the latter so closely resemble objects, printed words represent an entirely different kind of symbol.

Figure 3.7. Flash cards designed for transfer of meaning from pictures (hat and car) to printed words. From Symbol Accentuation™ Reading Program. Copyright 1989 by A. Miller. Used with permission.

Before children can understand that a printed word conveys the meaning of an object to which it bears no physical resemblance, they require an interim means of "fixing" words with object meaning. In a series of experiments (Miller & Leuthold, 1964; Miller, A., 1968; Miller & Miller, 1968, 1971), it was demonstrated that transfers could be made with children and adults who were able to speak but could not identify printed words. If pictures and printed words were fused on one side of a flash card, and that flash card was flipped to the other side revealing the word in its conventional form, children could transfer picture properties to printed words. Then, subsequently, they could identify the printed words without needing further transfers (see Figure 3.7). These procedures have been developed further in the Symbol Accentuation™ Reading Program so that, with the help of animated motion pictures to make the transition from picture to printed word and from letters to mouth movements, many children previously unable to read and write have learned to do so.

SUMMARY

This chapter uses Fred, an autistic boy with a closed-system disorder, to illustrate the distinction between lateral and vertical development. Systematically, Fred's developmental problems are related to normal developmental progressions. When he is stuck at a certain point, the methods used (Elevated Square, minispheres, multispheres, integrative spheres) to help him are described in some detail.

The chapter also considers the factors involved in the shift from multisensory involvement with objects to the ability to visually identify objects. Citing work with children whose vision was restored after the removal of cataracts, it is concluded that systems involving body involvement with the object are indispensable to the ability to identify objects distally with vision alone.

Illustrations from work with Fred are presented to concretize the strategies used and the kinds of developmental changes that occur in the course of cognitive-developmental systems work. Interspersed with these illustrations are discussions of methods for expanding various spheric arrangements until children are able to transform them into internal systems. Expansions of spheres discussed include location, position, object, and person. The view is offered that only when disordered children can grasp the nature of the object in all contexts does the object exist for them as a permanent, continuing entity independent of their involvement with it.

The next section of the chapter deals with the importance of weaning disordered children from elevated board structures to the ground so that they can learn to transfer their board knowledge. The manner in which Fred copes with this process and gradually achieves greater autonomy is described in some detail.

The final section of the chapter discusses Fred in terms of his vertical development. It then considers various gaps that all children must cross as they move from active involvement with objects to representations of these experiences, such as between the heard word and its action–object referent, between the three-dimensional object and the picture that represents it, and between the picture and the printed word. Various strategies are described to help disordered children with these gaps, including the use of Tableau Calendars to help children with the *what, when,* and *where* of their daily experience; 3D/2D strategies to help children shift from object to picture recognition; and fusion strategies to help children who can speak but not read, shift from pictures to printed words.

CHAPTER 4

Developing Social Systems

A Framework for Communication

The infant who holds out arms to be picked up and the 8-year-old who agrees to take turns with a classmate in riding a bicycle are both engaged in social systems. Each participant in the system has a felt inner need, a vehicle for expressing that need, and some awareness of the other. The integration of these three components—affect, cognitive means (action, gesture, language), awareness of the other—is an indispensable aspect of all social systems. But suppose the infant, although experiencing a need to be picked up, has never learned to reach out to the care giver. Or, suppose the child with the bicycle, although vaguely understanding the notion of taking turns, finds the prospect of giving over the bicycle intolerable. Each child would require a different kind of intervention: With the infant the task would be to construct an interactive system involving infant and care giver in which the child *could* reach out in recognizable fashion; the reluctant turn-taking child would require only the repair or reconstruction of a partially understood but inoperative social system. This chapter examines aberrations in the development of both kinds of systems and the constructive and realization strategies needed to build or correct them.

CONSTRUCTING INTERACTIVE AND SOCIAL SYSTEMS

Before discussing building social systems it is necessary to distinguish between two kinds of systems: interactive and social. *Interactive systems* develop first and refer to infant–care giver exchanges in which the infant is able to relate *either* to the care giver *or* to objects but cannot include both within the system. Initially, the infant's mode of interacting involves the care giver as a mere extension of needs—appearing in times of distress and disappearing when no longer relevant, in the same way that objects "disappear" when the infant does not actively engage them. However, as a function of repeated interactions, the infant gradually builds confidence in the continuing existence of the care giver just as he or she has been building confidence in the permanence of objects even when they are out of sight. Out of these interactions the infant gradually achieves *social systems*. They differ from interactive systems in that the child has now internalized the care giver enough to tolerate turning away to include an object in the relationship, as in giving and taking an object. Once this new pattern of relationship has been established, at about 9 to 10 months of age (Trevarthen & Hubley, 1978), the child has a framework not only for object exchanges but for various kinds of reference (gesture, words) to objects and events quite remote from the ongoing relationship.

Disordered children have major problems in two areas: building interactive systems with care givers, and moving from interactive to social systems that require the integration of care giver with objects.

INTERACTIVE SYSTEMS: CONTRASTING NORMAL WITH DISORDERED DEVELOPMENT

Perhaps nowhere is the contrast between normal and disordered—particularly autistic—children more poignant than in the area of early interactive contact. Where the normal infant eagerly reaches out for the care giver, the autistic child remains inert; where the normal infant smiles and gazes into the eyes of the parent, the autistic child avoids eye contact and rocks in a self-absorbed manner or becomes preoccupied with an object. Parents of autistic children report behavior from the earliest months that suggests an impairment in the child's ability to send and receive emotionally laden signals. Often they report that their children did not seek physical comfort from them (DeMyer, 1979) and that affective signaling was infrequent: "He was such a good baby . . . never fretted"; and that the response to the care giver was poorly acknowledged: "He didn't seem to know me," or, "He seemed to look right through me."

Such failure to signal emotional state or to respond to others has important implications not only for the development of social interaction but for all forms of communication. Thus, unlike newborn babies, who can adaptively signal the care giver via a broad range of emotional expression (Izard, 1977; Provence, 1978), disordered children are often affectively inert. Lacking both affective expression and preverbal communicative gestures—reaching to be picked up, pointing (Curcio, 1978; Wing, 1971)—they remain emotionally isolated and often seem to prefer objects to people. This behavior becomes more intelligible with the realization that a disordered child who cannot make emotional contact with a care giver cannot deliberately draw on that person to have needs met. Without a felt need for the care giver why should the child try to communicate with that person through action, gesture, or spoken word?

The Influential Infant

Two capacities present in normal infants but not in many disordered children enable reaching out and making interactive contact with the care giver: (a) the ability to translate inner states of comfort, distress, and anger into affective expression; and (b) the recognition by the infant that his or her actions or expressions have in some way influenced someone to do something with regard to them. Such influential interactions begin shortly after birth as the infant's affectively laden signals—body movements, screams, smiles, cooing, crying—become part of interactive systems related to particular interventions by the care giver. For example, the held infant moves to better reach the breast, and the mother adjusts her posture to accommodate; the screaming infant is picked up, and the distress ebbs; the infant's smile is returned, and the infant smiles anew. The mutuality inherent in such contingent exchanges may be responsible for the finding that as early as 4 weeks of age the normal infant begins to prefer the adult face to the object (Wolff, 1987).

Experiments document the capacity of infants shortly after birth to both influence and expect certain things to happen in a manner entirely consistent with the formation of interactive systems. Investigators (Blass, Ganchrow, & Steiner, 1984; Watson & Ramey, 1972) found that not only can very young infants systematically influence external events, they experience it as pleasurable when they do so and are distressed when once having succeeded, they then fail. Watson and Ramey found that when 8-week-old infants were exposed to a mobile that would turn when they pressed their heads against their pillows, they produced an increased number of head-presses and showed—in contrast to a control group—distinctive cooing and smiling behavior when the mobile turned. Blass, Ganchrow, and Steiner (1984) found that infants as young as 2 hours old who were given sucrose and whose heads were stroked, subsequently showed more head orienting and sucking responses when later stroked without sucrose than did control groups who were stroked and given sucrose unrelated to the stroking. Further, during extinction trials (stroking but no sucrose) 7 of the 9 experimental infants cried (suggesting that they expected the sucrose), whereas only 1 of the 16 control infants cried.

The results of these and similar studies strongly suggest that *infants shortly after birth have the capacity to form systems that tie their body functioning to external events.* Further, when these interactive systems are interrupted in a way that precludes the infant from using compensatory responses that might maintain the system, they become distressed. That these systems are fully operational by 2 months of age is suggested by the way infants respond (Tronick, Als, Adamson, Wise, & Brazelton, 1978) when their mothers experimentally *interrupt* their customary involvement with their infants by remaining still and expressionless. A clinical description of one infant's response follows:

> As in the normal interaction, the infant orients toward the mother and greets her. But when she fails to respond, he sobers and looks wary. He stares at her, gives her a brief smile, and then looks away from her. He then alternates brief glances toward her with glances away from her, thus monitoring her

behavior. He occasionally smiles briefly, yet warily in less and less convinced attempts to get the interaction back on track. As these attempts fail, the infant eventually withdraws, orients his face and body away from his mother with hopeless expression, and stays turned away from her. None of the infants cried, however. (Tronick et al., 1978, p. 8)

Following interruption of the usual interactive infant–mother system, the infant *expected* a response, as evident in his seeking for a time to compensatorily maintain the interactive system with brief smiles and glances. But then, because the system required the mother's response to his signals— and this did not occur—he unhappily turned away from her, perhaps so he could adaptively orient, engage, and form a system with a more responsive partner.

The Disconnected Child

This sense of both influencing and being responsive to another, so necessary for the formation of interactive systems, is often absent among disordered children. According to Ornitz (1987, pp. 148–165), the kind of social and language impairment found among autistic children is consistent with "dysfunction of brainstem behavioral systems *and* further distortion by selected neural structures that are themselves influenced by the brainstem and its dysfunction" (pp. 160–161). If there is impairment in "gateway" structures in the brainstem, these must negatively influence the manner in which sensory input from inside the body, for example, hunger, can be felt and related to the care giver's feeding. Lacking the ability to relate such events, the infant may not readily include the care giver as part of an interactive system.

Consistent with this view are the findings by Condon (1975) and Condon and Sander (1974). In contrast to the normal infant who "moves in precise and sustained segments of movement that are synchronous with the articulated structure of adult speech" (1974; p. 99) disordered children—particularly autistic children—have body responses that are consistently delayed and out of synchrony with the spoken word.

Deprived of the capacity for contingent interaction with their care givers, disordered children may develop striking preferences for objects over people. After all, objects tend to be more predictable than people and maintain fixed or relatively fixed positions so that the child can form systems with them with some certainty as to their locations and thing-of-action properties. Further, even when objects are in motion, their trajectories often become predictable. Whereas a disordered child may have initial difficulty pushing a swinging ball, with enough repetitive experience of the ball's trajectory the child succeeds in influencing the ball's motion and establishes a system with it. People, on the other hand, present the infant a complex array of changing stimuli that can, for example, be seen, felt, sucked, grasped, heard, and tasted all at once. People also intend action in a way that things do not and exhibit changing facial properties with opening and closing parts, some of which produce an array of intermittent sounds. How, by 4 weeks of age (Wolff, 1987), does the normal infant bring this assortment of diverse stimuli together into a coherent gestalt recognizable as a person and more interesting than even a moving object?

The normal infant is capable intrinsically of pulling together these different sources of input into one responsive entity, that is, a person who can be influenced with signals such as a hunger cry. As indicated in Chapter 1, once the normal infant becomes engaged by the nursing aspect of the care giver, the infant incorporates within the interactive system not only the nursing aspect but any secondary or background input that accompanies engagement with nursing. Thus, the crooning or stroking stimulation from the care giver that the infant experiences during nursing becomes part of the composite pattern organized into a system. Subsequently, when only the care giver's sound or stroking stimulation occurs, the infant may recognize it (and thus that aspect of the care giver) as part of the nursing experience by beginning to suck as if nursing. In the course of varied interactions such as being held and played with, the infant inadvertently takes in other properties of the care giver and organizes them into an identifiable person whose presence the child anticipates and recognizes even at a distance.

Following this integrative process, it is not this or that property of the care giver that becomes important, it is the infant's action upon the entire moving gestalt that the care giver has become and the response of that moving gestalt to the infant that creates an infant–adult system and not merely an infant–breast system, and so forth. And because this infant–care giver system is more relevant to the infant's survival it generally forms prior to that of infant–object systems (Decarie, 1969). For the disordered child, however, who has difficulty relating one source of input to another, interacting influentially with such a stimulus complex may be like trying to alternately throw and catch a small object through the partially opened window of a train moving erratically through the mist. Like the train, a person's start-and-stop sound making and body movements provide a window through which the other has an opportunity to respond to or initiate a communicative statement. The disordered child's inability to participate in systems structured by such rapidly shifting exchanges may forecast later difficulty in communicating with others.

Just as brainstem dysfunction can account for the delayed or aberrant response to pain in a way that interferes with the construction of the body schema (Chapter 2), so does the delayed (Condon, 1975) or aberrant response to inner or outer sources of input interfere with the formation of interactive social systems. If, for example, a child is still processing one source of input while being presented with another—whether object or person—he or she may be unable to take in the second source. Or, alternatively, the child who shifts from a precipitating event to the event precipitated may have no sense that the first event caused the second. Such a failure to form a system that relates a triggering act to the event caused by it is evident in the following case study of Jim, a 6-year-old nonverbal autistic boy, who, although unable to swim, persisted in following a group of children in jumping off a dock into 8 to 9 feet of water.

CASE STUDY: JIM—A DISCONNECTED CHILD

Seeing and hearing the contagious excitement of other children jumping off the dock may have induced Jim to leave his shallow area and jump off with them. Unable to swim, he went under and then rose to the surface in acute distress; gasping and sputtering, he swallowed water while his arms and legs flailed the water. The lifeguard quickly lifted him back onto the dock where he sat panting for about 10 seconds. Abruptly, as another child jumped in, Jim again followed and experienced the same distress. At that point the lifeguard removed him entirely from the situation.

Presumably, the contagious clamor of the jumping children induced Jim to jump. However, his readiness after being pulled out to jump in again suggests that he had not formed a system relating his jumping action to the distress that followed. He gave the distinct impression that he would, if permitted, continue to jump in and nearly drown an indefinite number of times without ever relating his action to the distressing outcome. Jim's *system-forming disorder* had important implications for the manner in which he sought to communicate his needs to people. Jim's problem in this area became apparent when staff at the Center's special camp for disordered children reported that they were unable to cope with his unpredictable biting and scratching.

Staff initially interpreted the biting and scratching as an aggressive "attack" on them. After a number of attacks, they had decided to deal with this behavior by systematically ignoring him after each such incident, the notion being that ignoring this undesirable behavior would "extinguish" it. In their view, any effort to make much of him following his attack would only lead to "reinforcing" his distressing biting behavior. To their dismay, however, they found that instead of diminishing, the biting and scratching behavior increased in intensity every time they turned from him.

Observing Jim in his cabin, we noted that the attacks seemed to follow a worker's becoming concerned with another child. We were also struck with the urgent and unblinking manner with which he looked at the person he bit, maintaining a fixed stare at them even as his teeth sank into an arm or hand. We knew that his parents were beginning to consider a residential placement for him and had been increasingly investing their hopes in a younger child. From the observations and this information it was hypothesized that the underlying meaning of the behavior was not to attack but to achieve and maintain reliable physical contact with a caring person in the only way available to him, just as a drowning person might clutch a piece of lifesaving driftwood to stay afloat.

To cope with this inferred contact need, staff were instructed to turn toward, not away from him, when he attacked and, while avoiding his teeth as best they could, to cup his face gently in their hands, look directly at him, and tell him tenderly what a beautiful child he was. This was done, not with the expectation that he would understand, but with the hope that the physical contact and affection expressed by staff would meet his contact need. This proved to be the case. When a staff person behaved in this way he would abort his attack and become calm. Attacks diminished from a high of 50 a day to 2 or 3 a week by the end of the summer. When the child's mother was informed of the methods that had proven effective, she wept. She and her husband had not previously grasped the relationship between their inadvertent turning away and his attacks.

Discussion

Jim's desperate need to resort to biting and clinging occurred because he could not form a system in which he could indicate through readable signals that he needed someone to attend to him. Lacking the sense that he could influence someone to nurture him, he could only react to the feeling of deprivation. To help him, the worker needed to behave *as if Jim had correctly signaled his need* in the same way a parent interprets the hunger or "colic" cry of the infant and acts accordingly. Once the parent's action completes the system, the distress abates and the child becomes calm.

In creating such a system for Jim, it was noted that his sense of feeling cared for, although derived from being attended to and held, never became related to a particular person. Any worker who behaved as requested was effective in helping him become calm. Presumably his diffuse systems did not allow him to relate his being nurtured to the particular person attending to him any more than he could relate jumping into the water to the distress that followed. Thus, in contrast to the normal infant, who from 6 to 12 months of age becomes acutely aware of the mother and any separation from her, children with system-forming disorders like Jim often continue to find one worker as acceptable as another. Only as a child begins to improve does one caring person become more special than another.

Given the difficulty many disordered children have in forming systems, what prospects exist for helping such children form interactive and social systems? The next section discusses one area of response shared by both normal and disordered children that *does* permit disordered children to develop interactive systems and to transform them gradually into social systems that include reference to objects and events.

Contagious Interactions among Normal and Disordered Children

One area common to both normal and disordered children is the capacity to react to contagious, affectively arousing input. Such responses are evident in the vocal interchanges of normal infants and their mothers. Researchers (Anderson, Vietze, & Dodecki, 1977; Stern, Jaffe, Beebe, & Bennett, 1975) found that infants and mothers interchange through "duets" or "chorusing" as well as alternations. Stern et al. found that alternations were more frequent when mothers were in a teaching mode, whereas duetting and chorusing were more characteristic of contagiously happy arousal states that the authors felt contributed to mother–infant bonding.

Such contagious systems, however, are not merely vocal. They often involve the infant's entire body in a highly exciting and contagious exchange. Brazelton, Koslowski, and Main (1974) nicely described such an interaction between a mother and her 3- or 4-month-old infant. The mother first tried to engage the infant by making sounds, jouncing, or moving the baby in different ways (vestibular stimulation). Once the infant was engaged by this stimulation, the mother slowly increased the intensity and variety of her actions with the baby. The infant responded to this with a parallel increase in excitement—arms and legs moving, smiling, vocalizing—which reached a peak intensity accompanied by tension and jerky actions. Then, gradually the high excitement decelerated; the infant looked away and went into the negative part of the cycle—performing actions while looking at nonsocial objects. Then, as mother again gained eye contact with her infant, the entire cycle of synchronous mother–infant behavior repeated itself.

Such sequences constitute an early form of interactive system referred to as diffuse, contagious systems—*diffuse* because there is no clear definition of behavior as in turn-taking systems; *contagious* because the quality of positive arousal "carries along" the infant; and a *system* because the infant and care giver are concurrently influencing each other and sudden interruptions at points of maximal excitement would dispose the infant to maintain the system by continuing the activity for a time. Such contagious systems are important because, just as mothers bring their infants into vital emotional contact with them, so can even very remote, behavior-disordered children be brought into more meaningful contact with people by stimulating body-to-body contact. The following incident, which occurred early in the Center's existence, speaks to the importance of contagious body contact as a source of diffuse interactive systems.

Workers planned to take a group of 5 nonverbal autistic children, ages 5 to 7, swimming in a new location. However, because the children had been together only for 3 months and had not formed any obvious bond with each other or the workers, it was feared that the new swimming situation might trigger panic, upset, and major tantrums. However, after adding additional staff, it was decided to risk the trip, and workers transported them by station wagon to the new swimming site. To the delight of staff neither the trip nor the new location troubled the children. Watching them giggling as they repeatedly collided with each other and climbed over and through each other's arms and legs in a happy tangle both going and returning, workers concluded that the children were comfortable because their contagious physical interaction with classmates enabled each child to bring along his or her own supportive emotional context.

Such body-to-body contagious activity provides disordered children—as it does normal infants—a way of relating emotionally without specific awareness of self–other distinctions. Brainstem dysfunction impedes contagious input less than turn-taking input because it requires less precision. Contagious activity may serve disordered children as a diffuse source of emotional support, as a means of establishing interactive systems, or as a means of helping disordered children transform interactive into social systems.

CONSTRUCTIVE INTERVENTION WITH CONTAGIOUS SPHERES

Establishing Interactive Systems

The ultimate goal of establishing social systems that include both emotional contact with a care giver and reference to objects requires first helping disordered children establish systems that accent one or another aspect of social systems. This approach parallels the course of normal development described by Trevarthen and Hubley (1978). These investigators found a pattern in which the infant interacts vigorously with the care giver the first 3 to 4 months and then becomes relatively unresponsive from 4 to 6 months of age. They suggested that this dip in interpersonal reactivity is caused by the infant's preoccupation with prehension of objects during this period and the inability to deal simultaneously with both object and care giver. But by 6 months of age the interest in relating to the care giver reasserts itself to the point that the child begins to express distress at being separated. Between 9 and 10 months of age the child begins to integrate person with object in a way that presages future social and cognitive development.

To parallel this progression the disordered child learns to cope first with action and objects, then with people, and finally with objects *and* people. The child achieves this through contagious spheres of activity. These spheres are repetitive, engaging patterns consisting of worker-guided actions that the child performs. For example, if a child has some emotional relationship with the care giver but is quite scattered and unable to establish systems involving action and objects, first efforts may be directed toward developing systems involving action and objects. The guiding notion is that by introducing spheres involving repetitive, contagious body activity with actions and objects and then with people, the child moves closer to developing systems with people that include reference to objects.

Contagious Spheres with Objects

When a contagious sphere turns into a system involving objects, for example, rapidly and excitedly picking up and throwing objects into a box, there is a blending of affective and cognitive components. The affective component helps generate the pattern of activity (picking up and throwing objects), whereas the redundancy provides opportunities for the child's cognition to gradually take in and distinguish one part of the system (picking up and throwing objects) from another (throwing them *into a box*). If the system remains purely affective, the child may throw anything that comes to hand without respect to location. On the other hand, if the system is prematurely too cognitive—"Little objects go in the red box and big objects go in the blue box"—disordered children may never "get into it." The contagious aspect is most essential to begin establishing the system. Once it is partially established (parts internalized), contagion becomes less necessary.

Because an organized approach to objects is essential in forming social systems that include reference to objects, a scattered, hyperactive child unable to engage objects requires help. Contagious spheres are designed to develop the required organization.

> A 33-month-old, nonverbal, hyperactive child, when not fixated on stereotypic behavior, would dart around aimlessly, apparently incapable of any functional, age-appropriate involvement with objects and toys. He had frequent temper tantrums accompanied by loud, shrill screams but was able to seek affection from his parents and respond to the emotionality in their voice commands.
>
> To help him organize his behavior, closed, contagious big-body spheres (climbing up steps and jumping off or sliding down and then repeating the sequence) drew on his motoric capacities. These spheres were presented in an unusually fast tempo and did not allow any unstructured, open components. This kept the child engaged by the physical structure of the spheres and effectively forestalled the hyperactive jumping from one salient object or event to another. Gradually these motoric spheres were opened up with new tasks, and the child began, on his own, to integrate them.
>
> In the course of 13 months of cognitive-developmental (C-D) systems work, attention span increased and random motoric behavior and tantrums decreased. Although not yet able to communicate with signs or spoken words, the child responded to parental requests and directions in a far more differentiated way and showed increasing understanding of the words, gestures, and facial expressions of others.

More frequently a disordered child may have considerable capacity to deal with objects but have little or no awareness of his or her parents. A variety of contagious spheres, with their expansions, develop this awareness.

Contagious Spheres with People

Developmentally, the contagious spheres introduced to develop awareness of the care giver are analogous to infants' social interactions up to about 12 months of age. They involve exchanges within a dyad consisting of child and worker or care giver. By introducing spheres involving repetitive, contagious body activity with another, disordered children gain repeated opportunities to orient toward and relate to the person with whom they are participating. The intent is to make it possible for the child, through this kind of arousing activity, to develop a relationship with a "special" person.

Because early development begins with face-to-face physical (proximal) involvement with the parenting person and gradually becomes a distal engagement between the infant and the parent, the first spheres for very withdrawn, isolated children (autistic, neurologically impaired, emotionally deprived) seek to parallel this process.

With the use of a *Rocking sphere,* many disordered children who rock by themselves can transform it into an interpersonal activity. The worker or care giver sits on a stool, with the child either lying infant-style in the adult's arms or sitting astride the adult's legs. Typically, the adult's arms and hands are supporting the back and head of the child. This is necessary so that, as the adult moves from Position A (tilted back) to Position B (leaning forward), the rocking movement does not interfere with the eye contact so necessary for interaction.

The adult's intent is to establish a rocking game by starting slowly with a quiet voice, gradually building up the rocking tempo and the voice to a level of excitement, and then abruptly interrupting the motion. Prior to interrupting the sphere, the adult observes the child for signs that he or she is beginning to anticipate the forward rocking motion. When this is evident, the adult, on returning to the leaning-back position, abruptly interrupts all motion. If the child responds to interruption by seeking to continue the rocking sequence (compensatory response)—as shown by intense eye contact, incipient rocking motion (or any sounds such as "Whee!" that the adult has been producing)—then the child is successfully internalizing the sphere *with another person.* After repeating the sphere 10 or 12 times, the sphere may be expanded.

Expansions may be developed by applying the same procedure with the child and adult seated face to face in a *rocking chair.* Here, the rocking motion of the chair substitutes for the adult's motion described earlier. As before, the sphere should be interrupted when the chair is in its leaning-back position. This may be followed by a *Rowing sphere,* in which the adult and child face each other while seated on the floor. The adult takes the hands of the child and places his or her feet against the child's feet. Again the sphere begins quietly with slow rocking as the adult repetitively pulls the child from a supine to a sitting position and gradually picks up tempo and excitement, the adult saying "Pull!" each time pulling occurs. When the child begins to pull, the adult interrupts by becoming immobile in the leaning-back position. The child's tendency to continue the rowing sphere by either pulling or saying "Pull" indicates that further expansion of the sphere is appropriate.

Still another expansion requires a loop of elastic cloth within which both adult and child can sit facing but not touching each other. Because the cloth is looped around the torsos of both adult and child, the expanded rowing sphere can be established merely by leaning alternatively against the elastic cloth. Again, when the child seems engaged with the adult in a repetitive, rhythmic pulling by leaning against the elastic cloth, the adult interrupts the sequence while in the leaning-back position. The adult should then be alert to the child's pulling action as an indication of need/wish to continue the sphere.

In the *Bouncing sphere* the worker, holding the child under the arms, helps the child bounce in place. After starting slowly, the pace quickens and builds in excitement until the worker suddenly interrupts to determine if the child seeks to continue the system. Typically, the sphere is accompanied by rhythmic comments such as "Up, up, up we go!" in synchrony with the bouncing movements.

Expansions may include the use of a small trampoline that the worker carefully monitors when bouncing with the child. As before, periodic interruptions permit assessment of the child's engagement in the sphere and disposition to continue.

A *Mutual Touching sphere* involving body-to-body interaction, provides systematic efforts to make interactions between child and care giver more deliberate. As they sit facing each other on stools, the worker or care giver touches the child's cheek, while taking the child's hand and placing it on the adult's cheek. This procedure is repeated with nose, ears, eyes, mouth, hands, in a rhythmic but somewhat unpredictable fashion. At various points, the worker interrupts the procedure to determine if the child compensatorily reaches out to the worker without support (see Figure 9.3, p. 348).

A *Swing sphere* helps the child develop in another way the notion of the stability (constancy) of people even though the stimulus properties that fall upon the child's retina are changing as the swing moves away from the adult and then comes closer. The other feature of this sphere is the possibility of understanding the causal relation between the adult pushing the swing and the effect of that pushing on the trajectory that the child in the swing experiences.

After placing the child in an enclosed swing, the adult faces the child and begins to push the swing gently while saying "push." As the child becomes comfortable with the rhythmic motion of the swing, the adult abruptly stops the swing (interruption) to determine whether or *how* the child seeks to continue the swinging motion.

Expansions of this minisphere include varying the extent of the trajectory, changing its shape (inducing a lateral or slightly curved trajectory), and touching the child each time he or she approaches the adult who is pushing. Periodically, each expansion is interrupted to assess the manner in which the sphere is being internalized.

Useful as these spheres are, the child cannot develop them into conventional social patterns until more aware of interdependent relationships with others. Two ways of bringing this about that combine contagion and enhanced awareness of the other are illustrated in Figures 4.1 and 4.2. The first figure shows procedures used in the *Grand Central Station sphere—*

Figure 4.1. Grand Central Station sphere.

Figure 4.2. Buddies sphere.

given its name because it involves an oppositional crowd—in which two or three children go in one direction across sturdy boards suspended between two sets of steps, and another two or three go in exactly the opposite direction. At each end a staff person noisily exhorts two or three children starting from that end to work their way past two or three children coming from the other end. Because space is limited, the children have to make rapid judgments and self-protective maneuvers that take into account the press of oncoming traffic. This is repeated three or four times. Children selected for this procedure are carefully screened for adequate physical stability and coordination, and sufficient staff are on hand to prevent accidents.

Another interactive sequence—the *Buddies sphere*—was designed to establish a more conscious interdependence between children who are relatively unaware of each other. It consists of three adjacent, narrow inclined planks that three children simultaneously climb from ground level to 3 feet above ground (Figure 4.2). Because the inclined planks are quite steep, each child is naturally quite eager to gain support and balance by holding the hand of the child on the plank next to him or her. Typically, the youngest or most vulnerable child is placed on the middle plank so that he or she has an opportunity to have a hand held by the child on either side. After the children reach the top, they walk down the stairs and repeat the process in spheric fashion, perhaps with a different child on the center plank. Following the use of this procedure, children hold hands more readily in walks or excursions outside the Center.

Still other ways in which contagious spheres may be introduced to further the development of one or another aspect of social systems are evident in work with Fred (the child presented in Chapter 3). Contagious spheres were first used with Fred to develop intentional sign or word-guided action and sound making in an interactive context.

CASE STUDY: FRED—CONTAGIOUS SPHERES

A contagious sphere referred to as the *Walk, Jump, Fall, Get-up, Around a Circle sphere* consisted of the worker, Fred, and his father. They formed a circle and rhythmically but in a rapidly paced manner performed various actions as the worker chanted and signed various action-related terms. The manner in which Fred assimilated this sphere is apparent in excerpts from his sessions:

Sessions 67 and 68

Fred showed no response to interruption after having been led through the Walk, Jump . . . Around a Circle sphere.

Session 69

In the Walk, Jump . . . Around a Circle sphere, Fred, following interruption of the jumping activity, jumped by himself. Further, when his father did not immediately join the activity, he pulled on his father to do so.

Session 70

As soon as the worker took Fred's hand to start the Walk, Jump . . . Around a Circle sphere, Fred spontaneously started jumping, a clear indication that he had assimilated that part of the sphere from the previous session a week earlier.

Session 71

As Fred, his father and the worker stood in a circle, Fred again spontaneously began to jump. Also, for the first time he fell (deliberately) by himself and got up, in this way indicating that he was now responsive to this part of the sphere as well.

Session 75

When the worker hesitated before initiating the next sphere, Fred made clear his wish to do the Walk, Jump . . . Around the Circle sphere by repeatedly jumping in place.

Developing Shared Meanings and Reference within Systems

The ability of the child to deliberately play object games with the care giver marks the appearance of social systems among normal 9- to 10-month-old infants. Often, a disordered child has considerable ability to cope with objects but seems to have little awareness of people, particularly of his or her parents. The following case study describes how strategies with contagious spheres enable the child to include care givers within object systems, resulting in enhanced awareness of the care givers.

CASE STUDY: TOMMY—FINDING MOTHER VIA SHARED MEANINGS

Initially, Tommy, a 30-month-old nonverbal toddler, preoccupied with objects, was quite oblivious of his parents' leaving the room; he continued to remain involved with opening and closing boxes or picking up and dropping objects. In the course of a year of C-D systems work, many contagious shared meaning spheres were developed that included the mother and sometimes the father as an integral part.

Noting that one of his favorite stereotypic activities involved sending small objects down a ramp, a worker rapidly collected all the objects and rapidly began passing them to him so that he could continue this activity. In a short while, his mother and father were stationed on each side of the ramp with a quantity of small objects that they would constantly pass to him. After a time, they were instructed to present the object in different ways so that the child had to look up at them to see where their hands were. This continued for about 10 minutes.

In another situation, Tommy would be vigorously involved in scribbling on a paper at one of the stations on the Elevated Square. In the middle of his activity, in spite of his protests, a worker would take his crayon and toss it to a parent at one of the board stations opposite him. This made it necessary for the child, in order to continue scribbling, to walk to the parent and reach for the crayon. As before, the crayon would be oriented in a variety of fashions—in front of the parent's face, to the right, left, and so forth—requiring the child to adjust to the change and notice the parent in order to get the crayon. This procedure was repeated several times.

After a year of work with such spheres, Tommy was retested by having his mother again leave the room while he was occupied with objects. This time he headed straight for the door through which she had left, and, when he could not open the door by himself, went to the examiner and pulled him by the hand to the door so that it might be opened.

Although interventions such as the one with Tommy help include the adult with the child's action–object systems, a true social system requires the capacity to deliberately take turns in an agreed-upon manner. This capacity emerged in Fred (Chapter 3) when, after months of intervention, he decided that he wished to play "chase me" with his worker instead of taking part in the usual, ritualized intervention fare. The infant who achieves this notion about self and others has established the prerequisite conditions for communication with another about objects and events in the world, first through action, then through gesture and words. Although opinion differs about the origin of this "secondary intersubjectivity" (Trevarthen & Hubley, 1978) and the degree to which it is influenced by prior learning, there is general agreement that it occurs in all cultures toward the end of the child's 1st year.

An interesting article on the origins of social games (Ross & Kay, 1980) supports the view that by 12 months of age infants are able to establish reciprocal relationships with adults (social systems) involving objects. It also provides specific support for the present view that social systems form as the infant becomes engaged with the care giver and that *interruption* of these systems results in *compensatory* behavior to maintain them. Further, these compensatory behaviors rapidly assume a referential function as the infant becomes aware of them and of his or her ability to initiate them in an interpersonal context. Ross and Kay described a study in which sixteen 12-month-old infants spent an average of 12 minutes playing with one of two adults (one male, one female) who were strangers at the beginning of the study. Typical games included playing peekaboo, passing a ball back and forth, and alternately throwing blocks in a tub. The adults did not interrupt the game until the pattern of turn-taking intrinsic to each game had been established. Interruptions lasted for 10 seconds during which the adults maintained relaxed facial expressions, seldom spoke, and watched the infants; during interruptions adults refrained from any game-relevant acts. The findings were as follows:

> During the interruptions, the infants were more likely to use referential gestures (gestures that could draw the adult's attention to the toy, such as looking alternatively at the adult and toy, pointing, reaching, and giving) than during the games. Infants were also more likely to partially or fully retake their own turns, or compensate in some way for the adults' turn taking failure during interruptions, than they were during the games. Compensations included acts that were normally part of the adult's turns, such as lifting and dropping a blanket in a game of peekaboo, or behavior that would facilitate the adult's actions, such as placing a tub in the adult's hands when the adult's role included holding the tub out to the infant. The infants watched the game toys and the adults' hand as they manipulated the toys more during games than interruptions; they watch the adults' faces more during interruptions than games. Finally, the infants showed more positive affect during the games than during the interruptions. These differences were all statistically significant. (p. 22)

Clearly, children at this stage of development establish social systems around games that entail shared meanings. Further, the establishment and the maintenance of these systems seem to follow principles of orienting, engagement (system forming), and compensatory action to maintain systems, as described earlier (Chapter 1). The findings reported by Ross and Kay (1980) indicate that this formulation has relevance not only for the development of the body schema (Chapter 2) and the formation of the object (Chapter 3), but also for the development of interpersonal communication. Drawing on such systems, as Bruner (1977) pointed out, enables the developing prelinguistic infant to work out the structural requirements of language communication by sharing meanings in repeated game actions that require a grasp of agent (subject), action (predicate), or object. This same capacity for shared meaning is evident as the infant points to indicate (to another) objects that are beyond reach or in a picture form (Bates et al., 1979; Ninio & Bruner, 1977).

The importance of shared meanings for the development of referential communication is further suggested in a study by Brenner and Mueller (1982) of two play groups of male toddlers observed over a 7-month period—one starting at 12 and ending at 19 months, the other starting at 16 and ending at 23 months. Brenner and Mueller found that the number of shared meanings by dyads significantly increased in the younger group between ages 12 and 18 months; the most dramatic increase was between 15 and 18 months, jumping from 9 (16%) to 39 (40%). No such significant increase was evident in the older group. Instances of shared meanings between toddlers included *run–chase* (or *run–follow*) games—"They both indicate that this is enjoyable (and social) interaction by laughing, screeching happily, or looking back over the shoulder"; *peekaboo*—"Where one child hides and appears suddenly and the other acknowledges this by smiling or laughing"; *rough and tumole—* "Both acknowledge the play with smile and shrieks"; *object exchange—* "The children exchange an object, utilizing the behaviors of 'offer' and 'receive'"; *object possession struggle—*"The children struggle over possession of an object"; and *shared reference—*"The children name or label an object or set of objects by mutual pointing and vocalizing" (pp. 384–385).

The surge in shared meanings directly preceded the surge in naming that occurs at about 18 months as a function of the naming insight (Nelson, 1985) and that introduces the symbolic-sign stage (see Chapter 5) in which the child discovers that "each thing has its name" (Stern, 1914, p. 108). The implication is that the acceleration of shared meanings between 15 and 18 months provides the prerequisite social framework for the naming insight and the spoken reference it fosters. Specifically, it is in accord with the view of Bruner (1975, 1977), Dore (1975), and Halliday (1975) that such shared meaning contexts between care giver and infant, as well as between peers, provide the interpersonal framework within which functional and referential communication first develops.

Taking Turns in Contagious Spheres

Once disordered children achieve systems enabling appropriate interactions with others, they advance to spheres that address the problem of shared meanings both with care giver and peers in increasingly more sophisticated forms. Contagious spheres were used with Fred to help establish such systems.

CASE STUDY: FRED—SHARED MEANINGS

These spheres were designed to develop the notion of turn-taking, which is such a critical part of communication. Reciprocal spheres included the Peekaboo sphere. Here, the worker, after placing a cloth over Fred, would—on removing the cloth—delightedly "discover" Fred and sign and say "Hi!" Then, to develop reciprocity, the worker would put the cloth over her head to see if Fred would "discover" her and, if so, whether he would say and sign "Hi!"

Sessions 67–72

During these six sessions Fred showed no response to the peekaboo procedure.

Session 73

After the worker placed the scarf over his head, Fred, for the first time removed the scarf by himself.

Session 84

Fred was fully involved in the sphere. Not only did he pull the scarf off the worker's head and his own head, he spontaneously patted his head when he wanted the scarf put on his head so that he might be found. When found, he produced the sign for "Hi!" in conjunction with waving.

Session 89

Fred clearly signed "Hi!" both at the *beginning* of the session when he responded to the worker's greeting and in context of peekaboo following his discovery under the scarf.

Expansions

Instead of cloth, the worker could have introduced cardboard and wood screens. Unlike cloth, however, these rigid materials are not placed directly on the child's face but are presented as the child is sitting upright. To introduce location expansions, the adult brings the various screens closer to his or her face disappearing behind the screen. Each time the adult reappears, he or she says, with great delight, "Hi!" or "Here I am!" Location expansions also include the adult's appearing on one side or other of the screen or at top or bottom of the screen. The adult can develop temporal expansions by changing the rhythm of appearances from quite rapid (short delay) to slow (a longer delay).

Having achieved the ability to reciprocate with another, the child now needs only to learn how to include reference to an object within the interactive system. This is accomplished with integrative spheres that systematically involve objects in a manner paralleling the same capacity as it begins to develop among normal 9- to 10-month-old infants.

Often children who do not relate to each other directly can relate through an object that requires them to interact in a prescribed manner. The utility of objects for this purpose was demonstrated by two 8-year-old boys (limited verbal, partially recovered autistic) riding a crudely made wooden car down a grassy hill. Abruptly, a front wheel came off the axle and the car stopped. Because the children wished to continue riding the car down the hill, the abrupt interruption was disconcerting and they kept placing the loose wheel ineffectively against the axle. Subsequently, workers had one child lift the car off the ground and hold it until the other child could attach the wheel. After a time both children began to adjust their movements in order to accomplish this. Later, when the wheel again came off (workers took pains to ensure that the wheel was not *too* secure) each child began to assume the correct role to get the wheel back on. After a time workers tried reversing roles and met with resistance. However, they persisted, and the children eventually learned both roles as well as a useful way of interacting with each other.

Workers also exploited objects while building a clubhouse for the children in a rather dense wooded area. To get the needed planks to the site, several pairs of autistic children carried planks from their source about 50 yards away through the wooded area to the club site. Initially, each child carrying the end of a 10-foot plank seemed quite oblivious of the child at the other end. When they went into the wooded area, the plank would get wedged between trees. Then, as staff exhorted, "Get that plank here. We need it!" the children—with some staff assistance—began to adjust to each other so that they might get the plank around the trees. This procedure was repeated many times with staff carefully indicating routes that would require the children to recheck the position of each other constantly to get the planks to the club site.

Because of the utility of these kinds of "forced" interactions, this situation has recently been adapted for the classroom by having the children build a simple house. This entails bringing in about three dozen planks 5 to 6 feet in length and 5 to 6 inches wide and requiring the children—two to each plank—to rapidly move the stack from one location in the classroom to another. Once accomplished, they form a rectangle frame above the ground by using four planks to connect each of four portable stations (each station is about 4 feet high). They then build a roof to their house first by laying planks across the frame and then by leaning planks around three sides. As the children bring the planks to the house, the teaching staff place various obstacles in front of them—a table, some stools, and so forth—that require the rapidly moving teams to constantly adapt to changing circumstances. As one team places its plank and goes back for another, it is immediately followed by the second and then the third team. When the house is built, the children can eat their lunch inside.

Other devices that require the collaboration of two children have been built. An example of such a device—the broken table—is illustrated in Figure 4.3. The table can best be assembled when two children work together. Typically, the incompleteness of such a familiar structure induces within some of the children a strong need to complete the interrupted system.

If broken objects are not available, the worker uses systematic interruption of contagious spheres involving action toward or with an object. The interruptions induce the child to maintain or restore the emerging system by referring through sign or word to the object or event that has suddenly become unavailable. The following examples of spheres and their expansions are taken from sessions with Fred.

CASE STUDY: FRED—INTERACTIVE SPHERES

The *Giving-and-Getting sphere* involved arranging Fred with a variety of objects in his lap. The worker, sitting opposite, then said and signed "Give" (tapping the extended palm) and required Fred to give her an object. After this sequence was well established with the help of rapid, worker-guided

Figure 4.3. Broken Table device to encourage interaction.

exchanges, the worker placed assorted objects in her lap and required Fred to sign and/or say "Give" at which she would give him the requested object.

Session 77

Fred participated in the reciprocal *give* sphere in which, with a pile of objects in his lap, he faced the worker. Each time she produced the *give* sign (accompanied by the spoken word "Give!") he would give the worker one of the objects. Subsequently, when the roles were reversed, Fred, for the first time, was able to produce the *give* sign to get objects from the worker.

Session 79

Fred, although cranky, participated in a give sphere with father and worker. He produced a *give* sign that was a fusion of "give" and "open."

Session 80

Fred made the *give* sign (touching hands together) to receive a block from his father or the worker. He was then to put the block in a mailbox, request that the mailbox be opended (with *open* sign), and give the block to the father or worker as requested. He did not produce the *open* sign but complied with requests for blocks from others.

Session 81

In context of the give sphere previously described, the worker added the term *more,* that is, *give more.* Fred immediately imitated the sequence. Fred would first do the *give* sign, worker would add the *more* sign (bringing tips of fingers from one hand to the tips of the other), and finally Fred made both signs together.

In the *Interactive Object-Down sphere,* after the worker and Fred had learned to alternate sending objects down a slide, the worker required Fred to pause until she said and signed "Down!" at which point Fred would release the object. Then, Fred was required to say and/or sign "Down!" to the worker or to his father, and one of them would release an object down the slide. This alternation of command was repeated a number of times.

Session 81

Fred produced the *down* sign as part of an interactive sphere. First, Fred would send a car down a slide, then the father would alternate by doing the same. Next, the father made the *down* sign to Fred—indicating that he was to send a car down. Following this (at first with assistance), Fred produced the *down* sign, directing his father to send a car down. This

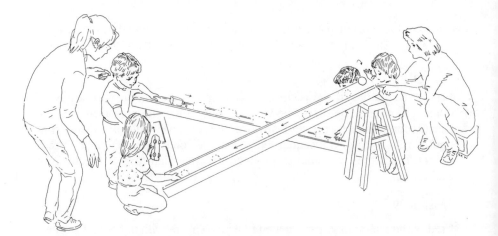

Figure 4.4. Interactive Object-Down sphere involving four children with varied objects.

interactive sphere continued for a number of cycles. Fred also took part in the same sphere in a classroom context with other children, as indicated in Figure 4.4. In that setting, with four children involved, the task required far more staff guidance to ensure that each child promptly either picked up objects or released them down the ramp. When the children were paced properly, staff could remove all support and watch the four children continue the system by themselves for several minutes.

These sequences demonstrate the importance of various spheres to assist disordered children in their developing ability to interact with each other in a productive fashion. The work is *constructive* in the sense that the interventions help create entirely new social systems. Such interventions differ from those in which the child demonstrates fragments of social systems that fail to operate in any cogent fashion. Here, the task is referred to as *realizing social systems* because the worker's task is to help the child fully realize and complete or pull together the parts into a functioning social system.

REALIZING SOCIAL SYSTEMS

Establishing Predictable Human Contact

The following case study describes a behavior-disordered 6-year-old boy who, although possessing a number of fragmentary skills—part-systems— such as the ability to label various objects and even to sight-read and sound out words, had not learned how to integrate those skills in his relations with others. Because he lacked a working repertoire of skills and functional language to express his needs for nurturing and guidance, he was, when he came to the Center, regularly wracked by severe tantrums. He was viewed as an autistic child with a system-forming disorder.

CASE STUDY: ROY—A FRAGMENTED CHILD

Roy came to the Center after having spent 3 years in a behavior modification program that stressed food rewards for performance and "time out" for control of unacceptable behavior, particularly tantrums. He was referred after staff at the previous setting had found him to be unmanageable; he had bitten, pinched, and scratched both staff and children in the midst of his tantrums. During these tantrums he would frequently pound against the floor with his head and use it as a battering ram against people trying to help him. Tantrums often lasted 30 minutes to an hour, ending only when he was totally exhausted.

Roy was a tall, aquiline-featured boy who toe-walked around the room, occasionally uttering a few words. He would pull a worker toward a desired object, and the slightest delay in getting what he needed could trigger a savage tantrum lasting for an hour. A site visit revealed that at home, Roy lived in a shadow world—shades drawn—with his family moving carefully around him. Few demands were made of him for fear that he would tantrum. At home he was typically "on the move," running between living room and bedroom, pausing for a few seconds to watch TV before resuming his endless pilgrimage.

During the first few weeks after his enrollment at the Center, his mother frequently kept him home because the effort required to get him on the school bus was too great. She also hesitated to wake him up for fear that this alone would precipitate violent tantrums. Once he was levered into the bus, he would become calm until he got to school. Then he would have to be pried out of the bus—screaming and flailing his arms and legs—in order to be brought into the building, a scene that would be reenacted when he had to leave school for home.

It was first hypothesized that Roy's difficulty—exacerbated by time-out procedures—came from inability to connect disparate spaces; that his sense of self did not yet allow him to internalize a notion of home when he was brought to a new place. Consequently, home no longer existed for him when he came to the Center. Workers, who observed him repeatedly taking 2 to 3 steps forward, hesitating, then taking 2 to 3 steps back, doubted whether he could "keep" events that had occurred only a few moments before. His retracing of steps seemed to be an adaptive effort to "fix" the new space in which he found himself so that he was not constantly moving from one unmarked space to another.

Following Roy's first tantrum of the day (as he entered his classroom), workers decided to keep him within the boundaries of that room and to introduce a ritual (sphere)—going up steps, walking across a board, going down a slide, and then repeating the sequence—to engage and provide him with a notion of where he was and what was to happen next. For a brief period (perhaps 5 minutes) he seemed to be engaged by this activity. Abruptly, however, he would strike out, kick, or go limp in an effort to thwart staff efforts to keep him moving through the sequence. Efforts to continue resulted in wild-eyed escalation of his upset requiring that he be held to prevent him from hurting himself or others.

When he was held securely and spoken to reassuringly, his lashing about gradually subsided, and he would stare intently at the person holding him. Often, however, as soon as he was released—no matter how gradually— the tantrums would resume.

After observing him in several tantrums, staff concluded that his upset came not only from the absence of predictability but from the loss of a bond with an important person—presumably his mother. Because it was not feasible for the mother to be in school at this time, it was decided to have the teacher stay close to him, to avoid his lunges whenever possible, and to mimic all his behavior. Then, should he respond to her mimicry with new behavior directed toward her, she was to mimic that also. The goal was to establish a bond as an infant might with the mother, through mimicry and minute mutual adjustments. At the same time demands for performance from Roy were reduced to a minimum.

This modified approach was partially successful. As the teacher tracked and mimicked his behavior, he would watch her with fascination for extended periods of time. However, if the teacher delayed too long in the tracking of his behavior, he might suddenly lash out by biting or scratching her. In self-defense the teacher began to wear arm paddings that reduced bruising. After a time Roy would sometimes initiate new behaviors at a distance from her (raising and lowering eyebrows) that he clearly expected her to mimic.

Noting an increased stability in his behavior, his class was increased from two to three children. The introduction of a new child—and the teacher's necessary shift of attention from Roy to this child—triggered a whole series of new tantrums, suggesting that he had regressed to his prior state. Roy's upset appeared to be based on his inability to keep the teacher as a special person when she turned toward someone else.

We sought at first to provide Roy with articles of clothing from the teacher that might serve as a transitional object (Winnicott, 1953). However, these had no apparent effect. The only thing that seemed to calm him was holding him securely, probably because of the increased experience of his body boundaries, and thus of his own existence, that this provided. To capitalize on this possibility, an upholstered device, called a ''Snug Box'' was constructed with a movable wall that could be pressed against him by the teacher (Figure 4.5), similar in purpose to the ''squeeze machine'' designed by Temple Grandin (Grandin & Scariano, 1986). This device calmed him almost instantly and he was able to again make contact with the teacher who resumed interactive tracking of his behavior.

Figure 4.5. Using the Snug Box with interactive tracking.

Soon, Roy would spontaneously go inside the Snug Box and seek to pull the walls close to him, perhaps so that he might better feel the boundaries of his body. At times the teacher would enter the box with him so she could sensitively mimic his behavior when he was feeling more secure. With the combined help from the Snug Box and interactive tracking, Roy began to bond with the teacher as evident in his sometimes touching her gently after striking out at her.

During this period Roy began to be fascinated by the sign and spoken language program. He would teeter on his toes in front of the video presentation of the signs and words (see Chapter 10), as well as in front of the reading program (see Chapter 11). Soon he was using more of his words in context. This was particularly true when he saw printed words. Yet, neither spoken or printed words could guide his behavior, and he could not use words to influence the behavior of others.

The most recent intervention with Roy entailed teaching him to share word meanings in an interpersonal context, in a sphere where teacher and Roy alternated word–action sequences. First the teacher would place words on the board, say them, and then perform the relevant act, for example, jumping after reading "jump" or falling after reading "fall." Roy would laugh when this happened and soon would perform the actions himself after reading them. The next phase concerned the use of words by the teacher to direct Roy to perform certain actions followed by Roy's use of the same and then different words to have his teacher perform actions. Gradually, out of this procedure, Roy learned that he could cause someone to do something by using both printed words and signed or spoken words.

Staff resumed introducing Roy into various spheres, both on elevated board structures and on the ground and found that he could now accept them—particularly when guided by his special teacher. His reality was systematically expanded by having him use the Tableau Calendar (see Chapter 3) and then a picture calendar, so that he might develop a notion of how his day was organized and realize that at the end of each day he would go home. Consultations with his mother emphasized the importance of carrying through the calendar at home as well as at school. Soon Roy could tolerate increased demands for performance and was able to leave the bus to walk into the building without tantrumming. At this point his mother began to participate regularly in the school program. She rapidly adapted the various school procedures for use at home. Currently, although Roy remains a very vulnerable child, his tantrums are much reduced in frequency and duration.

Discussion

A variety of body-related interventions helped Roy achieve social systems that enabled him to function and to learn. In retrospect, the single most important factor was the establishment of a bond, through interactive tracking of his behavior by the teacher—a strategy that closely paralleled mother–child exchanges during the 1st year of life. This replaying of the contingency relationship between mother and infant may have helped establish the sense of efficacy between him and his teacher so important in establishing a bond in any social system. A second important factor concerned the accenting of body boundaries, first through the physical containment that was necessary to protect him and others, and secondarily through the Snug Box.

The teacher's innovative combining of both the Snug Box and interactive tracking clearly accelerated the formation of social systems. Another important intervention concerned sharing the meanings of spoken and printed word fragments, first to self-referring body functions (*jump, fall,* etc.), and then to statements that influenced the teacher's actions—leading finally to his ability to use words reciprocally for communicating needs and intentions within stable social systems. Finally, the mother's involvement in his program was important because it allowed her to learn effective strategies, such as the Tableau and Picture Calendars that she could use with him at home. Then, with his mother's help he was able to generalize social systems developed with his teacher to home and elsewhere.

However, not all incomplete social systems need to be worked with so intensively for effectiveness. Occasionally, a child, although developed in cognitive areas, seems not to have grasped the social system that allows the notion of sharing or turn-taking. This was the case for the following child.

Development of Turn-Taking within a Social System

CASE STUDY: PACO—UNABLE TO SHARE

After 5 years at the Center, Paco, a dark, handsome 8-year-old, although formally diagnosed autistic, was operating at a near normal level in all but interpersonal areas. He had great difficulty working out relationships with the other children in the class. If anyone tried to use a toy he was playing with, he would scream and tantrum. This was particularly true in the play area when he was riding a bike around the path. The school routine—because there are more children than bicycles—requires each child after riding once or twice around the path to get off and give the bike to the next waiting child. This, Paco flatly refused to do. Pressed, he screamed and tantrummed for a half hour.

Asked, when calm, why he was so concerned about giving another child a turn, he replied that he knew he never would get the bike back. In other words, Paco only had a system involving himself and the bike. To allow someone else to take a turn would require an expanded system including Paco, the bike, and the other person. It would also require the bike to be part of a social system involving the abstract notion of turn-taking, which contrasted sharply with the immediacy of his physical engagement with the bike. Lacking such an expanded system, he experienced each demand for the bike as an interruption that triggered a powerful compensatory drive to maintain the original system. Then, when the bike was taken away, seeing no way that he could get it back, he responded with catastrophic tantrums.

Paco was seen in conventional psychotherapy, and efforts were made to help him play out his concerns and to reassure him that he would get the bike or toy back for another turn if he gave it over. None of these interventions worked. What did work was the use of hypnotic inductions that enabled him to vividly visualize and experience himself first riding around the playground path, nervously turning the bike over to another child, and watching the child ride the bike around the path, get off, and return the bike to him. Paco then—with a happy smile on his face—saw himself get on and again ride the bike. This visualization of a successful turn-taking experience was repeated on three consecutive occasions with Paco relaxing noticeably each time he saw the bike being returned to him. After the second induction, Paco's teacher reported that he was able to yield the bike in the play area for the first time without distress. After solving the bike exchange, Paco spontaneously generalized turn-taking to other situations in the classroom. Even when concerned about another child taking his things, he no longer fell apart but could, both with and without the teacher's intervention, handle the issue effectively.

Discussion

The intervention was effective because, although Paco was unable to expand his system with the bike spontaneously, he could do so in a trance state when he literally saw himself giving the bike to another and felt the relief of getting it back. Thus, the quasi reality of the trance state established the system expansion that he was unable to establish by himself. There is a direct relationship between the use of spheres and rituals for nonverbal children and the use of hypnotically induced "image spheres" for verbal children. Preverbal children engaged by spheres are experiencing a form of sensorimotor hypnosis in that they are often absorbed by the events within the sphere to the exclusion of all else. This engagement parallels that induced among verbal children and adults who show a similar exclusive engagement within the hypnotic state.

In Paco's case hypnosis helped present an expanded social system so vividly that it provided a transition to real-world functioning for him. In the following case a verbal child with a seizure disorder was helped, without hypnosis, to compensate for the traumatic loss of a key figure—an interrupted social system—by creating a substitute social system.

"Creating a Family" to Compensate for a Traumatic Loss

Sometimes, when the child's family system breaks down, it is desirable to introduce a make-believe family with its social systems to provide the emotional support and nurturing a child requires.

CASE STUDY: BARNEY—LOOKING FOR A FAMILY

A physically abused and emotionally deprived child with a seizure disorder, Barney became a ward of the court at 3 years of age and was assigned to a foster home while attending the Center. During this stable period in his life he developed an important relationship with his foster mother and began for the first time to speak in two- to three-word sentences. Unfortunately, this period came to an end when, after 3 years, the foster mother, for reasons of health, felt that she could no longer keep him and returned him to the Department of Social Services. He was then placed in a temporary foster home.

Barney became seriously distressed and refused to defecate to the point that he required periodic hospitalization so his impacted feces might be removed. At school his behavior deteriorated; he would throw over desks, tear papers from the wall, and without provocation assault children near him. To help him through this difficult time the staff decided to create a make-believe family for him—a social system that would build on and accent in family terms his already existing relationships at the Center. He was helped to notice that his teacher (with whom he had a good relationship) was looking after him in many ways as if she were his mother (she bandaged his cuts and bruises and gave him hugs), that the other five students in his class were like brothers and sisters (they shared toys and played with him), and that the directors of the Center who checked in on him each day and gave him little cars were like grandparents to him.

With the introduction of this family-accented social system, Barney's chaotic behavior rapidly stabilized. He began to defecate normally, to accept little cars from the directors to take home, and to stay in touch with his classmates after school. When another foster family accepted him and began the process of adopting him, the emphasis on his make-believe family was reduced. Currently, except for periodic instability when a teacher or child leaves or a new child comes into his home, he is able to sustain himself emotionally. The staff anticipate that within the next year he will return to a regular public school setting.

Discussion

Particularly interesting in Barney's case is that all the features that made up his "school family system" existed during the period of his greatest upset—but were ineffective. They only became effective when they were cast and brought to his attention as a family system, that is, "Teacher takes care of you *like* Mother," and so forth. Only then was he able to draw on the school relationships in a way that permitted him to partially reestablish the lost family system and achieve stability.

In a sense, Barney's case demonstrates one way in which a state (feeling part of a family) may be generalized to a new setting (school). The case study of Connie, a schizophrenic girl with a syncretic system disorder, demonstrates other ways in which systems developed in one setting may be transferred to another.

Generalizing New Learning to All Social Systems

CASE STUDY: CONNIE—LEARNING TO CONNECT DIFFERENT REALITIES

Connie, now 28 years old, was diagnosed as a childhood schizophrenic at the age of 5. Staff members have worked with and followed her in the clinic for about 22 years. At first she was unmanageable, tantrummed frequently, spoke in word salads, and had completely intimidated her mother and father (a paraplegic) with her bizarre behavior. They were ready to institutionalize her but came to the Center as a last resort. The parents were helped to set limits and to expect performance of basic spheres that soon became internalized systems. These included emptying the trash, cleaning her room, and setting the table; they received reassurance that they were not harming Connie by requiring that she do these things. Her regular therapy sessions involved discussion, demonstration, and role play of basic social systems having to do with "playing fair" and taking turns. Soon she began to look forward to the sessions.

With the help of the Symbol Accentuation Program (Chapter 11) she learned how to read and write. At first she was quite resistant and would come in saying she was a truck or a cat. Told with some firmness that trucks or cats couldn't learn to read, that teachers worked only with children, and that teachers at the Center hoped she would be a little girl so they could teach her to read, she started crying, saying she was a little girl and wouldn't be a truck or a cat any more. At the next session she came in saying she was a little girl and began to learn how to read. However, although she progressed during her clinic sessions, her reading failed to generalize to her public school setting. There, she was still a "truck" or a "cat."

This problem was handled by inviting Connie's teacher to a clinic session. Then, when Connie was reading appropriately for a staff member seated next to her, that person beckoned her teacher to take that seat. Connie continued reading until she looked up and saw her teacher. At this, she stopped reading. The staff worker then walked over to her and chided her saying that she wasn't playing fair—that if she read for workers at the Center she should also read in the same way for her teacher and for her mother and father. She was then asked to play fair by reading for her public school teacher, which she did. Subsequently, she generalized her reading to all settings without further difficulty.

Later, her mother reported that Connie was having difficulty learning how to swim in a pool used by her school and that she was refusing even to take part in swimming lessons. After adjusting schedules, one of us (AM) appeared at poolside and indicated, after Connie had recovered from the shock of seeing him in that unexpected setting, that he had every confidence that she could learn to swim and, indeed, that he expected her to do so. Apparently, because she had internalized her worker as someone who expected her to do things and would help her find ways to do them, she began to learn and faithfully reported her progress. She weathered adolescence with specific instruction from one of us (EE-M) on menstruation and is now in a group home. She commutes each day to her job in a sheltered workshop. It has not been necessary to place her on drugs or to institutionalize her. She has, however, required and will undoubtedly continue to require structured support on a weekly basis indefinitely.

Discussion

The application of C-D systems theory has been important at each stage in Connie's development. Initially, it helped her develop daily rituals at home, providing some organization to her life and communicating to her parents that she *could* respond to demands and carry out tasks. It came into play again to correct syncretic systems ("I'm a truck, . . . I'm a cat") by pitting her aberrant systems against her increasingly important relationship with workers at the Center ("Trucks or cats can't learn to read . . . we work only with children"). And, finally, in getting her to use her new reading ability, application of C-D systems theory expanded her "play fair" social system to include reading for her teacher and others.

SUMMARY

Dividing early social functioning into interactive and social systems, this chapter defines interactive systems as those covering the period from birth to 9 or 10 months of age, during which the infant interacts with either the care giver or the object but cannot include the object within the social interaction. Social systems begin with the achievement of an infant–care giver relationship at about 9 to 10 months of age in which one adult is more special than another. These new systems permit the child to receive and give an object to the care giver and to develop progressively more abstract ways of sharing meaning with the care giver. These include the shift from directed action to gesture signs to spoken words.

Many behavior-disordered children—particularly those termed autistic—fail to achieve these developmental sequences because brainstem dysfunctions interfere with their ability to process input from inside their bodies so that it can be related to external events. These children behave as if they are perpetually out of synchrony with the messages sent them. Lacking the capacity to interact effectively, many such disordered children cannot develop the sense common to normal infants that they are able to influence people to meet their needs. One consequence of this failure may be an obsessive preoccupation with objects, which have more predictable properties.

Each disordered child requires specific spheric interventions to remedy deficits that get in the way of meaningful interaction with another. For Fred, the spheres were designed to teach him to intend action toward people in both a contagious and a reciprocal fashion. Contagious, reciprocal, and integrative spheres were used with Fred to help him develop social systems that include reference to objects and events in the world.

The last part of the chapter describes work with children who require intervention to build in or to realize inoperative social systems. For one autistic child with a system-forming disorder, the intervention established a bond with another that became the framework within which the child's language fragments could be used in a functional manner. With another partially recovered autistic child, the task was to build in a turn-taking system that could generalize to other situations requiring this interpersonal skill. For a third child, traumatized by separation and loss, a make-believe social system was constructed to serve as a transitional family until the child could "root" in a real family. Finally, a schizophrenic girl, unable spontaneously to generalize her new learning from one site to another, was helped to do so by expanding her "fair play" social system to include not only her workers but her school teacher and other significant people.

CHAPTER 5

Developing Spoken Language

A PERSPECTIVE ON LANGUAGE: CONTINUITY VERSUS DISCONTINUITY

Recently, parents concerned about the language development of their 5-year-old seizure-disordered daughter brought her to the Center for an evaluation. The parents had worked intensively to get the girl to speak and, when requested, demonstrated that she could repeat certain words—"cup," "ball," "cookie," "mama." However, the child's evaluation established that she used spoken language in a very limited way, relating some words to their objects in an extremely restricted manner and grossly overgeneralizing others. For example, she could use the word *cup* to relate to a cup only if she could pick it up and raise it to her lips. When the cup was placed on its side and out of reach, she could not call it "cup," even when pressed. On the other hand, the word *cookie* was used to refer to anything that she could eat.

The limited nature of their daughter's speech was explained to the parents as a kind of conditioned response in which, for example, the word *cup* was a signal that compelled her to act toward the cup in much the same way that Pavlov's dogs on hearing a buzzer were directed toward food. However, she lacked an understanding of words as symbols that represented objects. If she understood words as symbols, she would know that *cup* represented not only a particular cup in all possible situations but any of a variety of cups that shared certain features in common. Further, she would know that *cookie* related to one kind of edible and not to anything that could be eaten. The parents calmly agreed and then the father, who had studied the origins of language, added that they were not concerned because spoken language is on a continuum and his daughter was now on that continuum, so he saw no reason why she would not eventually understand the meaning of words in the manner that had been described.

The view of language development expressed by this father bears on a controversy as to the continuous or discontinuous nature of language development that has important implications for helping disordered children develop language. If language development is continuous, then getting the words formed and somehow linked to a relevant object becomes the primary task. From there, the more symbolic meanings of the word would gradually develop. However, if language development is discontinuous—and the representational function of words is qualitatively different from words as conditioned signals—then there is an apparently impassable chasm from word as signal to symbol. Perhaps the best known proponent of just such a discontinuity position is Cassirer (1970) who stated his position as follows:

> All of the phenomena which are commonly described as conditioned reflexes (signs) are not merely very far from but even opposed to the essential character of human symbolic thought. Symbols—in the proper sense of the term—cannot be reduced to mere signals. Signals and symbols belong to two different universes of discourse; a signal is part of the physical world of being; a symbol is part of the human world of meaning. (pp. 34–35)

From the vantage point of Cassirer's distinction, achieving words as signals is quite irrelevant to the achievement of words as symbols. The user of words as signs shows three important characteristics: a compulsion on hearing or using the sign-word to relate it to its immediate referent; a lack of any specific awareness of the sign as a separate and independent entity in relation to its referent; and an overgeneralization of the sign to events that have only a single property or function in common with the original referent.

The child described earlier used words in a manner generally consistent with this definition. For example, the word *cup* was so closely tied to her use of the object that when it varied from this immediate use (lying on its side away from her), it was no longer understood as a cup. That same tendency to tie words to immediate body function also accounted for her overgeneralizing *cookie* to anything that she could eat.

With the achievement of symbols, words no longer trigger a compulsion to act nor are they tied so closely to body function. Instead, they now act as surrogates of objects or categories of objects. Words entail an awareness of not only the separate natures of these forms (words) and their referents (objects and events) but also the arbitrary relationship between the two. And just as this awareness guides the use of such symbols in varied syntactical or mathematical relations, so it makes possible a deliberate detaching of word from either action or object. More broadly stated, it is the alternating of directed awareness from symbolic forms to action–object relations that makes it possible for a child to look on his or her own body or thought processes. This awareness further enables the child to determine how to use particular symbolic forms or body actions to relate to reality.

In the attempt to understand the relation between sign and symbol several questions arise: Is the discontinuity between sign and symbol as sharp as Cassirer (1970) stated or do sign-words gradually become more like symbols? How can the relation between sign and symbol be more accurately described? Further, is there evidence that suggests that signs or sign functioning contribute to the development of symbol functioning?

DO SIGN-WORDS GRADUALLY BECOME MORE SYMBOLLIKE?

Cassirer (1970) viewed all signs as having the same general properties. His formulation provides no room for a gradual or continuous evolution of signs into more symbollike forms. Thus, if there is evidence that signs exist on a continuum from those that are most restrictive and context bound in their reference to those that are least restrictive, the notion of an absolute dichotomy of signs and symbols must be modified. Such a view seems inherent in the work of Kol'tsova, cited by Luria (1981), which shows that as the child develops from 6 months to the latter part of the 2nd year, there is a progressive or continuous detaching of the referring word from the body action context in which it first assumes significance. In this study Kol'tsova would name an object in the child's presence so that the child typically turned his or her eyes in the direction of the designated object and stretched a hand toward it:

> In the early stages, the child acquired the object reference only if he/she was placed in a certain position (e.g., in a lying position), if the word was pronounced by a certain person (e.g., by his/her mother), if the word was accompanied by a specific (pointing) gesture and if the word was presented with a certain intonation. . . . Hence, if a child of 6 or 7 months was lying down and heard his/her mother's voice naming an object, the child responded by turning its gaze toward the object. However, the child failed to respond if any of these conditions were changed (e.g., if the child was in a sitting position).

> During the next stage, the child's position (e.g., lying or sitting) was no longer important for retaining the object reference of the word, but the identity of the speaker, the intonation of the voice, and the gesture accompanying the utterance continued to have a decisive influence. If the word "cat" was pronounced by the mother, the child turned his/her gaze toward it. However, if the same word was uttered by the father, the child did not respond in the same way.

> At later stages, the identity of the speaker ceased to be an important factor in evoking a response to a word, but the child retained the object reference only when the utterance was accompanied by a pointing gesture. . . . It is only . . . by the end of the child's 2nd year that the word is completely emancipated from these attendant conditions and acquires its stable object reference. (pp. 46–47)

The sign influence can also be determined in the use of a child's first uttered words. When a spoken word and its action continue to be merged— and independent use of one without the other is not yet possible—the child is still functioning within a sign orientation even though some degree of representation occurs. Thus, McNeil (1970, p. 21) cited Leopold's report that his daughter at 20 months said "walk" as she got out of a cart to walk; "away" as she pushed an object away; and "blow" as she blew her nose. The gradual manner in which overgeneralized words become more restricted to their appropriate object meanings was clearly shown by Lewis (1936) as he charted the gradual manner in which Ament's niece Louise restricted the term *mammam*. From about 12 to 17 months of age the term *mammam* was used to refer to aunt, mother, sister, bread, cakes, cooked dishes, and milk (presumably because aunt, mother, and sister were actively concerned with preparing and giving her various kinds of foods). By 17 months the term *mammam* had changed to *momi* to designate mother, *desi* (Daisy) to designate sister, and *brodi* to designate bread and cakes, although *mammam* was still used to designate cooked dishes and milk. A further restriction of meaning was evident at 20 months when milk was referred to as *mimi,* and *momi* had changed to *mama* to designate mother.

TWO MAJOR DISCONTINUITIES IN THE DEVELOPMENT OF LANGUAGE

Although the preceding examples support a continuity position, both the literature and our own observations of children suggest the occurrence of two major discontinuous achievements in the development of language: the discovery of symbolic-signs (naming), and the discovery of symbols.

The Discovery of Naming

If the hallmark of sign functioning is the merging of utterance with body action and/or an engaging object, in the manner described, then the first *significant* departure from sign functioning occurs when the child becomes aware that the word—as a name—has an existence at least partially separate from its original system. Stern described the discovery of naming during the 18th to the 24th months of life as the insight that "each thing has its name" (Stern, 1914, p. 108; Stern & Stern, 1928). With this discovery children learn to communicate and define the unity of objects through certain utterances (words). They also learn that if they point to an object, request its name, and receive an answer designating it, that object can exist as a separate entity in their world. With these names as parts of sentences, children can then communicate the nature of objects and their intentions with regard to these objects, to themselves and others. Given the great utility of naming, it is not surprising that dramatic increases in spoken language vocabulary regularly occur, following its discovery, during the 2nd and 3rd years of life (McCarthy, 1954; Nelson, 1973; Stern, 1914; Stern & Stern, 1928).

Names as Symbolic-Signs

At first glance, children seem to achieve with the discovery of names a full grasp of symbols—terms completely detached from their respective systems. Contributing to this impression is the ease with which children can, after this discovery, accumulate the names for objects and events simply by pointing and asking, "Wha' dat?" Opposing this impression, however, is the finding, for example, that when 18-month-old children name objects, these names are not arbitrary symbols assigned to particular objects but *required* responses to the problem that each new object poses for the child. This *required* aspect is evident in the child's continued demand (Piaget, 1929; Vygotsky, 1962) for the names of things as well as the need to use these names and not others to designate particular objects or events. The child, as Bühler (1928, p. 54) pointed out, solves the problem of the object's existence by naming it. Lacking the special name for that object, the child demands it from adults. *The newly naming child, engaged by an unnamed object, experiences it as an interrupted system that requires completion through the act of naming, thus substituting the compulsive demand for a name for the prior compulsion to act toward the object. The feeling of incompleteness induced by the unnamed object explains the urgency of the child's demand for its name and reveals the name's sign heritage. For this reason the term* symbolic-sign *characterizes naming.*

It is, however, a mistake to assume that children's naming, once achieved, maintains the initial level of requiredness between name and object. On the contrary, just as Kol'tsova (cited in Luria, 1981) found a gradual detaching of the sign-word from its original context until the rather dramatic achievement of naming, so do we find a similar lessening of requiredness following the discovery of names. We were able to mark two points on this continuum by observing our son Ethan's response at different ages to the question of whether he could call his favorite toy—a blue station wagon—"milk." At the age of 28 months he firmly asserted that his station wagon was not *milk* because "You drink milk." However, asked the same question at 4 years, he agreed, after a pause, that he could name his car "milk" because "This thing [pointing to a white plastic trailer hitch fastened to the rear of his station wagon] is *white* like milk."

In other words, whereas at the earlier age he required a relatively fixed relation between name and object, by age 4 the requirement had so diminished that a tiny feature of his car, a white trailer hitch, that bridged the two objects by having white in common, was sufficient to achieve the transfer. At this point he was close to accepting, without perceptual support, the arbitrary linkage between word and referent.

The Discovery of Symbols: The *Fiat* Insight

If naming—the discovery of symbolic-signs—represents children's first major insight into words and leads to the gradual liberation of names and actions from their objects, then the ability to use symbols as arbitrary forms represents a second major insight into the nature of words. This latter achievement is referred to as the *fiat* insight because it enables the child, now fully aware of the distinct separation between words and their referents, to achieve reference, not through a sense of requiredness between word and object, but merely by the speaker's inner intent that a particular word form shall henceforth be represented by any of a variety of meanings. This insight into the nature of words and the new functions that flow from it allow children to accept the notion that one can designate a table by the term *hat,* and so forth, *without* having to perceive a physical similarity between the two.

The *fiat* insight develops between 5 and 6 years of age as children are increasingly confronted by forms—insignia, printed words—that convey meaning without an iconic relation between form and referent. However, even in the context of symbolic functioning, there is evidence of continuity. For example, the achievement of the first symbolic relations between arbitrary graphic forms and their referents does not mean that symbolic function is automatically conferred on all symbolic forms (see Chapter 6, p. 204). Children who can assign meanings to printed words do not automatically understand that letters are also symbols. There must be a gradual generalization of symbolic capacity to varied forms serving a variety of different functions before symbolic functioning can be truly established. Further, even when this occurs, as Werner (1948) points out, earlier modes of reference (sign and symbolic-sign functioning) continue to coexist and may, under certain circumstances, be drawn on to facilitate or enrich symbolic functioning.

Evidence for this position was derived from a study (Miller, 1959, 1963b) in which normal college students were required to rapidly repeat the word "push" while concurrently performing pulsing actions. Under ordinary conditions, the rapid repetition of a spoken word results in a lapse of meaning within 5 to 7 seconds. However, when the subjects repeated "push" while performing a pushing activity the word maintained its meaning significantly longer. On the other hand, when the word was repeated with an activity conventionally thought of as pulling, most subjects experienced the meaning lapse more rapidly. Subjects also actively pushed against a spring-loaded drawer while looking at themselves performing that activity and then performed rapid pushing gestures with their eyes closed.

The condition that most closely simulated sign functioning, the word "push" with a pushing action against an object *while* the subjects observed their own actions, resulted in the best maintenance of word meaning. Presumably this occurred because the system involving the lapsing word could draw most contextual support in this situation. On the other hand, the influence of symbolic functioning was also evident. Although the large majority of the subjects experienced more rapid lapses of meaning when "push" was accompanied by an action toward the body conventionally thought of as pulling, a few maintained meaning as well with the pulling activity as they had with the concordant pushing activity. Questioned about this, they replied that when the meaning began to lapse, they transformed the discordant pulling activity into a "pushing *toward*" themselves and then experienced the support they had previously gained from pushing. In doing this, they demonstrated awareness of the arbitrary relation between symbol and referent that characterizes symbolic functioning and behaved in a manner not unlike the aphasic patient who, unable to retrieve the abstract term *remember* (Head, 1926), was able to exploit a more sign-related term by simulating the action of digging something up in a way that brought with it the desired substitute phrase "dig it up."

A MODIFIED DISCONTINUITY POSITION

The study of signs, symbolic-signs, and symbols suggests that both continuity *and* discontinuity are in play in the course of language development. Within each early phase a progression (continuity) operates that enables the child to gradually detach words from their original system contexts. Thus, words as signs become gradually less dependent on a rigid context as the child matures until, with the discovery of names, a qualitative shift from sign to symbolic-sign develops, marked by a dramatic increase in speaking vocabulary. Then, in similar fashion there again develops a gradual process of detaching names from their required objects until with the fiat insight there is another qualitative shift evident in the ability to assign meanings to forms (printed words) that bear no physical resemblance to their meanings. At this point reading and writing become possible.

The point being made—which qualifies Cassirer's (1970) position—is that even though the gap between word as sign and word as name (symbolic-sign) is reduced by the continuous detaching of signs from their system contexts, a gap still remains. *Similarly, although symbolic-signs gradually become more like symbols, a discontinuity still exists between even the most advanced name and the first use of symbols. It is possible to improve the likelihood that a child will cross the gap from sign to symbolic-sign or from symbolic-sign to symbol but the insight that permits the qualitative shift cannot be taught. This insight must, in the final analysis, come from the child.*

To characterize the child's changed experience of reality in moving from sign to symbolic-sign to symbol functioning, it is helpful to imagine sign functioning as a narrow corridor that leads, after crossing a chasm, first into a large room (symbolic-sign functioning) and then, after crossing another chasm, into a great hall of infinite extent (symbol functioning). This metaphor suggests the expanded vista and sense of new possibilities occasioned by transitions from sign to symbol. It also directs attention to the important issue of *how* children progress from earlier to later forms of representational functioning. In particular, how two prenaming forms of reference—"natural signs" and words used as signs—contribute to the development of naming and thus the development of spoken language.

THE CONTRIBUTION OF SIGNS TO THE DISCOVERY OF NAMING

Prior to the naming discovery, the functions of naming are distributed between two representational forms—*natural signs* and *sign-words*. Natural signs include gestures or utterances that derive from engagement with salient properties of objects and events and that help the child self-represent various situations posed by reality. Natural signs, such as "rmm" that expresses a car's motor sound, are valuable to the child because they capture a property of an object or event in a way that enables the child to communicate with himself or herself in a limited way about the object or event. In that sense, they forecast the later-developing naming function, that also permits self-communication. Natural signs, however, are not very useful for communication with others because they are frequently idiosyncratic and reflect only a facet of the object or event to which they relate.

Sign-words also herald naming but in a different way, by using conventional word forms that promise the possibility of shared meanings between people. The following sections, first consider the formation of natural signs and their varied coping functions and then the manner in which such signs and directed action become integrated with word forms, leading to the discovery of naming.

Developing Natural Signs

Children's production of natural signs first comes from interrupted engagement with certain problems posed by reality. Johnny, interrupted in his play by his ball rolling into a sewer drain, *repeatedly reaches* for the ball as if that would somehow bring it back; Diane, trying to think of a shortcut to get home in time for dinner, closes her eyes and *moves her head from left to right* as she mentally follows different routes. Each child is engaged in "fixing" and expressing the nature of a compelling but distal object or event. In each case, the necessary natural sign emerges from interruption of the child's engagement with a particular object or customary way of doing things.

If natural signs express the child's effort to cope with various problems posed by reality, then the kind of problem should relate directly to the kind of natural sign that emerges and the role it plays. For example, if the child's engagement with a particular object is completely interrupted by its sudden *loss,* then the natural sign that emerges should enable the child to represent and communicate both the nature of the lost object and the need to retrieve it. Johnny's natural sign of repeated reaching for a clearly lost object expresses both his wish for the object and the nature of the object. However, if the child's engagement with a particular object is interrupted by an *obstacle* that denies the child access to the goal, then the natural sign should communicate the nature of the obstacle to the child and—as in Diane's case—a means of bypassing it. Finally, if a child engaged with a dynamic entity suddenly finds that some of the dynamism is missing, for example, if a noisy, moving train suddenly stops, a natural sign may develop from the child's compensatory effort to restore the lost dynamic property and, in so doing, to represent and fix the object so that it is available for later reference.

Natural Signs and Reference to Lost Objects and Events

Complete and partial interruptions of the child's engagement with objects and events contribute to the solution of certain problems through the formation of natural signs. One such instance was evident in the behavior of our 8-month-old son, David, who, when rocked in his crib, would utter small grunts with slightly accented body movements in cadence with the rocking (Chapter 1, p. 16).

David's ability to initiate "grunt-rocking" behavior to get us to rock him stemmed from new awareness of the distinction between *his* self-initiated rocking activity and the body motion induced by us rocking him. Prior to this phase, the two sources of rocking stimulation were merged within a syncretic system composed of our influential and his own slightly accented rocking. Together, the sources of stimulation (our rocking and his own) constituted the figural experience for him. When we stopped rocking him and he initiated his grunt-rocking to compensate for the deficit, reafferent stimulation from his own movements led to their becoming salient as well as oriented toward our rocking, with which they had previously been merged. Because his own activity, occurring by itself, became figural, David could become aware of both the body source of his behavior *and* its relation to our rocking, whose form it shared. With this new awareness, he could soon use this behavior regularly as a natural sign to get others to rock him.

A similar instance of natural sign formation from a completely interrupted proximal system and its subsequent use seems inherent in Pavlovitch's report (1920) that his 5-month-old son indicated his wish for a pacifier by making a clicking and smacking sound. For this to occur, the child had to first engage—act upon or with—the pacifier with sucking movements that incidentally produced clicking and smacking sounds. Then, during the sucking, the pacifier must either have fallen or been removed from his mouth; this complete disruption (interruption) triggered a compensatory searching for the object expressed by sucking with clicking-smacking sounds. The child's ability to initiate these sounds in the absence of the pacifier suggests that, like our son David, he had become sufficiently aware of his compensatory sound making to spontaneously express his wish for the desired pacifier.

Among deaf children, similar complete interruptions of proximal systems and the consequent salience of certain compensatory behaviors may account for the formation and use of natural signs that were later codified as manual signs in the American Sign Language (ASL) of the deaf. For example, the manual sign for *eating* (placing hand to mouth) may first have emerged from a compensatory hand-to-mouth action following the sudden unavailability (interruption) of food being eaten. Similarly, *spoon* (a scooping motion using two fingers as a spoon), *ball* (hand motion consistent with holding or catching a ball), *cup* (simulation of picking up a cup), and many others may first have appeared as compensatory reactions to interrupted engagement with these objects. In each instance, the compensatory action, because of its salience as well as its shared relation with the functional action system from which it derived, made it available as a natural sign for the object and the actions involved with it.

Self-Communication with Natural Signs

Another function of natural signs that presages the later role of spoken language concerns children's use of such forms for self-communication and thought. Self-communication allows children to anticipate an impending event by relating it to their own position in space; to maintain goals by representing the goal to themselves; and to solve problems by representing the nature of the problem to themselves.

Natural signs for self-communication occur quite early. Such signs were evident, for example, in the behavior of the 13-month-old boy referred to earlier (Werner & Kaplan, 1963) who, on approaching a staircase, "lifted his leg in a climbing fashion fully three feet before he reached the first step" (p. 93). The boy, engaged with the newly learned task of walking, suddenly experienced the steps looming in front of him as an interruption to his forward progress. This interruption induced a compensatory climbing response that served as a natural sign with the self-directed message: "Get ready to climb steps!"

A few months later, the same child at 15 months used another natural sign when, while looking for his sand spoon, he made shoveling movements with his right arm as he held his hand in a scooping position. Clearly, the child had stored a compensatory shoveling reaction (to his lost shovel) that had become sufficiently salient for him to use as a natural sign to guide him in his search for that shovel.

Piaget's (1952a) account of the manner in which his daughter Lucienne solved the matchbox problem (see Chapter 1, p. 17) is a graphic example of the use of natural signs to help solve problems through self-communication.

Lucienne's compensatory reaction to her impeded access to the chain in the box became a creative natural sign. As Lucienne opened her mouth slightly, then wider and wider, she represented to herself both the obstacle (narrow opening) and the direction she had to take with that obstacle (make it wider) in order to get the chain. She could not have found this solution without having first directed her compensatory reaction to the unavailable (interrupted) chain to *act upon* the obstacle (small opening of matchbox) that prevented her from getting the chain. During this confrontation she developed a natural sign (opening her mouth) uniquely designed to reflect both the obstacle and the understanding required to bypass that obstacle. In a somewhat similar instance Piaget (1952a) described how his daughter Jacqueline, aged 15 months, developed a unique natural sign to solve a different problem:

> Jacqueline was playing with a clown with long feet and happened to catch the feet in the low neck of her dress. She had difficulty in getting them out, but as soon as she had done so, she tried to put them back in the same position. . . . As she did not succeed, she put her hand in front of her, bent her forefinger at a right angle to reproduce the shape of the clown's feet, described exactly the same trajectory as the clown and then succeeded in putting her finger into the neck of her dress. She looked at the motionless finger for a moment, then pulled at her dress, without of course being able to see what she was doing. Then, satisfied, she removed her finger and went on to something else. (p. 65)

As in the previous instance, the nature of the interrupted engagement—the feet of Jacqueline's clown getting stuck in her dress—provided the impetus to make a natural sign with her finger that simulated the stuck clown feet. She then used this natural sign to communicate to herself by experimentally acting out and solving the nature of the interruption.

Natural Signs Relating to Distal Objects and Events

Another function of spoken reference that first appears in children's use of natural signs is that of designating or fixing the experience of a particular object or event so that it may subsequently be referred to at a distance and used for thought or communication.

The shift to distal reference was evident in two small girls who developed different natural signs from their individual ways of blowing out a lighted match. One, 21 months old, used the expletive "pooh" (Jesperson, 1922/1964) as she blew out a match, whereas the other, 17 months old, used the repeated fricative "f-f-f" (Werner & Kaplan, 1963) for the same purpose. Subsequently, each child was able to use her own sounds as natural signs to refer to distal, light-related objects, including a match, cigar, pipe, candle, and lamp.

The natural signs "pooh" or "f-f-f" that emerged from blowing out a match in a particular way derived from the girls' partial shift of awareness from the act of blowing out the lighted match to the *breath-sounds* that accomplished this act. Both sound and act shared the same influential vector as the children noted that their *breath-sounds* caused the lighted match to flicker and go out. This process permitted each child to experience her own compensatory sound making ("pooh" or "f-f-f") and the feeling of efficacy it conveyed, independent of the lighted match toward which the *breath-sounds* were originally directed. The children were then disposed to direct these natural sound signs to other distal objects that shared a light-related property.

Not all natural sound signs develop from direct body involvement with an object. Examples of natural signs deriving from distal engagement are evident in the "r-r-r" response of the Sterns' small children to a manually turned coffee grinder and their "s-s-s" response to a flower syringe (Werner & Kaplan, 1963). Also included in this category is the "ft" utterance for soda water used by the 2-year-old boy cited by Jesperson (1922/1964) and the "tch-tch" response of Piaget's 1-year-old daughter (1962) to the sound and motion of a train.

Once a child has become engaged with a dynamic, distal event and the event is interrupted (e.g., the coffee grinder stopped, leaving only the static grinder visible; the train disappeared, leaving only the rhythmic sound to be heard), he or she feels compelled to restore the integrity of the partially interrupted distal system by producing the sound pattern consistent with that event and by compensatorily investing the event's significance within that sound pattern. Subsequently, the child is able to use this sound pattern to retrieve or capture the object or event property that was previously marked by only distal involvement.

"Error-Generalization" of Natural Signs

Natural signs that derive from distal events generalize erroneously to new objects in much the same way that the girls proximally engaged with blowing out a match generalized their natural signs to new distal referents. Thus, Piaget's daughter generalized the term *tch-tch* from moving trains to moving cars and carriages, and then to a man walking and her father playing peek-aboo with her. Clearly, the manner in which the *motion* of varied objects acted upon her, like the manner in which *light* acted upon the two girls, dictated the generalizing of *tch-tch* to new referents. The similarity in a central property of each object and not the differences between objects was the significant factor.

At times, the dynamic property of an event may induce an extension in two ways—by *acting upon* another object and by inducing with a new object the same impression produced earlier. Werner and Kaplan (1963, p. 107) cited examples that include Stumpf's report that his son, aged 22 months, initially used the utterance "tap" to represent opening a bottle with a snapping movement and sound. Later, the child used the same utterance to refer to the bottle *acted upon* as well as to scissors and pliers that produced a snapping movement and sound like the original bottle opening. In similar manner, Gregoire reported that his 22-month-old son responded to the hammering of a nail by saying "pigne" (*p-i-ñ*), soon extending it to include the nail acted upon as well as a key and metallic pencil that impressed him as being identical to the nail.

Although such extensions of natural signs to quite varied objects are "errors" because they take into account only the most salient, dynamic, or figural properties of an object or event, it is important to note that these "errors" constitute children's earliest basis for generalizing meaning to new forms. Early extensions of natural signs occur without children being aware that they are including not only the most salient or figural property of particular objects but, inadvertently, the objects that provide a ground for these properties. The children behave as if they are merely applying their sign forms to their required referents; for example, a train *moves* and a walking man *moves* so it is appropriate to say "tch-tch" for both the train and the man. Or, the hammer acts on the nail, thus the nail and anything that resembles it must be designated by the hammer sound "pigne."

This mode of inadvertent error-generalizing occurs because small children's single-track manner (Werner, 1948) of experiencing their surroundings allows them to process only the most salient or figural facet of an object or event at a time. However, because this salient facet occurs simultaneously with or transfers its impact to the less impressive aspects of the situation, and because the child is disposed to organize all stimulus arrays into figure–ground relations, each single-track processing of figural properties necessarily includes the less impressive ground properties of the objects. As a child uses a natural sign to designate the same figural property with a variety of different object-grounds, he or she inadvertently extends reference to include both the salient properties *and* their varied object-grounds within the same system.

This inadvertent extension of reference is an example of the *principle of inclusion* and can be stated as follows:

> Whenever the child, engaged by a figural property of an object or event, is concurrently stimulated by a ground aspect of the situation, that ground aspect becomes part of a total, engaging system. Subsequently, when only the ground part of the system appears, the child compensatorily reacts to it as if it were the original, salient engaging property.

Both the promise and limitations of natural signs are readily apparent. The promise lies in the ability of children to derive referential forms from objects and events with which they are engaged and to use these forms to refer to properties of objects and events both near and far through gesture and sound making. The natural signs themselves are limited because children are unable to communicate the notion of a distinct object or event with certain properties that set it apart from other objects or events.

Natural signs from proximal systems are helpful because they convey facets of reality directly related to the child's immediate, pragmatic, and problem-solving activity with objects or events; natural signs from distal systems are helpful because they capture properties of objects or events at a distance. Both kinds of signs are limited, however, because they extend reference based only on the most dynamic property of an engaging object or event, and both fail to integrate varied properties of objects and events into coherent entities that can be distinguished from each other and categorized.

HOW SPOKEN WORDS FIRST BECOME MEANINGFUL

Concurrent with the development of natural signs, children begin to use conventional words in signlike fashion. The difference between natural signs and conventional words used as signs is that the latter can readily accumulate meanings from different action–object systems in a way that the natural sign, bound by its form to a particular salient property, cannot. Words can accumulate different aspects of an object's meaning because their vocal-auditory structure permits a certain detachment while remaining temporally related to that object. This makes it possible for a word to relate over time to all facets of an object and, ultimately, to the object itself. However, before this process can be adequately described, it is necessary to account for the manner in which conventional word forms—initially quite alien to action–object systems—become part of these systems. This process is referred to as the "naturalizing" of conventional spoken words.

Naturalizing Conventional Spoken Words

It seems likely that the naturalizing process occurs as an adult or parenting person introduces a spoken word in context of the child's engagement with a particular object or event. How the process develops depends on whether the child has a natural sign that already expresses engagement with that particular object or event. If a sign exists, the manner in which a child extends its meaning to a new spoken word follows the *principle of system extension* previously stated (Chapter 2, p. 48):

> Whenever one engaging system acts upon a new property of an object or event, . . . that property becomes an expanded part of the original system. The [child] then maintains the integrity of the newly expanded system when it is interrupted just as if it were the original system.

Thus, just as the hammer sound "pigne" transferred and extended its significance to the nail that the hammer acted upon, so a natural sign used in combination with a new spoken word may transfer and extend its significance to include that word.

There is evidence at very early ages that certain natural signs pass on their significance to new utterances with which they are used. Carter (1975), in this regard, found in her intensive study of a single child that at first the 10- or 11-month-old child's natural deictic gestures—pointing, holding out, or holding up an object while vocalizing "la" or "daet [that]"—were more important for reference than the vocalizations, but gradually reference began to depend more on the utterances. From this it is inferred that the gestural intentions were transferred to vocal expression. That natural sound signs operate similarly to help establish the reference function of parent-introduced spoken words seems evident in the finding by Stern and Stern (1928) and others that small children spontaneously merge such symbols with conventional word forms: "shu-shu *train*," "wah-wah *dog*," "muh-muh *cow*," "diddle-diddle *clock*," "tate-tate *scissors*." All such combinations allow the child to use the rhythmic and uniquely patterned quality of the natural sign to *act upon* the conventional spoken word in a way that enables the child to naturalize and thus possess the word as a meaningful entity.

Subsequently, because the word can incorporate a variety of part-meanings expressed by natural signs, such signs lose their utility and disappear, and the more serviceable word remains in use. Frequently, however, a child lacks a natural sign to *act upon* a newly introduced conventional spoken word. How then does that word become part of a meaningful system? The major distinction between the two kinds of situations lies in the manner in which word and meaning system are juxtaposed. When children have natural signs, they—in accord with the *principle of extension*—actively transfer the signs' inherent meanings to the forms of the new words. However, when natural signs are not available, children depend on the *principle of inclusion* to transform the external chance pairing of new spoken words *into* the action–object systems with which they are engaged.

The *principle of inclusion* (see p. 155) as it applies to introduced spoken words operates as follows: *When a spoken word is paired with an action–object system, the word, as a ground property that accompanies the child's engagement with a more salient property, becomes part of a total engaging system.* Just as the child's engagement with a figural property results in the inadvertent inclusion of accompanying ground-objects, so may it also include the forms of conventional words. For the child, the simultaneity of the auditory pattern "pin" with input from the dominant picking-up-tiny-item system, ensures the word's incorporation as a ground part of the picking-up system in the same way that *cigar* or *lamp* became ground parts of "pooh" or "f-f-f" light-related systems; or that *train, car,* and *man* became part of "tch-tch" motion-related systems. The "error" of incorporating an object or alien word occurs because the child's single-track functioning requires the processing of both the salient event and any secondary pattern accompanying that event *as if they both came from the same (salient) source.* The child functioning in this way is literally unable to discriminate between the two sources of concurrent stimuli, whether they impact the same or different sense modalities. *The identical processing of diverse inputs because of failure to discriminate between two sources induces the child to invest* cigar *and* lamp *with light significance;* train, car, *and* man *with motion significance; and* pin *with picking-up-tiny-objects significance.*

Once the word *pin* is incorporated into the now expanded action–object system concerned with picking up tiny objects, "pin" operates as a sign that *requires* the action–object part of the system. Thus, when the child hears only the "pin" part of the system (partial interruption), there is an immediate compensatory disposition to search for and pick up a small object to complete and maintain the system's integrity. Similarly, the child who sees a small object at a distance, has a compensatory disposition not only to pick up the small object but to utter "pin" while moving to do so. The self-produced utterance "pin," because it occurs when the child is not yet physically involved with picking up tiny objects, gives the child an opportunity to experience the term "pin" as figural, somewhat detached from but related to the action–object system with which it had become merged. This detachment—and the greater awareness of the sound "pin" which it brings— enables the child to use the term "pin" with more deliberation to relate to other objects that possess the required tiny size.

This formulation has relevance to Pavlov's findings (1927; 1928; 1962) in his studies of conditioning with animals. Pavlov found that stimuli (light, sound) previously incapable of eliciting food-related salivation became capable of doing so after having been concurrently paired with the presentation of food that did elicit salivation. However, where Pavlov and his followers accounted for this phenomenon as the outcome of a *connection* that the animal forms between *two separate entities,* for example, buzzer sound and food, we account for it by the animal's inadvertently *including* and thus transforming an objectively unrelated stimulus into one that is subjectively experienced as an intrinsic part of the eating food system. From the present point of view, the conditioned response involving sound (or light) and food develops as follows:

> When it first hears the sound the dog orients *toward it*. Then, as the food appears, the dog initiates a new orienting response *toward the food* prior to eating it. (It can be inferred that the dog experiences two separate entities at this time). However, as the animal repeatedly hears the buzzer sound both before and during presentation and ingestion of food, these separate orientings transform into a unitary engagement toward the food and the sound that accompanies it. The expanded system, that develops as the dog simultaneously ingests both food and the background sound, changes the sound's status from background sound to part of the figural experience of eating food.

> Then, when the sound is presented by itself (partial interruption of the system), the dog's salivation implies recognition of the sound's participation with the sight and ingestion of food in the same way that the term "pin," because it had become part of a picking-up-tiny-objects system, triggered a disposition on the part of the Sterns' daughter to pick up a tiny object.

If the dog's salivating in response to a buzzing sound (or flashing light) reflects its experience of a newly expanded system in which the sound (or light) is part of food ingesting, then once the sound or light is presented, any delay in producing the food part of the system should induce a compensatory effort to maintain contact with the part of the expanded food system that *is* available, that is, the buzzing sound or light. Pavlov's fascinating account of the dog's behavior when sound or light was presented, but food was not immediately forthcoming, provides striking support for the present view. Pavlov wrote (1962):

> The conditioned stimulus (buzzer/light) now becomes a pure substitute for the unconditioned stimulus (food) . . . the animal may lick the flashing electric bulb, or attempt to take the air into its mouth, or try to eat the sound itself; in doing this the animal licks its lips and grinds its teeth as if dealing with real food. (p. 89)

The dog's effort to eat the sound or light is a compensatory effort to restore its interrupted contact with food by directing its eating movements toward the most salient part of the food system still available, the sound or light stimulation. Just as Pavlov's animals soon perceived a buzzing sound or flashing light as part of their experience of food, so may small children experience the sounds of conventional speech as part of previously established systems concerned with acting toward or manipulating various objects. For both animal and child, the *external* condition that makes expansion of systems possible appears to be the presentation of the sound or word slightly before and during the engaging activity that follows.

The effect on children, who incorporate words within their action–object systems in the same way that animals incorporate previously unrelated stimuli, is that sign-words develop that require the child to produce the action now experienced as part of the word. It is this expanded sign system that required the child (McNeil, 1970) to walk after saying "walk" and "blow" as she blew her nose. However, with words related to objects, the situation is somewhat different. The reason is that in contrast to action words that relate to a single vector—*push, walk, blow,* and so forth—words that relate to objects are driven by various salient properties of the objects and may shift from one property to another within the same or different objects. Before children learn to integrate these properties into a single named object, their terms are quite global and holophrastic. However, it is the very diffuseness of words in relation to object properties that brings the child closer to the discovery of names.

Holophrastic Word Use

Whereas natural signs are limited because they are subjectively organized around a salient property of an object and not the object itself, holophrastic speech, which develops during the same period, is limited because it too diffusely includes an array of objects. One instance of a holophrastic word (Lewis, 1936) is 12-month-old Louise's use of *mammam* to refer to aunt, mother, sister, bread, and cakes as well as cooked foods—all entities concerned with preparing and giving her various foods and thus, through the principle of system extension, transmitted person and food quality to the word in one way or another. Although limited, holophrastic words are important because they are conventional in form and thus lend themselves more readily than natural signs to communication with others. The general nature of holophrastic terms is well characterized by De Laguna (1927):

> A child's word [during this period] does not . . . designate an object or a property of an act; rather it signifies loosely and vaguely the object together with its interesting properties and the acts with which it is commonly associated in the life of the child. The emphasis may be now on one, now on another, of these aspects, according to the exigencies of the occasion on which it is used. Just because the terms of the child's language are in themselves so indefinite, it is left to the particular setting and context to determine the specific meaning for each occasion. In order to understand what the baby is saying you must see what the baby is doing. (pp. 90–91)

Both the global reference of holophrastic terms and the role of the child's concurrent actions are evident in the observation by the Sterns (1928) that their 11-month-old daughter used the term *doll* to refer not only to her doll but to a variety of small objects (toy rabbit, toy cat) that she had access to and played with in the same manner. She also used the term *pin* to refer not only to a pin but to a bread crumb, fly, and caterpillar—all small objects that she acted upon in the same manner by the pincer movement with which she picked them up from the floor. Documenting similar word–action relations, Werner (1948, p. 277) cited Sully's observations of a child who used the term *hat* to indicate anything he could place on top of his head, including the hairbrush.

This same dependence on overt action to momentarily *extend* and make diffuse word meanings more specific was evident in the language used by the isolated and developmentally delayed 5-year-old twins studied by Luria and Yudovich (1959). These two children often used the same term to indicate different but related facets of a situation. For example, the term "to drink" was used by them at different times to indicate a teapot, a cup, the act of drinking, and water. Consequently, to provide the term "to drink" with the specificity required for having needs met, the twins had to use the term while *acting upon or toward* that part of the drinking situation that best met their needs at a particular time.

The preeminent role of action in establishing reference at this stage is evident in two experiments conducted by Luria and Yudovich (1959, pp. 78–79) with the children. In both experiments the role of action and the feeling of efficacy it conveyed momentarily transformed the physical nature of the objects with which the twins were engaged. In one experimental situation they were given everyday objects for a game in which they were asked to designate familiar objects by new names: a penholder was designated "papa," a pencil, "mama," a box, the "tram," an ashtray, the "workplace." Using the name-assigned objects, the children could relate the familiar words in the sentence: "Papa traveled to work on the tram" to entirely new referents (pencil, box, ashtray) *as long as the words were accompanied by actions* that acted upon and thus extended and momentarily transformed the meaning of the objects, that is, by having the "penholder-father" *climb aboard* the "box-tramcar" which then *traveled* to the "ashtray-workplace."

Similarly, when the experimenter took a small metal spoon, acted upon it with chopping movements, and asked the children what it was, they answered "an ax"; when the experimenter swept the floor with the knife the children said "brush." However, when the experimenter gave the children the knife *without* acting upon it and said it was "brush," they started sharpening the pencil with the knife. In this way they indicated that the word's fusion with dynamic actions and the causal impressions these actions conveyed, and not the word–object relation per se, still dictated the extension of the word's meaning.

These examples make clear that holophrastic expressions are composed of two parts—a conventional word form and a variety of previously developed sign systems concerned with functional action toward or with a particular object. The apparent diffuseness of holophrastic expressions stems from the same conventional word form, at different times, expressing intention via different action–object systems. However, each new reference draws on the principles of both inclusion and extension. *Inclusion* comes into play when the child accepts a particular word, for example, "ax," as part of a chopping action system; *extension* comes into play when the "ax"-chopping action system transfers its significance to the small metal spoon being used as if it were an ax.

Holophrastic terms and natural signs are similar because both are guided not by the object as a total entity with various properties *but by its most salient property*. Thus, when the natural sign "pooh" or "f-f-f" is extended by error-generalization, the extension is based on light as the salient property common to very different objects. Similarly, when the holophrastic term "pin" is overextended, it is based on how various tiny objects are picked up and not on the character of the objects themselves. With both terms reference is dictated by a single, dynamic property of an object (light, motion, small size)—a reference that includes, quite accidently, the object or event with which this dynamic property happened to act upon. During this phase of language development each time a child refers to a salient property, both the salient or figural property *and* the ground-object or event with which it is related become incorporated within a system dominated by the salient property of the object.

The difference between natural signs and conventional words used as holophrastic terms is that the latter can accumulate meanings from different action–object systems in a way that the natural sign, bound by its form to a particular salient property, cannot. Words can accumulate different aspects of an object's meaning because their vocal-auditory structure permits a certain detachment while remaining temporally related to that object. As a result a word can relate over time to all facets of an object's properties and, ultimately, to the object itself.

THE PROCESS OF NAMING

As children use the described procedures to naturalize a word and then to invest the salient properties of the object within its form, there begins to exist for the first time the possibility of true naming. Such naming allows the child to represent and group objects not on the basis of a salient attribute but on the basis of those combined characteristics that distinguish one object or event from another. This new advance also permits the child to at least partially detach the word from its syncretic systems and use it to communicate the nature of the object to others. Then, for example, the term *train* refers to a particular vehicle that moves and not, like "tch-tch," to anything that moves.

However, before children can use a conventional word to designate an object, and not merely its most salient property, various proximal and distal systems including properties of the object must be integrated with that word. The two vehicles for this integration are the *extensions* carried out by natural signs and the *inclusion* of reference properties within spoken words made possible by juxtaposing spoken words with action–object systems. With the term *ball,* for example, as a child uses the natural sign "bu-bu" coupled with a bouncing-ball hand motion (i.e., "bu-bu ball"), the rhythmic bouncing property of the natural sign transfers to the term *ball.*

Subsequently, the child hears the term *ball* while engaged with various proximal and distal functions related to it, such as rolling the ball, throwing it from a distance, and catching it. Finally, the child uses the term *ball* to refer only to objects which have the potential for being treated in a ball-like manner. Similarly, the term *cup,* after accompanying and incorporating different cup functions, elicits the notion of a certain object—a cup—with a certain shape that can be poured into, picked up, and drunk from and which maintains its identity even when not in use on a shelf. With an originally distal object, the term *bird,* for example, begins to signify a quick-moving, chirping entity that flaps or pecks, perches quietly on a branch, digs for worms, or may come close and eat from one's hand. When a stable relation develops between a number of utterances and their objects, the child has a basis for the discovery to which we have previously referred—that "each thing has its name."

In figure–ground terms, what occurs with the naming discovery is a shift from salient property as figural to the object itself as figural. As long as a single, salient property or quality, such as a distal movement, a light, or the gingerly way an object is picked up, is figural, all generalizations are dictated by that salient property and include by error the varied object-grounds that either accompany or produce the salient property. However, with the progressive storing of salient properties—for example, of a bird, its chirping, pecking, or flying properties—within the spoken word, the child can generalize the meaning of *bird* to other entities that possess the required multiple properties or functions.

The child who calls a cow "dog" or an ambulance "car" has partially achieved this process. In such instances the child has integrated within the name some but not enough of the object properties to achieve accurate reference and generalization. At a slightly later stage, the child will have incorporated within the spoken word enough unique properties or functions of a cow (horns, udder) to distinguish it from a dog; similarly, as the child integrates the term *ambulance* with its hospital-related function, it too will be distinguished from an ordinary car. With each new function integrated within the spoken word, the object itself begins to be experienced as more definite and figural with regard to its surroundings. Finally, as the full naming relation becomes established, each name–object relation becomes quite segregated from other name–object relations.

The naming discovery implies awareness by the small child that certain utterances (names) and certain objects constitute a system such that the appearance of one invokes the other. To the extent that the child becomes aware of the name as a separate, portable entity, subject to individual initiatives, the name is a symbol; to the extent that the child experiences an imperative relation between name and object it functions as a sign. During the initial phase of naming the sign emphasis is quite strong. A name for the early naming child is not an arbitrary form casually linked with its object, but part of an imperative relation that cannot be violated without the name losing its power to convey object meaning. Once this point is understood, the necessity the child feels to buttress the name–object relation with action becomes clearer. Murphy (1978), in this regard, found that by 20 to 24 months of age, names and pointing actions are still so closely related that children are more likely to name pictures in a book while they are being pointed at than at any other time.

As the child learns to fix the object by naming it, new ways of elaborating the object's relation to its surroundings and intention toward the object become possible. These new ways develop because the word is no longer dependent on a particular overt action–object system in order to establish reference. For example, whereas previously, actions were overt extensions of the word, as when a child felt compelled to walk on saying the word "walk" or to pick up a cup on saying "cup," after naming, these imperative actions become *covert* action dispositions (muscle action potentials, or maps) that express the word's meaning by accenting the body schema in a manner appropriate to that word (see Chapter 2, p. 36). Now, the child on saying or hearing the word "walk" will—instead of walking—produce covert actions related to walking (maps) in feet or legs; similarly, the utterance "cup" after naming might convey meaning to the child via the same picking-up-cup action but in diminished form (via maps) in the manner reported by Jacobson (1931) and Shaw (1940) for subjects thinking of performing various actions. Because a name such as *cup* now has a critical aspect of its meaning expressed through maps within the body schema, the name maintains a stable relation with its object and provides the child with the freedom to establish a category for the name *cup* by relating the term to various cups in all sizes, shapes, positions, and locations.

The feeling and continued requirement by small children that a particular name and object "go together" stems from the name's continued fusion with covert action dispositions (maps) derived from prior overt action–object systems. This feeling of relation is so potent a force in early naming that, once a child knows the name for a particular object, the name cannot be assigned arbitrarily to another object. This imperative feeling is evident in Vygotsky's (1962) report that when small children were asked, "Can you call cow 'ink' and ink 'cow?' they responded with "No, because ink is used for writing and a cow gives milk." Here, although the child no longer feels compelled to milk a cow or to write on hearing the terms *cow* and *ink*, the feeling of relation between these words and the object functions fused with them is still so strong that the words cannot be assigned referents that diverge from these objects.

The relation between words and their action referents was investigated (Miller, 1968b) as part of a larger study with 16 retarded people (mean mental age: 4 years 4 months) who were able to name objects and events and communicate in simple 2 to 3 word sentences. The procedure required each subject, on hearing a spoken word ("mop," "cup," "car," etc.) to perform an action that the experimenter demonstrated. Each subject was presented 13 common words with actions considered *relevant* to these objects and 13 common words with actions considered *irrelevant* to them. The number of presentations (trials) a subject required before being able to produce the required action on hearing the spoken word became that subject's bonding score.

It was hypothesized that if each child's meaningful use of spoken words was related to covert action dispositions (maps), then introduced relevant actions would blend quite rapidly with these maps and be better retained than irrelevant actions which were presumably at variance with the covert dispositions (maps) triggered by the name.

Support for this view was evident in the finding that relevant actions were significantly more rapidly acquired by 14 of the 16 retarded subjects than words paired with irrelevant actions. Subjects were tested for retention of their word–action pairs 4 to 5 weeks after the experiment. Although it had taken them far fewer trials to reach the criterion of one successful pairing of spoken word with action in the original experimental situation, they retained significantly more relevant than irrelevant actions.

Such findings are consistent with the view that spoken reference develops from a phase in which action dominates word meaning to one in which the name, with the help of covert action dispositions (maps), relates in an imperative manner to clearly defined objects and events. From this, the next step in word–object ontogenesis concerns the progressive diminution of the imperative aspect of the word–object relation and the increasing substitution of perceptual as well as conceptual operations for action dispositions. However, this progression from more to less dependence on action–object systems is not immutable; under certain conditions the progress may be aborted. This result occurs with many behavior-disordered or autisticlike children.

DEVELOPING REFERENCE AMONG BEHAVIOR-DISORDERED CHILDREN

Over the years, the present formulation has guided our work with severely disordered nonverbal children through two distinct phases. In the first (Miller & Miller, 1973) we documented the importance of sign language to help develop communication and spoken language, as shown in the film, *Edge of Awareness* (Miller, 1974). In the second phase (Miller & Miller, 1982), we demonstrated how minispheres, multispheres, and integrative spheres contribute to the emergence of sign and spoken language, as illustrated in the film, *Ritual to Repertoire* (Miller, 1982).

The First Phase

When we first began working with nonverbal behavior-disordered children, we were struck with the relative disinterest—since confirmed by Curcio (1978)—that many of these children showed in objects or events away from their bodies. Typically, they would neither point at objects nor produce natural signs related to the sounds that different objects make. Their general lack of reactivity to distal objects or events as well as their difficulty intending action toward objects seemed to occur because they become so completely engaged or "captured" by proximal aspects of their environment that they could not break out of their closed systems to act toward or refer to objects or events remote from their bodies. Once captured, each response sequence developed integrity as a system and engaged the child's sensorimotor activity in a single-track manner so that the child was quite oblivious to any object or event outside that system. For example, one 3-year-old autistic girl, after being verbally directed to toilet herself at a bathroom plainly in view some 20 feet down the hall, required repeated prompting during her journey as she became engaged first with a swinging door (one system), a bicycle in her path (second system), the turning of a doorknob (third system), and so forth.

We reasoned that children who could not respond to and use words because of overinvolvement with proximal action–object systems might be enabled to do so, through procedures that helped them naturalize and thus include spoken words within their proximal systems. To bring this about a variety of procedures were used: First, intentional action was developed by strengthening the vectors of those pragmatic actions already within their repertoire. Then, we systematically introduced manual signs adapted from the American Sign Language (ASL) for the deaf, which resembled various functional activities, to serve as natural signs. As the signs were introduced, we also introduced spoken words in a contagious manner, allowing the words to share the rhythm and pace of actions and signs.

Elevated Boards

The most effective means we had at that time of strengthening the action meanings of spoken words required the use of boards elevated 3 to 6 feet above the ground. Autistic children who were quite unresponsive on the ground became, on these boards, more alert, responsive to their surroundings, and directed in their behavior. The boards helped achieve this, in Lewinian (1935) terms, by exerting a "pull" (positive valence) on the child's body to move in accord with the manner in which they were organized. For example, an autistic child's presence on a board 10 inches wide, situated 4 feet above the ground, and extending a distance of 8 feet from point A to point B, helped induce him or her to *walk* from A to B. When an obstacle (a box 1 foot high) was placed in the middle of the board, the child would walk from A to the obstacle, *stop*, step *on* or *over* the obstacle, and continue to B. Situations constructed to induce such directed behavior included objects that had to be *pick*ed *up*, doors that had to be *open*ed as well as a bridge that had to come *down*, objects that had to be *push*ed or *pull*ed, and steps from which the child had to *jump*.

The boards strengthened the intentional act because the child could not avoid directly confronting the problem and, at the same time, found it difficult to lapse into one of the autistic maneuvers or unintegrated behaviors readily available on the ground. We sought at all times to naturalize conventional words by keeping them both temporally and vectorially related to natural signs and the systems from which these signs emerged. We chose sign language to relate directed action to spoken words after reasoning that children who could perform such directed actions on the boards might be able to transfer the significance of these actions first to manual signs that, like natural signs, resembled these actions and then to the spoken words accompanying the manual signs. To facilitate the transfer of meaning and function from action to sign, we selected 50 functional signs closely related to everyday activities. A number of these were taught quite readily in elevated board situations. For example, to teach the sign for *open* (hands parting) the worker said "open" and interposed parting hands in front of the door the child was opening.

In similar fashion, the worker said "walk . . . walk" while walking hands (sign for *walk*) in step with the child, as he or she walked from place to place on the boards, or said "push" and "pull," with the appropriate *push* and *pull* signs, as the child performed these actions. To teach the concept *come,* the worker repeated the word while beckoning to the child from the end of the board's length; for *stop* the worker emphatically said the word "stop" just as the child met an obstacle in the middle of the board. In this way board vectors, signs, and utterances shared the vectors common to particular action–object systems.

Training Films

Other concepts were taught with the help of specially prepared training films (see Chapter 10) designed to help the child blend everyday functions (eating, washing, etc.) with signs and words. For example, the hand sign for *break* (two hands simulate breaking something) was readily blended on film with two hands breaking a stick. Similarly, manual signs for *eat, drink, fork, knife, spoon, pour, plate* and many others were juxtaposed on film with their action–object referents in such a way that the sign and its referent shared the same quality. As each child observed these relations a worker in back of the child would utter the appropriate word while helping the child to form the relevant manual sign in coordination with the film sequence. Then, during the snack period that followed the film sequence, teachers actively attempted to generalize these concepts by saying food-related words—"cup," "knife," "fork,"—just prior to and while the child was using these objects in a functional manner.

To facilitate the transfer from "natural gesture signs" to spoken words, whenever possible the rhythmic pattern of the gestures was closely related to the syllabic structure of the spoken words and to the child's total body involvement. For example, as a child went *up* a ladder or went *up* on a seesaw, the teacher, in the course of performing the relevant sign (upward gesture), uttered the word "up" with a rising vocal inflection timed to coincide with the child's upward movement. Conversely, with the word "down," a downward gesture and dropping vocal inflection were paired with the child's downward body movement. When a sign was paired with a two-part utterance like "Get up!" or "Sit down!" the worker would fragment the sign (palms moving upward or downward) to correspond with both parts of the phrase.

To help develop expressive use of gestures and words, various functional activities were periodically interrupted so that the children inadvertently transformed a relevant action toward or with an object into a natural sign representing this system. For example, a worker would say "push" when a child was pushing an object and then repeat the word while abruptly moving the object out of the child's reach so that the child pushed against open space. Then, should the child compensatorily reproduce the pushing act the worker would push the object as if in response to the child's command. Similarly, to develop the sign for cup, the worker would say "cup" as the cup was removed from the child's hand in a way that left the child's hand formed as if still holding the cup. When the child compensatorily produced the cup sign (moving cupped hand toward the mouth), the worker would hand him or her the cup.

To make the utility of signs more evident to the children, related procedures were used on the elevated boards. For example, a child poised 3 feet above ground and wishing to get through a box enclosure with doors on each end had to produce (with little or no help) the sign for *open* before the teacher would open the door and let him or her through. In similar fashion, the child had to perform a *down* sign before a bridge would be lowered to permit crossing a gap in the structure. Once children could respond to and use signs effectively in training situations, they were helped to generalize this understanding to everyday settings on the ground.

Evaluation

To evaluate their effectiveness, these procedures were applied with 19 (median age: 11 years) severely disordered nonverbal autistic children in several institutions. After a median of 14 months' training during which 50 word–action–object systems were developed in the manner described, the children were tested for receptive understanding and expressive use of signs and words. The results indicated that the efforts to naturalize conventional spoken words so that they became part of proximal systems had been successful. The children for the first time were able to receptively grasp and act out the meanings of signs and words presented together *as well as words presented by themselves—without accompanying signs*. After training with 50 signs and words presented together, the autistic children responded correctly to a *median* of 27. Moreover, to the same words presented *without* signs they responded correctly with a *median* of 26 -correct responses. This latter achievement clearly indicated that the functional significance of many directed actions and signs had been extended to words in a way that enabled the children to follow purely verbal directions—"Get up," "Sit down," and so forth—and to produce and use objects such as a knife, fork, and spoon when requested.

At times, a child would abruptly grasp the relationship between his or her own gestures and the responsive actions of the staff person and would look with wonder at hands, worker, and object. Notable was the behavior of one 12-year-old autistic girl who, having been taught "get up" and "sit down" by physically raising and lowering a staff person into a chair, suddenly, after her actions were transformed into gestures by the worker's slightly anticipating them, realized the power of her hand movements. With evident glee, she commanded him to get up and sit down a dozen times in rapid succession.

Results also indicated that the training was less effective in developing the ability to use gesture signs expressively and least effective in teaching expressive use of spoken words. Although all the children achieved some expressive signs, the median use did not surpass 8 gestures of a possible 50. The children accomplished least with regard to spoken words; only 3 of the 19 children learned to use words expressively, and only 1 child achieved speaking in short sentences. The progress of these autistic children most resembled that of normal children in receptive gains and diverged in their difficulties with expressive, particularly spoken, language.

Limitations of the Earlier Approach

Results of the earlier work with behavior-disordered children suggested that the strategies used were likely to be most effective in enhancing understanding of signed and spoken terms and less effective in developing expressive use of signs and spoken words. The children did best with receptive responses to signs and words precisely because the principle of inclusion did not require them to be aware of words or signs as entities separate from their proximal systems. Thus, when the children heard the word "cup" they tended to respond to it as part of the action–object sequence concerned with picking up and drinking from a particular cup.

In accounting for the children's limited development of expressive signs and spoken words, we hypothesized that the more that use of a symbolic form required specific *awareness* of its existence as a symbol separate from but related to its object, the more difficulty the children had responding to and/or using it. Because the children could see themselves using signs, these were more available to them than ephemeral spoken words. Further, because the children tended not to produce sounds with any predictability, they were less likely to use natural sound signs to reflect properties of objects. The sound forms they did produce often seemed to have an ethereal or echo quality unrelated to any relevant context. Consequently, although spoken words produced by others could become meaningfully related to the children's actions, expressive use of these words was unavailable; the children had no basis for experiencing them as separable parts of their systems. To deliberately express words they had to view themselves, and particularly their sound-making mechanisms, as subject to their own intentions. Finally, they had to know that the sounds they uttered could be directed toward and represent objects and events both near and far.

If spoken reference (naming) is defined as the ability to use a symbolic form to designate and represent an object on the basis of its distinguishing characteristics, relatively independent of its function or context, then only one autistic child in this study achieved naming. For example, the children "knew" and were able to identify a spoon as long as it was "properly" located in a bowl or other food-related context, but they could not identify it at a distance or in an unfamiliar context, such as hanging from a hook. Nevertheless, two or three children seemed to gain some inkling of the naming process through their use of manual signs. This was evident in their increased interest in both collecting and using signs once they understood— like the autistic girl who commanded the staff member to rapidly get up and sit down—that the signs allowed them to cause certain things to happen. In this behavior they were like normal 18-month-old children who achieve a similar understanding with regard to spoken words. However, such "sign-naming," at least with the very disordered population described here was limited to action-verb usages where the sign and the action to which it referred shared a similar direction. Unlike normal children, all but one of these children were unable to capture the varied properties of an object within a name in a way that would allow them, eventually, to discover that all things had the potential for being named.

This analysis of the difficulties these children had developing expressive spoken language has implications not only for the development of spoken reference to objects and events, but for the manner in which reference becomes part of a social context. As shown in Chapter 4, in order to make reference part of a social situation the child must be able to share meanings with another on an action level. The child must then be able to include symbolic forms within the shared action context. Finally, the child must be able to detach the symbolic form from its original context and, while retaining its referential significance, present it in an entirely different context to another. Bates et al. (1979), in reporting observations of language development among normal 9- to 15-month-old infants, suggested how this socialization of language becomes evident: They described how one small girl first pointed to and made sounds related to an object and then, at a later time, was able to swing her pointing arm from object to adult—indication of an intent to make the designated object part of commerce between them.

Such behavior suggests the manner in which the child's distal systems begin to include not only the single-track child–object relation but the double-track relation the child must achieve between object and other as well. It is the child's ability to cope with such dual reference situations that establishes an important prerequisite for communication. Bates et al. suggested two important social contexts in which these dual reference (object–adult) problems must be solved before normal expressive language can develop: One designated "protoimperative," refers to children's tool use of adults to gain desired ends, for example, pulling an adult toward a desired object. The other, designated "protodeclarative," concerns the infant's ability to use objects to gain the adult's attention at a distance either by showing or pointing at a remote object. This latter capacity was unavailable to the disordered children we studied.

In general, the strategies used in the study left the autistic children with access to proximal but little or no access to distal systems. The absence of distal systems underscores their importance in the normal development of language, cognition, and human relatedness. Distal systems permit children to rapidly and easily use their sound making buttressed by ocular-motor input and gesture or pointing to act upon and thus relate to a broad range of stimulating objects and events. A natural consequence of this capacity is the enhanced polarity between the child's sense of his or her own body and the external world. Until this develops, children can neither represent nor have commerce with objects or people except as they intrude within the proximal space defined by their pragmatic activity. Without distal systems, autistic children are confined to a reality based only on what they experience directly with their body or on what is within arm's reach. In this reality, objects and people tend to exist upon entering their proximal space and disappear upon leaving it.

The Recent Phase

The major emphasis of our more recent work has been to systematically expand the realities of disordered children with minispheres, integrative spheres, and multispheres. This approach enables them to learn to use language interactively in different contexts both near and far from their bodies. A related goal has been to help the children detach signs and words from original system contexts—without loss of meaning—so that they can use signs and words more effectively to communicate needs and intentions. Fred's achievements of *first signs, sound making, first spoken words, combined signs,* and *combined spoken words* illustrate the approach.

CASE STUDY: FRED—DEVELOPMENT OF LANGUAGE

Fred's *first signs,* like those of many behavior-disordered children, developed in the context of contagious minispheres that were systematically interrupted by the worker. At first the signs were "natural" in that they derived directly from actions performed within spheres. A bit later, however, Fred began to reproduce conventional signs that the worker introduced within various minispheres.

Natural signs in Sessions 69 through 73 resulted from Fred's anticipation of contagious action sequences within minispheres. For example, in Session 69, after prior exposure to banging on a drum, he tapped on his father's knee to indicate his wish to continue this activity. In Session 70 he spontaneously started jumping, and in Session 71 he spontaneously fell down just prior to starting the Walk, Jump, Fall . . . Around the Circle sphere. Session 73 was notable in that Fred produced two natural signs as well as his first conventional (introduced) sign. To illustrate the emergence of natural and conventional signs Sessions 73 through 75 are summarized:

Session 73

The first conventional sign appeared during the Walk, Stop sphere between the classroom and the therapy room. Fred, interrupted, produced the sign for *walk* (moving hands in walking motion) which the worker had consistently introduced during their daily walks.

As part of an informal routine, Fred, after removing his own shoes, *reached over to assist the worker in taking off her shoes*. Later, during the Peek-aboo sphere, after the worker placed a scarf over Fred's head and then her own, Fred, for the first time, removed the scarf from his own head and then from the worker's head.

Session 74

Fred produced the *pour* sign during a pouring minisphere in which, after the worker repeatedly signed and said "pour" while pouring juice, a jar of juice was brought next to Fred's cup and poised over it. Fred immediately and then subsequently made the *pour* sign over his cup.

Session 75

Fred produced the *walk* sign when the worker stopped walking and signing (interruption). Then, when he approached a door, the worker was able to elicit the *open* sign by bringing his hands in close proximity to each other. As he parted his hands, she opened the door.

Later, during a multisphere that included pouring a drink into a cup, cutting clay, and banging on a drum, he produced a *pour* sign and then poured a drink into his cup. Then, while cutting clay, he *spontaneously interrupted his own sphere*, got up, got a truck located on the other end of the room, and brought the truck to the worker so that they could do a pushing-pulling (with string attached) truck sphere—rolling it back and forth between them.

At the end of the session the worker was able to elicit a *bye-bye* wave.

During Sessions 69 through 75 Fred acquired four new signs—*walk, pour, open,* and *bye-bye*. But, perhaps most encouraging were indications that he was increasingly able to initiate spontaneous behavior toward the worker. This was evident when he tried to help the worker take off her shoes and particularly when he interrupted his own spheric activity (cutting clay) and supplanted it with another sphere (pushing-pulling truck).

Using Signs to Communicate Needs Spontaneously

Fred's most impressive effort to communicate his intentions through signs occurred when, ready to leave Session 77, he spontaneously grabbed the worker's arms in an effort to have her get up. This action was transformed into conventional signs during the following session:

Session 78

Fred, finding it difficult to leave the classroom, cried as the worker led him to the therapy room. As soon as the worker sat down, Fred attempted physically to get her up from her chair. When that failed, he signed "get up," went to the door and spontaneously signed "open" at the door.

In the following sessions Fred grasped new signs and demonstrated his ability to use them in interactive spheres involving one or more people:

Session 80

Fred produced the *down* sign as part of an interactive sphere that went as follows: First Fred would send a car down a slide, then his father would alternate by doing the same. Next the father made the *down* sign to Fred, indicating that he was to send a car down. Then (at first with assistance) Fred produced the *down* sign directing his father to send a car down. This interactive sphere continued for a number of cycles.

The worker had found that Fred remained better engaged in activities if she periodically "toned him up" by gently rubbing and tickling his arms and legs and by playfully pulling his toes. . . . At one point during the session he lifted his foot toward the worker indicating that he wished more play with his toes.

Sound Making

Many behavior-disordered children lack the ability to spontaneously initiate sounds. Consequently, the worker must use a variety of means to bring this capacity under the child's control. Sometimes vocalizing can be elicited in the course of contagious activity such as jumping or running. When this happens, the worker abruptly interrupts the activity and—while the child is still vocalizing—pats the child's mouth in uneven fashion so that the child has repeated opportunities to note the source of the sound and how variably blocking the mouth interrupts and changes the pattern of vocalizing. This process can then be cast within an interactive system by having the worker and the child alternate patting each other's mouth and noting the sound changes produced. A similar strategy can be used when a child begins to cry. Then, the worker takes the child's hand and brings it to his or her mouth in an uneven patting sequence that interrupts the emission of sound and creates an "Indian call." Often, as was true with Fred, a child becomes oriented by the changing sound pattern and begins to notice that the movement of the hand on the mouth influences sound production. Some children become fascinated by this discovery and begin by themselves to experimentally influence their sound making with different mouth-patting sequences.

In another useful procedure to develop sound-making awareness, the worker pats the child's back or brings the child's knees repeatedly against the chest in a way that gently compresses the diaphragm and lungs and helps produce sound as the child expels air. Once sound is produced in this way, the patting mouth procedures just described may be used to enhance awareness of sound making.

A third procedure entails the use of sound–action spheres. One such sphere, called the *Ba . . . Ba . . . Boom/Bang sphere,* was designed to encourage intentional sound making. The worker hits a drum with a stick first lightly and then more intensely, while saying, in tempo, "Ba . . . Ba . . ."; then, after an interruption to build up anticipation, he or she says "Boom" or "Bang," and strikes the drum sharply. In using this sphere with Fred, the worker would note what part of it he responded to and spontaneously produced. The results of this intervention with Fred over a number of sessions follow:

Session 69

One behavior that suggested beginning assimilation of a sound sphere had to do with Fred banging on his father's knee, which his father said meant that he wanted to bang the drum—part of the Ba . . . Ba . . . Boom/Bang sphere previously introduced.

Session 70

Again, as in the previous session, he signaled his wish for the banging drum sphere by repeatedly banging his fingers on the table (not on his father's knee) while looking at the worker.

Session 74

Fred participated in the Ba . . . Ba . . . Boom/Bang sphere and, at the end of this activity, for the first time he said, "Ba . . ."

Session 75

During the Ba . . . Ba . . . Boom/Bang sphere Fred did not produce a sound. However, when, after saying "Ba . . . Ba" while striking the drum, the worker hesitated (interruption) with stick poised in the air, Fred looked directly at the worker and completed the sequence by striking the drum with his hand.

During the next 15 sessions Fred seemed unable to produce sounds within the sound sphere. However, during this same period he became increasingly preoccupied with the manner in which his mouth produced sounds. Excerpts from Sessions 80 and 81 describe this interest:

Session 80

Fred produced much vocalizing this session as he looked at his mouth movements in the mirror. He continued his sound making—"Baba . . . Deedee"—when the worker imitated him but did not imitate any new sounds offered by the worker.

Session 81

Fred continued to be interested in sound making. This was evident as he watched both his and the worker's mouth movements in the mirror. At times he resisted the worker's attempts to help him form certain mouth movements. . . . There was much babbling but still no imitation of new sounds offered.

It may be that Fred's mouth interest coupled with the sound expectation developed in the Ba . . . Ba . . . Boom/Bang sphere contributed to increased ability to intend sounds evident in the following sessions:

Session 91

Fred produced "Ba!" sounds each time the Ba . . . Ba . . . Boom/Bang sphere was interrupted. The sound was made with the clear intent that the sphere be continued.

Session 93

During the Ba . . . Ba . . . Boom/Bang sphere, following interruption after *ba . . . ba . . .* , he produced "Mang!" with the gesture for bang (the drum).

In subsequent sessions he produced relevant sounds in this sphere without difficulty.

Combining Signs

Fred's first combined signs—*give more* and *give "i"* (in)—suggested that he was better able to combine signs that expressed his intention with regard to objects than signs that related to the objects themselves in noun–verb or verb–noun phrases. The *give more* sign developed during Session 81 in context of a *give* sphere: Fred would first do the *give* sign and receive a block; the worker would then add the *more* sign (bringing tips of fingers together); and finally Fred made both signs together and received more blocks.

The *give "i"* sign developed during Session 83 in response to interruption of a well-established integrative sphere (Doll-in-Car, Car-Down Slide). Following interruption of the Car-Down sphere, Fred immediately signed "Give" and got the car. Then, when prevented from immediately sending the car down, he spontaneously used the sign *give* with the "i" sound—meaning, "*Give* me the doll so that I can put it *in* the car." Following this, after being prevented from sending the car with doll down the incline, he produced his first combination with a noun–verb intent—*car down*.

In spite of the *car-down* achievement, Fred demonstrated considerable confusion between the object as an entity and its function—or between subject and predicate. This made it difficult for him to respond accurately to certain two-sign phrases such as signed and spoken requests to pick up different objects on the table or to distinguish between one named object and another.

Session 84

In repeating the Cup, Pour, Cup-on-Hook sphere, Fred demonstrated confusion between *cup* and *pour*—sometimes using the *pour* sign for cup and the *cup* sign for pour. However, after many repetitions of the sphere he began to use the appropriate signs. He demonstrated a similar confusion between the signs for *apple* and *raisin*. Further, when required to carry out specific commands in a familiar context, for example, "Pick up apple," "Drop knife," and so forth, as part of cleaning up the table, he would pick up or drop any item that came to hand. His dependence on the immediately available referent, at least for some signs, was evident when, directed by spoken word and sign to turn out the light (without it being part of a sphere), he could not do so unless he was placed directly in front of the light switch.

Fred's confusion between signs for *cup* and *pour,* on the one hand, and *apple* and *raisin,* on the other, are "good" errors in that they are characteristic of early, syncretic levels of language development (perhaps between 12 and 14 months) when name and function are still merged or when categories are not well developed. In Fred's thinking, because pouring is a function of a cup, why should the signs *pour* and *cup* not be interchangeable? Similarly, because he eats both raisins and apples, why should their signs not be equivalent? Only when Fred grasps the naming insight that "each thing has its name," will he be able to discriminate with precision between different objects.

Before disordered children combine signs in two- or three-unit phrases, they produce them sequentially in relation to different parts of integrative spheres. Thus, each sign derives from a component (subsphere) leading to a particular outcome. Once children can use signs in this step-by-step fashion they seem better able to combine them in phraselike combinations. The manner in which this occurred for Fred is described:

Session 87

The Traveler device (Figure 5.1) was introduced in an integrative sphere that required Fred to consecutively respond to and produce signs for *pull,*

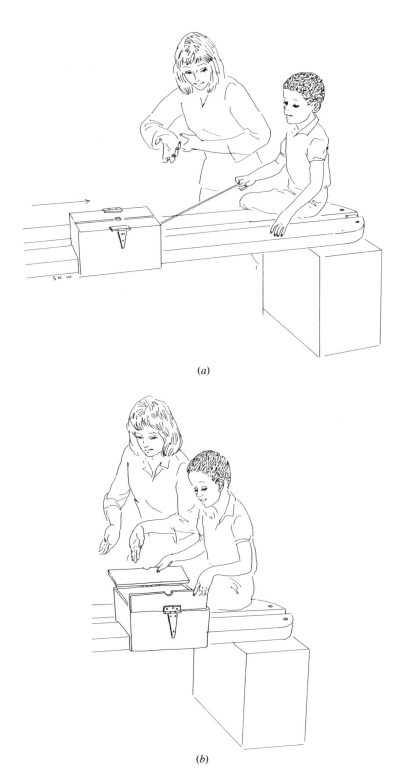

(a)

(b)

Figure 5.1. Fred using the Traveler in response to sign-words (*a*) ''Pull''; (*b*) ''Open.''

open, pick up, give, and *close* in the course of performing the task. . . . Fred seemed fascinated by this game and made excellent eye contact with the worker while both responding to and producing the relevant signs.

Precursors of Shared Reference

Before Fred could share reference with another he had to be able to interact using conventional terms, to communicate meanings to himself, and to designate objects away from his body. Fred had developed capacities in the first two areas but needed specific help with the third—pointing at things away from the body.

Session 89

During this session Fred clearly signed "Hi!" both at the beginning of the session when he responded to the worker's greeting and in context of the Peekaboo game after his discovery under the scarf.

Following this, he demonstrated that he could both receive sign commands from and give commands to the worker in context of the Walk, Jump . . . Around the Circle sphere. Of particular interest was his new tendency, when given a command by the worker, *to sign that command to himself* before performing the required act. . . . Here, for the first time was evidence of the development of self-communication.

The closing activity of the session was designed to help Fred develop a pointing gesture—a pragmatic act that could help him define objects away from the body. This was done with the help of the Pointing Board (Figure 5.2), which consisted of a 1/2-inch groove in an 18-inch board. The groove enabled a person to put the index finger in it. The worker and Fred alternately pushed a peg down the groove with the index finger. Once the

Figure 5.2. Fred using Pointing Board to develop pointing ability.

peg reached the end of the board, the recipient was required to pick it up and put it in a hole in the peg board. With only modest support Fred was soon able to alternate pushing pegs down the groove and putting the pegs in their holes.

Working with the Pointing Board he was able without assistance to use a pointed finger to push a small peg, a marble, and other small objects along the groove. This procedure helped train him to extend his index finger as he pointed at objects in imitation of the worker. At times, however, his pointing would lapse into reaching for the object with fingers outstretched. He also used the extended finger to activate a Jack-in-the-ball by pressing the index finger on top of the ball. He enjoyed the causal relation between his finger pressing and the sudden effect it produced as Jack popped out of the ball. Subsequently, the distance from this object was extended so his pointing could serve a designating function and supplant reaching.

First Spoken Words

Given Fred's confusion between objects and their function and his apparent preference for signs that related to action meanings, it is not surprising that his first spoken words, like those of many disordered children, also related to actions. How these first words came about is described in the following session summaries:

Session 85

The sphere began with both Fred and the worker seated and facing each other. Then, the worker would sign and say "Get up!" Following this, Fred was to command the seated worker to get up. The worker would then, grasping both Fred's hands, set up a contagious, alternating pulling sequence accompanied by the command "Pull!" After a series of such alternations first the worker and then Fred was to sign and say "Sit down!"

In the course of several repetitions of the sphere, Fred for the first time appropriately signed and said "Get up!" "Pull!" "Sit down!"

The worker was struck by Fred's growing involvement in the sphere, evidenced by his constant eye contact, his smiling and laughing, and his evident delight in keeping the game going. Fred's first spoken words occurred less as a function of interruption than of the excited contagion that developed in response to the reciprocal pulling.

In the sessions that follow, the spoken words sometimes emerged directly from a contagious sphere and sometimes they resulted from interruption of integrative spheres.

Starting with Session 85, Fred began to use utterances with his signs—largely as a function of interruption of an ongoing sphere. All utterances were sign related. As is true with many disordered, nonverbal children, *in no case did Fred achieve a spoken word unless he had previously been guided by it as a sign-word and had learned to use the sign.* Fred's use of spoken words, however, was largely restricted to action reference. Not having grasped the name–object relationship he had great difficulty distinguishing and relating one object to another as evident in the session that follows:

Session 90

The worker seated Fred at a table and presented him with one of two foods; the implements needed to ingest the food were placed out of his reach. Thus, he had either a bottle of juice (which required a cup) or a dish of pudding (which required a spoon). To drink the juice or eat the pudding he needed to ask the worker for the cup or spoon.

Fred could not at first indicate with either sign or word that he needed the cup or spoon. Only after several hand-over-hand repetitions, during which the worker named by sign and word the needed articles, could he begin—with sign only—to correctly designate the appropriate object.

Although Fred had difficulty choosing between two objects in the situation described, he had no such difficulty when asked at various points in the transition from the therapy room to his classroom, *"What should we do?"* *"Where are we going?"* He would respond to these questions by signing and saying, "walk" "down" "up" quite appropriately.

Fred's difficulty with signing or saying which of two implements he required in contrast to designating "What should we do?" tasks, stems from the nature of the two situations. The first situation required Fred to distinguish between one set of two objects (cup and spoon) then between another set (juice and pudding) before relating one of the two implements to one of the two foods. In contrast, no such complex relational process was involved in Fred's response to "Where are we going?" because here he coped one at a time with the events he confronted on the way to the classroom. This same response pattern was confirmed in the next session:

Session 94

The worker introduced some additional word–object relations within the Climb-Stairs, Objects-down-the-Tube sphere. Thus, after Fred went up the steps he had to designate the object—ball, car, or cup that was to go down the tube. . . . Fred had difficulty designating the object. When focused directly on the object, and when he was not shaking his head from side to side, he usually produced the correct sign-word. Other times, he tended to get stuck on the word *cup* even when the worker changed to another object. However, he had no difficulty with action sign-words and correctly produced "up," "drop," and "jump" whenever interrupted in context.

Fred was finally beginning to include in his spoken vocabulary the names of two familiar objects—*ball* and *cup*. Both objects had been used in a variety of spheres and with many expansions. The next task was to help him use these terms in meaningful two-word phrases.

Working toward Two-Word Phrases

Among the two-word phrases that normal children accumulate during the 2nd year of life (Brown, 1973) are stereotypic social phrases such as "all gone" and "bye-bye" in which the meaning is quite diffuse. Such phrases contrast sharply with the later developing noun–verb (cup falls) or verb–noun relations (give cup). Although we include in our work pragmatic terms such as "Hi!" and "Bye-bye!" and "I" and "You" to develop the self–other reference so important in establishing social contact, noun–verb and verb–noun relations are stressed to make syntax available to the children. Accordingly, the next session illustrates the development of these relations within an action sphere before the attempt is made to elicit syntax concerned with objects:

Session 102

As part of a continuing effort to develop syntactical relations, the worker attempted an integrative sphere entailing different actions centered around the cup. At Station 1 Fred was given a cup; at Station 2 he washed the cup; at Station 3 he dried the cup; at Station 4 he put the cup on the hook; and at Station 5 he dropped the cup. *Following* Fred's involvement in this sphere, interruptions were used at each station to elicit "give cup," "wash cup," "dry cup," "cup on hook," "drop cup."

Fred was very organized while engaged in this sphere although he waited until the worker used sign and word to guide him to the next station. When interrupted, Fred provided one word at a time but could add others when queried. For example, at Station 2, interrupted by being asked what he was going to do, he replied "Wash." Asked, "Wash what?" he would say "Cup." He could not, however, say "Wash cup" intentionally without such prompting.

Following the cup sphere, the worker sought to develop syntax around the term "box," a concept Fred could grasp receptively but which he had not yet produced expressively in either sign or word. To develop this capacity, the worker set up five stations arranged in circular fashion around the room. The first station entailed Fred being given a box, the second, opening the box, the third, closing the box (a different box), the fourth, dropping the box, the fifth, putting an object in the box. Following Fred's sign-word–guided actions, the worker, through interruption, sought to elicit the terms "give box," "open box," "close box," "drop box," "in box."

Fred performed each action in sequence, guided by sign-words related to each station. When interrupted, he said "give," "open," "close," "drop," and "in." He repeated the sign-word for box but would not name it like other familiar objects (like "cup" when shown a cup). In short, where the term "box" was concerned, Fred would mimic it but would not use it to designate that object.

Session 103

The worker continued trying to develop syntactical relations. She first established a bubble-blowing task and then had Fred pop the bubbles with pointed finger. In this context he was able to combine the worker's name and then his own name with the term "blow," for example, "Fred blow (bubbles)."

Following this, the worker developed an integrative sphere having to do with combing the hair of a baby doll and of adults, brushing the baby doll's teeth, brushing Fred's teeth. In this context, following interruptions, Fred initiated signs for comb and brush. Then, when the worker tickled Fred, he spontaneously said "Tickle" and offered his foot to the worker.

Finally, in context of spheric activity—walking across the Primary Board to and from worker and father—Fred was able to request with sign and word, "Mary walk," "Poppa walk," "Mary jump," "Poppa jump," with the expectation that different people would perform these different actions.

Here, for the first time, Fred demonstrated the ability to vary subject and verb to achieve different outcomes. He demonstrated this, however, only in a highly structured, spheric setting after prior experience with the different participants performing these acts. Only when he can use words spontaneously in this way outside of spheric contexts can we say he has achieved this capacity.

Fred has reached an interesting point in his social and language development. He has clearly progressed dramatically from the mute, stereotypic, and twiddling child described in Chapter 3. Perhaps most indicative of his progress is the parents' report of an episode that occurred one morning when Fred went into his parents' bedroom and signed and said "Get up!" Startled, the parents got out of bed at which point Fred signed and said "Walk! . . . walk! . . . walk!" as he moved toward the kitchen. With both parents following him, Fred walked to the refrigerator and signed and said "Open!" Father opened the door and Fred pointed to the box of eggs and said "Break!" At that point, hearing a sizzling sound on the stove, they turned and saw that Fred had put butter in the frying pan and had turned on the stove. Now he waited for someone else to complete the task of making breakfast.

That Fred had generalized the language learned at the Center to his home is indisputable. He clearly sensed that his signs and words were tools that had to be used with people if his ends were to be met. That the language, although spontaneous, was still quite limited is apparent from a number of perspectives: First, Fred could not fully depend on words to forecast his intentions. He could only use the words in context *as he moved* from bedroom to refrigerator. At a more advanced stage he would be able to stand in front of his parents and say, "Get up! I'm hungry! Make scrambled eggs for me!" Instead, he had to depend on his body actions toward desired events (moving to the refrigerator, pointing inside) to substitute for the syntax he lacked. Further, although he could initiate words he still had to pair them with signs. Beyond this, he could not combine action words with nouns. In fact, all the spontaneous words used in the incident were action words with the object meaning carried by some physical action directed toward the desired objects.

These aspects of the episode indicate that Fred's language was still part of his sign stage functioning and that he had not achieved the insight that "each thing has its name" in a way that would allow object meanings to become portable and usable independent of particular contexts. Lacking this understanding, the action words were still fused with their objects in a manner that precluded the development of true syntax. Whether or not Fred will be able to cross the gap from sign-words to names remains to be seen. He possesses one important prerequisite in his knowledge that signs and utterances must be used as part of his relationship with people if they are to be influential. However, even with his limited language, he now lives in a more predictable social world, in which he can share meanings and influence what happens to a significantly greater degree than he could before treatment.

SUMMARY

This chapter presents a modified discontinuity view of language development that maintains the notion of discontinuity between sign and symbol proposed by Cassirer, but which also includes a role for continuity. Continuity is implicit in a proposed symbolic-sign stage, which helps bridge the gap between sign and symbol.

Children must bridge two major discontinuities if they are to achieve full language capacity. The first is the gap between sign and name, which is bridged by the discovery of naming (symbolic-sign stage); the second, presaging the achievement of symbols has been termed the *fiat* insight because it entails the ability to arbitrarily assign meanings to symbolic forms even though these forms do not resemble their referents. Just as the naming insight makes possible spoken language, so the fiat insight makes possible the development of reading and writing as well as the ability to observe one's thoughts, actions, and their relations.

A solution to the problem of naming is proposed in which the child collects the varied properties of an object within the form of the conventional word that relates to that object. This "collection" process begins as the child hears a particular word—"cup," "ball,"—while using the object in a variety of cup- or ball-related functions. In this way the words begin to refer not only to the most perceptually salient property of an object but to its secondary properties as well. For example, the term "cup" refers to a certain object that can be poured into, picked up, and drunk from, and that maintains its identity even when not in use on a shelf. Then, when a stable relationship develops between a number of such utterances and their objects, the child has a basis for the discovery that "each thing has its name."

Following this, the earlier work is contrasted with the more recent approach. The chapter describes the limited effectiveness of the earlier approach—using signs adapted from the American Sign Language for the deaf with spoken words while children performed clearly defined actions on elevated board structures and in various everyday contexts (eating, dressing, etc.). The major finding of the earlier work was that profoundly disordered children who were previously unable to understand either signed or spoken words could learn to do so after these terms were introduced within functional action contexts. Equally important was the transfer of signed meaning to spoken words evidenced in the posttraining ability of these children to respond solely to spoken words used without signs. Whereas a number of children learned to use signs to designate certain objects only three of the children learned to use some words expressively.

Although the early insights developed in working with elevated boards and sign language have been maintained, in recent years a more flexible approach has been followed that, with the help of minispheres, integrative spheres, and multispheres, allows workers to intervene more precisely in accord with the child's needs. After a discussion of the earlier approach, therapy with Fred is used to illustrate the more recent approach.

CHAPTER 6

From Speech to Reading and Writing

A BRIEF HISTORY OF THE SYMBOL ACCENTUATION READING PROGRAM

We first confronted the relation between speech and reading in 1960 when we tried to teach Barrie, an 8-year-old learning-disabled youngster, how to read. Barrie's classroom teacher, after unsuccessfully trying phonic and whole word approaches, and knowing of our interest in language and perception, had referred Barrie's mother to us at Montana State University (now the University of Montana). Watching Barrie, shoulders hunched over her primer, index finger frozen under each word, we were struck with the great difficulty she had identifying and retaining the forms of printed words. Even when repeatedly given the correct terms for words, she would promptly forget them when they reappeared in the next sentence. Yet Barrie spoke in normal sentences and, when tested, demonstrated that she could designate pictures in a manner only slightly below age expectations.

We speculated that because printed words did not resemble their objects, it was difficult for her to invest meaning in them. If that were so, making the words more physiognomic in the manner described by Werner (1948) might enable her to better invest words with meaning and distinguish one word form from another. We began to pencil in changes in the forms of words in her book in a way that both focused her attention on certain unique features in the shapes of the words while providing her with cues to the words' meanings. We put dots inside the *oo* in the word *look* to designate looking eyes, curled the end of the word *come* so it could be construed as beckoning, turned the word *dog* into a more doglike form by making the *d* headlike and adding a tail to the serif on the *g*, and so forth. With these kinds of additions, Barrie began to sight-read the words successfully and, later, to distinguish them from each other even without picture accenting.

The work with Barrie led to a series of experiments with retarded and normal preschool children—first with flash cards, then with stroboscopic slide presentations, and finally with motion picture sequences—to determine just how important it was for children to have "bridges" to cross the gap from objects and pictures to the arbitrary forms of printed words. Ultimately we discovered that many children not only needed transitions from objects and pictures to printed words, they also needed transitions that would guide them toward an understanding of how letter–sound relations allow one to discover the meaning of an unfamiliar printed word by sounding it out.

Returning to Boston in 1964, we were invited to share our findings—which we had already presented at meetings of the American Psychological Association (Miller & Miller, 1962; Miller, 1963a)—at the Wrentham State School for retarded children and adults. There, following the presentation, the superintendent invited one of us (AM) to establish a language development laboratory to translate our research into a reading program capable of helping even very limited trainable retarded people learn to read. The laboratory was established, and experiments with this population were conducted. After several years of research and field testing, a reading program—Symbol Accentuation™ (Miller, 1968/1989c)—was completed. In Chapter 11 the program is described in some depth, and its application with different kinds of children is considered.

COGNITIVE-DEVELOPMENTAL SYSTEMS APPLIED TO READING AND WRITING

Reading and writing entail a symbolic process that depends for success on the ability of children to expand their systems of spoken words to include graphic forms. Once children have extended certain meanings to these graphic forms (printed words), they can later derive these meanings from them. Like spoken language, reading and writing follow a developmental progression in which the graphic forms used to convey meaning become increasingly remote from their objects. Thus, just as humans progressed from an ability to find meaning in pictures to more arbitrary ideograms (Huey, 1908/1968) and then to phonetically organized written forms, so too, the developing child first "reads" and "writes" pictures and then more arbitrary forms (trademarks, insignia, printed words) before being able to cope with phonetic reading and writing.

This progression occurs because each earlier developmental stage contributes to the formation of the next more advanced stage. Just as the sign stage contributes to the formation of naming—the symbolic-sign stage—so does the symbolic-sign stage through naming contribute to the formation of reading and writing and the development of the symbol stage. In emphasizing the importance of one stage's contribution to the next, we take issue with the general concept of "reading readiness." Typically, this poorly defined term holds that if children have not been able to learn how to read with conventional procedures, then they are maturationally not "ready" to do so.

Although not disputing the importance of age, genetic, or neurological factors in language development, we maintain that the ability to learn how to read and write is *also* a function of the methods used to teach it. When the methods used are consistent with the developmental stage of the children or adults being taught, many who appeared to lack the readiness to learn will be found able to do so. However, before investigating the role that stage-related methods play in the development of reading and writing, it is important to note the influence of two factors—the cognitive demands posed by different kinds of graphic symbols such as pictures, printed words, letters—*and* the stage of symbolizing capacity available to a particular child. Only when the demands posed by particular kinds of graphic symbols are consistent with the symbolizing capacity of a particular child will that child be able to read and write with those forms.

The Symbolic Demands of Our Written Language

Because the words of our written language convey meaning both through their total configuration (the word's entire form) and through their internal structure (letter forms) related to sounding-out the word, one of two very different kinds of symbolic demands may be in play as a child confronts a particular printed word. To clarify the nature of these demands, it is desirable to contrast the printed word as a total form—as used in early sight-reading—with its apprehension as a phonetically organized sequence.

When this contrast is made, it becomes apparent that the child reading phonetically requires a fuller awareness of words as symbolic forms than does the child reading by sight or configuration (before understanding phonics). For example, the new sight reader addresses printed word forms as if they were objects and events or *pictures* of them (see Figure 6.1). The stance toward these forms is *outward* oriented, with emphasis placed on the printed word's shape because, just as changes in the form of a picture change its significance, so changes in the overall shape of the printed word form change its meaning. Such a reader deals with printed words essentially as if they were pictures. And just as a child reading pictures does not have to be

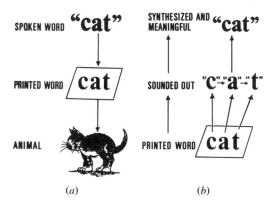

(a)   (b)

Figure 6.1. Differences in orientation between (*a*) sight-reading and (*b*) phonetic reading. From A. Miller, 1968/1989c. Copyright 1989 by A. Miller. Used with permission.

conscious of the picture as a symbol that *represents* an object or event, neither does the early "picture-word" reader. Phonetic readers, on the other hand, have to be aware that both printed and spoken words are arbitrary symbols that represent each other as well as their object meanings. Grasping this reciprocal relation, they are able to deal with printed words in terms of two vectors: *inward* from letter forms to utterances that compose the word (permitting children to sound-out words); and *outward* to the entire printed word and to the object or event it represents, as the sound form they create in this manner becomes a spoken word.

Assigning meanings by *fiat* comes into play when, after discovering the meaning of a printed word by sounding-out its parts, children have to assign that meaning to the entire printed word form. Unless children are able to assign meanings in this way, they find it necessary to sound-out the same printed word laboriously each time they encounter it. In contrast, having assigned meanings by *fiat* to entire printed words, they can read these words as units. And, although the advanced sight reading that emerges from this process bears a superficial resemblance to earlier sight-reading because both deal with the entire word, only the advanced sight reader possesses the ability—on confronting unfamiliar printed words—to shift to sounding-out a word to gain its meaning.

The nature of the obstacles to reading and writing depend on the kind of reading attempted. When the goal is phonetic reading and writing, it is far more difficult for the child to solve the cognitive problems involved than is the case with early sight reading. However, even for early sight or picture-word reading, children must still address the disparity between the shapes of printed words and the forms of objects whose meanings they convey. How children cope with printed words—and whether or not they succeed with them—depends on the reading method used and the symbolic capacities available. The relevance of stage-related symbolic capacity for early sight-reading may be illustrated by a hypothetical reading lesson in which the demands of the lesson interact with children possessing different levels of symbolic capacity.

A Hypothetical Reading Lesson

In this lesson the words are taught by the "look-say" method in which each printed word form is treated as a unique visual pattern that the teacher flashes while uttering its name. After a number of such repetitions, the printed word is presented in silence and the child is required to produce the appropriate spoken word. The assumption behind this procedure is that the child can grasp the notion that the printed word, like the spoken word paired with it, conveys meaning and, further, that the meaning of the spoken word can be *assigned* to the printed word. Because many 5- to 6-year-olds have achieved this understanding, they generally have little difficulty attributing, for example, cat significance to the printed word *cat*. They can do this because they treat the printed word as one of a group of symbolic forms—like trademarks—that represent things or events even though they bear no physical resemblance to them.

This is not the case for many developmentally delayed or disordered children who, although able to name objects and pictures of objects, do not yet understand that certain forms may represent objects without in the least resembling them. Assume that such a child has just recently achieved naming, and thus the level of "requiredness" between name and object is rigidly fixed; the child is quite intolerant of the name *cat* referring to anything that does not look like a cat. To assist this analysis, such a child will be referred to as functioning at the *primary naming* level. This child, confronted with the printed word *cat* after repeated pairings with the spoken word, has no basis for grasping the notion that the graphic form *cat* can convey cat meaning. Consequently, just as Ethan at the age of 28 months rejected the possibility of the term *milk* for his station wagon "Because you drink milk," so must the child at this stage reject the printed word *cat* because it does not look like a cat.

However, in the same way that Ethan by the age of 4 years had progressed to the point where he *could* call his station wagon "milk" because he found a milklike property in the white trailer hitch, children eventually are able to use names to transfer meaning to forms that bear little resemblance to the names' usual referents. Children with this ability are referred to as having *secondary naming* capacity, which allows them to find cats, dogs, and so forth in the shifting forms of clouds or in rock forms, merely by applying the appropriate names to them (Figure 6.2). Then, for example, by using the

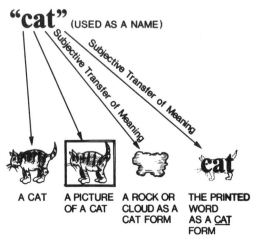

Figure 6.2. The name-guided transfer of "cat" meaning to various forms. From A. Miller, 1968/1989c. Copyright 1989 by A. Miller. Used with permission.

same process to selectively stress a curve in one place and a line in another, the child in school is able to "find" the required cat properties within the printed word *cat* when the teacher asserts that it means "a cat."

The child, without understanding the symbolic relation intended by the teacher, can—after repeated pairings—find the designated animal within the word's contours by viewing the *c* as the head, the *t* as the tail, and so forth. If the child succeeds in subjectively transforming (accenting) salient portions of the printed word's contours so they "fit" the object required by the name, he or she extends the meaning to include that word. This helps the child mentally "etch" the word's contours so that he or she can sight-read it when the teacher next presents the printed word by itself. Whereas children at the *primary naming* phase (approximately 18 to 36 months) would fail the sight-reading lesson, those operating within the *secondary naming* phase (approximately 3 to 5 years) would eventually achieve this extension. The *secondary naming* child uses the name to guide the search for extended meaning within the contours of potential referents in a manner that is unavailable to the *primary naming* child, bound by name–object relations.

Children operating at the *secondary naming* phase of the symbolic-sign stage, may, even though they lack knowledge of the function of arbitrary symbolic forms and the ability to establish relations by fiat, achieve an early form of sight-reading by finding required object properties within the forms of conventional printed words. Then, over time, as they scan named word forms to find contour points that extend the name's meanings, they have repeated opportunities to note that printed words do not really resemble their objects. As they become more fully aware of the distinct separation between words and their meanings, they also become aware that the transfer of meaning to printed word forms depends not on finding object properties within the words, but solely on their inner intent that certain words shall represent certain meanings.

Symbol Accentuation: A Bridge to Sight Reading

Although the preceding formulation provides a plausible account of the manner in which normal children first achieve sight-reading, it remains speculative. For a test of this formulation, we chose a population of retarded people who could designate objects and pictures that resemble objects yet were unable to read, even though they had been exposed to years of reading instruction that included both configuration and phonetic approaches. We hypothesized that they could not derive meaning from printed words because they were functioning at the *primary naming phase* of the symbolic-sign stage and had not been able to advance to the *secondary naming* phase that would have allowed them subjectively to invest object properties in the forms of printed words.

If this proved to be correct, then these retarded people could not sight-read because they lacked the symbolic capacity to *deliberately* extend the meanings of names to unfamiliar forms. They could spontaneously extend names to objects within the same category, for example, cups of different shapes were still called *cups* because they could act toward them as cups that could be picked up and drunk from. The printed word *cup*, however, lacked the cuplike properties required to extend its significance to that printed word. Consequently, retarded people who could not deliberately extend meaning to printed words might be able to do so if, following their engagement with a particular name-related object, the extension of meaning was enacted for them.

The manner of accomplishing this extension was suggested by an observation of our son David's (aged 21 months) early use of names. Sighting the sudden movement of a bird perched in the fork of a tree, David pointed at it while exclaiming, "Bird!" . . . Bird!" During the course of these exclamations, the bird abruptly disappeared within the tree fork. Still pointing and peering at the tree fork, David continued to say "bird" but with a questioning intonation as if asking where the bird had gone. On subsequent visits to the tree he would point at the tree fork and exclaim "Bird!" possibly anticipating that his utterance would induce the bird's reappearance on the branch.

Apparently, under certain conditions, a name may, independent of the child's volition, be invested in a form totally disparate from the object toward which it was originally directed. In the example given, the shift seemed to depend (a) on the system involving the name "bird," the pointing activity, and the engaging bird poised in the tree fork; (b) on the sudden disappearance (interrupted system) of the bird; and (c) on the child's compensatory impulse to maintain the system by imposing bird meaning on the site where the bird had last been seen. The combination of all these circumstances resulted in a figure extension in which the fork of the tree assumed bird meaning; the tree fork, previously a ground for the figural bird, became, on the bird's sudden departure, part of the bird system because of the bird that *had* been on the fork.

There is a similarity between the inadvertent manner in which the bird meaning was error-generalized to the tree fork and the inadvertent manner in which natural signs are error-generalized. Thus, just as the term *tap* was used by Stumpf's child (Werner & Kaplan, 1963) to refer both to opening up a bottle with a snapping sound and, later, to the bottle which had been *acted upon*, so did David inadvertently transfer bird meaning to the forked branch which the bird had acted upon. An additional feature that may have facilitated the transfer was based on the *persistence of vision* phenomenon (Montagu, 1964), which makes moving pictures possible. Thus, it is well known that if a card has a picture of a bird on one side and a picture of a cage on the other side, persistence of vision results in the bird being seen in the empty cage as the card is rapidly flipped from one side to the other. Because such persistence of vision is strongest in small children, it is quite probable that David's compensatory disposition to maintain the bird in that location was enhanced by a tendency to "see" the bird on the branch after it had left.

We used this principle of inadvertent extension of meaning in a series of studies with retarded people (Miller & Miller, 1968, 1971; Miller, 1968). The hypothesis in these studies was that just as David extended the bird's meaning to the tree fork, so might a retarded person engaged with an object be taught to extend the object meaning to the form of a printed word within which that object seemed to disappear.

Inadvertent Perceptual Extension of Meaning from Name to Printed Word

We first sought to enact such extensions (Miller & Miller, 1968) by blending object properties with printed word forms using flash cards in one experiment and a stroboscopic projector in a second. In each instance we sought to extend object or motion properties to the printed word by carefully relating and sequencing object or event properties with word contours. Then, when the accentuated form of the word (with its built-in object or action properties) was suddenly replaced by the conventional form of the word, it provided a perceptual transfer of meaning from accentuated to conventional form of the word.

We hypothesized that *primary naming* retarded people would, because of their tendency to experience names as part of the designated objects, more readily identify words that had been perceptually merged with their objects than printed words that had not been treated in this way. The first experiment was conducted with 10 retarded people (mean age 15 years, mean IQ 55) who could neither read nor recognize the printed word forms used in the experiment.

As Figure 6.3 indicates, the presentation of words under the accentuated condition consisted first in showing each person flash cards on which the words had been carefully changed to partially simulate their referents (e.g., the letters of *walk* appeared to walk, *wood* seemed to be made of wood, etc.) and then flipping the flash cards over to show the words in their conventional forms. A single trial consisted of the experimenter naming the accentuated form followed by a flip to the other side of the card where the same word in its conventional form could be seen. During the conventional procedure, in contrast, the same procedure was followed, with the exception that the words on the flash cards were presented *only* in their conventional forms. In both conditions, subjects were given the name of each printed word and a verbal description of its meaning—for example, when *walk* was presented, the experimenter would say, "Walk. You go for a walk."

Eighteen common words were presented, one at a time, to each person until he or she could correctly name and recognize each word; 9 words were presented with an accentuated procedure and 9 with a conventional procedure. Lists of words presented under the two conditions were alternated and randomized. Because each child was used as his or her own control, it

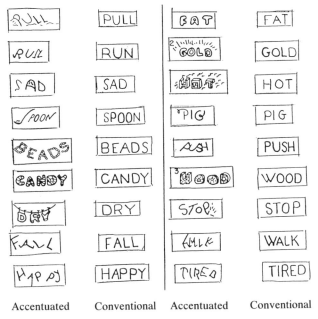

Accentuated   Conventional   Accentuated   Conventional

Figure 6.3. Lists of accentuated and conventional words. From A. Miller and E. Miller, 1968. Used with permission of American Association on Mental Retardation.

was possible to determine the relative effect of each procedure by examining the total number of trials a child required before successfully identifying words under each procedure.

The results indicated that the 10 retarded people required a mean of 11.7 trials to correctly identify 9 accentuated words in contrast to a mean of 26.2 trials for 9 conventionally presented words. This difference was significant ($p < .005$). Following the successful identification of all 18 words, each child was asked to find and correctly identify them in a series of short conventional sentences averaging five words in length. Findings from this procedure demonstrated that the words taught with accentuation could be discriminated within these conventional sentences (mean of 7.0 correct word discriminations) as easily as those taught conventionally (mean of 6.2 correct word discriminations).

A second study was performed to test the replicability of the initial findings with a larger group of retarded children. In this study a stroboscopic projector was used that enabled the accentuated and conventional presentations of the words to be projected on a screen located in front of the subjects. In projecting words for the accentuation procedure, a slide with the word in its accentuated form was placed in one projector and a slide with the word in its conventional form was placed in the other. This procedure resulted in

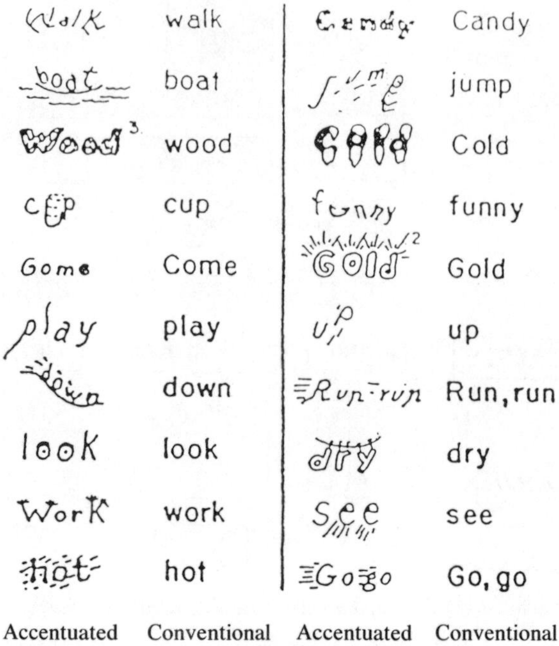

Accentuated	Conventional	Accentuated	Conventional
(walk)	walk	*(Candy)*	Candy
(boat)	boat	*(jump)*	jump
(wood)	wood	*(Cold)*	Cold
(cup)	cup	*(funny)*	funny
(Come)	Come	*(Gold)*	Gold
(play)	play	*(up)*	up
(down)	down	*(Run, run)*	Run, run
(look)	look	*(dry)*	dry
(work)	work	*(see)*	see
(hot)	hot	*(Go, go)*	Go, go

Figure 6.4. Lists of accentuated and conventional words used in stroboscope experiment. From A. Miller and E. Miller, 1968. Used with permission of American Association on Mental Retardation.

the illusion of motion when the words were alternated at a rate of 2.7 times per second. Then the word *walk* appeared to walk, *jump* to jump, the words *up* and *down* to follow those vectors. More static terms like *cup* and *candy* merged with accentuated forms possessing the required object properties. During the conventional presentation both slide projectors projected the word in its conventional form.

The subjects were 38 severely retarded children whose mean age was 17 years and mean IQ was 45. Children were individually screened to preclude prior knowledge of words to be taught and to make certain they had sufficient vision, hearing, and speech to participate. Sixteen of the 20 common words listed in Figure 6.4 were presented in random order to each subject; 8 words were taught with accentuation and 8 conventionally. After the successful identification of each word, the child's capacity to discriminate that word was tested by having him or her select it from among two other words of similar length projected on the screen.

Again, as in the previous study, the accentuated condition was favored. At the end of 5, 10, and 15 trials under the accentuated condition 5.2, 6.8, and 7.1 mean words respectively had been correctly identified in contrast to 1.9, 4.2, and 5.0 mean words under the conventional condition ($p < .0001$).

Ability to discriminate words presented in conventional form from an array of 3 words of similar length did not differ significantly. Among those words taught with accentuation, there was a mean of 3.8 correct word discriminations in contrast to a mean of 3.2 for words taught in their conventional forms.

The consistent finding that the participants in the studies could read conventional printed words more readily after the stroboscopic procedure helped them transfer accentuated (object) properties to them, supports the view that the prior failure to sight-read stemmed from inability to find object meaning in these forms spontaneously. Possibly this occurred because the children's use of names and actions was so tied up with conventional objects (primary naming) that they were unable to use a name as a guide for finding its properties in the printed words. Thus, the same continuity between name action and object that may first have made naming possible, may also have prevented its extension to printed word forms. To gain more understanding of the role of action in the transmission of meaning from name to printed word, another experiment was conducted that kept the accentuation conditions constant for the subjects but varied the manner in which actions were paired with names.

THE ROLE OF ACTION IN EXTENDING MEANING FROM NAME TO PRINTED WORD

In the following study (Miller, 1968) it was hypothesized that *primary naming* children were influenced in their extensions of meaning from name to printed word not only by the perceptual blending of object properties with the forms of printed words, but by the action dispositions that names induced toward printed word forms.

If this hypothesis was correct, then the introduction of *relevant* or *irrelevant* actions or gestures that either strengthened or disrupted the name's action dispositions, should have influenced the name's transmission of meaning through accentuated sequences to printed words. If, as we proposed, action is an important part of the *primary naming* person's functioning, then inserting name-related actions within the previously developed accentuation procedure should, by better establishing meaning transmission between name and printed word, facilitate the acquisition and retention of printed words. Thus, in contrast to the previous model of name–inadvertent perceptual extension (accentuation)–printed word, the new model was of name–*action*–accentuation/printed word. The dependent variable was also different in this experiment. Whereas the first two experiments varied the presence or absence of accentuation, this study kept accentuation constant but varied the kind of action introduced with the name. Thus, if action or gesture is a significant variable in the acquisition and retention of printed words necessary for reading, it should manifest a facilitative effect when it is relevant and an inhibitory effect when it is irrelevant to particular names.

To test this view, 16 retarded people with a mean mental age of 4 years 4 months were divided into two matched groups (Group A and Group B). In the course of the 12-week experiment, they were taught first to *bond* 26 common spoken words with gestures—13 with relevant and 13 with irrelevant gestures—and then to use these word–gesture relations with accentuated sequences that showed objects acting on or transforming into printed word forms. Subsequently, they were asked to read (correctly identify) the 26 words in their conventional printed forms. Retention of words *and* actions was tested 1 week and 4 weeks after the words had been taught.

Bonding

As a first step, names were paired with either relevant or irrelevant actions. Actions or gestures were considered relevant when they reflected a central meaning of the name with which they were paired and irrelevant when the action or gesture chosen seemed quite divergent. Thus, a circular mopping motion was considered a relevant gesture for the spoken word *mop*, whereas the gesture that simulated lifting a cup to one's mouth was considered irrelevant for mop. The bonding measure was based on the number of word–action pairings a subject required before he or she could, on hearing the spoken word, produce the gesture that had been paired with it. The results showed that the actions that had been designated relevant were successfully bonded by the retarded subjects significantly ($p < .001$) more readily (mean of 1.5 trials per word–gesture bonding) than those under the irrelevant gesture condition (mean of 2.4 trials).

Name + Action + Accentuated (Object to Word) Sequences

The intent of this part of the study was to determine the importance of extending the name's meaning through action to a picture that transformed into a printed word. If relevant action was an important part of this transfer of meaning, the subjects should have sight-read significantly more words taught with relevant than with irrelevant actions. Once they had bonded a set of 4 or 5 spoken words with either relevant or irrelevant actions, they were helped to use these word–action combinations to identify unfamiliar printed words.

Instead of flash cards or stroboscope to enact the perceptual transfer from object to printed word, animated motion picture films were used. Unlike earlier procedures, the films could portray the object in different dynamic relations with the printed word. It could show one entity merging with, acting upon, disappearing within or being supplanted by another entity in a way that permitted a full range of possible transfers of meaning. Notable also, in the use of animation, was the possibility of combining several strategies, for example, acting upon *and* supplanting (sudden replacement of object with printed word form) to establish the most effective transfer of meaning from objects and events to the forms of printed words.

Instances of the way in which the retarded subjects coordinated their relevant or irrelevant gestures with animated film sequences is described for the words *hat* and *mop*:

> As the subject saw a film sequence of a hat being placed on a person's head under the relevant condition, he or she was required to say "hat" and actively simulate putting a hat on his or her own head. Then, as the hat transformed into the printed word *hat*, the subject was again required to say "hat" and perform the relevant hat gesture. A subject under the irrelevant gesture condition would follow the identical procedure with the exception of the action used—for "hat" it was a scanning action with hand shading eyes.
>
> For *mop* under the relevant action condition the subject, while watching a sequence in which a mop was being used with a circular mopping motion, said "mop," and performed the same kind of mopping motion seen in the film. As the lower part of the mop turned into *mo* and the handle of the mop into *p* the subject again said "mop" and performed the relevant mopping motion. In contrast, a subject under the irrelevant action condition would say "mop" and, while observing the mopping motion on the screen, bring hand to mouth as if drinking from a cup.

Not all film sequences depended on direct action upon or with the printed word forms. Some exploited certain cause–effect relations common to everyday life involving objects at a distance from the subject. In these situations, the movements of a figure in the foreground of the screen were followed by certain actions in the background—providing the illusion that the first set of movements were the *cause* of the second.

This principle was used with the words *near* and *far*. *Near* was developed by a film sequence in which each time animated hands moved toward the foreground person's chest, a tiny and faint version of the printed word *near* seemed to come closer. Gradually, as *near* came closer it grew larger and clearer. The moment it became conventional in size and clarity, the gesturing figure abruptly disappeared, leaving only the word *near* on the screen.

The opposite gesture sequence was used to develop an appropriate sequence for *far*. (Figure 6.5) Each time the foreground animated figure produced a "go away" movement (simulated by the subject) the word *far* appeared to retreat into the distance until, just as it disappeared from sight, the gesturing figure in the foreground was abruptly supplanted by the conventional word *far*. In this way, because spoken word and relevant gesture were "magically" related to a vector central to the word's meaning, the printed word had the opportunity to become invested with this meaning in a way not possible with irrelevant gestures.

Figure 6.5. Illustration of gesture–word relation for *far*.

Acquisition of Printed Words

The results of these procedures showed that when the subjects used spoken words bonded with relevant actions in concert with the animated sequences described, they were subsequently able to identify more printed words than when they used irrelevant actions. The difference, however, was not at first statistically significant. Examination of subjects' response to the six sets of words on film (one set of 4 or 5 words on each film) revealed that the animated sequences for four words—*I, rat, jump, see*—on Film Set E, accompanied a significantly higher designation of printed words ($p < .001$) than any of the other film sets. Further, with words on this film and no other, subjects' use of irrelevant action was followed by more correct designations than that following relevant action conditions for all four words. When data from Set E were removed, retarded subjects' performance for all other sets under relevant action conditions (mean of 21.7 correct word designations) proved to be significantly greater ($p < .03$) than their response (mean of 17.2) under the irrelevant action conditions.

Certain characteristics distinguished Film Set E from the others. First was the appearance within the film sequence of an animal—a scurrying rat that transformed into the printed word *rat*—which may have triggered an aversive reaction. Each remaining word in the set (*I, see, jump*) and its accompanying irrelevant gesture may have been integrated around this affective state—producing in effect a rat-related narrative around each term. These narratives may have been facilitated by presenting the entire sequence of 4 words in different order two more times after each word was developed. Relevant gestures that related directly to each word as a separate entity—*I* with a self-reference gesture, *see* with a shading eyes gesture, *jump* with a slight jumping action, *rat* with fingers moving rapidly on arms—may have been less effective because they provided little gesture opportunity to express the emotional response.

Viewed in this manner, it is understandable how supposedly irrelevant gestures when related to an affect around the rat sequence were actually more facilitating than supposedly relevant gestures designed to facilitate each printed word by itself. Because the words in all other film sets fit the pattern of unrelated printed words without an organizing affect, it is not surprising that in these sets relevant gestures facilitated more correct printed word designations than irrelevant gestures. An interesting note is that the four subjects most able to exploit irrelevant gestures in Set E and, presumably, to use them for expressive purposes had higher mental ages (mean mental age of 5.2 years) whereas the four least able to do so had notably lower mental ages (mean mental age of 3.9 years).

Retention of Printed Words and Gestures

The ability of the subjects to retain printed words and gestures they had been taught during this 12-week-study was tested both 1 week and 4 to 5 weeks after completion of the experiment. Retention scores were based on subjects' ability to correctly designate, on flash cards, words previously taught under one of the two action conditions with animated film sequences.

The results indicated that, 1 week after the training sequences, retarded subjects retained significantly more words ($p < .05$) under relevant (mean of 5.0 words) than under irrelevant (mean of 3.6 words) gesture conditions. However, 4 to 5 weeks after the experiment, the significant difference favoring relevant gesture had disappeared, with words last taught being best retained independent of action condition.

The retention pattern was very different with regard to the actions that had been bonded to spoken words. Both 1 week and 4 to 5 weeks after training, significantly more relevant than irrelevant actions were retained. After 1 week subjects retained a mean of 9.2 relevant actions and a mean of 3.6 irrelevant actions ($p < .001$). Subjects still retained a mean of 7.2 relevant actions in contrast to a mean of 1.6 irrelevant actions ($p < .02$) 4 to 5 weeks after the experiment.

These findings support the view that names constitute systems encompassing action dispositions that may be extended to include printed word forms. Printed words, however, are more susceptible to "drifting" from the system than are relevant actions. The results also indicated that one could not always predict which actions a person would experience as relevant or irrelevant. When, inadvertently, a series of animated film sequences lent themselves to organization around one sequence—a scurrying rat—actions originally designated irrelevant seem to have been experienced as relevant as they contributed to a series of affectively driven narrative statements about the rat. This suggests that the role of action changes radically when children begin to understand that printed words, like the spoken words that preceded them, contribute to such a narrative. At that point, action may serve less to facilitate a spoken or printed word than to express its significance.

CONTRASTING SYMBOL ACCENTUATION WITH "LOOK-SAY" PAIRING OF PRINTED WORDS AND PICTURES

In the previous study we tested a model: name + action + animated (accentuated) sequence that united object properties with a printed word form. That study showed that, when the name-guided significance extended to blend relevant action with animated object–word sequences, retarded people acquired and retained more printed words than when name-guided significance was partially diverted by irrelevant action. The next study (Miller & Miller, 1971) further tested the importance of the model on a new group of nonreading retarded people by comparing the effect of a name-guided + accentuated sequence versus a name-guided approach that presented the printed word separate from its object ("look-say" approach).

If the look-say and the accentuated methods of teaching early sight-reading are contrasted, a greater conceptual demand seems required by the look-say procedure. It is implicit in the separation between printed word and the picture referent with which it is paired, requiring the child to understand that one of the two forms (the printed word) represents the other (the object pictured). The achievement of this act of reference and representation goes beyond symbolic-sign stage capacity—during which the child establishes reference by finding required object properties within a potential referent—to symbol stage capacity that entails the deliberate intent that one entity shall henceforth refer to another.

Applied to reading, once object meaning is conferred on a particular word by fiat, the child can use that word as a surrogate for the object with which it had been paired. In contrast, no such fiat is required to invest meaning within a word taught under the accentuated condition. To invest meaning in a printed word, the name-guided subject need only see the object (or its properties) transform or disappear within that printed word. The extension of meaning is automatic, requiring no deliberate intent, because it derives from a perceptual illusion that conveys a sense of the object within the printed word form.

Whereas the separation between printed word and object in the look-say presentation seems to require an inner intent to refer a printed word to its object before that word could assume the meaning of its object, the accentuated condition allows a printed word to assume object meaning by virtue of the externally realized relation between the object and the printed word into which it transforms.

Nonreading Retarded People with Look-Say and Accentuated Conditions

If the preceding analysis is correct and most retarded people who cannot read are operating within the *primary naming* phase of the symbolic-sign stage, then, when they have the opportunity to learn new printed words

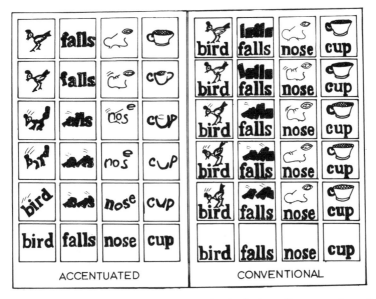

Figure 6.6. Comparison of accentuated and conventional ("look-say") presentations of printed words. From A. Miller and E. Miller, 1971. Used with permission of American Association on Mental Retardation.

under look-say and accentuated conditions, they should learn to read significantly more words under the accentuated conditions.

In order to test this hypothesis, the general method followed was to present each of 40 retarded subjects (mean age 13 years, mean IQ 44) two different kinds of training films (see Figure 6.6 for excerpts from these films). The film with accentuated sequences showed animated objects that seemed to transform into their conventional printed word forms; the film with look-say sequences, presented a printed word with its object and showed the object going through similar animated sequences but remaining separate from the conventional printed word that appeared below it on the screen.

The words taught during this experiment included for List A, dog, table, falls, and car; and for List B, walk, cup, bird, and nose. Each group of words was filmed in both accentuated and look-say formats that were closely matched for all factors (animation, duration) except for the separation factor. Twenty subjects (10 male, 10 female) had List A in accentuated form and List B in conventional form, whereas the remaining 20 had List B in accentuated form and List A in conventional form. Conditions were counterbalanced for possible order effects so that each condition was presented first an equal number of times. Both lists were presented with a 16-mm projector, with the subject seated approximately 2 m from the screen. The subject saw words about 15 cm high projected at eye level on the screen.

At the end of either an accentuated or look-say training condition, after four words had been presented under one of the two conditions, the subject was presented each word in its conventional form, by itself, for 5 seconds. The number of words the subject correctly identified during this period became the score for Trial 1. Subsequently the same words were shown in a different order leading to Trial 2. The same procedure was followed for the third and fourth training sequences. On the following day, each subject was taught a new group of four words for the remaining condition. Scores for the identification trials were obtained for the second condition in the same way as for the first condition.

The results clearly supported the hypothesis that retarded people would do significantly better under the accentuated condition—consistent with their primary naming capacity—than under the look-say condition. During the four identification trials, retarded people under the accentuated condition were able to read a mean of 1.9, 2.5, 3.0, and 3.2 words. In contrast, under the look-say condition they were able to identify a mean of only 1.2, 1.9, 2.3, and 2.6 printed words. The differences favoring accentuated over look-say conditions were significant ($F = 19.56$, $1/39$ df, $p < .001$).

However, to gain a sense of how each of the 40 retarded people fared on the two conditions, we compared the total number of words each person correctly read under accentuated and look-say conditions. We found that 27 of the 40 people read more words under accentuated than look-say conditions, whereas 13 did as well or better under look-say.

In considering these results, we speculated that the central aspect of the 27 retarded subjects' functioning that made it possible to benefit from the accentuated condition was the name-guided "requiredness" with a particular referent—a requiredness that expressed itself in a single-track engagement with the animated object that appeared on the screen. This disposition to be engaged by *one* compelling object to the exclusion of all else, characteristic of the *primary naming* phase, may well have facilitated the extension of meaning from object to printed word. On the other hand, the 13 subjects may have done better under the look-say condition because of their ability to deal with *two* separate entities in relation to each other, a double-track capacity characteristic of symbol stage functioning.

Testing for Single- versus Double-Track Dispositions

To test this view, we sought a situation that might independently discriminate between those retarded subjects who operated in a single-track manner and those whose double-track capacity permitted them to establish reference between two separate entities. Through such a situation, we hoped to determine whether the subjects disposed to operate in a single-track manner were also the ones who had done best with the accentuated conditions. Similarly, we wanted to determine whether the subjects generally disposed to operate in a double-track manner (capable of establishing reference between two separate entities) were the same people who had done as well or better with the look-say condition.

A way of discriminating between those retarded people who were disposed toward single- or double-track functioning was suggested by Piaget's doll experiment (1948), one of a series he conducted to explore the problem of egocentricity. In our version of the experiment, two dolls were placed on a table about 30 cm apart so that one doll faced the back of the head of the doll in front of it. The subject, after walking around the table and observing the dolls and their relation to each other, sat down and, while looking at the face of the foremost doll, was asked what the doll in back of it saw.

Single-Track Response. If the subject reported that the doll in back saw the eyes, nose, mouth, or part of the face that *he or she* saw in the doll facing him or her, the response, in present terms, reflected a single-track disposition because the subject was apparently unable to detach attention from the face of the foremost doll.

Double-Track Response. However, if the subject answered correctly that the doll behind the one he or she was looking at saw the back of the head of the doll in front, it demonstrates a double-track capacity that permitted establishing reference between two separate entities. Such subjects, it seems clear, could not correctly report what the doll in back saw without detaching their attention from the doll facing them and establishing a reference relation between the two dolls.

Of the 36 subjects able to participate in the second part of the experiment, 24 had previously done best under the accentuated condition, and the remaining 12 had done as well or better with the look-say condition. Each subject was scored single- or double-track depending on whether he or she gave a correct or incorrect response to the doll test. Children who gave incorrect responses by referring to some part of the doll's face were scored single-track, whereas those who correctly solved the problem by referring to the back of the doll's head were scored double-track.

As shown in Table 6.1, of the 24 subjects who had previously preferred the accentuated condition, 16 scored single-track and 8 double-track on the

TABLE 6.1. Single- or Double-Track Responses among Retardates Favoring Accentuated or Conventional Conditions[a]

Response	Accentuated	Conventional
Single-track	16	3
Double-track	8	9

Note. From A. Miller and E. Miller, 1971. Reprinted with permission of American Association on Mental Retardation.
[a]$\chi^2 = 4.02$, $p < .05$ (two-tailed test).

doll test. In contrast, of the 12 subjects who had previously done as well or better with the look-say condition, 9 scored double-track and 3 single-track on the doll test. The relation between prior condition preference and single- or double-track disposition was significant ($\chi^2 = 4.02$, 1 df, $p < .05$).

Thus, most of the people who did best with the accentuated condition turned out to be the same people who were unable to disengage themselves from the impression made by the doll in front of them. The single-track tendency appeared to have impeded their grasping the correct relation between dolls but facilitated their success under the accentuated condition. In that context, single-track engagement with the animated object as it blended into a printed word probably helped them transfer meaning to that word and to identify it later when it appeared by itself. However, in the look-say condition, this same single-track tendency, just as it impeded grasping the reference relation between the two dolls, may also have impeded grasping the reference relation between the printed word and the separate object with which it was paired. This was not the case for those retarded nonreaders who were able to solve the doll test correctly. The double-track capacity of these subjects to deal with reference between two separate entities in this situation was entirely consistent with doing as well or better with the look-say condition.

Taken together, the results support the view that accentuation procedures were most effective with those people who had not yet achieved the symbolic attitude that made it possible for them to simultaneously cope with two separate entities, whether this entailed the reference relation between two dolls or the relation between a printed word and its object. For example, to solve the doll problem correctly, a subject had to symbolize himself or herself in the position of the rear doll. Once this was done, he or she could "see through the doll's eyes" the rear of the doll's head. Similarly, to find meaning in printed words taught under look-say conditions, the subject would have had to credit the printed word with the symbolic capacity to "see" its object—even when, with the word presented by itself, the object was invisible. In each instance the symbolic attitude required the subject to use a symbolic vehicle (rear doll, printed word) to refer to a part of the situation that could not be perceived directly.

Testing for Developmental Stages in Sight-Reading Capacity

To determine whether the findings reported were restricted to the retarded population or characteristic of different developmental stages among normal children, the same experimental procedures (Miller, 1968) were applied to two groups of normal preschool children aged, respectively, 3 to 4 and 5 to 6 years. We reasoned that if differences found among retarded people reflect two different stages of symbolic functioning, then the single- or double-track dispositions common to each stage should be apparent in the manner in

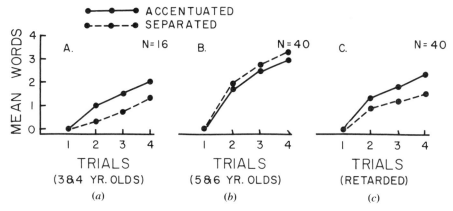

Figure 6.7. Comparison of words identified under accentuated versus separated conditions for (a) normal 3- to 4-year-olds, (b) 5- to 6-year-olds, and (c) retarded children. From A. Miller, 1968. Used with permission.

which the two nonreading groups of normal children responded to accentuated and look-say presentations of printed words.

To address this issue the same accentuated and look-say conditions used with the retarded population were presented to a group of 16 normal 3- to 4-year-olds and a group of 40 normal 5- to 6-year-olds. It was found, as Figure 6.7(a) shows, that the performance of normal 3- to 4-year-olds was very similar to that of the retarded group. In each group the relative difference favoring the accentuated over the look-say condition was the same. The difference between conditions for 3- to 4-year-olds was significant ($p < .03$), as it had been for the retarded group.

However, when the same conditions were presented to 40 normal 5- to 6-year-old children who had not yet learned to read, the difference between the two conditions disappeared. As shown in Figure 6.7(b), the children did equally well under both conditions with a mean of 2.8 words under the accentuated condition and a mean of 2.9 words under the look-say condition.

The finding that normal 3- to 4-year-olds but not normal 5- to 6-year-olds were significantly more responsive to accentuated conditions supports the notion of a progressive shift by the latter toward a more differentiated relation between symbol and referent. However, the finding that 5- to 6-year-old children did about as well on accentuated as they did on look-say conditions suggests that they were still in a transitional phase that enabled them to comfortably attribute significance to printed words both by finding object properties within the word's contour (accentuated condition) and by deliberately attributing object significance to them by fiat (look-say condition). The use of both procedures—one deriving from the symbolic-sign stage, the other from symbol stage functioning—makes early sight-reading readily available to normal 5- to 6-year-old children. Whether these capacities are sufficient for phonetic reading and writing, however, requires further consideration.

It is useful to reiterate the discussion earlier in this chapter, contrasting the symbolic demands posed by early sight-reading and phonetic reading. Early sight-readers, we suggested, need to be aware of printed words only in terms of their outward vector toward objects and events. To sight-read effectively, however, readers must attend to the word's total configuration, because slight differences in the total form of printed words relate them like pictures to different referents. In contrast, phonetic readers have to be aware that *both* printed and spoken forms of words are symbols that represent each other as well as their object meanings. This awareness permits phonetic readers to cope with two vectors: *inward* from letters to mouth-sounds permitting them to sound-out words and discover their meanings as part of spoken language; and *outward* from spoken word meaning to total printed word form by fiat.

This analysis raises interesting questions with regard to normal 5- to 6-year-old children who did equally well on accentuated and look-say conditions. Would such children have sufficient grasp of the nature of symbols to establish reference between letters and sounds as well as they did between printed words and their objects? Or would the shift in kind of symbol (a letter instead of a printed word) and the kind of orientation (inward to mouth-sound making instead of the customary printed word–object *outward* orientation) prove a problem? Certainly, if children of 5 or 6 could cope with letter sounds by fiat—without the kind of external continuity provided by accentuated conditions—this would mean that they had generalized their understanding of symbols to a variety of orientations and relations. However, if they could not readily achieve these new symbolic relations and benefit significantly from conditions that merge symbol with referent, it might be concluded that the growth of symbol stage functioning is gradual and must be learned in multiple contexts before the notion of symbolic functioning is quite generally grasped.

LETTER–SOUND REPRESENTATION AS
A DEVELOPMENTAL PHENOMENON

To answer these questions and further clarify the nature of the symbolic capacity of normal 5- to 6-year-old children, a study (Miller, 1968) was conducted with 20 normal 5- to 6-year-old children attending a kindergarten. In this study, the accentuated condition for each of 5 letters (*b, f, s, t, o*) consisted of a mouth appearing on the screen and going through those lip and tongue movements normally required to utter one of the sounds represented by these letters (Figure 6.8). As these mouth movements progressed on the screen and extraneous parts of the face disappeared, they merged imperceptibly into the appropriate letter until only the letter remained visible. For the separated condition, the mouth went through the same movements but did not transform into the letter. Instead, the letter remained at the right

| ACCENTUATED | SEPARATED | ACCENTUATED | SEPARATED |

Figure 6.8. Accentuated versus separated presentations of *f* and *t*. From A. Miller, 1968. Used with permission.

of the screen. The figure indicates the different manner in which the same letter was treated under accentuated and separated conditions. The following procedure was used:

> In both conditions the experimenter uttered the appropriate sounds each time the filmed mouth movements reached the point where the sound would naturally be uttered. Thus, when the screened image of teeth biting into the lower lip occurred under both conditions, the experimenter would utter "fff" for the *f*; when the tongue touched the palate and flicked outward the experimenter would say "*t*uh;" when the lips pursed and performed its plosive motion, the experimenter would say "*b*uh;" when the lips formed a circle, the short "o" sound would be uttered; and when the lips extended and the flattened tongue paralleled the palate, "sss" would be uttered.

> All children were screened to rule out those with prior knowledge of sounds related to letters. Accentuated and separated conditions were presented via two 16-mm films, one for accentuated and one for separated presentations of

b, f, s, t, o. Each mouth–letter sequence lasted for 5 seconds and was shown three times (15 seconds) before the next mouth–letter sequence was shown. After all five mouth–letter sequences were shown, there was a recognition trial during which the child had opportunity to produce the appropriate sound while looking at each of the letters as they appeared by themselves for 5 seconds in their conventional forms. This procedure was repeated for a total of six training cycles, each cycle followed by a recognition trial. Running time for each of the two films was 12 minutes. Ten subjects were randomly assigned to the accentuated and 10 to the separated condition.

The results of this study with normal 5- to 6-year-old children indicated that significantly more letter–sound relations were learned under accentuated than separated conditions ($F = 103.56$, $df = 1,19$, $p < .001$). The means for the six recognition trials under the accentuated condition were, in the order of their occurrence, 1.9, 2.4, 3.7, 2.9, 3.3, 4.2. Means for the separated condition were .4, 1.4, 1.6, 2.0, 2.5, 2.4.

These results support the view that symbol stage functioning, even though grasped as an insight in one area of functioning, must be grasped again in other areas before it is fully established. In that sense, symbol stage functioning is only gradually acquired. Therefore, the relative success of normal 5- to 6-year-old children with the look-say method does not imply the immediate extension of the ability to letter–sound relations. If this capacity had generalized, the children should have done at least as well under separated as under accentuated conditions. Instead, the results clearly indicated continued dependence on syncretic systems concerned with blending mouth function with letters when unfamiliar letter–sound relations were involved.

The difficulty 5- to 6-year-old children had with letter–sound relations may have been related to the shift from the outward orientation implicit in printed word–object relations to the inward orientation required to produce sounds for certain letters, it may have been the result of the nonobject nature of the referent (sounds instead of objects), or it may have been caused by a combination of these factors. What seems most clear is that normal 5- to 6-year-olds readily shift from a symbolic to a more primitive syncretic organization *when they are confronted with unfamiliar relations.*

The experiments described support the view that reading method and symbolic capacity interact with each other as well as that "reading readiness" is partly an artifact of reading method. Beyond this, they suggest that a person's mode of symbolic functioning may express itself in certain general styles of coping with reality. Words presented in a manner consistent with the limited, *primary naming* capacity of a person—whether retarded person or normal preschool child—should enable that individual to achieve early sight-reading of printed words well before being ready for the conventional look-say method.

From another perspective, our findings and stage formulations (sign, symbolic-sign, and symbol) roughly agree with Piaget's sensorimotor stage (0–2 years), preoperational stage (2–7 years), and concrete operations stage (7–11 years). Certainly, in both our symbolic-sign stage and Piaget's pre-operational stage, children are characterized by a dependence on single-track perceptual experience in their cognition. It is this tendency that in Piaget's system accounts for the inability to conserve, and in our formulation accounts for the effectiveness of accentuation as a perceptual bridge from name to printed word. Piaget refers to the stage of concrete operations as best characterized by the child's new ability to internalize relations in a way that enables the child to keep in mind two aspects of a situation at the same time. This capacity, in Piaget's system, accounts for the child's ability to conserve number, volume, and so forth; in both systems it enables the child to establish symbolic relations by virtue of the inner intent to establish them.

SUMMARY

The development of reading and writing is conceptualized in terms of cognitive-developmental systems theory. It is argued that the ability to read and write is a function of both the child's developmental stage and the method by which reading is taught. The requirement of a fixed relation between name and object is so strong for children at the symbolic-sign (primary naming) stage that they cannot accept as meaningful any form that deviates from the one the name induces them to expect. However, for children at the later phase (secondary naming) of the symbolic-sign stage, the name–object relation is sufficiently flexible for them to "find" named objects in various forms—clouds, rocks, printed words. Such children are relatively close to achieving the *fiat* insight that makes it possible to assign meanings to novel forms simply by intending to do so. These children have entered the symbol stage of functioning and can now readily deal with the relation between printed words and their object and picture referents.

Following this discussion, a series of experiments are described with both nonreading retarded children as well as normal 3- to 4-year-old and 5- to 6-year-old children. In the first test of the theory, a group of 10 retarded children previously unable to learn to sight-read, were presented a group of 18 words. Half the words were presented under accentuated conditions in which properties of an object or event were blended with the form of the printed word; the remaining words were presented in their conventional forms. All retarded children acquired significantly more words under the accentuated condition and retained those words that had been accentuated as effectively as words presented only in their conventional forms. When the experiment was replicated with a stroboscopic presentation, and with a larger population of retarded people, essentially the same results were found.

The next study tested the effect of including body action or gesture within the accentuated sequence. To examine this effect, two kinds of actions—*relevant* and *irrelevant*—were related to certain names. Once these actions were bonded to names, the attempt was made to determine if the inclusion of relevant action facilitated acquisition and retention of printed words over a sequence that included irrelevant action. All other conditions were held constant. In general, printed words taught under relevant action conditions were retained significantly longer than those taught under irrelevant action conditions. Relevant actions that had been bonded with spoken and printed words were retained significantly longer than irrelevant actions.

The next experiment contrasted look-say pairings of printed words and their picture referents with accentuated sequences showing pictures of objects blending into their printed word forms. Retarded people learned significantly more words under accentuated than under look-say conditions. Examining the findings more closely, it was found that those retarded people ($n = 27$) who did better under accentuated conditions tended to operate in a single-track manner consistent with fixed name–object relations. In contrast, those people ($n = 13$) who did better with the look-say task tended to operate in a double-track manner consistent with the ability to relate printed words arbitrarily to their referents.

When the accentuated and look-say conditions were presented to normal 3- to 4-year-olds and normal 5- to 6-year-olds, the writers found that 3- to 4-year-olds, like most of the retarded people, benefited significantly more from accentuated than from look-say conditions. In contrast, 5- to 6-year-olds did just as well with look-say conditions as they had with accentuated conditions. This finding suggested that many children were in a transitional state just prior to grasping the fiat insight that makes it possible to arbitrarily assign spoken or printed words to their referents.

The final experiment introduced a procedure for accentuating letter–sound relations by relating them to mouth movements. In these animated motion picture sequences the mouth movements necessary to form certain sounds were seen to transform into letters that represented these sounds. A "separated" condition presented these mouth movements separate from the letters to which they related. Normal 5- to 6-year-olds who did not require accentuation where printed words were concerned did benefit from accentuation significantly more than from separated conditions. These findings were consistent with the view that symbolic capacity extends gradually to new domains after children first establish the fiat insight.

Applying Cognitive-Developmental (C-D) Systems Theory with Behavior-Disordered Children

Part Two of this book describes the application of C-D Systems theory to the enormous but often subtle disabilities presented by profoundly disordered children. These disabilities are dealt with—whether in body schema, interaction, or language—by trying to understand how they impact a child's experience of reality. Only then do we intervene.

Each successful strategy or piece of equipment described (after discarding many that were unsuccessful) emerged from an effort to solve a particular reality problem confronted by a child. These days, after evaluating a child, we have a sense of direction and a set of tools with which to help a child solve problems. In the following six chapters we share what we have learned about evaluating and working with such children and their families. In doing this we present, not a prescription, but a compass course for persons trying to help behavior-disordered children develop their capacities.

CHAPTER 7

The Umwelt Assessment

WHAT IS AN UMWELT ASSESSMENT?

An Umwelt—following Uexküll's (1934/1957) use of the term—refers to the subjective "world around one." Applied to behavior-disordered children, it refers to the unique reality constructed by each child and within which the child functions. An Umwelt Assessment, therefore, is an effort to sort out the nature of this reality in order to introduce the interventions most helpful in resolving that particular child's reality problems. This chapter—which may serve as a manual—introduces those tasks that over the years have been most helpful in this regard.

The necessity for a new way of evaluating behavior-disordered children became apparent as we noted the inadequacy of conventional standardized tests. The Stanford-Binet, Bayley, WISC-R, McCarthy, and other similar tests were not designed for behavior-disordered children; in fact, their structure actively works against evaluating their true capacities. The history of these tests (Sattler, 1974) indicates that their major goals were, first, to define the nature of intelligence and, second, to study individual differences between people. Useful as these tests were in identifying retarded children, they were not designed to assist the remediation of deficits. Consequently, when behavior-disordered children take the tests, the sharp disparity between the required reality contact and the manner in which these children address reality obscures both their true capacities and the best means of tapping them.

One important source of difficulty in conventional tests is that tasks are presented in a disconnected manner to the already "disconnected" child with a *system-forming* disorder or the overly engaged child with a *closed-system* disorder (pp. 41–43). For example, with the Bayley, Stanford-Binet, WPPSI, and so forth, the child is asked to perform as many as 25 different tasks, most of which require ability to process, a high degree of verbal capacity, and an ability to stay focused and attentive while sitting in a seat. In the Bayley and the Stanford-Binet, bead stringing may be followed immediately by putting a spoon in a cup, and then by building a block tower.

Material in this chapter is taken from the *Miller Umwelt Assessment Scale*. Copyright 1989 by A. Miller. Used with permission.

Whereas normal children can handle such rapid shifts from one unrelated task to another, they are very difficult for children with system-forming disorders who have trouble "getting into" a particular task. Rapid shifts are also a problem for children with closed-system disorders who, having become engaged by a particular task, have great difficulty detaching and relating to a new one. Consequently, any scores derived from such tests are quite irrelevant to the main issues that prevent these children from functioning more appropriately.

Selecting Tasks for the Umwelt Assessment

We have tried to avoid these pitfalls by having fewer tasks (16) and by having more layers to each task so that the examiner can assess the shift from the most circumscribed reality to more expanded realities. In addition, there is a "testing limits" procedure that not only suggests how far the child is from being able to participate in more expanded realities, but also indicates how useful such "testing limits" procedures are as interventions.

The *tasks* tap *sign, symbolic-sign,* and *symbol stages* of functioning and involve relatively familiar situations that require the child to cope with an object (Swinging Ball) moving toward him or her, with climbing up steps, and with walking over, across, or around various obstacles such as the varied holes in the elevated Swiss Cheese Board. The tasks also entail dealing with a step-slide arrangement; blocks; rakes to get objects, both with and without the interference of obstacles; and cups and bowls that must be stacked in a variety of ways. Other tasks involve symbolic play, picture recognition, reading and number capacity, and awareness of people.

The *expandable* nature of each task becomes apparent as a child interacts with it and the person introducing it. For example, in the most expanded reality of the Swinging Ball task, the child notices the adult repetitively swinging a ball toward him or her and enters into a game whereby the two alternately push the swinging ball back and forth. To take part in such a game the child must have an awareness of the adult, an awareness of the moving ball, and a knowledge of the social system that makes adult–child play with the swinging ball possible. However, a child who has not achieved this most expanded reality may show a more circumscribed reality system. Such a child, may, for example, push the ball away each time it comes *without* noticing the adult who is sending it. Or, even more circumscribed, a child may only react to the ball when it bumps into his or her body. Finally, most removed, a child may not notice or react to the ball even when it does collide with the body. In similar fashion, each of the tasks lend themselves to solutions involving more restricted as well as more expanded reality systems. Thus, the examiner is interested not only in the "correctness" of the child's solution, but in how it helps characterize his or her unique way of making sense of and coping with the world.

Systems of Disordered Children

Typically, the children evaluated at the Center come with deficits in the area of social and emotional contact with others, in their ability to cope effectively with their physical surroundings, and in their ability to communicate their experience to themselves and others. A proper assessment of the kinds of systems these children possess and how these systems fail to bring them into adaptive contact with their surroundings permits planning interventions most likely to help them develop expanded Umwelten within which they can perform and grow.

In using the Umwelt Assessment it is assumed that even the most disordered child is striving to find a way to cope with a confusing world. Thus, the emphasis on the child's experience and how he or she copes with and construes reality is an integral part of each evaluation. To achieve this, staff at the Center try to determine what kinds of systems or fragments of systems the child brings to the evaluation and what must happen to those systems before they can help the child understand and adapt to his or her surroundings. For example, a nonverbal child with a system-forming disorder tends to orient in scattered fashion to various aspects of the surroundings but rarely moves beyond orienting to significant engagement that could lead to better coping. Staff try to determine what it takes to develop such engagement. Similarly, if a child with a closed-system disorder presents closed stereotypic systems, workers try to determine how permeable these systems are and how readily they can be expanded. If it is noted during the evaluation that a child can stack cups in the upright position, it is also necessary to determine if he or she can stack them upside down. The child, while stacking cups right side up, is presented with a cup upside down to see whether he or she turns the cup for right-side-up stacking or futilely pushes the upside-down cup against the right-side-up cup in an effort to get it to stack. Similarly, does the child stacking blocks require that only he or she pick up the blocks being stacked, or can the child accept a block from the examiner? Beyond this, can the child tolerate having the examiner modify the block structure?

In addition to evaluating the systems the child brings, it is important to determine the extent to which the child can become engaged by the spheres that are introduced by the examiner. Thus, if the child can accept a repetitive slide sphere that involves going up steps, sitting down, going down a slide, returning to steps, and so forth, and can gradually take over the slide sphere, this suggests capacity to assimilate other introduced spheres that can lead to more appropriate functioning.

Setting

The examiner brings the parents with their child—usually between 18 months and 7 or 8 years of age—into the large evaluation room which contains attractive structures for climbing in, through, and around various obstacles. A big red ball hangs from the ceiling. Remotely controlled video cameras are on opposite walls. The parents are invited to sit on one of the structures as the examiner explains the various tasks and the parents' roles in the evaluation. The examiner also states that by the end of the hour he or she will have some preliminary comments about the child and the relevance of the Center's program for that child. The examiner requests that the parents sign a release permitting videotaping before the session begins.

Procedure

During the evaluation the examiner often asks a parent to assist with the different tasks. Sometimes this means holding the child so that he or she can focus on a particular task, sometimes it means calling and beckoning to the child from across a structure, and sometimes—when the parent feels the child can improve performance on a task—the examiner turns the task over to the parent. Through such participation the examiner has opportunity to note not only the capacities of the child as he or she copes with the various tasks, but the manner in which the parents work with the child. A scale in Chapter 12 characterizes parents in terms of the *support–demand* stance they have toward their child. The assessment of parental stance is part of the overall evaluation of resources available in working with a disordered child. However, we defer discussion of this scale to a later chapter so that it does not interfere with the present description of child assessment procedures.

MILLER UMWELT ASSESSMENT SCALE

The following sections describe the bits of reality—tasks—that are used to assess each child, the understanding that can be gained from each task, the responses of different kinds of children to these tasks, and, most important, the ways in which the child's responses on these tasks guide staff members toward interventions most likely to be effective.

The Miller Umwelt Assessment Scale includes the following tasks:

1. Swinging Ball
2. Primary Board Demands
3. Swiss Cheese Board
4. Slide Sphere
5. Unstructured Period A
6. Blocks
7. Stacking Cups and Bowls
8. Reciprocal Pull Toy

9. Symbolic Play
10. Unstructured Period B
11. "Croupier" (Rake–Obstacle) Sequences
12. Graphic Expression
13. Object and Picture Designation
14. Reading and Writing
15. Number Relations
16. Parent Separation

To facilitate the use of these tasks, each section includes a statement of purpose, a description of materials, and a detailed explanation of procedures. A scheme for scoring performance on each of the tasks as well as the response to limit-testing is at the end of the procedures material. Finally, an evaluation section describes the manner in which children with different system disorders tend to function on the task.

TASK 1. SWINGING BALL

Purpose

The Swinging Ball task evaluates the child's awareness of and ability to cope with a large object that regularly approaches and moves away. On the most basic level the examiner wishes to determine whether the child can visually *track* the changing direction of the ball as it approaches from left, right, and center. The next determination is whether the child is able to *anticipate* the arrival of the ball as he or she follows its excursions. If so, can the child coordinate his or her *pushing* activity with the ball's arrival? Finally, can the child integrate pushing ball activity with awareness of the examiner who is pushing the ball, as in a reciprocal ball-pushing game?

Materials

A large rubber ball 12 to 18 inches in diameter attached to a rope hanging from the ceiling in a room that allows the ball to swing freely. It should be possible to adjust the ball to the child's eye level.

Procedure

ORIENTING BY TRACKING.   The child and parent face the hanging ball from about 3 feet away, the parent behind the child. The examiner is opposite the child and parent and gently swings the ball toward the child from three directions: right, left, and center, each time saying, "Here it comes!" The maximum number from each direction is five. The examiner varies the directions in a random fashion. Using more than five swings per direction may be thought of as testing the limits.

The eye movements of the child are noted to determine if they follow the motion of the ball. Also note if, as the ball approaches, the child lifts arms to anticipate its arrival.

ENGAGEMENT WITH THE BALL.   Following this, the examiner begins in the course of three or four trials to push the ball directly toward the child. When the child tracks and anticipates the arrival of the ball with lifted arms, the examiner says, "Push!" The examiner notes if the child begins pushing the ball as it arrives. If the child does not push the ball, the examiner requests the parent to position his or her hands over the child's and help the child push the ball each time it arrives. After three or four hand-over-hand pushes, the examiner requests the parent to interrupt support to see if the child will now push the ball when it arrives.

RECIPROCAL ENGAGEMENT WITH THE EXAMINER.   For those children who are able to push the ball on the examiner's request, either without help or after the parent has removed support, the examiner seeks to determine the nature of the pushing. Is the child merely pushing the ball when it arrives, or is he or she engaged in a pushing-ball game with the examiner? The game aspect can readily be determined by the child's glances at the examiner before or during pushing, and/or by the child's playful demeanour.

Swinging Ball

	Response			Limit-Testing		
Status of Reality Systems	Yes	No	Marginal	Yes	No	Marginal
Visually tracks ball						
Anticipates ball						
Pushes ball						
Pushes ball reciprocally						

Evaluation*

Two general kinds of responses are common. In one, characterized by children with *closed-system disorders*, the child may show little or no ability to track the ball and is repeatedly surprised as the ball looms closer. An important prognostic indication is whether the child learns—either with repeated approaches of the ball or with assistance—to coordinate body activity with the ball's arrival. Children who learn to do so within the assessment typically respond more rapidly to intervention than those who do not. Sometimes a child who is not responding to the ball shows a tendency, following the *interruption* of hand-over-hand assistance, to slowly lift a hand in the direction of the ball—positive indication of a beginning ability to cope with the object.

*Because the behavior patterns of children with syncretic system disorders are so variable and idiosyncratic, they are not discussed in this and other task evaluation sections of this chapter.

Children with *system-forming disorders* respond quite differently, often tracking the ball as it moves toward them in one part of its trajectory and losing it entirely as it arcs away. Once they spot the ball coming toward them, they will self-protectively—but in a delayed manner—lift their arms. Parents often have to hold such children in place, or "pulled" by some other transient stimulus, they would leave the situation. These children often lack the staying power to engage the examiner in the pushing-ball game.

Both kinds of children have significant body schema problems. The closed-system child is unable to adequately differentiate his or her body from the moving ball in a way that would allow rapidly initiated activity in synchrony with the ball's motion. On the other hand, the child with a system-forming disorder has difficulty because his or her "stimulus-driven" response pattern makes it difficult to experience the body as other than a set of fragmented parts that the child attends to episodically as circumstances require.

TASK 2. PRIMARY BOARD DEMANDS

The *Primary Board* refers to a structure—a board suspended 3 feet above the ground between two sets of steps. The *Demands* refer to circumstances that each child confronts while engaged with this structure. The *first demand* concerns the child's repeated performance climbing up the steps, walking across the board, and climbing down in terms of *motor coordination, system-forming capacity*, and *response to the care giver*; the *second demand* concerns the child's response—as the structure is modified—to a *gap* running the length of the board that the child must *straddle* while walking; the *third demand* refers to a vertical insert on the structure (the Anticipation Board) that the child must climb over to get to the beckoning care giver on the other side.

Purpose

The Primary Board Demands determine the child's capacity to use the body to engage in an increasingly differentiated and complex manner in the service of certain goals. The first demand requires the child to *climb a set of stairs*, walk across a plank that is 15 inches wide and 6 feet long to another set of stairs, and *then walk down them*. The examiner is interested in how the child climbs steps: Is it one foot at a time, or can the child alternate feet? Once on top, how does the child react to being three feet above the ground? Does the child respond to the beckoning and calling parent at the other end of the board? If the child can move only when strongly supported, does he or she require less support as the sequence is repeated? Also noted is whether the child—in repeating the sphere of climbing the stairs, walking across the board, going down the stairs—begins to assimilate and to anticipate various

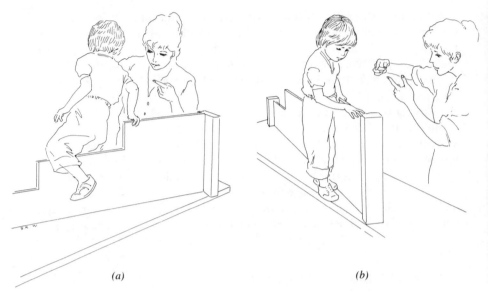

(a)   *(b)*

Figure 7.1. The Anticipation Board: Child (*a*) successfully crosses obstacle; (*b*) child fails to cross over and reach the parent.

steps in the sequence. In other words, to what extent does the child tend to transform the sphere into a system?

Once the child has completed the preceding sequences, a second demand is introduced within the sphere: This, accomplished by removing a plank inserted in the middle of the board, requires the child to *straddle the gap* and proceed as before across the board to the parent. The last demand, called the Anticipation Board, is placed diagonally across the board (Figure 7.1 (*a*),(*b*)) so that the child must climb over it to get to the beckoning parent on the other side. How children respond to these demands says much about their resources and the manner in which they experience and cope with their immediate surroundings. In Figure 7.1(*a*) the child successfully crosses and in (*b*) fails to cross over and reach the parent.

The Primary Board Demands assess different kinds of capacities: gross motor, body awareness, problem solving, awareness of the other, and system-forming capacity. By guiding a child into this protected but moderately stressful situation and introducing structures that the child must confront, it is possible to learn a great deal about how the child copes and relates to care givers and to the immediate environment.

Materials

A board (15 in. by 6 ft) is suspended above the ground between two sets of steps. The board is constructed so that a 4-inch center plank can be removed, leaving two boards parallel to each other with 5 inches for each foot as the child straddles the 5-inch gap. The structure also permits diagonal insertion of a fencelike board over which the child must climb to reach the beckoning care giver on the other side.

Procedure

THE FIRST DEMAND: TESTING FOR MOTOR COORDINATION, SYSTEM-FORMING CAPACITY, AND RESPONSE TO CARE GIVER. The child climbs up the stairs with one hand on the banister while the care giver provides minimal physical support and both signs and says (finger pointed upward) "Up, up!" As the child walks across the board, the examiner signs and says (walking motion with hands) "Walk, walk, walk!" in tempo with the child's walking. Both care giver (on one side) and worker (on the other) provide physical support as needed to keep the child safe and moving. On reaching the steps, the child descends with one hand on the banister while care giver, providing minimal support, signs (pointing downward) and says "Down, down!"

After reaching the ground, the child is immediately oriented and guided toward the first set of steps and the entire sphere is repeated for at least three cycles. During this phase the examiner notes whether the child is beginning to assimilate the sphere as evidenced by looking toward the first set of steps on reaching the ground, stepping on the board without help, initiating going down the stairs, and so forth.

Next, the child climbs the stairs with the examiner while the care giver goes to the other end of the board and signs (beckons) and calls "Come, come!" to the child. As the child (with examiner hovering) moves toward the person calling, the examiner notes *whether the child glances at the care giver and/or alternates looking at him or her with looking down.* Once the child arrives, the care giver hugs the child briefly, then walks to the other side of the board, and again beckons and calls.

THE SECOND DEMAND: STRADDLING THE GAP. Children next demonstrate whether or not they have achieved a differentiated awareness of the sides of their body. This is tested by removing the center piece from the board so that the child straddles the 5-inch gap. A child who has not adequately distinguished one side of the body from the other remains "stalled" in this position until the examiner touches the feet or teaches the child how to unweight one leg in order to move the other. Once the child is moving, it is possible to determine whether the child can *respond to the calls of the parent at the other end* without losing contact with the foot movements required to avoid stepping in the gap.

Attempting additional trials, leaning the child from side to side to help unweight each foot, or touching feet to provide cues as to their location should be viewed as testing the limits.

THE THIRD DEMAND: THE ANTICIPATION BOARD. The final Primary Board demand tests the child's ability to solve the problem of the Anticipation Board, a fencelike obstacle placed diagonally across the Primary Board, in order to get to the beckoning care giver on the other side. To succeed the child must climb over the board or eventually be forced off the Primary Board because there is no further space on which to stand. The earlier in the sequence the child anticipates the need to step over the board, the more developed the child. Normal 18- to 24-month-old children can meet this demand with little difficulty. In solving it, the child *demonstrates understanding that to reach the parent he or she must climb over the fence.*

To succeed, the child must integrate two disparate but related events: getting over the fence and getting to the parent. Often, disordered children can address one task—walking toward the parent—but are quite unable to integrate climbing over the fence, as shown by their tendency to be forced off the board.

However, even in failing, the child provides important cues as to the reason for the failure. For example, a child may understand the problem as shown by looking at and reaching toward the care giver on the other side of the Anticipation Board but may lack the perceptual-motor coordination to climb over. For some, the problem stems from their "losing touch" with the parent as they become engaged by the obstacle. For still others the problem does not exist, either because they accept the configuration that the Anticipation Board imposes or because they are unable to relate to the beckoning parent from a distance and consequently have no reason to climb over the obstacle.

The task for the child once the center board has been replaced and the Anticipation Board erected, is to climb over the board to reach the beckoning and calling person on the other side. The examiner positions the child on the wide side of the primary board and stands behind the child to minimize the child's use of the adult for support. If necessary, the examiner provides support, first by holding the child's hands and then by stabilizing the child's body.

Perfect performance—full awareness of the way the Anticipation Board divides space—is evident when the child alternates glances toward the barrier and the care giver on the other side and, immediately, steps over the low end of the Anticipation Board and walks to the care giver. Complete failure is evident in the child who, in spite of the calling and beckoning care giver, follows the vertical board until there is no further room to move without being forced off. Such a child lacks the ability to anticipate outcomes of his or her actions.

Once the child has addressed the board with one side of his or her body, the board's position is reversed so that the child has the opportunity to perform the task with the opposite side of the body. The examiner notes any differences in crossing the barrier from the left and right sides.

Any additional trials, support, or cues provided by the examiner to help the child should be noted and viewed as testing the limits to determine how close the child is to success.

Primary Board Demands

	Response			Limit-Testing		
Status of Reality Systems	Yes	No	Marginal	Yes	No	Marginal
The first demand						
Alternate steps						
Alternate looking at care						
giver and obstacle						
Form system						
The second demand						
Straddle gap						
The third demand						
Solve Anticipation Board						

Evaluation

Typically, autistic children with closed-system disorders do quite poorly on this task. Although they may climb the stairs with alternating feet, they tend to be preoccupied with the space directly in front of them. Consequently, they do not tend to look at the care giver when that person is beckoning and calling them. On the other hand, they tend to form systems from the sphere quite rapidly—often after two or three circuits of the Primary Board sphere. Initially, they tend to remain stalled when the center board is removed. However, with modest support they are often able to move and soon no longer require support. They do most poorly with the Anticipation Board, often following the contours of the board until they are forced off. Further, even when assisted in solving the task, they tend not to understand the necessity of climbing over the board to get to the person.

Children with system-forming disorders typically climb and go down steps one at a time with support. On the elevated platform they tend to be guided by it from one end to the other. They may look either at what they are doing or at the care giver but they do not alternate glances from one to the other. When they are straddling the gap, they often seem unable to move, even with substantial cues, although eventually they learn how to cope with the gap. The same poor body organization that makes it difficult for them to move when straddling the gap is also responsible for their inability to climb over the Anticipation Board even though they seem to grasp its nature as a barrier, as shown by their pausing in the middle as they look at the beckoning care giver.

TASK 3. SWISS CHEESE BOARD

Purpose

This task tests the disordered child's ability to cope with events that impinge directly on his or her body. The events are a series of different-shaped holes that the child has to walk around or over to get from one side of an elevated board to the other. If the child steps into a hole, does the child learn from the experience or continue to make the same misstep over and over? If a parent calls at the other end of the board, can the child shift attention from holes to parent calling without mishap? This test taps the resources of a disordered child so one can determine whether high demand tasks such as these elicit adaptive behavior not otherwise available.

Materials

Swiss Cheese Boards are 3 feet wide and 8 feet long. They include a variety of holes varying in size from 8 to 16 inches. One board is composed solely of free form shapes; a second board (used for retesting) includes geometric forms (square, triangle, rectangle) in various combinations.

Procedure

The examiner first tests the child's ability to perceive and walk around variously shaped holes in a platform 3 feet above the ground. Next, the examiner tests the child's ability to integrate the beckoning and calling parent at the far end of the board with the task of avoiding holes. Highest perform-ance consists of looking down at the feet and up at the parent repeatedly. Children who solve this task on the highest level demonstrate awareness of

Figure 7.2. Child withdrawing foot from hole in the Swiss Cheese Board.

space both near and far from their body as well as the capacity to use their body in a highly differentiated manner to reach a goal (usually a parent) at the other end.

During the Swiss Cheese Board task (Figure 7.2) the examiner is sensitive to the child's concerns about being 3 feet above ground and confronted with variously shaped holes. The examiner takes every precaution to prevent the child from falling once he or she steps into a hole, becomes startled, and momentarily loses balance.

There are two parts to the procedure: In the first, both examiner and care giver, on each side of the usually barefoot child, hold the child's hands and guide the child from one end of the board to the other. During this journey *the examiner notes the child's response to the holes and whether he or she steps into them. If this happens, the examiner notes whether the child subsequently learns to walk around holes. The examiner also notes whether the child consistently needs to feel the contours of the hole with extended foot or is able to anticipate the next hole with only visual contact.* Two trips suffice to test these issues.

Following this, the care giver goes to the far end of the board and beckons and calls "Come! Come!" to the child while the examiner hovers near the child. During this part, the examiner places the child's hand on a guide rail for support and attempts to determine how the child manages the Swiss Cheese Board with minimal support. Again, the child makes two such excursions with *the examiner noting whether the child integrates (alternates glances) between the immediate task of avoiding holes and the goal of reaching the care giver.*

Swiss Cheese Board

	Response			Limit-Testing		
Status of Reality Systems	Yes	No	Marginal	Yes	No	Marginal
Child avoids all holes with visual or visual-haptic contact						
Child walks around holes *after* stepping in them						
Child shifts glances from holes to beckoning care giver without mishap						

Evaluation

The most disordered children, operating at an early sign stage, repeatedly step into holes and show little if any capacity to adjust to their presence. Children with somewhat greater capacity step into holes at first but then begin to feel for them carefully with their feet. Still more advanced, they demonstrate the ability to cope with the holes by noting their presence visually and by walking around them.

TASK 4. SLIDE SPHERE

Purpose

This task determines (a) if the child can transform an introduced sequence of physical events (integrative *sphere*) into an integrative *system;* (b) if the child can accept expansions of the newly formed system; and (c) if the child can *spontaneously* expand the new system. These issues are vital in assessing the teachability of a disordered child. For example, if a disordered child at first cannot take in the several steps of an integrative sphere—climbing steps, sitting down, going down a slide at right angles to the steps (Figure 7.3), and returning to the steps—it is necessary to determine the effectiveness of rapidly paced, repetitive, physical activities as well as sign- and word-guided activities in establishing the introduced sequence as an integrative system.

The examiner knows that a system is forming when the child is observed completing some or all facets of the sphere with little or no support. Then, because many disordered children who have finally formed a system are resistant to modifying it in any way, the examiner must determine if the system can be expanded or changed in a way that the child can accept. This is evaluated by introducing variations within the system such as having the child stop and send blocks down before going down the slide. Prognosis is best for those children who can both readily form and accept expansions of the system.

Materials

A set of steps (3 or 4) leading to a 30- by 30-inch platform on which a child can sit down. The platform places the child about 3 feet above the ground.

Figure 7.3. Testing for system-forming capacity on the Slide Sphere.

Attached to the steps at right angles is a 5-foot slide. Also available are a half dozen blocks.

Procedure

ESTABLISHING AN INTEGRATIVE SYSTEM.   The sequence begins with the care giver at the base of the steps and the examiner at the base of the slide. The parent guides the child up the stairs, assisting the child as necessary and signing and saying "Up, up, up!" until the child reaches the top. Then, the parent helps the child sit down while signing and saying "Sit down!" Following this, the parent helps the child place feet and legs on the slide and signs and says "Down, down!" as the child slides down. When the child arrives at the bottom of the slide, the examiner signs and says "Get up!" and rapidly assists the child to his or her feet. As soon as the child is standing, the examiner orients the child's head toward the care giver at the steps, who beckons and says "Come! Come!" If the child hesitates, the examiner physically guides the child to the care giver. The moment the child reaches him or her, a second cycle begins.

In the course of four rapidly paced cycles, the examiner and care giver attempt to reduce physical support to a minimum to determine if the child can carry through the sequence with only sign and word guidance. The locations where the child most clearly displays intention to continue are just prior to climbing the steps, sitting down, going down the slide, and turning toward the parent.

INTRODUCING EXPANSIONS.   Expansions are introduced at the point of *maximal tension* in the sphere—just before the child starts down the slide. They are introduced only if the child has indicated by hitching forward in anticipation of going down the slide, that he or she has assimilated that part of the sphere.

"STOP!" AND "YOU [NAME], DOWN!"   This expansion determines if the child can accept and be guided by a new sign and word within a newly formed system. Just as the child begins to hitch forward to go down the slide from the sitting position, the examiner stops the child by firmly signing and saying "Stop!" in front of the child's face. If the child persists in trying to go down the slide, the examiner says "Stop!" again and physically prevents the child from going down. The examiner then points at the child and says, "You [name], down!" If the child does not immediately go down the slide, the examiner provides just enough assistance for this to happen. This expansion is repeated two more times. *The examiner carefully notes whether or not the child responds to "Stop!" and "You [name], down!" by pausing and then continuing down the slide.*

"STOP!" "BLOCK DOWN!" AND "YOU [NAME], DOWN!"   This second expansion is introduced only if the first one is successful. Here the purpose is to determine whether the child can accept another term, "Block down!" can accept and send a block down the slide, and can distinguish the command

"Block down!" from the command that directs the child to go down the slide.

Immediately after the child follows the stop directive at the top of the slide, the examiner hands the child a block to slide down, saying "Block down!" and pointing down. This is repeated three or four times until the child clearly seems sign and word guided. Abruptly, the examiner shifts to pointing at the child and saying, "You [name], down!" to determine how readily the child grasps the new intention and slides down.

During the next three cycles the examiner varies the procedure by saying "You [name], down!" after only one or two commands to send the block down. *The examiner carefully notes whether the child turns toward the examiner to receive the message and how readily the child shifts from one message to the other.*

SPONTANEOUS EXPANSIONS.   Of particular interest, in the course of the structured Slide sphere, is whether the child will introduce his or her own expansions. Common spontaneous expansions include trying to walk up the slide and sliding down on the stomach or sideways.

Slide Sphere

Status of Reality Systems	Response			Limit-Testing		
	Yes	No	Marginal	Yes	No	Marginal
Forms integrative system						
Accepts at least one expansion						
Produces spontaneous expansions						
Signs or words						

Evaluation

Because signs and spoken words accompany each component in the system, a child, when interrupted, frequently produces the relevant *down* sign or spoken word (compensatory reaction) as an expression of need to maintain the continuity of the developing Slide system. A normal 2½-year-old child will almost immediately integrate the varied components and then spontaneously begin to expand the system by going down the slide headfirst, sideways, backward, and so forth. Such a child also shows no difficulty including the blocks and other expansions within the system.

A great deal can be learned by determining how many cycles the disordered child requires to put this system together and how difficult it is for the child to integrate expansions within the system. Of interest is not only the manner in which the child solves the tasks of climbing up steps, sitting down, going down the slide, and turning around to go back to the beckoning parent at the steps, but the manner in which the child copes with the demand to expand the task. Children with closed-system disorders may form the slide system rather rapidly but then, tend to encapsulate their experiences resisting the request to send a block down the slide before they go down themselves. Other children with system-forming disorders never even get to the expansion part of the test, requiring as many as a dozen repetitions before they can sit down by themselves or make the turn at the bottom of the slide to go back to the person at the slide steps.

TASK 5. UNSTRUCTURED PERIOD A

Purpose

An unstructured 2-minute period immediately follows the Slide sphere, while the blocks used in that sphere are lying on the floor. It is used to determine how the highly structured intervention of the Slide sphere influences subsequent behavior when structure is removed: Will the child, as many autistic children do, perseverate with the last task introduced by continuing to go round the slide? Will the child become preoccupied with particular objects or show an interest in the care giver or examiner by bringing objects to them or by trying to sit on their laps or involve them in a particular task? Will the child remain within a very circumscribed space or tend to use the whole room? In the absence of structure, will the child begin to twiddle and rock, be "caught" by a variety of stimulating things in the room, or explore the properties of familiar objects by examining and playing with them in quite unexpected ways?

Materials

Objects intrinsic to the assessment situation should be left within the child's reach. This includes the Swiss Cheese Board, the Primary Board, and the Slide sphere with blocks.

Procedure

The examiner and the care giver cease all activity and remain quiet for 2 minutes. The examiner and care giver sit at opposite sides of the room and respond only to direct initiation from the child or to the child's being in a potentially dangerous situation. If the child approaches and acknowledges an adult's presence in some way (e.g., with glances, pointing, sounds), the adult makes eye contact and nods in acknowledgement. If the child asks the adult a question, the adult briefly responds. During this period the adults do not initiate any activities.

Unstructured Period A

Status of Reality Systems	Spontaneous		
	Yes	No	Marginal
Child investigates objects in the room in terms of their functional properties			
Child uses and explores large portions of the space available			
Child brings objects to people			
Child is more interested in people than objects			

Evaluation

Often, autistic children with *closed-system disorders* either continue the last structured activity with few spontaneous expansions, begin to twiddle, or become repetitively engaged with one object. They usually remain in a limited sector of the available space and do not initiate social exchanges.

In contrast, children with *system-forming disorders* tend to use all the space available and frequently flit from one object or event to another. Although they may show more interest in people than children with closed-system disorders, this interest is usually fleeting.

TASK 6. BLOCKS

Purpose

This task has several parts designed to determine the following capacities:

1. Can the child accept blocks handed to him or her from a variety of orientations? Children unable to accept blocks or to do more than hold them are operating on the earliest sign level of functioning. Objects, at this level, trigger reflexive reactions that the child has not yet learned to modify to permit releasing the object much less handing it to someone.

2. Can the child stack blocks and anticipate that they may fall down when the stack gets wobbly or the examiner threatens to knock them over?

3. Can the child get involved in the contagious activity of throwing blocks in a box and, if so, has the child grasped the social notion of taking turns, as evident in a readiness to alternate with the examiner in throwing blocks in a box?

Materials

Ten natural wood blocks: five square and five rectangular blocks.

Procedure

The examiner and the child sit facing each other. The care giver sits behind the child to assist the examiner in maintaining the child's focus on the activity.

STACKING BLOCKS.   The examiner first firmly stacks three rectangular blocks, making a clapping sound as each block is stacked in order to orient the child. The examiner then says "Here!" as he or she offers the child the fourth and fifth remaining rectangular blocks, followed by the five square blocks. Each block is offered the child for stacking, but if the child does not follow through in the placement of the block, the examiner directs and assists the child in the stacking so that a standing tower gets built.

ANTICIPATION OF TOWER FALLING.   As the tower becomes taller the examiner assesses the child's sensitivity to the possibility of the tower falling. If the child seems insensitive to this possibility, the examiner playfully threatens the tower and pretends to push it over saying, "It's going to fall. Here it goes!" If the child still seems not to anticipate the fall, the examiner knocks the tower down and observes the child's reaction. The examiner then pauses for a moment to see if the child starts rebuilding the tower or makes any motion related to awareness of the tower falling.

If there is no response, the tower is again built up as before and the same process repeated.

THROWING BLOCKS IN A BOX.   Next, the examiner attempts to get the child to throw blocks by throwing one or two blocks with much clatter into a plastic box and encouraging the child to join the activity (contagion effect). If the child does not respond, the throwing task ends. If the child does throw one or two blocks, the examiner divides the blocks into two piles of five and attempts to engage the child in a game of alternately throwing the blocks in the box. The examiner says "I go!" and taps self before throwing the block and pausing. If the child has not moved, the examiner points and says, "You go!" Alternation continues with the remaining blocks.

In the event that alternation does not develop, the examiner may test the limits by exaggerating the throwing of a block into the box and then encouraging the child to do the same. This may be repeated a few times to see if the child can get the pattern of alternation as evident in his or her pausing when it is the examiner's turn.

Blocks

	Response			Limit-Testing		
Status of Reality Systems	Yes	No	Marginal	Yes	No	Marginal
Accepts blocks						
Stacks blocks						
Anticipates tower falling						
Joins contagious throwing						
Alternates throwing						

Evaluation

Nonverbal autistic children with closed-system disorders are usually able to accept blocks and will stack but are often insenitive to the falling tower. Although they may participate in contagious block throwing, they rarely alternate block throwing with the examiner. In contrast, nonverbal children with system-forming disorders often respond well to the examiner's structuring of the task. Their attention often wanders, but when brought back to the task, they can typically accept blocks and, although they have trouble stacking because of eye–hand coordination problems, they often anticipate the tower's falling. They may momentarily join in contagious throwing of blocks into the box, but it is difficult for them to alternate block throwing with the examiner.

TASK 7. STACKING CUPS AND BOWLS

Purpose

To cope with surroundings, a child must adjust his or her approach to changing circumstances. This task evaluates the child's ability to shift his or her approach. A particular set is first established toward a task and then the child's ability to adaptively shift—to break set—is tested by changing the nature of the task.

The task is graduated from the simplest stacking sets, involving stacking cups with their openings facing upward, to sets involving progressively more complex adjustments—for example, the child is given the cups one at a time upside down and is required to turn them over for right-side-up stacking. At the most complex level the child is required to alternately stack cups and bowls, with the bowl presented upside down over the cup and the cup presented right side up over the bowl. In this instance the child must take into account both the position of the cup or bowl (whether it is right side up or upside down) and its location (over cup or bowl). After the child has successfully completed all the cup-and-bowl-stacking sequences, the examiner introduces a sequence in which stacking is abandoned entirely and the child must take each cup and place it upside down inside a bowl, resulting in six cup–bowl combinations spread out on the floor.

Materials

Six heavy plastic cups with handles and six heavy plastic bowls of the same color.

Both cups and bowls can be readily stacked.

Procedure

A. CONVENTIONAL STACKING. The task begins with the child and examiner facing each other with the parent sitting in back of the child to help focus his or her attention. The examiner then stacks two cups right side up, saying "Here!" each time the child is handed another cup.

The examiner holds the base two cups firmly so that the child does not scatter them. If the child accepts cups 3 to 6 and stacks them, the examiner goes on to the next part of the task. If not, either the examiner or the care giver working with the child hand-over-hand guides the child into stacking cups 3 and 4. The examiner then provides the child opportunity to stack cups 5 and 6.

After the cup stacking, the same procedure is followed for stacking six right-side-up bowls. If the child, after hand-over-hand support, is unable to stack either cups or bowls, the examiner ends the task.

Expansions

For children who have stacked at least two cups or bowls, the task continues with systematic expansions of the general procedure.

B. INVERTED STACKING.   The examiner says "Here!" as he or she hands the child upside-down cups, one at a time, for inverted stacking.

C. OPPOSITIONAL STACKING.   The examiner stacks two cups right side up, then hands the child upside-down cups, one at a time, for right-side-up stacking. *The examiner notes whether the child immediately inverts the cup before attempting to stack, touches the inverted cup against the right-side-up cup before righting the cup, or persists in futile efforts to force the inverted cup to stack.*

D. OBJECT DISCRIMINATION STACKING.   The task for the child is to alternately accept a cup and a bowl for stacking in their own stacks placed 6 inches apart. The child is handed, in alternation, right-side-up cups and bowls over the corresponding stack (i.e., cups over cups and bowls over bowls).

E. LOCATION CONFLICT IN STACKING.   The variation here is that the examiner hands the child the cup *over* the bowl and the bowl *over* the cup. This means the child must overcome the "pull" to stack in the same location and *note that the form of the objects requires them to be stacked in the opposite location.*

F. LOCATION AND INVERSION CONFLICT.   The same procedure is in Expansion *D*, except this expansion requires that the cups and bowls be *inverted* as well as displaced when handed to the child.

G. Asymmetrical Inversion and Location Conflict.   This time both cups and bowls are stacked upside down. However, although the cups and bowls continue to be handed over opposite stacks, the bowl is handed the child in the upside-down position (as before), whereas the cup is handed in a right-side-up position. *The examiner notes the readiness of the child's response to the unique adjustment the cups or bowls require before they can be stacked properly.*

H. Breaking the Stacking Set.   Until now the basic formula guiding the child has been that a way must be found to stack either cups or bowls. This final task challenges that formula: The examiner leaves all six bowls and six cups spread out in front of the child and then takes a cup, inverts it and places it inside a right-side-up bowl. The examiner does this twice and then says, gesturing toward the child, "You do it!" *The examiner then notes whether the child, confronted by all the cups and bowls—with the examiner's new cup–bowl model in the middle—can ignore all previous stacking sets and relate to the new model.* If the child is unable at first to follow this new pattern, the examiner may test the limits by adding a third and fourth cup–bowl set, pausing each time to determine at what point, if any, the child can follow the new pattern.

Stacking Cups and Bowls

	Response			Limit-Testing		
Status of Reality Systems	Yes	No	Marginal	Yes	No	Marginal
A. Conventional stacking						
B. Inverted stacking						
C. Oppositional stacking						
D. Object discrimination stacking						
E. Location conflict in stacking						
F. Location and inversion conflict						
G. Asymmetrical inversion and location conflict						
H. Breaking the stacking set						

Evaluation

This task discriminates sharply between different kinds of disorders. Non-verbal or limited-verbal children with closed-system disorders have substantial difficulty with this task. When the disorder is most severe, a child may persistently try to force the inverted cup to stack in right-side-up cups (i.e., Expansion B). But even when a closed-system child has mastered Expansions A through G, the difficulty may become apparent in Expansion H when the stacking set is challenged.

The following example taken from the Umwelt of a 13-year-old autistic boy with a closed-system disorder suggests that the sudden shift from stacking cups and bowls separately to combining them in separate cup-in-bowl arrangements spread out on the floor (H), may sometimes present too radical a change in circumstances.

Presented the cup- and bowl-stacking sequences, Tim immediately showed resistance to change. For example, having stacked cups right-side-up, he at first resisted righting a cup offered upside down and tried unsuccessfully to force the upside-down cup into the cups stacked right-side-up. With hand-over-hand work he learned to adjust the cup properly and soon could cope with a task (F) requiring him to take an upside-down bowl offered over a right-side-up cup and turn it over so that he could place it with other right-side-up bowls. However, when the examiner, seeking to test the limits of his flexibility, required him to reorganize the task by placing a cup in each bowl, he started the task, then abruptly groaned and lashed out, scattering the cups and bowls.

The sudden shift from one kind of organization to a completely different kind was clearly beyond Tim's capacity and signaled that expansions had to be carefully planned if he was to include such shifts in his repertoire without breaking down. Tim could cope with the task as long as the examiner maintained the vertical stacking orientation and required him to change only *one* factor in each sequence (shifting from right-side-up to upside-down stacking, etc.). However, when there was *too radical* a departure from the vertical stacking set, that is, when the shift from vertical stacking of cups and bowls was replaced by combining cups with bowls in a lateral pattern, he could not adjust. The implications for teaching Tim successfully were clear.

In contrast, children with *system-forming disorders* have a different kind of problem with this task. When they are firmly guided and distractions are reduced, they can cope with most of the stacking tasks. The final task, however, often gives them difficulty because they must ignore the competing stimuli provided by *all* the cups and bowls laid out in front of them and focus only on the cup–bowl pattern established by the examiner.

TASK 8. RECIPROCAL PULL TOY

Purpose

In Chapter 4 it was noted that at about 9 to 10 months of age the normal infant learns to cope both with the care giver and with an object at the same time (Trevarthen & Hubley, 1979). This happens every time a parent and child play together in relation to a toy. Prior to this, the infant either relates to the object or to the care giver, but not to both within the same system.

To test for this capacity the child is given a pull toy—a small dog on wheels—with a string at both ends permitting the child and examiner to have a tug-of-war around who gets the dog. Several aspects of the pull-toy situation are of particular interest (see Figure 7.4). Does the child grasp the string and pull the dog closer, demonstrating a means–ends understanding of the causal relation between pulling on the string and the dog's movement? Does the child understand that, when the examiner pulls a string attached to the other end of the dog, the examiner is responsible? The child's awareness of the examiner's role is evident in eye contact and in participation in a playful teasing game of unexpectedly pulling the dog away from the examiner. The child who is aware of the examiner's role and gets into the game has achieved the social system described by Trevarthen and Hubley.

Materials

A pull-toy dog that makes some noise and has moving parts when pulled. The toy should have strings of equal length on both ends so it can be pulled forward and backward by child and examiner.

Procedure

MEANS-ENDS.   The examiner, seated opposite the child, places the dog on the table and presents the string attached to the dog's head to the child. If after a few seconds the child does not pick up the string, the examiner models by pulling the toy up to the child two or three times and saying playfully "Woof-woof." If the child still does not pull the string, the examiner

Figure 7.4. Child and worker pulling dog in Reciprocal Pull Toy task.

puts the string in the child's hand and guides the pulling activity two or three times before releasing the string. Should the child still not pull the string, the examiner ends the task.

RECIPROCAL PULLING.   If the child is able to pull the string, the examiner attempts to engage the child in a tug-of-war around who gets the toy. If the child immediately pulls back the string while looking at the examiner, then the child has demonstrated understanding that the examiner is the agent of the tug.

Reciprocal Pull Toy

Status of Reality Systems	Response			Limit-Testing		
	Yes	No	Marginal	Yes	No	Marginal
No response to string						
Pulls string to bring dog closer						
Pulls back without looking at the examiner						
Participates in tug-of-war (looks at examiner)						

Evaluation

Autistic children with most profound closed-system disorders are unable to pull the string (see description of Fred, Chapter 3). Even as they learn to do so and to pull back when the toy is pulled away from them by the examiner, they look only at the dog and *not* at the person responsible for pulling. In general, however, children with closed-system disorders seem, particularly when given hand-over-hand support, to grasp means–ends but not reciprocal play relations more readily than children with system-forming disorders.

TASK 9. SYMBOLIC PLAY

Purpose

Sometimes the capacity of the child to engage in symbolic play provides the earliest indication that the child is close to moving from sign stage to symbolic-sign stage functioning. To evaluate symbolic play capacity the examiner first gives a toy dog something to eat and then simulates putting the dog to bed by placing a blanket over it. Following this, the child is requested to reproduce the two sequences. This approach is based on the finding (Watson & Fischer, 1979) that children who can mimic the symbolic play of the adult possess symbolic play capacity.

The examiner tests the child's symbolic play capacity on two levels by *first* presenting items that bear little similarity to the real objects and *then* presenting objects that look like their objects. For example, a block (representing the dog) and a flat lid (representing the bowl) are used by the examiner who states, "Doggie drinks water," and then, "Doggie goes to sleep" (with blanket as a prop). If the child fails to mimic this demonstration, the same procedure is repeated with a toy dog, a bowl, and a dog's sleeping basket (see Figure 7.5).

Materials

A toy dog, sleeping basket, small blanket, bowl, rectangular block (to simulate dog), a flat lid (to simulate bowl), and an 8- by 12-inch piece of cardboard (to simulate basket).

Procedure

There are two parts to this task: abstract symbolic play; concrete symbolic play.

ABSTRACT SYMBOLIC PLAY. The examiner begins with the sequence using the block, lid, and cardboard. The examiner takes the block and says "Woof, woof" while petting the block-dog and then adds, "Nice doggy." Then the examiner says "Dog is thirsty," takes the dog to the lid simulating a bowl, and holds the block next to the lid while saying "Dog drinks" and making drinking sounds.

Next, the examiner says "Dog's tired" and carries the block-dog to the cardboard representing a basket, which is a foot away. The examiner then places the block-dog on the cardboard-basket, saying "Night-night, doggy," and covers the block with a blanket.

Immediately following this, the examiner gives the block to the child and tells the child, "Take care of the dog!" The examiner notes whether the child repeats the preceding sequences. If the child repeats the relevant parts

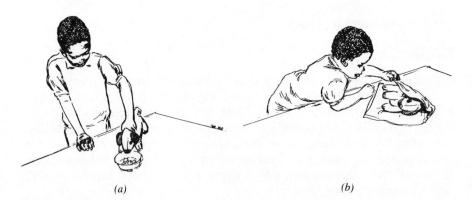

(a) *(b)*

Figure 7.5. Symbolic play with toy dog. (a) Child pretends to feed the dog, (b) Child pretends to put the dog to bed.

of the dog-drinking or going-to-bed sequences, it is not necessary to continue to the next part.

CONCRETE SYMBOLIC PLAY.   This sequence, for children unable to succeed with abstract forms, is identical to the preceding one, with the exception that the examiner introduces a toy dog, a bowl, and a basket. The examiner repeats, as before, the drinking and going-to-bed sequences. Again, immediately after modeling the sequences, the child is given the toy dog and asked to take care of it.

Symbolic Play

	Response			Limit-Testing		
Status of Reality Systems	Yes	No	Marginal	Yes	No	Marginal
Child achieves abstract symbolic play with at least one sequence						
Child achieves concrete symbolic play with at least one sequence						

Evaluation

Often children who cannot cope with the more abstract representation of the situation can do so with toys that resemble real things. Sometimes a child who demonstrates no symbolic play in both parts of the test demonstrates some symbolic capacity indirectly. Thus, one child who failed to cover the sleeping dog climbed up on the table and simulated going to sleep next to the dog.

It is interesting to contrast the performance on this task of children with closed-system disorders with those having system-forming disorders. Typically, when language development is roughly equivalent, both kinds of children develop symbolic play. However, the symbolic play of closed-system children tends to be more circumscribed and object-dependent than the symbolic play of children with system-forming disorders. Verification of this view awaits more data.

TASK 10. UNSTRUCTURED PERIOD B

Purpose

Following the symbolic play tasks the child is given another 2-minute unstructured period. The setup is identical to that described earlier with the exception that the dog, basket, bowl, and blanket are left available instead of the slide and blocks that are available after the slide task. Repeating the unstructured period provides information with regard to the reliability of the child's behavior when demands are withdrawn.

Unstructured Period B

Status of Reality Systems	Spontaneous		
	Yes	No	Marginal
Child investigates objects in the room in terms of their functional properties			
Child uses and explores large portions of the space available			
Child brings objects to people			
Child is more interested in people than objects			

TASK 11. "CROUPIER" (RAKE–OBSTACLE) SEQUENCES

Purpose

In this graduated series of tasks the child has the opportunity not only to demonstrate a grasp of the instrumental function of tools, but to solve an increasingly complex set of obstacles that interfere with getting a desired object (cracker or small toy). Of particular interest is the child's ability, when a desired object lies inside a U-shaped obstacle, to push the object away before pushing it sideways and then toward himself or herself. Such integrative ability indicates capacity to conceptualize a solution and to delay gratification in a way that favors more advanced learning (the less mature move is to try to pull the object over the barrier toward oneself).

Materials

A large flat surface (a table) covered with a rug, at the child's waist level. Three rakes are also used: one with a short handle, one with a long handle, and one with a rectangular piece missing from the arm.

Also available are a series of obstacles with Velcro on one side so that they will remain stable on the rug covering the table.

Procedure

The Croupier tasks are presented to the child in an ascending order of difficulty. The examiner presents the child the rake and target object in a variety of arrangements. The examiner provides support only on the first-level task. On the remaining tasks, if the child does not successfully solve the task as presented, the examiner models the appropriate solution *once* and then sets up the task for the child to try again. If the child is unable to successfully solve the first level of the task, the examiner stops. Beyond the first task, the examiner should *stop* expansions only after the child shows three consecutive failures.

A.   The task for the child is to pull the rake toward himself or herself so that the object placed just inside the rake's arm will be brought closer. The rake is within easy reach of the child's hands, that is, at midline. The examiner first waits to see if the child will pull the rake. If not, the examiner models pulling the rake.

If modeling does not have the desired effect and the child does not grasp the handle, the examiner puts the child's hand on the handle. If this action does not provide sufficient help, the examiner then guides the child through the rake-pulling sequence until the object inside the rake arm is brought closer.

If, after several such supportive efforts have been made, the child is still unable to use the rake, the examiner stops the task.

B.   The examiner places the target object in front of the rake arms and about 6 inches to the lower left side. To succeed, the child must first make a lateral movement and then pull.

C.   The object is behind the rake surface and about 6 inches to the upper left side. To succeed, the child must move the rake away from his/her body and make a lateral movement before pulling the rake and the captured object inward.

D.   The object is positioned about 4 inches behind the rake arms. When the rake is lifted up, the child is momentarily unable to see the target object. To succeed, the child must lift the rake and place it behind the target object before pulling inward.

Figure 7.6. Child trying to adapt to cut-out rake in Croupier task.

E.   The examiner gives the child a rake with the inside of the arm cut out, leaving narrow sides. To succeed, the child must either use one of the sides of the cut-out face, turn the rake on its side, or completely turn the rake so the edge that has not been cut out is available (see Figure 7.6).

F.   The child must make a choice between two rakes, one of which is shorter than the other, in order to obtain an object that is beyond the reach of the shorter rake when it is extended as far as possible. The examiner seeks to determine if the child grasps the need for the longer rake and uses it to get the object.

Figure 7.7. Child must turn wrist in order to insert rake between the parallel barriers to get object.

In arranging the rakes on the table for the child's use, the examiner places the long rake to the left of the short rake if the child is right-handed or to the right of the short rake if he/she is left-handed.

G.   The task for the child is to use the rake to push the object to the left (or right) of the barrier before attempting to pull the object closer.

H.   The task is to pull the object placed between two parallel barriers on the table. The child, in order to gain access to the small object, must turn the rake to its narrow side, insert it behind the object, and then pull it closer (see Figure 7.7).

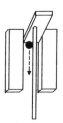

I.   The task is to get the small object, placed within the horseshoe-shaped barrier, by pushing the desired object away from the body, then to the side of the barrier, and then toward the body.

J.   The task is to retrieve the small object from its location within a small horseshoe-shaped barrier that is within a larger horseshoe-shaped barrier.

Croupier Sequences

Status of Reality Systems	Response			Limit-Testing		
	Yes	No	Marginal	Yes	No	Marginal
A						
B						
C						
D						
E						
F						
G						
H						
I						
J						

Evaluation

Nonverbal children with closed-system disorders typically have substantial difficulty with the rake tasks (see Figure 7.8). Often, when given the rake, they bang it on the table and have little sense of its function as a tool that might bring desired objects closer. Like very small children, they tend to ignore the rake and reach for the desired object—a car, cracker, and so forth—with outstretched hand. Even when closed-system children have acquired some tool use and can solve some of the problems, they often fail when the task requires more deliberate use of the tool. For Tim (cited earlier in the cup–bowl task), this capacity was beyond his reach:

> Tim has a rudimentary sense of how tools work. He could use a rake to bring a piece of cracker within hand reach. In using the rake he again demonstrated, as he had with the cups and bowls, the ability to cope with changed circumstances when these did not differ too radically from each other. For example, not only could he use a rake to get a cracker at Level A with the cracker placed inside the arm of the rake, he could also get the cracker at Level B with the cracker at some distance to the left of the rake. Further, when at Level H he had to turn the rake sideways to retrieve the cracker from the narrow channel, he succeeded after a few trials. However, he was completely unsuccessful at Level I where he had to push the cracker *away from himself* (a 3-step task) before he could get it. He could, it is interesting to note, "solve" the task without insight when directed by his father in a rote manner ("Push cracker away—push sideways—pull toward you").

The closed-system child can be contrasted with the system-forming disordered child in the following way. The closed-system child often has the motor skill to manipulate the tool in a relatively precise manner but lacks the concept of how to use it to push an object away from the body (Levels I and J). Children with system-forming disorders, on the other hand, may

Figure 7.8. Child solves multistep maze problem to get object with rake.

sometimes grasp the concept involved but even then have great difficulty sustaining attention and coordinating eye with hand so that they can implement that understanding to manipulate the rake in relatively precise ways.

TASK 12. GRAPHIC EXPRESSION

Purpose

At the most basic level the examiner assesses whether the child has any sense that the movement of the crayon on the paper produces marks that vary with movements of the hand. In other words, does the child possess a sense of self as a source of intentional activity related to making marks? At the next level the kinds of marks produced by the child are analyzed, both in terms of their relative complexity and in terms of the flexibility the child shows in moving from one kind of mark making to another. In this context, an assessment is also made of the child's ability to mimic the examiner's marks. At the most advanced level the task demonstrates the child's ability to represent reality to the self and to others through drawings of things and people.

When a child is operating in a certain fashion—perhaps producing only lateral line scribbles—the examiner attempts to introduce a series of expansions by working hand-over-hand with the child at right angles to the lateral scribble. Then, the staff person *interrupts* (removing hand-over-hand support) and watches to determine whether the child persists in the new pattern. A child who performs a single lateral scribble, is tested to determine if he/she can tolerate crossing the lateral scribble with scribbles at right angles to it. If the child produces a circle, the examiner tests to see if the circle can include dots, and so forth. From this kind of evaluation, guided by the developmental data provided by Werner (1948) and by Kellogg (1970), it is possible to gain a sense of both the child's developmental drawing level as well as the child's capacity to learn.

Materials

Several sheets of 7- by 11-inch white paper as well as black and red crayons or magic markers.

Procedure

A. PRELIMINARY GRAPHICS.   The examiner presents the child with a blank sheet of paper and the black and red crayons and observes what the child does. If the child after 30 seconds does nothing with the crayons, the examiner draws two or three vertical lines with the black crayon, then pauses to see if the child will copy these lines. If the child still does not use the crayon, the examiner places the black crayon in the child's hand and, guiding the child's hand, rhythmically produces seven or eight vertical lines and then interrupts the activity by releasing the child's hand. If the child still fails to produce any graphic activity, the examiner ends the task.

B. VARIABLE GRAPHICS.   When a child produces markings, the examiner next assesses the child's ability to vary the markings, either through copying, or *compensatorily* after hand-over-hand guided markings. Thus, if the child produces verticals, the examiner introduces lateral markings and determines the condition under which these are produced. Following this, circles are introduced. In the final part of this section, the examiner assesses the ability of the child to combine the various parts by forming a cross surrounded by a circle.

C. REPRESENTATIONAL GRAPHICS.   Children who have some verbal ability should begin with this task. If they are able to draw an object or person and can designate at least two relevant parts of the object or person and the examiner can discern basis for the child's designation, the child need not be evaluated on A and B.

The examiner asks the child to "Draw something." If the child complies, the examiner then asks "What is it?" Should the child designate the drawing— for example, house, cat, man, boy,—the examiner asks the child to designate two or three relevant parts of the drawing.

For children who cannot initiate a drawing, the examiner draws a round circle and asks the child, one item at a time, to put in the eyes, ears, nose, mouth, and hair of the person's face.

Graphic Expression

Status of Reality Systems	Response			Limit-Testing		
	Yes	No	Marginal	Yes	No	Marginal
A. Preliminary graphics						
1. Spontaneously draws either vertical/horizontal lines or circle						
2. Copies examiner's graphic (at least one)						
3. After hand-over-hand training is interrupted, continues drawing without support						
B. Variable graphics						
1. Shifts from one form (vertical/horizontal or circle) to another by copying the examiner						
2. Continues introduced pattern developed through hand-over-hand guidance when it is interrupted						
3. Combines at least 2 forms by copying examiner						
4. Combines 2 forms after hand-over-hand guidance is interrupted						
C. Representational graphics						
1. Spontaneously produces a picture of something and can identify 2 parts of it						
2. Completes at least 2 parts of introduced circle-face						

Evaluation

Children with closed-system and system-forming disorders can, with appropriate intervention, eventually achieve representational drawings. The developmental path this takes, however, seems consistent with the nature of their disorders, with closed-system children being more likely to use less space on the paper and to represent things and events close to the body than children with system-forming disorders.

TASK 13. OBJECT AND PICTURE DESIGNATION

Purpose

This task assesses the child's ability to recognize and designate several familiar *objects* as well as *pictures* of these objects. Depending on whether the child fails to recognize and identify objects or pictures, he or she participates in either a brief object-training or picture-training sequence to determine the utility of certain interventions.

Materials

Three objects that can be taken apart and reassembled as well as three forms that have properties of both pictures and objects (3D/2D) (pp. 106–108).

Procedure

A. OBJECT DESIGNATION AND TRAINING.   In this task the child must identify three familiar objects—*dog*, *hat*, and *cup*. The examiner says, "Show me the _____." If the child successfully points to or picks up the designated object, the examiner changes the order and asks for another object until all three are either referred to by the child or the child fails to comply.

For children who fail to designate objects, the examiner takes each object and demonstrates something about it. For example, the examiner says "hat" while removing the hat from the doll's head and says "hat" again as the hat is put on the doll. The hat is then given to the child to put on the doll's head as the examiner again says "hat." The examiner then takes the cup and demonstrates how the cup can be pulled apart and put together again, and then used for drinking. Each time the examiner puts the cup together and brings it to the mouth, he or she says "cup." Then the cup is given to the child in its pulled-apart state, and the child is assisted—if necessary—in putting the cup together and lifting it to the mouth as if drinking. As the child does so, the examiner again says "cup."

A similar procedure is used with the dog. The examiner takes off and then replaces the dog's head. Each time the head is replaced, the examiner says "dog." The dog with its head off is then given to the child for "fixing." As the child, with or without assistance, places the dog's head on its body, the examiner says "dog."

Following this procedure, the child is reexamined on ability to designate the three objects. Children who are able to designate objects after functional training with them demonstrate their responsiveness to this kind of intervention in expanding their knowledge of objects.

B. PICTURE DESIGNATION AND TRAINING.   Children who are able either before or after training to designate the three objects are then presented pictures that closely resemble the objects and are asked by the examiner, "Show me the _____." Each time a child designates a picture, it is replaced in the array in a changed order and the child is asked to show another picture, until he/she either successfully designates or fails to designate the three pictures. Those children who fail the picture designation take part in the following picture-training session.

Picture training is provided by first showing the child a picture version of the object that includes a three-dimensional element (Figure 7.9). For example, the child sees half of a cup secured on one side of a card and is invited to remove the part cup and restore it on the card, the examiner saying "cup" each time it is restored. Following this, the examiner says "cup" after flipping the card to show a two-dimensional version of the cup. In similar fashion, as the child is presented a picture of a dog with a three-dimensional head attached to the picture, the examiner says "dog"; the child removes and restores the dog's head as the examiner says "dog"; and then again as the card is flipped to its two-dimensional side. The identical procedure is followed with hat.

After the training procedure, the child is again tested on his or her ability to designate the pictures. If a child succeeds after previously failing to designate pictures, this supports the utility of 3D/2D procedures in providing a transition from objects to pictures of objects.

Object and Picture Designation

	Response			Limit-Testing		
Status of Reality Systems	Yes	No	Marginal	Yes	No	Marginal
A. Object designation and training						
1. Identifies at least 2 of the 3 objects						
2. After training identifies at least 2 of the 3 objects						
B. Picture designation and training						
1. Identifies at least 2 of the 3 pictures						
2. After training identifies at least 2 of the 3 pictures						

Evaluation

For all kinds of disordered children who have not yet learned either to distinguish one object from another or to recognize the symbolic relation of a two-dimensional form—a picture—to a three-dimensional object, these test procedures provide a useful preliminary indication of receptive understanding of spoken words as they relate to objects and pictures. For those children who lack this understanding, the training sequences show how close they are to grasping this understanding, and whether functional involvement

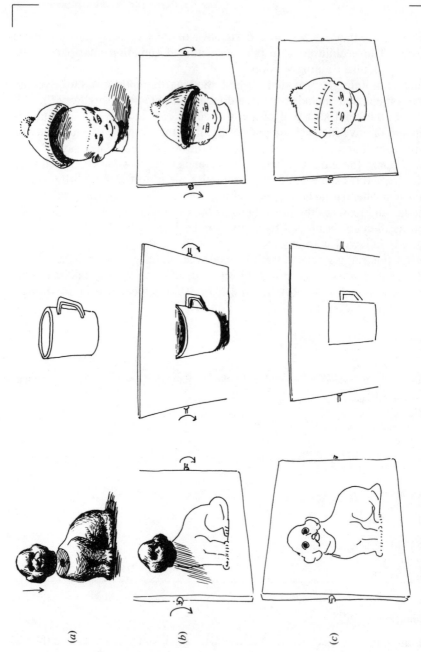

Figure 7.9. (a) Objects (dog, cup, hat); (b) Part objects/part picture transitions from objects to pictures (3D/2D); (c) Pictures.

with the object or careful transitions from object to picture are likely to be helpful. Children who can use spoken words to designate objects and pictures may proceed to the evaluation of reading and writing status.

TASK 14. READING AND WRITING

Purpose

By sampling the child's capacity on key aspects of the reading and writing process, it is possible to determine where the child requires help. A sample training session to help the child in a deficient area then provides a sense of the usefulness of certain interventions for that child.

We have isolated four critical facets of the reading process that must be assessed to determine the child's capacity to read and write: (a) ability to *sight-read* a few common words, (b) ability to relate certain *letters to sounds*, (c) ability to *blend letter sounds into sound forms*, and (d) ability to translate heard sounds into letters and printed words—*dictation*. As in the preceding test, when the child fails a particular section, brief training is provided to determine how relevant the intervention is to the function being taught.

Materials

Four words on flash cards from Lesson 1 of the Symbol Accentuation Reading Program (see Chapter 11). Each word is on a set of three flash cards, with Card 1 showing the word in conventional form while Cards 2 and 3 show the word with progressively more properties blended with the form of the word (Figure 7.10).

Procedure

A. SIGHT-READING AND SYMBOL ACCENTUATION TRAINING.   The child is presented 4 common words in printed form on flash cards. These words are *bird*, *cat*, *gun*, *cup*. If the child fails to identify the words and indicate knowledge of their meaning, the examiner provides a brief training session.

In back of each conventional word card are two cards with altered forms of the words, each form having properties of both the conventional word and the object. Thus, after a child fails to identify the conventional form of the word the two accentuated cards are briefly shown as the examiner designates each card and then flips back to the conventional word form. As Figure 7.10 shows, the prospects for the child to successfully identify the accentuated card are greater because the word looks more like a picture of the object represented by that word. Following this training, the child is again asked to identify the conventional words in a different order. If the child succeeds, it suggests that accentuation procedures may help the child establish sight-reading.

Figure 7.10. Testing the effect of transitional picture-word forms on ability to recognize *cat* and *gun*.

B. LETTER–SOUND RELATIONS.   The child is shown five different letter forms—*sh, m, b, f, c, oo*—(from Symbol Accentuation Lesson 16) and is asked to utter the sounds (not the letter names) of these letters. If the child fails to do so, he/she is taught the sounds with accentuated cards in back of each conventional letter form. As Figure 7.11 shows, these accentuated cards fuse the mouth position required to utter the sound with the letter that represents that sound. As each accentuated card is shown, the examiner utters the relevant sound. Following this, the child is again shown the letters in conventional form to determine whether letter–sound accentuation is effective.

C. LETTER–SOUND BLENDING.   If the child successfully relates sounds to letters, the examiner seeks to determine whether the child can sound out

Figure 7.11. Testing the effect of transitional mouth–letter forms in assisting the production of "f" and "m" sounds.

these letters when they are placed together in wordlike form. Here, the child combines consonants previously presented (*sh, m, b, f, c*) with the strong vowel *oo* to create *shoo, moo, boo, coo*, as each letter derives from mouth movements in left-to-right sequence. For example, a student who has been producing the "m" sound in coordination with the transformation of compressed lips into the letter *m* is required to shift with the examiner's pointed finger to the vowel form *oo* to create "moo." In similar fashion the examiner tests for the ability to create "shoo," "boo," "foo," "oof," "coo" by blending the individual sounds (Figure 7.12).

Children who cannot blend these letters into sound forms are given brief training—placing fingertips to mouth—so that they can feel each sound they

Figure 7.12. Testing with flash cards for blending of individual letter sounds into meaningful sound forms.

utter and relate that feeling to the mouth-accentuated flash cards that help guide the child's utterances from left to right. Then, following retesting, the examiner can determine how useful such procedures are for a particular child.

D. DICTATION.   The final phase of the evaluation concerns the child's ability to transpose heard sounds into letter forms. First the sounds for letters *sh, m, b, f, c, oo* are dictated, giving the child the opportunity to print the letters (without looking at their printed forms). Subsequently, the examiner dictates "shoo," "moo," "boo," "foo," "oof," "coo." On the basis of the child's performance, particularly with regard to "foo" and "oof," the examiner can determine how close the child is to fully grasping the notion of translating sounds into graphic forms in a way that permits their meanings to be deciphered.

Reading and Writing

		Response	
Status of Reality Systems	Yes	No	Marginal
A. Sight Reading and Symbol Accentuation training			
1. Sight-reads 3 of the 4 words			
2. Sight-reads 3 of the 4 words after training			
B. Letter–sound relations			
1. Produces sounds for 4 of the 5 letters			
2. Produces sounds for 4 of the 5 letters after training			
C. Letter–sound blending			
1. Correctly blends at least 4 sound forms, including "foo" and "oof"			
2. Blends at least 4 sound forms, including "foo" and "oof," after training			
3. Blends 2 sound forms, e.g., "moo," "shoo," but not "foo" and "oof"			
4. Blends 2 sound forms, but not "foo" and "oof" after training			
D. Dictation			
1. Hears 6 individual sounds and correctly writes 4 letters, e.g., m, b, f, c			
2. Hears 6 individual sounds and correctly writes 4 letters after training			
3. Hears 6 sound forms ("moo," "boo," "foo," "oof," "shoo," "coo") and correctly writes 4 without a model			
4. Hears 6 sound forms and correctly writes 4 words without a model after training			

Evaluation

Using these simple tests, the examiner can quickly define those aspects of the reading process that are most difficult for a particular disordered child. Typically, those areas are the shift from picture to printed word, the blending of letter sounds into sound forms, and the ability to accept dictation—translating heard sounds into written forms. By introducing a brief training procedure after each area, the examiner can also determine the likely readiness of a particular child's response to interventions that provide careful transitions. The application of these procedures with different kinds of children is discussed in Chapter 11.

TASK 15. NUMBER RELATIONS

Purpose

This test assesses certain aspects of the child's grasp of numbers. Areas examined include *seriation*, *number concepts*, and *number conservation*.

Materials

Ten large bolts and 10 large nuts.

Procedure

A. SERIATION.   The examiner lays out 10 bolts about an inch apart on a table in front of the child and asks him or her to count them. If the child succeeds, the examiner then lays out 10 nuts and asks that these be counted. Should the child not be able to start counting either series, the examiner may count the first 3 items and then pause. Should the child still not continue, the task ends.

B. NUMBER CONCEPTS.   After scrambling 10 bolts into a pile, the examiner—holding hand palm upward toward the child—asks consecutively for 2, 6, 3, and 7, of them. If the child succeeds, the task is repeated with 10 nuts, only this time the child is asked for 3, 5, 2, and 8. Then, to determine if the child grasps the notion of quantity independent of *kind* of object, the examiner puts 4 bolts and 4 nuts on the table, scrambles them together, and asks the child for 4, 6, and 7 without specifying kind of object. The examiner notes how readily the child includes two kinds of objects in the count, observing whether he or she has to exhaust one kind of object completely before including those of another kind. Children who respond correctly to this task continue with the conservation test.

C. CONSERVATION OF NUMBER.   This task, adapted from Piaget's (1952b) work on conservation, tests for conservation of quantity by lining up 10 nuts in two parallel rows with 5 nuts in one row and 5 in the other. Each nut is separated by about 2 inches from the next one. The child is then asked to count the items in each row. After completing the count, the child is asked if the rows are the same or if one row has more. If the child says the same, the nuts in one row are placed close together whereas the nuts in the remaining row are left as they were. Then the child is again asked if the same number of nuts are in the two locations or if one row has more nuts.

Number Relations

Status of Reality Systems	Response		
	Yes	No	Marginal
A. Seriation			
1. Counts both rows accurately			
2. Counts one row accurately			
B. Number concepts			
1. Responds correctly to at least 6 of 8 requests			
2. Responds correctly to at least 4 of 8 requests			
3. Responds correctly to 3 of 4 requests with 8 mixed objects			
C. Conservation of number			
1. Reports "same amount" independent of configuration			

Evaluation

Children who accurately count objects (A) demonstrate knowledge of the one-to-one correspondence between number and referent—and that with each additional object the number must change. Children who can count mixed objects. (B) demonstrate that their number concepts transcend counting one or another *kind* of objects. Finally, children who answer that both rows have the same number (C) demonstrate a grasp of conservation of quantity independent of the way the items are configured. Incorrect answers indicate that concepts are still influenced by the perceptual context in which things appear.

TASK 16. PARENT SEPARATION

Purpose

This task, adapted from the "Strange Situation task" (Ainsworth, Blehar, Water, & Wall, 1978), tests the extent of a child's special relationship with a parenting figure. In the task the parent says goodbye and then walks out of the room for 30 seconds.

Procedure

The examiner takes the parent(s) aside and informs him/her or them of the following procedure:

> We would now like you to play a favorite game with your child. It should be repetitive, like Pat-a-Cake, or have a rocking motion, like Row, Row, Row Your Boat, and you should face your child while playing.

> We would like to see how your child reacts when you stop this game and leave the room and so, when we cue you (after 2 minutes), tell your child that you will be going bye-bye. Act as if you are really leaving. Take up any belongings that you have, hug and/or kiss your child, and then wave and say "bye-bye."
>
> You will only be out of the room for less than a minute so stand just outside the door in the corridor. We will cue you when to come back in by rapping on the door. When you return or your child comes out the door, verbally greet him/her and then slowly walk over to meet him/her.

When the parent(s) leave the child, the examiner monitors the child's reaction to the separation. Unless the child attempts to engage the examiner, the examiner remains motionless and says nothing, in order not to influence the child's natural reaction. Should the child go to the door at any time and appear to have difficulty turning the knob, the examiner assists the child. If the child succeeds in opening the door, the reunite-greeting sequence should be allowed to take place there.

Parent Separation

		Response	
Status of Reality System	Yes	No	Marginal
A. Separation–departure			
1. Acknowledges departure with verbal expression or by waving bye-bye			
2. Attempts to maintain contact by holding, following, or staying near the parent(s), or by crying			
B. Coping after initial separation			
1. Either seeks to locate parent or verbally establishes parent's whereabouts			
2. Shows great distress or turns to examiner			
C. Separation–reunion			
1. Upon reunion, actively seeks parent; soothed if upset			
2. Upon reunion, does not seek contact with parent but accepts it when offered			

Evaluation

Typically, autistic children with closed-system disorders ignore parents' leaving and become preoccupied with objects. Children with system-forming disorders may register a diffuse distress but seem to lack any coordinated means of dealing with the situation. In contrast, normal 2- to 3-year-olds will protest and immediately run to the door through which the parent has left and try to open it. This differentiation is also evident when the parent returns. Closed-system autistic children tend to ignore the parent's arrival whereas more related children run to the parent for comfort.

UMWELT ASSESSMENT FINDINGS RELATED TO MAJOR DEVELOPMENTAL AREAS

This section describes the manner in which findings from different tasks may be brought together to provide in-depth understanding of disordered children in four major areas. These areas are *body schema development*, *contact with the environment*, *social contact*, and *representation/communication*.

Body Schema Development

A number of tasks provide important information about the developmental status of a disordered child's body organization. These tasks include, for example, the Swinging Ball task or negotiation of the gap on the Primary Board. When a child grabs and hangs on to the swinging ball but cannot coordinate pushing activity with the ball's swinging motion or when—on the Primary Board—a child stands "frozen" unable to move a foot on either side of the gap when the center piece is removed, a lack of body awareness is inferred. This is also true of a child who can cross the Swiss Cheese Board only by feeling the contours of each hole with his or her foot (haptic input). The limited body awareness inherent in all such responses is consistent with early *sign stage* body organization.

More advanced *sign stage* body organization is evident in the child who is able to capture the nature of events away from the body purely by vision and can use this information to anticipate and physically coordinate the body with these objects or events as they come closer. For example, the child can anticipate the approaching swinging ball in order to push it away or can anticipate the holes in the Swiss Cheese Board through vision before physically confronting them. It is also evident in the child who can include objects within his or her relationship with another (Trevarthen and Hubley, 1978), as described in Chapter 4 and as revealed in the Reciprocal Pull Toy task in the Umwelt Assessment.

Contact with the Environment

Here are included tasks such as Croupier Sequences (tool use), Blocks, Stacking Cups and Bowls, Reciprocal Pull Toy, and problem-solving tasks such as the Anticipation Board (one of the Primary Board Demands). The tasks elicit functioning that is either sign stage (child seems to ignore, react in a limited way, or fuse with the object); late sign stage or early symbolic-sign stage (child can differentiate self from reality sufficiently to use tools and to maneuver objects around an obstacle, e.g., Croupier sequences); or systematically explore the nature of his or her surroundings (Unstructured Periods A and B); or symbol stage functioning (child can represent events in the immediate environment to the self as seen in symbolic play, graphic play, or use of sign and spoken language).

Social Contact

Sometimes the same task, for example, the Swinging Ball task, may have relevance not only for body schema development and contact with the environment but for *social contact* as well. Thus, the child who can push the ball *to the examiner* in contrast to merely pushing the ball, demonstrates social contact at the late *sign stage*. A similar inference may be derived from the turn-taking part of the Blocks task and the Reciprocal Pull Toy task. Social contact may also be evaluated from the child's spontaneous preference for people over objects during the periods of unstructured activity, as well as through the Parent Separation task. During the latter, failure to respond to the parent's absence is consistent with the early *sign stage* (out of sight means out of mind) whereas *persistent* distress, coupled with efforts to open the door along with delight on discovering the parent is consistent with the later sign or early symbolic-sign stage.

Representation/Communication

Tasks that reflect representational capacity include Symbolic Play, advanced Croupier sequences Stacking Cups and Bowls, Graphic Expression, Object and Picture Designation, Reading and Writing, and Number Relations. Here, *sign stage* performance is characterized by triggered response to objects and events and an absence of representation. For example, an early *sign stage* functioning child may be able to stack cups in the manner in which they are oriented—either upright or upside down—but not be able to stack an inverted cup on an upright stack. At the *symbolic-sign* and *symbol stages* the nature of the object is grasped in all orientations, and reality can be not only represented but also interpreted and selectively transformed to meet the needs of the child, as when a child decides to use a particular wooden block as a train or truck.

Ability to communicate is picked up during the Umwelt by noting the child's responses to signs and words as well as any communicative signs—reaching, pointing, raising arms to be picked up, pulling the adult to get a desired object or words—that the child produces during any part of the evaluation. Signs or words are evaluated sign stage, symbolic-sign stage, or symbol stage depending on the extent to which the child's use is independent of the immediate context. The more context-bound usages are evaluated as sign stage, whereas the more independently used terms are viewed as symbolic-sign or symbol stage depending on how they relate to reality.

SUMMARY

This chapter presents the Miller Umwelt Assessment Scale—a series of tasks designed to sort out the manner in which disordered children experience reality—so that interventions can be designed to help them solve their reality problems. The text describes how the various tasks help characterize the kinds of systems available to a particular disordered child and how the systems bring or fail to bring that child into adaptive contact with people and surroundings. The tasks provide information about the child's current status, and also—through testing of the limits—show how close the child is to a more adaptive stance in various deficit areas.

The areas of a child's developmental status that the tasks help clarify are body schema development, contact with the environment, social contact, and representation/communication. The first four tasks (Swinging Ball, Primary Board Demands, Swiss Cheese Board, Slide Sphere) provide important information about the child's use of the body to organize and cope systematically with large objects in his or her immediate space. Information about the child's immediate contact with the environment is derived from another group of tasks (Blocks, Stacking Cups and Bowls, Croupier). These tasks help elucidate the relative flexibility of the child's systems in problem solving with small objects. The nature of the child's social contact is clarified by a third set of tasks (Reciprocal Pull Toy, Blocks, Unstructured Periods A and B, Parent Separation). Finally, information about representation and communication is derived from the following tasks: Graphic Expression, Object and Picture Designation, Reading and Writing, and Number Relations.

CHAPTER 8

Individual Applications of Cognitive-Developmental Systems Theory

The goal in this chapter is to convey—from a number of perspectives—the nature of individual work with systems-disordered children at the Language and Cognitive Developmental Center (LCDC). To do this, we report the experiences of both relatively new and more experienced practitioners of the C-D systems approach, as well as the experiences of parents who work with them. Beginning with interviews of several staff members, the chapter then details the treatment of two system-disordered children from the vantage point of the staff and parents involved.

INTERVIEWS WITH STAFF USING THE C-D SYSTEMS APPROACH

One of us (AM) interviewed Dr. B, a developmental psychologist who has been at the Center for 3 years. She had not previously worked with profoundly disordered children.

First Impressions

AM: What was it like when you first came to LCDC?

DR. B: The biggest problem was integrating textbook theory and research with these very different kinds of children. It was a scary feeling when I first went into a classroom and M, an autistic child I was assigned to work with, climbed into my lap. I had been trained in textbook theory that didn't transfer at all to the real child I had to work with. It was a shock. At first the disordered children weren't quite people. Later, they became people with serious problems.

There wasn't a lot of room to mess around here. There is a pressure to get going with the kids and get them moving. And to do it with the tools that have been developed here. Then you have people like K who

---

The interviews in this chapter are edited transcripts of tapes from the files of the Language and Cognitive Development Center. Names and identifying details have been altered to protect the anonymity of the participants.

applies C-D brilliantly and makes you feel like two cents when you watch her work. For me—even after my PhD in developmental psychology—being here has been an exercise in humility. I think the trick is to find a way to sustain yourself during the learning period.

Mastering the C-D Systems Approach

AM: Was it difficult to learn the C-D systems approach?

Dr. B: C-D systems theory provides an enormously useful structure for working with the disordered child. But the other critical part comes from the person. I felt pressure and at first I left out a lot of my abilities and talents in my quest to master these concepts. And I approached the children in a fragmented way. For a time I was so caught up with the procedures that I forgot what I already knew about children.

  I kept trying to understand various elements . . . the integrative spheres. You never quite understood why I didn't just "get it" and had to have you spell it out. To me the end point and the starting point made sense. But I didn't understand the means, how to get from one point to another. It is a complex structure with different aspects to it. It was always a matter of understanding . . . like what is a sphere? What does it consist of? For me I had to understand the concept in general terms as opposed to a construct used only in a therapy session. For example, with the multisphere it was clear to me what you were doing. And I could always understand it while watching it, but when I was faced with the situation, I couldn't use it creatively. It was like being able to read and make music without being able to do variations on the major themes.

AM: What finally brought the approach together for you?

Dr. B: Reading your book and attending the C-D systems seminars helped conceptually . . . but nothing is going to help you with the child you face if you can't relate to the child. You just can't go in there with your map. You have to be able to change and adapt C-D strategies to *that* child. You need a repertoire of coping when the kid tantrums, withdraws, or gets into a stereotypic loop. A manual won't help you with each child. It's going in there, throwing yourself into the water, messing up, dragging yourself to your supervisor, getting help. You can't sit there with a manual and do it. It requires the experience of living it and making sense of what you have lived.

AM: Given your experience, how would you go about training a person in the C-D systems approach?

Dr. B: You need a dedicated person. Given that, the person should be comfortable with children and should probably start with a young child who is not so profoundly disordered. With such a child it might have been easier for me to apply the developmental ladder that I already knew. I could have applied C-D systems theory more rapidly because

I would have seen the gains and quickly understood the relevance of the different procedures. But starting with older, enormously disordered children, it was harder for me to see the gains and thus more discouraging.

But even with a profoundly disordered child like A, what I found enormously helpful was getting into his stereotypy. He would repetitively do what looked like picking up and dropping . . . but I couldn't interrupt it. If I did, he would have glorious tantrums. I couldn't transform his stereotypy into picking up and dropping or into throwing. Those functions seemed too far ahead of him. So I tried to get closer by putting something else into his fingers that he could drop. I used clay and when he dropped his bit of clay I dropped mine. Then, one day when he dropped the clay, I caught it. Right after that, he caught *my* clay when I dropped it. He had finally accepted a change in his system that I had introduced. Then I expanded the system so that his mother would catch his clay. Then I would roll the clay and do something functional with it, and he would tolerate some of that. Bit by bit, stretching what he was doing, he began to look at me . . . to take notice of me.

So, even though I didn't have a younger child to learn with . . . what worked for me was having some way to get into and modify this very disordered child's stereotypic systems. Once I could do this it was like a dance. You have the structure and you integrate it with the emotional being of the child. And that helped me learn C-D.

AM: What does it take to get a profoundly disordered child moving?

Dr. B: It really is everybody coming together around a child. It's the C-D therapist and the speech person applying C-D in her particular way; it's the classroom teacher and assistants building new functions; it's the movement therapist and the adaptive physical education person and it's the family following through on school gains. When that happens . . . and everybody has the same goals, it really works. And then it feels very good.

The next person interviewed was EC, a speech and language therapist who had spent 5 years in the field before coming to LCDC. She was interviewed by EE-M after she had spent 2 years at the Center.

First Impressions

EE-M: What were your initial reactions to the C-D approach?

EC: What struck me most poignantly when I first observed K working was how functional everything was. The other thing that struck me was the way she used incredibly small steps to give a child experience of an object. She seemed to know all the ways that a very small child or infant experiences a particular object and how to expand on it. For example,

I remember how she taught Anna (an autistic child with a system-forming disorder) how to make sense of a cup. Very slowly she started out just having her drink from a cup and hang it on a hook, pour from a cup and hang it on a hook, drink from a cup and then stack it . . . a variety of things. And eventually she got her putting a broken cup together and filling it so that the child got the idea of a cup that holds things; she had her turning the cup in different positions for stacking and hanging. She had her use it to fill with marbles, beans, rice. She used the cup to pour different items; she put it in different places—called location expansions. Anna had to go get a cup and put it in a little cupboard. Many more things than I ever thought were possible with a cup.

When I thought about it—what children do when they are learning— you really do use items in so many different ways. And you do gain that experience of *cupness* or that wholeness of the object that makes the cup a thing with many facets through those varied functions organized around that object. So that's what struck me in the beginning.

Mastering the C-D Systems Approach

EE-M: Was there any part of this approach that was difficult for you?

EC: I found it particularly difficult at the beginning to decide what were the right small steps to take. I puzzled about things like—How many steps do you present at a time? How quickly do you move? What does the child show you that indicates that this is the right time to move from A to B? Timing was very difficult for me at first.

Also, the notion of minispheres, multispheres, and integrative spheres took me a while to fully understand. The way I finally organized it for myself was to think of the minisphere as one small step or piece of behavior. You start out with one piece of behavior—the minisphere— that has to be repeated. Then the multisphere is a couple (or more) pieces of behavior that the child needs to learn how to move between. Then the integrative sphere becomes a more complex system in which there are a couple of steps that involve the same item—as when you pick up a cup and open the doors of a cupboard so you can put the cup inside. And that's how I broke it down for myself.

And then the other things that struck me were the dramatization, K's way of using her voice, her timing when she interrupted. . . . Knowing when to interrupt was one of the most difficult things for me. And that's still something I'm working on. Knowing when the child is *just ready* to continue an activity or behavior and to stop it at that highest point of tension to get the language or to get a sign. That was very interesting for me. And it took a long time for me to see that that was what she was doing. I didn't really see it at first.

Contrast with Behavior Modification

EE-M: In what ways does our approach differ from your former way of working—before coming to the Center?

EC: I noticed that there wasn't any use of M&M's and that constant "Oh, good for you!" each time the child did something. What seemed particularly important for this child (Anna) was contagion and the way that contagious activity helped the child connect different parts of a sphere. And that has become more important to me as I've learned about timing and interruption. And I learned more about contagion by watching K get a child to *need* to continue by interrupting a contagious activity.

Previously my approach was very behavioral. Someone would stand behind the child and help the child perform a desired sequence of behavior. The child's successful performance would be rewarded with social praise or a hug. That approach differed most from the C-D systems approach by the way sequences were broken down. There was nothing like teaching the child an object by introducing the varied functions of the object. It was a laying on of an entire sequence without any effort to establish the meaning of that sequence. But the part that *did* transfer to my C-D work was knowledge about the importance of "hands on" work with disordered children in teaching them things.

What was new in this Center, in addition to the things we've talked about, was the emphasis on redundancy to form ritual-systems. That was discouraged in my other settings. Now I realize how important such repetition is in helping a child grasp the meaning of a particular sphere. Previously, the pressure on me was always to introduce something new—so repetition was somewhat frowned on. Also, the notion of expansions. There was none of that, so one never really knew what the child had learned. Now, with expansions of a particular function, you know that the child can generalize understanding because you have taught the child to do just that.

I have also learned a lot here about how children learn to see and the importance of the body schema. I never really knew that many disordered children do not have a sense of their body boundaries. Once I understood that, I knew why objects dropped out of their hands or why the object seemed to disappear for them when they turned away. Your example about children who had sight restored after cataract removal (see Chapter 3, pp. 80–82) but still had to learn how to perceive objects by handling and working with them brought home how important it was for the child to build up an experience of the object. I found the whole notion of trying to see the world the way the disordered child sees it extremely helpful in working with them.

The next interview was with K, a master C-D systems therapist with an MA in Early Childhood Development, who has been with the Center for 9 years. She was joined in the course of the interview by Dr. EW, a clinical psychologist, who has been with the Center for 10 years.

Evolution of the C-D Systems Approach

AM: How has the C-D systems approach changed over the years?

K: Well, for one thing it's become more complex. We are now much more aware of the individual child as evident in your concepts of closed-system, system-forming, and syncretic system disorders. We didn't have that in the beginning. These formulations give one a sense of what to expect from a particular child. We are also much more sensitive to what engages a child: With closed-system children we look at the quality of the movement . . . the stereotypic patterns, their interest or fascination with visual patterns and with pictures. And we know how to expand these perseverative patterns and fascinations into functional behavior.

AM: What about children with system-forming disorders?

K: M provides a good example of a *system-forming disorder*. M's language is quite good. But M cannot look at a balloon and pump it up at the same time. She looks at the balloon and stops pumping or she pumps and doesn't look at the balloon. There are a number of reasons for such system-forming disorders. Sometimes it is because the children just do not have the cognitive capacity to put systems together. With other children it happens because of neurological problems. . . . These are children who live in a very chaotic world. With such children one must begin with minispheres that involve a strong causal element so that they can begin to understand that what they do has an effect. When, after much repetition, M understands the causal link between her pumping and the balloon getting bigger, or understands that the thing she dropped in the water caused the splash, her actions and their outcomes become linked into a system. Without this kind of repetitive intervention these children remain scattered—orienting indiscriminately to everything around them. In working this way we help the children do what they could not do by themselves.

AM: What is it like to work with a child with a syncretic systems disorder?

K: With a child like L, with a syncretic systems disorder, I work harder to engage the child so that I control the environment. And, as with system-forming disorders, I work repetitively to establish systems involving clear cause-and-effect relations. If L comes up with something bizarre such as "My foot is crying," I might first try to see if she is trying to tell me something about her foot hurting. If her foot *does* hurt and there is a bruise or something, then I would transform her sentence into "L's foot hurts. L wants to cry." However, if there is no immediate reality to relate her comment to, I might introduce a compelling event such as giving a doll baby a bath that she could organize herself around. Always my concern is that the child not drift off into bizarre fantasies unrelated to the immediate surroundings.

In other words, with closed-system children we are trying to build functional aspects of reality into their systems; with system-forming disordered children we are helping form systems; but with syncretic children we are trying to correct mixed-up ways of experiencing reality—to make sure that they don't drift off into issues totally unrelated to the here and now. With the syncretic systems children, it is very important to have a long-term relationship because they organize themselves through their relationship with you. This is far less important for closed-system children because of their usual preoccupation with objects. To assist work with syncretic children, it is important to have the same people work with them for extended periods of time.

Dr. EW entered the conversation here and elaborated further on children with syncretic system disorders. She explained how she dealt with P, an 8-year-old boy with a syncretic system disorder, when he persistently misinterpreted events.

Misinterpreted Cause and Effect

DR. EW: Sometimes, what seems bizarre in such a child is an incorrect interpretation of cause and effect. P, for example, had this notion that smoke detectors going off cause fires. At home, every time a smoke detector went off near the stove he was terrified because he thought it was causing a fire. He couldn't get the notion out of his mind. I corrected it by drawing picture sequences showing how heat from the stove triggers the alarm in the smoke detector and by having his parents demonstrate how a flame near the detector triggers the alarm. His abnormal response was directly related to how he confused an effect—the sound of the smoke detector—with the heat or fire that triggered it. A similar misinterpretation of reality was behind some of the unusual interpretations which T, a 9-year-old boy with a similar disorder, made. T was frightened one night at home by the sound of angry, loud voices transmitted through the walls of his room. Later, during one of our sessions at the Center, he heard voices in the corridor and fearfully stated that there was someone in the wall. I had to show T that the sounds came from outside the room and not from inside the walls and that there was nothing he need fear. In other words, my task was to show him that similar appearing events do not have to have similar sources. Because the sounds at home frightened him did not mean that he had to be frightened by the sounds at the Center. For a while, after this, every time he heard a sound he needed to have it interpreted and made harmless. By repeatedly emphasizing the different ways in which sounds came about, he gradually became comfortable about sounds outside the clinic door.

Developing the Sense of Self-Efficacy

AM: Can you expand on your work with T?

DR. EW: Of course, this is only one facet of my work with T. Before he could readily accept correct interpretations of reality, he required a stronger sense of self. I helped establish this stronger sense of self in my C-D work with him by accenting his role as an agent able to make things happen. For example, at first T was fascinated by the way the wheels of his bike turned, and he would follow their motion, mesmerized. But when I put him *on* the bike he became the agent . . . the mover of the pedals. As he began to experience himself as the agent in this and similar situations, he began to feel stronger. He no longer felt that his legs were likely to "fall off" when he got tired and he is literally "more together." His progress was much accelerated when other kids in the neighborhood (see Chapter 2, p. 72) saw him riding his bike and pronounced the previously weird kid okay and invited him to do "wheelies" with them.

   The syncretic child's shift from passive involvement with the object to active engagement—making the bike go—feeds back the sense of mastery that strengthens the sense of self and helps establish a more valid understanding of cause and effect.

AM: (returning to K) How does C-D systems work differ from that of other professionals?

K: Well, we do not use time out or punishment to control a child's behavior. Our emphasis is on transforming or helping the child organize behavior. People who are captured by the technology of behavior modification often seem to impose their procedures from "outside-in" whereas we try to work from "inside-out" as we fit our strategies to the biological and psychological need of the child to make sense of the world. We are also more sensitive to the way in which each child processes information. Sometimes it is primarily visual, sometimes it is more tactual. For many of the children it is auditory, and for some children it varies. Sometimes, certain children are hypersensitive to certain stimulation— to certain colors, for example—just as certain children are acutely reactive to sound or to being touched. All this must be taken into account in trying to help disordered children form functional systems.

Expanding Existing Systems versus Introducing New Ones

AM: When do you find it desirable to expand a child's existing systems rather than to introduce new ones through spheres?

K: In my work I do one or the other depending on the needs of the child. For example, in R's case I elaborated systems he already had. R is a child with a very complex repertoire of systems for dealing with objects but who *totally* lacks a repertoire for dealing with people—or with people *and* objects. All his object systems were closed off from people. Watching him intelligently explore and make sense of his surroundings, you would think he was a normal child. But if you tried to *play* with him as he examined his surroundings, he would totally ignore you. For him, an adult entering his closed world of object systems becomes an intruding, confusing object. My task with him, therefore, was to insert myself into his transactions with objects in a way that he could accept. You might say that I had to get inside his object systems by becoming necessary to his doing what he needed to do with things. In this expansion of his object systems he learns that some of the things he cannot do by himself he might be able to do by turning to me and to his mother for help.

For other children, who lack the rich repertoire of object relations that R has, my first task is to help them build systems by introducing minispheres that can be progressively expanded and which I then combine into integrative spheres that help them develop more complex and functional ways of dealing with objects. With such children, the first very visible gains become apparent as I systematically expand a child's closed object systems. But to get this gain, you must help the child get beyond a particular object or picture fixation. We will be discussing how this happens when we talk about my work with Jack.

AM: Do you think C-D systems therapy will become highly enough developed that a therapist will be able to go step by step in a prescribed format?

K: I think we will have a more developed set of guidelines for those working with disordered children. But, because each child—even a child who falls within the closed-system category—is different, it will always be necessary to adjust the interventions to the specific needs of that child. It seems unlikely that we will be able to anticipate the tremendous variety of ways in which disordered children function. What we have are a set of principles that guide a variety of effective interventions.

The rest of this chapter deals with the collaborative work involving practitioners and parents of two children with different kinds of system disorders. It begins with Jack, an autistic child with a closed-system disorder. After a developmental history and Umwelt Assessment, an interview with K provides insights into her work with Jack—now 3 years old—and his mother and father. She has seen Jack with his parents for one or two sessions a week for the last 6 months. Following this report are excerpts from an interview with Jack's mother and father. The transcript reflects the C-D systems work practiced collaboratively by K, C-D systems therapist, and Mr. and Mrs. H, Jack's parents.

JACK, AN AUTISTIC CHILD WITH A CLOSED-SYSTEM DISORDER

Jack's Developmental History

Mrs. H reported that Jack was born at full term via a vaginal delivery without complications. He weighed 8 lb 6 oz with Apgar scores around 9. The mother said that she had as much access to the baby as she wished and that he nursed strongly although without rooting. He ate voraciously, and spit up often from eating so rapidly "as if he didn't know when to stop eating" and almost doubled his birth weight after two months.

In the hospital, nurses told the mother that he was the quietest, sweetest little boy they had ever seen. One of us (AM) asked Mrs. H to describe Jack as a newborn.

MRS. H: He was very, very passive, very quiet, not at all demanding. He behaved as if he never really wanted to be here. He never really had excitement about being here. Nurses also told me—on the two nights I wanted a full night's sleep without having to nurse him—he refused to take a bottle. He didn't reach out to take a bottle until he was 14 months old. When he was hungry, he smacked his lips. He was very patient and might wait for up to 20 minutes to be fed.

Failure to Explore

AM: What was he like during the early months?

MRS. H: Unlike his older sister, Jack never really explored his hands or feet. He would just sit there . . . and that was it. He never wandered away to check out things and then come back. You could take him to a store in a carriage but, while other children would be grabbing at things as they went down the aisles, he never did. He was satisfied to just sit and rock for hours and hours at a time. He never squirmed . . . just seemed happy . . . just looking.

Unusual Response to Stimuli

Mrs. H became concerned about deafness because, in spite of their pediatrician's reassurance, she felt his response to sounds at 2 months of age was unusual.

MRS. H: You could smash something behind him and he would never turn around. But he might respond to a very soft sound—music or a jingle on TV. He wouldn't respond to kootchy-koo or peekaboo. He might laugh but never participate. Only in the past 6 months has he started responding when I say, "I'm going to get your belly button."

If he fell or bumped his head, he would cry and put his hand to the hurt spot. On the other hand, when at 6 months he began from time to time to repetitively bang his head on a wall, bedpost, or door, he showed no signs of pain or distress. During this period he also began to rock his head from side to side. He would clutch me when he was frightened by a new event, but I don't recall his going to anybody for comfort when he hurt himself. The only thing he took an interest in when he was around 18 months of age was a spring horse. First thing in the morning—even before juice—he would get on that horse and pretty much be on it for 3 or 4 hours at a time during the day. And he would yell happily as he rode the horse in different ways—frontward as well as sidesaddle. He would get very "high" from jumping on the horse and continue being high after jumping down.

Response to Father

Jack's father became very concerned about his inability to establish a relationship with his son.

MR. H: At first I spent a lot of time with my little girl trying to offset any problems that she might have with a new brother—so when Mom was holding Jack I would be holding my daughter. But later when I saw I had no relationship at all with him I felt this was a bad mistake so I tried to move toward him. But he didn't have any interest in me—would look through me like I wasn't there. I would never get any response at all from him when I came home. I assumed that he was jealous, was still nursing so he didn't respond to me. I remember a few times he hurt himself and I went over to pick him up and he wouldn't let me pick him up. He would pull away and then get over the upset fairly quickly and walk away. He seemed fairly tough and didn't seem to want comfort from me.

Motor and Spatial Functioning

AM: How was his coordination? And when did he learn to walk?

MRS. H: He just got up at 7 or 8 months and did it. He was not like my older child who did it more gradually by 9 months. He was also a climber. At 15 or 16 months he would just climb up a piece of furniture if he was standing next to it. Fortunately, his balance is outstanding so he wouldn't fall. On the trampoline he bends his knees and jumps way in the air much better than his older sister. He is also able to use a bar mounted on the door. He watched once or twice, then started doing it dramatically better than his sister.

MR. H: If he wanted to get from one side of the bed to the other he wouldn't walk around. He would walk right through . . . walk over whatever was there . . . a chair, anything. If a person was in his way he'd walk over the person as if he were an object.

Events Leading to Referral

When Jack was about 6 months old, the parents began to think about seeking help because they noted his difficulty adapting to new things (such as accepting the bottle) as well as his father's inability to start a relationship with him. His mother commented that "Getting him to adapt to different things—like putting on his winter coat—meant screams. To put shoes or boots on was a horror show as was getting a snowsuit on him to take him outside."

He also resisted changes in his feeding. Mrs. H could not feed him from a spoon, and he wouldn't eat baby food. He ate with his fingers—cereal, bread, and cauliflower—basically only white foods. He seemed threatened by different-colored foods. The mother tried, by modeling, to get him to stick out his tongue, but "He never seemed to know he had a tongue." The parents also could not get him to throw, to pick up, or to roll a ball. He could not handle crayons of any kind. At most he would take a crayon, try to balance it under his chin, and walk away. Starting at about 6 months of age he always kept something small in his left hand such as a toy bear, which he might exchange for another small toy figure every 2 or 3 months.

Finally, when he was almost 2 years old, the family pediatrician referred him for an evaluation at a large medical center. The speech pathologist at the hospital said he was not processing language and referred him to a developmental pediatrician who immediately diagnosed him autistic. The pediatrician recommended LCDC and within a week the parents had arranged for an evaluation.

Umwelt Assessment

Jack, a sturdy 2½-year-old, had great difficulty organizing himself and accepting the spheres offered him in the evaluation room. He kept a plastic toy clutched in his hand throughout the session and would typically respond briefly to tasks, then either collapse into a screeching tantrum or cling to his mother. For example, after pushing the swinging ball once or twice (although not reciprocally), he clung to it but then abandoned it when it bumped into him. On the Swiss Cheese Board he first fell through a hole, briefly walked around others to his mother, then collapsed into tantrums and refused to address the task further.

Jack's failure to turn spheres into systems was strikingly evident on the Primary Board Demands. Here, after crumpling, screaming, and stamping his feet, he eventually walked across the board. However, once he got on the ground he seemed unable to connect one set of steps with the other and thus never completed a full cycle of going up, across, down, and so on. This failure to accept introduced spheres was also evident in the Slide sphere. Even after several experiences of going down the slide and being brought back to the steps he failed to connect steps with slide. Released, he tried to climb up the slide and quite ignored the steps.

Perhaps his best achievement was pulling the string that brought the toy dog closer. When the examiner pulled the dog back, he responded several times by pulling the string to bring the dog closer. However, at no time did he indicate any awareness that the examiner was pulling on the other end. His gaze was completely focused on the dog. He refused entirely to address the Stacking Cups and Bowls task or the Croupier task—turning away to burrow his head into his mother's shoulder.

In summarizing her findings the examiner commented that "Jack seemed not to focus on anything away from his body although he was extraordinarily reactive both to any changes directly affecting his body or the visual field near his body." His mother reported that even changing his clothes caused great upset as she replaced one shirt with another. Reporting on his unusual reactivity to change, the examiner commented:

> I observed his visual reactivity directly: While clinging to his mother he kept looking at an object near his feet. When I moved that object only a few centimeters he totally lost contact with it and became very upset. After the Umwelt I *did* get him to take part in a sphere that had to do with dropping blocks down the slide. I would take one block, gently put it on the slide, and push it down as he followed the motion with his eyes. Then I put the blocks near his hands before sending them down. Finally, he began to accept the blocks and send them down himself. I gave blocks to each parent so they could continue the process. He became noticeably calmer as he continued to take and send blocks down the slide—accepting his first sphere.

Commenting on Jack's behavior with people, the examiner said:

> He had no communication. And his father seemed not to be a person for him. His mother seemed to exist for him only as something to cling to. In his difficulty going beyond his own systems and accepting spheres he is among the most closed-system–disordered children I have seen.

C-D SYSTEMS THERAPY* FROM THE PERSPECTIVE OF THERAPIST AND PARENTS

Treatment Goals

There were several interrelated goals:

1. To help Jack gain functional relations with objects both close to and away from his body

*A documentary film, *A Small Awakening*, (Miller, 1989) that follows Jack's treatment and progress has been produced.

2. To enable him to develop a predictable space within which he could move between objects

3. To help him relate to people without catastrophic tantrums or excessive clinging to his mother; and

4. To assist Jack in developing a means of representing reality to himself and others.

AM: How did Jack tantrum?

K: Well, a tantrum was to lie down and scream very, very loud. His face would turn red and he would kick—the screeching was most pronounced—and his hands and feet would move in a disorganized way. His face would be up but you couldn't reach him. You had no way of comforting him, and he had no way of comforting himself. It was almost as if the sounds he produced kept his tantrum going and enveloped him. And sometimes he would even scream and put his hands over his ears. It was the closest he came to some kind of self-comfort. He couldn't stand his own screaming. And he clearly didn't know the screaming came from him.

AM: How did you deal with the tantrum?

K: I didn't try to deal with the tantrum directly. I sought instead to think of what I could do to engage him. I had to somehow get him to sustain himself without tantrumming when separated from his mother . . . because as long as he was clinging to her I could do nothing. And I had to get him to leave that object that was frozen in his hand. And the block sphere that had started so nicely on the slide didn't go anywhere because I couldn't make any expansions on it. If he had to *move* any distance to get the block he would get very upset. So I started by having him sit on his mother's lap and required very little movement from him. I also shifted from that original sphere of dropping blocks down the slide to a much more visually oriented sphere.

I decided to work with his visual reactivity because I had seen his reaction to even very small visual changes and because he seemed to get confused and lost when he had to move his entire body even a few feet from one point to another. Also contributing to this decision was the mother's excited report at the end of the second session that Jack had, for the first time, taken her hand and directed it toward a picture. Mrs. H connected this new initiative to his C-D sessions with me.

AM: Had you shown him any pictures during the first or second session?

K: I had begun to show him a few pictures. But what I now did was to *systematically* hand him pictures. I found that I could keep him calm by presenting him with colorful, high-contrast pictures of animals . . . not too big. Invariably, looking at the picture and holding it would calm him down. I wanted him to accept and hold each picture I gave him in his hand. And he did. Then, I would very quickly guide his hand to drop the picture in an open jar right next to his hand. To keep the sphere going I then introduced the next very clear picture. I had to pace this very carefully. If I gave him a new picture *before* he was through saturating himself with the first picture, he would get very upset. If I waited too long before giving him the next picture, he also got upset. In general, he needed 4 to 5 seconds of peering at the picture and then I had to help him drop it in the jar with a very light hand-over-hand movement before he could accept another picture.

Within 10 minutes he was dropping the pictures in the jar by himself and coming back to get a new one. You must realize that when he came back for another picture he wasn't coming back to me but to the new picture he needed to complete the sphere. At first, I would have to *creep* each new picture into his visual field. And then I would slowly pull it out of his visual field to get him to follow it and he would then take it. Following this, I would gradually increase the distance from the picture to the bottle—inch by incremental inch. At this time he was still sitting in his mother's lap.

Separating from Mother

AM: What was your goal at this point?

K: My goal was to have him separate from his mother. I had Mrs. H sit in my place so that she could do the same thing that I did. But this he could not tolerate because his mother in a way was an important picture for him. And removing him from that big picture was not acceptable. I solved this by having the mother sit across the table from Jack where he could *see her* but not reach her. He snuggled into one of the bays on one side of the table and his mother into a bay on the other side (Figure 8.1).

Then, I had the mother *send the picture to him* in a truck. And he would take the picture and put it in the jar. Now, I made the task more difficult by having him put the picture in a slit on top of the jar. Then, after a few sessions he would send the truck back to his mother by himself to get another picture. It wasn't easy for him. He started to connect the notion that he had to touch the truck to make it move to his mother in order to get the picture. It had to be done very gradually over a few sessions. He would touch it very lightly. And luckily the truck would move a little bit toward the mother just by his touching it. But what I was really trying to do was to force his distal perception—getting him to look across the table. To help him with this I had Mrs. H hold the picture up and point to it—as in a TV commercial—and name the parts of the picture as she had done before when he was sitting in her lap. Soon he expected that each time he pushed the truck to his mother she would hold up a picture, point at different parts, saying, "Here is the *tail* of the monkey [his *eyes*, his *feet,* etc.]." and then put it in the truck and send it to him.

And the picture that his mother held across the table—about 3 feet away—would consistently engage him from a distance in a manner that it had not previously done. Then he learned, with the help of her pointing, to scan different parts of the pictured object. At first she didn't understand why she had to sit so far away and point at the picture and began to ask questions. I didn't want to lose the momentum just gained, so I said, "Do it! I will explain later." Then, bit by bit, Jack became slightly more assertive about pushing the truck to his mother and she would very slowly point to and verbalize the different parts of the picture before putting it in the truck and sending it to him so that he could pick it up and put it through the slit in the cap of the bottle.

From Pictures to Objects

AM: In addition to pictures, you needed to get him to deal with objects. How did you accomplish this?

K: That took about 10 or 12 sessions. I used dominoes with pictures on them instead of dots—I was trying to get him involved with three-dimensional objects instead of only pictures. In doing this I broke the usual pattern of moving from objects to pictures (3D to 2D) and moved instead from pictures to picture-objects (from 2D to 3D). I had him push the domino pictures into another bottle with a rectangular hole and very soon he was able to discriminate between the two; he carefully dropped the plain pictures into the slit and the domino pictures into the rectangular hole. Both bottles were located fairly close to each other to one side of him.

Expanding Use of Objects

AM: How did you help him expand his use of objects?

K: I introduced a peg—a simple cylinder—that he would put in another jar. I used a transparent jar for each of these objects so that once the objects left his hand and dropped inside the bottles he could still see them. It was important that each object leave his hand so that he could address the next object. Otherwise he would keep holding it in his hand, and there would be no opportunity for him to get the next object. The beauty of the transparent jar was that he could dispose of the objects and pictures and still *see* them through the jar. In contrast, when I tried him with a pegboard, after he got two or three pegs in the board he would become so involved with each peg that he would not accept any additional pegs. So without the jars to help him get rid of the different objects—one at a time—we certainly could not have proceeded further.

The "Mechanical" Therapist

AM: Did introducing new objects require special care on your part?

K: At this point, each time I introduced an object, I felt like a mechanical crane slowly bearing significant, highly salient objects that he would take from the crane-hand, and examine carefully, before disposing of it in the appropriate jar. When he did not receive an object from me, he was quite assertive in pushing the truck to his mother to get an object or a picture to put in the jars. He was also able to turn away from the jars to me and wait expectantly for the next object. And I had to move slowly and very predictably, again like a crane, for him to reach toward and get the object from me. The spatial geometry had to be consistent. His very fragile reality consisted of the jars on one side of him, me on the other side, and his mother across the table. In this space, his movements consisted only of pushing the truck to mother, receiving an object or picture and putting them into the appropriate transparent jars.

Jack's Hand Function

AM: You were concerned about Jack's limited hand use. How did you help him develop more hand function?

K: Jack's hand use deserves some comment. At first there was very little deliberate use of the hands. Given a picture he would hold it because it was so engaging, much in the same reflexive way he would hold his bottle—he was not yet weaned. But only as he pushed the truck was there some deliberate and intentional use of an object—the truck—to gain a particular end—the picture. And then, rather quickly after this, I started with small animals. Some of these were similar to the pictures, but others—like dinosaurs—were quite different. But all these small objects—ducks, giraffes, zebras, lions, and so on—were highly carved and visually very distinct and interesting (Figure 8.1).

   I held these objects up, just as I had the pictures. In fact, for him, I'm sure that they were more pictures than objects. Perhaps it was a bas-relief for him. But at first he would treat these objects as if they were the pictures. There were certainly no animal sounds, such as "Woof, woof," with the dog, consistent with the animals they represented. He merely held each object and became saturated with it just as he previously had done with the pictures. But then, in order to develop more functional use of his hands and to accent the properties of these picture–objects I had him open the door of a toy barn and put these objects inside.

Coordinating Vision with Hearing

AM: Did you have any problems with coordination of Jack's hearing and vision?

Figure 8.1. Sequence showing Jack sending truck to his mother. Mother names an object and sends it to Jack for placement in the toy barn.

K: Yes. To help him develop coordination, I introduced his first integrative sphere. He would readily open the door of the toy barn to put the animals inside but would not permit the door to be closed—perhaps because he needed to keep the objects under visual surveillance—just as previously he may have needed a transparent jar so that he could continue to see the objects that he had dropped in them. And he would look in the door. But when I called him for the next animal he would not at first orient to me. Sound and vision were still not coordinated. So then I would put another animal within his visual field, and gradually I moved the animal toward myself and kept saying, "Jack . . . it's here . . . here . . . here!" inducing him to connect the jerky movements with the spaced sounds.

I didn't name the object at that time. But very soon after that he indicated by taking his mother's hand and pointing at the object that he wanted it named. So now he was moving beyond a *something* in his visual field that gratified him visually to a certain something with a particular name. At first only the mother could "bless" the object by naming it. Later, he allowed me to name the different objects.

Jack's Rigid Spatial Relations

AM: Can you expand on Jack's rigidity?

K: At one point I had used up the various objects so I asked his mother to "steal" objects he had previously placed in the barn so I could continue the process. This was impossible. He would immediately notice if an animal/object was missing from the barn and begin to screech. Similarly, if he had put the animal/object halfway into the barn and I tried to push it all the way in, he would again screech with protest. I could not rearrange anything. This was also true with the placement of the jars. I had to be very careful when I first set them up. Sometimes he would tolerate it, and sometimes he wouldn't. So it was very shaky. Those expansions—spatial expansions—sometimes didn't work because they changed the visual pattern too much.

For example, if I started with two jars—one on each side of his body—he would tolerate them. And he would not then tolerate having *these* jars closer together than they were originally. In other words, the starting position of each pattern seemed to determine its own rightness of position. At first it was as if each pattern became fixed as in a still picture. And to move aspects—the jars or animals—was to violate the picture's integrity. Once the relations were structured, any movement of any part would cause him upset. The relations between objects seemed almost to have been cast in cement.

On different days he could tolerate different distances between the objects. On any one day, however, the objects had to maintain the relations that were first introduced. It felt as if he had formed an attachment with the objects—had bonded with them—in a certain way and to change their relations was to violate this attachment. Perhaps he had invested in the objects and the relations between them the way normal children invest in their parents. Fortunately, as the work continued, he began to permit expansions if they did not deviate too radically from the familiar space he had constructed.

I then sought to humanize his contacts with objects by bringing in human figures—little doll figures—instead of the animals. Mrs. H helped a great deal by constantly bringing in an array of new figures, each slightly different from the others, so that Jack might take these dolls and put them in the barn and close the door . . . although he still had trouble closing the door—losing sight of the object. So there I was . . . still having a problem getting him to expand his systems. I had him push and pull a wagon to get the new human figures from the mother, which he did. *As long as he could see the figure on the wagon, he would pull to get it.* He still wouldn't pull a pull toy lying around but he would pull a string attached to the wagon to get the visual satisfaction of bringing the new object closer. When he did this, I sensed his driving need to get that object so that he could peer at it.

Developing Jack's Use of Symbols

AM: How did you move him toward representing objects?

K: I did this by carefully drawing pictures of objects and putting them on paper bags that contained the objects designated by the pictures. Here, I was trying to help him develop symbolic capacity so he could begin to carry objects cognitively and not always have to clutch them in his hand. I drew exact copies of the objects he particularly liked—the little elephant, the little zebra—painted in with water colors on the paper bags. And I would hand him the paper bag with the object inside and show him the picture. First I got him to orient to the picture on the paper bag—a step that was absolutely necessary because otherwise he would not even look at the paper bag much less put his hand inside to get the object. Then, while he was looking at the picture, I would open the paper bag and show him the same object inside. Then, I took his hand and slowly put it inside the bag—he fought me a bit at first. After a few times he would do this on his own and match the object with the picture on the bag in a way that suggested that he now knew the picture represented the object. He could then, guided only by the picture on the bag, directly open the bag to get the desired object inside.

I then systematically began—although his mother had already been doing this—naming the pictures and the objects in the bag. "Ah, a giraffe!" and match it with the object. Shortly afterwards at home he came out with his first word, "bear." Then, when he saw a picture of a bear at the Center he said, "bea . . . r" with a sense of wonderment. His second word was "deer" and his next words were "pig" and then "ebra" (for zebra)—all but bear being presented as pictures on bags.

AM: Did you ever use manual signs with this child?

K: I attempted a few signs but for this child, at this time, manual signs seemed totally irrelevant. He doesn't look at you, he doesn't see the signs, and he will not let you touch his hands to help him form them.

AM: Would it be fair to say that for Jack pictures served the role that signs played for Fred (described in Chapter 3)?

K: Yes. Unlike most of our children, the pictures—not the signs—served the function of organizing him. It was the only way he could organize. And eventually pictures began to represent real objects. He was very different from Fred who needed the signs to organize and who had to learn subsequently to recognize pictures. This child developed an interest in objects through the pictures, not the other way around. It was only when he began to match objects to pictures that they really became for him pictures *and* objects.

AM: Did you ever use 3D/2D with him?

K: I used it several times with him. But I used it from 2D to 3D, not from the object to the picture. He did not like to touch the object part of the picture—putting the dog's head on, for example—but clearly recognized the dog picture and through this developed more interest in the three-dimensional object-picture of a dog on the other side.

Developing Means–Ends Capacities

AM: How did you *build* on his interest in pictures to get more functional and integrative behavior?

K: At this point the objects had become just as interesting to him as the pictures. The next session when I gave him the bag closed he had to pry it apart to get the object inside. Eventually, I put a string around the bag that he had to pull off in order to get the object inside. Using bags, I could expand the functions needed to open them and get the objects which completed the picture–object system. Then, after pulling the string off the bag, he learned to turn away from the bag and put the string on a hook. Alternatively, he would take the string and crumple it so he could push it through the hole in the jar. Having disposed of the string he could turn back to the bag. Then he would open the bag, take the object out, and put it in the house. For a while he would allow the door of the house to be closed, but then he decided he needed the door to remain open. After using the string, I began to close the bag with clothespins—the kind that pinch things shut mechanically. Given the bag, he had to apply a pincer grasp to the clothespin, remove it from the bag, drop the clothespin in a little bucket for clothespins—not on the table—then open the bag, get the object, and put it in the house.

   To further complicate his life, I began to randomly close some bags with string, others with clothespins, and others by merely folding them. This meant that he sometimes had to pull the string, crumple it, and stuff it in the bottle or put it on the hook, and at other times he would remove the clothespins from the bag and drop them in the clothespin bucket. I even got him to fit the clothespins to the rim of a can, although he didn't care for this—perhaps because it had no particular function for him. Removing the clothespin had served its function so why should he have to bother with it anymore?

   While I was doing this, I also systematically expanded six to eight spheres—all different but with components that he had already learned. Not only did he have to cope with different ways of opening the bag, he would find different things in the bag—an object or a picture or a cord—that he would have to deal with in different ways. If he found a picture, it had to go through the slit in the transparent jar; an animal object would go in the house; a domino would have to go through the rectangular hole on top of the jar. I would keep feeding him these slightly different integrative spheres using many, many variations during the weeks.

AM: Was Jack's mother aware of why you were doing this?

K: Absolutely. We were both slightly euphoric. He was focused, doing things with objects—and it looked nice—almost as if he was playing . . . although an unusual kind of play. Everything was going quite well. And I had vastly expanded the range of integrative spheres he would accept: Many different jars with different shapes—also magnetic alphabet pieces placed in their different carved-out places in a metal board—blocks, dies with numbers on them, pennies for penny jars, purses that he had to unzip to get a penny that he would put in the penny jar, and so forth.

Applying Multispheres to Help Jack Incorporate New Functional Relationships

AM: Up to now, Jack's limited behavior was directed toward getting the object for purely *visual* gratification. How did you get him to explore the functional properties of objects?

K: I now felt that he needed to learn other cause–effect relations so that not everything he did was organized around pictures. He also needed to learn more about himself as an agent able to make things happen in a way that went beyond pictures.

So I now began to focus more on functional, causal relations such as pushing the pump on top of a jar so that water would come out of the spigot. I began this by suddenly interrupting a familiar sphere that he loved to do—putting alphabet pieces in their proper places—and substituting a causality toy or a functional task. One causality toy I used was a jack-in-the-box which he just had to press and out would pop a highly painted face. And he would use it a few times. However, as soon as he got "itchy" with the causality toy, I would interrupt its use and return him to the familiar objects and pictures that he would drop in jars. I would then introduce another causality toy—like a spatula that fans out into three spatula parts: You push it and it fans out, then you push it again and it contracts (Figure 8.2). And he liked this although he wouldn't do this for very long. And then I would abruptly introduce within his more familiar spheres functional items like an eggbeater that he had to turn or a tape measure that he had to pull out. Always I would interrupt the functional tasks before he lost engagement with them and return him to more ritualized spheres.

AM: Actually, as you did this, you were adapting the multisphere concept to his particular needs.

K: That's right. I was training him to shift from one kind of repetitive visual sphere—putting letters into their places—to a more causal type of sphere such as the jack-in-the-box or opening and closing the spatula. In real life this might be like shifting from watching cartoons to sharpening a

Figure 8.2. Jack opening and closing spatula.

pencil or turning on the water for a drink and then going back to watching cartoons.

AM: Did he always remain at the table?

K: No. At about the same time I began to work with pictures on the bags, I began to do integrative spheres around the Elevated Square. About two thirds of the hour sessions would be around the table and a third on the Elevated Square. The first two times I put him on the Elevated Square it was a total catastrophe. He would tantrum and cling to his mother as he had earlier and would not do anything. It was too big . . . and he seemed to get lost.

   The Elevated Square began to work when I took the most salient and engaging object he had been working with at the table—the magnetic alphabet pieces—and used them on the square. His task was to place a magnetic letter within the correct outlines on the magnetic alphabet board. I put the letters on one station of the Elevated Square and the alphabet board on another station: I had him get the "A" and focused him on the outline for that letter on the alphabet board at another station about 5 or 6 feet away. When I released him with the magnetic letter, he ran like a shot to that station so that he could fit the letter within the correct outline. Then I would move the alphabet board to different stations and started pointing to its location. He would first look at me and then follow my pointing finger so he knew exactly where to run to fit the letter.

His interest in following my pointing had previously been developed at the table for shorter distances when I would hide objects for which he had the picture in his hand and would point at one of a series of identical containers in which that object was located. My intent was to have him relate to me to get information about the location of the object that matched his picture. Or I would have six opaque glasses turned upside down with the desired object under one of them. And I would point to the one concealing the object so that he had to be guided by my gesture before he knew which glass to turn up. It took a long time. It was not easy for him.

AM: Does he now point at objects by himself?

K: He now points at pictures and objects. It started as he began to point to pictures to get their names. At first he would use his mother's finger to point to pictures. Now he points by himself.

Incomplete Puzzles Used as Broken Objects

AM: Did you use any other techniques with the Elevated Square?

K: The letters were 90 percent of getting him to master the Elevated Square. He would go around it to get the letters that he needed to fit into outlines on the alphabet board. I did not use broken objects on the square, but I did use puzzles with missing pieces on the square in the same way. In going through these exercises he learned how to scan. For example, eventually at one station I might have a magnetic letter, a peg, and a puzzle piece. And he could pick up any one of these items. On the remaining three stations I would have the alphabet board for the letter, a pegboard with an empty hole for the peg, and a puzzle board with a missing piece. He had to scan each of the three other stations to see where his particular item should go. Then, when he found the right station to receive his item he would go directly to that station and put it in. To keep the sphere going I would try to covertly remove a puzzle piece from a completed puzzle. So, after he had just "solved his world" by completing a puzzle, his mother and I would conspire to selectively disrupt it again. After a while, he began to visually check what we were doing at the other stations while he was completing a puzzle. And, if he caught one of us removing a piece, he would screech loudly. Using these procedures we not only taught him to scan and to cope with different pictures with missing parts, we taught him how to deal with the space of the Elevated Square.

The Emergence of Object Hunger and Naming

AM: What other changes in his functioning did you help bring about?

K: Along with the above procedures I kept introducing new objects. I would get him to accept these objects in two ways: I would just sneak it in so quickly that he had no time to react negatively to it and then swiftly return to the more familiar object; and I began to print the word on the bag instead of the picture.

Suddenly, after several weeks of this both at the table and on the Elevated Square, he lost interest in the old, familiar objects. Now, he wanted only new objects. And he "used up" each new object quickly by peering at it and by exploring its functions. He now in an excited way took real pleasure in new objects—how they looked and how they worked. He was interested in wind-up toys—how they moved and the sounds they made—whereas previously such objects would have sent him screeching and clinging to his mother.

Now he needs new objects constantly, and he uses them functionally. This is a major change. He runs into my toy closet, takes up objects, works them, puts them back. He could get in my toy closet and remain there for the entire session. In addition, he is now increasingly seeking the names from us for the various items in the closet, and his vocabulary is increasing. At the same time, the relative order and calm which had developed at table and Elevated Square has disappeared. He gets very excited running from one place to another, climbing on things and jumping from them—much more than he had previously. . . . His behavior clearly suggests that he has discovered a new way to experience his surroundings but does not yet *fully* understand how he relates to objects, how one object relates to another, or how to use the names of objects to communicate with people about them.

PARENTAL INVOLVEMENT—JACK

In this section, AM interviews Jack's parents, Mr. and Mrs. H, to better understand their experience and collaborative role in their son's program.

AM: What were your first impressions of the program?

Mr. H: We knew within 20 minutes of having been at the Center that this was the program for him. This was the first time I had seen him engage in any kind of play. Using rituals, K was able to get him to do things within a half hour that we hadn't been able to get within 2½ years. And it wasn't because we hadn't tried. But she knew the approach and how to handle him. As a result, when we left—we had just gone through a fairly devastating period—we were very, very encouraged by what we had seen K do and felt that this was not an absolutely lost cause. So when we left we were much more optimistic than when we came. That's for sure.

Mrs. H: The first hour was thrilling. She got him to do things that he had never before done. She got him to send blocks down the slide. She used his name softly . . . and he seemed to be responding to his name. It was the first time I had seen him respond to his name. Then she gave me blocks and my husband blocks so he would keep sending them down the slide. The other thing that amazed me was when she took some round paper plates and a marker and showed him how it worked on the plate and put the marker down. Then she said "Jack" and he picked up the marker and drew a circle on the plate. I had tried unsuccessfully all summer to get him to draw. The closest I had gotten was to have him put the marker in my hand. And she did this without putting it in his hand. . . . That sort of amazed me.

Parents' Reaction to Therapist

AM: What was your reaction to K, your C-D therapist?

MRS. H: She's wonderful . . . but all business. She smiles a lot and doesn't seem to get frustrated. The humanness is there. A couple of times he would crawl over to her and she would say, "Oh my darling. But if I hug you now I will lose the whole thing." And so you know the humanness is there. And at other times when he does something really exciting like when he says "pig" for the first time when presented with an animal she runs over and gives me a hug. It is as exciting for her as it is for me.

MR. H: I felt the same way. It was very much a team. You can't fake sincerity. You can't fake feeling. And you can't fake love where children are concerned.

MRS. H: And when I told her things, she would listen to me, make suggestions. She would also explain things to me. If she couldn't explain to me at the moment why she was doing something because she needed silence for him, she would make sure to explain it to me later.

What impresses me also is that she really seems to know him. She's not just adapting a program that she uses with every child. She knows *where* he's different. She knows when an object is too far from him, when it is too close, when you can start calling his name a little bit louder, when he is getting distracted so that she has to move him into another sphere quickly. She just knows him better than I do.

MR. H: It was never just a notion of an hour session. If we were on a roll and K had time available, sometimes the session would go on another 15 or 20 minutes—no problem—because we were on a roll. We would run into her lunchtime many, many times. K's personality seems to be similar to most of the people that we've met here. Perhaps not as—well she's a pretty marvelous woman—but just about everybody we've met in the program has this type of personality. We really have a sense of belonging. The other thing was that it was all business the whole 60 minutes or more . . . I was amazed that she wasn't exhausted at the end of it . . . because it was just go, go, go . . . very intense.

MRS. H: And she uses physical strength to bounce him up and down to get him to jump that not everyone might want to do. He's a pretty big boy.

MR. H: And she used to like when I came because I could help him jump up and down.

MRS. H: She would often do it instead of me because she wanted him to develop more separation from me . . . so she did a lot of real physical work with him.

AM: How did you understand the work on the Elevated Square with K?

MR. H: My understanding was that it was requiring him to think through a way of accomplishing certain things. When he took part of a puzzle and the rest of the puzzle was on the other side of the square, his job was to figure out the best path to get there and complete the puzzle. Then the thing was repeated with different puzzles—how was he going to solve it—learn how to get from one place to another.

MRS. H: We helped him figure out space relations at home by opening up the gate that we used to keep closed upstairs in the daytime. We kept gates closed and you suggested that we open them. And we did and never had any problem at all. As if things were opened up now and he knows how one place is connected with another. And he never had any problem going up and down the stairs. His balance is great, and he likes the idea that he can go up and down the stairs now. When he's tired, he goes upstairs and lies down on the bed, pushbuttons the TV on, picks up a book, and just stays there. It's not a punishment; it's just a very relaxing time for him.

MR. H: He knows what he wants, and when he needs to get away he does exactly that.

MRS. H: K told me he was suddenly very interested in painting for the first time with the paintbrush on the Elevated Square. And that was amazing. He actually dipped the brush into the paint (at one station) and painted by himself for 10 full minutes. And he really enjoyed that. He also enjoyed breaking the spaghetti (at a second station). And she kept taking him away from one object and taking him to the next. And she explained that the reason for this is that he doesn't know that he can come back to something that he was working on. When you take him away he thinks it's forever. So although that's something she does, I don't know if I can do that at home, but I will try.

AM: Did it bother you when K interrupted what he was doing to take him to another task?

MRS. H: I know she knows what she's doing. He has tantrums all the time. So if he has one at the Center. . . . It bothers me when he cries because he is in distress. It doesn't bother me when he cries because he is frustrated because he's going to have to get over the frustration.

I do continuously tell her of things that he is doing at home. And make sure that she is aware of any new thing that he is doing—such as putting the clothing on our daughter that started 3 months ago. I tell her when the tantrums are increasing and when they are decreasing.

AM: Are they increasing or decreasing now?

Mrs. H: Actually they are stronger. I spoke to her, and she said that's probably because he is beginning to open up to the world and starting to experience things more like other 3-year-olds. But that his frustration is much greater because he doesn't yet have the words or ways of dealing with these new experiences.

Mr. H: What we found is that K would try to get him to do certain things and he would do a number of them. And then she would try to get him to do a few more things. Then the session would end and he would go home and finish the things she had started with him at the Center.

Generalizing the Program

AM: How about the work at home? How would you decide what you would do?

Mrs. H: At first I was pretty much trying to carry on at home what we did during the sessions. I bought cards with animal pictures similar to the cards K used. I got a container and had him drop them into it. I got a toy truck like the one at the Center and if I had another person helping me—would pass the truck back and forth like at the Center. And at home, I would continue the naming. Any time he wants the name for something—for a picture—I immediately give it to him.

Mr. H: You would know when he wanted something named because he would take your finger and lead it to a picture in a book. . . . I, of course, was going in another direction. I had visions of him becoming a great baseball player so I would get him to play with a ball rolling it to him—but not much success with him at first. . . . Before I forget—about the signs—you should know that they are starting to work.

Mrs. H: This is happening the past couple of weeks that he is starting to use signs. He is more responsive to signs. In the past week I have been doing the signs right in his face. And he has begun to make the *give* sign when he wants something.

AM: In working with him would your daughter take part?

Mrs. H: Ann is about 4½ years old now. I would try to get her to pass cards back and forth so that sometimes he was handing her the object, she would give it to me, and then I would reverse the sequence. And the three of us would play Ring-Around-a-Rosy. And even though at first he never touched or held her hand, she would grab him around the wrist and I would grab the other wrist. He may have only fallen down once (to the words *All fall down!*) but he was getting a lot of enjoyment out of it. And this was early on—shortly after I had started with K.

Generalizing Jack's Symbolic Capacity

AM: In what other ways did you carry over the LCDC program?

MRS. H: We also carried over to home the idea of getting him to use pictures to represent things. One way we did this was to put pictures on the walls of his room as you had done at LCDC instead of just in his hand. It worked for a few weeks and then he would take them down and make piles of them. I bought a bunch of animal calendars and would have a room full of frogs one day; the next day a room full of bears. The first time it lasted 3 or 4 days, and then he took them down and put them in piles. Piles that you couldn't disturb. And then I might put up a bear calendar around the room. This might last 2 days, and he would then take them down and put them in another pile.

He also began to make piles of other things at home. And that was new after K started with him. He would take everything out of the food closet after once seeing me take a can out of that closet. He would put everything from the food closet on the counter and protect that uneven pile of cans and so forth with his body. It became his and you couldn't touch it. Three or 4 hours later, when he was into something else, I could start moving things back in.

He did the same thing with the refrigerator—taking everything out—especially the jars. At first he would mix up what belonged in the food closet with what belonged in the refrigerator. But within a month and a half he was able to take everything out from both food closet and refrigerator and put them back again in exactly the right spot: Refrigerator foods would go back in the refrigerator; canned foods would go back in the closet.

But he still has some of that quality. Even now, when he doesn't want something to change—like he's afraid I'm going to change something on the TV—he will literally push me away from it.

AM: So the connection between the way certain things go together—certain pictures with certain objects—that K started working on with him at the Center continued at home with the notion that the food closet represented canned foods while the refrigerator represented other kinds of food.

MRS. H: Yes. And the clothes. . . . He would take all my clothes out of the closet and try to get me to wear everything at once—whether or not they fit. Then I discovered that I didn't have to put them on but just had to touch my body with the clothes. But he would keep doing this at any time so that if I took a bath he would come after me with the sweater he needed me to put on. I'd say "No!" and he would go through a half-hour tantrum, screaming. . . . Then he would go to his sister's clothes and do the same thing. But what I noticed was that after a short time, he wouldn't let me put his sister's clothes against my body; they had to be placed in contact with his sister's body. And this was very frightening to her. I had to tell her it was a little game and not to worry.

MR. H: I remember the day he dragged my shirt downstairs.

MRS. H: He dragged it down in the middle of the night . . . his workshirt.

MR. H: He knew. . . . He brought down my shirt for me. He needed to connect each person's clothes with them just like he had to connect each picture with the right object.

MRS. H: And this went on for a couple of months and now he no longer does it.

Now, if he wants to go outside and he thinks I'm ready, he will get me my jacket and his jacket. So he has some associations with the need to put jackets on before going outside.

Another thing that happens to him now that didn't happen before he started the Center is around his hearing. Before he started here, if I snapped my fingers in back of his head, he would turn toward the sound with a very unhappy look on his face. But if I were to bang my fist against a sheet-metal slide he probably wouldn't even blink his eyes. After he started at LCDC—as he became more aware of sounds—his hands would go up to his ears. Previous to coming here they would not go up to his ears except when he was screeching in a tantrum.

It may be that sounds are more disturbing because he is opening up more and more. Before he came here—at age 2—we felt that he was withdrawing into himself more and more.

MR. H: But as he started to open up, it seemed to me at any rate that the more he opened up, the more problems he had with sound sensitivity.

AM: As if he suddenly started to notice a whole universe of sounds.

MR. H: Yes. But K told me to speak to him softly and to try to keep the object close to him—which wasn't hard because he generally wanted a book on his lap and he wanted the characters named. I would move things to be named a little distant from him after a time. Yesterday, for example, he was all the way across the yard and I—just out of curiosity—loudly yelled, "Jack!" And he turned around. Previously he would never respond to loud sounds. So I don't have to whisper his name anymore.

MRS. H: Another thing K did was to give special sounds that went with each animal: This is a cow it goes "moo"—giving separate sounds to help identify each animal.

MR. H: We carried that over at home. . . . The first word that had significance for him was *bear* so we got him a pull toy with a bear in it and he pulled it at home just as he had at the Center. He recognized it immediately and began to pull it around the room. It was his bear on wheels. But he still wouldn't pull other similar toys around the house.

AM: K described how she used the pictures to transfer his interest to objects—using the pictures on bags. Did you do anything like that at home?

MRS. H: I didn't do anything with the bags. What I try to do if he is pointing at the picture of an object, *I try to run and get that object so that he can see the relation between picture and the thing it represents.* If he points to a picture of a screwdriver I say "screwdriver" and run into the kitchen and get a screwdriver. So we carried through what K was doing with pictures on the bags by getting the real objects for him—whenever possible—all through the house and outside like with tools. We still try to do this.

MR. H: We bought him an Eeyore doll so now he can relate Eeyore in three dimensions to both the pictures in his book and on television. Before he was only interested in the pictures. Then he would push the three-dimensional objects away. But once he caught on how pictures stood for objects he got more interested in objects. As soon as he got the Eeyore doll he immediately said "Eeyore!" So now he can name the object directly without having to have the picture first.

AM: Has his interest in objects continued?

MRS. H: Yes. But it hasn't increased. He has many more activities now. For example, now he likes to go upstairs with his picture book by himself. And he likes his little quiet time so he sits down on his bed and reads his picture book.

AM: What about object hunger—needing new objects all the time?

MRS. H: He still has that . . . even with the pictures. . . . But after a few weeks he's used them up and he puts them under the rug. He just doesn't want to see them anymore and I have to get him a new batch.

MR. H: Now, whenever you bring something new in the house he gets very, very excited. When we buy something for Ann and for him, he now not only has to look at his own new thing, he has to look at her object too. And that sometimes leads to problems.

AM: What about naming things?

MRS. H: His vocabulary keeps increasing. With each week there may be 2 or 3 new words. It's not clear yet how consistent these words are. The day before yesterday somebody brought a cake and I put two plates on the table and I said, "Here, cake!" and he walked right over to the table and said "Cake!" And that's the first time he said "cake." Our experience is that the words are not yet stable. One day he will have the word, and the next day he may not. But from a child who last September had not one word, he now has 10 or 15 words and *all* the letters of the alphabet. He not only names the letters of the alphabet, he can recognize them by shape on the page . . . right through the whole alphabet.

AM: Does he ever use any of his words to get something he wants?

MR. H: The only time he did anything like that was when I had taken his bottle away. Then, he used the *give* sign so that I would give it back to him. Another time I asked him if he wanted a banana and he said "nana."

MRS. H: He can now also make a choice between two objects. If I leave two or three boxes of cereal out now, he will choose a specific box and bring it to me. And I will sign and say "Give!" and then he gives it to me so that I can pour it in his bowl. So I say and sign "pour" as I pour it in the bowl. Before we started at LCDC if we presented him with a choice, he immediately started to tantrum. Now, given a choice between milk and juice, he will push away the one he doesn't want and take the other. The other day when I offered him toast, he looked at it and then walked over to the closet, got the cereal box, and brought it to the table.

AM: When you first came, you were much concerned with how he related to people—and with his eye contact . . .

MR. H: Both K's and your suggestions have been very helpful.

MRS. H: At first he had no eye contact with me. If I held him in front of me, he would look away or look through me.

MR. H: One of the things that works for me is that if I lie on my back and pick up Jack—almost like weight lifting—he looks directly at me. We keep eye contact like that for a couple of minutes. And it really works. Another thing we did that was consistent with K's work was setting up a sphere in which he gave me an object and I would give him one—he having to put the object in my hand before he got another one. And we did this very successfully with blocks, small animals. I might first have to get him to put his hand in mine a few times before he would do it. But pretty soon he would do it when I tapped my hand and said "Give!" At first this happened without eye contact but then he started to look at me.

MRS. H: Later, I discovered that if he was jumping up and down on the bed and I stood in front of him that he would begin to look at me each time he jumped up and down. This happened when he was excited and I was with him and held his hands as he jumped up and down (while the mother remained still).

MR. H: And I learned also that if he wanted a cookie—my wife reminded me to do as she had learned at the Center—to get right down to his eye level and say his name softly so that when he looked up he would look both at me and the cookie. And through this we started getting the eye contact. . . . It just started to develop.

MRS. H: And even with the bottle, K said, "Don't just leave the bottle on the table. Make him see—by presenting it so he looks at you and the bottle—where it is coming from." And another thing she suggested: "Don't give him a whole bunch of food at one time. Give him a little bit so that he has to keep coming back to you for more." So I do that with different foods that he enjoys.

Improved Social Contact

AM: Have you noticed any changes in his relationships with other people?

Mr. H: At first he very much enjoyed being a spectator. I would chase my little girl around the house, and he thought that was the greatest. But I could not get him to join in. He would laugh and hoot and howl and think that that was terrific stuff but not join in to go around. A couple of times though when we did it, he would join in a little bit. He would go halfway around the room and stop. But primarily, he enjoyed watching it and jumping up and down on his trampoline.

Mrs. H: In the past 2 days—where it's been very hot—I've taken him and his sister into the little wading pool in the backyard. And this is *the first time he ever chased his sister around the backyard with the garden hose, trying to get her wet.* He was doing to her the same thing she had done to him in the past. And that was the first time I had seen him chasing her. And he was enjoying himself. This was not to hurt her. This was actually the first time that *he* was the one who initiated the game.

Also he and his sister now hug a lot. She has taught him to hug. And he loves to hug her. Unfortunately, at the playground, he now goes to girls the same size as his sister and tries to hug them. And they don't know what is going on. But I look at it this way: He's a 3-year-old boy. And he's certainly allowed to hug other children. And if the other children want to get freaked out, then it's their thing.

AM: Earlier, you said that any change of clothes or touching him would cause upset. How does that tie in with the hugging?

Mrs. H: The hugging is only 3 months old.

Mr. H: He now hugs me too. He enjoys coming over and being picked up by his dad and being very, very much hugged.

Mrs. H: But earlier on we couldn't get a jacket on, boots, or anything that touched him. I wasn't able to get boots on him until the end of the season. I would get them big so they would go on easy. With regard to the hugging, there are *still* times when he doesn't want to be touched. Especially at night when he's tired. And he will push his father away. And he will push his sister away. And this happens very quickly. She doesn't always understand this. She never listens to me. And eventually she'll engage him in play. But he really doesn't want that play. He wants to be left alone. So he pushes her away.

Mr. H: This happens when he is tired. I can play with him. He can enjoy the roughhousing and everything. But then you can tell. Or usually my wife can tell. And that's it. He wants to lie down on the bed and he doesn't want to be touched.

AM: Earlier, Mr. H, you commented that *now* you had a son. When did you begin to feel that way?

MR. H: When he came here 6 months ago, I had no relationship with my son whatsoever. None. No matter what I tried to do, I just did not exist for him. If I went into the back room where he was playing with an object and I started playing with that object—nothing. He wouldn't even turn away and go to some other object. He wouldn't even give me *that*. He would just stand there until I went away and then he would continue his play. It was like my presence was part of a dream for him. And if there was a block on the other side of my body that he needed, he would just step on me to get it as if I were stairs or something. I was nothing more than part of the sofa if I was sitting there. When I came home from work, if he was in the kitchen, there was never any response related to whether I had come or gone. I could've been hanging upside down. It wouldn't have made any difference. There was absolutely no contact whatsoever, no recognition, no anything.

MRS. H: And there was no name for you either.

MR. H: I really totally did not exist. And he would not allow me to snuggle up with him, give him a hug or pick him up.

MRS. H: What he would do. . . . His grandfather came once a week to visit and my father would be more aggressive with him and reach out and want to pick him up to hold him. And Jack would get fearful and run in a corner whenever he came in the house.

MR. H: I didn't want that to happen so I didn't push it too much. You know, you try subtly to insert yourself but that didn't work.

Only after we started at LCDC did things start to change. We learned how to get eye contact by using the object at eye level with him while saying, "Here! (offering the object) Jack!" But most progress started to happen when you suggested that I be physical with him, bounce him up and down, do Rough and Tumble with him. That was very important. We found that he loved that and that it broke down the barriers. And now he enjoys a very physical contact with his dad. He likes to hug his dad. . . .

MRS. H: To jump on and ride on your shoulders . . .

MR. H: And I notice now a lot of times if I'm lying down, napping before I go to work, he will get up and snuggle next to me for a while.

AM: So you began to exist for him through the Rough and Tumble.

MR. H: Very much so. Now, I feel—considering Jack's disability—that I have a very, very good relationship with him. I am very, very happy with it. There is no question in my mind that the Rough and Tumble was the turning point . . . I had started to make some small progress as he started to open up a little bit. But it was the Rough and Tumble—the physical contact—that within 3 or 4 days changed his entire attitude toward me. He started coming over to me and wanting to play with me while before (laughs) I just wasn't there.

MRS. H: Before, when I walked into the house, I literally had to pick him up and put his eyes in front of mine. And then I would get a hug. Now, not only does he come to me when I come in the house but when his father comes to the door, he jumps up and down saying "Da-da, Da-da, Da-da."

MR. H: (smiling) We've really come a long way. I mean . . . I understood the problem . . . but that doesn't make it easier. It really doesn't. So I am absolutely thrilled now that I have a little boy—in spite of his problems—with whom we have a close, feeling relationship. We can touch and hug, and he gives us back a lot.

ANNA, AN AUTISTIC CHILD WITH A SYSTEM-FORMING DISORDER

The next child, Anna, was diagnosed autistic with a system-forming disorder at the age of 4 years 8 months. Anna has been attending the Center's school with various individual C-D system-related services for 22 months. She demonstrates a form of autism very different from Jack's and, prior to beginning with the Center, she showed a familiar pattern of first gaining and then losing language. Finally, the work with Anna demonstrates how C-D systems intervention varies with the kind of system disorder a child presents: An autistic child with a system-forming disorder such as Anna's must be treated very differently from Jack, an autistic child with a closed-system disorder.

The section begins with excerpts from an interview with Anna's mother, Mrs. J, relating to her daughter's early developmental history. This is followed by descriptions of collaborative C-D systems work with Anna and her current status.

Anna's Developmental History

AM: Can you describe Anna's birth and early development?

MRS. J: Anna was born at term, weighing 5 pounds 15 ounces, after an uneventful pregnancy. She was born quickly . . . in less than 5 minutes. The first concern I had was that she did not have a very strong sucking instinct. I was a new mother so I didn't know much about breast feeding either. She certainly didn't suck like my next two children did and that's for sure. She didn't want to take the nipple. She'd slobber a little bit there but didn't make any effort to latch on. You hold it there and you hold her, but she has to do the job finally. And she didn't. . . . So in that sense there already was some difficulty in making contact. . . . Anna became jaundiced the 2nd day after she was born so they put her under the lights for 3 days. I think what was there was there before (referring to Anna's autism), but who is to say that that didn't exacerbate things.

AM: Did her light treatments interfere with you seeing her?

MRS. J: I was in the hospital and I was looking at her and holding her sometimes but not what. . . . Now, looking back again I wouldn't let them do it. I would insist on being under the lights too if we had to do it.

AM: You would've wanted to hold her more?

MRS. J: Yes . . . it was horrible. I was crying all the time. They're telling you it's nothing serious, but meanwhile they're taking your baby away. Not a very nice experience.

Subsequently, Mrs. J reported motor milestones that suggested a slight delay, with Anna crawling at 8 months and walking at 16 months. Verbal development was more delayed with the first use of syllables at about 15 months of age and up to 20 words used inconsistently up to about 24 months of age. Between 30 and 42 months she lost the ability to use these words, and phrase speech did not develop. She would become unusually excited riding in an elevator or when tossed up into the air, and particularly before 4 years of age she often seemed unaware of bumps or falls that would be painful to most children.

Mrs. J also described Anna's difficulty sleeping and her need to rock and walk with her for hours to comfort her. When she finally fell asleep for a couple of hours, she would "jolt awake—screaming."

MRS. J: "I didn't think it was abnormal, but I remember my mother saying later that it scared her because she had had 5 kids and none had been like that."

AM: She was very slow to take comfort.

MRS. J: It sounded like terror. . . . Eventually she would become exhausted . . . and that continued for about a year. When she was 11 months old, I remember her crying inside her room and me sitting outside, crying. I think it made our relationship different. I was not as connected to Anna as I am to my other kids—between the problems with breast feeding and the screaming. . . . Your child teaches you how to parent. And Anna didn't teach us how to do it. So it didn't happen the way it should have. We were gone more than I would ever be from my other two kids because she didn't seem to mind. She was oblivious to who was holding her, basically. Or sometimes she would seem to prefer you but it didn't bother her to have you replaced. So you just continued about your life—particularly if you are not breast feeding.

Comparing her with my youngest daughter makes me realize how different she was. My youngest daughter is 7 weeks old and for the past week or two she has just been actively seeking communication with me. It's really amazing. I know Anna didn't do that. Because that's what builds up the closeness. She smiles at you and makes lots of sounds in her effort to keep you with her. And you get a conversation going. And it's clear that she's determined to keep you with her. And if you turned away she would try to get you back either by crying or trying to entertain you. And Anna never did that.

AM: So you felt like you were always giving but not getting much back.

MRS. J: Yes. With Anna that's how it was. She was so little that people expected less of her. She lagged, but it wasn't so apparent because she was so tiny. But there were moments . . . another child was born a month before Anna so we got together with the family on his birthday. He would go to a radio and turn it on and off, explore it, try to take it apart a little bit. And Anna never did anything like that. She never had that desire to really look into something. She'd go around to things and kind of touch things and see things and run around a lot. But I never saw her sit with something and get into it in a kind of intellectual way I guess . . . I became increasingly concerned.

AM: What was the main alarm signal?

MRS. J: The main thing was she didn't understand anything. She didn't speak. . . . She used some words—"Mama," "Dada," and "bye-bye"—appropriately. And sometimes she said, "Hi!" or "Hi there!" But receptively she was not good. She started getting some, but her ability to be word guided or to follow your gesture or intention wasn't there. We never knew whether she would do what we asked or not. You call her but can never be sure whether or not she will come. Her response was very inconsistent to any sounds or noises. Little sounds would set her off, but big sounds she would quite ignore. The predictability was always uncertain. If she was tuned in at that particular moment she might do what you asked her. But she could just as well be tuned out.

Events Leading to Referral

Mrs. J then described the manner in which she and her husband had sought help for their daughter from various professionals. Her pediatrician, after repeatedly telling her not to worry, finally referred her to a psychologist (Anna was aged 2 at the time) who diagnosed the difficulty as a parent–child problem. Mother described the traumatic effect this diagnosis had on her (discussed in Chapter 12) and how she withdrew completely from Anna for fear that her contact would only harm her child further. Further complicating the situation were marital difficulties and plans for a divorce. The family separated for several weeks—the father going to the West Coast with Anna in the care of a nanny—while the mother remained on the East Coast.

Mrs. J reported that Anna seemed very dislocated in her new home and, even after the mother returned, tantrummed a great deal and seemed depressed. It was in the year that followed—from 30 to 42 months of age—that Anna gradually lost the 20 or so words that she had acquired. During this period another psychologist diagnosed her as mentally retarded, which somewhat relieved Mrs. J's feeling that she was responsible for her child's disorder. Following this, Anna was evaluated at a major West Coast facility and diagnosed as autistic. Her mother then contacted the Autism Society of America, attended the annual conference, and was impressed by a presentation there (Miller & Miller, 1986). As a result, Mr. and Mrs. J arranged for an evaluation of their daughter at LCDC in Boston and then decided to move to Boston so that Anna could be enrolled in the Center's cognitive-developmental systems program.

In the next section Anna's Umwelt Assessment is summarized.

Umwelt Assessment

Anna, a petite, beautiful child, possessed minimal system-forming capacity. She had learned some motoric things—and could run, jump, climb, and (according to her parents) even swim and roller skate—but she couldn't organize herself around objects unless she made direct body contact with them. When she collided with something, like a step when going up the stairs, she could deal with it. Thus, she successfully avoided most holes on the Swiss Cheese Board although she couldn't integrate that with attending to her mother calling her at the other end. She didn't throw things like Fred or clutch objects in her hand like Jack, nor did she have any obsessive interest in objects. She would just flit or float with a sweet smile from one thing to another, never engaging with the object. If she picked up something, she would at the same time be looking at something else. And when that happened, she would lose contact with, and allow to fall, anything she had in her hands. Eyes and hands rarely got together. Also what she picked up seemed to have little meaning or function for her—it had momentarily caught her eye and so she picked it up. Periodically, she would get stuck looking at something—like an exit sign or a pattern on a curtain—away from her body.

In an important sense she behaved as if she were both blind and deaf, even though these sense organs were intact. Even when she picked up an object and looked at it, she did so like a blind person (see Chapter 3, p. 81). She didn't seem to attend to the properties of the object. For example, when stacking cups, if she couldn't immediately get the upside-down cup that had been given her to go into the right-side-up cup, she would keep pounding cup against cup in a futile effort to get it to stack. There was no real interest in the contours of the cup as a unique form although after a number of repetitions, she *did* learn to invert a couple of bowls so they could stack. And she wasn't interested in pictures or, in general, in patterns or colors. Analogously, she often failed to respond to loud sounds: One could stand directly behind her and shout her name and she would fail to turn toward the sound source. Yet, at other times according to her parents, she would delight in funny sounds made by a kazoo or a toy guitar.

Striking, also, was her slack eye–hand coordination to achieve a particular end. In putting a cup on a hook, for example, she would put the cup in the general vicinity of the cup hook and then look away as she hit all around the hook, the cup handle getting together with the hook only by accident. A similar lack of eye–hand precision, as well as understanding of how tools and detours work, was evident on the Croupier task where she could pull an object closer only when it was placed within the arm of the rake. She was quite unable to adjust the rake to pull closer an object to one side of the rake or to use the rake to work the object around a barrier. Allowed to do as she wished for 2 minutes, she gravitated to the elevated boards and efficiently climbed to their highest position 7–8 feet above the ground. During this period she was totally preoccupied with the climbing and showed no interest in people.

She seemed to vaguely recognize her parents and to be mildly pleased when they were around. But Anna did not cling to her mother like Jack, or tantrum when the parents left the room. That she could anticipate events to some degree was evident in her ability, with support, to climb over the Anticipation Board to get to her mother or father. However, on one occasion while straddling the board preparatory to crossing, a slight lateral movement of the board diverted her into rocking from side to side so that she lost contact with her goal of reaching her parents. She lacked picture recognition, but her behavior on one occasion suggested symbolic capacity as she put a cloth (simulating a blanket) on her head before putting it on the toy dog she was supposed to cover and put to bed. She uttered no words during the session.

C-D SYSTEMS–RELATED THERAPIES

Treatment Goals

The various C-D systems related therapies in which Anna participated included two 1-hour sessions per week of C-D systems therapy in which the mother or mother and father participated, 30 minutes per week of speech therapy, and two 30-minute sessions per week of movement therapy. During the remainder of her school week she participated in a language-oriented curriculum (Chapter 9). Although there is overlap among the different therapies, each has its particular emphasis. All therapies related to the following treatment goals for Anna:

Because Anna lacked functional systems with objects, a primary goal of C-D systems therapy was to help her organize her scattered behavior around and with objects. Once she had an improved framework of object relations, a second goal was to help her find meaning in signs and pictures related to objects. A third goal was to help her relate to people and to people–object combinations.

Speech and language-oriented C-D systems work was introduced to improve her sound making and to help her operate reciprocally using sign, sound, and pictures to understand and communicate intentions.

Movement therapy was introduced to enhance her reactivity to people and to promote those reciprocal exchanges that provide the framework for social and language exchanges between people.

Movement Therapy

The following summary, written by AG, movement therapist, and edited for this chapter, suggests the utility of this approach and its compatibility with C-D systems theory. These sessions began after Anna had attended LCDC for a year.

Initial Impressions

I meet Anna as she is accompanied into the school by her mother. She often has her hair done up with a ribbon and wears a smock which adds to her doll-like delicacy. Anna does not look at me directly during the transition from outside to the therapy room. At times she takes my hand but often leads the way—gingerly navigating her way through several changes of direction—to my therapy room. As she approaches my room, she often quickens her steps and scampers past the door and into the adjacent speech therapy room. However, there are days that she walks directly to the right room.

Anna's Use of Unstructured Space

During the first few weeks of therapy Anna wandered around the room not paying any attention to the empty space in the middle. She tended to walk around the periphery wiping her hand along the walls; the mirror was treated as just another wall. She tested and manipulated anything that moved, other than the therapist, including toys, chairs, the table, and the shelves. During the first few weeks there were several objects purposely left in the room such as two balls, two telephones, a drum, and two chairs. Anna would focus all of her attention on these objects, their surfaces, and their range of movement, and showed no interest in other aspects of the room. However, as these objects were gradually eliminated over the weeks, Anna began to explore the more permanent aspects of the room. She climbed onto the empty shelf and onto the table. She looked into the one-way mirror and the other large mirror and used the middle of the room to gallop and spin.

Anna's Interaction with Objects

When there is an object that attracts Anna in the room, she studies it intently. Although she is doing this less at the present time, Anna takes every object to her mouth first, feeling it with her lips and tongue, and often gnaws at it with her teeth. She would take a chair, for example, tip it over, tap on all of its surfaces, scratch it, and suck on the vinyl seat covering. With the balls and the drum she would bang them into her face. (It seems that this sort of intensive, sensory collision is what Anna needs to take in and get to know an object.)

Response to Mirroring

I play the role of a mirror of Anna's movements and vocalizations, using my own body. At first Anna seemed oblivious to my presence. Her systems include only her own actions and her episodic involvement with objects. Working close to her, I would mirror her various actions. After I had mirrored Anna for 10 sessions, her systems began to include me:

Before, in Anna's "jumping system" she jumped and I jumped. We were not connected. Now her jumping system includes me. She takes my hands, and we jump together.

Before, Anna would play with the light switch. Then in the darkness she would gallop in circles around the center of the room. Now, once the light is out, she takes my hand and gallops with me.

Before, Anna would merely look at the colorful cloth picture on the wall. Now she puts her arms up for me to lift her to the picture. Once she has access to the picture, she taps on it with her hand. I answer by tapping her hand from the other side of the picture. She taps my hand in return . . .

Before, Anna would lie under the cloth picture and tap on the floor. And, although I was lying right next to her, she would not look at me. Lately, Anna has begun to gaze into my eyes. This sort of interaction occurs one to three times during the course of a session.

Expanding Anna's Interactive Systems

Initially, Anna made no response to my attempts to expand her interactive systems. Recently, however, she has accepted some expansions. Two examples of this follow:

Previously, Anna would climb on the table and then attempt to get down on her own. To expand the getting-on-and-off-table system, I spun around with Anna before putting her back on the floor. As I spin her, she hugs me while smiling and closing her eyes. . . . Now, when she wants to get down from the table she motions for me to help her down.

Previously, Anna galloped around the room on her own and stopped when she felt like it to go on to something else. I expanded upon Anna's galloping system by tapping the rhythm of her gallop on the floor. Now Anna is able to use this galloping sound as a signal to resume her galloping and to leave a different activity in which she has been engaged.

Summary

Anna now uses the whole room, the middle and the walls. She has begun to initiate interaction with me and is increasingly responsive to my attempts to expand her interactive systems. Further, she now shows greater awareness of herself—approaching and reacting to her reflection in the mirror with smiles and touches.

C-D Systems Therapy

This section includes the key points of AM's interview with K, C-D systems therapist, concerning her work with Anna and her mother.

AM: What was your primary concern with Anna when you started with her almost 2 years ago?

K: Because she was so scattered and unrelated to either things or people, my primary concern was to get her involved with her surroundings. She had such little interest in doing things that we had to generate some kind of excitement for her. We had to introduce a contagious quality for her. If you got her excited and focused on a particular task, you could get her to do things. With Anna you spent a lot of time setting up contagious activity to get her built up to the point that her motor was turning over. And then you tried to connect her up to different things.

One way of generating this contagious excitement was through Rough and Tumble, which she loved. I soon learned that she did best with all those things that impinged directly on her body and required a strong, whole body response. My task was to build on this kind of experience so that she could eventually deal with objects without requiring total body involvement. In trying to get her to do various tasks, I always had the sense of her having "limp hands." But if I did hand–over–hand and guided her, she would get upset. Then she would make her "all finished" gesture. And people took that very seriously. If we did not, she could become self-abusive—banging her head on the ground and biting. But you could bring her back by compressing her and working her around with swinging and Rough and Tumble.

Initial Spheres That Exploited Anna's Need for Whole Body Response

AM: What were the first spheres you used with Anna?

K: One of the things she was interested in was the car. And she became interested because I used to pull up her shirt and "drive" the car across her stomach going "brrrr." She liked that, and then I would interrupt by quickly putting the car away—hiding it. And then she would try to get the car, and I would pull up her shirt and go "brrrr" again. This procedure helped her anticipate an event that was going to be repeated. When I started with her, she had no anticipation. She then, after a number of repetitions, began to lift up her shirt so the car could be run with sound across her stomach. That was one of the first intentional things—around the car—but it had to be exciting.

Another task that engaged her in this way was dropping blocks in a bucket of water so it would splash vigorously. She seemed compelled to put herself—her foot, her hand—in the water rather than merely to drop the block. When she poured sand in a bucket, she needed to put her hand in the sand stream so she could feel the flow. She was less interested in the more remote throwing or pouring the objects into a container than she was in feeling the flow on her body or in having direct experience of the water or sand by putting her body directly in it. Nevertheless, we did get her to throw the object a few times. Just as she did better when the car was directly on her body, so she seemed drawn to experiencing other materials directly on her body before she could somewhat detach from them. Apparently, seeing others perform an activity—or even herself performing the activity—did not provide strong enough feedback for her. But seeing-feeling the event was more effective for her and gave her more a sense of that event. This was particularly true when the event had a contagious quality.

AM: Where did you go after these initial spheres?

K: Once she became more focused, we started by engaging her in two-step *integrative/interactive* spheres. The base activity consisted of Anna orienting to a parent, receiving an object—block, peg, or small toy—and turning to me for guidance in throwing or dropping it into a bucket of water. Anna quickly began to internalize the sphere as evident in her anticipating both receiving and throwing the object. In the beginning, we would work on only one object–one action at a time. She would, for example, get pegs and put them in the pegboard, or cards and drop them in the mailbox, or pennies and put them in a jar. Then, during the first 2 months, we gradually expanded to seven or eight objects, all with their different containers and somewhat different actions. Her success depended on keeping the distance between the steps (getting and dealing with the object) very short, keeping distracting stimuli at a minimum, and maintaining a relatively fast tempo of getting and dealing with the object. If the distance between steps was too great, she would revert to infantile engagement with the object by shaking or mouthing it or allowing the object simply to drop from her hand.

Following this, we began to introduce three- or four-step integrative spheres such as picking up a toy dog, opening the door of a toy house, and putting the dog inside, or dealing with the same object in different ways so that Anna could experience a familiar object in terms of its varied properties. For example, she learned that she could pour from a cup, hang it on a hook, and stack it.

AM: When did she begin to use signs?

K: Signs developed a couple of months into our work when we interrupted well-established systems. I remember Mrs. J's amazement and disbelief when she saw her daughter make her first intentional sign—*open*. But soon Anna could use other signs such as *give* and *come* in a variety of settings and activities and always with the intent of getting an object. Other signs that rapidly followed were *up, down, drink, eat, cracker,* and *shoe*. Toward the end of our first year of work she added new signs—based on interruption of her actual contact with objects—for *guitar, jack-in-the-box, bird, drums,* and *whisk*. I remember when she was playing the guitar, we would take the guitar away and she would produce the strumming sign that was similar to the gesture she used to play the guitar. And that was the way we got all of the signs. However, she could maintain these signs only by daily and systematic repetition in the classroom during speech and language sessions and in the C-D work parents conducted at home.

AM: Earlier, we spoke of Anna's functional blindness. How did you help her see better?

K: The work described earlier, where she had to do different things with objects that helped define their properties, certainly helped her see the objects better. But one particularly useful task was working with a balloon. By pulling, blowing, pushing the balloon, and holding it in her hand while the air went out, Anna learned to see it in different ways. Often she had to collide with an object before it existed for her. It had to be dramatic. She had to feel it on her body. Then, once she had dealt with the object in these dramatic terms, she could *see* it. Before that work if she came into the room and the balloon was on the floor, she might ignore it; or if you put it in her hand, she would let it go and drop it. So she really didn't see the balloon until she experienced its various properties . . . in very much the way you have described functional blindness (Chapter 3, p. 81). The object's various properties have to be experienced before it exists as something that can be seen out there in space by itself.

But that by itself was not enough. She needed to find a way to separate her body involvement with an object from the object itself. And for that the Elevated Square was of great value.

AM: How did the Elevated Square help her see?

K: The issue for Anna was never just seeing—but seeing herself in relation to the object as she dealt with the same object differently. The Elevated Square was important because there she could establish a system with an object in a contagious manner and then separate parts of that system. For example, working contagiously at one location, she would rapidly pick up and drop blocks as part of one excited glob of activity. During such activity she had no sense of what it meant to pick up an object *deliberately* and drop it. So once she could contagiously pick up and drop blocks in one location, I sought spatial separation between each part of the task: picking up blocks at one station, then dropping them at another station a few feet away.

Working with her like this on the Elevated Square—making her pick up *and then delay* the dropping by walking from A to B—helped her see and anticipate the things that she was going to do before doing it. It also helped her understand that the block that she picked up in one place had the potential for being dropped in another. What normal children gain quite automatically, she had to have structured for her in this way. The picking up had to be distinct from the dropping. If she did it too closely together, then there was no picking up and no dropping—it was just a doing something that she couldn't keep and transfer to other situations that were not contagious.

Prior to C-D systems work with her, such fusions were the rule: She did a lot of mouthing with objects and a lot of bodily excitement that went nowhere. Only when we began to help separate her body actions from the objects with which these actions were engaged did she begin to "keep" these objects and the actions that went with them. It certainly was the beginning of getting behavior that helped her both function with and see the object.

AM: Did anything else help her see and deal with objects better?

K: The use of broken objects also played a part. Each time she had to put together a broken object—a cup, ball, dog—she had to notice how one part of the object related to the other. We accented the object parts even further by dividing them between stations (Figure 8.3). For example, if she had the handle part of the cup on one station and the remainder on another station, she had to rush from one to the other to restore the cup. She did the same thing with the head of the dog on one station and its body on the other. Even though she did it in a rather fuzzy way, she did know where the head of the dog should go. And that helped her put together the object.

But contagious activity always made it easier for her to connect different parts of the object. Because she was readily caught up by the contagious activity of pouring rice from a cup and she couldn't pour rice from half a cup, she developed an even more urgent need to put the cup together. Similarly, there was some contagion around rolling a ball and she couldn't roll half a ball, so she felt compelled to restore the ball and then roll it. But really she got most excited about the dog and putting the head on the body.

Because she continued to have difficulty accurately coordinating eye–hand activity so necessary in putting together parts of an object,

Figure 8.3. Anna completing a broken cup on the Elevated Square.

you and I designed a series of object puzzles on wires—where she needed only to push the object parts along the wire for the object to come together (Figure 8.4). In this way we sought to train eyes and hands to work together more effectively. Objects we built for this purpose included a car, a person, a hand, and a face. Once Anna could put the various forms together on the wires, we removed them so she could put them together without this support.

The strongest puzzle we did was the one with the face. About a month ago—working without wire support—she started getting one eye in the right place and the mouth in the right place. But the first time I picked up the face and held it in my hands she went "Da-da-da!" very excited. So that crazy-looking puzzle has turned out to be useful. But she did it first on the wires with a lot of gusto when she put it together.

The Role of Drawing and Painting

AM: How did drawing help in her development?

K: She did a lot of wall drawings with the markers. She would go to her mother or father to get a marker, take off the cap, then start scribbling on the paper stretched across the wall. Then I would take her marker so that she would have to get another one. And she really did become more aware of the whole causality—that she's making a mark. . . . And those markings changed from scribbles to nice circles and lines and with bright colors. And she has gotten to stay inside the paper; she knows very well when she strays and I say "On the paper!" so that she colors the paper instead of the wall. And so she learned about visual properties and boundaries through spheres involving the markers.

This new awareness came about—at least in part—from the way she learned to translate body actions intentionally into marks on the paper. She was holding a marker, and it had to be a big marker that made a really heavy mark on the paper. And I let her have a large area so that

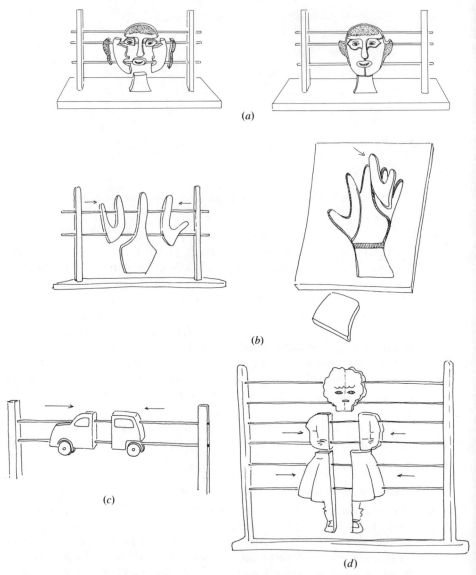

Figure 8.4. Broken objects and body parts on wire frames: (a) Head; (b) Hand (on and off wire frame); (c) Car; (d) Doll.

she could hold the marker and see the mark as she ran across the length of the room—paper covered the entire wall—with a crayon or marker in her hand. And I did it with interruptions. I would get her going, then stop her abruptly and take her crayon or marker away from her so that she would have to go to the mother to get another crayon or marker.

And I used markers that were very responsive to pressure so that even the slightest pressure left a big mark on the paper.

Now I conceal the paint under different items in the room and instruct her verbally and with signs, "Pick up the hat and get the paint." She really has begun to follow those directions very carefully and accurately. And I will also do things like giving her a paint brush and having the paint jar on the floor in front of her. . . . Her immediate impulse, of course, is to put the brush in the jar. I now require that she delay that impulse by first picking up the paint jar and putting it on the table before she can put the brush in. At first I really had to hold her because she so urgently needs to put the brush in the jar. . . . You could feel the tension of her body driving toward putting the brush in the jar—which conflicted with my direction—and she would at first resist. . . . And now I have gotten her to defer that need and pick up the jar *before* putting the brush in.

Another thing I did was to put six paint jars in a row and five would be empty. So she would have to scan and assess each jar to see which one had paint in it before she ran to it. I have also put tape over the holes in the paint jars so that she can't put the paint brush in. So she has learned very quickly to remove the tape in order to put the brush inside.

Now we see how directed and focused she is painting on a smaller area . . . less scattered and more form properties to her painting in contrast to even last month. And I think that her visual awareness— the ability to see things away from her body—has been helped by her drawing and that it might have been one of the turning points in helping her begin to distinguish the shape of one thing from another.

Picture Recognition

AM: In what ways have you used pictures in treating Anna?

K: Along with this, we worked on picture recognition. But I really don't think the interest in pictures came until she first had more of an interest in the object. If you can't see the object, you certainly can't see the picture. She was excited first by certain pictures because of their patterns or because they moved . . . but they didn't have much meaning. Thinking about it, I think the 3D/2D shift from dog to dog picture was probably—if not her first picture—among her first.

Now pictures are going very well—quite a large picture vocabulary. I work it like this. I put up pictures of an orange, a knife, a squeezer, and a cup. And now I ask her what she wants and she usually goes to the orange first—pointing. And then I randomize the order. Then I ask her what she needs. And she points to a cup. Then I ask her again, and she points to the knife and makes the knife sign. And she is just starting to get the function of the knife and to press down and see the knife cut the orange. Before you would have to take her hand and do it, but it was meaningless because she wasn't engaged with the task—the hand would be on the knife, but her eyes would be elsewhere. So then the orange is in half. And I ask again, what she needs and she points to the squeezer. Then she helps to squeeze it, and when I ask again she points to the cup.

AM: How does her use of signs compare with her use of pictures?

K: It's funny. Her expressive use of signs is not as well grounded as her response to pictures. It's almost as if she has difficulty with the recall. Sometimes she goes through all her signs when she wants a particular one. But with pictures she doesn't do that. Even though the signs might seem to be more grounded in the body than pictures—action being a body function—they are not. She has trouble retrieving signs in the same way she has trouble retrieving the sounds or words she needs for a particular situation. She has made a lot of specific sounds at specific times but does not yet *own* them. Perhaps because she never knows when she is going to be capable of producing them. But then, she gets the sign when it is in the context of the visible object to which the action relates—such as the strumming sign for the guitar—but she has great difficulty bringing it up in the absence of the object.

AM: With pictures she doesn't have to retrieve the meaningful symbol to derive meaning from it—it's given—but with signs and spoken words she does. The proof of this is that when someone else produces signs or words to guide her behavior she has no problem relating signs or words to the relevant objects or events. So it's clearly an issue of retrieval.

K: You're right. Her receptive understanding *has* become much stronger. And she's holding the meanings of signs and words much better. Therefore, I think with work the other stuff will come. Today, for example, she wanted to continue banging so I took the little stick she was using and put it under a hat and asked her with sign and word to pick up the hat. Then she went to the hat and picked it up to get the stick. Then I had it in a purse. I said, "You go and open the purse . . . open . . ." And she would go and open the purse. There is no way she could've done this even 2 months ago.

Anna's Sign-Word Guidance Outside of Repetitive Spheres

AM: Do you feel her understanding of sign-words is being expanded beyond its use in spheres?

K: You know her actions are not sign-word guided as part of a repetitive sphere. These tasks are really quite arbitrary and she does them without the support of a repetitive context. It is out of the system. Without redundancy I say "Go to the purse and open it," and she is now able to do it. I just hide it arbitrarily all of a sudden. And that is very new.

Before she would have a block in her hand and I would repetitively say "It goes in the box" after having done it 10 to 15 times. So for the *first time* she follows one-shot directions—like a normal child—without sphere support. Although I understand, of course, that it has to be a familiar object.

AM: Are there other objects she can do this with?

K: Well, she has done it when I hide the brush when she is painting. I would say, "The brush is in the pot." First I would assist by pointing, but later I would not and simply say, "Pick up the lid of the pot." And she would scan the room to find the purse, the tube, the pot, in the house, under the hat. Before she can do this, however, she must be engaged with the object; otherwise, removing it has little meaning, and she will not make the effort.

AM: Her use of the brush means that she was in the painting system and now needs to find the brush in order to continue that system. If you removed the entire system—paint, paper, and brush—it's not clear whether she could retrieve the various parts. However, as long as she is oriented toward painting (paper and easel present) she has a framework for being sign-word guided to find the paint or to get the brush. . . . So she is still system related. But what you are doing is teaching her how to retrieve things from the environment. It is easier to retrieve things from the environment than it is to retrieve things (signs, words) from within oneself. She must first learn how to retrieve things from outside herself before she can retrieve things like signs and words from inside herself.

K: Then she may well be on her way to solving her retrieval problem. She certainly shows increased intentionality, improved sign-word guidance, and better picture recognition. And she uses what she has learned to get the things she needs. Unlike Jack who wants the name but doesn't yet use it to get things, Anna is using what symbol structure she has to guide her functioning and to communicate.

AM: One of Anna's major difficulties when she started with us concerned the detached quality of her relationships with people. How have you tried to help her with this?

K: I have tackled this problem indirectly by getting her involved in tasks that require her going to people. Even in the earliest spheres she had to go to her mother or father to get something and then bring it to me so she could find out what to do with the object.

Certain objects were particularly useful in getting her to relate and to use her mouth functionally. The best such object was the balloon. In the beginning she could not blow the balloon up although she clearly wanted to do so. To get it blown up, therefore, she had to hand the balloon to her mother or to me. In this way we fostered some important interactive behavior around the balloon, handing it to one of us, getting it blown, handing it back to her. She started to put the balloon to the mouth of one of us. She knew that the mouth (not the person) had something to do with getting it blown up. And that was a very good interactive sphere for her.

Following this we got her to take turns with blowing bubbles and using the kazoo. We started with the musical instruments—she liked music. She learned how to blow bubbles. The balloon picked up more meaning because she was starting to develop a blowing function. And she enjoyed it. The excitement around the balloon was such that she would open things to get it. Then, she would hand it to you for inflating. Once it was filled with air, she would slowly let the air out. Then we would put it somewhere else—away from her body—and she would get it and bring it back to be blown up again, and so on.

AM: The balloon was clearly an important vehicle for developing more complex interactive/integrative spheres with her.

K: It certainly was. She would turn to the person, get the object, and do something with it. It got to be quite intentional. When I started hanging up the balloons on the rope that's when I got very, very intentional pointing from Anna. She would point to that balloon with great urgency saying, "bu . . . bu . . . bu . . ." And then when she got it she would be very happy. And she would hold it and let the air out. And then I could expand it by having her untie things to get to the balloon, and I got her to blow it up and we hung up the balloon with the clothespins. So I did some spheres around the balloons. And the spheres were around balloons and bubbles that got integrated both with the puzzle and with the objects.

Interactive Window

AM: Have you used any other kinds of equipment that have produced similar responses?

K: Another important tool for helping her interact more appropriately is the Interactive Window that you designed (Figure 8.5). The window has been good because it taps into her own body actions of moving and drawing. When the other person starts to move with her . . . it makes a certain tension because of the glass between the two people. It's like the distance between the stations. It separates the people but it cuts out the fusion . . . makes the other person more distinct. . . . It just outlines the other person.

AM: Does she react to the other person's movements on the other side of the window?

K: To some extent. It's helped her become much more aware of her mother. . . . She becomes more aware because Mrs. J (on the other side of the window) is isolated from physical contact and only presents a moving image for her to relate to. It makes the mother a moving picture. Its first effect has been to have Anna stay with the task longer.

Figure 8.5. Mother and Anna drawing on the Interactive Window.

It has made her watch her mother. It has resulted in her making partial imitations or responses to her mother's movements. And, when the mother makes something really exciting—like dot patterns on her side of the window—Anna sees and hears it and is drawn toward producing that pattern.

Mrs. J is really very imaginative in play with Anna. Everything has to be exciting for Anna . . . by sound, by color, and by movement. Sometimes the mother would follow her and play little tricks on her . . . unexpected moves. And in this way Anna has gotten very interested both in her mother and in painting on that window.

AM: How would you now describe Anna's relationship with her mother?

K: Anna shows dramatically improved contact with her mother and very much comes to her. She snuggles into her lap. Her whole awareness of her mother is different. When she is sad, she goes to her mother, throws her arms around her, and she looks at her much more. There is a difference in quality. She has much more attachment with her mother. It is now easier for Mrs. J to keep on giving because she is getting something back.

Speech and Language Therapy

This section discusses the course of speech and language therapy by EC, speech and language therapist, which began 5 months after Anna started LCDC and which has continued systematically over the past 17 months. She was interviewed by her supervisor (EE-M).

EE-M: What was your first goal with Anna and how did you attempt to realize it?

EC: My first goal with Anna was to get reciprocal activity from her. I did this by handing her things—musical instruments in which she was really interested. I had harmonicas, kazoos . . . I also had causal toys that involved her mouth: little spinner toys that she could blow and cause to spin around, . . . I had jack-in-the-boxes, I had cymbals, I had drums, I had a banjo . . . a variety of instruments. And I would involve these in a trade: You give me this one, and I will give you that one. Just to get some back and forth going.

First it was just handing her things and letting her play with them. Then, as she became engaged with these things I began to play with something different—in effect competing with her interest in the thing she had at hand. If she looked up and expressed some interest, then I would pull her hand from her thing and put my instrument in it.

This was not as smooth as it sounds. Anna was difficult to engage. She had a very short attention span. She was easily distractible, didn't stay with anything, and things would drop out of her hands.

EE-M: How did you get her to hold the things you gave her?

EC: It just started to happen as a result of the C-D work she was having with K. Also K and I would coordinate a lot. Sometimes I would repeat some of the sequences that K did. And, as she gained the ability with K to use certain objects, I would bring them into speech C-D. And vice versa . . . So if I got something going with her, K might pick it up. We traded a lot of the same materials back and forth.

Although we both used C-D strategies, my focus was more on vocalization and hers was more on the actual behavior and the functional use of the object systems. Often, I would take the same systems she was using and try to expand them by adding gesture and vocalizations.

Around April—after 3 or 4 months of speech—she was becoming more easily engaged, for longer periods of time. All that time we were working on developing signs from functional actions and she began to have the *pour* gesture. Also she could use the *give* gesture to get a particular object and then use the *open* gesture to get me to open a box to get a particular object. So that was happening.

EE-M: Did she learn these signs with you, with K, or with both of you?

EC: Hard to say. I think she learned a lot of them with K but then generalized them in her communication work with me. After a while she had gestures for *open, give, clap hands* for cymbals, *bang-on-table* for a drum, *squeezing gesture* for a squeeze toy, *shake* for a rattle, *strumming sign* for the banjo, *turning gesture* for a hand eggbeater as well as a jack-in-the-box. As she gained more signs, these were used continuously in the session. And I continuously made sounds with the signs and used words with the signs.

I started using gestures to get musical instruments out of boxes. She was interested in opening boxes and cabinets. And that's still a favorite thing to do so I just used it. And I started using a sphere with interruptions for opening up the cabinet doors. First to get the gesture and then the vocalizations.

Interrupting Anna's Object Involvement

EE-M: How did interruptions help with therapy?

EC: We would sit in front of the cabinet door. This was her favorite thing to do. She would sit cross-legged in front of the cabinet. And I'm sitting right next to her. And then I would scoot her around to face me asking, "What do you want?" And wait for her sign. And then she would make the sign for *open*. Then she would get into the cabinet. But then as soon as she started touching and playing with something—as soon as she got engaged with the object—I would close the cabinet. Then, I would turn her toward me again and ask her, "What do you want?" And then I would pat her and jiggle her a little bit. Then, I would sometimes break it up with body work to get that vocalizing going again. Eventually I would get that vocalizing going again, coupled with the sign. Then, I would open the cabinet door again so that she could get the object and play with it a little bit, and so on.

EE-M: How else did you exploit her involvement with objects?

EC: At first I had a lot of stuff in there. But then I started controlling things more. There was a movable dog on the string, there were drums and instruments—things that she wanted badly. So I did this many, many times. And there were some days where I really got consistent vocalizations plus the signs and some eye contact—looking upward at me.

Later on I would actually let her take the objects out . . . drum, guitar, and so forth. Then, when I interrupted her engagement with the object, I would get the sign. She would be playing with the instrument and then I would take it from her and begin playing it. And then she would make the *give* sign to me and I would give it back to her. So in the course of working with her around an object I would use multiple interruptions with her.

EE-M: What about two-sign combinations?

EC: During this work I started getting two-sign combinations: *give blow* for *kazoo, give bang* for *drum, give squeeze* for *squeeze toy*. To get the kazoo, for example, she would sign *give* and then *blow* (with her mouth). I would not say that she was on a two-sign level, but she certainly has that capacity.

Just the other day . . . on the computer she spontaneously signed *more cheese* during the cheese sequence. It's in spurts. Just as the words and signs pop out unpredictably so some of the two-sign combinations pop out in the same manner.

EE-M: I understand that sometimes she runs through her entire repertoire of signs to get a particular object.

EC: That happens sometimes. Although at other times she picks exactly the sign she needs. I get both kinds of behavior from her. Right now I have her so structured that she is giving me the sign that I want. But she definitely has a retrieval problem. When she is tired or frustrated, she loses the connection between sign and object. At those times all she expresses is wanting something.

EE-M: To keep each sign related to its object, your strategy is to keep her in some kind of touch with the desired object and then to remove it.

EC: Yes. Or I may briefly help her start the sign with her hand . . .

EE-M: How do you view the future with regard to her retrieval problem?

EC: It's going to be a tough one. But some specific sound/object relations are coming back. "Bu-bu" is back for bubble or balloon, and she no longer has any trouble retrieving that. And she has the *give* sign.

EE-M: Do you relate new sounds to their objects?

EC: At first they are systematically related to their objects: "plink-plink" for the banjo; "bang-bang" for the drum. In other words, onomatopoeia first and then a combination of object sound with the word form such as "bang-bang drum" (see Chapter 5).

She also started to hand things to me. She would be blowing something; then I would say "E (therapist's name) blow," and she would hand me the object to blow. At first I had to say "E blow" and help her hold the object up to my mouth; and when I handed it back to her, I would hold it to her mouth and say "Anna blow." Eventually she learned to give me the instrument to blow immediately after she blew.

I also did some spheres with her on the Elevated Square. On her initial effort she fell off—a soft fall—but for the first time that I knew of Anna cried in response to being hurt. And she cried and put her arms around me and let me comfort her. And that was pretty amazing. That was the first really human contact she had with me. She let me take her to the bathroom and wash her face and let me comfort her. And we could return to work—but not on the Elevated Square for that session.

EE-M: That certainly suggests some increasing closeness.

EC: There was definitely increasing closeness. By that time she was running pretty consistently down to my therapy room—running on her own to look for me. And she still does that. Whenever she has an opportunity, she "escapes" down to my therapy room.

Either I'm a person for her or the things in my room became important to her or—more likely—a combination of the two. This past spring a couple of times when she saw me in the hallway she would use the sign *come* and babble and of course I would come to her. And she did this just on seeing me.

Increasingly through the year and a half there has been much more of an attachment—particularly as I started doing some body work with her. You and I have both worked with her. That meant bouncing, patting, jiggling, and tapping her and pushing her knees up on her tummy and jiggling her tummy to get "ahhhs" and doing sound spheres with that.

EE-M: Describe the sound spheres.

EC: Sound spheres are started when you introduce a repetitive sound rhythmically and then interrupt it to see if she will continue it. For example, with the drum we do "ba-ba-boom, ba-ba-boom" and then do "ba-ba . . ." to see if she will fill in the missing sound. I use a lot of different sound spheres. I also use a tube with her that elicits a lot of reciprocal sound making from her . . . it amplifies and focuses the sound for her: One end of the tube is in my mouth and the other end is in her ears. And I would do sound spheres into the tube and we would almost get alternating: I would do some, then Anna would do some. And she would laugh a lot with the tube and become really engaged.

With Anna you have to introduce things and take them away—otherwise she will very rapidly drift away from it. She satiates very rapidly—physically, vocally, or with objects—and there are not really many objects that she likes.

EE-M: Did you introduce broken objects and 3D/2D?

EC: I worked with broken objects, and they definitely engaged her: She had a definite need to put the dog's head on its body and to put the cup and the ball together. And that was consistent with what K was doing with them. I used the cup, the ball, the lady, and the dog; and I also used the cup and dog with 3D/2D. And I think that was the real beginning of her picture recognition.

EE-M: Did your work with pictures go beyond that?

EC: Yes. I began putting pictures of things on boxes, on language master cards, holding up pictures for her to point to in order to get the object the picture represented. I also used that to encourage pointing for choices. Often K in her C-D sessions would set up a picture series—say using pictures on bags—which I would carry through in a somewhat different way. She now has a vocabulary of 30 or 40 meaningful pictures.

She developed pointing as she worked with both objects and pictures. Her pointing started with her taking my hand and pushing it toward something—or just batting at something in a kind of diffuse manner. This was about 6 months into my work with her. And then she started taking my hand and pushing it toward something she wanted. And then she allowed me to mold her finger and push it toward one or the other thing that she wanted. And her pointing has gotten much better—much more discriminating. And eventually, by holding really large pictures far apart I began getting her to both face and point in the direction of the picture. Then, when she pointed at the picture, I gave her the object the picture represented.

EE-M: When she pointed at the picture did she expect to get the object?

EC: I don't know . . . I think so. If she got the dog when she pointed at the picture of the dog—something she was really interested in—she got real excited. She would vocalize, play with it . . . I would pick pictures and objects she was highly interested in. And I would combine a picture she wasn't interested in with one she was in order to get a definite choice. Like grapes against the dog. Once she got object recognition, she very quickly got picture recognition. She certainly recognizes and can sign for a number of common objects: *cup, cheese, knife, orange, grape;* and she has become fascinated with people's faces.

EE-M: How does she show this new interest in pictures of faces and objects?

EC: She has now gotten fascinated with faces—simple faces with eyes, nose, and smiling mouth on plates and on balloons. And she really does follow them and become excited by them. Today, in fact, she held a balloon in one hand while painting on the balloon with the other after seeing that done in a lot of ways.

So we went from very basic reciprocal behavior, signs and sound making, lots of play with objects, using gestures with a variety of objects then using pictures on bags and boxes and on Language Master cards. Lots and lots of stuff. With Anna, like with a lot of disordered kids, the important thing is the drama. And knowing when to interrupt, knowing how not to satiate too much verbally.

EE-M: How did you dramatize your contact with her?

EC: Using your voice urgently like "up, up, up!" And you're going to go "down, down, down!" Really having to act it out with her with a lot of vocal gesture accompanied by the relevant signs. You dance on tables with this kid.

EE-M: And when you did that?

EC: Sometimes she responded extremely well. And sometimes she didn't. It really depended on where she was that day. She could be in and out in a moment. She could be having a wonderful day and could very easily be put into contagious activity to get her going; and then I could stop—

interrupt her—and get signs and sounds from her. And at other times she would be very sleepy and very easily frustrated.

She went into a slump this past spring (a few months before her mother gave birth to another child). Before that she had a consistent "oh" for "open," and "ba" for "balloon" with signs, and then for a time she seemed to lose everything. Now she's getting them all back again—so it seems she didn't lose them. They just became less available to her.

And periodically through all the therapy once in a while a word would pop out distinctly like "apple" or "egg." I was doing a little sphere with her—a little sequence with an egg slicer and a hard-boiled egg. And she wanted that egg so badly and I was withholding it. She was so angry with me and so ravenous that she began making all kinds of sounds and suddenly she yelled out "Egg!!" And of course I gave her lots of eggs at that time. And there was egg all over Anna and egg all over me—but she never said it again. She signed *egg* but wouldn't or couldn't say it.

Contagion and Body Work

EE-M: It sounds like you built up so much affect that it just popped out. I've seen you run with her back and forth in the hall to build up that kind of contagious excitement.

EC: Yes. That was part of the body work I started last June (6 months into speech C-D). We would run up and down the hall. And I would be vocalizing and she would be vocalizing. We would bang on the door and then run to the other side of the hall, bang on the door again and then repeat it over and over. And then I would interrupt right in the middle of it and wait for her to sign *run, run, run* to continue the system.

At first I helped her start the sign but then she began to make the sign spontaneously the moment we stopped running. She hasn't said "run" yet but we're getting rhythmic vocalizing. I was more interested at that time in her signing and gazing at me as she made the sign.

EE-M: How did you get her to look at you?

EC: I certainly didn't say "Look at me. Look at me!" I got her to look at me by constantly and abruptly changing my physical relationship with her—by moving in and moving out. "Look at me!" doesn't work with these children. They don't understand the term for one thing and for another, children like Anna do best when you work with them indirectly—like suddenly changing your body position with respect to them. You cannot approach directly and say "Talk. Say this. Do this." You have to provide a context. You have to get a contagious activity going. And it seems the more I work with other things the more there is to expand on.

EE-M: What other things have you used?

EC: I started with the Language Master, for example, but using it as a sphere. And I am also using the computer with touch screen and picture sequences in a spheric manner and she is vocalizing more. And I'm not asking her to vocalize. But I am patting her tummy and looking at her saying, "What, what, what, what do you want?"

EE-M: How does she respond to picture sequences?

EC: She does well with pictures—particularly when they are colored. She needs a better auditory-verbal connection. Pictures now seem to stimulate more vocalizing. It has also been useful to develop choices and picture sequences using the computer.

EE-M: How do you use picture sequences on the computer?

EC: The computer—with a touch screen—has been useful in helping Anna develop pointing and choices, associations, sequencing, and naming. I can illustrate its use with a cheese sequence that I developed because Anna is unusually fond of cheese:

Anna touches the computer window, which has a picture of cheese. The computer says "cheese." She is now pointing with greater specificity at the window—and these are smaller pictures. Then, in addition to the picture of cheese, I introduce pictures of a knife, a person cutting cheese, and a person eating cheese. First we run through all these pictures. She points and touches the screen and hears "cheese" from the computer when the cheese is shown, "knife" with the knife, "cut cheese" with the cutting-cheese frame, and "eat" with the picture of the person eating; and she says "ee, ee, ee"—for eat—with that. Then I say, "What do you need?" So she points at the cheese. Then I ask her what she needs, and at first I tell her "knife, knife, knife." Then she points to the picture and gets the knife. Then, "What are you going to do?" and I answer for her "Cut cheese, cut cheese." Then she starts to cut cheese. For the last part of the sequence she points to the picture of the person eating cheese by herself without any help and signs and says "ee, ee, ee."

So with the help of the computer I accent an integrative sphere that she has started to internalize so that she knows first this, then this. She is getting the notion of a functional sequence through pictures which builds on her sequence work with K with big body actions on the elevated structures.

I also use an "orange eat" sequence where she learns to quarter an orange and an "orange drink" sequence where she learns to make juice from the orange and drink it. And she is signing right along. She has also started approximating the sounds of "orange" and "drink."

And she now anticipates sequences. The other day she placed the pictures on the computer by herself. She now knows that there is a system—and that when she touches the picture on the screen she'll hear a word that relates to the picture and its object. When this happens she starts making sounds.

EE-M: Compare Anna today with how she was when you started with her.

EC: The gains described may seem small, but when I think of where Anna was—the changes are huge. When Anna first came she had zip functional play with objects, very little sound coming out of her, you could barely engage her in anything. Everything was "finish"—her all done sign—in 2 seconds. But now—while there are still periods where she is difficult to engage—the majority of the time I can engage her solidly for a half-hour session. I can really get her doing things. But sometimes I have to flit around with her—where I run around the room like a crazy woman—trying to figure out what to do because nothing is working.

She has much more capacity to use objects in a functional manner, has gained picture recognition, vocalizes more, seems happier, and makes more of a connection. She's truly developing a strong prelinguistic base. And she looks at you more and more. There are more periods where she looks right at me and I am less and less surprised when that happens.

And at the end of a session I can hug her—and when I pull back she moves forward. She's a real person for me now, not the way she was—a manikin flitting around—and it was very frustrating. And, at times, it still is but there is so much more of her there. And you have to like her, her bounce. And she shows so much more emotion. She jumps up and down, she's smiling more, and she's laughing out loud and she giggles in anticipation of . . . if I'm going to do something she absolutely adores. She loves the big cones I use for a megaphone. I'll just start to pick it up, and she will start laughing even before I start making noises—just in anticipation. I never saw anything like that when she first came . . . never.

PARENTAL INVOLVEMENT—ANNA

This section is an excerpted interview with Mrs. J. regarding her collaboration with K during C-D systems therapy.

AM: Do you recall Anna's first gain?

MRS. J: She got her first sign at home—although we had been working on it at the Center. She was at the door and she did the *open* sign and everybody started to scream. It's funny . . . because now it's such a part of her life you forget how significant that was and how overwhelmed we were. We couldn't believe that she was actually intending something. And we hoped she would rapidly build spoken language but that hasn't happened yet. . . . But I feel that if Anna can get signs and pictures she may get spoken language. Now of course we are dealing in speech with sound making and with the problem of how capable her mouth is and we feel that much more than we used to. After 6 years of not shaping her mouth to words it's very hard for her to do.

AM: Often you would watch K engage Anna in a repetitive activity—such as strumming her toy guitar or making sounds with the kazoo—and then interrupt the activity by removing the object. How did you understand this?

MRS. J: The basic thing of interrupting . . . I think the interrupting taught her the signs she got. That is how we got them . . . doing it enough times then interrupting her . . . which basically forced her. . . . She could practice it but then interrupting really made her *need* to do it. With Anna you first had to build the impetus for doing things . . . and that was with contagion. Trying to get her to a level where it meant something that she wanted to go on with the activity. Or that the task was so interesting that she had the desire to do it. And certain objects always elicited intentional activity: the guitar, the balloon, bubbles because they are exciting objects for her. We were able to build on those.

AM: Do you recall when she began to point at things at some distance away from her body?

MRS. J: I remember it being a big deal. And it was. I remember her going from throwing her hand at the object to actually using her index finger to point. We had been working on it for a long time. We had physically shaped her finger and tried in different spheres to help her distinguish between one object and another. . . . With her, sometimes you work and work and just manage to push her up to the next level and *pop!* you have it and there she is pointing . . . a real *decisive* point—with no fooling around. She suddenly got it—the fog cleared and suddenly her finger went thrusting through it toward the object.

But there were physical things that contributed to her successful pointing. Before she could point she would—when we refused to give her an object she needed—throw her arm out in the general direction of the object. And that was her primitive way of saying I want something. But that was different from looking at something you want and pointing at it.

AM: When she threw her arm at the object—often while looking elsewhere—she was expressing herself in a very fuzzy manner. But with pointing she was saying, *It's this one . . . no other.* Now she could make her eyes and hand work together to pinpoint a particular object at some distance. And that's what is exciting about that. . . . But what about working with Anna at home?

MRS. J: My husband and I used to do C-D with her every night. It was a good thing. Particularly at the beginning of the program. It gave us a chance to interact with her in a way that we hadn't been able to before that. . . . It had been hard to be with her. Hard to know what to do with her. And she's very difficult to structure because she'll do something for about 1 minute and then you have to find something new for her to do. Like you have to keep feeding her new things to engage her, otherwise she runs out of gas.

And even with C-D. But as you learn how it works, you know how to create that engagement from the basic idea that you started with. And it was really very good for about 20 or 30 minutes. She would do the same basic tasks: pick up an object, put it in a wagon, pull the wagon with it, then repeat it with another object, then pile a block here, stack something there, throw a block, or pick up a piece and put it in a puzzle. And it was primarily about linking up spaces and developing a sense of purpose.

AM: And doing sequential tasks.

MRS. J: Yes. And finishing the sphere. We do a lot of that still with K— putting the block in the square part and the ball in the round part, cutting an apple, and drinking from a straw in a cup.

AM: Aside from the things we've talked about, how would you now describe your relationship with Anna?

MRS. J: Anna now is much more responsive than she was. She doesn't cry when you leave the room, but she will get fussy and she will get upset in general. And on her own she'll come and hug you a lot now. And she laughs with you. And she's much more there with you. Now I don't get surprised when I'm talking to Anna and she *looks* at me. It doesn't shock me anymore. But that would've been a shock to me before. . . . I could count on one hand during her first 4 years the number of times I saw Anna behind her eyes. And when it happened, it was just the most exciting thing. And she looks at you with such direct clarity. It's delightful. You suddenly get washed in her eyes. Yes. And you realize, just because it was so rare, how intense it is—as if she's intensely trying to take you in.

DISCUSSION OF JACK AND ANNA

This chapter has presented interventions for two autistic children with different system disorders. One child, Jack, made very dramatic progress during a 6-month period with only two 1-hour C-D sessions per week; the other, Anna, with far more intensive intervention (3.5 hours of individual sessions plus 25 classroom hours per week) in the course of 22 months, made important progress but at a far slower rate. How can we account for this difference?

Certainly, the most obvious difference is the age at which each child started the program: Jack began at 2½ years, whereas Anna started at 4 years 8 months. We, like others working with disordered children, have consistently found that interventions are far more effective with children under 3 years than they are with older children. However, beyond the age difference, certain emotional factors inherent in the mother–child relationship may have played a role in shaping the underlying autistic disposition present in both children into a closed-system disorder in Jack's case and a system–forming disorder in Anna's case.

There is, first, the difference in early postnatal contact between Mrs. H, Jack's mother, and Jack, on the one hand, and Mrs. J and Anna, on the other. Mrs. H reported that immediately after Jack was born, she had as much access to her son as she wished and that he nursed strongly although without rooting. In contrast, Mrs. J reported that Anna lacked much of a sucking reflex and didn't seem to want to take the nipple. Subsequently, both mothers sensed in their babies the unrelatedness so characteristic of autism. Mrs. H described it "as if he never really wanted to be here," and Mrs. J commented that "she [Anna] was oblivious to who was holding her." Clearly, the mothers interpreted the unrelatedness differently: For Mrs. H it was a somewhat sad but objective comment on his state, but for Mrs. J there was the possible implication that she felt unwanted, because she didn't seem to matter to Anna more than anyone else mattered to the infant. Certain behaviors by each child may have eased or strengthened these attitudes. For example, when Jack was frightened by a new event, Mrs. H recalled him clutching her—providing her with at least some indication of her importance to him. However, when Anna jolted awake screaming, Mrs. J would spend hours trying to comfort her with little or no effect until, exhausted, Anna fell asleep. Mother commented that the problems with breast feeding and the screaming made her feel not as connected to Anna as she was to her other children and that she was absent from her more than she would ever be from her other two children "because Anna didn't seem to mind."

Further complicating Mrs. J's relationship with Anna was a psychologist's assessment that Anna's problem was due to a faulty mother–child relationship. The psychologist—picking up Anna's unrelatedness—made the error of assuming that the entire problem was due to "faulty mothering." The negative impact on the mother's self-confidence, coupled with serious marital problems, led to her mistaken notion that if her mothering was "wrecking" her child, she had better not have anything to do with her. Anna's consequent depression and her loss of tenuously gained words correlate closely with her mother's withdrawal.

Anna's underlying autism with its scattered, flitting style of relating to her surroundings may have become patterned by circumstances immediately following her birth. Anna did not bond with her mother in the way that normal infants do. The normal infant (Chapter 1, p. 17), after orienting to the touch of the nipple on his/her cheek, engages it with vigorous sucking movements. In doing so, the infant forms a system that entails ingesting not only milk but unique qualities of the mother as well. Initially, interruption of the sucking system—loss of breast or bottle—results in compensatory sucking to restore the system. Later, the sight of the mother at a distance may trigger sucking and arm-reaching behavior for the same purpose. Still later, as Mahler et al. (1967) has described, the child learns to expand his or her own systems by moving away from the main life support system that the mother represents to orient and engage with (explore) new objects before returning to mother for "refueling."

Anna's development never followed this model. Just as she failed to bond (orient toward and engage) with her mother, so was she unable to orient toward and fully engage objects and events in her surroundings. Instead, she oriented and engaged fleetingly: Momentarily caught by an object she picked it up but let it drop almost immediately as she looked elsewhere and moved to another object. Always the incoordination between what she was looking at and what her hands were doing interfered with her fully "getting into" the object's unique nature, as when she failed to turn over an upside-down cup in order to stack it right side up. Such failures suggest that her relations with objects were as superficial as her contacts with people. Only when she collided with objects and events (stairs, climbing equipment, immersion in water), was she able to function more appropriately and adaptively.

In contrast, Jack *was* able to bond with his mother, although the unusual nature of his nursing was evident in his inability to know when he had enough—as if faulty "wiring" interfered with proper feedback from his stomach. However, once having bonded to her, his autistic disposition precluded the exploratory leaving and returning for refueling described by Mahler et al. (1967). During the assessment, although he possessed the ability to adapt when pressed to do so, he could not tolerate moving around in new spaces and resisted participating in spheres the examiner introduced. Instead, he expressed his autistic disposition by clutching small objects in his left hand, by excluding all others (including father), and by being unable to spontaneously expand or to tolerate expansions of the few systems that he had formed. This left Jack overly invested in a few objects and needing to keep the relations between objects rigidly fixed. Thus, captured by his originally formed systems, he too, but for different reasons, could not develop.

Anna's slower rate of progress in contrast to Jack's—stems not only from her age when work with her started at LCDC—but from the nature of their respective system problems. Jack began with *some* systems, including an extremely important one with his mother. Anna, on the other hand, had *no* extremely important systems with people *or* with objects. Without important relationships with others there is not much reason for a child to grope toward ways of communicating with them. We propose that Anna's rate of progress has been slower because she first had to learn *how* to form and maintain important systems with people *and* with objects before she had a basis for communication with people about things in the world. Because Jack already had a system with his mother and with a few objects, it was simpler to help him expand these systems so they included other important figures, for example, his father, other objects. Then, strategies were oriented around helping him solve the relations between things in space and the notion of representation so that he too could communicate his needs.

Differential Treatment of Jack's Closed-System and Anna's System-Forming Disorder

The difference in treatment strategies for the two children is perhaps best seen in the attempt to help them develop functional relationships with objects. Jack already had a bond with his mother and cared intensely about objects—clutching his plastic toy in his left hand—while for Anna objects had little value. So, for Jack, the therapist had to find ways to help him release objects so that they might become part of transactions. In direct contrast, for Anna the problem was one of *heightening* her interest in the unique properties of the object. Thus, the solution for Jack was to begin with pictures that interested him but were less likely to elicit clutching behavior than objects. The pictures of animals then became used in increasingly elaborate spheres that started by giving him a picture, letting him assimilate it, and then putting it through the slit into a transparent bottle where he could still see it. Subsequently, he learned to push the truck to his mother who would pick up a picture, point to, name, and describe it and then send it via truck to him for disposal—all capacities that swiftly transferred to objects. For Anna, the very different intervention was to include the object in a contagious activity in which she could involve her entire body, such as running the car across her bare stomach or placing her hands or feet in the flow of sand or water she was pouring into a bucket, before she could deal with the car or pouring in more conventional fashion. Beyond this, Anna required a variety of spheric techniques involving the repair of broken objects and the use of the same object in a variety of ways before she could experience its varied properties.

Interventions to help develop symbolic capacity also differed. For example, Jack was keenly interested in pictures, whereas Anna was not. With Jack, therefore, it was a relatively straightforward matter to demonstrate the correspondence between pictures and the objects they represented. He grasped this very quickly and was soon on his way toward establishing and generalizing the notion not only of correspondence but of the notion of categories represented by pictures. Anna, on the other hand, after developing an interest in a few objects such as the dog and the cup had to be carefully shown, through 3D/2D transfers and by juxtaposition of pictures with their objects, how pictures related to objects. This was a much longer process because she had to become keenly interested in the objects before she would try to find their replicas in the contours of pictures.

Only in the area of developing important relationships were some of the strategies similar: For example, both children drew on contagious physical activity and Rough and Tumble to help establish new relationships. With

Jack this intervention was critical in establishing a relationship for the first time with his father. With Anna, it became the "juice" that helped start significant relationships with her different therapists. With her, however, contagious activity had to be supplemented with specific strategies such as the use of the Interactive Window and many others listed in the appendix at the end of this chapter.

Anna's Major Gains

The most important gain Anna has achieved during the past 22 months is the formation of much more substantial relationships with people—particularly with her mother—expressed in part by improved eye contact. This is confirmed by all therapists and her parents. Next most important is her substantially improved ability to see and engage more appropriately with objects. There is a beginning development of communicative systems, currently including a few spoken words, 40 to 50 signs, and well-established picture recognition.

Currently, she is far better sign-word guided than she is with regard to expressive use of signs or spoken words.

Prognosis

Anna's prognosis is good for continued development of social systems and the development of some spoken language—perhaps buttressed by signs and pictures to more completely communicate her intentions. She functions currently at the advanced sign stage of development (12- to 18-month range). Although she now has a number of the prerequisites for naming, for example, significant people, ability to point at objects, she has not yet grasped the catalytic function of names as a means of holding objects even in their absence. When she does so, she will live in a much larger world.

Jack's Major Gains

Jack's gains include dramatically improved social contact (particularly with father), improved eye contact, recognition of pictures as symbols, increasing vocabulary of names (spoken), ability to move from place to place with less distress, and improved means–ends relations. Indications are strong that Jack is currently crossing the threshold from sign to symbolic-sign stage functioning (Chapter 5, pp. 146–147). This is evident in his recent object hunger and need for such objects' names. It is also evident in his increasing spoken vocabulary and in his new awareness of the relation between pictures and their referents as well as the notion of categories. For example, he now has categories for all clothes belonging to father, mother, and sister. Future work will emphasize the use of names in interpersonal transactions in a way that will lead to a more functional use of spoken language.

Prognosis

Jack shows excellent prospects for full development of spoken and written language with appropriate social interactions.

SUMMARY

This chapter communicates both the quality of the C-D systems approach and the manner in which therapists and parents have applied the procedures to meet the system needs of two very different children. Interviews with staff suggest that even with prior training and experience in developmental psychology or speech and language therapy, workers require the conceptual framework offered in this book, observation of experienced C-D systems therapists, participation in the Center's ongoing C-D systems seminar, and regular supervision before they feel they "own" the approach and can use it effectively with different—closed, system-forming, and syncretic—system-disordered children.

Two disordered children and their families are described, including their developmental histories, Umwelt assessments, and the C-D system interventions used. The first child, Jack, an autistic child with a closed-system disorder, began the program at age 2 years 6 months and has achieved dramatic gains in both social and cognitive functioning. His behavior strongly suggests that he is in transition from sign to symbolic-sign stage functioning. Interviews with the parents demonstrate the manner in which the work at the Center generalizes, through the parents' efforts, to the home and elsewhere.

The next child, Anna, diagnosed as an autistic child with a system-forming disorder, began treatment at the Center at the age of 4 years 8 months. Anna's early developmental history revealed inability to breast-feed and jaundice that required her, after she was 2 days old, to be physically separated from mother for 3 days. Complicating her development were her mother's preoccupation with marital problems and a psychologist's incorrect diagnosis of Anna's problem as caused primarily by the mother–child relationship.

Anna's scattered way of relating to her surroundings required that treatment goals be organized around helping her invest in the world around her so that she could both relate to objects in a more functional manner and establish more meaningful relationships with her parents and the people that cared for her. Interventions focused first on object relations so that she could form basic systems from which—with the help of interruptions—she could form functional signs. Subsequently, she learned to find meaning in pictures. Most recently, C-D systems therapy has focused on interactive systems and, with the close collaboration of her mother, has contributed to her ability to respond to and return affection and eye contact to important people in her life.

The final section of the chapter discusses why Jack has made significantly more rapid progress than Anna even though she had substantially more intensive intervention. In addition to the age at which intervention began, there is speculation that early bonding—or its failure—shortly after birth may have shaped the nature of the underlying autistic process into a closed system for Jack and a system-forming disorder for Anna. From this perspective, Jack has made greater progress because he already had important systems with his mother that Anna had to establish with her mother.

Appendix

This appendix summarizes the variety of interventions used to work toward the goals for Jack and Anna. Goals and interventions are organized under four categories—Body Organization, Contact with the Environment, Social Contact, and Representation/Communication.

GOALS AND INTERVENTIONS FOR JACK

Body Organization

Goals

To develop improved body awareness
To deal with Jack's tantrums

Interventions

Therapist works with Jack on the Elevated Square.
Father engages in Rough and Tumble with Jack on regular basis.
Therapist copes with Jack's tantrums by engaging him with use of pictures.
Therapist makes no demands for him to move into new space until the space becomes familiar.
Therapist allows him to sit on mother's lap initially.
Therapist establishes a security ritual for Jack by beginning each session in the same way.
Therapist is careful to present pictures at the pace Jack requires to assimilate them.
Therapist touches Jack the minimal amount required for him to complete a sphere, such as when he put the picture through the slit on top of a transparent jar.

Goal

To help Jack develop improved coordination between his vision and his hearing

Interventions

Therapist moves object in jerks, while coordinating a sound with each movement.

Mother, at home, names object softly while she brings it close to Jack's body. Mother also calls Jack loudly from a distance.

Both therapist and parents constantly narrate his behavior so that he begins to include what he hears with what he sees and does.

Contact with the Environment

Goals

To move Jack from rigid to more flexible spatial relations

To encourage scanning of objects in different spatial locations

To encourage pointing

To encourage increased interest in the nature of objects

Interventions

Therapist gradually introduces location expansions of objects with which Jack is involved (moves jar from accustomed position).

Therapist introduces multispheres involving disparate objects so that Jack learns he can shift from first to second or third object without losing ability to return.

Therapist works with Jack on the Elevated Square with interrupted systems so that he must move from one station to another on the square to complete systems.

Both therapist and parents attempt to "feed" Jack's "hunger" for new objects.

Parents open upstairs gate at home so that Jack can connect downstairs space with upstairs.

Therapist and mother conspire to remove parts of objects or puzzles on Elevated Square so he must scan all stations before moving toward station to complete interrupted object or puzzle.

Therapist requires that Jack first point to and retrieve hidden objects at short and then longer distances.

Goal

To help Jack develop means–ends capacities (use of hands, tools)

Interventions

Therapist helps Jack repetitively push truck to mother and later receive it from her.

At home, father rolls ball back and forth with Jack.

Therapist introduces various causal (wind up, etc.) toys.

Therapist requires that Jack open bags closed in a variety of ways (string, clothespin, top folded down) to get desired objects.

Social Contact

Goals

To develop distal perception of mother

To develop integrative/interactive systems involving mother

Interventions

Therapist helps Jack send truck to mother sitting opposite him. Mother names picture or object, designates (pointing and describing) varied parts, and returns picture or object via truck to Jack for appropriate placement (jar, barn, etc.).

Goal

To help Jack improve his eye contact and expand his social systems

Interventions

Therapist and parents offer objects to Jack at eye level while these are held in front of the offerer's face (Jack looks at person while looking at object).

Therapist and parents introduce rapid trading of objects using similar strategy.

Father, while lying down, "weight lifts" Jack, who faces him.

Jack jumps repetitively while facing stable parent.

Mother and sister involve Jack in "Ring-Around-a-Rosy."

Father involves Jack by playing contagiously with his sister.

Parents support Jack's chasing his sister with hose to wet her.

Father engages in Rough and Tumble with Jack on regular basis.

Representation/Communication

Goal

To expand Jack's interest from pictures to objects

Interventions

Therapist sets up minispheres involving dominoes with pictures on them. Jack puts the dominoes into a rectangular hole through the cap of a transparent jar.

Therapist sets up minispheres—pegs and blocks go through appropriately shaped holes in transparent jars, and animals and people figures go into barn and house respectively.

Goal

To develop Jack's understanding of how symbols represent objects

Interventions

Therapist repetitively places pictures on paper bags (or boxes, etc.) with the objects represented by them inside and requires Jack first to point at the picture, then open the bag and discover the object inside. Following this, he places the object in its appropriate location.

Therapist works repetitively from 2D to 3D by having Jack attend to the picture on one side of a card and then to the partially objectified object the picture represents on the other side of the card.

At home, when Jack points to pictures, the parents supply the object to which the pictures refer (whenever possible).

At home, parents support Jack's matching clothes to the people who wear them and support his removing and replacing food from food closet and refrigerator.

At home, parents periodically introduce new pictures for the walls of Jack's room and when he eventually takes them down and puts them in piles, they replace them with new pictures.

Parents keep track of the new words Jack learns and try to elicit them in relevant contexts.

Parents encourage use of sign *give* coupled with pointing at desired object, picture, or spoken word.

GOALS AND INTERVENTIONS FOR ANNA*

Body Organization

Goal

To develop body awareness

Interventions

C-D systems therapist introduces Rough and Tumble to foster body awareness.

---

*This list is representative only of Anna's individual therapies. It does not include the substantial array of interventions used in her regular classroom. Obviously, the gains achieved are a function not only of her individual therapies but of her classroom work as well. For a description of classroom interventions, see the curriculum described in Chapter 9.

C-D systems therapist introduces Anna to a range of elevated structures for the same purpose.

Parents introduce a moving bed (not referred to in case discussion) at home for vestibular stimulation and improved body awareness.

Goal

To develop improved eye-hand coordination

Intervention

By engaging Anna with provocative objects and then interrupting her, C-D systems therapist and speech and language therapist seek to improve both eye-hand coordination and awareness of objects.

Contact with the Environment

Goal

To develop Anna's interest in and ability to anticipate objects and events

Interventions

C-D systems therapist repeatedly and contagiously runs car with "brrr" sounds back and forth on Anna's bare stomach and then abruptly interrupts the activity.

Mother or C-D systems therapist painting on one side of the Interactive Window (Anna painting on other side) periodically makes unexpected moves or patterns that, following interruptions, Anna begins to anticipate and follow.

Speech and language therapist makes "funny sounds" through megaphone which Anna begins to anticipate.

C-D systems therapist introduces 6 paint jars of which only one has paint. Anna has to scan all jars to locate the jar that is filled with paint before she can run to it.

Goal

To develop transition from whole body contagious involvement with objects and events to functional activity with them

Interventions

Prior to requiring her to pour water or sand into a bucket, C-D systems therapist supports her need to experience the water and sand flow first on her hands or feet.

C-D systems therapist introduces the Elevated Square with stations: Anna develops contagious picking up and dropping at one station; then she divides the task into picking up at one of the stations and dropping at the other.

C-D systems therapist keeps distance between stations short, minimizes distractions, and maintains fast tempo to enable Anna to perform the preceding activity.

Goal

To help Anna see objects better in terms of their unique properties

Interventions

C-D systems therapist introduces balloon and encourages Anna's pulling, blowing, pushing, and letting air out of it.

C-D systems therapist uses division of function between stations to help Anna deliberately cope with the same object in two ways—picking it up and dropping it.

C-D systems therapist introduces broken objects (cup, dog, bowl, shoe, ball) by placing parts on stations on the Elevated Square; another broken object is a table that Anna needs to put together.

C-D systems therapist also introduces broken objects on wire frames that guide Anna in completing the objects. These include a car, a hand, and a face.

C-D systems therapist introduces repetitive drawing and painting on paper stretched across the wall of one side of the room.

C-D systems therapist helps Anna distinguish between painting on the wall and on the paper.

Goal

To help Anna develop means–ends relationships

Interventions

C-D systems therapist introduces markers very responsive to pressure so that even the slightest effort leaves a big mark on the paper.

C-D systems therapist conceals paint (a desired object) in different parts of the room and requires that Anna remove the obstacles in order to find it.

C-D systems therapist tapes over the holes in the paint jar so that Anna can't put the paintbrush in until she first removes tape.

C-D systems therapist encourages use of knife to cut an orange and to squeeze juice from the pieces in an orange squeezer as part of an integrative sphere.

Speech and language therapist uses multiple interruptions to enhance Anna's investment in desired objects and to motivate her to open various doors to get desired objects.

Social Contact

Goal

To develop interactive and social systems (see Chapter 4, p. 159 for definition)

Interventions

Movement therapist helps Anna establish interactive systems by mirroring her behavior, for example, tapping in response to her tapping.

Movement therapist expands Anna's interactive systems by inserting new behavior, for example, whirling her around before helping her down from the table.

C-D systems therapist develops interactive systems via contagious activities: bouncing her, playing Rough and Tumble, swinging her, tossing her from person to person, and so forth.

C-D systems therapist introduces integrative/interactive spheres involving people and objects.

C-D systems therapist introduces painting on both sides of the Interactive Window.

C-D systems therapist introduces bracelets and necklaces (not included in K's account of her C-D systems work with Anna) that Anna puts on mother and that mother puts on Anna.

Mother introduces interactive sphere requiring Anna to orient her squirt bottle toward mother's moving plate.

Mother carries over integrative/interactive spheres from Center to home.

Speech and language therapist introduces reciprocal sphere by trading desirable objects (harmonica, kazoo) with her.

Speech and language therapist introduces body work and contagious excitement to foster more interaction as well as to encourage sign and sound making.

Speech therapist encourages Anna's emotional response to her (hugs, interesting toys, "fun" play).

C-D systems therapist encourages Anna to hand balloon to her (therapist) to get it blown up.

C-D systems therapist and mother take turns with Anna blowing bubbles and blowing the kazoo.

Representation/Communication

Goal

To help Anna develop communication and representational capacity

Interventions

C-D systems therapist encourages the development of functional signs by interrupting her engagement with certain objects (guitar, jack-in-the-box, kazoo, bubble blowing, etc.).

Parents, at home, and C-D systems therapist, at the Center, use spoken word "come" with the sign to get Anna to come to them. Anna then is supported in using the sign to get parents or therapist to come toward her.

Parents carry over to home all sign-word sequences used with Anna at the Center.

C-D systems therapist and parents use 3/D 2/D procedures to help Anna grasp the symbolic function of pictures.

C-D systems therapist introduces sign-word guidance without a repetitive context; for example, Anna is required suddenly to find the brush with which she has just been painting.

Speech and language therapist develops improved eye contact by abruptly changing her physical relationship with Anna, for example, unexpectedly moving in or out.

Speech and language therapist also elicits improved eye contact by interrupting contagious activities such as running back and forth in the hall with Anna.

C-D systems therapist at Center and parents at home introduce pictures of common objects that Anna must consistently identify by pointing or sign even when presented in random order.

Speech and language therapist addresses Anna's retrieval problem by keeping sign in close touch with its object and, at times, by helping her start the sign.

Speech and language therapist uses sound spheres, for example, repeating "ba-ba-boom" by banging drum and voicing sounds, then leaving out the last sound to elicit a compensatory "boom" sound.

Speech and language therapist vocally mimics the sounds that objects make in conjunction with the conventional word, for example, "plink-plink banjo" or "bang-bang drum."

Speech and language therapist dramatizes and repeats with much vocal gesture words she uses with signs.

Speech and language therapist consistently uses contagious activity, for example, running back and forth that is unexpectedly interrupted, to elicit relevant signs and sounds.

Speech and language therapist makes use of Language Master—placing pictures on the cards—so that Anna sees picture and hears relevant word at the same time.

Speech and language therapist uses touch screen of the computer in similar fashion although here Anna must touch the relevant picture to hear the spoken word. Pictures are used in this way both by herself and in integrative sequences guiding activity.

C-D systems therapist encourages pointing by hanging desired objects, for example, a balloon, on a rope just above Anna's reach.

C-D systems therapist uses picture sequences to guide an integrative sphere (pictures include an orange, knife, juice squeezer, and cup) that ends with a cup of orange juice she drinks.

Speech and language therapist generalizes signs learned in C-D sessions coupled with relevant sounds and words.

CHAPTER 9

Classroom Application of Cognitive-Developmental Systems Theory

Teaching and working with disordered children in a group—although having points in common with individual work—presents unique challenges and opportunities. Working with a single child is much like parenting an only or first child. At first, the parent focuses exclusively on all the child can or cannot do. The manner in which the child attends or babbles or grasps an object is of consuming interest. However, with the birth of the second child, all changes. Then, suddenly, the parent must accommodate and attend quite differently to the two children. Now *both* require attention. If the parent neglects some aspects of care for one child, that child suffers; if the other child's needs are not met, then that child is unhappy. What must emerge is a new arrangement or perspective that permits attending to the needs of more than one child at a time. The parent who achieves this—like the successful teacher—has a vital, interacting group with the emotional support needed to make important developmental gains. The next section considers the classroom ambience and the ways that different teachers confront this essential condition for effective teaching.

THE CLASSROOM AMBIENCE

The nature of a classroom can be determined at a glance simply by observing how the head teacher works with aides and children and structures the physical layout. At the Center, there is provision for making these observations without interrupting the natural flow of events in the classroom. An observation room equipped with a one-way vision screen and sound capacity (Figure 9.1) is adjacent to every two classrooms, allowing parents, professionals, and supervisors to have access to a view of the classroom without disrupting the class. These observation rooms are an important learning tool for both parents and staff.

Role of the Teacher

The following vignettes contrast two hypothetical classrooms, with particular emphasis on their teachers and how they influence the emotional climate.

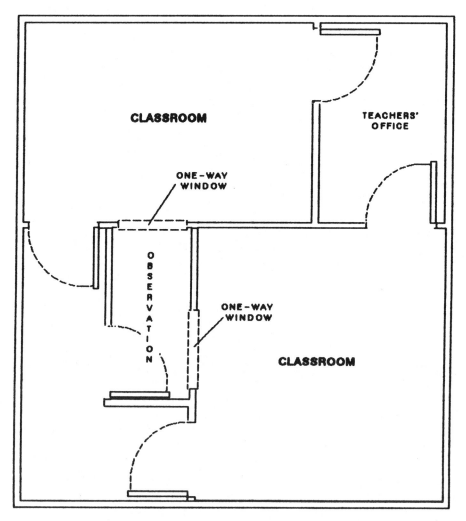

Figure 9.1. Schematic showing relation of observation room to two classrooms.

The First Classroom

This room seems cluttered: Desks and chairs with haphazardly stacked papers, pencils, and notebooks parallel a wall. Various pictures and calendars hang on the walls; mobiles with dangling objects hang from the ceiling.

The teacher, her voice trailing off when she speaks, directs her class as if from a great distance. She motions tentatively to a rocking child. The child, unresponsive, continues to rock. Her aides stand apart from the children with arms folded, gazing pensively at her. The teacher attempts to present her lesson but has not collected all the materials she needs. She leaves the children to get the remaining material while the aides inertly wait and the children begin to drift. One waiting child begins to sag against the nearest aide; another slowly rises from his chair then—feeling released from constraint—catapults across the room, glides along the wall, then lunges across the room's open space to the solidity of another wall, which he again glides along. Unobserved, another youngster moves to a sunny spot on the floor, curls up, and begins to suck his thumb.

The teacher—nervous about having left the children—hurries back to the room, hair streaming behind her. Immediately, the gliding child snatches at and pulls her hair. She shrieks at him to sit down. He prances about laughing giddily. One child puts her hands to her ears and starts rocking back and forth; another child cries. A third child begins to wander around the room making odd, meaningless sounds while methodically tearing the pictures hanging from the walls. Aides and teacher are all talking at once, trying to get the children back to the work table in order to continue the lesson. The two aides attempt to lead one of the agitated youngsters back to his chair. He kicks out at them. The chaotic situation continues.

The Second Classroom

In contrast, this classroom is brightly lit, with spare furniture painted in crisp, primary colors. The teacher stands before the children who are seated on stools, their bodies fitting neatly into bays carved in the table. Aides hover, seated behind the children and poised to help them attend. The teacher, voice urgent but calm, signs and speaks crisply, telling the children what is to come next. The children follow the teacher's movements. When a child attempts to leave the group, the teacher quietly signals the aide who swiftly moves the child back to the table. The materials she is about to present are neatly stacked out of the children's reach on an adjacent table.

Still speaking in her direct manner, she picks up and brings her materials to the children and begins the lesson. She speaks and signs about the events of the day, pointing to each picture or object as she goes on. When she requires a group response—holding her materials so that all can see and raising her voice somewhat—the children sign or speak in response. Periodically she focuses on one child whom she questions, and then she reengages the group. She smiles as she carefully follows the response of each child, her body stance commanding attention, yet her alert glances toward the other children suggest that she is constantly aware of the group as a whole.

When one child tangles with another, she brings both children into the lesson by having them hold the class material for one another. From time to time her voice quality changes from excitement to quietness to pleasure at a child's response. One of the children starts to "glom" against her;

she grins and pats him on the head while shifting her weight so that he has to sit up. Another child begins to slide from her stool during the lesson; the teacher rests an arm on the child's shoulder and keeps it there, saying "Your turn is coming," and then continues the lesson.

Obviously, the latter classroom is preferred for the education of behavior-disordered children. Several factors make this kind of classroom possible.

The Effective Teacher

The head teacher is the one essential feature in implementing the Center's program. To achieve this the teacher must be healthy and strong—emotionally as well as physically—and able to "be there" for the children. If a child conquers a difficult task, whether putting on shoes and socks or learning to use a sign, the teacher can express delight; on the other hand, if the child bites, scratches, or spits, the teacher can react and confront the child. Beyond this, the teacher must have a sense of possibilities for each child and be challenged by the way he or she functions. The teacher constantly tries to "read" the children's intentions and capacities and to probe and test for ways to enter into and expand their realities. Effective teachers do not have to "sentimentalize" the children or "keep" the functioning the children finally produce. Trained teachers understand that their task is to turn over to the children's care givers the "magic" that makes the classroom functioning possible.

Good teachers are always seeking effective tools to bring about positive change in the classroom. They understand the use of drama and contagion in presenting material and may change voice pattern in order to orient the children or change the pace of presenting the material so that the group gets caught up in the activity. An effective teacher also possesses the knack of being able to focus on one child without losing emotional touch with the group. Always the teacher is able to move in and out—perhaps briefly hugging one child and speaking directly to another.

The effective teacher can handle the close scrutiny that goes with being videotaped regularly and can use the feedback gained through supervision and study of the tapes to alter approaches with certain children. Although pleased with recognition for performance, she or he can work without constant feedback. At the same time the effective teacher's strong proprietary feeling for her or his class never interferes with the ability to accept supervision and guidance in the use of new strategies. Able to take intelligent risks and resilient enough to take inevitable setbacks in stride and try again, this teacher couples a sense of mission with a sense of humor and does not permit feelings of compassion for the children to interfere with making appropriate demands for performance. The effective teacher understands that to make an appropriate demand on a child is to honor the possibility of growth just as being overly solicitous may mean to give up on that child.

The effective teacher does not have to "do it all" and soon learns that aides—tuned in to the needs of a child—can enhance the impact of the program on a child. Consequently, the teacher rapidly learns to work with and train aides or assistants so that they know how to provide necessary backup. He or she teaches them to help faltering children in a way that does not diminish them nor detract from the material being presented. For example, when the teacher is requesting a sign or word from a child who is suddenly "caught" by the movement of another child in the room, the aide knows how to deftly position the child's head so that she or he is again looking at the teacher.

The effective teacher has to know curriculum materials, understand how to present them, realize what the children know and almost know, sense how they relate to one another and to adults and, most importantly, have a sense of when teaching strategies are getting through and when they are not.

Alliance with Parents

The teacher who successfully establishes a working relationship with the child's parents has more resources available than when working alone with the child. Such teachers understand that whenever a child is accepted into the Center, the Center also accepts the child's family. A sturdy alliance between the school and the home meets the child's needs better both at school and at home. If each setting handles the child differently, then the child has difficulty understanding what is *really* expected and the program loses impact. For example, after finding it difficult to teach a child to urinate in the toilet, the teacher learns that grandmother requires him to stand whereas parents tell him to sit while urinating.

Such a finding suggests that there are important gaps in the ongoing alliance and communication with the family. How to bridge these gaps without compromising a professional attitude requires a delicate balance of openness and reserve. The first step in this direction is to encourage parents to take advantage of their unlimited access to the observation room, preferably accompanied by the child's C-D therapist, who can interpret the behavior and comment on the teacher's goal for that particular lesson and his or her handling of the parents' child. In this context, both parents and staff can indicate to one another differences or similarities in the behavior that they are seeing and, more importantly, how they deal with the child in a particular situation.

The Classroom Environment

While attending to these issues, the teacher tries to structure the classroom so that it is a safe but engaging setting. The room should reflect a calm, structured setting with few distractions. Too many stimuli can distract disordered children from orienting toward and engaging material. This does not

Figure 9.2. Children sitting on stools around table with cut-out bays.

mean that the classroom is bare of all furnishings—but it does mean that furniture is functional, well designed, and painted with bright cheerful colors. The rooms should be well lit and have good capacity for the storage of play materials and educational supplies. This is important because materials that are too visibly displayed can make learning difficult for children with problems inhibiting or focusing attention.

To that end, as Figure 9.2 shows, circular and semicircular tables with bays help children stay within the group and oriented to the teacher; they sit on stools that dispose them to maintain an erect, attentive posture rather than on chairs with backs against which they can slump. Disorganized, nonverbal children sit at a large circular table that has bays (niches) cut into it, large enough to allow the child's body to fit comfortably. The teacher stands before them or sits with them depending on the kind of lesson. Seated aides hover behind the children but do not permit the children to lean on them indiscriminately. Excessive leaning, or glomming, can cause a child to become engrossed with a particular feature of the aide's body or apparel such as earrings, moles, or loosely hanging hair, to the exclusion of the lesson.

Floors are carpeted so that activities can take place there without need for cushions. The windows have curtains so that daylight does not enter the room when children are viewing the Sign and Spoken Language (SSL) or Symbol Accentuation (SA) training tapes. A closed cabinet houses the video for the SSL and SA tapes. The cabinet doors open from the center and are kept closed when not in use so that the children will not attend to the many inviting buttons and knobs. Other cabinets or closets hold the children's belongings or toys. Each child's cubby for personal belongings displays his or her photograph above the coat hook. Next to the child's own photograph are photographs of family members.

As the children grow in their awareness of themselves, the classroom takes on a somewhat altered appearance. The following sections indicate the nature of classroom and curriculum for two groups operating at different cognitive levels: Children in the first group are nonverbal and operating at the sign stage; those in the second group are verbal and operating at a symbolic-sign stage.

DESIGNING CURRICULA FOR TWO KINDS OF CHILDREN

Grouping the Children

Our experience suggests that it is unwise to include only children with the same disorder, for example, autism, within a class. Such a grouping tends to deprive autistic children of more functional ways of relating. A mix of children who are autistic (closed-system disordered), aphasic (system-forming disorder), and schizophrenic (syncretic system disorder), results in a more upbeat classroom because both aphasic and schizophrenic children often relate spontaneously to each other and to autistic children. This does not occur when the class consists only of autistic children. In mixed classes teachers have the opportunity to pair children (e.g., autistic with aphasic, schizophrenic with autistic) in a way that makes possible more challenging relationships and new learning not otherwise available. However, in organizing a mixed class, care must be taken that the disparity in physical and cognitive capacity between least and most advanced child not exceed 3 years.

Designing the Daily Program

C-D systems theory, translated into curricula and effectively introduced by teachers, becomes a powerful means of advancing the cognitive and emotional development of disordered children. However, to bring about desired developmental change, teachers must craft their daily programs so that they address the needs of both nonverbal, sign stage children as well as verbal, symbolic-sign stage children. In designing programs for each population, teachers find it useful to refer to the five areas of development discussed in Chapters 2 through 6. These areas are *the body schema* (Chapter 2), *coping*

(Chapter 3), *interaction with people* (Chapter 4), *communication* (Chapters 4 and 5) and *representation* (Chapters 5 and 6).

However, as teachers include the different areas in their programs, they rapidly find that their emphasis on a particular area must vary with the developmental status of their children. For example, *body schema* work means one thing when teaching nonverbal, sign stage children, and quite another when teaching verbal, symbolic-sign stage children. For the former it implies emphasis on body awareness and body efficacy, whereas for the latter it implies, in addition, emphasis on the self-concept. Similarly, although *coping* is vital for both kinds of children, the sign stage child is largely learning about how objects work and how to dress, use utensils, and find the way from one place to another, whereas the verbal, symbolic-sign stage child is dealing with maps of the environment and solving more abstract multistep problems. Further, nonverbal, sign stage children must learn to *interact* reciprocally with another first without and then with objects; verbal, symbolic-sign stage children develop "best friends" and participate in both competitive and cooperative activities. Finally, nonverbal, sign stage children learn to *communicate* and *represent* their experience via direct expressions of the body such as actions, gestures, and scribbles leading to pictures; verbal, symbolic-sign stage children learn to do so via progressively more abstract modes that involve pictures and spoken and written words as well as symbolic play.

Within the curricula for nonverbal and verbal children, any one procedure may address several of the five areas at the same time. In general, tasks that involve several areas, for example, *body schema, coping,* and *interaction,* justify longer interventions than tasks that involve only one area.

CURRICULUM FOR NONVERBAL (SIGN STAGE) CHILDREN

As the sample daily curriculum (Table 9.1) indicates, the nonverbal sign stage child has ample opportunities during the day to develop awareness of the body—body schema—and to respond to and use signs and spoken words as well as to deal with those problem-solving tasks that contribute to cognitive and language development.

The day is generally divided into 10 to 12 periods. Each period brings into play one or more of the five areas referred to earlier. The periods are short—generally 20 to 30 minutes in length. Shorter time periods enable staff to structure activities in the intense manner most likely to engage the children. The relatively short periods permit each activity to be highly structured, yet avoid isolating it from the adjacent activities. This is particularly important for distractible children with system-forming disorders.

Although the activities appear quite diverse, there is a high degree of connectedness in the content of a single day's activities. Children find that concepts that they dealt with in one period surface again in subsequent

TABLE 9.1. Sample Daily Curriculum for Nonverbal (Sign Stage) Children

Time	Activity	Areas Developed
	Orienting	
8:30	Handing over the child	Interaction
	Massage/compression with voice modulation	Body awareness
	Rough and Tumble and selective tickling	Body awareness
	Narrating and predicting imminent events	Body awareness
	Reciprocal touching, exploration and part naming	Interaction
	Tableau Calendar for structured transitions	Interaction
	From One-on-One to Group	
9:00	Circle spheres—contagious activity (teachers and children)	Interaction
	("This is the way we pat our head [rub nose, run, walk,	Body awareness
	jump, fall, stamp feet, etc.]")	Communication
	Sign and Spoken Language Program	
9:30	Training Film 1 (action signs/words: *walk, run, jump, fall,*	Communication
	come, go, stop, etc.—receptive and expressive)	Interaction
	Generalizing action concepts to others settings	
10:00	Toileting/Washing	Coping
	Snack Time	
10:20	Child uses signs/words *give, pour, eat, cookie, drink,*	Coping
	spoon, fork, etc., for desired objects/events	Communication
	Elevated Board Spheres	
10:40	Using Bridge or Template Tunnel and combined board	Body efficacy/
	structures including Grand Central sphere	awareness
	Using multiple orienting to revitalize an inert system	Interaction
		Coping
	Reciprocal Spheres	
11:15	Using Traveler with terms *push, open,* pick up, close	Interaction
11:45	Reciprocal ball pushing sphere	Coping
12:00	Lunch	Coping
		Communication
12:30	Rest Period	
	Cooperative Building Spheres	
1:00	Boards to build large and small Velcro house	Coping
	Cooperative repair of Broken table and chair	Interaction
	C-D Art Program	
1:30	Repetitive circles, lines and dots as minispheres and inte-	Representation
	grative spheres	
	Symbolic Play Spheres	
2:00	Using Elevated board replicas (small) with dolls	Representation

activities. The generalization of a learned concept from one setting to another and from one activity to another is an integral part of each day's and also of each week's curriculum development. It is not sufficient, for example, that a child understands the concept of *pull* only on the boards or only with the training tapes. The child must be able to understand and use this concept in all situations.

The program deliberately overlaps activities to emphasize certain areas of program content. Many of the daily activities address two or more key areas of functioning. Typically, the program for a nonverbal child focuses on *body schema* development (including mini- and multispheres, or integrative spheres emphasizing gross and fine motor coordination) *coping* with surroundings (including problem solving, tool use, grasp of spatial relations), *interaction* (with adults and peers) as well as language acquisition and play for *communication* and *representation*.

Disordered children who show uncertain body–world differentiation are often able to walk, run, and climb without conscious awareness of the body parts involved. However, such children—as observed in Chapter 2—seem only marginally aware of their own existence and that of others and are either totally or variably unresponsive to sounds or words. Nevertheless, such children often can respond and adjust to certain kinds of intrusive stimulation or to collisions with their immediate surroundings. Consequently, one important task of the teacher is to find the best way to *orient* such a child as he or she struggles to bridge the gap between the reality of home and the different reality of school.

Orienting the Children

There are few things more disruptive for a child with a poorly developed body organization than to start the day in a room of adults and children without a structured transfer to a specific person. To establish this important transition and to help "ground" the child first joining the class, the parent or driver literally "hands over" the child to the teacher or aide by taking the child's hand and putting it firmly into the teacher's hand, saying, "Time for school with Marvin [teacher's name]," or "Go with Diane." This emphasis on direct physical interaction communicates the notion that the child has arrived in a space (the classroom) where he or she has a special place.

After the transfer, the teacher further grounds the child by leading him or her to the area for taking off outer clothing while quietly repeating, "It's time for school, . . . time to take off coat and hat." Then, before the child can drift off—the teacher or aide begins to prepare him or her for the school day. At first, the teacher may find the child resists vigorous body work. With such children, as Ayres (1979) points out, leading with a gentle approach may be more effective. However, for those children who enjoy and *need* more intrusive work to help establish body definition, the teacher or an aide may introduce Rough and Tumble play, selective tickling, and guided collisions with obstacles and people. The use of all such strategies entails the formation of systems to build up the child's anticipation of something that is getting ready to happen—a tickle, a hug, bouncing—through repetition followed by interruptions of these systems to stimulate compensatory body reactions.

The teacher initiates Rough and Tumble activities (described in Chapter 2) with the child lying on the floor facing upwards. Playfully rolling the child from side to side, the teacher interrupts periodically to determine whether or not the child seeks to continue rolling. Another useful technique entails *body massage* in combination with *body compression*. To do this the teacher sits on the floor with the child sitting across the lap, preferably *facing* the teacher. The teacher alternately stimulates by gentle and vigorous massage of the head, shoulders, arms, trunk, legs, and so forth, while *naming* these body parts for the child. The teacher's voice should rise from a soft whisper to somewhat above a normal speaking voice, continually modulating the voice so that the child is constantly oriented to the sound and to its source. The teacher follows with compression in which—with back to the teacher —the child's knees are held securely against his or her chest and then abruptly released. The alternation between compression and release provides a contrasting experience that seems to enhance body–world awareness.

A teacher or assistant may physically enclose the child who enters school *tantrumming* or in a highly disorganized state, prior to moving him or her into the day's activities. This is done sitting on the floor, with the child in the teacher's lap facing the teacher. The teacher wraps legs around the child's body and restrains the child's flailing arms while avoiding being bitten. At this point the child cannot contain or structure himself or herself, so the teacher temporarily provides this structure. Again, there are varying *degrees* of structure. As soon as the child becomes calmer and more organized, the teacher eases constraint. The teacher talks to the child during this time, continuing to say that he or she is "in school," naming the other staff in the room, telling the child that he or she will "see mama or daddy later," "see mama or daddy after school," and so on. When the child calms down a little, the teacher, while still maintaining physical contact, continues to "ground" the child by narrating what is happening in the room, what other children are doing, and what the disorganized child is going to do next.

If the child is still so disorganized that the preceding methods are ineffective, the teacher introduces the child to a repetitive sphere on an elevated board structure. Children introduced to such spheres typically require no more than six to eight circuits before they become more organized. Structures elevated 2 to 4 feet above the ground, with various intervening obstacles that require immediate adaptation, are quite compelling (Chapters 1, 2, and 3). However, the teacher has to briskly guide the child through the board spheres. As the child becomes calmer and more engaged with the sphere, the teacher interrupts the sphere at various points, asking "Where are you going?" "What are you going to do next?" in an effort to elicit a sign or word in the sphere context. Often, the disordered child's ability to anticipate with sign or word what he or she is going to do next, contributes dramatically to improved organization and calmness. When the child has become more organized and responsive, the teacher immediately brings the child back into the group while carefully describing ("narrating") the next activity in which the child will participate.

Once a child feels more established, another body activity, that of swinging the child between two workers, may appropriately provide enjoyable vestibular and kinesthetic stimulation contributing to better body definition. The workers hold the child's hands and feet and swing the child from side to side; a variation entails another staff member waiting to "catch" the child when the workers swinging the child release. The contagious nature of this activity quickly pulls in the entire group. Alternatively, a worker can pick up a child and laughingly toss him or her to another worker while naming the worker (to make certain he or she is ready to receive the child). A typical verbal comment is, "Ready or not here she [or he] comes . . ."

Following this kind of general arousal activity, the teacher may seek to help the child define specific body parts. This may best be done through a combined teasing-tickling approach. The teacher slowly approaches the child in a teasing manner saying, "I'm going to tickle your . . . [pausing to build up tension] . . . foot [nose, hand, tummy, . . .]," moving unpredictably to each part before tickling or touching that part and then interrupting to watch carefully for signs that the child is attempting to anticipate the location of the next tickle. This procedure may be supplemented by hiding parts of the child's body—a foot, hand—with blocks or a cloth and then asking, "Where is [child's name] foot [hand]?"

Another means of orienting the disorganized, unrelated child is the "tracking" procedure. The staff member tracks the child simply by reproducing what the child does or says. This can be effective if the child occasionally glances back to see if the worker is still tracking. If the child does not glance back at the teacher while being tracked, the teacher then taps the child lightly, makes a throat-clearing sound, or calls the child's name in order to attract his or her attention. Before long, the child may be focusing more and more on the tracker, and not simply wandering around the room. When the worker finally "catches" the child, the teacher may make a big fuss, tickling and laughing with the youngster.

The teacher can then move into more subtle interactive spheres by sitting quietly with the child and imitating the child's hand movements and body posturing (see Roy, Chapter 4). Often, the child becomes aware that he or she is controlling the adult's reactive movements. Occasionally, the child may begin altering the hand (or other part of the body) movements, such as by playing pat-a-cake or touching different body parts. In this case the teacher should follow the child's lead, continuing to imitate. If the child remains involved in repetitive movements, the teacher should first follow and then slowly vary the exchange. For example, if the child has been patting a hand on the floor, the teacher should subtly change the sequence by

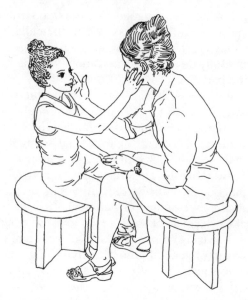

Figure 9.3. Mutual Touching sphere to encourage interaction.

occasionally patting the wall. If the child follows, the interaction is well on its way. The important aspect of this flow of interaction is its *reciprocal* nature—the child performs an action, then the adult, and so forth—yet both parts of the sequence constitute a system in which the action of one dictates the action of the other.

These actions readily expand into reciprocal exploration, touching, and naming of parts of the child's and teacher's faces, an activity that the teacher usually initiates. Figure 9.3 illustrates the nature of this activity and indicates how the teacher and child *simultaneously* place a hand on each other's cheek. As this is happening, the child can both see and feel the interaction. The child will often spontaneously elaborate this routine by moving on to explore the teacher's teeth, nose, hair, and eyes. Eye contact tends to increase substantially during these exchanges. As the teacher participates, he or she notes whether the child begins to take over the activity.

The final phase of the orienting procedure entails the use of the *Tableau Calendar,* a device that enables the children to anticipate major activities in the course of their day. The notion, here, of course, is that the children become far better grounded when they have a sense of what is going to happen next and how one event follows another.

One of the most frequent causes of tantrums at the Center is the children's inability to understand in concrete terms just what is going to happen next. For children who have limited understanding of verbal language and who deal with the world in haptic or visual terms, each move from one location

Figure 9.4. Child using the Tableau Calendar to note next activity.

to another is a threat that can break down the tenuous organization achieved in one setting. The systematic use of the Tableau Calendar (Figure 9.4) tends to preclude such breakdowns. The calendar consists of a series of three-dimensional replicas, somewhat larger than doll furniture, of salient features of several major activities common to each school day. The children can see this miniature series of detachable replicas (each can be slid into a different slot depending on the day's sequence of events) and soon learn how each section represents a particular activity.

Thus, before the children move to the sign and spoken language films, the teacher shows them a small replica of the TV monitor on which they see this program; prior to lunch they see a replica of their table with stools. As the children progress in their understanding of time, the teacher may introduce more than one event at a time until the child grasps the notion of a sequence of events (with tableaus closer to the left signifying those events that come first). With frequent reference to the Tableau Calendar the children increasingly anticipate what is going to happen next and, in doing so, establish a more functional orientation toward the school day.

In short, the most important functions of effective orienting are to provide the disordered child with a structured *transition* to the school setting, to develop his or her *body awareness*, to encourage pleasurable *interaction* between teacher and child, and to prepare and focus the child for the highly structured work to follow.

FROM ONE-ON-ONE TO GROUP

The Use of Circle Spheres

The orienting brings the child into school; the next important step is bringing the child into relationship with other children in the group. Circle spheres help make this possible. Following the morning orientation, the teacher and aides begin to guide the children into the more highly structured circle spheres. The teacher might begin by softly singing the tune of one of the songs so that the children anticipate the circle sphere. The circle spheres provide a transition from a lesser degree of structure—orientation—to a more demanding degree of structure—the language or board sessions immediately following. During circle spheres the class begins to come together as a group.

Circle spheres should generally begin with large body, gross motor activities. Everyone holds hands while standing in a circle. Then, to the tune of "Looby-Loo" (or something similar) teacher and aides help the children move *in* . . . then *out,* for example, "Here we go *in* again. Here we go *out* again!" This should be done both gently and vigorously so that the children collide with each other as they go in and suddenly separate from each other as they go out. (In a sense this is a compression–release exercise involving the entire group.)

Following the more vigorous *in–out* circle sphere, it is useful to shift to the quieter "Hello" song in which teacher and aides as well as children sing "Hello" to each child by name. Again, as with all spheres, the activity must be rapidly paced so that children do not drift away. This is also true at the end of the day, when the children are assembled together in order to sing the "Good-bye" song. Often, to ensure that each child is making contact with another, it is desirable to have the greeted child touch or shake hands with the teacher or a designated child. Assistant teachers are constantly alert to orient each greeted child to the appropriate person.

After the "Hello" sphere, the teacher and aides circling with the children to the tune of "Ring Around-a-Rosy," alternately *run, jump, walk,* and *stamp* their feet, with sudden *stops;* they then *turn* in the opposite direction and repeat the body actions. While doing this, children and staff sing, "Walk around the circle, walk around the circle," "Walk, walk, walk," or "Run around the circle, run around the circle." Then, alternating voice quality, the teacher says, "Run, run, run," corresponding to the children's actions at that time. (See Fred's response to "Walk, Jump. . . . Around the Circle" sphere in Chapter 4.)

The teacher and aides use all of the action verbs developed in the Sign and Spoken Language (SSL) tapes (see Chapter 10) in this sphere. Whenever possible, the teacher requires the children to hold hands without a teacher between them, because this provides the opportunity for one child to relate to another. Often, when one child will not hold another child's hands, they will hold on to a 12-inch dowel (about 1 inch in diameter) held by the other child. As dowels are made progressively shorter, the child approaches hand-holding without difficulty. The contagious quality of the songs and the body actions involve even very isolated children in the spheres. To further this, it is useful to shift from fast, exciting, and loud songs and actions to slowly paced quiet ones. This is a lively and enjoyable time of the day for the children and easily provides them with transitions to the next activity.

Visitors observing the children during this phase of the program often comment that they have difficulty distinguishing them from normal preschoolers. Spheric songs that explore large and small motor activities, encourage interaction, and help develop the body schema include the following:

1. *"This Is the Way We Pat Our Head* [rub nose, clap hands, stamp our feet, wave our arms, tickle (name), etc.]." This circle sphere works best with the children and staff seated on the floor. The melody "This is the way we go to school, so early in the morning" is of use here. The teacher helps the children learn their body parts either through hand-over-hand help by assistants or as the children mimic the movements of others. To fully participate, the child eventually should be able to pat head or other body part without the aid of the teacher. The teacher interrupts the activity at different times to assess system forming and the child's need to continue the activity.

2. *"Where Is [child's name]?"* This sphere is a variation on the "Where is Thumbkin?" song. While the teacher is singing this song, she or he gently places an opaque cloth over the child's head. When the chorus comes to "There she or he is!" the teacher or another child lifts the cloth and with surprise and delight "discovers" the child. Each child has a turn under the cloth, and all the children simultaneously point to the child whose turn it is. If necessary, teachers and aides help the other children point at the discovered child. After the cloth is lifted from the child's face, the teacher may tickle the child, singing, "Let's give [child's name] a tickle." This sphere is good for recognition and identification of the children as well as an exercise in object (child) permanence. The cloth used may be opaque or transparent, depending upon the child's concern with having his or her face covered.

A number of important areas are involved in circle spheres of this nature. These include *body awareness, interaction,* and *communication* as the child learns to respond to the words built into the contagious circle spheres. Following these circle spheres the children take part in the Sign and Spoken Language Program.

The Sign and Spoken Language Program

Typically,* after the children have concluded circle spheres (approximately a half hour), they next, with forecasting provided by the *Tableau Calendar,*

*When children first begin the Program, they work on the Elevated Boards *before* addressing the Sign and Spoken Language Program.

move to the *Sign and Spoken Language Program*. In doing this they find additional means of generalizing concepts from circle spheres to other aspects of reality. At first, the teacher presents one or two signs. Then, as these are assimilated, the teacher, in the form of organized play, consistently expands their range of reference. Further, because each sign with its expansion is accompanied by the appropriate spoken word, the sign as well as the word assumes expanded reference. For example, because the first training tape in the program involves action signs and words (walk, run, jump, fall, etc.) used earlier in the circle spheres, the teacher can further develop the range of reference related to these words as the children see and hear the combined sign/word sequences in other contexts. This process occurs quite rapidly with many disordered children because—with help from staff sitting behind them—they accompany with their own sign making the tape's action sequences for each sign and spoken word. Following exposure to the training tape, teachers often introduce the Simple Simon game to help the children act out the signed and spoken sequences just presented on the tape. Chapter 10 presents a more complete description of the Sign and Spoken Language Program as well as the manner in which the children interact with the content on the training tapes.

Following this sequence, teachers and staff help the children toilet themselves.

Toileting

Guided by the teacher, the children refer to the *Tableau Calendar* before toileting and note the three-dimensional replica of a toilet and sink to help them forecast the next activity. Many of the children come to the Center unable to toilet themselves—an issue of much concern for parents who frequently have younger children in addition to their disordered child. We explain to parents that toileting is a relatively complex integrative system encompassing a number of important coping skills that they—working with staff—can help their child master. Toileting involves recognizing an inner signal, approaching the toilet, lowering or unzipping pants, sitting down, defecating and/or urinating, wiping, getting off the toilet, adjusting or picking up pants, flushing the toilet, washing and drying hands, returning to the classroom—a total of 11 components. Typically, with parents carrying through the program at home, within 3 to 4 months after their arrival at the Center most children are fully able to toilet themselves.

The teacher begins this process by first carefully evaluating the child's status with regard to forming the toileting system. The teacher needs to know, for example, how many parts of the toileting system the child has mastered. Because this is a rather elaborate system, the child may at first take in only the more salient, flushing-water part. If the child cannot carry through other portions of the system, the teacher assists the child hand–over–hand until the child can do so. Teachers and aides help the children complete the toileting system by flushing the toilet, adjusting clothing, and washing and drying hands *even though the defecation or urination may not have occurred.* In developing this system it is important that the child perform each step in the proper sequence. At first, the child is not required to sit on the toilet for more than a moment before getting up, picking up pants, flushing water.

Formation of the system can be tested by interrupting it at key points such as after pants are lowered while the child is still standing or just before flushing the water. If, following interruption, the child *needs* to sit down after lowering the pants or to flush water after getting up and picking up pants, then the system is forming.

Once the system is forming, the child may sit longer on the toilet but not so long that the rest of the system is lost. It is helpful also for the child to notice the performance of a child on an adjacent toilet. To encourage urinating or defecating, the worker gives the seated child a squirt bottle with water inside that the child squirts between his or her legs into the toilet. As the child completes parts of the system, the worker expresses pleasure with a pat or a hug *whether or not the child has urinated or defecated.* The notion here is that as the system gets stronger, it will increasingly require that the child defecate or urinate. In order to help the most disordered children achieve and generalize these systems, the children have several opportunities to practice toileting systems in the course of the day. In addition, it is important that parents carry through the same procedures at home.

Snack Time

After washing, the children proceed to Snack Time. The snack serves two functions: (a) to teach children to use eating tools (knife, fork, spoon), and (b) to generalize the food-related language presented earlier on the Sign and Spoken Language training tape, to a real-life eating situation. This generalization is also sought during the lunch period.

Concepts such as *eat, drink, fork, spoon, knife, plate, glass,* are used. Often, the first use is the one that mimics the one shown on the training tape so that, for example, after seeing the tape showing "cookie," children have a cookie snack. Then by interrupting the snack, children have the opportunity to continue it by signing or saying "cookie." For a description of the techniques used, see Chapter 10.

After Snack Time the children again refer to the Tableau Calendar for reference to the elevated board activity.

ELEVATED BOARD SPHERES

There are four major uses of elevated board spheres: To help develop the *body schema, coping* behavior (including problem solving), *communication,* and *social interaction*. Although any one board sphere may involve several of these areas, certain spheres accent one or two areas more than the others.

Developing the Body Schema via Body Efficacy and Coping Activity

Earlier (Chapter 2) we discussed how enhancing the child's *body awareness* via intrusive stimulation contributes to the formation of the body schema. We now consider the role of *body efficacy* and *coping* activity in furthering the development of the body schema.

Only when the child experiences his or her body as able to move, carry, lift, push and/or pull resistive things, does the child's sense of body efficacy combine with body awareness to establish a more organized body schema. Perhaps the importance of body efficacy in defining the body as a source of intention can best be brought home by describing an experience as a 3-year-old that one of us (AM) remembers quite vividly:

> We lived in an apartment house with a large, heavy metal door with decorative scrollwork that I found enormously difficult to open. Reaching up toward the brass handle and pulling, I could for a time only pull the door open a few inches—not enough for me to slip inside before the door would close. One day, after tugging at the door handle with all my strength, the door opened wide enough for me to enter. Later, long after I could open that door with ease, I continued to recall the pleasurable sense of competence that moving that heavy door had induced within me.

Analyzing this event, it is possible to distinguish between *body efficacy* and *coping*. Body efficacy was in play as the child felt the heavy door yielding to his physical effort, whereas coping occurred as the child performed the more complex task of slipping inside *after* opening the door. Staff seek to establish a similar sense of body efficacy and coping among behavior-disordered children by encouraging them to perform big body tasks in which a change becomes evident as a function of their activity. One body efficacy and coping task entails the children moving a large table from one side of the classroom to the other. Another task used at the Center (with close supervision) entails the children carrying chairs down a flight of steps to new locations. Still another entails the children carrying planks, trays (with food on them), or large boxes from one place to another. As the child participates in these activities, he or she begins to experience the body not only as a separate entity, but as one that can directly act on objects and produce noticeable changes.

Body efficacy and coping are easily brought into play when a child performs tasks on elevated structures (L. Miller, 1989). The structures physically restrict the child so he or she can move only from one specific place to another along a well-defined path. The elevated board spheres, therefore, not only structure the child, they structure where the child is going and what options for action are available. In such spheres, because of the need to attend to the space around his or her body, the child is less likely to engage in autistic mannerisms or be diverted by extraneous events. Consequently, the child is better able to act upon and cope with the various tasks he or she confronts.

For example, on one elevated structure—the *Bridge* (Figure 9.5)—the child must deal with a demanding situation by pushing a board (the bridge) from the vertical to the horizontal plane (body efficacy) to close the gap in the structure so that he or she can walk across (coping). That motion is identical to the "down" sign. The child first learns how to perform the task alone before the teacher moves the board ahead of the child's motion. In this way, the child's functional action transforms into a meaningful sign to the teacher (communication) to lower the board.

Another demand situation that combines *body efficacy* with *coping*—the *Created Stairs* task (Figure 9.6A)—located 3 feet above ground on the Primary Board, occurs as a child *pushes* one block to a taller one (body efficacy), creating stairs on which the child can step *up* and then, after pulling another step closer, step *down*. Thus, the task requires adaptive motions of pushing, going up the stairs, pulling another stair closer, and then climbing down in order to get to the other side of the board (coping). These movements are adaptive not only in enabling the child to cope with the situation but in helping to learn sign-words *push, on,* and *pull* in the course of building and climbing the stairs. If a child does not pull the rope, a teacher or aide assists.

The *In-Out Box* (Figure 9.6B) variation derives from the *Created Stairs* task. The difference is that instead of a tall step in the center, there is an open box that allows the child to climb *in* and then *out*. This is secured directly to the planks of the Primary Board. While walking on the Primary Board, the child confronts the box and guided by sign and word goes *in* and then comes *out*. If the child is small enough to fit into the In-Out Box, he or she may be commanded with sign and word to "Sit down!" and subsequently "Get up!" before getting out of the box. The *push* and *pull* steps may be added to the In-Out Box if the child is small enough to make their use functional.

Combining Elevated Structures

After the child has acquired the ability to cope with elevated board structures as single units (minispheres)—for example, going up and down stairs—the child's range of intentional activity should be systematically extended. One way of doing this is to create integrative spheres composed of two or more elevated structures that have been combined in different ways. Thus, the board spheres can be expanded, one component at a time, so that they form a two and then three or four component integrative spheres. Teachers, however, need to resist a general tendency to combine all board structures at once. The child is far more likely to assimilate the capacities inherent in

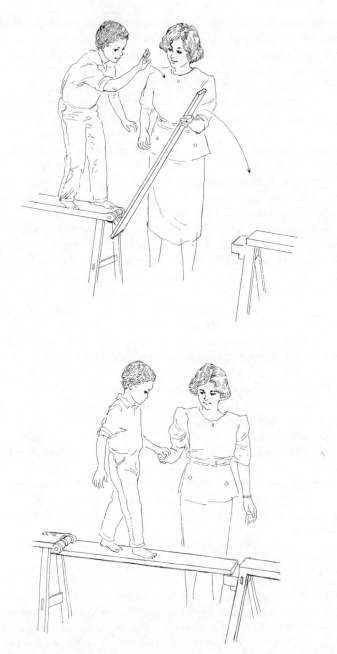

Figure 9.5. Developing the "down" sign from the coping act of putting the bridge down.

each sphere if they are added one at a time as the child turns each into a system.

Having the child work with combinations of elevated board structures (integrative spheres) is particularly useful because through them the child both accents body boundaries in different ways and experiences the body as an effective manipulator of objects. Figure 9.7 shows the manner in which a teacher induces both *body awareness* as well as *coping* behavior by combining elevated structures that require deliberate changes in the postural model of the body as the child learns to adapt first to each structure separately and then to the combined structures. Thus, the child learns to negotiate the *Mini-Maze,* and the body adjustments it requires, before addressing the *Slide* sphere and *its* changing body requirements. In doing this the teacher helps the child parallel the natural flow from one body activity to another found among normal children. The Primary Board is placed so that the Slide is parallel with it, the movement of the children is clockwise, and a teacher is at each end of the whole system. The teacher directs the children up the stairs, signing and saying "Up!" repeatedly after which the aide at the opposite end of the Primary Board animatedly signs/calls "Come!" to the children as they advance along the board. The teacher then directs them down the steps and onto the steps of the slide, whereupon, the children have to go up, sit down, and slide. Teacher and aide repeat the combined sphere until the children can do it with a minimum of help. At that point, the teacher might place the slide so that it is facing the other direction, forcing the children to shift their body orientation to a counter-clockwise direction.

Two additional combinations of structures that help develop the *body schema* and *coping* are illustrated in Figure 9.8. In Figure 9.8(*a*), the integrative sphere combines the Primary Board with the *Template Tunnel* (see Chapter 2) and the *Tip Stairs.* This combination helps disordered children experience their bodies more vividly by virtue of their repetitive adjustments to the different structures. Entering the Template Tunnel accents body boundaries as the child adjusts the body differently to get through the opening; the other structure—the Tip Stairs—helps develop *body efficacy* as the child becomes acutely aware of how deliberate shifts in body weight cause the top of the stairs to tip and induce the child to jump. The second integrative sphere (Figure 9.8(*b*)) provides a variation that helps generalize body awareness by placing the Template Tunnel on the ground and by introducing a different device with doors on the Primary Board that the child must open (body efficacy and coping) before going through. Other body-accenting devices that may be integrated within such spheres (the Crawl Board, Mini-Maze, Swiss Cheese Board, etc.) are described in Chapter 2.

Developing Interaction and Communication with Elevated Board Structures

In addition to the *Grand Central Station* and *Buddies* spheres already described in Chapter 4, elevated structures assist teachers with other inter-

A.

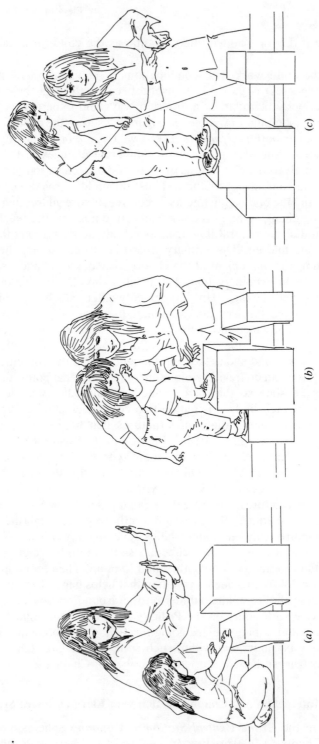

(a) (b) (c)

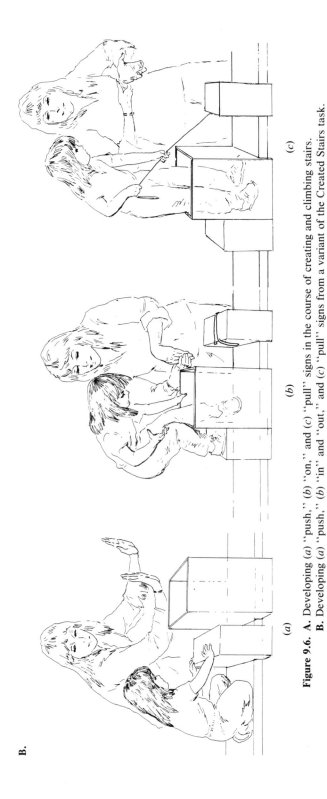

Figure 9.6. **A.** Developing (*a*) "push," (*b*) "on," and (*c*) "pull" signs in the course of creating and climbing stairs. **B.** Developing (*a*) "push," (*b*) "in" and "out," and (*c*) "pull" signs from a variant of the Created Stairs task.

(*a*)   (*b*)   (*c*)

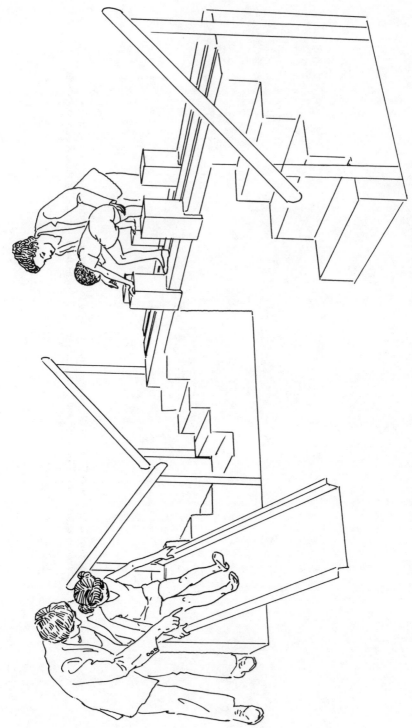

Figure 9.7. Combining two structures—Mini-Maze and Slide—into an integrative sphere.

Figure 9.8. Additional integrative spheres to develop the body schema: (*a*) Tip Stairs and the Template Tunnel on the Primary Board; (*b*) Template Tunnel on the ground and an open-close device on the Primary Board.

active and communicative strategies such as *multiple orienting* and activities with *Choice Boards*.

Multiple Orienting

From time to time, a disordered child who has mastered all parts of a particular structure, seems to "go dead" in the system. When this occurs, the child no longer seems engaged but will either become floppy or try to run away at every opportunity. Such behavior suggests that the system in its current form is no longer relevant for the child, that it adds nothing further to the child's body organization, language or cognitive capacity. The *multiple orienting* technique corrects this situation by helping the child to participate within the sphere in a way that energizes the child and encourages a more interactive relationship with the teacher. This procedure is never used during the initial phase of turning a sphere into a system but only when a particular system has gone dead or when it becomes important to augment interaction and sign-word guidance.

Assume that the "dead" integrative system consists of the child going up a set of stairs, walking across a split parallel board, going down a slide, and then repeating the process. The usual meanings inherent in this sequence are *up, walk, down, around* (back to the stairs), and so forth. Although these meanings may—through repetitive use—become inert, they can be revived by *partially* detaching them from their usual sequence. For example, although going *up* the stairs is usually followed by walking across the board, the *multiple orienting* procedure entails the teacher suddenly—when the child is halfway up the stairs—signaling with sign and word for the child to turn around and go *down* the stairs. Then, just before the child reaches the bottom, the teacher may again require the child to abruptly shift direction and go *up* the stairs. Similarly, while walking across the board—and just before the child is getting ready to sit and slide down—the teacher suddenly requires the child to *jump off* the board and then return to the steps.

The principle guiding *multiple orienting* is that by violating expectations within the sphere, the child begins to experience the *too familiar* meanings in a different way. Cognitively, the surprise elicited by these partial violations of the system often results in the child orienting more to the teacher. The teacher then observes that the child looks expectantly at him or her to see what the next surprise will be. Once the child consistently looks at the worker for guidance as to the next change, the teacher may ask the child which of two alternatives the child wishes, for example, to go down the slide or jump off the board. The child's ability to make such choices marks an increased ability to use signs and words to direct his or her own functioning first inside and later outside of familiar systems.

In short, the gains from this procedure are evident in the renewed vitality of the child within the system and in the revived way the child now orients to both the teacher and the familiar physical sequence. Stated differently, the procedure helps the child internalize the teacher as a meaningful part of his or her functioning within the system. This occurs because there is now no way in which the child can function without constant attention to the next change the teacher initiates. On a more long-term basis, the gains are implicit in the child's taking in the notion that familiar meanings may be generated in unexpected ways without losing their meanings and that knowledge about these unexpected ways can be gained by careful attention to the teacher.

In the next procedure the situation is reversed because now *the child commands the teacher, assistants, and/or the other children* to perform sequences on the elevated board structures that the child has just successfully performed with sign and verbal guidance. Typically, a teacher will begin by going halfway up the steps of the Primary Board and then turn to the child questioningly. The child, initially assisted by an aide, either signs or says *up,* to which the teacher immediately responds. The teacher then goes a bit further, confronts a new component on the structure, pauses, and again looks at the child for guidance, and so forth. In an additional variation one child, after successfully crossing the board in response to the teacher's guidance, then sign/calls "Come!" to another child before continuing down the steps and onto the slide. The language concepts *up, walk, go, come, down, sit,* and *slide* correspond directly to the children's physical activity within the sphere.

Choice Boards

Still another useful interactive procedure entails the use of *Choice Boards* (shaped like a V and attached to the Primary Board or a set of steps). A child standing at the apex of the V 3 feet above the ground is then instructed to go to one of two people whose name and sign is given him or her. The child must then scan the two people—one at the end of each leg of the V—and then walk on the plank toward the named person. This procedure can be repeated many times with teachers, parents, and aides changing their positions when the child is not looking so that the child learns to relate a person's name and sign to the unique characteristics of that person. (At other times this same structure is useful in helping the child learn to choose between two different objects by substituting objects for people at the end of each leg of the V).

A variation on the use of Choice Boards involves a setup in which the child, standing on the Primary Board, is asked to choose which of three possibilities he or she wishes to address (Up-Down Stairs, Slide, or Tip Stairs). The child may indicate choice by pointing, sign, or word. Having made a choice the child may immediately go to and use the designated device. This procedure should be paced rapidly with each child returning to the start position for another choice. With adequate pacing of the children this procedure may be cycled six to eight times before it is desirable to move to another activity.

(a)

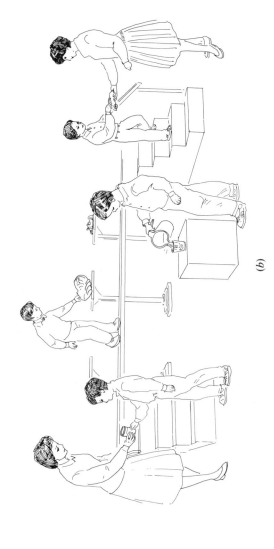

(b)

Figure 9.9. Child learns (a) to bring objects from stations to the teacher; and (b) to further complicate the sphere by adding pouring water and bringing the filled glass to the teacher.

Before introducing specific tasks that involve the elevated board structures, the teacher first develops them as separate entities. *Only then* may they be used in more elaborate integrative spheres. Thus, when the child is involved with another in a reciprocal act such as a shared chore, he/she already has some of the required skills in his/her repertoire.

For example, before a child can take an object from a station and give it to the teacher at Station B (Figure 9.9(a)), the child must already have demonstrated the ability to give an object when face to face with another. Similarly, before a child attempts to integrate pouring water into a glass (Figure 9.9(b)) prior to bringing it to the teacher at Station A, the child must first master the minispheres of pouring water into a glass and of carrying it from one location to another.

In Figure 9.9(a) after the child climbs the steps on the Primary Board, he or she picks up one of the items on the stations (car, glove, shoe) and brings it to the worker at the other end of the board. If three children are in this sphere each one may take and bring a different object to the worker. This sphere is expanded (Figure 9.9(b)) by requiring the child to pour water into a glass at a station on the ground and bring it to the teacher in Position A before resuming picking up objects from the stations and bringing them to the teacher in Position B.

Other relevant expansions include changing the objects on the stations, changing the positions of the teachers, reversing direction, and introducing new activities to intervene before the child makes contact with tasks involving another person. In this way the child learns to generalize his or her capacities and to maintain an inner sense of direction even though other events interfere. The child's augmented ability to interact with people around objects in an increasingly complex manner is an important outcome of these spheres.

THE LCDC PLAYGROUND

Although the elevated board spheres developed *within* the Center enable the children to use their bodies in a relatively small, structured space, the children still need to learn how to cope with structures in the larger spaces of the Center's *outside* area. To make this possible we designed and carefully spaced various elevated structures in our outside play area.

The playground consists of a number of structures—the *Sandbox,* the *Square-Diamond,* the *King's Castle,* the *Maze*—of varying complexity. Our general strategy is to introduce and have the children fully experience—as parts of spheres—all aspects of *one structure* before introducing them to the next structure. Then, to ensure that the children do not lose touch with earlier structures, staff frequently interrupt their involvement with a later structure and guide them back to earlier ones. As a result of this multisphere strategy the children gain a conception of the spatial relations between as well as within the different structures.

Because of the urban nature of the setting, the Sandbox (Figure 9.10(*a*)) created for the children is surrounded by a fencelike structure with cut-out footholds that allow the children to climb in and out. Thus, the sand remains clean and free of debris from animals and has the added advantage of making a demand on the children in terms of problem-solving and body organization.

Adjacent to the Sandbox is the Square-Diamond. Developmentally, it is one of the earliest pieces of equipment to which we introduce the children. The Square-Diamond (Figure 9.10(*b*)) ranges from 3 to 4 feet from the ground and pitched so that the children are either slightly leaning forward or leaning back slightly as they walk along its path. They can reach the path by climbing up the steps at either end. If they take the steps at the lower end, they will have to adjust their bodies in order to negotiate the uphill climb; if they take the other set of stairs, they will have to adjust to the downward incline. There is enough room for the children to pass one another on the path, thus

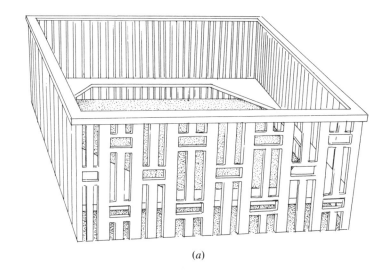

(*a*)

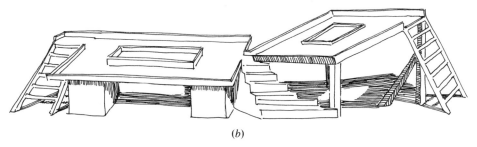

(*b*)

Figure 9.10. (a) Sandbox; (b) Square-Diamond structures in the LCDC Playground.

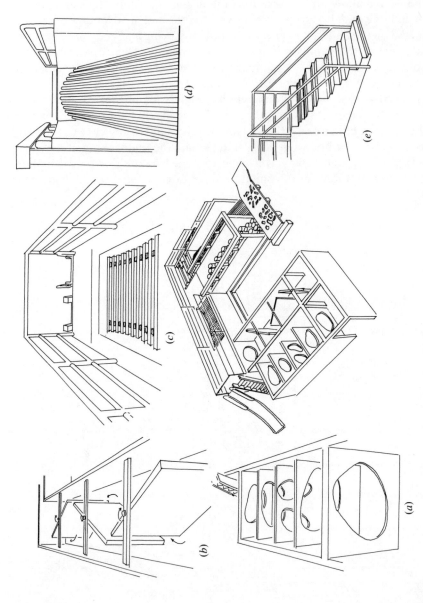

Figure 9.11. Maze with component structures: (*a*) Template Tunnel; (*b*) Swinging Doors; (*c*) Swaying Bridge; (*d*) Pipe Slide; (*e*) Asymmetrical Stairs.

requiring them to acknowledge the existence of each other while taking care not to fall. A child may also take an alternate route if the path is blocked by an oncoming child. In this way, problem solving involving various body adjustments play a role in the use of the Square-Diamond.

The Maze (Figure 9.11) offers the children a number of possibilities to further develop their body schemas and coping ability. The Maze incorporates within its form a series of different substructures. For example, as Figure 9.11(a) shows, it includes on the bottom left a long template tunnel requiring many body adjustments to get through. Above that structure (Figure 9.11(b)) it shows large swinging doors, which move only when pushed on one side. To the right of this (Figure 9.11(c)) there is a swaying bridge that enables the child to gain access to (Figure 9.11(d)) a semicircular pipe slide that abuts the Swiss Cheese Board. Then, at the right end of the structure (Figure 9.11(e)) the child finds a set of asymmetrical steps that require the children to take into account the changing relation of each step to the next so that they must adapt their movements accordingly.

This complex structure often attracts many children at the same time. Often when two classes are on the playground together, a substantial number of the children converge at this structure. Those who have had experience with the Swiss Cheese Board as part of their training find that they can repeat and then generalize their newly acquired facility. Coming down the slide after crossing the swaying bridge, the child has a relatively long distance to go in order to find the steps that will lead him or her to the slide again. To keep this in mind is a rather complicated task for a child who in order to

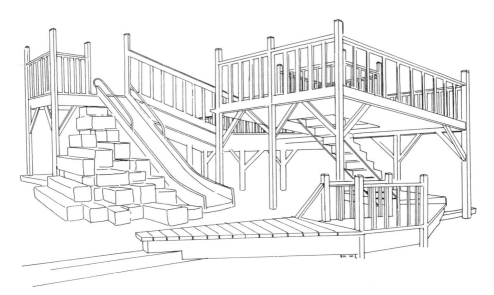

Figure 9.12. King's Castle structure in the LCDC Playground.

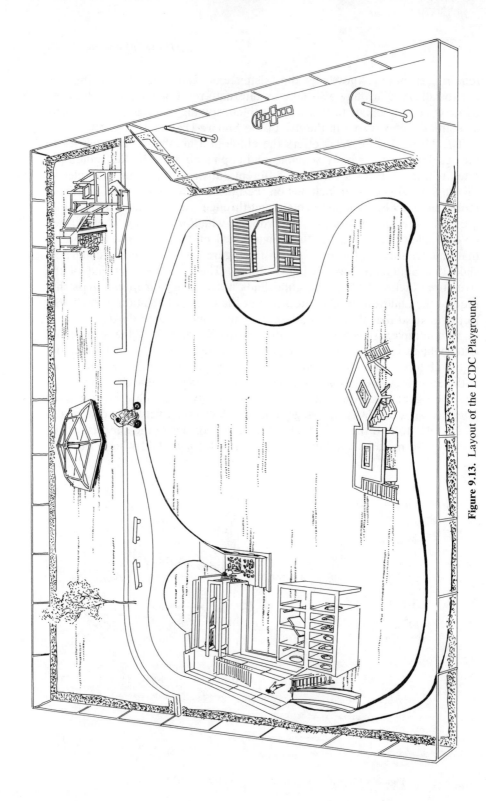

Figure 9.13. Layout of the LCDC Playground.

function usually has to have the outcome immediately apparent. The Maze with its swinging doors, cutout forms and asymmetrical stairs helps develop body awareness and efficacy as well as coping ability in the children who repetitively engage with various parts of the structure. The Maze tends to keep children engaged for a relatively long period of time, with many opportunities to interact with one another in a productive manner.

The King's Castle (Figure 9.12) has the quality of a lookout tower. It contributes to more advanced functioning because, if it is used to its fullest, it permits children to survey the entire playground area from a height. Typically, the less developed children remain preoccupied with the space in their immediate vicinity whereas more advanced children become concerned with the physical relations between the structures. If a previously self-involved child can climb up the steps (also asymmetrical) to the top of the platform, look around, and respond to someone calling his or her name from across the playground, that child has made significant improvement. This structure also contains a slide that is immediately apparent upon completing the climb up the steps. In order for the children to overcome the pull of the slide and go on to the top of the tower, they have to understand the possibilities inherent in this structure, including the ramp leading to the top deck and the "secret ladder" directly under the structure.

The LCDC Playground has spaces within it for large group games of chase, running, tetherball, volleyball, basketball, and so forth. In addition to these games, a path throughout can be used for bikes, trikes, skating, walking, and pulling wagons and carts. Figure 9.13 provides an overview of the relationship between various structures and activities.

RECIPROCAL SPHERES

At first, only rarely do system-disordered children spontaneously play with each other. For most of the children, play with another—like other forms of interaction—must be carefully structured before the child can learn to initiate activity independently. To attain this goal, the staff work with the children both in pairs—as dyads—and in the larger group. In the following section are some of the activities that the children engage in, at first with the support of the teacher and assistants and then by themselves.

Ball Pushing

The teacher sets up a *reciprocal ball-pushing sphere* by placing the children on stools facing each other with a large ball between them suspended from the ceiling. Staff place the children's hands on the ball directly in front of them and help them push it to each other. The placement of the ball prevents it from escaping the orbit of the children's reach and keeps it within their visual field. With the help of the teacher and aides they learn to push and

Figure 9.14. Children engaged in reciprocal ball-pushing play.

guide the swinging ball back and forth. A variation on this would be to push a ball to one another across a table (see Figure 9.14). They may also pass the ball around the table to one another. This must be done quickly and with a degree of urgency in the teacher's voice (either by whispering or singing a fast-paced tune) in order to establish the contagion that will keep the sphere going.

Block Building

The reciprocal block-building sphere is also an activity that requires the teacher, initially, to help the children participate hand-over-hand in placing the blocks on top of one another. A teacher sits back of each child helping him or her alternate block building by loudly placing one block on another. Often, the loud smack of one block landing on another helps orient the children to the blocks and to each other.

Another block sphere involving two children in a turn-taking sequence entails arranging the blocks in a row at the edge of a table and then having each child alternate knocking the blocks off the table into a metal pan below.

The teacher and an assistant—one behind each child—pace and monitor the alternating behavior of the children until they grasp the notion "First you, then I . . ."

Blowing

Reciprocal blowing—with the children facing each other—may be done with a cotton or Ping-Pong ball. The object is for the child to blow the object across the table to the other child and to keep the other child from blowing the ball on the floor. To structure the game properly, the teacher makes a channel out of several long blocks so that the ball remains oriented properly between the two children.

Exchanges

Reciprocal exchanges are set up between two seated children facing each other. One child has a bucket of small plastic balls, whereas the other child has an egg carton capable of receiving those balls. The teacher helps the child take one ball from the bucket and give it to the other child, who then puts the ball into the egg carton. When one egg carton is filled, the child closes it, takes another egg carton, fills it, and so forth. The teacher helps so that the activity takes on a continuous paced rhythm, saying "Pick-up, give, put in" for many cycles. The teacher interrupts to see what the children will do spontaneously. Subsequently, the children reverse roles to ensure that both experience the activity in all its aspects.

The following activities, ordered in terms of difficulty, help the child to engage with and acknowledge the existence of the other.

1. *Hand-to-Hand Transfer.* An engaging object—a small car, an enclosed bell, a candy—is located next to each child's hand on the table. The child picks up the object and must put it in the hand of the other. The child giving the object points to or touches (and names when possible) the other as the child receiving is making reference to the self. The action is then reciprocated.

2. *Passageway Transfer.* Using a narrow passageway that is located at eye level, the child must pick up the object and push it to the other, again naming the receiver. The action is then reciprocated.

3. *Using an Instrument to Pull to Self.* Using an instrument such as a plate, the sender picks up the object, makes reference (reciprocal), places the object on the plate; the receiver must now act by pulling the instrument towards the self.

4. *Using an Instrument to Push to Other.* The sender must now use the plate to push the object away from his/her body and to the other. Before the receiver acts, self and other references are established. Sender and receiver roles are then reversed.

5. *Using an Extended Instrument to Push to Other.* Using an instrument (rake) as an extension of the body directly from the hand, the sender must push the object (losing sight of it) to the other. Reference is made before sending the object. The other child then repeats the process.

6. *Using an Instrument (Vehicle) Not Directly Extended From the Body (Traveler).* The sender picks up the object, opens a box, puts the object in the box, closes it, and then pushes the box away from him/herself to the receiver who begins pulling the box with a string toward him/herself. Roles are then reversed.

7. *Using a Vehicle Requiring Problem Solving.* The child must place the object (small car) on a slope (a board) so that it will roll down to the other child. The child must make the board slope by lifting up the board to enable the object to roll. The other child repeats the process so that the object rolls in the opposite direction.

8. *Using Hands to Push an Object around Detours to the Other.* Given a series of detours, the sender must solve the problem of detours and plan a path to the receiver. The receiver then becomes the sender.

9. *Using Instruments to Push Candy around Detours to the Other.* Using an instrument (rake) as an extension of the hand, the sender must solve the problem of detours to push the object to the receiver. Again, the roles of sender and receiver change.

To help develop large group interaction, the Interaction Boards (Chapter 4, p. 132) and Swinging Ball are used. Teachers also encourage group interaction by requiring the children to hold hands while running in a line, much the same as the children hold each other's hands when they perform the Buddies sphere (see Chapter 4). The following interventions are introduced in order to further expand their existing interactions.

Swinging on the Large Ball

The entire group can push one child seated on the large Swinging Ball. Each child should have a turn pushing or being pushed. This can be done either as a group activity or with as few as two children.

Interactive Spheres with Broken Objects

When using the broken objects (see Chapter 4) in order to promote reciprocal play, teachers and aides initially help the children. With the large table, for example, the teacher and an aide help two children push it together so that it forms a complete table surface. When trying to place the legs on the table, two or more children may put the legs in their sockets so that the table can stand upright. With the broken chair, the back may be attached by one child while another child installs the arms or legs. Once children repair broken objects, they immediately use them—putting things on the table and sitting in the chair.

Interactive spheres may also be used with the smaller broken objects (cup, bowl, shoe, ball, dog) described in Chapter 4. To implement spheres with these objects, each child is given a part of the object and must approach the other child in order to complete the object. Once one object is restored, the children proceed to another, and so forth.

Turn-Taking Spheres with Objects and People

Before introducing specific tasks, the teacher analyzes them into their component parts and uses them in mini- and multispheres or integrative spheres so that the child begins to learn all the parts of a task as well as the language that accompanies it before sharing it with another. Thus, when the child is involved with another in a reciprocal act like a shared chore, he/she already has some of the required skills in his/her repertoire.

For example, before a child is asked to take turns carrying a passenger on his or her trike or pulling a child in a wagon, the teacher has already determined that this skill is in each child's repertoire. Knowing this, the teacher has no concern about the rider in the wagon taking a turn pulling it, or the driver of the trike taking a turn as passenger while the former passenger "drives" the trike.

The same kind of reciprocal pattern may be introduced with dressing, either with children's clothing or adult dress-up and makeup play. Children may comb each other's hair or put hats, necklaces, and bracelets on each other. The participating adult turns over control of these tasks to the children as soon as they begin to perform the activity successfully. Repetition of these acts coupled with periodic interruptions typically results in children performing with increasing autonomy.

Spheric Involvement in Everyday Tasks (Chores)

This is an area often neglected as a means of having the children relate to and work with each other. Often normal children are given those jobs that make for a smoother running classroom. Children clean blackboards and erasers, pick up chairs and place them on desks, or run errands for the teacher. When teachers introduce these same activities with disordered children, they find that—after initial support—many can perform them with increasing effectiveness. For example, after the children clear the lunch utensils, they learn to wash the table. This may entail one child spraying water on the table by means of a spray bottle while the other washes with a sponge. Other tasks include helping one another carry a bucket of water (each child holding onto the handle), washing a very dirty blackboard (a group effort, so they can see their effect), carrying trays filled with objects to another part of the room, carrying bags of groceries, emptying them with the help of another child, and placing the objects on a shelf in the cupboard.

Functional activities around the home or classroom can be used as a basis for teaching the children many functional tasks in a social framework. Such tasks also provide a useful and systematic basis for language usage that can readily transfer to comparable situations at home and elsewhere.

Toileting and Washing

After working on reciprocal or interactive spheres the children, again guided by the Tableau Calendar, toilet and wash themselves in preparation for Lunch.

Lunch

Lunch provides additional opportunity for coping, interaction, and communication as the children—with support from the teaching staff—carry the food and table settings into their room, set the table, hand out food, open boxes, use utensils to cut and pick up food, and clear and wash the table. Following the meal, the children take turns vacuuming the area so that all crumbs and food debris are removed. They may also, at the end of the meal, clean plates and cups in a preliminary manner.

Rest

During this period the children lie quietly on their cots in a semidarkened room while listening to nonintrusive music. Often the children have soft animals with them. A skeleton teaching staff is in the room to respond to the children as needed.

Cooperative Building Spheres

Following the rest period the children engage in one of several different cooperative building spheres. One of the earliest involves the children, two by two, picking up planks (6 ft long by 5 in. wide and 1 in. thick) stacked in one location in the room and bringing them to another location to form one of several structures. For one structure the children lay the boards across a set of stools to form a large table that they sit around and on which they play with blocks and other toys. At first a pair of children may resist picking up the planks and carrying them to their new location; however, with staff support, adequate pacing, and repetition, the children fairly rapidly learn to do so. It is quite rewarding to observe children who previously had been unable to either cooperate or do anything functional, begin to jointly lift up the planks, move to the proper location, and place them in the correct pattern.

Once the children can make a simple table, they soon learn how to make a crude house (staff provides the framework) by laying planks across the roof and stacking them on the side for walls. After this project, the children

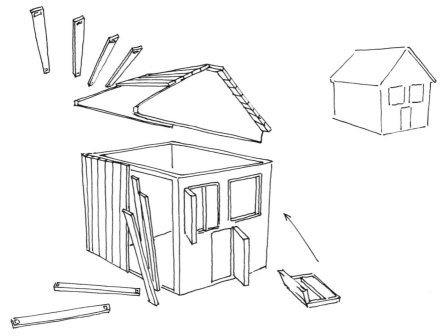

Figure 9.15. A Velcro house structure.

can also make ramplike structures that they can both walk on and send toys down.

A variant of this sphere entails making a house with Velcro to keep the parts in their proper places (see Figure 9.15). This integrative sphere requires the children to help one another construct a house that they can later furnish or enter and in which they pretend to sleep or eat. The large Velcro house is put together by having the children carry parts to a house frame; they then attach the parts by means of the Velcro. The teacher securely places the child's hands on the part to be carried and slowly removes support while allowing the child to begin to carry it until the child can completely take over the teacher's role.

A small Velcro house can be constructed by having all the pieces in one corner of the room with one child, while another child has the frame. The teacher then requires the child with the house parts to pick up a part, walk to the other child and hand it to that child, who then places it on the frame. All this is accompanied with appropriate language. At times, the teacher may wish to include the Velcro furniture in the play with the houses. These, most frequently, are viewed as individual problem-solving devices that can be taken apart and put together. However, they can also be used so that one child is holding one piece while the other adds the missing part to complete the structure. All the cooperative building spheres involve *body efficacy* (lifting, carrying objects), *coping* (building a multistep structure via integrative spheres), as well as *interaction* (lifting and carrying planks with another or giving parts to another).

During the final period of the day the children participate in either the Cognitive-Developmental Art Program or a Symbolic Play Program.

COGNITIVE-DEVELOPMENTAL SYSTEMS ART PROJECT

Based on the work of Kellogg (1970) and her belief that scribbling offers a way to discern more clearly children's developing vision and mental processes, we decided to use scribbling spheres as a way of encouraging the development of representational processes. We did this by assuming that just as interruption of a sphere results in compensatory actions that become more intentional, for example, compulsive object throwing can be transformed into deliberate dropping (see Fred, Chapter 3), so may rote scribbling be transformed into deliberate drawing which may then be progressively complicated and expanded. It seemed likely that a C-D art program could help disordered children develop (a) intentional activities in a graphic sphere, (b) provide the graphic transition from a variety of scribbles to a combination of two or more scribbles, and then (c) provide a basis for representional drawings. In proceeding in this way, we assumed that scribbles were to graphic symbols what babbling was to spoken words. Accordingly, just as meaningful language emerged from babbling, so meaningful drawings could emerge from scribbling.

Spheric activities were developed around the various scribbles that Kellogg had identified as part of the normal progression toward representational drawing. Younger and nonverbal children and those whose drawings are in the basic scribble stage are introduced to graphic interventions drawn from Kellogg's list of scribbles (curve, dot, line, zig-zag, loop, and circle) (see Figure 9.16). After establishing these scribbles with crayon or finger paint, teachers introduce different media such as clay, paint, and collage to generalize the scribble. With all media, however, the emphasis is on helping the children convert an introduced sphere into a system (established ritual) that they can continue without support. The main procedure to establish this is the interruption of a graphic sphere of scribbling so that the child may compensatorily continue and thus "own" the scribbles he or she produces.

The Cognitive Developmental Art Program (C-DAP) proceeds in three stages: (a) the formation of a *range* of scribbles, (b) the production of a *combination* of scribbles, and (c) the development of *representational* drawings.

Range of Scribbles

Each week the teacher introduces one of a range of scribbles. For example, Week 1 might introduce the children to the concept of the "line." The

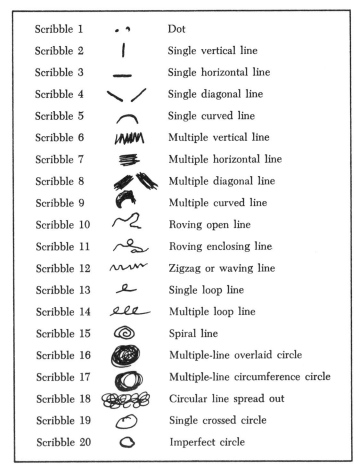

Scribble 1		Dot
Scribble 2		Single vertical line
Scribble 3		Single horizontal line
Scribble 4		Single diagonal line
Scribble 5		Single curved line
Scribble 6		Multiple vertical line
Scribble 7		Multiple horizontal line
Scribble 8		Multiple diagonal line
Scribble 9		Multiple curved line
Scribble 10		Roving open line
Scribble 11		Roving enclosing line
Scribble 12		Zigzag or waving line
Scribble 13		Single loop line
Scribble 14		Multiple loop line
Scribble 15		Spiral line
Scribble 16		Multiple-line overlaid circle
Scribble 17		Multiple-line circumference circle
Scribble 18		Circular line spread out
Scribble 19		Single crossed circle
Scribble 20		Imperfect circle

Figure 9.16. Scribbles used in LCDC's C-D Systems Art Program. Adapted from Kellogg, 1970. Copyright 1970 by R. Kellogg. Used with permission of Mayfield Publishing Co.

process to be used could be (a) drawing on paper (markers, crayons, or pencil), (b) using line strips of paper to be pasted in collages, (c) working with clay, or (d) using paint on paper. The method of introducing the particular "scribble" might involve the teacher working hand-over-hand with the child while saying "Line, line, line . . ." until the child takes over the activity. When the teacher judges that the ritual has been established, that is, it moves from an introduced sphere to a system of repetitive line making, he or she interrupts the ritual to help bring it under the child's deliberate control. The interruption used to bring about intentional action on the part of the child might be (a) for the teacher to suddenly release her control of the child's hand in order to see if the child will continue to make the line, dot, and so forth; (b) for the teacher to obstruct the continuation of the ritual by means of blocking the child's activity; or (c) for the paper to be removed and another sheet of paper substituted.

Combining Scribble Spheres

If each introduced scribble is considered a minisphere, then combining different scribbles produces a multisphere, in that each scribble is arbitrarily related to another. In helping children achieve scribble combinations—lines going through circles, dots inside circles—each scribble must be interrupted at the point of maximal tension and the child introduced to an entirely different scribble. Once the child becomes engaged by the new scribble sphere, that sphere, too, is interrupted and the child is brought back to the first scribble where the process is repeated.

As indicated in Chapter 3, the rationale for the multisphere procedure is that by interrupting and shifting engagement from one minisphere (scribble) to an entirely different sphere, the first sphere continues to remain "alive" in the child's psychological economy even while the child becomes engaged by the second sphere. After a number of cycles involving interruptions to each of the two spheres, the child begins to demonstrate, by glancing at the second sphere while still engaged by the first, a sense of relation between the two spheres. This combinatory process is assisted by the first scribble remaining within view *while* the child is performing the second scribble.

Representational Drawing

Just as it is impossible to predict precisely when a child will cross the gap from signs to names (see Chapter 5), so there is no way to know when the child will shift from even the most elaborate complex of lines, dots, and circles into the first representational drawing. Staff can, however, sometimes prod the process by suggesting and even accenting the combined scribbles that the child produces. Thus, if a child has produced circles and line combinations, the teacher might suggest that the circle is the head and the lines the legs and then put in the eyes. If this engages the child, the teacher might then ask where the mouth or hair should go. If the child accepts the notion that graphic marks can represent a person, representational drawings quickly follow.

Symbolic Play Spheres

In this part of the program the children are supplied with small replicas of some of the elevated board structures with which they were engaged earlier in the day. These may be used either in the presence of the full-size elevated structures or alone with other relevant objects. Children then have the opportunity to make small dolls, walk, jump, or sit in situations similar to the ones that they themselves have experienced on the elevated board structures. The intent, here, of course, is to help the children represent their earlier experiences in play and, in a more general sense, to develop their ability to represent their own experiences to themselves.

The Tableau Calendar can also be used for this purpose as children sit small dolls around the table for a make-believe snack or put the dolls on the toilet or place them around the TV set to simulate participation in the Sign and Spoken Language Program.

To further assist the development of symbolic play, the children have the opportunity to assist the teacher in driving a toy car to the gas station, getting fuel, driving the car to school, letting a child out, then bringing the child home, and parking the car in the garage. In another guided play sequence, the teacher washes, dresses, feeds, toilets, and later, puts a baby doll to bed. Periodically, during these sequences, the teacher will interrupt her actions to ask a child what he or she should do next. As the child indicates through gesture or word the appropriate action, he or she moves that much closer to spontaneous, symbolic play.

CURRICULUM FOR VERBAL (SYMBOLIC-SIGN STAGE) CHILDREN

Each of the five factors that were relevant for the nonverbal child are relevant—after certain adjustments—for verbal children at the symbolic-sign stage of development. For example, whereas for nonverbal children the development of the body schema was central, for verbal children at the symbolic-sign stage of development, the development of the *self-concept* is the primary issue. However, for both nonverbal and verbal children, the concept of *coping* continues to be important. The difference is that for the verbal children the concept extends beyond the immediate environment to knowledge and use of tools, and maps, as well as geography and history. Similarly, the concepts of *social interaction, communication,* and *representation* reflect the child's increased symbolic capacity. This section, shows how the curriculum for these children relates to these major areas of their development.

Self-Concept

Just as there are two major aspects involved in the formation of the body schema, so are there two major aspects to the formation of the self-concept. One, has to do with the development of self-consciousness or *self-awareness;* the other has to do with the formation of *self-efficacy.*

Self-awareness develops as significant adults act upon and define the child by referring to his or her characteristics—being handsome or pretty, "taking after" a parent, being stubborn, hardworking, strong, being able to run well, and so on. Self-efficacy expands as the child experiences his or her own significance when performing competently in a play, building a model, doing well in school, washing dishes, painting a mural, or helping someone do something. What counts here is not the performance of the act per se but the feeling of having played a significant role in the achievement of that task.

For example, just as a stonemason or a steelworker will pass by a skyscraper and point with a proprietary feeling at "my building" because of having worked on it, so do all children—and particularly disordered children—develop a sense of themselves when they relate it to specific achievements. Consequently, throughout the day, in all parts of the curriculum, teachers and staff find ways to make visible the children's personal, academic, or athletic achievements in ways that help them develop both positive self-awareness and the sense of their own efficacy so critical in all functioning. The manner in which self-awareness and self-efficacy as well as other important systems are realized in the course of the curriculum is evident in Table 9.2.

Coping

Orienting the Children

Just as nonverbal children need to be oriented to the events of the day in the class, so do those children who have some measure of spoken language. However, given the more advanced status of the children (symbolic-sign stage), orientation need no longer be organized around direct body action with situations—as with the Tableau Calendar—to communicate sequences of events. Now, each child can receive a warm verbal greeting and perhaps be placed next to another child, after removing outer garments and placing them in the cubby. Frequently, the children play song games that introduce one to the other. Although circle spheres may still be played with this group of children, the emphasis is on requiring more spoken language. Children now not only touch the teachers to get their attention, they call their names. The sign–name relation taught by teacher and aides often helps the child recall the relation between a teacher and her or his name.

With this newly verbalizing group of children, the teacher may at the beginning of the day narrate the day's events indicating each activity and requiring children verbally to elaborate the nature of the activities. The next step in organizing their day is the *Picture Calendar*. The children no longer need three-dimensional replicas of the structures of their day; however, they still need help forecasting how one event follows another. The teacher prepares a calendar showing the events of the day simply drawn on a large sheet of oaktag or on the blackboard. She or he draws salient events and then adds those events that are new or are specific for a particular child (such as a birthday). The teacher displays this calendar so that the children can refer to it whenever a change in activity is about to occur. In this manner, the children learn to anticipate and narrate forthcoming events of the day. When parents develop similar calendars for their children at home (see Chapter 12), tantrums and upsets by children (who have difficulty with the sequence of events without visual support) often diminish.

When the children have begun to understand the Daily Picture Calendar, the teacher introduces the Weekly Calendar, describing the children going

TABLE 9.2. Sample Daily Curriculum for Verbal (Symbolic-Sign Stage) Children

Time	Activity	Systems Developed
	Orienting	
8:30	Acknowledge peers and adults Establish group identity (This is the Big Kids' Class) Language: Greetings ("Hi [name]." "How are you?" "How do you feel?")	Self-awareness Group awareness Interaction Social awareness
	Show 'N Tell	
8:45	Description of salient features of object, event, person (could include description of yesterday's lunch). Method: question–answer or narration	Communication Representation
	Reading	
9:00	Group I: SA Lessons 4–6 involving 2–3-word sen- tences using flashcards Group II: SA Lessons 17–19. Phonics, worksheets, dictation of single sounds, words, sentences; read short paragraph for comprehension (combine sight and phonic approaches) Group III: Combine SA with Advanced Phonics Read- ers; review *WH* words (who, what happened; where, when did it happen; why?)	Representation Communication
	Exercise	
9:30	Calisthenics: Windmills, jumping jacks, and so on Giving directions: Teacher and child take turns in giv- ing directions ("Everybody stamp your feet!" "Everybody clap hands!")	Body awareness Self-efficacy
	Snack	
10:00	Children help prepare snack by bringing trays to class, serving (crackers and juice), and cleaning up Children take turns performing tasks and follow rules ("No grabbing the crackers." "It's his turn to pour.")	Coping Social awareness
	History/Geography/Story	
10:30	*History* (2× per week): Personal histories of the chil- dren and their families; history of LCDC and the surrounding community *Geography* (2× per week): Geography of room, Cen- ter, and relation to home of each child; learning to use maps to find locations during trips to library and other locations *Story* (1× per week): Children listen to and discuss story (e.g., *Black Beauty*) from week to week	Self-awareness Coping

TABLE 9.2. *(Continued)*

Time	Activity	Systems Developed
	Free Choice	
11:00	Various games, activities made available with rules determining who plays with what, whom, and where Vote: on agreeing to play or not play with certain games and whether to share	Social awareness
	Science/Art	
11:15	*Science* (3× per week): Learning about and practicing with levers; studying how an ant farm works *Art* (2× per week): Using different media (paint, clay) to represent their experience	Coping Representation
	Lunch	
12:00	Children, backed up by aides, bring hot lunches from second floor to classroom; distribute food, napkins, utensils; eat their lunches while conversing with each other and teacher	Social awareness Communication
	Rest	
12:30	Children rest, nap, or listen to quiet story	
	Adaptive Physical Education	
1:00	*Outside Individual Games:* Bikes, skates, scooters around playground path *Cooperative Games:* Catch, relay races, tetherball, basketball	Self-efficacy Social awareness
	Arithmetic/Money/Time	
1:30	*Arithmetic:* Addition, subtraction, and word problems; applying knowledge to money use on class visits to stores *Clock:* Demonstrating hourglass, and then modern clock; relating numbers on clock to events (lunch, time to go home, etc.); explaining short and long clock hands	Representation Coping
	Handwriting	
2:00	Translate printed words learned in reading to cursive forms; write a letter (with assistance) to a friend	Representation
	Preparation to Leave	
2:15	Children organize and categorize papers to bring home; recall events of the day with help of Picture Calendar; prepare for next day's events; say goodbye to each person using social phrases	Coping Communication

to sleep, then waking and beginning the new day. She or he indicates the activities that are repeated as well as some new event that makes each day different from the ones preceeding and following it.

Teaching Geography and History

When teaching the concepts of space and time to behavior-disordered children, the C-D system strategies developed at the Center build on the child's most immediate experience. For example, in order to teach youngsters the geography of the classroom, school, and neighborhood, the teacher might, with the aid of the Picture Calendar, take the children for a walk, and pointing in the direction that they are going, name the destination. The teacher also has the children look back and designate the site from which they came. Typically, when normal children enter a room, they explore the space by walking around and asking about some of the objects in that space. Teachers attempt to encourage such interest in surroundings with both verbal and nonverbal children in the classroom. With the nonverbal child, the teacher places more emphasis on gestures and in walking alongside and indicating by sign and spoken word the nature of new objects. However, this is more frequently done by the object's function rather than its name. For example, a chair might be labeled "sit-down," the table might be "place to eat," and so forth.

However, because verbal children have a name for the object, the teacher need only point to and name the object for such a child to move in the desired direction. Often, in order to grasp spatial relations the newly verbal child benefits from relating various spatial locations to different people who occupy these locations. For example, since Gus, the building coordinator, has his office on the first floor, the child might be instructed to "Go down the stairs and give this to Gus," or "Bring this bowl to another [class, teacher, or child]." Generally, an assistant teacher will follow at a distance seeing that the child does not get lost while performing the task.

GEOGRAPHY.   Teachers help the children understand spatial relationships by having them draw and use simple maps. With the child seated, the teacher first indicates the child's location on paper and then indicates some salient feature in the room (perhaps a window) and draws this on the map. Following this, the teacher represents on the map the location of a favorite toy or food next to the window. Guided by the map, the child finds the food by the window. Variations of the game—a form of treasure hunt—involve the teacher indicating the hidden locations of various items on a map that the child has to follow in order to discover them.

Once the children have mastered the geography of the classroom and of the three-story building that houses the Center's school and clinic, it is a small step to take these principles and expand them to the school neighborhood, city, state, and country. Children are taken on short walks, with teachers indicating markers along the way, perhaps a fence that the children can touch while walking, or a small incline that they can walk down more rapidly, or a curbing that is painted in a bright color. These features or markers might be considered the "road map" on the way to the neighborhood store to buy some food to prepare when the class returns to the school. Even while pointing out the markers, it is important for the children to keep their destination in mind by pointing in the appropriate direction and talking about it, with the help of judiciously narrated comments by teachers and aides. When using narration, the teacher might speak about what the child is doing at that particular moment, for example, "John is walking quietly, holding Dora's hand. Now he is stepping off the curb. Now he looks both ways before crossing. Now John crosses the street holding Dora's hand."

After narrating the events exactly as they are happening, the teacher begins to help the child *anticipate* events that will soon happen. A teacher might say, for example, "*Soon,* not right now, but *soon* we will come to the store." By helping the children anticipate events the teacher combines notions of time and space with further exercise in the way that language can guide expectations. Teachers introduce these notions in a quiet, reassuring manner. Immediately after experiencing the activity, simple maps can be drawn in class and can then be used in subsequent walks. Clearly, a walk is not merely placing one foot in front of the other while leading a dully compliant child. It is, instead, a shared experience in which the teacher is constantly alert for means of marking aspects of reality for the child, so that it can be represented through language.

Scavenger walks in which the children discover, pick up, and bag small items such as a twig, bottle cap, or rusty bolt are particulary helpful in organizing space for the children. To help locate and "fix" these discoveries, teachers armed with Polaroid cameras photograph the general location in which the item was discovered. Brought back to class and shared with classmates, the objects can be described by function, named, and the precise location designated with the help of the photograph. Items may then be properly displayed with descriptive labels for later scrutiny and review.

HISTORY.   Teaching *history* to the children begins with the teaching of time. Here, the Picture or Tableau Calendar is helpful because it helps the child relate the passage of time to an activity that has occurred, is occurring, or is about to occur. With a combination of sign and spoken word the teacher talks to the verbal child about the nature of past, present, and future. In order to communicate the notion of the future, the teacher starts with the concept of tomorrow. In order to teach "tomorrow" the teacher may have the children begin an engaging event at the end of one day and finish it on the morning of the next day. If the children have unusual difficulty (as some closed-system children might) in not finishing the activity, the teacher may want to begin an event in the morning and finish it *later* in the afternoon.

One of the many activities the children enjoy is making things to eat. Having children mix the dough for cookies and then place the cookies in the oven to eat later at snack gives them a beginning notion of the passage of time. Having them prepare the cookies on one day and eat them the next may initially exceed their capacity to "hold" the event. While waiting, the teacher can introduce the notion of *drawing* what they are waiting for, for example, circles might represent cookies, while dots within the circle would be chocolate chips. Or, if preparing popcorn, the children—with guidance from staff—can draw each step in the sequence: pouring oil in the pan, putting corn in the pan, turning on the stove, popping the corn, and eating the popped corn.

Another activity is to have the children "watch" the food as it is baking in the oven. At this time, concepts such as "later," "wait," "first this, then that," and "now" may be meaningfully introduced to expand the systems concerned with such events so that they may include substantial delays. Here too, *narration* and *prediction* are employed so that the children remain engaged with the event. However, usually the mere interruption of the integrative system of making and eating cookies is enough to keep the children engaged. Narration and prediction help calm the children if the time elapsed is difficult for them to tolerate.

Ritual events that occur with regularity, such as birthdays, holidays, and the changing seasons, give the child a beginning notion of what a year is. Birthdays and special parties are celebrated for each child to mark the passage of time in a way that enables the children not only to understand and share the ritual but to anticipate the coming event.

When undertaking the formal study of history in a class of verbal students, the teacher starts with discussion of the children's own beginnings. Each child is requested to bring in a baby picture. With the help of parents, the child also brings in pictures of the whole family. Pictures of the child at varying stages of growth help the child discuss how he or she looked as a baby or as a toddler, and how long ago it was. Pictures of the family can stimulate discussions of where they lived previously, or how people dressed, or how people looked compared with the present day.

One of the next steps is for the children to observe a class with children who are younger or older than themselves. In this way, they can compare their place in the growth cycle to others and talk about what it is like to be younger or older. Discussions of growth and competency can be addressed. Charts indicating the child's growth in height over a period of time provide a graphic symbol of the difference in the child's height on entering the class as compared to the present. The teacher who points this out to the child, commenting on the child's gain in strength and on how big the child is getting to be, is often rewarded with a glowing grin and a visible show of the child's enhanced self-esteem. Competency charts indicating growth over a period of time in areas such as reading, math, and physical education are indicators not only of the passage of time but the child's increasing growth in ability.

The child's personal history easily flows into histories provided by parents and grandparents who come to class and recount—accompanied by maps, pictures, and so forth—their experiences as children, and, if of foreign birth, how they came to this country. Such histories help the children relate to the reality of lives that extend back in time before they were born. From this point on, although with frequent references to their own backgrounds, teachers introduce history in more conventional terms. Even then, emphasis is at first on the neighborhood, city, and state before moving into larger notions of countries and their varied relationships, as, for example, the nature of the United Nations.

Science Projects

Another aspect of coping entails the systematic exploration of different aspects of physical reality. This may entail studying how inclined planes and levers work, how the application of heat to water causes boiling, evaporation, and precipitation, and how wheels work. Science projects also include the study of insects and animals as well as their propagation. Beyond this, children are taught the nature of sexual differences, maturation, pubescence, and how babies come about.

Social Interaction

Rules—Ethics

When the children are not able to speak and have a great deal of difficulty in understanding what is said to them, we establish interactive systems by working with the child "hand-over-hand" and by example. When the children behave in ways that are destructive to themselves or others, we help them transform the behavior into more acceptable patterns. The system of interactive and social spheres described in Chapter 4 is an important part of this transforming process. With verbal children, the socializing process begins to take on a more conventional tone. Early on, the attempt is to form a strong alliance within the group so that the children begin to identify with one another. Sometimes, the class chooses a name, for example, The Big Kids' Class, or Kids on the Move.

One of the first rules is safety—not getting hurt or inflicting pain on anyone else. This is stated often in class and is also written and displayed on a classroom wall. The teacher indicates that in her or his class no one is permitted to get hurt, that each must look out for the other. If a child hits another child or hurts a child's feelings, the teacher confronts the situation by finding out the source of difficulty and helps the children solve the problem by not only the rules but by using the notion of fair play. To elicit empathy with the child who is crying because he or she is hurt or feeling dejected, the teacher says to the culprit: "He [she] feels bad, how would you feel if you got hurt?" Usually, the teacher dramatizes this to impress the child with the seriousness of the behavior. The teacher then urges the child to apologize and/or take care of the child who is hurt.

Possessions and Sharing

Another established procedure is the Buddy System. Each child walks with a buddy and each is responsible for the other's safety in the street. Early on, the teacher establishes the notion of sharing, but only after the children have a notion of possession. Each child has a cubby to keep personal possessions such as pencils, markers, or toys. Children share only what is class property and then with the stipulation to take turns. In order to demonstrate this further, they play the *Territory Game* with the following rules. Sections marked out with tape on the floor are given to each of the children for toys that are for his or her personal use (not for sharing) as well as for toys that must be shared. When a child begins to use one of the group toys, he or she starts a preset timer. When the timer goes off, the child must return the toy to the group section for another child to use. The rules are established beforehand and the children have to demonstrate that they understand the rules. If the rules are not followed, the teacher restates them once again and demonstrates what the children must do.

Often, the children do not fully understand the rules. It is important for the teacher to make certain that there is full understanding before going on with an activity. For example, when establishing turn-taking, the teacher has to spell out every aspect of the game; that is, Paco will ride the bike around the playground two times and then it will be Andy's turn. During the event, the teacher calls to the children indicating how many times each child has to ride before turning over the bike. It is a good idea to give the children some choice in the activities that they are about to engage in and then spell out the rules for them. Along with that comes the injunction, ''Play fair.'' The teacher must state the rules very clearly for the children. It is helpful to write the rules and display them prominently so that they may be referred to when necessary. Every minor rule need not be listed, only the major ones that make for consideration of one another.

Serving as Big Brothers and Sisters

One important socializing experience for the older, better organized children at the Center—a number of whom are in transition to normal classrooms—is the opportunity the Center provides for them to spend time with the smallest, least able children. For perhaps 30 to 45 minutes, several times a week, these children spend the rest period or part of a play period with the more disordered children. Often the smaller children develop bonds with the older children in much the way that younger sibs relate to older ones. For the older children, the relationship is protective and even includes some ''bragging'' about what my ''little brother'' or ''little sister'' has learned to do. On a more subtle level, these interactions help the older children understand what a long distance they have traveled since they came to the Center and that they can help others travel the same route.

Communication/Representation

Once the child begins to make his or her needs known verbally, even though it may be not be a frequent occurrence, the curriculum is adjusted to meet this change. Signing although not predominant during the day, is still utilized, particularly when introducing new concepts or when attempting to teach sequencing or syntax. For a youngster who has difficulty in processing auditory information, signing is still a very important tool. Signing or gesture is also useful to the child so that he or she can retrieve words that are fused with the sign but are unavailable unless the child is given a sign (body) cue.

Frequently parents and teachers are so delighted with the child's new acquisition of speech that they want to discontinue immediately the use of signs and present only spoken words. We often caution against abandoning the signs prematurely because the children tend to be weak in audition and still rely heavily on visual and body actions to process information. If we can convince the parents that signs continue to provide an important adjunct to their child's development, then often the child will learn more rapidly. Signs are also important in the first stages of teaching disordered children to read. For example, as steps on the way to reading (see Chapter 11), we introduce signs with objects and pictures and find that this combination helps recognition. Then, when we use signs and gestures with pictures as they turn into printed words (Chapters 6 and 11), we find that sight reading of printed words improves.

Expanding Pragmatic Skills with Verbal Children

When system-disordered children first begin to use spoken language it is often poorly directed. Frequently the children announce their needs to the air, magically expecting them to be met. Although they may now have better eye contact and point to objects, they may still not fully understand that they can reach someone at a distance by speaking and no longer have to physically tug at them to have them attend. Establishing the pragmatic force of language generally begins in a group setting. All of the children are seated facing the child who will be the one issuing commands. Because all of the children know the action commands—jump, fall, clap hands, kick your feet, laugh—the teacher introduces them first.

The child who is issuing commands is helped to state: "Everybody [command]," to which the whole group responds. Commands such as "Everybody [with the appropriate gesture] laugh!" or "Everybody cry!" or "Everybody clap your hands!" usually keep the children happily engaged in this contagious activity. All the children have a turn in the command position, and all must try to choose different actions. The teacher assists by quietly cuing the children with a whispered word or picture of the action. As the teacher calls upon the child by name, members of the group have a chance to become familiar with the name of each person.

At a later point in the game, the children begin to call not only upon the group but on individual children to perform a specific action. As an alternative, the child who is issuing commands is placed behind an obstacle such as a door or hanging blanket so that he or she is hidden from view, whereupon the children in the group are urged to call the child's name. When the child comes into view, the children repeat his or her name with the command. By keeping an action component within this context, the teacher ensures that the children enjoy playing the game.

Another method of eliciting calls is to have the child call from a distance with the use of a small megaphone (or rolled core from paper toweling) to one member of a group of children who are seated on the other side of the classroom. The teacher helps the child to choose the person he or she wants to call by assisting the child to point to the other as well as by cuing with the child's name. If the child is speaking too softly, the others in the group should be helped to say, "What?" to encourage more projection. Sometimes, the teacher may want to teach the child to cup hands to mouth while calling, for this method works nicely in the playground.

During snack time a child often addresses the rote expression "I want [cookie, milk, etc.] please" to no one in particular while looking in the general direction of the food. In order to further socialization, the teachers require that the children call them by name when requesting something. In this manner, person–object relationship is stressed. In order to effect this, the teacher is custodian of all the food items; she or he waits expectantly, looking at the child to see if this alone will elicit the desired response. If not, the assistant teacher helps the child to point to the teacher and say that person's name, or whispers to the child to say it, or tells the child to call the person by name and then repeat the remaining sentence. If the child has difficulty, the teacher may then hide face with hands (peekaboo style) until the child uncovers the face and/or names him or her. The teacher might also stand up, holding onto the snack items with back turned to the children, who must then say the teacher's name before she or he will turn around. The teacher then requires the children to repeat the name along with the desired phrase. These strategies can be used with the children as guardians of the snack items as well, so that one child may be in charge of handing out the crackers and another is in charge of pouring the juice. Each child then gets a chance to relate to the other in pragmatic terms; that is, "John, please give me cookie." It is also helpful for the child to learn "Thank you, [John/Susan, etc.]."

It is also useful in this context, to teach the children choice and the use of the words, "yes" and "no." The teacher, for example, provides a choice between crackers and drinks so that when the items are held up, the child has a chance to indicate his/her preference. With the nonverbal child we teach the child the head gesture for "no" and "yes" and then add the pointing or outstretched hand to the desired object. When the child is verbal, the pointing or outstretched hand with a cue from the teacher to say the word is generally sufficient.

Another method of expanding the pragmatic use of language is *Language Sequences*. These are events that are within the child's experience and that are "acted out" with the help of teachers and pictures of the sequence. A modified role play of such sequences describe a logical sequence of events through spoken language. The children dramatize the event and are helped to either sign or speak the appropriate content. In order to help them retain the sequence of events further, the pictures are placed in sequence in front of the class. Usually events have to have a certain dramatic consequence in order to appeal to the children. One of the earliest language sequences involves a child blowing up a balloon and then stepping on it to make it burst. This has been a popular and exciting part of the curriculum and has helped elicit a fair amount of spoken language. These and similar sequences are described in Chapter 10.

The Symbol Accentuation ™ Reading Program

Once the children have begun to speak in simple two-word constructions, the Symbol Accentuation (SA) Reading Program is introduced. With the help of gesture, objects, and films, the children are introduced to the initial sight-reading phase of the program. Upon completion of this phase, they then go onto the phonetic aspect of the program (see Chapter 11). The SA Reading Program prepares the children to read at a first-grade level and is easily integrated with any linguistic series that permits the children to read at more advanced levels. One important virtue of the SA Reading Program is that it teaches the children the regularities of written language early on without confusing them with irregularities. It also begins at an earlier developmental level than other reading programs.

SUMMARY

This chapter describes the Center's cognitive-developmental systems approach with nonverbal, sign stage children as well as with verbal children operating at the symbolic-sign stage. After a discussion of the role of the effective teacher there is a discussion of the curriculum for the nonverbal child.

This curriculum emphasizes the importance of developing the body schema, coping, interaction, communication, and representation. Various strategies are discussed in the context of orienting the child to the school setting, and helping the child to interact with children in groups and to use sign and spoken language in the context of elevated board structures and during the Sign and Spoken Language Program as well as during snack and lunch time. Also discussed is the role of the Tableau Calendar to forecast the various activities within the day so that the child does not get "lost" going from one place to another.

The use of elevated board spheres—including structures in the LCDC

Playground—is described with indications of how each structure contributes to the development of cognitive, social, or communicative capacities.

Special attention is given to reciprocal play and problem solving as means of developing interactive systems with a variety of progressively more complex interventions. These include pushing objects to each other, alternately building structures or pushing over blocks, blowing Ping-Pong balls back and forth across the table, and using instruments (Traveler) to send objects back and forth.

Following this, there is a discussion of the Cognitive-Developmental Art Program (C-DAP) and the manner in which scribbling—viewed as a spheric activity—may be systematically interrupted to develop intentional combined scribbling (circles + lines or circles + dots) before moving toward representational drawing. Scribbling is compared to babbling with the point being made that just as it is impossible to predict when a child will move from use of signs to naming (symbolic-sign stage) so is it impossible to predict precisely when the child will advance from scribbles to representational drawing.

Curriculum for the verbal child follows next with a discussion of how the self-concept, coping, and social interaction as well as communication and representation are realized through the curriculum. The self-concept is nurtured through interventions that enhance self-awareness and self-efficacy. Coping is encouraged via curricula that systematically build from the child's personal experience of space and time. Geography—building from the child's immediate experience of his or her surroundings—gradually expands to include the Center, the neighborhood, the city, state, country, and relations between countries. History follows the same pattern by building from the child's personal history to history of parents and family, of the Center, the region, and so forth. In this way, the children begin to have a sense of the manner in which they fit in a time and space bound to a certain social-cultural fabric.

Coping also entails the manner in which things (levers, wheels, and so forth) work, and the nature of insect, animal, and human organisms. This is followed by a discussion of social interaction and the manner in which rules and ethical principles provide a framework for relationships between people. The rules and ethical principles refer to not hurting, protecting, and being protected as well as to fair play—in terms that the children can understand. There is also a discussion of the manner in which older, better organized children spend time with younger, nonverbal children in a way that contributes to bonding between younger and older children and an enhanced sense of self for all the children. Finally, there is a discussion of communication and representation that considers the manner in which spoken language becomes more functional and pragmatic and the general nature of the Symbol Accentuation (SA) Reading Program.

CHAPTER 10

The Sign and Spoken Language Program

Children learn to communicate with signs or words when they experience such signs and words as *influencing* not only their own actions but the actions of others in a desired manner. For example, the child who signs and says "Come!" and experiences another coming closer, extends the guiding meaning of that term to one that can also be used to *act upon* and guide the behavior of another. The child's sense of efficacy when this occurs unites both sign-word user and respondent within a social system in which shared meanings conveyed by these forms mediate increasingly complex interactions. However, to reach this stage of functioning with nonverbal, disordered children, it is necessary to proceed in a systematic manner from relatively simple action meanings to more complex meanings related to objects and events expressed in sentence forms.

Accordingly, this chapter charts basic steps in the progression toward receptive (sign-word guided) and expressive communication among system-disordered children functioning at the sign stage of development. The use of signs adapted from the American Sign Language for the deaf (ASL) with spoken language, derives directly from the view that gesture language is a transitional phase in the development of language and thus may, initially, be more available to disordered children than conventional spoken language. Support for the utility of signs with disordered children has accumulated over the years as shown in the findings of the following researchers: Miller and Miller (1973); Creedon (1973); Brown (1977); Konstantareas, Oxman, & Webster (1977); Bonvillian, Nelson, and Rhyne (1981); Konstantareas (1984, 1987). The effectiveness of sign language and its capacity—when presented concurrently with spoken words—to transfer meaning to these words, indicates that it may serve not only as a means of communication in itself, but as a means of facilitating the development of naming (symbolic-sign stage) and thus the understanding and use of spoken language.

Central to the Center's language program are four training tapes that introduce sign and spoken language to nonverbal disordered children. Each of the training tapes presents a cluster of concepts and helps establish certain linguistic functions. The concepts introduced with the training tape are shown in Table 10-1.

Material in this chapter is taken from the *Sign and Spoken Language Program* (Miller, 1970/1989a). Copyright 1989 by Arnold Miller. Used with permission.

TABLE 10.1.   Concepts Introduced by Sign and Spoken Word in Four Categories on Videotape

Category 1 Action	Category 2 Food Related	Category 3 Objects/Events	Category 4 Two Sign/Two Word	
walk	chair	boy	apple	eat apple
run	table	man	orange	eat orange
jump	eat	sleep	cookie	break cookie
fall	glass	awake		eat cookie
come	pour	wash		more cookie
go	drink	comb	chair	my chair
stop	knife	toothbrush		big chair
get up	fork	hat		little chair
sit down	spoon	sweep		chair falls
open	plate	house	fork	big fork
close	cookie	tree		little fork
pick up	bread	cat	spoon	big spoon
drop	egg	car		little spoon
push	salt	boat	falls	hat falls
pull	ketchup	ball		glass falls
break	roll	bird		orange falls
up	pie			apple falls
down			table	table falls
				pick up table
				table up/down
			egg	pick up egg
				drop egg
			cat	cat in (bag)
				cat out (bag)
				cat jumps
				cat eats

OVERVIEW OF CATEGORIES ON THE SIGN AND SPOKEN LANGUAGE TRAINING VIDEOTAPE

Why Training Tapes?

The use of training tapes relates directly to the use of manual sign language with disordered children. One of the reasons for using manual sign language is that it serves as a "bridge" between the spoken word and its referent; specially prepared training tapes make the bridge easier to cross. This bridge, consisting of the resemblance between many signs and their referents, makes signs far more available to disordered children than the arbitrary forms of spoken words. However, even with manual signs, in everyday life a variety of distracting stimuli and difficulty in relating one thing to another often divert the disordered child from the intended relationship between sign and referent. Careful editing minimizes such diversions of attention by perceptually marrying or interweaving the sign and its object or event meaning in a way that highlights the sign feature with the closest resemblance to the most salient aspect of the referent. For example, the sign for *run*—rapid patting of one hand with the other as the hands move from left to right—relates to the act of running *primarily* in the rapid patting rhythm. Editing that interweaves this rapid patting with the similar rhythm of one or more people running gives the disordered child a far better chance of relating sign to referent.

The iconic relationship between sign and referent benefits also from the manner in which the manual sign for *pour* (hand simulates holding a glass with thumb pointing down) interweaves with the image and thus the meaning of pouring a liquid from a glass (see Figure 10.1); the hand sign for *jump* (two fingers of the preferred hand jump off the other palm) blends with the action of a child jumping off a stool; and the sign for *break* (two hands simulate breaking something) is interwoven on tape with two hands breaking a stick. The iconic relationship that facilitates interweaving is also apparent with such manual signs as *eat, drink, fork, knife,* and *spoon.* These signs simulate everyday functions or use of objects in ways that intimately relate a sign, its meaning, and the conventional spoken word accompanying the object or event. Then, because the spoken word (on the tape's sound track) accompanies this interweaving process, the viewing child begins to experience the manual sign *and* the spoken word paired with it as *part* of and directly related to the referent action or object.

Because disordered, like normal children, initially experience reality solely from their own perspective, the training tape first parallels this disposition by presenting manual signs and the actions or objects to which they relate as they would appear to the child producing the sign. Only after this does the tape present the sign from other perspectives—including how the sign would look when presented by someone directly facing the child. For example, when the concept *come* first appears on tape, the sign (beckoning arms and fingers) is interwoven with a child coming directly toward the signing viewer. Later presentations of the concept gradually shift from the subjective to the objective viewpoint—separating sign from referent in the process. The child then begins to understand that the relation between sign-word and outcome is independent of perspective, that is, two people at right angles to the viewer may communicate certain meanings to each other independent of their orientation to the viewer. Other command sequences on tape seek to generalize meanings to varied situations. Thus, the child learns that concepts such as *come, fall,* or *jump* may relate either to a single person or to a group of people who perform as requested on command. Here again, the training tape dramatizes the cause-and-effect relation between sign-word and referent, and helps generalize it.

Another feature of the training tape concerns the manner in which contagion is built into the various sequences. Disordered children respond well to contagion; the training tape, therefore, combines visual and auditory images in the highly contagious manner most likely to engage them. The tape achieves this by pacing actions briskly, with vivid sound effects, and

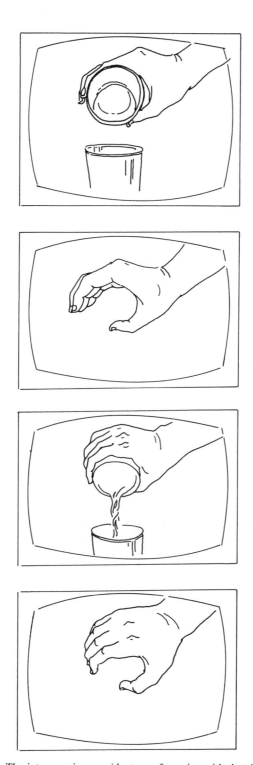

Figure 10.1. The interweaving on videotape of pouring with the sign for *pour*.

by generating excitement and urgency through different voices. For example, as the children observe the manual sign for *stop* (the edge of one hand strikes the palm of another) appearing in rapid succession in front of bike riders, a car, and so forth, and hear the urgent "Stop!! Stop!!" coupled with the shriek of brakes and the skidding of tires, they are better able to take in the significance of sign and word. The teacher can then exploit this contagion for further learning in the real world (see next section).

The training tape also dramatizes the potential of signs to influence others by clearly demonstrating the relationship between the *use* of a particular sign (command sequence) and its impact on another, whether this concerns concepts such as *come* and *stop* or familiar functions such as *eat* and *drink*. Finally, tape permits a clear and vivid account of the manner in which syntax works to communicate varied aspects of reality. Once these concepts have been introduced on tape in a way that disordered children can accept, they can learn with help to extend them to the real world.

Expanding Concepts Presented on Videotape

One of the major problems of system-disordered children is that they do not readily expand specific learning related to one object or situation to include the same or similar objects or situations in other contexts. It is necessary, therefore, to help the children achieve these expansions by teaching and reteaching a concept's meaning as it relates to many different objects, actions, and situations. Only when the child can appropriately attach sign-word meaning to objects and events in a variety of settings does the child fully understand these meanings. In other words, the child must learn that the meaning of the concept *jump* goes beyond the particular child jumping off a chair as shown in the action category of the training videotape. The child must learn that the concept *jump* has specific meaning that may refer to the child jumping off a table, to a classmate jumping down the hall on a pogo stick, and so forth.

When sign-word expansions begin, the aides turn the children from the tape to face the teacher and various props that have previously been set up. The aides tell the children through sign and word to "turn around," making the sign in the direction they wish the children to move. If a child does not respond, the aide crooks his or her finger to indicate the desired direction. Added pressure in the same direction from the aide's leg on the child's knee also helps orient the child in the proper direction. Now the children are seated facing the teacher, with the aides stationed behind them.

Some expansions involve the entire group, whereas some focus on a single child. While the teacher engages a child for individual work, other aides keep the remaining children oriented toward the teacher and his or her work with that child.

The Sign-Word–Guided Child

Guidance by a sign-word precedes the child's ability to communicate intentions through the same sign-word. Obviously, a child cannot use a sign or word meaningfully until he or she knows what the term means. Initially, contextual cues play a major role; the child first derives meaning and support not only from the sign-word but from the perceptual organization of the setting. For example, when the sign-word "Come!" is first introduced, the child responds not only to the sign and word but to the movements of the other children as they respond to any physical structures such as the Primary Board that might focus their movements.

However, before crediting a child with true receptive understanding of a concept, there must be evidence that the sign-word guides the child's actions even when detached from such familiar perceptual and contextual cues.

To help this occur, the child needs to vividly experience the relation between each sign-word and outcome as a unique system independent of circumstances. If the sign-word "Drop!" is being taught, the child needs to relate it to the notion of something being released that plummets to the ground. In other words, the sign-word must trigger a strong body response of a certain kind. A child who learns—on seeing and hearing the sign-word "Drop [it]!"—to suddenly release any object being held—is well on the way to responding independent of particular settings. To help bring this about, staff provide strong sensory feedback to amplify the effect on a child of each sign-word–guided action. For example, if a child is being urged to respond to the command "Drop!" (an object) the teacher helps the child hold the object high above the head and then drop it into a noisy metal container. Although all dropped objects will produce some clatter, larger objects will produce more racket than smaller objects. In this way the child not only gains enhanced proprioceptive and auditory feedback while performing the exaggerated action, he or she learns that the "release" action related to "drop" applies to a range of objects.

Another strategy that adds to the impact of sign-word sequences stems from the systematic use of voice modulation. Often, system-disordered children habituate or "tune out" voices (or any sounds) that are repeated on the same frequency or intensity level. Thus, in order to better capture and guide the child's attention through sign and word, staff continually change the voice quality and intensity of their spoken words. If the teacher shouts initially to gain a child's attention, he or she may subsequently repeat the verbalization in a whisper. In general, variations in both voice pitch and intensity help engage system-disordered children.

Related to and coupled with voice modulation is the systematic use of *contagious activity* to help the children both learn and generalize action meanings. Contagion generates a high level of anticipation and excitement in the children and promotes active group participation. An example of the use of contagious activity to teach and generalize the concept *run* follows:

The aides—with excited, rapidly paced signs and utterances "Run, run, run! . . . Run, run, run!"—nudge *all* the children into running toward the teacher. When they reach the teacher, they are hugged, turned around, and required to "Run, run, run!" back to the urgently signing/speaking aides.

The effectiveness of this procedure derives from the group excitement and the expectations built up in the children while waiting for the command. After the children perform the action several times as a group, the teacher focuses on individual children by quickly—rapid pacing is vital—using the sign-word with each child. As the teacher commands each child by name, the aide helps that child *immediately* perform the required action. In this way the teacher exploits the contagious group excitement generated during the previous activity. This same procedure lends itself to other action concepts such as *crawl, roll,* and *jump.*

Typically, extremely disorganized, resistant, or distractible children require more external structure to achieve sign-word guidance. To build more structure into the activity, staff place boards or slightly elevated ramps on the floor which guide and provide a "running start" for the children. The ramp provides a natural pathway from each child to the teacher and to the aides. This additional support exerts a "pull" on the children to follow the vector of the board.

Just as children incorporate sign-word concepts that accompany the actions seen and heard in the training tape (principle of inclusion) so do they incorporate these same signs and words when they accompany activities that they perform during the school day. Thus, signs and words accompany mini-, and multispheres and integrative spheres set up for the children as well as the natural integrative sequences such as eating lunch, dressing or undressing, going for a walk, and playing. When the child engages in more complex activity sequences, the worker's accompaniment with signs and words is referred to as *narration* because in effect, the worker—like a sports announcer—tracks the child's behavior with signs and words that relate to and describe the child's actions. As children assimilate such narration within their action systems, they begin to communicate with themselves through signs and words in a way that furthers their ability to think and plan ahead.

Communication: A Two-Way Process

Before children can communicate with adults or with each other, they must be able to both receive and send messages. Developmentally, as indicated earlier, the ability to receive and be guided by messages—whether conveyed by gesture signs or spoken words—precedes the ability to use them with others. In our work we find that children's guidance by sign-word sequences is often closely related to their beginning use of signs. For example, a child who starts with help to use the *jump* sign while watching the jump sequence on tape is far more likely to jump when someone directs the *jump* sign to him or her than the child without this training. Before using signs to influence others, the child must first use them to self-communicate, for example, by performing the *jump* sign before jumping. Consequently, the general procedure in working with disordered children at the Center is to help them perform the signs *while* watching the training tape in a way that allows them to experience their sign making as part of the observed sequences.

To develop the child's ability to be both guided by sign-word sequences and to use them to guide or influence the behavior of others, the child participates with each taped concept as it goes through two sequences: an *interweaving sequence* and a *command sequence*. As the child makes the sign (with help) while watching that sign interweave with its referent, the child begins to experience both the sign and the spoken word accompanying it as related to the referent (principle of inclusion, see Chapter 5). The intent is to have the child use his or her hands in synchrony with the subjectively presented hands on tape, to perceptually merge them with the hands on screen as they interweave with the referent.

When this occurs, the child begins to experience his or her own hand movements as invested with the meaning of the referent. Then, during the *command* sequence that follows (also from the subjective perspective), the child begins to experience the sign separate from but related to the referent, as the use of the sign triggers an immediate reaction from someone at a distance from the sign maker. Subsequent command sequences show the sign being used effectively at right angles to the observing child and, eventually, directly opposite the child in the face-to-face stance that generally accompanies everyday communication.

Once the child experiences both *interwoven* and *command* sequences for a particular concept on tape, the teacher turns the child around to use the sign-word sequence with others so that the child can begin to learn that the *intentions* conveyed on tape are effective not only in the training tape, but also in the real world. Excerpts from the four categories on the training tape demonstrate the pattern of instruction that helps the child expand tape training to the real world.

CATEGORY 1. ACTION CONCEPTS

To begin our training, we chose sign-word concepts related to 18 everyday actions for several reasons: First, the sign–action relationship is often very clear, relating to a single vector (push/pull, come/go, pick up/drop) or kind of action (open/close, stop, break) in contrast to the multiple properties intrinsic to objects. Consequently, we reasoned, sign–action relations should be easier for the children to learn. Second, sign–action sequences involve big body activity, which lends itself to contagious activity whether running, jumping, falling, and so forth. Finally, we wished to include two action concepts—*come, stop*—essential to the safety of the children. Once disordered children can respond to these two terms, parents and staff are far more able to protect them. Sign-word action concepts taught with the videotape include the following:

come	close	pick up
stop	push	drop
get up	pull	walk
sit down	go	run
fall	up	jump
open	down	break

Presenting the Videotape

To work with the tape, the children are seated on stools in a semicircle in front of the video monitor (see Figure 10.2). The teacher alternately stands

Figure 10.2. Children sign and say "*eat*" with the Sign and Spoken Language (SSL) training tape.

to the side of the monitor to control the stop button (for still pictures) and shifts position to work the backup role along with the aides. The session runs smoothly and effectively only if the teacher and aides understand their roles and constantly adjust to each other's needs.

The aides sit behind the children in a way that allows them to closely track the responses to the concepts on tape. Although bending quite close to the children, aides must take care that the children do not lean into them or rest against their bodies in a manner that engages them more with the aides than with the training tape. If a child does this, the aide quickly backs away until the child regains balance, and then returns. Staff also avoid the distraction (and possible loss) of loose hair or jewelry while working with the children.

The aide's task during tape presentations is to focus the child's attention on the screen while modeling the child's hands into the appropriate manual sign when it appears on the screen. In order to make it most likely that the videotaped sequences engage the child's attention, the aide orients the child by physically turning his or her head and body in the direction of the screen and by holding the child's arms outstretched as in pointing toward the screen, or by a combination of these methods. As the interwoven sequence (sign and referent) appears on tape (while the child hears the spoken word) the aide helps the child form the sign from the child's perspective, when it appears. For example, with the concept *break,* the aide shapes the child's hands into the sign for *break* (hands simulate breaking a stick) while the training tape first shows the sign (a) *interwoven* with breaking an actual stick, then again after the person on the tape has been (b) *commanded* by the sign maker, "Break!" and is shown breaking the stick from the child's subjective viewpoint (see Figure 10.3 (*a*) and (*b*)).

In using the sign training tape it is important to tailor the amount of external support to each child's level of functioning at any given time. Staff must be sensitive to very subtle cues (body movements, posturing, facial expressions) in order to respond to the children's current needs in terms of the amount of support they provide. As a child begins to take over a sign the staff person gradually reduces support. For example, if the child makes no attempt to sign or speak along with the tape, the aide firmly and repeatedly adjusts the child's hands into the appropriate sign. However, if the child begins to move hands with the taped situations but still does not make the sign, the aide decreases the firmness of the support—gently molding the child's hands, but leaving the opportunity for the child to take over. The next step in reducing support entails the worker seated behind the child backing his or her hands to the child's wrists—providing just enough support for the child to move hands into an approximation of the manual sign. Finally, as the child does more of the signing, the aide may only nudge the child's elbows to induce sign making at the appropriate time.

During the tape presentations the aides do not speak the words along with the sound track as it is distracting for the children to hear speech from behind

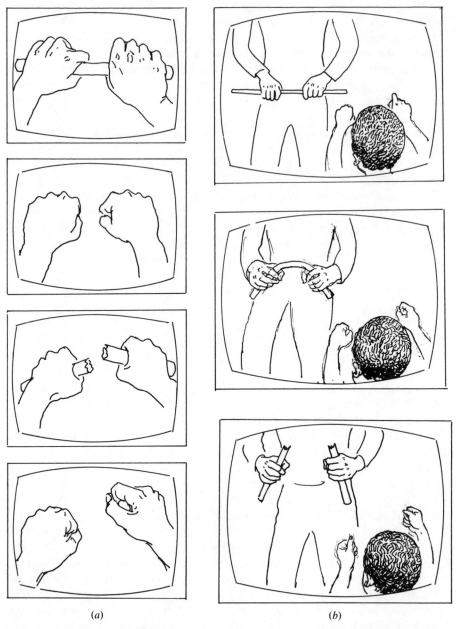

Figure 10.3. The term *break* in (*a*) interwoven and (*b*) command sequences.

their heads as well as from the tape and the teacher at the same time. In the initial use of the sign training tape, pacing is extremely important both in coordinating the child's activity with the tape sequences and in shifting the child from videotape to real world. Delays of only a second or two between the child forming a sign and seeing it on screen in relation to its referent often make the difference between the child gaining and missing the relation between sign making and outcome. The teacher shows only one repeated concept in interwoven and command sequences (lasting about 1 minute) on tape and then halts the tape so that the sign-word meanings may be generalized before returning to the tape to show another concept.

Come! and *Stop!* Concepts

Come and *stop* concepts are taught first because of their survival implications. Many disordered children are at constant risk because on entering dangerous situations—such as crossing a busy street—they not only fail to heed the approach of cars or trucks but also fail to heed the care giver's command to "come!" or "stop!" To remedy this, staff both teach the concepts as described and generalize them vigorously to varied real-life contexts.

Come

The tape sequence for *come* shows beckoning hands from the viewpoint of the sign maker. As these hands beckon, the viewer notes someone coming closer to the signer. Subsequently, the sign for *come* is made at right angles and then from the position of someone opposite the viewer. The sign *come* is also shown inducing more than one person to come closer to the signer. On the sound track, the viewer hears the spoken word "Come . . . come!" uttered with varying degrees of urgency by different people. The viewer also hears walking and running sounds as people beckoned walk or run toward the person signing and speaking.

Children viewing the tape, with aides assisting them, repeatedly make the sign in coordination with the sign maker on tape. Periodically, the teacher will freeze the image of a person signing on the tape and then release it so that the signing child has the illusion that his or her sign was the occasion for the person on tape to come closer. After completing the videotape sequence, the teacher introduces the following generalization procedures.

To develop *sign-word guidance* for *come,* the teacher establishes both *location* and *person* expansions so that the child learns to respond to the term in varied locations and with different people. The first step in teaching this concept after viewing the tape is to use an elevated board structure (Primary Board) to provide structure and a direct pathway (vector) to the teacher beckoning at the other end. The child stands on the board facing the teacher, with the aide directly behind. In this way the teacher reduces the number of alternative responses available to the child, and the board's vector guides the child toward the teacher. Each time the teacher gives the signed and verbal command "Come!" the aide—when necessary—nudges the child to move toward the teacher.

The teacher establishes *location expansions* by systematically shifting position, beginning fairly close to the child and gradually moving back or to left and right as the child comes closer. When he or she finally reaches the teacher, aide, or parent, the child receives a hug. The teacher modulates voice pitch and intensity while calling out the command. When the teacher's use of sign-word "Come!" consistently brings the child on the elevated structure closer, it is necessary to extend the sign-word's power to situations on the ground. The teacher then uses the command on the floor with progressively greater distances between teacher and child and from various locations until the child responds from all parts of a large room. The teaching staff continually extends the situations in which the child can respond to the command (hallway, outdoors, etc.) until the meaning has generalized across all settings, and in spite of competition from other sights and sounds.

After establishing location expansions the teacher begins to establish *person expansions*. The imperative meaning of the sign-word must derive from more than one person. In addition to the teacher and aides, the child must learn to respond to his or her parents. This is achieved by having different people in the classroom—aides, parents—use the term first on the elevated board structure and then on the ground in all parts of the room. Parents learn to use the same procedures at home in varied locations and with different family members. In this way the child achieves both location and person expansions for that particular concept.

EXPRESSIVE USAGE.   The next task involves helping the child understand that he or she can *use* the term to guide and influence the behavior of others. To achieve this the teacher tries to respond in an exaggerated, sign-related manner immediately after each sign use by the child. The setup involves the aide behind the child serving as his or her voice while helping the child make the sign for *come*. The teacher faces the child about 6 to 8 feet away. Then, immediately after the child (with help) signs and says "Come!" the teacher takes an exaggerated step toward the child, stamping feet, coughing, and so forth, to be more visible to the child. Each time the child signs (beckoning motion with both hands), the teacher takes another step until he or she reaches the child and makes an excited fuss.

This "fuss" coupled with the teacher's exaggerated and repetitive response to the child's signing helps establish the influential awareness between child and other so necessary for communication. By repeatedly exaggerating response to the child's sign the teacher attempts to accent the child's power to bring someone closer. As the child gives indication that he or she is spontaneously aware of the effect of the sign-word—perhaps by slight beckoning movements of the hands—the aide gradually decreases support for sign making until the child performs the sign independently. When a child has acquired some ability to use the sign expressively, the child uses it alongside the teacher in a contagious exercise in which the entire class comes closer as the child uses the sign. Staff utilizes many opportunities throughout the day for additional work on *location* and *person* expansions so that the child fully grasps the power of the sign-word sequence to bring people closer.

Stop

The training tape conveys the power of the sign-word sequence "Stop!" to bring about a sudden stopping of action by showing a moving car (as well as people walking, riding bikes, and so on) with relevant sound effects. As with *come*, the training tape presents *stop* from subjective and more objective viewpoints and in interwoven and command sequences. Again, as with *come*, the teacher starts and stops the tape to induce the illusion that the child's sign making is related to the sudden cessation of activity.

After videotape training, the teacher and aides help expand *stop* by using it in the context of the elevated board structures. As the child moves toward the teacher on an elevated board structure in response to "Come!" commands, the teacher abruptly and vigorously changes the command to "Stop!" while making the stop sign directly in front of the child's face and body in a way that simulates a barrier. The aide's task—immediately after the teacher's command—is to pull the child's harness or shirt firmly from behind to ensure that the child stops on cue.

Then, the teacher systematically develops both location and person expansions for *stop* so that the child can respond to it in a variety of situations on the ground and when the term is used by different people. The child has not acquired consistent receptive understanding of the concept until he or she is able to respond to the command "Stop!" without assistance in a variety of situations and in response to different people.

As the child achieves some receptive understanding of this concept, the teacher introduces the group contagion method. While the children are running, crawling, or walking toward the teacher, he or she shifts from an action command to the signed and spoken command "Stop!" before they arrive. For example, "Come, come . . . STOP!" or "Run, run . . . STOP!" or "Walk, walk . . . STOP!" This generalization typically requires two or more aides/backup persons to ensure that the children follow the commands appropriately.

EXPRESSIVE USAGE.   One way of teaching the children to use the command *expressively* is simply to reverse the roles of teacher and student. The aide assists the child to give the signed and spoken command "Stop!" to the teacher (or another child) as he or she is running or walking toward him or her. The teacher dramatizes the causal relationship between sign-word and action by stopping immediately and with much noise as soon as the child produces the sign or utters the word "Stop!" This can be done with individual children and then with the group contagion method as the children begin to show more intention in their use of the sign-word.

The *Body Press* technique can also be useful in eliciting the expressive use of "Stop!" If, for example, while the child is engaged in a sphere on a board structure, the teacher restrains the child by grasping a leg or ankle, the child will feel compelled to remove the teacher's restraint in order to continue the sphere. An aide can then help the child direct the sign-word "Stop!" to the teacher, who immediately releases the child's ankle or leg.

There are many opportunities to generalize *stop* meaning within various daily school activities. For example, an interaction game of riding bicycles in a sphere can be useful in highlighting the influential nature of the sign-words, relating sign-words directly to body action, and dealing with the notion of sharing or turn-taking. As several children ride around the pre-scribed sphere, an aide can help the child without a bicycle to give the command "Stop!" directly in front of another child as that child approaches. When the child stops, they can trade positions and repeat the sequence.

Expanding Concepts

Get Up!/Sit Down!

Following presentation of the get up/sit down sequence on videotape—organized like the other sequences—the teacher moves down the line of seated children quickly giving the sign-word command "Get up!" to each child. Aides moving in back of each child help them rise immediately after they receive the command. When all the children are standing, the teacher moves in front of each child and signs/says "Sit down!" at which point the aide helps the child sit. As a useful variation involving contagion, the teacher may command the entire group to "Get up!" and "Sit down!"

In using these manual signs it is important to coordinate the verbal double syllable in each concept with both the action it refers to, and with the manual sign component. Since the term "Get up!" has two parts, the manual sign is presented in two parts so that spoken sign and word are closely coordinated. For example, "Get [hands rise in one motion] up! [hands rise again to complete the motion in synchrony with *up*]." It is also helpful in the first phase of teaching the concept for the teacher facing the child to place his or her hands (with slight pressure) under the child's arms before making the sign for *get up* (which closely resembles this act) and on the child's shoulders (with slight downward pressure) as the teacher makes the sign and speaks the words "Sit down!" The staff's voice should also show rising intonation with "Get up!" and dropping intonation with "Sit down!" These procedures seem to help merge sign and spoken word with the referent action.

A useful game that helps extend both the *get up* and *sit down* concepts is musical chairs. In this game the teacher commands the children with sign-word sequences to "Get up!" when the music begins and "Sit down!" when it stops.

EXPRESSIVE USAGE.   At the beginning of a seated activity, with only the exact number of stools available for the children, a staff member casually sits on one of the children's chairs before he or she reaches it. An aide helps the child (whose chair has been taken) to tell the usurper, "Get up!" It is helpful initially to use the method of placing the child's hands under the teacher's arms to dramatize the causal relationship between sign-word and another's action, and to better merge the manual sign with its referent action. Subsequently, the child commands the worker to get up without touching.

Other useful settings for generalizing the terms include the *Bicycle* sphere and the *piggyback* game. In the Bicycle sphere the teacher helps the child say "Stop!" and "Get up!" to the child who is riding so that he or she can take a turn on the bicycle. In the piggyback game the child learns to tell a staff member to "Sit down!" so that he or she is low enough for the child to climb on shoulders. The staff member remains in the crouched position until the child signs/says "Get up!" at which the worker rises slowly with small, jerky movements following each command.

Fall

Following presentation of the videotape that provides the children with a preliminary understanding of the sign-word's meaning for *fall,* the children stand on their stools with the aides behind them. They see on the floor in front of them a mattress or thick gym mat. The teacher gives the sign-word command to "Fall!" focusing on individual children. Immediately following the command, the aides use the mock "fall" technique—by holding onto the child's leg and arm, it is easy to help the children gently fall onto the yielding surface. Other opportunities for establishing the concept occur when the children are riding bicycles. The aides can carefully tip the child off balance while signing and exclaiming loudly "Fall!"

Also useful are broken or fall-apart objects such as a chair that is designed to collapse when the child sits in it. These outcomes relate the concept directly to the child's body. The surprise value of this and similar carefully monitored generalizations both engages the child and begins to embed the sign (two upright fingers of one hand "stand" in the outstretched palm of the other and suddenly fall) with the spoken word "fall!"

When the children have acquired some understanding of the concept as it relates to their bodies, staff begin to extend the concept's meaning as it relates to objects and to other people. They arrange the room so that a box of blocks or some cups and plates are conspicuously teetering near the edges of tables, shelves, and so forth. Then, while passing by the table, the teacher or an aide unobtrusively bumps the objects causing them to fall. Items are chosen that make a lot of noise as they hit the floor to dramatize the effect and meaning of the action. As the objects fall, the teacher and aides turn to the children and sign/exclaim with great surprise "Fall!" The teacher can model the sequence described and then replace the object(s) near the edge of the table and tell a child "Make it *fall,*" or "*Fall*—you do it."

EXPRESSIVE USAGE.   After any of the mock accidents, the teacher can ask the child "What happened?" "What is that?" and so forth. The aide assists the child to sign/say the term appropriately. Children are generally intrigued with the fall sequences, and the term usually becomes part of their sign-word repertoire rather quickly. With support from aides as necessary, children sign/say "Fall!" and teacher and/or aides respond by falling dramatically to the ground. Other activities that help bring the concept under the children's control entail the children commanding peers to "fall" or commanding staff to cause other objects such as cups and plates to "fall."

Open/Close

Following the videotape sequences in which the child participates with various openings and closings of doors and boxes, the teacher helps the child generalize the sign for *open* (two hands move from palms down and touching each other to palms facing each other) and *close* (the opposite motion of *open*) to real-world situations.

This begins with spheric activities on the elevated board: As the child goes through the sphere on the board the teacher requires the child to sign/say "Open!" before opening a door to a small tunnel placed on the elevated board. The child then crawls through the tunnel. Subsequently, the teacher introduces different containers that the child must open on command to obtain desired objects. Typically, the worker begins with transparent containers to allow for the possibility that the child might not keep the memory of the object inside the container. To firmly establish the *open* meaning, the teacher uses jars, boxes, milk cartons, drawers, chests, cupboards, and elevated board structure equipment.

When moving from activity to activity throughout the school day, the teacher exploits the many opportunities presented by doors, elevators, and similar objects to generalize the *open/close* concepts.

EXPRESSIVE USAGE.   A variation of the body press technique is an effective means of eliciting expressive use of *open*. Seated on the floor or in a large chair, a worker literally wraps his or her legs around the child's body so that the child feels some degree of constraint. As the child seeks to get loose, an aide helps the child transform this intention into the *open* sign. As the child makes the manual sign, the staff person quickly releases the child without, however, permitting "escape." As the teacher repeats this procedure, the child must assume progressively more of the signing function in order to win release. In going through this procedure, the child has repeated opportunities to form an interpersonal system that includes his or her influential sign and the teacher's response to it.

To help establish the meaning *close,* we have constructed a set of steps in which the top of the middle step can be opened from the center—leaving an empty gap between the first and third steps. The child needs to close this step in order to climb to the top of the steps. In closing the step, the child produces hand movements that are identical to the sign for *close,* making the transition from action to sign very clear. After several cycles of a climbing-jumping off sphere during which the child must repeatedly close the second step, the teacher interrupts the sphere by preventing the child from closing the step. Often, with only minor assistance, the child begins to sign *close* in order to continue the sphere.

With some children it is helpful to first place the child's hands on both sides of the flaps that, when closed, form the step, to merge the action and the sign as he or she responds. As the child repeats the process, the teacher progressively increases the distance between the child's hands and the flaps until he or she is able to attach meaning to the manual sign even when it is physically detached from the referent action.

Teachers also find an "open-close box" is useful. In this box teachers place, in clear view of the child, engaging objects that invite manipulation. The aide, standing behind the child, places the child's hands on either side of the flaps and continues with the procedures described earlier. Timing is extremely important in helping the child make sense of the relationship between sign and action: The teacher's response in opening and closing the flaps must immediately follow the child's productions of the sign. The aide must be sensitive to the child's body cues in order to vary support quickly.

Still another procedure for generalizing *open/close* entails use of a cardboard box into which the children can climb. After the child has developed a system—opening the box, entering it, closing the flaps—the teacher interrupts the system just as the child is ready to climb into the box. To continue the sphere, the child must first produce the *open* sign or word. When the child is inside the box, a peekaboo game can be effective in engaging the child and in eliciting an alternating "open" and "close" response in reference to the flaps of the box.

Push/Pull

First the child participates with videotape sequences showing children pushing (a car, a box, some children) or pulling. In one tape sequence the child pulls a rope attached to a bell so that each pull causes the clamor of a ringing bell. The tape presents pushing and pulling accompanied by and preceded by sign-word sequences shown in various perspectives. Following the tape, the teacher generalizes these concepts to the real world.

In order to stress the iconic nature of the signs and to avoid confusion between their meanings, children need to learn the sign—as it is in the tape— from their own perspective, that is, the teacher faces in the same direction as the child while using the sign-word command "Push!" and relating the sign to the object being acted upon. It is inappropriate for the teacher initially to make the manual sign while facing the child. Such a radical shift in perspective, as stated earlier, makes it difficult for the child to "read" the sign. It is also helpful to use *vocal gesture* to simulate effort in performing the action (e.g., "puuuush!").

It is useful to arrange an individual or group generalization similar to the one described for *come*. A piece of rope or cloth is looped around a staff member's waist. An aide alternately gives the command "Pull!" (while standing beside the child) and helps the child pull the staff member close to his or her body. The aide can assist the child by giving a short pull on the rope each time the command is given. As part of an elevated board sphere or in means–ends training, the child pulls himself up a sharply inclined plane with the aid of an attached rope. The staff person stands beside the child, signing and saying "Pull!" as the child performs the action.

Staff also place the table in an obviously inconvenient position. At mealtime the children are lined up on one side of the table. Staff then give the sign-word command "Push!" and assist the children—with appropriate vocal gesture—in pushing the table back into position for their meal.

To further develop "push" they use the hanging ball, either with one or more children riding on top of it, or simply as a pushing back and forth game. Staff gives the command to "push" before the children are allowed or assisted to do so. (This procedure can be easily modified by having the child on the ball use the manual sign expressively to another child in order to receive a push.)

EXPRESSIVE USAGE.   Wagons, shopping carts, tricylces, scooters, and swings are used within spheres. These objects provide good opportunities not only for developing interaction skills but also for receptive and expressive language development. The children alternate roles, first being the agent or performer of the action (e.g., pushing/pulling another child in the wagon), then being the commander of the action (e.g., telling another child/adult to push or pull him or her in the wagon). Again, the child learns to signal intention with the manual sign or word to the child or adult before he or she gets pulled. Interrupting the pulling action is an excellent way of inducing the signing child to sign or speak again.

Another means of eliciting *push/pull* commands derives from the use of the Traveler (see Figure 5.1, p. 177). The Traveler—a rectangular box on wheels—has a length of rope tied on each end. The children exchange various objects by alternately *pulling* the Traveler or *pushing* it to the other child. For example, Child A must tell the staff member he or she wants to "pull" before being allowed to do so and acquire the object that Child B has placed in the container. In a more elaborate and advanced exchange Child A must tell Child B directly to "push" the Traveler to him or her in order to acquire the object. This is an excellent generalization for receptive and expressive language usage as well as basic interaction skills.

CATEGORY 2. FOOD-RELATED SITUATIONS

We developed this training tape to provide disordered children with signs and word meanings that would allow them to function more appropriately in food and food-related situations. Except for three action verbs (*eat, drink, pour*) the 17 concepts referred to in this videotape are familiar nouns encountered in mealtime settings. Teachers begin by teaching the action verbs—concepts that relate directly to the child's body because children seem to learn these words more readily than signs for objects. The teacher must accent the functional properties of objects in a manner that relates directly to the signs representing them. This is possible because many signs seem to have emerged from the way in which people use objects. Sign-word concepts employed in this training tape are the following:

glass	plate	ketchup
eat	table	roll
pour	chair	cookie
fork	drink	egg
knife	bread	pie
spoon	salt	

Expanding Concepts

To exploit this characteristic so that disordered children can more readily gain the use of signs, the children need first to engage—form a functional system with the object—so that when the system is interrupted, the child will compensatorily produce the related action function. For example, the sign for *glass* (hand holds an imaginary glass) may emerge when a child who is holding a glass in preparation for drinking from it, suddenly has the glass removed (interruption) from the hand. At that point, the shape of the child's hand (as if still holding the glass) becomes a sign as the child compensatorily moves it toward the mouth. By quickly alternating between inserting and removing the actual object from within the child's hands, the object and its sign become fused or connected in a way that invests the sign with *glass* meaning.

However, to achieve a more complete understanding of *glass*—that it is possible not only to drink from a glass, but to pour liquid into it—the child needs to become engaged with glass function in varied contexts. For example, the receptacle aspect of a *glass* becomes most evident when the children around the table see the teacher holding a pitcher of juice in a tilted position, as though to pour. Here, the tilted pitcher is part of a functional system that *requires* for completion a glass to receive the liquid. For some children the need for a glass to complete the system becomes imperative only after the teacher has repeatedly poured the juice onto the tabletop, or into their empty hands.

In the early stages of teaching sign-word sequences for objects, it is essential to have the object physically present. It is impossible for a nonverbal disordered child to achieve the sign or word for an object without first becoming involved with a salient, functional aspect of that object. As in Category 1 action concepts, unless the signs generalize from use with the videotape to the real world, they have little value for the child. The following activities for generalizing signs are used after the children have participated with the relevant taped sequences.

Eat

The teacher holds a food item directly in front of the child. As the child reaches and grasps for the object, the aide (behind the child) transforms this motion into the *eat* sign (hand moves toward mouth). Beginning approximately 2 feet away from the child's mouth, the teacher moves the food item closer and closer each time the aide helps him or her make the sign. The aide molds the child's hands into the *eat* sign just before the teacher pops a small piece of the food into the child's mouth. To help the child experience the sign as causing the food to come closer, the action must immediately follow the sign. As the child repeats and begins to initiate the sign, the aide lessens the amount of support. Acceptable early variations of the sign include the child touching a finger to cheek or mouth as a signal to eat. As the child establishes the function of the sign, the teacher may require a more precisely formed sign.

Pour

As the teacher commands with sign-word "Pour!" the children—armed with containers filled with water—pour water into the water table they surround. Aides prevent the children from pouring until they see and hear the command.

In teaching the expressive use of the *pour* sign, the teacher uses the notion of merging the action with the manual sign; the pitcher from which the liquid is poured is close to and moves in the same direction as the child's signing hand. Each time the aide molds the child's *pour* sign (relating it directly to the container), the teacher immediately pours a small amount of liquid into the glass on the table. As the child repeats this procedure, he or she begins to initiate more of the signing. As this occurs, the aide reduces support.

Fork

After the training tape, several "pokable" objects (raisins, small marshmallows, apple bits) are placed in a tall thin jar. The child is told to get the item while someone holds the jar so that it cannot be tipped over. The child soon realizes he or she cannot reach the item with fingers. An aide models the action of getting the object with a fork. Then the fork is placed in the child's hands so that he or she can experience the function of the fork. The teacher allows the child to repeatedly spear food objects with jabbing motions of the fork. The teacher or aide then removes the fork and helps the child make jabbing motions with two fingers of one hand into the open palm of the other (the sign for fork). As the child does this, the teacher gives the fork in order to relate the jabbing motion directly with the fork's function.

When the children are sitting at the table for mealtime, the teacher withholds the forks while telling them to begin eating. (Aides are in position to prevent recourse to fingers.) At this point the teacher may *teasingly* hold up the fork or use it to sample the food on a plate while asking, "What do you want?" If the child does not initiate the *fork* sign, an aide helps the child make the sign. The child gets the fork and uses it with the meal.

CATEGORY 3. FAMILIAR OBJECTS AND EVENTS

This videotape helps extend the child's vocabulary by teaching familiar objects and events. Of the 16 words on this tape, 5 are verbs dealing with daily activities and the remaining 11 sign-words have familiar object referents. The teacher begins by introducing the verb concepts. The following sign-word concepts are included in the tape:

sleep	hat	car
awake	ball	boat
wash	house	bird
comb	cat	man
sweep	tree	boy
toothbrush		

Expanding the Concepts

Sleep/Awake

After the training tape, the children lie down on a large mattress with pillows and blankets. The teacher signs/whispers "sleep," "close eyes," in a hushed voice and turns off the lights. Then an aide turns on the light while the teacher and other aides simultaneously give the sign-word "Awake!" and get the children to their feet. Staff sharply vary their voices in order to dramatize the contrast between the two states. This activity is conducted in the same way as others using the contagion technique. As a variation, and to encourage expressive usage, one or more of the children may substitute or give the commands along with the teacher and then switch roles.

When the children respond to these terms, it is useful to vary the activity by having the children put large dolls to "sleep" and then wake them up. This activity readily extends to play with others and even more advanced parent–child role playing.

Wash

The generalization for this concept is obvious. Immediately after the training tape, the teacher brings a large tub of water and soap into the classroom. The children are seated around the tub on the table. Staff rub some dirt or mud on the part of each child's body to be washed, beginning with hands, then feet, arms, and so forth. When dealing with invisible body parts (face, neck), it is necessary to use a mirror. It is important to notice whether the children are aware of dirt on their bodies and clothing, how they react to dirt, and whether they spontaneously attempt to wash it off and clean themselves.

It is inappropriate to conduct the activity in the bathroom the first several times. The reason for this is pacing. If even a few minutes elapse between viewing the wash sequences on videotape and acting it out, the activity becomes disconnected. When the sign-word "wash" guides the children's behavior, the teacher begins to use dolls in the generalization by putting dirt on various parts of the doll while telling the child to alternately wash the doll's hand, foot, and so forth.

The *wash* and *dry* concepts are also stressed during toileting time. The dirt applications dramatize the necessity for washing and the contrast between dirty and clean. Later activities may include cleaning other objects, but as with all new concepts, it is best to begin with the child's immediate body experience.

Comb

After the training tape, this sign-word is taught both as a noun and as a verb concept. The teacher performs the manual sign (fingers simulate combing hair) in the same direction as the action is performed on tape, in order to better merge the sign with its referent action or object. Staff help the children to comb first their own, and then other children's and staff's hair, while signing and saying the word. They begin with a dramatically oversized comb (sold in joke stores) illustrated in Figure 10.4. This is also a good activity for teaching *I/you* distinctions and simple interaction skills.

The teacher accentuates the hair and the necessity for combing by presenting unkempt hair, or sprinkling powder in staff's hair. This activity is performed in front of a mirror so that the children can see what they are doing and the effects of their combing. The activity can be varied and complicated by raising it to the level of symbolic representations, using dolls.

Sweep

After the training tape interweaves a broom sweeping with the manual sign (one hand whisks another), staff further dramatize the concept by relating it directly to the real world activity of sweeping. They spread piles of sawdust, woodchips, or other "messes" on the floor. As the children sweep and see the immediate effect of their actions in the contrast between the unswept

Figure 10.4. Child using oversize comb to dramatize the function and sign for comb.

and swept portions of the floor, staff accompany the children's actions by
signing and saying "sweep!"

When the children begin to understand the term, staff help them sweep
the mess into the dustpan and dump it into the garbage. They vary this
activity by having one child sweep while another holds the dustpan at the
proper angle—an excellent cooperative interaction sequence.

Toothbrush

Following the tape sequence that interweaves actual brushing of teeth with
a very large brush with the sign for brushing (one finger simulates the use
of a toothbrush), the children are given a very large toothbrush (also from
the joke store) similar to the one shown in the tape. Then, as staff sign and
say "toothbrush" the children brush their teeth. Generalization of the concept consists of staff and then children signing "toothbrush" as other children's and dolls' teeth are brushed.

To elicit the sign, staff periodically "steals" a child's toothbrush while
he or she is brushing teeth.

Hat

After the tape sequence in which various hats are supplanted by the sign
for hat (patting one's head), children with staff help learn to use the sign.
To help the child experience the sign for hat in relation to the object, staff
uses the disappearing object strategy described earlier for *glass*. An aide
holds the child's head and helps him or her make the manual sign over the

hat. As the sign and the object are merged for the child, staff removes the hat, holding it just outside the child's grasp. The aide provides enough support to help the child form the sign at which point the hat is rapidly replaced. This sequence is repeated a number of times with different children until it becomes clear to the child that head tapping rapidly brings back the hat.

Ball

After the training tape shows how a ball and two cupped hands meeting interweave with each other, staff introduces a variety of balls with the children. Staff plays catch with one child at a time, demanding that the child sign for the ball each time he or she is to receive it. As the child holds the ball, the aide molds the child's hands around it and periodically removes and gives it back so that the child inadvertently forms the ball sign (two hands together as if holding or catching a ball).

Subsequently, staff plays catch or kick-the-ball with each child in a circle, calling the child's name out before throwing or rolling the ball to that child. Children also learn that the sign applies to the use of a ball for knocking down blocks, as in bowling, or they throw the ball into a box or net, as in basketball. Timing of questions ("Where's the ball?" etc.), contagious excitement, and swift backup are important in sustaining this activity.

Requisite Skills for Developing Syntax

After the children have developed a reasonable repertoire of single concepts from Categories 1–3 of the training tape, staff begins to plan ways of combining these terms into simple sentences. Before doing so, however, it is helpful for the children to have acquired the basic distinction of self and other reflected in the terms *I* (self-patting sign) and *you* (pointing at *other*). Another requisite skill closely related to combining sign-words in meaningful syntactical constructions is the ability to follow simple two-step action sequences. Procedures for developing those skills are outlined in Chapters 8 and 9 (see particularly Choice Boards, Chapter 9, p. 365).

CATEGORY 4. TWO-SIGN/TWO-WORD COMBINATIONS

This category helps children learn basic syntactical constructions involving two-sign/two-word combinations. Constructions introduced on the tape include verb + noun (*eat apple*); noun + verb (*chair falls*); possessive pronoun + noun (*my chair*); adjective + noun (*big spoon*); and noun + preposition (*cat in*). See Category 4, p. 397, for 2 sign/2 word combinations.

Verb + Noun

Samples of verb + noun syntactical forms presented on the training tape include *eat apple, break cookie, eat cookie, pick up table, drop egg.* Here, the tape presents in vivid form the action performed on the object. In a typical sequence, the child, while hearing "break cookie" on the sound track, sees a cookie appear on the screen suddenly interwoven with hands making the *break cookie* signs. This is immediately followed by the image of the cookie being broken. The same pattern is followed with different verb + noun relations. When the object concept is presented alone, the teacher can stop the tape to check whether the children can discriminate and identify it. When they have done so, the teacher releases the stop button, and the aides help the children sign the complete two-sign/two-word sentence while the action is being performed on tape.

In this category staff follow the same pattern developed with the earlier taped categories: The children participate with a particular sequence on the tape, then turn around to practice that new sequence with staff and each other. In generalizing verb + noun sequences, many children have difficulty fixing the object component. They may grasp the action part but fail to know where to direct it. With such a child, immediately after the child expresses the action term, for example, *eat,* the aide working with the child helps the child point at the intended object. This serves to locate that object in space and to connect it meaningfully with the verb component of the message. For example, with the *eat apple* sequence, the teacher begins by first requiring the eat + *point* (at apple) response. When this technique becomes a part of the child's repertoire, the aide begins to transform the pointing into the sign for *apple* (moving knuckle in cheek). At first, the sequence is eat + point + sign for *apple*. However, as the pointing and the *apple* sign become fused, the child begins to drop pointing and depends on the sign to carry the apple meaning.

Again, when introducing or generalizing any new skill or concept, the teacher begins with those concepts that relate directly to the child's body. In the case of the syntactical constructions, this means starting with "eat apple," "eat orange," and "eat cookie." Before the child can combine the signs-words into a meaningful syntactical construction, the child must already understand—at least to a limited extent—the meanings of both component terms. The pointing procedure provides an important transition for many children who cannot yet designate objects as part of a two-sign/two-word sequence.

Noun + Verb

Noun + Verb sequences shown on tape (*orange falls, plate falls, hat falls,* etc.) help the child respond to these terms and tell others about the occurrences described. In generalizing a syntactical construction such as noun +

falls, it is useful to involve the child directly by mixing the names of people (including the child's name) with the names of inanimate objects + *falls* to highlight the change in meaning that occurs when one noun replaces another. As the children realize that changing the noun while keeping the verb constant determines the entity that falls, they begin to achieve a basic notion about this kind of sentence.

As with single sign-word terms, sign-word guidance precedes expressive usage. To begin teaching the meaning of a two-sign/two-word term referring to various objects falling, the teacher might "accidently" knock a glass off the table, sign and exclaim loudly, "Glass falls!" Then one child is called up front to perform the same action on command; for example, while the glass is teetering on the edge of the table, the teacher gives the sentence in command form—"Glass Falls!"—by accompanying it with "Now *you* do it." If the child does not respond, the aide helps the child push the glass off the table to make it fall. As it falls, and then again after the sequence, the teacher and child emphatically both sign and/or speak the sentence.

Varying the object that falls or is otherwise acted upon helps the child begin to understand the notion that two signs/two words combined have a different meaning from either sign-word by itself. There are many opportunities throughout the day for generalizing these concepts. Staff take advantage of situations in which things fall, break, and are otherwise acted upon to work on developing two-sign/two-word syntax.

Adjective + Noun

In teaching adjective + noun constructions (e.g., *big/little chair*, etc.) it is important to dramatize the relevant meaning by using extremes to illustrate the notion. This is done on the tape as the child sees a big pitchfork next to a little table fork. In generalizing the concept *big/little* the teacher might give the child choice of soda in an oversized glass or a doll-size cup. At table time the teacher might arrange the situation so that there are not enough chairs for certain children so they are given tiny chairs. In expanding the child's vocabulary it is desirable to choose those concepts that are clearly contrasting, such as, *fast/slow,* and *hot/cold.*

The Cat Story

In addition to the vignettes described in the preceding paragraphs, the training videotape introduces a brief story about a cat. This story is interwoven with two-sign/two-word sequences to describe the actions. In one scene a cat is shown on a table going into a large paper bag followed by the sign-word phrase "Cat in!" Then, when the cat goes out of the bag the phrase "Cat out!" follows. Subsequently, the cat jumps off the table ("Cat jumps!") and begins to eat ("Cat eats!").

This simple story line can then be acted out by the children, using a cat doll to simulate the various events. At first the children follow the sign-word commands of the teacher; but as the sequence becomes more familiar, they are able to command the teacher or others to carry through the various steps with the cat doll. Work with this story provides a nice transition for the staff's use of natural events and picture sequences to further develop the children's language capacity.

EXPLOITING NATURAL EVENTS FOR LANGUAGE

The systematic use of natural events to develop language first developed after a hurricane that uprooted many large trees near the Center. Observing the children's awe with the gaping holes left in the ground—and noting in particular how fascinated they were with one mammoth tree that had, as it fell, largely flattened an automobile—we decided to turn it into a language sequence with the following steps accompanied by signs and words:

A Tree Falls

Wind pushes.
Wind pushes tree.
Tree falls.
Tree falls on car.
Car breaks.

The advantage of such sequences is that they begin with the child's engagement with a real-life event. Capturing the causal sequence step by step with signs and words and acting out the sequence with models of a tree and car provided the children with important language practice. In reenactments, one child (assisted by teacher) was narrator, while another child responded by making the tree fall on the car. Then the children exchanged roles. Such play provides a natural transition to the use of picture sequences that the teacher can draw in cartoon fashion to depict the various events.

Still Picture Sequences

Once children have mastered the material in Categories 1–4 of the videotape, they are often responsive to still picture sequences. However, before beginning work with picture sequences, the teacher tests the child's ability to identify pictures of familiar objects. Further, it is unlikely that the child will benefit from prepared picture sequences unless he or she is able to follow the simpler sequences from the Tableau Calendar. If the child cannot identify routine activities, project at least one activity ahead, and order some of his or her daily activities in time with the Tableau Calendar, then the use of picture sequences for language development is not appropriate.

With a class just beginning to use picture sequences, the staff first dramatize or act out the sequence. This is done before the cards are shown in order to give the child some concrete reference for the pictures. When acting out the sequence, the teacher keeps language to a minimum; the phrases are descriptive of the action being performed. One of the earliest and most engaging sequences is the *Break the Balloon* sequence.

In the three-card sequence each card portrays a picture:

Break the Balloon!

1. Boy/girl *blow* balloon.
2. Boy/girl *step* on balloon.
3. Balloon *break!*

In beginning this sequence, the teacher first holds up a balloon and helps the child identify it (balloon sign is two hands expanding outward). Then the teacher makes a "production" out of blowing up the balloon, narrating as she or he continues. Aides, working behind the children, help the children reflect with sign and word what they see happening. Narrations typically include:

1. Blow!
2. Blow balloon!
3. (Name) blow!
4. (Name) blow balloon!
5. Big balloon!
6. Break balloon!

The length and construction of the teacher's narration should be geared to the language level of the children in the group. Whenever possible, the teacher and aides develop a contagious atmosphere by having the children sign/yell "Blow!!" or "Blow balloon!!" as the teacher or aide blows the balloon. Then, in response to "What should I do?" the children respond, "Break . . . break balloon!"

Following the dramatization the teacher presents Card 1 (showing a boy or girl blowing a balloon), describes it, then immediately presents and describes Cards 2 (child steps on balloon) and 3 (balloon breaks). While this is being done, an aide refers the child to each picture—the three pictures are laid out on the table—and helps the child act out the event. To keep the group involved, it is often helpful to have the group loudly repeat the appropriate response in unison. As they do this, aides move from child to child helping with signs.

A more advanced pictured sequence that lends itself well to this format is the *Car Accident* sequence. Seven cards portray a boy pulling a wagon loaded with groceries across a street. The boy gets hit by a car, goes to a physician, and is last seen walking with an arm in a sling. Again, the children first act out the sequence with assistance from teacher and aides before using each card to develop a dialogue about a part of the event. The following is a transcript of an exchange between teacher and students after they had acted out the event and while they were all looking at the first card—a boy pulling a wagon of groceries:

Card 1—Boy Walking with Wagon

Teacher:	What's happening?
Child A:	Boy walk.
Teacher:	Boy walk where?
Child B:	On road.
Teacher:	What's the boy doing?
Child C:	Boy pull wagon.
Teacher:	What's in wagon?
Child D:	Milk in wagon.
Teacher:	Milk and . . .?
Child E:	Bag.
Teacher:	Where's bag?
Child E:	Bag in wagon.

While the main action concerns the boy *walking and pulling a wagon in the road*, there is ample opportunity to expand vocabulary and to elicit prepositions. It is also appropriate to teach the children that they have to look for cars when walking across the street. The next sample indicates the children's responses to the card portraying the consequences of the accident:

Card 3—Accident Scene

Boy fall.
Wagon fall.
Boy hurt.
Car hurt boy.
Milk fall out wagon.
Bag fall out.
Boy fall on arm.
Boy hurt arm.

Card 6 shows the child receiving assistance and Card 7, the fixed arm. The following are children's language responses to these cards:

Card 6—Assistance

Boy gets up.
Lady helps boy.
Lady picks up wagon.
Lady and boy pick up wagon.
Pick up milk (and bag).
Put milk in wagon.

Card 7—All Is Well

Boy smiling.
Doctor fix arm.
No more hurt.

Another way of using the sequence cards is to help the children identify
and understand their own and others' expressions of emotion. In Card 5,
for example, the teacher may stress that the boy is crying because he is
hurt, afraid of the doctor, and so forth. To act out this event with toys, one
child is assigned a boy doll holding a string attached to a wagon; another
child has a toy car that hits the boy doll and upsets his wagon; a third child
uses a doctor doll carrying a Band-Aid.

When the children have demonstrated good understanding of the sequence
in role playing, it is useful to have them order the cards in the correct
sequence. At first the teacher uses only three cards portraying the main parts
of the sequence and asks the child, "First what? Then what happens?" Also,
the teacher points to the position on the slot board (the holder for cards
during presentations) where Card 1 should be. This helps the child order
left to right—a useful preparation for reading and writing.

SUMMARY

This chapter, devoted to early language development, considers in some
detail the utility of a specially prepared videotape. With tape, disordered
children have repeated opportunities to experience the relation of sign-word
sequences to specific events. Videotape allows signs to be presented first
from the viewer's subjective position and then later from a variety of other
perspectives. Tape also allows referent actions or objects to be interwoven
with hand signs in a way that helps the child invest action or object meaning
in hand gestures. Subsequently, the videotape helps the child understand
the command function of sign-word sequences.

The chapter describes four categories on the training tape used at the Center: The first category introduces 18 action concepts, with particular attention to *come* and *stop* because of their relevance to the safety of the children; the second category seeks to expand the children's functional use of language by introducing 17 food-related concepts; the third category introduces 16 familiar object concepts; and the fourth introduces two-sign/two-word combinations to help teach basic syntactical relations involving verb + noun and noun + verb structures as well as adjective–noun sequences, possessive pronouns, and prepositional relations. There is careful consideration of how best to help the children generalize their understanding and use of signs from training tape to the real world through the use of vivid sensory feedback and contagious activity.

Following discussion of the training tape categories, there is a section on the importance of exploiting natural events for language development. One method of doing this entails using an event—such as an uprooted tree—to stimulate language use. The same general strategy may be employed in a somewhat more focused manner through the use of still pictures of a staged event that the children can role play and then sign and talk about.

CHAPTER 11

The Symbol Accentuation
Reading Program

The Symbol Accentuation Reading Program was developed to teach reading
to children able to communicate in sentences of two to three signs or words
but who had been unable to learn how to read and write either with whole
word or phonic approaches. In Chapter 6 we described the circumstances
and research that led to the development of the program. This chapter describes the program and the manner in which it relates to the problems of
behavior-disordered children.

The Symbol Accentuation (SA) Program is divided into three phases.
Each phase requires coordinated use of training videotapes,* flash cards,
and workbook materials. Although the program can be used with only flash
cards and workbook materials, teachers find it is most effective with all three
components.

The *first,* or sight-reading, phase consists of 10 lessons oriented around
training tapes. These videotapes, flash cards, and the workbook materials
accompanying them help students sight-read 51 common words in all meaningful sentence combinations in large and small type.

The *second* phase provides students with a transition from sight-reading
to phonetic reading. It consists of five lessons in which additional
films, flash cards, and workbook materials help students divide words into
two parts so that they can begin to relate these parts to their component
sounds.

During the *third,* or phonetic, phase of the program, 15 lessons involving
videotape and associated materials help students read and write phonetically.
They first learn to read and to write words in which consonants combine
with the strong vowel *oo,* then to read and write words in which consonants
combine with the short vowels *a, i, e, o, u.*

Material in this chapter is taken from *Symbol Accentuation: A New Approach to Reading*
(Miller, 1968/1989c). Copyright 1989 by A. Miller. Used with permission.
*Formerly on film, the SA program has been converted to videotape because of its greater
flexibility for teaching purposes.

PHASE 1. ESTABLISHING SIGHT-READING

For behavior-disordered children to sight-read, they must be able to derive meaning from the forms of printed words even though these forms, unlike pictures, bear no resemblance to their objects. Many have trouble doing this, however, because of their strong disposition to use spoken words as part of action–object systems. For many disordered children, use of a particular spoken word *requires* direct reference to a particular object or event or at least to a picture that closely resembles that object or event. It is necessary, therefore, to provide a means for these children to extend their spoken word systems so that they can include not only objects and their pictures but the forms of printed words.

To achieve this we draw on the principle of extension (Chapter 5, p. 156) to the effect that whenever a child uses one system to *act upon* a new entity, that new entity will become part of the original system. Applied to the problem of sight-reading printed words, this means that if a way is found for the child to use a spoken word system to *act upon* the printed form of a word, the child will experience the printed word as part of its spoken word system. Then, subsequently, when the printed word appears by itself, the child will relate to it as if it were a necessary part of the spoken word system.

Children's early use of spoken language—with its object requiredness—favors this process of extending systems to include printed words. When normal adults or symbol stage children use the spoken word "cat" or "cup" to refer to a feline or drinking utensil in English, they know that the same meanings can be conveyed in another language by entirely different utterances; for example, the Spanish "gato" and "taza." Such knowledge implies awareness that the sound form of a word is detachable from its meaning. For many disordered children, however, the sound forms of spoken words are not detachable from their action or object meanings. Thus, the names "cat" or "cup," if they are to mean anything, must remain "fixed" to objects or pictures that manifest the required cat or cup properties. And, because the printed words *cat* and *cup* do not manifest the required properties, problems arise if teachers are unaware that many children expect this relation. Repeated failure to find the required relation (as indicated in Chapter 6) leads to a general disinclination to attend to any printed words and thus precludes the child's achieving either sight-reading or phonetic reading.

The SA Program resolves this problem by enabling disordered children, both with and without blatant neurological problems, to find meaning in printed words without requiring them to grasp the arbitrary symbolic function of these words. Children who can name things or pictures of things can gain sight-reading by learning to experience printed words as if they were pictures.

The first 10 lessons of the SA Program contribute to sight-reading by first meeting children's expectation of *seeing* certain objects or pictures of objects when they *hear* certain names and then helping them transfer the meanings of these objects to the forms of conventional printed words. In Lesson 1, when the teacher says "bird," he or she first meets the child's expectation by showing an animated motion picture sequence of a bird while the child mimics the bird's flying motion as it transforms visibly into and thus *acts upon* the form of the word *bird* (see Figure 11.1(*a*)). As this happens, the child inadvertently transfers the bird-meaning inherent in the moving animal to the word *bird* into which the animal has transformed.

After each such transformation, the acted-upon word contours take on heightened significance for the child, perhaps because having seen a living thing disappear behind or within these contours, the child seems to anticipate that it might at any moment reemerge. In other words, just as our son David (Chapter 6, p. 191) transferred bird-meaning to the fork of a tree because he had just seen a bird disappear behind and thus perceptually *act upon* that fork, so do many older disordered children inadvertently transfer bird-meaning to the printed word *bird* after seeing the bird disappear within the contours of the printed word. Figure 11.1(*a*)–(*c*) shows this transfer of meaning occurring for *bird, cat,* and *cup.*

(a)   *(b)*   *(c)*

Figure 11.1. Transformation on videotape of (*a*) bird, (*b*) cat, and (*c*) cup into their respective printed words.

During the first 10 lessons, different kinds of object or action-to-word transformations help disordered children transfer meaning to nouns, verbs, and adjectives. Always, the nature of the transformation is directly related to a central meaning of the word into which the object or event transforms.

Relevant Body Action with Animated Sequences

As each object transforms on the screen, the child both names the object and coordinates relevant body action with the taped sequences. Through body action the child gains continuity between the spoken word and the picture-to-printed-word part of the system. Thus, as the animated sequence for gun transforms into the word *gun,* the child holds arms as if holding the gun on the screen; as the child sees a cup transform into the word *cup* while being lifted, he or she simulates this cup lifting; as a cat pounces on screen, the child moves arms as if pouncing. This coordination of relevant body action with the animated motion picture sequence not only helps the child focus attention, it helps strengthen the meaningful relation between the spoken word and the conventional printed word into which the object has transformed.

Generalizing Words from Training Tape to Conventional Reading Materials

After a child has been exposed to a few printed words developed from animated objects or events, these words appear again at the end of each lesson in their conventional form. However, even if the child correctly names these words on the tape, this does not necessarily mean that he or she can identify them on flash cards, on the blackboard, or in smaller type size within sentences. The SA Program helps bring about this generalization through the use of "accentuated" flash cards and workbook materials.

Immediately after children have been exposed to a particular training tape, the teacher shows them the accentuated flash card sets for words on the tape. Thus, after the children have seen *cat, gun, bird,* and *cup* on the tape, they view card sets in which the words share properties with their objects. The teacher first shows the card with the conventional form of the word, then, if a student cannot identify it, the teacher rapidly flips to the least accentuated (least object properties) or to the most accentuated word before flipping back to the conventional word (Figure 11.2).

Students who can name even the most accentuated, or objectlike, form of the word have a basis for transferring meaning to the less accentuated form and, eventually, to the conventional contours of the word. This is important because it means that instead of only one chance, students have three chances to sight-read the printed word. Also, while helping children generalize from their training tape to words on flash cards, the different levels of accentuation enable the teachers to determine how much accenting or object similarity a child needs to achieve this generalization.

Figure 11.2. Flash cards of *bird* drawn from two points in the progression from picture to printed word.

Workbook materials coordinated with each lesson also play an important role in helping students generalize the forms of words to new contexts. Thus, for each of the words taught by training tape and flash cards, there is a work sheet that requires students to fill in and thus to complete the interrupted contours of a word they have previously identified on videotape and flash cards. As they do this, students find themselves focusing more precisely on the unique contours of each word. Other matching work sheets require students to recognize these contours in smaller print and to relate them to their appropriate objects (see Figure 11.3(*a*),(*b*)).

Sentence Meaning

Once a child can sight-read a few words, he or she can quickly learn how the meanings of single words change as they combine into sentences. To ensure that students grasp the meaning of the entire sentence, both teacher and students *act out* the meanings of sentences immediately after they have read them. For example, after sight-reading Lesson 2—*bird falls* (see Figure 11.6), *mop falls,* and *cup falls,* and so forth—the teacher, followed by the children, uses toy objects (a bird, a mop, a cup, etc.) that they cause to fall as soon as they have read the relevant words. Also facilitating students' understanding of the function of sentences are sentence work sheets that require them to relate two-, three-, and four-word sentences to the appropriate objects or events portrayed on the other side of the page. And, finally, at the end of Lessons 5, 8, and 10, there are pages of sentences in smaller

Figure 11.3. (*a*) Student fills in contours of word on work sheet. (*b*) Student matches words to their referents on work sheet.

type that combine all words taught up to those points. These sentences lack any picture support and thus test the ability of students to derive meanings from words that stand by themselves.

With the help of these materials, students not only learn how words are generalized to a variety of contexts, *they learn how the meaning of each word is qualified by its role in a sentence.* At the same time, *they become accustomed to reading from left to right,* a skill that has utility for the phonetic reading and writing they will achieve at a later phase. But, perhaps most important, they begin their achievement of reading in a framework of success that adds to their later willingness to attempt the more difficult phonetic relationships.

"Weaning" Printed Words from Their Objects

Children who learn to sight-read through the use of the procedures and materials described achieve this by viewing printed words more as pictures than as arbitrary symbols. This is not surprising, because it is the transfer of pictured object properties to the printed word's form that makes it possible for children to name these words. However, as long as they view words as pictures, they cannot divide them into letter–sound components in accord with the phonetic alphabet; pictures, after all, lose their coherence when they are divided into parts. Therefore, before students can read and write phonetically, they must be able to experience words as meaningful entities detached from and only arbitrarily related to their objects.

The SA Program helps bring about this understanding of words as separate entities *by steadily diminishing children's dependence on object to word transformation during the first 10 lessons.* Thus, from maximum dependence on transformation sequences (Lessons 1–4) in which the printed word exists

TABLE 11.1.   Words Taught by Transforming Pictures into
Printed Words

Lesson	Words
1	bird, cat, cup, gun
2	table, dog, falls, mop
3	hat, nose, cold, pat
4	I, see, the, rat, jump
5	stop, girl, hot, walk, boy
6	lady, man, he, she, and
7	eat, come, candy, car, hand
8	up, down, far, tree, go
9	big, little, we, sit, near, foot
10	sink, toilet, window, door, bed, shower, sleep, awake

only *after* the object turns into the word, the words in Lessons 5–9 are
visible *throughout* the sequence, but become most salient as objects and
events act on and merge with them. Finally, with Lesson 10, the printed
words maintain their separate identity *without any transformation from the
objects or events with which they are paired* (see Table 11.1).

Workbook materials are also useful in this "weaning" process. For example, each time a child successfully identifies printed words on a matching
work sheet and draws lines to the relevant pictured objects, the child experiences both the separate symbolic function of these words and their
physical dissimilarity from their objects. This detaching of words from their
objects accelerates as the child reads sentences that are clearly separate
from the absent events they describe.

Children who complete the program's first phase begin to experience
printed words more as arbitrary symbols than as pictures of objects. The 10
lessons of Phase 1 present the words in a way that makes it possible for the
child—by Lesson 2—to combine 7 nouns with the verb *to fall*. By the time
the child reaches Lesson 10 he or she no longer requires accentuation to
attribute meaning to the words.

Various stages in this process are illustrated in the following sample lesson
plans (Lessons 1, 2, and 9) from the first phase of the program.

LESSON 1

Purpose

To develop sight-reading of *bird, cat, cup, gun.*

Materials

1. Symbol Accentuation Training Film (Videotape) 1
2. Symbol Accentuation Flash Cards: bird, cat, cup, gun

3. Objects: a toy bird, cat, cup, gun
4. Work Sheets: Tracing; Matching

Procedure

1. Pair each spoken word with appropriate body actions. For example, pair "bird" with a flapping arm motion and encourage children to imitate you. Then perform only the actions and require the children to name the objects and events to which your actions relate.

2. Present the training tape of objects or events that children name as they transform into their associated words. Your assistant can help students coordinate their actions with the tape.

3. Use Symbol Accentuation Flash Cards after the tape presentation to help students transfer words from videotape to conventional print. These flash cards relate directly to the videotaped sequences.

4. After flash cards, work sheet materials help students to stress the contours of the printed words and relate them to their objects. They also help students sight-read sentences in smaller type.

Relating Spoken Words to Actions

Begin the lesson by preparing your students to name certain objects or actions that they will see on the screen. This can best be done by your saying a word as you perform a relevant action and having your students do the same: Say "bird" as you make flying motions (Figure 11.4(a),(b)) and have your students repeat both word and then actions. Subsequently the students' mimicking of the teacher's behavior will be understood. Say "cat" as you make a pouncing motion. Say "cup" as you make a cup-lifting and sipping gesture with a real cup. Then perform only the actions (without props) and

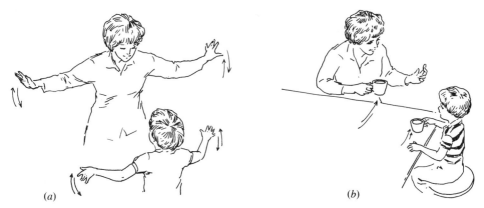

(a)   (b)

Figure 11.4. (a) Teacher says "bird" while making flying motions. (b) Teacher says "cup" while making a cup-lifting motion.

have your students name them. Vary the order in which you present the actions.

Videotape Presentation

BIRD.   The first accentuated sequence is a bird that appears to fly closer until it lands. As the bird flaps its wings and transforms into the conventional word *bird,* say "bird" and have students flap their arms like wings before and after the transformation. Encourage students to say "bird" during the second time around.

GUN.   As a gun appears on the screen, students say "gun" and relate their gun-action to the animated tape sequence for *gun,* both before and after it transforms into the printed word *gun.*

Follow the same procedure for *cup* and *cat* as they appear, having students relate their body actions to animated sequences as illustrated in Figure 11.5(*a*)–(*e*). For best results, the children's body actions should simulate as closely as possible the videotaped presentation.

At the end of the lesson, all words are shown, one at a time, in their conventional forms. This is a recognition series and, as the words appear on the screen, your students should attempt to identify them. If they cannot, you should do so and have them repeat the word after you. Immediately following the end of the tape, turn off the monitor and begin the flash card presentation.

Flash Card Presentation

You should, because four words are being taught, have four sets of flash cards, three cards to each set. The top card shows the conventional word, the next card shows the minimally accentuated word, and the last card shows the word with maximum accentuation (Figure 11.2).

First show your students the conventional word. If they are unable to identify this word, briefly show them the least accentuated form of the word and then flip back to the conventional word. If your students still cannot name the conventional word, flip to the most dramatically accentuated word card, then back to the conventional word. Help students who still find it impossible to identify the word by having them perform the relevant body action. It is always better for a student to utter the word from flash card or body cues that you provide than by your providing the word's name. Each drill should end with student identification of the word. You may at times wish to vary somewhat from the suggested procedure to more perfectly meet the needs of a particular child.

Work Sheets

TRACING WORK SHEET.   These work sheets are set up to help students attend to the contours of the words and to help them understand that words are separate from their objects. The work sheet for *bird* (Figure 11.3(*a*)) shows a picture of a bird on a branch with three versions of the printed word beneath it. The first word is intended as a model, the second word has its contours broken up in a way that allows the student to fill in and complete its form. The third, or outlined, version of the word provides less structure and, therefore, requires the student to attend more closely to the printed word's contours than previously.

Filling in the word should be done with black marker, if available, or with a thick black crayon so that darkness of the portion colored by the student will at least roughly correspond to that of the printed portion. Students should complete the letter contours rather rapidly.

After a student has completed the tracings for *bird,* point to the word *bird* and ask the child to name it. Finally, ask the student to show you what it means by pointing to the picture. It is desirable to do this to ensure understanding that each of the three words relate to the same object. Repeat this work sheet procedure with the words *cup, gun, cat.*

MATCHING WORK SHEET.   After the student has had the opportunity to do this with the four words, present the Matching Work Sheet (Figure 11.3(*b*)). This sheet provides training in word discrimination and in generalization from larger to smaller type sizes. To do this, have the student name each word and then draw a line from it to the picture it represents.

Frequently, students are so impressed by the pictures on this work sheet that they have trouble shifting their attention from them to the printed words. To cope with this, cover all pictures with a strip of paper or cardboard. Then have your students place a finger under the first word and name it. If they cannot name it, place the appropriate flash card set next to the word and have them name the word on the flash card and then name the word in smaller print on the work sheet. Following this, remove the strip concealing the pictures and have the students find the appropriate picture. Having done so, they should draw a line from the word to the picture. Repeat this process for each word to be matched with its referent.

Optional Board Work

When you reach this point, if your students are not too tired, you can test on the blackboard their ability to identify the words previously taught. Be careful in your board lettering to draw the words so that they look like the printed words they have previously learned to recognize. Pay particular attention to the *a* and *g* in this respect.

LESSON 2

Purpose

To teach four words, *table, dog, falls, mop.* To teach sentences based on words in Lessons 1 and 2.

Materials

1. Symbol Accentuation Training Film (Videotape) 2
2. Symbol Accentuation Flash Cards: table, dog, falls, mop
3. Objects: a table, a toy dog, a mop
4. Work Sheets: Tracing; Matching; Sentence Matching

Procedure

Prepare your students for the training tape by using the same procedure described in Lesson 1.

Say "dog" while holding your hands in a dog-begging posture, "table" while making a flat, outward oriented motion of your hands. Students repeat both the word and the action "falls" while you move your hand toward your left as if you were tipping over some object; "mop" as you make a circular mopping motion with the toy mop. After this, perform the actions silently and require the class to name your actions.

Videotape Presentation

Following the procedure described in Lesson 1, help your students name and coordinate their actions with each transformation of an object or event into a printed word. As the table appears, students should say "table" while they relate their actions to the videotaped sequence in which successive movements of hands across a table seem to uncover the printed word *table*.

As the dog assumes its begging posture, students say "dog" and assume the same stance.

As the mop appears, students say "mop" and perform the identical mopping action.

As a hand on the screen tips over the letters, students say "falls" and simulate the same gesture. Remember to stop the tape and have your students name each printed word immediately after the object has transformed into it.

Flash Card Presentation

Follow the same flash card procedure described in Lesson 1 to teach individual words. Then, use the cards to combine words into simple sentences. Given a student's ability to identify words in Lesson 1 and 2, it becomes possible to group flash cards so that they achieve the following sentence meanings:

bird falls	gun falls	table falls
cup falls	dog falls	mop falls
cat falls		

Figure 11.5. Child simulates with animated sequences (*a*) the flying motion before and after the animated bird transforms into *bird;* (*b*) cup-lifting motion; (*c*) begging dog motion; (*d*) mopping motion; (*e*) hand-falling motion.

In teaching these two-word phrases the teacher should not require actions specific to each word. The meaning of the whole sentence (subject and predicate) is different from the meaning of the individual words that compose the sentence.

To ensure that students grasp the meaning of the words in combination, do not encourage any body action until they have first sight-read both words. Then repeat what they have said, for example, "Bird falls?" in a questioning manner, as if to say, "Where is this happening?" Following this, pick up the toy bird, and as you show it to the class, say "bird"; then a moment later as you say "falls," allow the bird to fall from your hand.

Repeat this procedure with a shorter pause between "bird" and "falls." Then have a student read both words. As the student reads the word *bird,* suddenly move the toy bird toward the class. As the student says "falls," drop the bird, repeat "bird falls," and have the class repeat it (Figure 11.6). Have individual students read the words while you supply the appropriate action meanings. In some cases, the students will read, dramatize, and eventually be able to arrange sentences by themselves. Such variations of student participation will enhance the program. Repeat this same procedure with other word sequences presented in the workbook.

Work Sheets

Present Fill-In Work Sheets as indicated in Lesson 1. In Lesson 2 and in the following lessons, you will find both Word- and Sentence-Matching Work Sheets, which require students to relate first words and then sentences to the events that they portray. For example, Lesson 2 Sentence-Matching Work Sheet helps establish sentence meaning by requiring students to draw

Figure 11.6. Children observe a bird falling after reading *bird falls.*

a line from the word sentence to the appropriate pictures of a bird, cat, dog, mop in the process of falling. Check and correct matching sheets to make certain that words and objects are properly linked and that they understand the significance of this linkage—that the printed words signify certain events.

LESSON 9

Purpose

To teach sight reading of words *big, little, we, sit, near,* and *foot* and to extend sentence possibilities by introducing the pronoun *we,* with *sit* and with previously taught verbs like *pat, see, jump, stop, walk, come* and *eat.* This lesson also introduces the modifying functions of adjectives *big* and *little,* as well as the meaning of *near* in contrast to *far.* It also continues to reduce the amount of accentuation used to transfer meaning to each printed word.

Materials

1. Symbol Accentuation Training Film (Videotape) 9
2. Symbol Accentuation Flash Cards: big, little, we, sit, near, foot
3. Objects: none required
4. Work Sheets: Tracing; Matching; Sentence Building

Procedure

Videotape Presentation

The actions children perform with various videotape transformations of pictures into printed words are illustrated for *big, we,* and *little* (Figure 11.7(a)–(c)).

Flash Card Presentation

Drill as before and introduce the following sentence combinations. Require the children to act out the meanings in each sentence immediately after reading it:

we sit	we sit near the little foot
we sit down	we sit near the big boy
we sit near the table	we sit near the little girl
we sit near the big foot	we see the big boy

Substitute *I, he* and *she* for *we* to further establish the use of those pronouns.

Figure 11.7. Children perform relevant actions in coordination with relevant animated sequences: (*a*) big; (*b*) *we*; (*c*) *little*.

Work Sheets

Present work sheets to further establish sentence meanings.

PHASE 2. TRANSITION TO PHONETIC READING

Sight reading and phonetic reading—as indicated in Chapter 6—reflect two diametrically opposed ways of deriving meaning from and thus experiencing printed words. Sight-readers, on the one hand, derive meaning from printed words by relating them, as if they were pictures, to some external object or event. To do this effectively, they must attend to the word's total shape because slight differences in word shape relate the word to different object meanings. This means that sight-readers direct their interest, not toward the sounds they utter when they sight-read a particular word, but toward the unique form of the word and the object or event it designates.

Phonetic readers, on the other hand, derive meaning by systematically sounding out the letters within a word and synthesizing these sounds into a spoken word whose meaning they know. For this reason, their interest in printed words proceeds from the letter parts of a word to certain utterances. Or, put another way, the phonetic reader views the printed word in terms of its potential relation to his or her sound making, whereas the sight reader views it in terms of its direct relation to its object.

The problem, therefore, in preparing sight-readers for phonetic reading is to help them experience printed words not as pictures but as forms that signal them to utter sounds in certain sequences. And, although the "weaning" process described earlier may help detach the word from its picturelike relation with its object, it may still be necessary to help children direct their interest from word parts to sounds so that they can learn how these parts, when properly combined, become meaningful.

Phase 2 helps children develop this new way of experiencing printed words by having them divide and combine words already learned in the course of the first 10 lessons. The general procedure followed first requires students to recognize familiar words when these words are spoken in a divided fashion, for example, "b . . . ird," "b . . . oy," "c . . . at." After they can recognize spoken words in this way, they learn in the course of 5 lessons to coordinate the divided words they hear with the same words analogously divided on videotaped sequences, on flash cards, and on workbook materials.

On videotape, for example, they see the word *bird* with first the *b* blackening and then the outline form *ird* blackening. With repeated presentations they learn to say "b" when they see the *b* on the screen and "ird" with the *ird* on the screen. As they do this, they may achieve the general notion of a relation between the parts of printed and spoken words.

One of the risks that teachers face when they first begin to divide words into parts is that the students will find the divided word so unfamiliar that they will be unable to attribute meaning to it. To help students understand that the words they are dividing and combining continue to be meaningful, after each outline form of a word completely blackens, they see the appropriate object; for example, after the outline form of the word *bird* becomes completely blackened on the screen, a picture of a bird momentarily appears. Because such picture meanings appear only after the sounding out of printed word parts has been completed, it helps the children understand that the sounding-out process must precede the discovery of meaning.

Another procedure that helps establish this understanding requires children to relate the word being combined on the screen to a work sheet relating directly to the videotaped sequence. When the tape shows the word *cup* with the *c* blackened, a student with the work sheet can both say the sound "cuh" and trace with a finger the contour of the *c* on the work sheet. When the *up* part of the word fills in on the screen, the child can similarly say and trace this part of the word. Then, as the whole word blackens, the student combines the two sounds into "cup" while tracing the whole word. The picture of a cup on the work sheet relates to the cup seen in the tape. As a supplementary exercise, teachers may have their students blacken the outline forms of the words on their work sheets with crayons while producing the appropriate sounds.

Flash cards used with Lessons 11 through 15 follow the same format described for film and work sheet sequences. The first card of each four-card set shows the first consonant of the word blackened, and the rest of the word in outline form; the second card shows the remainder of the word blackened while the first consonant is in outline form; the third card shows the whole word blackened; and the last card shows a relevant picture. When using these cards, teachers have their students produce the appropriate sound with each card and then, by combining sounds, attempt to anticipate the picture meaning on the fourth card.

Phase 2 develops the general expectation in students that the first and second part of a printed word relates to the first and second part of the spoken word and, further, that the combining of these two parts results in a meaningful word. This phase helps those students who require transition to phonetic reading. Teachers present students with 48 of the 51 words they have just learned in a form that begins to approach phonetic reading.

LESSON 11

Purpose

To provide a framework for the phonetic instruction to be introduced in Word-Building Lessons 16–30.* To develop understanding that the sequential dividing and combining of a printed word coincides with the sequential dividing and blending of a familiar spoken word. To demonstrate that printed and spoken words may be separated and recombined without losing their meanings and that meaning emerges when their parts are combined.

Materials

1. Symbol Accentuation Training Film (Videotape) 11
2. Symbol Accentuation Blending Flash Cards: bed, big, boy, bird, cat, cup, candy, car, come, cold
3. Work Sheets: Blending

---

*These blending tapes and printed materials are not primarily designed to develop specific letter–sound relations. This is the task of Lessons 16–30. However, some preliminary learning of letter sounds may occur as a by-product of work with blending.

Procedure

The printed words to be separated and combined with their spoken forms in this lesson are *bed, boy, bird, big, cat, cup, candy, car, come, cold.* First utter them, one at a time, so that students can recognize them as familiar spoken words. Then have your students utter the appropriate sounds in coordination with the part-by-part blackening of the outlined word forms on Lesson 11. Finally, have your students trace word parts on their work sheets while viewing the film, and when you dictate word parts to them.

Auditory Blending

Begin by telling students that you are going to say a word in a "funny" way and that you want them to guess what it is. Then, say "b . . . ed." If they do not immediately understand, reduce the time between "b . . ." and "ed" until they suddenly say "bed." Make certain that the word is meaningful to them by asking what a bed is for. Follow this same procedure with "b . . . oy," "b . . . ird," and so forth.

A useful variant of this procedure involves assigning half the class a beginning sound—for example, "c" and the other half, the ending sound, "at." Then, have each half say their sound in close succession until someone hears the word "cat."

When you find that your students can both blend and understand the meaning of the words they hear, introduce the videotape.

Videotape Presentation

The first word, *bed,* appears in its conventional form. At this point, you and your students should say "bed." A moment later, only the *b* is seen in black, while letters *ed* are shown in outline form. Stop the tape, point to the *b,* make the "buh" sound for the letter *b* and have your class repeat it. Then continue the tape until *ed* darkens in at which point your students should say "*ed*." Immediately following this, your students will see an image of a bed and then the conventional darkened word *bed.* Have them say "bed" when they see the object and again with the final printed word. On subsequent presentations, help your students utter the appropriate sound in coordination with the left-to-right blackening of the two parts of the word. As with auditory blending, you may choose to vary the procedure by having half your class say one sound with one part of the printed word while the other half follows with the other sound. Follow the same procedure with all words to be blended.

Blending Work Sheets

Blending Work Sheets (Workbook I) may be used both in conjunction with tape and by themselves. Each Blending Work Sheet is headed by two pictures; one for each set of words beneath them. When working with the tape, the task for each student is to trace the outline forms on the work sheet in coordination with the manner in which they blend on the screen. Thus, on the first of the outlined forms for *cat,* the student traces with a finger only the *c,* as it appears on the screen, then the *at,* as that appears. Prior to the cat's appearance on the screen, students sound out the entire word. These work sheets are also used for dictation of the sound parts of the words. For example, after you utter a particular sound (e.g., "cuh"), have your students use crayons or markers to fill in the appropriate outline letters on the work sheet. Then, when you say "at," they do the same with the appropriate outline letters.

When you check work sheets, note whether the words have been crayoned properly and whether or not your students can produce the appropriate sounds with the relevant word parts. Also make certain that your students understand the symbolic relationship of the whole word to its picture.

Blending Flash Card Presentation

These cards are derived directly from the videotape sequences (see, for example, Figure 11.8). After briefly showing and saying the word conventionally, present the next card, which has the first letter shown blackened in while the remaining letters are in outline form. The next card reverses this relation; the following card shows the reference picture. The conventional word is then shown again. As you flip from card to card, students should sound out blackened areas of words on flash cards the same way they did with words on the tape. After sounding the two parts on the third card, they should indicate the meaning of the word. Then you can present the reference picture on the fourth card as confirmation.

The same procedure described for Lesson 11 is followed with Lessons 12–15.

PHASE 3. PHONETIC READING AND WRITING

In order to read and write phonetically, a child must understand how the letters that make up the words he or she reads and writes correspond to the sounds that make up spoken words. Thus, students must realize that letters symbolize certain sounds and that the left-to-right order of the letters relates to the order in which they must both utter and blend these sounds. Finally, they must discover that the sound forms created by sounding out letters correspond exactly to a conventional spoken word whose meaning they know. If they falter at any stage of this process, they find themselves viewing a meaningless set of printed marks.

The SA Program reduces the possibility of faltering by *teaching only the regularities of our written language;* by *eliminating the names of letters;* and by *using training tapes, flash cards, and workbook materials* to help the child first fix and then blend letter-sounds into meaningful words.

Figure 11.8. Blending sequence on flash cards for *bed* (derived from training tape).

Teaching the Regularities

There are two major sources of confusion in written English. One source stems from words whose letter arrangements do not directly correspond to the sound values most frequently associated with them, for example, the letters *gh* convey one sound in the word *light* and a completely different sound in the word *laugh*. Another important source of error stems from letters representing vowel sounds that have more than one value. Thus, whereas the letters *a* and *i* have short sounds in *man* and *fin*, they have long sounds in *cane* and *line*.

The SA Program makes two assumptions about this situation: (*a*) *Children more readily learn phonetic reading and writing with the regularities of the language than with these regularities obscured by exceptions; and (b) children who secure a firm understanding of regular phonetic relationships are better able to accept the irregularities when these are eventually taught.*

The SA Program implements this view by teaching only the most common sound for each letter. Thus, the Program presents the letter *c* only as it sounds in *cat,* the *g* only as in *gun,* and so forth. With regard to vowel sounds, the Program teaches only the *oo* sound as in *room* and the short sounds for vowels *a, i, e, o, u.* This means that with this Program children can learn to read and to write all words that can be created by combining all consonants (except *q, x, y, z*) with the vowels designated.

Letter-Sounds Instead of Letter-Names

The names of letters are not taught in the Symbol Accentuation Program because it is the sounds of letters, not their names, that combine into meaningful spoken words: the letter-names designate letters and are, especially during the early phases of phonetic instruction, a likely source of confusion. For example, it is confusing to tell a child who is attempting to derive cat-meaning from the printed word *cat* that the letter *c* is named "see." What the child needs to know is how to turn the letters of the word *cat* into the appropriate sound sequence. In short, particularly for many behavior-disordered children who have difficulty attending to more than one thing at a time, *teaching only the sounds of the letters precludes the possibility of confusing the letter-names with their sounds and makes more likely a successful synthesis of sounds into a recognizable spoken word.*

Letter-Sound Linkage, Blending, and Meaning

Even after the most confusing irregularities of our language are eliminated, children must still link letters to sounds, blend these sounds into a word, and expect that word to be meaningful.

The first step of this process—letter-sound linkage—may pose a problem to children because they do not understand how letters relate to the meaning of printed words. To really understand the contribution of letters to a word's meaning, children must first master the three-part phonetic process of which letter-sound linking is merely the first part. They need, therefore, an interim basis for linking letters to sounds until they can grasp the manner in which letters and sounds combine into meaningful words.

The SA Program uses several interim strategies to establish a few letter-sound relations that enable teachers to demonstrate quickly how these letter-sounds combine into meaningful words. Among the strategies are videotaped situations showing events compatible with sounds to be linked with particular letters. To help link the "m" sound to the letter *m* the child says "mmmm" while seeing on the screen the face of a boy licking his lips. Suddenly the boy's face is supplanted by the appearance of the letter *m*. To help fix the sound "oo" to the appropriate letters, children imitate the action of a woman first dipping her foot into cold water and then abruptly withdrawing it. As her mouth opens and she is suddenly replaced by the letters *oo*, the children shout "oo!"

A more important strategy, also using animated picture sequences, involves *articulation movement to letter transformations* derived from research reported in Chapter 6. Here, animated faces appear on the screen in process of uttering certain sounds. As a face produces the mouth movements needed to articulate a sound, these movements transform into the appropriate printed letter. On SA Lesson 16, for example, a mouth compresses into a nearly flat line from which emerges the letter *m* accompanied by the sound "mmmm." In another sequence the letters *oo* emerge from a rounded mouth accompanied by a drawn out "oooo" sound. In another, teeth bite into a lower lip and then teeth and lip transform into the letter *f*. The letters *sh* develop from a finger placed in front of the mouth with the appropriate "shh" sound.

Students watching such transformations *find themselves inadvertently emulating the articulation movements as the movements culminate in the appropriate printed letter form*. Initially, teachers and/or the sound track produce the appropriate sound as the letter emerges from the mouth. Later when shown only the conventional letter, students find themselves disposed to move their mouths in accord with the mouth function the letters trigger.

A third set of procedures entails the use of printed materials. Students use matching work sheets that require them to match either a letter form to a situation previously illustrated in the tape or a mouth formation to a certain letter. Accentuated flash cards related to the mouth-to-letter transformations on screen also help fix letter–sound relations. The cards do this by picking up two important steps in the transformation of mouth movements into the conventional letter form. These steps remind the child of the more engaging videotape sequence and thus guide the child to the appropriate sound for the letter. Finally, there are writing work sheets that both show the letters' conventional form and provide space for copying these forms with pencil or crayon. These same writing work sheets are also used with the videotape. Students see the letter on the screen, locate it on their writing work sheets, and finally copy it as they produce the appropriate sounds.

A second problem that children must solve concerns *the blending of sounds (signaled by letters in a word) into a single sound form*. They first do this with the help of the videotape for Lesson 17. Here, for example, they combine consonants previously developed in the videotape in Lesson 16 (*sh, m, b, f, c*) with the strong vowel *oo* to create *shoo, moo, boo, foo, oof, coo, boom* as each letter derives from mouth movements in left-to-right sequence. For example, a student who has been producing the "mmm" sound in coordination with the transformation of compressed lips into the letter *m* finds attention engaged by the sudden appearance next to the *m* of a mouth with the letter sound *oo* emerging. This new stimulus guides the child from the *m* to the *oo* while at the same time inducing mouth opening in a manner consistent with uttering the "oo" sound. In this way—almost without intention—the student utters the word "moo."

Although this procedure effectively induces students to blend consonants and vowel sounds into single sound forms, *they still need to know that the sound forms they produce are meaningful.* Unless students integrate these forms with an appropriate object or event, they are merely mouthing empty sounds. The Program deals with this problem by showing relevant animated picture sequences immediately after students complete their blending of a word developing on the screen. Thus, after the word *moo* forms, a mooing cow's face appears on the screen; after *shoo,* a voice on the sound track says, "Shoo!! Shoo!!" and a hand waves away flies; after *foo,* a mouth spits out food, and "Foo!" is heard. Students vigorously imitate these actions while saying the relevant words. In this way, they integrate word forms with their appropriate meanings. Later, these same relations become stronger as students use work sheets (directly related to the videotape sequences) that require them to first sound out a word and then draw a line to the picture illustrating its meaning.

The Program presents this same pattern of developing a few letter–sound relations and then exploiting them in various meaningful combinations in Lessons 16–30, not only with the *oo* vowel but with the short vowels as well. In the course of these lessons, students have sentences and short paragraphs in their workbooks providing consonant–vowel combinations.

Writing and Reading

When students learn that they can communicate through writing in a manner comparable to but different from the way that they can communicate through spoken language, the process of reading assumes new significance. Up to this point in the learning process, students often do not really understand how reading and writing differ from their spoken language. They may feel, for example, that printed words can communicate meanings only if they are read aloud. Or, they may believe that written words share the transience of spoken words; they are surprised that words placed in envelopes and opened at a later time still retain their ability to communicate information.

However, once they become aware that the words they write are independent from spoken usage, and that they can use written words to communicate with people out of sight and hearing range, the act of reading becomes a more personally relevant enterprise and students become more motivated. This seems to happen because the children can now view each new word whose meaning they decipher as a potential part of a writing vocabulary to express their own intentions on paper.

The SA Program helps establish this understanding by demonstrating to students that they can reproduce and thus control words they read and hear. The Program brings about student control of written language *by teaching phonetic writing in direct relation to phonetic reading.* This is done, initially, in coordination with the training tape. For example, as the *sh* of the word *shoo* develops on the screen, students refer to the screen, say "sh," and then write the letters. They do the same as the *oo* follows the *sh* (see Figure 11.9). Then the teacher requires them to place a finger first under their *sh* and then their *oo* and sound out and blend the word, *shoo.* Following this, the teacher refers them to the screen where they see the word *shoo,* followed by a hand shooing flies, so they can determine for themselves whether or not they are correct. This repeated process helps students establish a direct relation between conventional printed letters and the letters that they (the children) produce. In addition, it helps establish the left-to-right sequencing of letters and sounds so critical for reading and writing.

Once students master this process of sounding and copying words and checking with the meanings portrayed on the screen, the teacher dictates these words without any visual forms of the words. Students must translate the heard word into its written form. The teacher frequently assists this transfer *by helping the child place fingers of the free hand lightly over the mouth while slowly uttering the word. The mouth movements acting on the fingertips enable many students to isolate the sounds within the word more readily, particularly, the order in which the sounds emerge.* As soon as a student has isolated the first sound heard in a word, the teacher urges the child to immediately write the appropriate letter for that sound on the left-hand side of the page. The process is repeated as the child isolates subsequent sounds until the entire word is written.

After the child has written a number of such words, the teacher may request that he or she find a particular written word, then another, and so forth. Children searching for the words they have written, achieve several important things: They learn that they must form letters carefully or they will be unable to recognize them, and they learn that they must always begin sounding out the word from left to right or they will be unable to derive the meaning. But, equally important, they learn that they can write words, return to them later, and still find meaning in their own writing.

These procedures—letter-by-letter copying and sounding out of words with training tapes, translating of spoken into written words (dictation), and forced recognition and reading of their own writing—resolve most of the left-to-right confusions so common among children. Beyond this, they begin to provide children with the understanding and skills needed to use written language as naturally as spoken language.

Phase 3 begins phonetic reading and writing instruction by teaching children to fix a few letter–sound relations. They then learn to combine these letters into meaningful words and to write these words by themselves. This pattern of fixing, combining, and writing continues through Phase 3.

Figure 11.9. Children relating phonetic reading to phonetic writing.

During Lesson 16 children learn to utter sounds and to write the letters for *sh*, *oo*, *c*, *b*, *f*, *m*; in Lesson 17 they learn to combine these letters into the word forms *shoo, moo, foo, oof, coo, boo, boom* and gain their meanings through both reading and writing them. This pattern of a constant *oo* vowel combining with different consonants continues through Lesson 20. The man-

TABLE 11.2.   **Phase 3: Letter–Sound Relations Blended into Words**

Lesson	Letter–Sound Blends
16	sh, oo, c, b, f, m
17	shoo, moo, foo, oof, coo, boo, boom
18	t, h, r, p, l
19	toot, shoot, boot, hoot, roof, room, root
20	poof, poor, loop, pool, loom, tool, fool, cool
21	s, see, sink, sinks, boot, boots, room, rooms, boom, booms, roof, roofs, root, roots, cup, cups, bed, beds
22	a, ash, sash, fat, hat, pan, lap, tap, can, fan, sad, bad, dam, pal, mad, jam, bat
23	i, sit, lip, pit, hip, hit, bit, dish, fish, fin, lit, rip, pin, sip, tip, ship, rim
24	e, pep, pet, net, hem, men, hen, shed, bed, step, wet, j, jet, v, vest, beg, leg
25	o, shot, top, pot, hop, mop, hot, g, dog, pop, sob, pod, cot, dot, rob, lot
26	u, up, cup, rub, nut, bus, sun, mud, gun, shut, jug, gush, dug, tug, hug, rug
27	boom, bed, bell, bib, bit, bud, bun, bus, bad, bag, bat, coop, cat, cog, cot, cub, cut, cab, can, cap, cash, cast, dog, doll, dot, den, dim, dish, dug, dam, dash
28	fast, fill, fin, food, fish, fist, fan, fat, fell, fog, fun, gush, gum, hoop, hoot, ham, hat, hen, hill, hit, hip, hop, hug, hush, hut, jam, jet, jib, jig, jug, keg
29	loop, last, lap, leg, lid, lip, lit, lot, mad, mat, map, men, met, mob, mop, mud, mug, net, nip, nut, poor, pal, pan, pat, peg, pen, pep, pest, pet, pill, pin, pit, pod, pop, pot
30	room, rag, ram, rash, rat, rest, rim, rip, rob, rug, run, rut, shoot, shot, sad, sap, sag, sash, stag, shell, step, sip, ship, stoop, stub, tool, tag, tip, tub, van, vet, w, we, web, wet, win

ner in which the program systematically introduces new vowels and consonants can be seen in Table 11.2.

Lesson 21 teaches the letter–sound relation for *s* and demonstrates the way the number of objects increases when a word is changed from singular to plural. Lessons 22–26 teach, respectively, the manner in which consonants combine with short vowels *a, i, e, o,* and *u.*

Lessons 27–30 demonstrate the manner in which changing the vowel in the middle of a word changes the entire word; for example, *boot, bat, bit,* and *hoot, hat, hit, hut.* The final lessons also differ from Lessons 16–26 in that the words are developed with minimal accentuation. Although the videotape used in Lessons 16–26 accentuate all letters in order to provide sequential cues for the appropriate sounds, the videotape for Lessons 27–30 show the first two letters—a consonant and a vowel—as a unit (e.g., *ca, mo, ri*), leaving only the final consonant in its accentuated form. The purpose is to decrease the dependence on letter accentuation and, at the same time, to train students to cope with the first two letters of a word as a unit. Such combining makes blending the word into a meaningful entity easier than having to blend three or four letters separately.

Sample Lessons 16, 17, 22, 23, and 27 illustrate different facets of the Phase 3 phonetic program in teaching disordered children how to discover the meaning of words by sounding and writing them out.

LESSON 16

Purpose

To establish linkages between letters *sh*, *oo*, *c*, *b*, *f*, *m* and their sounds.

Materials

1. Symbol Accentuation Training Film (Videotape) 16
2. Symbol Accentuation Flash Cards: sh, oo, c, b, f, m, and their sounds
3. Work Sheets: Matching; Writing

Procedure

Students are helped to establish linkages between letters and sounds in several different ways during this lesson including dramatic situations that result in sounds consistent with the letter–sounds relation. Students also simulate animated mouth movements that transform into the relevant letter forms, copy the letters from a model, and write the letters on hearing the appropriate sounds.

Videotape Presentation

Prior to presenting the videotape for Lesson 16, utter certain sounds with certain gestures and have your students mimic them. After this, produce only the gesture and have your students supply the sounds. Because your gestures relate closely to the material on tape, you will, by doing this, prepare your children to utter sounds when they see comparable gestures or events on the training tape. For this purpose the volume can be turned down so the videotape's sound track cannot be heard.

The sounds and gestures are as follows:

Sounds	Gestures
shh	Place your forefinger in front of your lips, making a "hushing" motion as you say "shh."
oo	Withdraw your foot as if from cold water and make the "oo" sound.
mmm	Lick your lips and say "mmm."
fff	Make the "fff" sound as you simulate with your arms the diminishing diameter of a tire as it goes flat.
cuh	Lean your head back and lunge forward as you make a coughing sound "cuh."
buh	Utter a "buh" sound as you make ball-bouncing motions with your hand (one "buh" for each bounce).

After this, perform only the gestures and have your students guess the sounds that go with them. Remember to vary the order of your presentations.

Fixing Letters to Sounds

The videotape for Lesson 16 uses situations and mouth-to-letter transformations to help fix letters to sounds. The tape begins by having a "shh" gesture (forefinger in front of lips) transform into the conventional letters *sh*. Your students should mimic the taped gesture (as they did yours) and produce the appropriate sounds when they first see the gesture and after it has transformed into the conventional letters *sh*. Other letter–sound sequences on the tape involve both kinds of linkages. The vowel *oo*, for example, appears after a taped sequence in which a woman withdraws her foot from cold water and also derives from a mouth-to-letter transformation. Students should mimic actions (as they did earlier) and utter "oo" sounds at appropriate points. Other sequences are:

Letter	Tape Sequences
m	A boy licks his lips and is suddenly supplanted by the letter *m*. Students simulate the action and utter the sound during the picture and letter parts of the sequence. Then the letter *m* transforms from compressed lips needed to utter the "mmm" sound; students also simulate this sequence (Figure 11.10(*a*)).
f	Students make the "fff" sound with the animated sequence of a tire going flat and with the conventional letter *f*, which replaces the tire. Then, the letter *f* emerges from an animated sequence in which the upper teeth bite into the lower lip. Students should closely simulate the teeth–lip sequence portrayed (Figure 11.10(*b*)).
c	Students should lean heads back and produce the "cuh" sound as they see the head and mouth of a man produce the same motion on tape and then transform into the letter *c*.
b	Students should make a "buh" sound each time a ball bounces and is replaced by the letter *b*. They should utter the same sound as that from the compressed lips of an animated face as it explodes into the letter *b* (Figure 11.10(*c*)).

Writing

After students can produce the appropriate sounds on seeing the conventional forms of the letters, begin teaching them to write these letters. You can do this most effectively by coordinating your writing instructions with the tape sequence for a particular letter. For example:

1. Allow *sh* to unfold on the screen
2. Students say "sh"

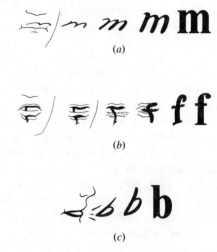

Figure 11.10. Transformation from articulatory movements into letters: (a) m; (b) f; (c) b.

3. Students copy the *sh* they see on the screen
4. Students look at copy and says "sh," then look at copy on the screen and says "sh"

Following the copying procedure, turn off the monitor and dictate the sounds for letters *sh, m, b, f, c, oo,* varying the order of the presentation. Have your students print these letters so that they resemble the letters on the tape. You and your assistant move among the students helping them form the shapes of letters.

After students have written each letter, ask them to point to the *sh* or *m,* and so forth, on their papers. Students who can find their own letters have clearly linked letters to their sounds.

Flash Card Presentation

Following the tape and writing procedures, the accentuated flash cards provide a supplementary means of buttressing the relation between these letters and their sounds.

1. Present letter on flash card in conventional form
2. If letter cannot be identified, briefly expose minimally accentuated form, then flip to conventional form
3. If this fails to elicit correct sound, present maximally accentuated form, then flip to conventional form

Work Sheets

The Matching Work Sheets follow the same format used during Phase 1 only now letters are related to sounds or mouth positions by drawing a line from the letter to the appropriate image. The Writing Work Sheet provides space for each letter in the lesson to be written three times by the student and includes a model of the commonly used handwritten forms of *a* and *g*.

LESSON 17

Purpose

To teach students to combine letter-sounds in Lesson 16 into *shoo, moo, foo, oof, coo, boo, boom* and to derive meaning from these words.

Materials

1. Symbol Accentuation Training Film (Videotape) 17
2. Symbol Accentuation Flash Cards: shoo, moo, foo, oof, coo, boo, boom
3. Work Sheets: Matching; Writing

Procedure

An effective procedure for Lesson 17 follows:

1. Vividly describe the meanings of *shoo, moo, foo,* and so forth; have students act out their meanings.
2. Present these words in a divided manner and have students indicate their understanding by saying the word conventionally and acting out its meaning.
3. Utter appropriate sounds as letters transform from mouth to letters on Lesson 17, (e.g., first *sh*, then *oo* combine into *shoo*). Then, students must correctly sound out words as they form on the tape and demonstrate knowledge of their meanings.
4. Have students copy the word letter by letter as it develops on the screen.
5. Dictate each word as a unit and require students to transcribe the heard words into written forms without the help of models.

Enhancing Word Meanings

Students sound out and discover the meanings of words *shoo, moo,* and so forth, developed from letters on the videotape for Lesson 17, if you first relate the spoken forms of these words to specific objects or events. Do this for each of the words in the following manner:

"Shoo (accompanied by shooing gesture)!" You say "Shoo!" and do this (gesture) when you want bugs and mosquitos to go away.

"Moo" says a cow.

"Foo!" You say "Foo!" when you taste something you don't like and want to spit it out.

"Oof!" You say "Oof!" if someone happens to hit you in the stomach like this (simulate this event).

A Coo Coo (cuckoo) bird comes out of a clock and says "Coo coo!"

If someone wants to scare you, they jump out suddenly and say "Boo!"

When a cannon goes off, you hear "Boom (use large expansive gesture of arms)!"

Then, describe the object or event and have your students produce the appropriate sound as follows:

"When you want bugs to go away (gesture), you say . . ."

"The cow opens her mouth and says . . ."

"If you get hit in the stomach, you say . . ."

"The bird that comes out of a clock says . . ."

"When you taste something you don't like (grimace), you say . . ."

"A cannon goes (make large, expansive gesture) . . ."

Dividing and Combining Spoken Words

Begin by saying to your students, "Now I'm going to say the words in a funny way. Let's see if you can guess what I'm saying and can show me what it means."

Then, scrambling the order of presentation, present the words in divided fashion, for example, "sh . . . oo," "m . . . oo," and have your students say the words properly and act out their meanings.

Sounding Out Words

During the videotape, letters previously related to sounds during Lesson 16 combine into *shoo, moo, boo,* and so forth. The tape begins with the development of *sh* from forefinger and mouth as on the videotape for Lesson 16. Have your students say "Shh," as the forefinger and mouth transfer into conventional print. The *sh* then remains on the screen while an open mouth appears to its right and rapidly transforms into the letters *oo*. As this happens, your students should say "oo." (Sometimes at this point it is useful to stop the image and point first to the conventional *sh* and then the *oo* so your students have an opportunity to sound out both parts from the fixed, conventional word). Then, ask the students what "that" (pointing to *shoo*) means. Allow the tape to continue so that they can see the meaning of *shoo* illustrated by a hand waving away flies. As the word *shoo* again appears, have your students repeat it orally.

Follow the same general procedure as *moo, boo, coo, foo, oof,* and *boom* transform from mouth movements to letters on the screen.

Writing Words

Students learn to write out words from the same animated picture sequences that first enabled them to sound out words. For example, as the *f* develops from the teeth–lip sequence, students say "fff" then write the letter *f* on the left side of their pages. They go through the same process as the *oo* develops to the right of the *f* (Figure 11.11(*a*),(*b*)). They may have to check the screen carefully to make certain they are writing their *oo* in the same relative position to the *f* as the letters on the screen.

Then require them to place a finger under and make the correct sound for the *f*, then for the *oo* until they hear themselves say "foo." When this happens, ask them what "foo" means. Start the tape again so that they can see the sequence that shows a man spewing out food. Work on the contrast between *foo* and *oof*. Congratulate your students if they have correctly anticipated this sequence.

Follow the same procedure with other words on the tape. After they have written three or four words, ask them to show you *shoo, moo,* and so forth. If they are having difficulty doing this, have them place fingers of their free hand over their mouths and slowly say the word they are looking for. As they utter the first sound of the word—"m" in "moo"—have them all point to the top left-hand side of the page and move their fingers from letter to

(*a*)   (*b*)

Figure 11.11. Sequences that contrast word forms: (*a*) *foo*; (*b*) *oof*.

letter (downward) until they find the letter *m* on the left. Have them continue sounding out the "oo" part of the "moo," then determine whether or not an *oo* follows the *m* on their work sheets. Then have them use this method to find the other words that they have written.

Dictation

Many of the procedures described for writing out words with the videotape are important when you dictate words as units without providing the children a model. Here, it becomes very important that they immediately write the letter on the left side of the page for each sound they utter, before uttering and transcribing the next sound. (Sometimes a fold in the middle of the work sheet, which divides the word into two parts, provides a helpful guide to them in their effort to keep the first letter on the left side and the next letter(s) on the right side). As with copying, many children can more readily relate sounds to letters by using their free hand on their mouths to help isolate the sequential sounds in a word.

Have your students print their words between 1 and 2 inches in height. Lines, lightly ruled every 2 inches across the page, tell them how large their letters should be and provide them with a base on which to place their words. After they have written four or five words, have them find these words by themselves.

Flash Card Presentation

If students cannot readily sound out conventional forms of the words on flash cards, allow them to work with the second card, which provides cues for the "oo" sound. You may also tell them the first sound and allow them to blend this with the "oo" sound by themselves. After sounding out the word, see if they can anticipate the picture meaning on the third card. If not, show this card to them and have them sound out the word again.

Work Sheets

Present Matching Work Sheets and require your students to sound out each word before attempting to relate it to its object by drawing a line from word to object.

Writing Work Sheets provide models for correct formation of letters. When they are using these sheets, you should periodically ask your students what they are writing and have them sound out their writing to preclude their working in a rote manner.

Note: If you find it necessary to stay on Lesson 17 for longer than 1 or 2 weeks, make certain that you vary the lesson components (videotape, flash cards, copying, dictation, work sheets) enough to keep your students engaged with the materials.

LESSON 22

Purpose

To teach the manner in which consonants combine with the short vowel *a* to create new words.

Materials

1. Symbol Accentuation Training Film (Videotape) 22
2. Symbol Accentuation Flash Cards: a, ash, sash, fat, hat, pan, lap, tap, can, fan, sad, bad, dam, pal, mad, jam, bat
3. Work Sheets: Matching; Writing; Sentence Reading

Procedure

As you say "aah" as in "hat," place a finger at either end of your mouth to highlight the lateral mouth stretching that takes place when you utter that

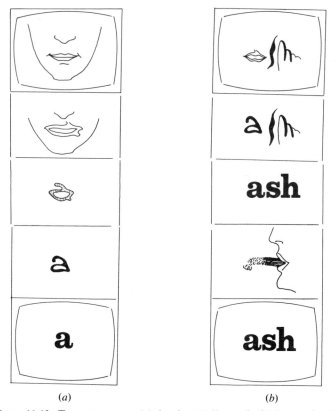

(a)   (b)

Figure 11.12. Tape sequences: (*a*) the short "a" sound; (*b*) the word *ash*.

sound. Then merely stretch the sides of your mouth several times and have your students provide the appropriate "aah" sound.

Videotape Presentation

As the tape begins, your students say "aah" as a stretched mouth transforms into the letter *a* (Figure 11.12(*a*)). A moment later, the stretched mouth serves as the first part of the word *ash* (Figure 11.12(*b*)). As it transforms into *a*, students say "aah!" then "shh." The same process occurs with words in which the stretched mouth appears in the center of words: *sash, fat, hat,* and so forth.

Flash Card Presentation

Follow the procedure described in Lesson 17.

Work Sheets

Follow the procedure described in Lesson 17.

LESSON 23

Purpose

To teach the letter–sound relationship for *i* and the manner in which consonants combine with it to create new words.

Materials

1. Symbol Accentuation Training Film (Videotape) 23
2. Symbol Accentuation Flash Cards: i, sit, lip, pit, hip, hit, bit, dish, fish, fin, lit, rip, pin, sip, tip, ship
3. Work Sheets: Writing; Sentence Reading

Procedure

Tell your students that the new sound you are going to teach them is "i" and that each "i" goes with a little broad jump. Then accompany a series of "i" sounds: "i . . . i . . . i . . ." with little broad jumps (feet together, body erect at the end of each jump) and have your students do the same. After this silently jump and have your class produce "i" sound effects. Divide words with "i" as you did in Lesson 22. For example, say "si . . . t, li . . . p, pi . . . t"; have students pronounce the words conventionally and indicate their meanings. Take care to pronounce the first consonant and the vowel as a unit because this prepares children to do the same on viewing the training tape.

(a)   (b)

Figure 11.13. Tape sequences: (a) the short "i" sound for the letter *i*; (b) *i* in partially transformed word.

Videotape Presentation

Have your students say "i" with each broad jump of the animated letter *i* (Figure 11.13(*a*)) on the training tape.

Later the *i* will appear in a bent-over position in a partially transformed word (Figure 11.13(*b*)). Then one at a time the letters assume their conventional shapes in concert with your students uttering the sounds that go with them.

Writing

Follow copying and dictation procedures described in Lesson 17.

Flash Card Presentation

Follow procedures described in Lesson 17.

Work Sheets

Note Sentence Reading Work Sheet for stories exploiting the "i" sound.

LESSON 27

Purpose

To teach the initial consonant and vowel of words as units to be combined with end sounds: shoo . . . t, sho . . . t, co . . . t, ca . . . t, and so forth. To teach how vowel sounds in the middle of a word change the word's meaning, for example, boot, bat, bit; hoot, hat, hit.

Three new things happen in Lesson 27 and continue through Lesson 30. One concerns the amount of accentuation. Whereas in previous lessons, all letters were accentuated sequentially to provide sound cues for the child, in Lesson 27, for the first time, the child sees the first two letters of the words as a unit, leaving only the last letter accentuated. The second new thing is that—in contrast to lessons devoted solely to one vowel sound in combination with previously taught consonants—now the child must shift from words with one kind of vowel sound to words with other vowel sounds in the course of the lesson. The third new feature of this lesson concerns the duration of the picture on the videotape following the sequential development of the printed word. Previously these referent pictures were on screen for several seconds. However, beginning with Lesson 27, the duration of these referent pictures reduces to less than a second.

Materials

1. Symbol Accentuation Training Film (Videotape) 27
2. Symbol Accentuation Flash Cards: boom, boot, bed, beg, bell, bib, bit, bud, bug, bun, bus, bad, bag, bat, coop, cat, cot, cub, cup, cut, cab, can, cap, cash, cast, cog, doll, dot, den, dim, dug, dust, dam, dash
3. Work Sheets: Matching Writing; Sentence Reading

Procedure

Prior to showing the training tape for Lesson 27 in which the consonant and vowel of each word are presented as a unit, present the words in their spoken forms to the children. For example, say "boo . . . t" and have your class repeat it in this fashion, then conventionally before having them guess its meaning. As you do this with the words to be shown in the tape—*boom, boot, bed, bell, bit, but,* and so forth—you also provide your students with practice combining consonants with the different vowels taught during Lessons 16 through 26.

Videotape Presentation

New words introduced for the first time in this tape are *bell, bib, bud, bun, bag, cog, cut, cub, cab, cap, cash, cast, doll, den, dim, dash.*

Flash Card Presentation

First present students with the conventional form of the word. Then, if there is any difficulty, flip to the second card. There, stress the first two letters as a unit and add the final accentuated letter, for example, "boo . . . t." The third card provides the reference picture.

Writing and Dictation

Follow copying and dictation procedures previously described in Lesson 17.

Work Sheets

Matching Work Sheets carry further the root emphasis on the words and provide matching exercises for all words.

Writing Work Sheets may be used by students who require more practice in forming letters. Sentence Reading Work Sheets exploit the different consonant vowel combinations presented during this lesson.

APPLICATION TO DIFFERENT DISORDERS

Trainable Retardates

The first field application of the Symbol Accentuation Reading Program was conducted at Wrentham State School in Massachusetts (Marko, 1968) with a population of trainable retarded residents who had not previously been able to learn how to read. The program was applied over a period of 18 months with 70 trainable retarded residents (mean chronological age (CA) 21 years, mean Stanford–Binet mental age (MA) of 4 years 8 months, and mean IQ of 38). These retarded residents learned to sight-read a mean of 28 words in all possible meaningful combinations, in large and small type. Twenty of the 70 were able, with the help of letter–sound accentuation (Phase 3 of the Program), to sound out and decode the meaning of words with different consonant-vowel-consonant combinations. They could also write words from spoken dictation (without models).

Disadvantaged Preschool Children

A doctoral dissertation involving a field application of SA was conducted by Messier (1970) with 5-year-old children enrolled in Head Start Programs in Brockton, Massachusetts. Using control and experimental groups (20 children in each), Messier found that children taught with the Symbol Accentuation Program achieved significantly higher gains on Metropolitan Readiness and Peabody Picture Vocabulary Tests than those children exposed to conventional readiness preparation for the first grade. He felt that preschool children could learn to read on this level because Symbol Accentuation was geared to their developmental level of functioning.

Autistic and Schizophrenic Children

A field application of SA with severely disturbed children (E.E. Miller, 1970) was conducted at the League School of Boston with 10 psychotic children (mean CA 8 years 7 months). Eight of the 10 children had been unable to achieve any measurable skill in reading and writing at the time the program was initiated. After 10 months of SA training, 7 of the 8 had made substantial gains in reading and writing and had improved their Metropolitan Readiness Test scores a mean of 23.6 percentile points (from 5.2 to 28.8) and their Peabody Picture Vocabulary Test scores a mean of 20 points (moving from a mean IQ of 55 to 75). It was believed that important factors in the SA program stimulating development with these children were the habit of directed attention and increased contact with others which this Program fostered.

Aphasic People

E.E. Miller (1968) reported on the meaningful multisensory stimulation that SA procedures provided patients with strokes who had lost large portions of their ability to speak and read. As a result of this intervention, Miller found that these patients showed increased ability to initiate both spoken and written language.

Learning Disabled Children

An informal report from the Reading Department of the Wellesley Public Schools (A. Miller, 1970) in Massachusetts indicated that SA had been an effective teaching strategy with 10 learning-handicapped children assigned to a learning center in one of the public schools for a 1-hour session per day during a 10-month period. All 10 first- and second-grade children assigned to this group scored substantial gains in their ability to read and write with comprehension as measured by the Stanford Achievement Test Primary I Battery.

Report on the Symbol Accentuation Reading Program by the Regional Special Education Instructional Materials Center (SEIMC), State University College at Buffalo

This federally funded instructional materials center introduced SA with three different groups of children. The SEIMC report (Brown, 1971) stated:

> Since it was not feasible to evaluate SA with all possible populations with which it might prove relevant, the Buffalo SEIMC limited its field evaluation of SA to Educable Mentally Retarded (EMR) children who have not been able to achieve first grade reading ability, to "High Risk" first grade children, and a deaf population. (p. 5)

Educable Mentally Retarded

This class of 10 students (4 girls, 6 boys) had a mean CA of 10 years 1 month, mean Stanford–Binet MA of 5 years 8 months, and a mean IQ of 69. Unsuccessful attempts to teach these children to read had been made for 3 years prior to exposure to SA instruction. The children were taught with SA for 10 months and evaluated on acquisition of sight-reading and phonics, as well as on Metropolitan Readiness and Peabody Picture Vocabulary Tests. Pre- and posttesting indicated substantial gains for 9 out of the 10 children both on sight-reading and phonics tests (53% in sight-reading, 45% in phonics).

Significant gains were also evident on the Metropolitan Readiness Tests (mean gain of 11.8 percentile points) and on the Peabody (mean gain of 10 months in mental age and 5.6 points in IQ). The report stated:

The Symbol Accentuation Program was effective in helping most of the students in the acquisition of basic reading and writing skills and improved listening skills. (p. 8)

"High Risk" First-Grade Children

This class was termed a "high risk" first grade because the 12 children in it had either spent 2 years in kindergarten, had low readiness scores, or were considered poorly motivated. The mean chronological age of the class (6 years 9 months) was closer to the norm for children beginning second grade than first grade. The teacher reported that by the end of the program all of the children were well into second-grade-level reading materials. The SEIMC report continued:

The Symbol Accentuation Program seems to have had some of its most dramatic effects on this "high risk" group. All 12 children showed gains in their abilities to sight-read words, sound letters, and translate the sounds they heard into the correct written letters. These results, coupled with the teacher's comments, support the view that most motivational problems which existed at the start of the program were eliminated. (p. 12)

Deaf Children

Two complete SA programs were made available to St. Mary's School for the Deaf in Buffalo with the open-ended instruction to use the materials in any way that might seem useful with deaf children at different ages. Subsequently, 4 teachers used the materials in highly individual ways with their children. The SEIMC report stated:

Teachers of deaf children were quite excited about the SA program's ability to induce progress among children they could not previously move. The teachers reported that the program's impact was impressive and that it had sufficient flexibility for individual use and/or in small groups. (p. 15)

The SEIMC report closed with the following statement:

It has been claimed that the SA Program helps children who cannot read and write to do so. Previous studies have shown this to be the case under very controlled conditions. The present study has found nothing incompatible with that claim nor with the findings of the previous studies. The results of instruction using the Symbol Accentuation Program, therefore, are entirely consistent with the claims that exist. Equally important are indications that the program's impact goes beyond effective reading and writing instruction; some of the subjects also acquired new confidence in their ability to learn and demonstrated this via increased academic competence. (p. 17)

SUMMARY

This chapter describes the Symbol Accentuation Reading Program designed to help children with 2–3-word sentence speaking ability to read and write. The program, divided into three phases, provides careful transitions from sight-reading (Phase 1) of 51 common words to phonetic reading (Phase 3) of consonants and vowels.

Innovative features of the program include the use of gestures and signs to facilitate the transfer of meaning from animated pictures to printed words or to letters. Subsequently, videotape recognition of words is transferred to flash cards that provide cues to the words when they cannot be recognized in their conventional forms. Once words can be read in large print, the children learn to read them in small print and as part of increasingly elaborate sentences.

The second phase of the program helps children divide and integrate words previously taught by sight so that they learn that words do not lose their significance when they are broken into parts. For some children this transitional phase makes possible a grasp of the third phase. In this final phase, children learn to blend a few consonants with the strong vowel *oo* and immediately see the meanings of the words they have created. The use of videotape sequences makes it possible for the children to visually shift from one letter–sound relation to another in a manner that favors meaningful blending.

The program has been effectively used with normal preschool, learning disabled, retarded, and deaf children. At LCDC it has been used for over 20 years to help system-disordered children—otherwise unable to read—to do so. The program integrates well with conventional programs that are organized linguistically and in which new relations are added one at a time.

CHAPTER 12

The LCDC Model

Behavior-disordered children often challenge a family's resources to the limit. The problem of how to "be" with a child who gives back little and behaves at times in frightening and unpredictable ways poses serious dilemmas. Frequently marriages are affected, and siblings feel neglected because of the parents' preoccupation with the disordered child. Sometimes professionals unwittingly add to the problem either by inappropriately reassuring the parents that the problem will resolve itself or by incorrectly diagnosing the disorder. By the time parents are referred to the Language and Cognitive Development Center, they usually realize that something is seriously wrong with their child and urgently need to know what can be done about it.

The LCDC model that has evolved over the years addresses these issues, first, by responding to the parents' need for clarity—as far as this is possible—about their child's situation and by indicating whether or not the Center's program is appropriate. Second, if appropriate, by collaborating closely with parents in their child's program. In the following we describe different facets of the Center's cognitive-developmental systems program and how it attempts to meet the varied needs that both child and family bring.

A PARENT'S REACTION TO THE LCDC PROGRAM

Umwelt Assessment

The first significant contact a family has with the Center is around the evaluation of their child. Typically, one of the directors (AM or EE-M) or one of the senior staff conducts the evaluation after relevant background material and previous evaluations—neurological, psychological, speech and language—have been received. Either or both parents participate in the evaluation (see Chapter 7). The manner in which the evaluation is conducted and its significance to parents seeking clarity is suggested by the remarks of Anna's mother, Mrs. J, when we asked her, recently, if she could recall her impressions of her child's first evaluation at the Center. She replied as follows:

MRS. J: We went in there and for the entire period it felt like time that was really. . . . It was the first time we had any period of time that we felt that anybody was understanding Anna. That there was some kind of system geared to understanding a child like mine. It was very exciting because from the first moment she was engaged. And the various tasks on the boards. . . . She really liked them, she responded, and they were at her level where you could make some real conclusions about her state of development. Some of the things she could do and some she couldn't do. And that's how you're able to tell where you're at. Whereas if you can't do any of the tasks, how are you going to make any kind of inference?

Any other time she was tested they tested her the way they test normal kids, and Anna is not a normal kid. And it was a very frustrating experience because she basically didn't or couldn't do anything. Even more upsetting was when she didn't do things she was capable of doing because she didn't choose to do them. And it's taken me some time to understand that that is what they are measuring in IQ tests. It's not your ability, it's your willingness to do it . . . which makes you have the ability you have.

And all the way through the evaluation you (AM) were explaining what was going on in a steady commentary. And at the end you summarized it, and it was so succinct. We went out of there just elated not because we felt that Anna was going to be cured but because you were people that understood and could describe what was going on with her. . . . It was really enlightening to me to be able to break down her behavior like that in a way which nobody had done. Before it was just a mass problem. And afterwards you outlined 2 or 3 things that she would have to do before she would be able to talk . . . not guaranteeing that she would talk although we were encouraged. But steps that had to be achieved. And nobody had done that for us before. Not even close. I felt that this was the first time somebody really looked at Anna.

After the assessment, we talk with the parents and share our understanding of the child, drawing on previous reports but depending mostly on the child's system-forming capacity as it becomes apparent during the Umwelt. Typically, there is enough data at that time to judge whether the child is appropriate for the Center and to provide some preliminary understanding of the child's disorder. We share this with the parents. When there are obscure aspects of the child's functioning, we defer sharing information until we have the additional understanding that further evaluations can provide.

Tour of Classrooms

Once we determine that a child is appropriate, we take the parents on tour of each of the Center's six classrooms, lingering longest at the one-way observation window that permits viewing of the most likely class for the new child. The fact that our program is open to such direct scrutiny seems to have special meaning for parents. Here, Anna's mother reports on her impressions of the tour.

MRS. J: It was a new experience to be able to look into a classroom and see kids that were either working on the elevated board structures or doing actual subjects and things. In other settings I couldn't really see what was going on. That open quality is not at all common and it was very important to me. . . . Particularly at that time because I didn't know as much about autism or feel able to judge . . . or know that she was okay. And Anna was a more vulnerable child then than she is now. I'm not as frightened for her as I used to be. She has a little more ability to stand up for herself. And I was able to go into the classroom with her . . . I wouldn't put her anywhere with people who weren't truly caring people.

AM: Soon after that you and your husband decided to move here from the West Coast so that Anna could attend the LCDC program. What went into your thinking?

MRS. J: We felt we had finally found a program for nonverbal children her age who were autistic and which could deal with her scattered behavior. And we were most concerned about her language. It is the most evident feature . . . that would affect her life enormously. We had to find a place that was good for her. And we hadn't found it where we lived. And I was biased against the public schools mainly because I am sensitive for Anna. I wanted her in a place that would be committed to working with her—a place that really cared about what happened to her and was willing to take a good look at her and accepted her all the way along the line.

Therapy Assignments

Once we accept a child and family into the Center's program, the family is assigned a C-D systems therapist who meets with the parent(s) and child once a week. The child attends school daily from 8:30 A.M. to 2:30 P.M., except for a short day on Friday (8:30 to 11:30 A.M.) so that staff conferences can be held on Friday afternoon. When appropriate, the child is also assigned speech and language, movement therapy as well as adaptive physical education work on an individual basis for weekly sessions. In addition, the parents meet weekly with a counselor—psychologist, psychiatric social worker, or psychiatrist—to deal with any or all issues that come into play around parenting a disordered child. As we make these assignments, we are careful to emphasize the collaborative nature of the work . . . that although we as professionals have accumulated a body of knowledge about disordered children, they as parents are the unique experts on what their child is like in a variety of situations. Our approach is consistent with the collegial stance with parents that Schopler (Schopler, Mesibov, Shigley, & Bashford, 1984; Schopler & Reichler, 1971) established a number of years ago. We also emphasize that we need each other to help their child develop. The manner in which Mrs. J perceived her role with the C-D systems therapist is captured in the following comments:

AM: What is it like working with K (C-D systems therapist) and Anna?

Mrs. J: Well, it's similar in feeling to the assessment. Because I feel immediately we are energized. We're working right at Anna again. There's someone enormously talented who is working right at Anna's level. For an hour Anna is totally engaged. And that is really something to see that happen. I feel like you see Anna's brain working when you are in C-D while at home you may only glimpse her ability. But during the C-D session for a steady period of time you see Anna think.

AM: Are you part of this?

Mrs. J: Yes. K really uses the parents from the beginning. K has a lot of respect for the parents and the role they play with the child. And she sets things up in order to give the maximum relationship between parent and child. And I never felt that I couldn't make suggestions, innovations myself . . .

AM: What about a suggestion from you? How would she respond to it?

Mrs. J: She would always listen. She would comment on whether it was a good idea or whether it seemed too advanced. Many times I think she . . . at the beginning when I was learning . . . did things she wouldn't have done on her own because she felt it was important to me. And I learned from that. She taught me how to do C-D and how to understand what level Anna was on and what would be more difficult for her.

AM: She speaks of you as a collaborator.

Mrs. J: Yes. And it has been that way although she taught me first and I'm learning much more from her than vice versa. But the more you do. . . . The latest one I've introduced was drawing the face on the plate that Anna sprays off with the squirt bottle. And Anna really, really likes that. . . . If you find something that interests her you've overcome that first big barrier.

Then you have a chance to see whether she can do it or learn. And she did. She was able to understand that you spray it, the face drips off, and that when you move the plate she has to follow it while squirting water. We've included that in spheres many times with variations. . . . That's probably the latest one.

Counseling Sessions

During weekly counseling sessions parents have the opportunity not only to gain practical information about what is known about their child's disorder, they can work through issues around their role in the disorder. The excerpts that follow indicate the kinds of issues with which parents struggle. This mother's feeling of rejection by her autistic child and an incorrect diagnosis compounded the child's problems and worked against her development. The mother describes her efforts to find help for her 2½-year-old daughter's unusual behavior and failure to develop language.

MRS. J: Finally we brought her to a pediatrician who recommended us to a psychologist. That was a big mistake. Because we went to her, and she did a number on us. And I do think it is very unprofessional of a professional not to explain what they are trying to see. What she was trying to see was my daughter and I interacting. I thought she wanted me to stay out of my daughter's way so she could study her. And that's what I did. I really don't think that was fair because it didn't show the way that Anna and I communicated . . . which wasn't normal . . . but there.

AM: You were entering with different assumptions.

MRS. J: Yes. I think some professionals do that quite frequently. They think of themselves as much more qualified to see what is going on than you. It's almost as if they are trying to trap you so that they could come up with a diagnosis. She didn't know what was wrong with her and what she did come up with at the end she called a parent–child problem. And I really got the feeling from her that she thought I was going to wreck my kid. And it came through. She called it a general developmental delay because it was. When you tested her, it was there. But she said the cause was a parent–child problem.

AM: That hurt you a lot.

MRS. J: It really did. Because we didn't know what we had done that was so awful. It was terrible. I was ashamed. I didn't want to show anybody that. I didn't want to put it in the record. I was ashamed . . . and I was afraid that it was true. And it made me withdraw from Anna. You don't feel you can forgive somebody for that because it was so much the wrong thing to do. And I was apart from her. What I needed was someone who could explain what was wrong and how you could do something a bit differently.

AM: Someone who would put an arm around you and say, "Look, try this or consider that . . ."

MRS. J: And that what you're doing is okay. You're loving her. And you're doing. . . . But it wasn't what we got. And it was a terrible thing. And time went on, and we moved to another city and I really, really drew back from her. And my husband and I at that time started having more problems. We never were without problems, but (it was) the worst period for us as well. We were going to get a divorce and neither of us was there for Anna. It was a terrible, terrible time.

AM: Something I don't understand. If this psychologist upset you and you felt she was wrong, why didn't you go to another one—or move closer to Anna—and show the psychologist that what she said was untrue?

MRS. J: No. I think that I was so insecure already because I knew something was wrong. And in the back of your mind you suspect that it is you and then somebody says it *is* you. I felt very guilty, very shamed, very afraid and I wasn't strong enough. Now I would say I know better about my kid. But at that time I didn't. I thought they did know. They were professionals. I thought they had seen kids like this and parents like me and they knew what they were talking about. And she acted like she knew. It wasn't like "I don't really know what's going on with your kid." Instead she said, "Here it is. I'll write it down."

Mrs. J then described her withdrawal from her child and the child's acute distress and sadness in the new setting. The mother kept her out of any program for a year, and Anna gradually lost most of the 20 or so words she had. In the next excerpt is the mother's description of her struggle to reclaim her child in spite of the child's intimidating screaming and Mrs. J's feeling that she was unable to comfort her.

MRS. J: Anna went through a period at night where she would wake up and be totally, totally out of control . . . just screaming and flailing. And you mentally struggle: Should I keep her in an enclosed space? Is it that she doesn't know where she is? Should we walk through the whole house? And it's scary to you. You can't get through to her. It might go on an hour . . . and she's terrorized and she's built herself up to it. And it looks like an anxiety attack that is just out of control . . . although she doesn't get paralyzed with fear. That isn't her way. She kicks and screams. It does't happen like that anymore, but it still comes up like that a little bit.

AM: How did you cope with it?

MRS. J: What helped was changing my way of looking at her. I had to say to myself that this child is frightened. And something inside of her has just ballooned and ballooned, and she doesn't have the mental means for dealing with it. And she doesn't reach out to get calmed. She doesn't have the ability to find someone to help her with that. She doesn't have the ability to comfort herself or to get comfort from anybody else . . . although sometimes it helps to keep her in a small space by holding her tightly (compression) and talking to her calmly.

But sometimes we're at a point where she really does need to walk through the house (reintroducing her to it) while talking calmly and telling her what we are doing (narrating), and then you can go back to the small space. Compression helps . . . but with her it's not the first step. You do it a little bit, walk her around, and then you come back to it. Compression by itself doesn't work . . . gets her even more upset.

It's also really a matter of your own inner sense of self. You say to yourself . . . I am the mother. I see this child. It is terror on her part. I can help her. I am going to help her. But I have to keep my own calm. Her upset doesn't look like other kids but it probably feels to her like your other kids feel. And you don't really do anything different. It's just harder to do it.

AM: You exaggerate what you would do with any normal, scared kid.

MRS. J: And what scares you is that it doesn't work right away. It's frightening to see your kid so frightened.

AM: And if you panic and your kid picks it up . . .

MRS. J: And that does happen. You really have to keep yourself calm all along—although there's nothing worse than a crying, upset baby. But I now know that if I "lose it," the attack will be prolonged because she does pick it up. Anna is very sensitive to the undercurrents going on . . . as are normal kids. But because you don't immediately see her responding to the undercurrents, you may tend to think that she is not. But she is.

AM: The other misconception about autistic kids like Anna is that they don't make relationships. They do . . . but slowly and one must work harder to establish them.

MRS. J: And you don't get the immediate proof that the relationship is there. But you just have to believe it and understand that it is there even if you don't get the proof of it very much . . . but if you just stop and take a deep breath and say, "I know it may take me 15 minutes. . . . It may take me an hour or two. But I will get through to my kid. I know that I will." And you will. And I believe this and it has never failed me.

It's really hard to believe in your own ability to matter when your child is not responding to you right away. And that it (her disordered behavior) is not bigger than you. It's not. And you have to have a relationship with the child you have. She may get better and hopefully they all will. But you don't let go.

SUPPORT–DEMAND RATIOS

In the courageous struggle of this mother to reclaim her daughter, we see the mother shift from one kind of stance toward her daughter to another. The first stance—triggered by her child's "rejection," and an inaccurate diagnosis—led her to pull back, or withdraw, from her child. We characterize this as a *low support–low demand* stance, in which the parent engages only minimally with the child and provides neither the nurturing (low support) the child requires (even though unable to reach out for it) nor the demands (low demand) for more adaptive behavior that all children require if they are to become social beings. The typical impact of such a stance on a child is the depression, loss of prior learning, withdrawal, and increase in disorganized, self-stimulating behavior described by Anna's mother.

Mrs. J's move to reclaim her disordered daughter, however, indicates that an important shift took place. Her determination to have a relationship with the child she has and not to "let go," coupled with her resourceful use of varied strategies—compression, narrating, staying relaxed—to help her daughter through her acute distress, testifies to this new stance. Now we characterize her stance as *high support–high demand* because she both nurtures and guides her daughter through her distress. In our experience, parents who can assume this stance, which staff also tries to achieve at the Center, help their disordered children move toward optimal development.

Unfortunately, other stances that parents assume toward their disordered children seem to work against their childrens' development. One such common stance is *high support–low demand*. We saw this stance in the behavior of a mother of an 18-month-old girl with a seizure disorder that followed a high fever. The mother irrationally felt that she had not taken proper care of her daughter and was therefore somehow responsible for her condition. The reactive, excessively nurturing, *high support–low demand* attitude that the mother evolved, gradually became the family standard for interacting with the child. At one point, when the father attempted to have the child use a spoon instead of her hands with her cereal, the mother snatched the spoon and protectively interposed her body between the child and her father. Unless the mother gets help for the emotional issues which contribute to this stance, her child's opportunity for development is severely limited.

Another counterproductive stance that characterizes some parents is that of *low support–high demand*. Essentially, this describes a parent who makes continuous and inappropriate demands for performance from the child without providing the support or nurturing that the child requires. A recent example of this was evident in the behavior of a mother of a lovely, elegantly dressed 4-year-old girl, with a serious, bilateral seizure disorder that was difficult to control with medication. The disorder would express itself in the child turning white, trembling, making sudden jerks, becoming "absent" in the middle of a task, and from time to time losing coordination and falling down. Sometimes the child—losing control in the middle of a seizure—would wet herself. If the mother were present, she would march her firmly to the bathroom, shriek at her for wetting in a way that echoed throughout the Center, change her, and march her out again. Efforts to interpret the gravity of her child's disorder and the need to pace demands in a manner that took into account her problems, fell on deaf ears. The mother (and father—although to a lesser degree) insisted that the girl was normal and was going to learn how to talk, play, and be like other children her age—and that she (mother) would not let up on her daughter until she got there. Our attempts to work with the mother to help her daughter develop were viewed with suspicion. Ultimately, the mother decided that she could not leave her child at the Center with "those other (disordered) kids," and removed her so that she could educate her by herself at home.

Clearly, unless it is possible to "get through" to a parent like this who is desperately denying the severity of her child's disorder and very likely fighting off an underlying panic about her child's survival, there is little basis for collaboration. And yet, this trust and collaboration is essential if the learning that happens at the Center is to transfer and generalize to the home and elsewhere. The first step in helping the family to correct a counterproductive stance toward the disordered child is to identify that stance. Toward this end certain parental characteristics have been useful in distinguishing one kind of support–demand stance from another during a child's evaluation.

High Support–High Demand

1. Parent verbally encourages the child while providing just enough assistance for the child to complete the task.
2. Parent applauds the child's performance and then sets a slightly more difficult task.
3. Parent relinquishes support as the child shows ability to perform a task.
4. Parent can accurately forecast what the child can do and can almost do.
5. Parent adjusts speech and posture to "get with" the child in different situations and induce optimal functioning.
6. Parent actively attempts to organize or transform the child's disorganized or inappropriate behavior.

Low Support–High Demand

1. Parent repeatedly stops the child's undesirable behavior without providing a channel for desired behavior.
2. Parent threatens physical punishment or restricts the child to achieve control.
3. Parent orders child to begin a new activity without attention to the child's involvement in ongoing activity.
4. Parent scolds and then turns from child.
5. Parent's demand for the child to perform overrides concern with how the child is feeling (e.g., tired, wet, or hungry).
6. Parent's need for the child to succeed is so strong that he or she takes over the role of the examiner.

High Support–Low Demand

1. Parent keeps worrying about the child's safety although the child seems quite able to cope.

2. Parent keeps ineffectively calling the child while the child continues the same unacceptable behavior.
3. Parent "protects" the child by interposing his or her body between the examiner and the child.
4. Parent complains about the examiner's demands.
5. Parent constantly "fusses"' with or "does for" child—wipes nose, toilets child, pulls up pants—usually before each task.
6. Parent tries to engage the examiner in conversation prior to each task.

Low Support–Low Demand

1. Parent ignores the child's behavior when the child reaches toward the parent.
2. Parent seems disinterested in expecting or requiring any performance from the child.
3. Parent seems unable or unwilling to assist the child as he/she struggles with a problem.
4. Parent remains in conversation with another while the child gets into a potentially hazardous situation.
5. Parent does not indicate desired behavior during task or does so ineffectively.
6. Parent frequently takes away from focus on the child by drawing the examiner's attention to self.

The sections that follow describe how we try to build the collaboration that enables a family to adopt a high support–high demand stance—not only through C-D systems therapy or through counseling—but by adopting an approach in which staff both teach and learn from parents and attempt to be sensitive to parents' concerns.

THE LCDC MESSAGE TO PARENTS OF BEHAVIOR-DISORDERED CHILDREN

One of the key problems for many disordered children is the generalization of their learning from one setting to another. Unless this happens, the child's learning remains restricted to the site in which it first occurred. The children lack the capacity to spontaneously extend systems from one location to another. Consequently, staff do a number of things to help bring about such extensions. Among the most important is providing parents with basic information about understanding and working with their children.

When disordered children come home from school they tend rapidly to fall into the pattern of behavior that the family expects. They have left the reality systems of the Center and are now in the reality systems of the home.

And, by themselves, the children cannot bridge the gulf between home and school. Typically, the child has no way of saying, "I'm beginning to understand the order of events in the schoolday," "I'm learning to clothe myself," or "I'm learning to sign and vocalize for something that I want." Consequently, unless the family knows about the child's progress—and how to bring it into the home—they tend to treat him or her exactly as they had before starting the Center's program. Then, for example, not knowing about the child's new ability to put on clothes, a parent continues to dress him or her. Similarly, not knowing that the child can now communicate intentions through sign language or pictures, parents miss out on chances to respond to this new learning and to help extend it to the home and elsewhere.

Choice of Attitude

A family attitude of high support–high demand makes it most likely that the child's school systems will extend to the home. To gain this attitude, parents often have to overcome the distress and disappointment they have concerning their child. Often, such feelings make a parent afraid to expect *any* progress or improved functioning from the child. However, our experience suggests that unless parents can reinvest in their disordered child and expect something back, they are unlikely to see the best that he or she can do or the progress achieved at school. Why, after all, should the child show how well he or she can set the table, remove dishes, use signs, pictures, or words to communicate needs, perform various tasks, or read and write unless family members provide opportunities for the child to use and "show" the new abilities?

Alternatively, it is possible that parents, on seeing some improvement, set themselves up for disappointment by expecting too much too soon. Or, in their need to see the child more like other children the same age, they ignore what he or she can do and fix their eyes only upon the distance the child still has to travel. Parents, for example, may view the few manual signs their nonverbal child can perform as trivial in contrast to the speech they want, therefore, they may not respond to these signs or use them when talking to him or her.

Parents who try to sense the way in which their disordered child experiences life tend to be more effective with their child than those parents who do not make this effort. What is it like to live as a profoundly withdrawn autistic child, or a scattered, flitting autistic child, or a schizophrenic child? Although no one can know with precision the life experience of another, it is possible, by carefully observing the behavior of such a child, or by reading the descriptions of people who have recovered from their disorders, to arrive at a general notion of how a particular child experiences or tries to make sense of the world. Temple Grandin, for example, who recovered from her autistic disorder, described in her book (Grandin & Scariano, 1986), what it was like for her:

I was well into adulthood before I could look people in the eye. As a child I remember Mother asking me time and again, *"Temple, are you listening to me?* Look at me."* Sometimes I wanted to, but couldn't. Darting eyes—so characteristic of many autistic children—was another symptom of my autistic behavior. . . . I had little interest in other children, preferring my own inner world. I could sit on the beach for hours dribbling sand through my fingers and fashioning miniature mountains. Each particle of sand intrigued me. . . . Other times I scrutinized each line in my finger, following one as if it were a road on a map.

Spinning was another favorite activity. I'd sit on the floor and twirl around. The room spun with me. This self-stimulatory behavior made me feel powerful, in control of things. After all, I could make a whole room turn around. . . . I enjoyed twirling myself around or spinning coins or lids round and round and round. Intensely preoccupied with the movement of the spinning coin or lid, I saw nothing or heard nothing. People around me were transparent. And no sound intruded on my fixation. It was as if I were deaf. Even a sudden loud noise didn't startle me from my world.

But when I was in the world of people, I was extremely sensitive to noises. . . . Today, even as an adult while waiting in a busy airport, I find I can block out all the outside stimuli and read, but I still find it nearly impossible to screen out the airport background noise and converse on the phone. So it is with autistic children. They have to make a choice of either self-stimulating like spinning, mutilating themselves, or escape into their inner world to screen out outside stimuli. Otherwise, they become overwhelmed with many simultaneous stimuli and react with temper tantrums, screaming, or other unacceptable behavior. Self-stimulating behaviors help calm an overaroused central nervous system. . . .

But as a child, the "people world" was often too stimulating to my senses. Ordinary days with a change in schedule or unexpected events threw me into a frenzy, but Thanksgiving or Christmas was even worse. At those times our home bulged with relatives. The clamor of many voices, the different smells—perfume, cigars, damp wool caps or gloves—people moving about at different speeds, going in different directions, the constant noise and confusion, the constant touching were overwhelming. (pp. 22–25)

No one disordered child is like another but parents of autistic children will most likely recognize some of their own autistic child's behavior in Ms. Grandin's description. From our perspective, the behavior and feelings she describes—and her great difficulty with change—suggests that her autism was of the closed-system type (See Chapters 2, 8). Now, consider what it might be like for 5-year-old Anna, the nonverbal, autistic child with a system-forming disorder (described in Chapter 8).

In Chapter 8 we said that

She would just flit or float with a sweet smile from one thing to another, never engaging with the object. If she picked up something she would at the same time be looking at something else. And when that happened she would lose contact with and allow to fall anything she had in her hands.

And later, from her C-D systems therapist,

She seemed compelled to put herself—her foot, her hand—in the water rather than merely to drop the block. When she poured sand in a bucket, she needed to put her hand in the sand stream so she could feel the flow.

From these observations we infer that Anna lives in a fuzzy world of fleeting images. Momentarily, when she touches or picks up one of these images, the fog clears for a moment and the image becomes more substantial. But then, as the item falls from her hand because another image has attracted her, the first one merges back into the fog and the new exciting image momentarily takes over. From time to time, an event becomes more real for her (she smiles and attends), when it collides directly with her. Then, when she can see, feel, and hear the objects as they collide against large portions of her body, the "realness" lasts longer. Similarly, the fog may open for a moment or two when some salient event intrudes (a loud noise, a sudden movement, a change in temperature, an obstacle) or when her bodily needs for food and drink or air impel her toward something outside herself.

What must it be like for still another kind of child—often diagnosed as having childhood schizophrenia—that we define as having a syncretic systems disorder? Such a child easily becomes convinced that there is someone in the wall or that the sound of the heat detector is causing a fire; a boy may have to show and look at his penis to make sure it is still there. Still other insights come from Renee's (Sechehaye, 1951) *Autobiography of a Schizophrenic Girl* as she describes the loss of object constancy and the reefication of objects common to this disorder.

One day we were jumping rope at recess. Two little girls were jumping a long rope while two others jumped in from either side to meet and cross over. When it came my turn and I saw my partner jump toward me where we were to meet and cross over, I was seized with panic; I did not recognize her. Though I saw her as she was, still it was not she. Standing at the other end of the rope, she had seemed smaller, but the nearer we approached each other, the taller she grew, the more she swelled in size. (p. 20)

. . . For some time I had been complaining bitterly that things were tricking me and how I suffered because of it. . . . As a matter of fact, these "things" weren't doing anything special; they didn't speak, nor attack me directly. It was their very presence that made me complain. I saw things, smooth as metal, so cut off, so detached from each other, so illuminated and tense that they filled me with terror. When, for example, I looked at a chair or a jug, I thought not of their use or function—a jug not as something to hold water and milk, a chair not as something to sit in—but as having lost their names, their functions and meanings; they became "things" and began to take on life, to exist.

. . . In the unreal scene, in the murky quiet of my perception, suddenly "the thing" sprang up. The stone jar, decorated with blue flowers, was there facing me, defying me with its presence, with its existence. To conquer my fear I looked away. My eyes met a chair, then a table; they were alive, too, asserting their presence. I attempted to escape their hold by calling out their names. I said, "chair, jug, table, it is a chair." But the word echoed hollowly, deprived of all meaning; it had left the object, was divorced from it, so much so that on one hand it was a living, mocking thing, on the other, a name, robbed of sense, an envelope emptied of content. Nor was I able to bring the two together, but stood rooted there before them, filled with fear and impotence. (p. 40)

Feeling uncertain about the distinction between their emotions, perceptions, and inner reality as opposed to what is really "out there," it is not surprising that such children are often in chronic anxiety states and feel very uncertain about the way their bodies are put together and what may happen to them. Parents can help children like these most by providing consistent emotional and physical support when the child requires it (not more and not less than the child needs at a particular moment), by correcting distortions of reality ("There is no one in the wall" or "Your penis will stay on your body"), and by actively structuring the world for their child. They can do this best by expecting or even demanding the functioning that is within or close to the child's capabilities.

For all disordered children, consistency, support, and structure do much to help construct a more orderly and less frightening world. To be able to *support and demand* appropriate functioning from the child, parents need, of course, to know precisely *what the child is currently doing in various areas, what he or she is close to doing, and what is still well beyond his or her capacity*. When parents have full information about these three aspects— not only with regard to academic or language functioning but also social, self-management, and chore skills—they are then in a position to both support and require desired behavior. Among the things parents need to consider are the child's ability to dress, use the toilet appropriately, wash, make his or her bed, set and clear the table, scrape the plates, deal with trash, help with laundry, stack groceries, and help clean house, as well as to follow directions by signs, pictures, and spoken words.

What Is Happening at School?

Before parents take their youngster home on school vacation, parents need an opportunity to talk with the key people concerned with the child's well-being. Ideally, this should include one of the directors, the various therapists, and his or her teacher. Parents should also, in addition to the suggestions in this chapter, have a specific plan for coping with their child's bizarre or unacceptable behavior. The more that parents become familiar with the current level of their child's functioning, the more likely they are to spend meaningful time with him or her.

Communicating

Almost all the children in the Center have major problems in both expressing themselves and in understanding what is said to them. There are, however, certain things that parents and families can do to ease these problems. What they do depends on the level of the child's ability to understand and use language. Thus, if the child is nonverbal, the child takes part in the Sign and Spoken Language Program (see Chapter 10) systematically used at the Center. Parents need to learn, therefore, what the signs are for "eat," "drink," "stop," "go," and so forth, as well as how to induce these signs from their child. (A sign class for parents is conducted weekly at the Center.) When using signs with their nonverbal child, parents sign and say the word and *use* the manual sign at the same time. When the child, for example produces a sign to indicate his or her desire for food, the parent should repeat the child's sign (indicating that the message was received) and say, as if to confirm the child's request, "Eat?" and then give him or her the food. During the day, whenever a parent or family member moves from one activity to another, the child will be less troubled by the shift if signs and words are used to communicate the change.

For children who have *some* spoken language it is wise at first to pattern speech to them in the manner in which they speak. For example, if a child is able to communicate only in 2–3-word sentences, it is not helpful for the parents to talk in sentences with parenthetical clauses. Rather, the parents should speak directly in concrete terms; even if the child has some spoken language, parents should not hesitate to use signs to buttress and help extend understanding. If a child is able to use only one word at a time, the supplementary use of pointing and expressive use of the face, signs, and pictures become most important to assist communication.

In general, whether a child is nonverbal or has some speech, parents should try to have the child oriented toward them when trying to communicate. The child is most likely to be oriented (attending) when looking directly at the parent. Often this can be achieved by abruptly moving toward or to either side of the child and by making an abrupt sound. (It is confusing to say "Look at me!" to the child.) Then, sign and speak briefly and concretely about the matter at hand. All the children have difficulty with other places and other times (past and future). Thus, if a parent wants the child to know that he or she is going to school or to a particular relative, it often helps to show pictures of the school, teachers, particular relatives, and so forth, to bind one space to another.

Often, when a child is out of school for several days due to illness, a parent can arrange for the teacher or children in the child's class to speak to him or her over the telephone. Regular calls can do much to keep a child connected to the reality of the school even when away for an extended period.

Going Home Each Day as a New Experience

Just as many disordered school children have difficulty "keeping" school when they are at home, so do they have difficulty keeping home when they are in school. This difficulty is just one expression of the limited way in which they experience their world. For them it is the here and now that is real. For this reason, their recollection of home, mother, father, brother, sisters, and relatives becomes very hazy. This observation is strikingly true for the nonverbal children, because language provides the major means of thinking about the past or anticipating the future. Because of this haziness, the Center staff, for several months with a new child, treat going home as an entirely new experience. And, because each new experience is both a possible source of distress and an opportunity for more progress, it is necessary to proceed carefully in introducing it. The following steps should prove helpful.

Leaving the School

A disordered child has more chance of absorbing the fact of leaving if the departure is deliberate and involves the child saying "Bye-bye" to significant people (teacher, assistants). If possible, it is desirable to take a picture of the school and of these significant people so that he or she can look at it on the way and at home. (These same photographs can also help prepare for the return to school.) Then, as the child leaves the school, adult staff in the bus try to orient the child toward the school and the people waving so that he or she can see them from the vantage point of the bus. They say things like "Wave bye-bye, Mrs. . . . " and "Bye-bye school."

On the Way Home

During the trip home, particularly when the parent takes the child home, it is useful to forecast and describe salient events in simple sign and spoken language before and as they occur, for example, "Bus (car) stops . . . go BM . . . wash hands . . . drink juice. . . ." Periodically, parents find occasion to mention "Going home . . . see brother, sister, friend, pet . . ." On stops it might also be helpful to point in the direction of the school and say ". . . school, Mrs. . . . ," and then point in the direction the car is going and say "Going home . . . see . . ." The "visit home" procedures described in this section apply also to the child's visit to any friend, relative, or situation with which he or she has not had recent contact.

The probability of this procedure being meaningful is even greater if the parent takes the child's arm and helps him or her point in the two contrasting directions.

Arriving Home

In many school situations the child is brought home by special school bus. On the child's arrival home, he or she may be quite disoriented. We recall one instance where a parent sought help for the acute distress her child showed on coming home. When we inquired, it turned out that as soon as the child got off the bus, mother—a very energetic and vital person—would come hurtling down the path with arms spread to sweep up her child. Seeing this "force of nature" coming down on him the child would place both hands in front of his face and begin to whimper. The situation corrected itself when his mother learned to wait quietly at the door until her son approached and give him the quick hug that was all he could tolerate at that time.

If, after coming home, the child wishes to go outside and inside the house a number of times, a parent should go along with it for a time as long as the child is relatively calm. The child may simply be trying to establish, in the only way possible, the reality of the house and that he or she is now in a different place from school. To ease this transition process, a parent might—as the child wanders from room to room—name the rooms for the child: "Mother and father's room," "Your [use child's name] room," "kitchen," and so forth. Some parents take the child's favorite toys and lay them across the bed to help the child's transition. If there are brothers and sisters, they are reintroduced one at a time. During the first hour or two after the child comes home, parents should try to keep the mood reasonably quiet. It is stressful for a child trying to readjust to home to have assorted relatives suddenly descend or to travel about very much.

STRUCTURING THE CHILD'S HOME EXPERIENCE

It is undesirable for a disordered child—home from school over the weekend or during a more prolonged vacation—to sit or lie around in front of the TV throughout the day. The child gains most when he or she carries over important routines (systems) from school to home. The following sections sketch out a day that will help keep the child meaningfully engaged during a weekend or vacation.

Getting Up and Body Play

When the child wakes up, it is helpful if a parent can be in the room, perhaps sitting on the bed. Then there should be some gentle tousling of hair while talking, followed by some body play: "Where's that foot? Where's that hand? I touch your nose. I pull your ear. I tickle your tummy," and so forth. (This procedure not only wakens him or her in a gentle playful manner, it also helps orient the child toward his or her own body and to the parent).

Showering

Once the child is more awake, the parent takes him or her to the shower (or bath, if the shower is frightening) and starts off, urging when necessary, "Wash that foot [pointing]. The other foot, too. Wash under your chin. Back of the ears . . ." Should the child be unable to wash, the parent puts soap or washcloth in the child's hand and guides it until the child begins to take over, then removes support. If the child is comfortable in the shower, parents may, on subsequent days, begin to move the shower's temperature from body temperature toward a cooler temperature. Then, the parent helps towel the child's body briskly, assisting or urging as needed, "Rub your cold feet. Rub your head," and so forth.

Dressing

Here, too, parents have new opportunities to press for more functioning. They can sign and say, for example: "Put on your socks." If the child has difficulty pulling them on, the parent puts one sock halfway on and then, making a pulling motion, signs and says: "Pull the sock on." (The parent should always test to see how much the child can do alone before moving in with support.) And, of course, when the child succeeds in putting on a sock or whatever, a big hug and expression of approval from the parent helps the child feel the loving presence of the parent even when he or she is not there to help with the task. The same general procedure holds with regard to combing hair, brushing teeth, tying laces, and other actions related to personal care.

In all these tasks, children may require much repetition before they start taking over the task-system. Parents do best when they are most sensitive to their child's beginning efforts at taking over. Often, a parent can test this by withdrawing support (interrupting) in the middle of the task to determine if the child now "needs" to complete the task.

Breakfast

If a child has been systematically setting table at school, he or she should certainly do so at home. (At school the process is facilitated by place mats that have the knife, fork, spoon, plate, and glass outlines stenciled in. Parents can replicate this at home by tracing such outlines on plastic place mats.) As the child sets the table for each person, indicate by sign and word what the child puts down and for whom: "Spoon for Daddy, spoon for Mommy . . ." If the child is new at table setting, it is best that he or she put down only one item at a time. Later, a parent can try with two spoons at a time, then three or four, and so on.

Some parents slyly set the stage so that many food items "happen" to be placed in front of the disordered child. This means that members of the family have to ask the child, "Please pass the butter [the milk, the bread, etc.]." Other members of the family should understand that they may have to repeat themselves or to point urgently several times before something is passed. Each family must decide for themselves whether they can sustain this kind of effort at each meal. If it seems to interfere too much with everyday family life, the parents can periodically determine when to follow these procedures. Each time a disordered child responds appropriately to such a demand, the child moves that much closer to acceptable functioning.

Using the Natural Environment

After breakfast, a walk might be appropriate. On the first or second day the child on these walks should remain within sight of home or not stay very long away from home. The parent and child can visit familiar neighbors, identify them by name (they might be alerted to the visit and have a cookie or two handy), go to the next place, and so forth. Parents should name appropriate landmarks near the home and always try to gauge the child's response when it is desirable to return home.

On these walks it is possible to exploit natural surroundings. If there is a park with a grassy hill, the parent can let the child run up the hill while pointing and saying, "Up, up. Run up the hill." At first, a parent or sibling may have to run alongside to get things going. Then, at the top, the parent pauses to see what the child does. If he or she wishes to run or roll down the hill, the parent lets the child do so while saying, "Down the hill. Run (roll) down the hill." If the child wants to walk on a stone wall, or on a plank across a stream, or on a curb with one foot on the sidewalk and one in the street, the parent can allow the child to do so as long as proper safety precautions have been taken. As the child does these things, the parent accompanies the actions with signs and words (narration) so that the child can learn to self-communicate. The parent should require a child who can speak to tell *what* he or she is doing *while* he or she is doing it (self-narration).

On returning home, particularly when home has been out of sight, it is useful to allow the child to lead the way to determine how effectively he or she is able to use landmarks and to keep the route in mind. When the entire route is too long, the child might "lead" the last part home.

Play

After the walk, it is desirable to play directly with the child. We recall one situation where parents gave their autistic child a certain toy—a Busy Box—and then were distressed when the child persisted in obsessively dealing with each of the various parts. At first the child absolutely refused to let anyone play with him as he played with the box, pulling away the adults hands. However, with persistence, he began to accept the adult playing with one part of his Busy Box while he played with another part. Eventually, he became involved in a turn-taking exchange in which he had to take into account what the other person was doing. This guided interaction—because it provided a framework for more normal interaction—was far more useful than allowing the child to remain totally obsessed with his box without any intrusion.

In other words, with closed-system disorders such as the one just described, parents may have to be gently but firmly insistent about their wish to interact with their child. Eventually, the child will accept the intrusion and more interactive play patterning becomes possible. Useful play includes anything that helps the child relate to another human being. A game of catch encourages interaction just as repetitive swinging or bouncing does when it occurs while the child is engaged with someone else (see Jack, Chapter 8, p. 295). Likewise, playing pat-a-cake and using a seesaw (teeter-totter) are beneficial because they involve another. Some TV, particularly "Sesame Street," "Captain Kangaroo," or "Mr. Rogers' Neighborhood," is helpful, particularly if others are present and comment.

However, parents need to closely monitor certain sources of stimulation. Disordered children with uncertain contact with reality need to have their access to "out of this world" shows or frightening horror programs closely controlled. If a parent is in doubt about a particular program, it is better to censor it. When this is not done, disordered children's preoccupation about things that might happen to them readily spreads to all parts of their lives, including school, dreams, and play.

Rough-and-Tumble Play

Frequently, parents of a disordered child mistakenly protect their child from the rough-and-tumble play that arises naturally among children. A certain amount of rough-and-tumble wrestling, pillow fighting, and so forth, can be a very positive part of the day's activity, as well as a way in which other children in the family can let off steam, stimulate responses, and relate pleasurably with a disordered child. Supervision should be available, of course, to see that such play neither lasts too long nor goes too far.

Sometimes, as was the case with Jack (Chapter 8), the systematic use of Rough and Tumble between parent and child, can help establish a positive relationship. In introducing vigorous and contagious body play, however, parents need to adjust their "roughness" to the child's ability to accept it. A parent intruding too quickly can set back the process for some time. At LCDC, parents with questions about how much to use can consult either the child's C-D systems therapist and ask for a demonstration or speak with the child's classroom teacher who physically orients the child each day.

Chores

After play, or periodically during the day, it is important to set up work projects. The more the disordered child can sustain efforts and complete jobs, the better for that child. Some chores that parents find helpful and that add to the child's self-esteem include washing the car (parents should make sure it is very dirty first so that the child can see the effects of his or her labor), raking and bagging leaves, breaking branches, shoveling snow, and carrying out the trash. Frequently, in order to get a child started in such work, a parent may have to guide the child's hands. But, as the child develops further, he or she will be able to do the chores without help. With more work the child will learn to bring requested things to a parent from different parts of the house, and still later, to do errands around the neighborhood.

Each chore should be viewed as a system with a number of component parts. For example, in putting away food just brought from the grocery, one component is removing the food from the paper bag, another is opening the closet or refrigerator, and another is putting the food away. Parents should first develop a single component (taking food out of the bag) before attempting to connect it to the other components. Parents can seek advice from the C-D systems therapist to help develop such chore-systems.

Academic Work

It is entirely appropriate to schedule a certain amount of academic work during weekends or vacation periods. This is an important way to communicate that the work done at school is not only for the teacher but for the parents and, further, that the parents expect their child to use this knowledge in everyday living. Prior to working with a child on signs, reading, writing, geography, history, or arithmetic, parents consult with their child's teacher with regard to both where the child is and how best to approach the work. However, should a parent get too tense in working academically with the child, it is best to ask someone else to do it until the parent deals with the internal issue that is getting in the way.

Sometimes the transfer of school attitudes to the home can be assisted by sending videotapes home with a child. One verbal child was extraordinarily proud of his new ability to work with a computer. Bringing a videotape home that showed how effectively he used the computer not only added to his self-esteem but gave the parents a better sense of his program at school.

A Picture Calendar

As the day ends, and the child prepares for bed, parents should review what the child has done that day and will do the next day. Disordered children need help in looking backward as well as forward and in developing the notions of yesterday, today, and tomorrow. Disordered children are most likely to grasp these notions if parents prepare a picture calendar for this purpose. Parents can then review with the child the appropriate picture for each completed activity and anticipate through the picture calendar what will happen the next day. For example, one day's calendar may include pictures of a child getting out of bed, showering, having breakfast with the family, doing chores, playing ball, doing academic work, going for a ride in the car, looking at TV, having dinner, going to bed.

Frequently, parents combine their own simple drawings with pictures from various magazines. Many of the children have some understanding of pictures as symbols of acts or objects, particularly if the pictures are immediately related to the real event or object. Certainly, they are more able to make sense of the passage of time by seeing a series of drawings related to changes—one after the other—than they are through someone telling them what is to happen next.

The importance of the picture calendar became apparent in Susan's case. Susan, an autistic 7-year-old girl of the closed-system type, had severe tantrums when she was unable to determine what was going to happen next. However, once her father prepared a picture calendar (Figure 12.1) and showed her what was going to happen—just before it happened—both parents reported a dramatic diminution in her tantrums.

Aside from structuring each day, parents seem to have concerns most frequently around dealing with bizarre or unacceptable behavior, with giving their other children enough attention, and with trying to understand what constitutes improvement.

Coping with Unacceptable Behavior

Many parents are uncertain about what to do when they observe their children "twiddling" objects, grimacing, rocking back and forth, masturbating in public, and so forth. Typically, they are unsure about the wisdom of intervening and, if intervention is appropriate, just how it should be done.

Our view is that intervention is appropriate. When a disordered child is twiddling, either hold his or her hand or the object being twiddled. The child often looks at the person who interrupts the twiddling. The interruptor then has the opportunity to direct the child toward some functional task: "Pick up the papers on the floor." If the child is masturbating in public, the parent should stop him or her and give a bundle to carry or a cart to push. In private, the child may be left alone for 5 or 10 minutes, then interrupted and required to do something else. At times, a child may withdraw into autistic rituals—twiddling, rocking, or masturbating—when feeling suddenly "left." This could happen when a parent finds it necessary to attend to the other children. Sometimes, if a parent merely touches the disordered child on the arm *while* turning toward other responsibilities, it is sufficient to "keep the child in the world." Other times, giving a familiar object such as a bracelet or eyeglass case can help the child stay in contact. A parent might also say, "I'll be right back," leave the room, and return as promptly as possible. This can be easily developed into an exercise to help the child tolerate such separations by staying out of the room for increasingly longer periods, always being sure to make clear that the return will happen as promised.

Frequently, parents of a disordered child tend to be overly protective and

Figure 12.1. A daily picture calendar made by a father for his disordered child.

condone behavior that they would not accept from their other children. For example, if the disordered child takes a favorite toy from brother or sister, a protest is likely to ensue. To allow the disordered child to keep the toy is unwise for two reasons: It precludes the possibility of the child discriminating between the concept of "mine" and "yours," and it creates unnecessary stress and resentment in the other child. However, should a parent require the return of the toy, it is an excellent idea to have a substitute at hand.

Part-Time Help for Parents

No parents, no matter how dedicated, should devote all their free time to the task of supervising or working with their disordered child. Not only is it undesirable for parents as human beings, it also precludes the possibility of the parents "being there" for the other members of the family when they require support. One way of easing some of the pressure that a disordered child inevitably places on parents is to hire part-time help, or if that is not possible, to seek volunteer help. Parents living near colleges or universities that offer special education programs might gain access to capable college students on either a paid or volunteer basis. Parents can also approach the Autism Society of America, 1234 Massachusetts Avenue, NW, Suite 1017, Washington, DC 20005 (or call (202) 783-0125) to gain a sense of possible resources in their area. For an organization concerned with the broad range of mental disorders including schizophrenia and depression, the reader may contact the National Alliance for the Mentally Ill, 1901 North Ft. Meyer Drive, Suite 500, Arlington, VA 22209-1604 (or call (703) 524-7600).

THE STRUCTURE AND PHILOSOPHY OF THE LCDC PROGRAM

Questions Asked of the LCDC Program

Over the past 25 years we have been asked many times by parents: Will you accept my child in your Center? Can you help my child develop? If so, how much can you help? How will you work with my child?

This final section of our book responds to these questions and, at the same time, describes the philosophy that guides the work of the Center.

Criteria for Acceptance

There are two interrelated programs at the Center. One, *the toddler program,* is for children from walking age (around 14 months) to 3 years; the other, *the school program,* is for older children. Children in both programs must have adequate (or correctable) vision and hearing, be able to walk and climb stairs (assisted), and be able to hold an object in one hand while doing so. They must also show a significant delay in important aspects of their functioning. Usually this is apparent in language delays or in thought disorders as well as in the unusual ways in which they make or fail to make human contact. These problems may or may not be directly related to diagnosable neurological issues.

Although a residential program for people in the 6-to-22 age range is currently in the planning stage, it will be several years before it is ready for occupants.

In the toddler program the C-D systems therapist works with the child and either or both parents for up to two 1-hour sessions per week. A model of this work is described in Chapter 8. The toddler program has a capacity for about 12 children. Children attend until age 3 at which time the problem is either resolved or they transfer to LCDC's school program or to another program. The Center is not equipped to work with cerebral palsied children or with children who have neuromuscular disorders such as muscular dystrophy.

LCDC's School Program

The school, a private day program licensed by the state, has capacity for 40 children ranging in age from 3 to 16, who attend 27 hours each week. The school accepts children with diagnoses ranging from severe developmental delay to autism, aphasia, childhood schizophrenia, brain-injury, seizure disorder, emotional deprivation, and severe learning disability. Once a child meets the criteria for acceptance, the next issue is an opening appropriate to the child's age and ability in one of the six classes.

Children on the waiting list who are over 3 years may receive C-D systems therapy once or twice a week until an opening becomes available.

How Much Will a Child Benefit from the LCDC Programs?

Before we can answer this question, we must know about the child. Much depends on how old the child is, whether there is substantial neurological involvement (as demonstrated by findings of neurological tests), whether the child has any relationship with the parents, the nature of the child's system disorder (see Chapter 2, pp. 41–44), and how able the parents are to work with their child.

Perhaps prospects will get clearer by referring to two children. The first child, Jack, came to the Center at 2½ years, tested over a year delayed, showed no gross neurological signs, was diagnosed autistic with a closed-system disorder, has a relationship with his mother, and has parents who readily adopt a high support–high demand stance toward him. This child, although showing many signs of abnormal development, such as tantrums, rocking, hand biting, inability to communicate, and great resistance to change, has made exciting progress in the course of 6 months of C-D intervention.

Now, at 3 years, he is crossing the naming threshold and has an excellent prognosis for near normal development as he enters our school program.

In contrast, another child, Karen, was accepted in the Center at age 7, tested 4.5 years delayed, suffered diffuse brain injury at birth (anoxia), has a system-forming disorder, and has parents with a high support–low demand stance. The child relates only to the teacher not to the group, has difficulty attending for more than a few moments, and easily becomes distracted. When she came to the Center two years ago, her language was almost completely echolalic. Now she can communicate her needs in sentences. Although staff anticipate further gains in the areas of academic achievement, (some basic sight reading), social development, and improved ability to care for herself, her prognosis is for limited development.

Of the five factors we consider important—age, extent of neurological involvement, relationship with at least one parent, type of system disorder, parental support–demand stance—Jack is favored by all five; whereas Karen is favored by only one (ability to form relationships).

Age

The literature and our own experience clearly supports the view that children who come to the Center younger (under 3 years)—other things being equal— do substantially better than those who come to us older. However, the literature also states that if a child has not developed language by age 5, prospects for achieving it afterwards are remote and prognosis in general is poor. Although we find this to be generally the case, we have seen too many exceptions to the rule to accept, categorically, that a 6–7-year-old nonverbal child can never develop language. Just this past year two nonverbal children at the Center—respectively 7 and 8—began to speak: the 7-year-old now speaks in complete sentences and the 8-year-old communicates with signs and spoken words.

Neurological Involvement

Often, damage to the brain is the decisive factor in determining how much can be accomplished. Although the literature suggests that below 3 years of age healthy portions of the cortex may substitute for damaged portions, the more damage that has occurred, the more impaired the functioning. When specific areas of the brain are affected, such as the left temporal lobe in aphasia, speech and language are directly affected and there must be careful training with multisensory strategies to help the child compensate for the injury.

Children with injury to specific areas of the brain affecting language, perception, and thinking processes have done well at the Center with the help of the Sign and Spoken Language Program (Chapter 10), the Symbol Accentuation Reading Program (Chapter 11), and the various strategies and devices described in Chapters 2, 3, 8, and 9. Children with more extensive injury—while generally developing improved body organization, problem solving, and some functional sign and spoken language—have done less well.

Relationship with at Least One Parent

By relationship we mean that the child shows a distressed reaction to the parent leaving the room, moves toward the parent when he or she is hurt or frightened, and becomes aware of and moves toward the parent when, after leaving, the parent returns. The absence of relationship, although noteworthy, is not irreversible. We have consistently helped parents make contact with children previously unavailable to them emotionally. Once a child has developed a special relationship with a parent, that child has increasing reason to communicate with that parent. However, the need to build or rebuild a special relationship with a parent or caretaker means that an important part of C-D systems work must be devoted to this task while cognitive and communication capacities are being developed. (For an illustration of this process see Chapter 8, section on Anna).

System Characteristics of the Disordered Child

In general, children with syncretic system disorders, for example, childhood schizophrenia, improve most rapidly because they generally enter the Center's program with an array of systems, including spoken language, that are more or less working. Their central problem often centers around the confusion between their inner life and the outer world—between what is fantasy and what is real. As staff help the children to differentiate self from world and to structure their relationships with others, many of the children learn to cope with their confusions and to move very rapidly in the Center's program. Staff anticipate that of the seven such children now in the Center, six will eventually return to normal classrooms in the public schools, although most may continue to require supplementary therapy in the Center's clinic.

Among autistic children, those with closed-system disorders seem to progress more rapidly than those with system-forming disorders. This may occur because the two kinds of children confront very different problems. The central problem for children with closed-system disorders is to learn how to *expand* and *connect* systems. On the other hand, the central problem for children with system-forming disorders is how to build systems. Because only when the system is *there* can the child learn to expand and connect it, it follows that it will take longer for children with system-forming disorders to progress than children with closed-system disorders.

Parental Support–Demand Stance

Parents are a major resource in the work of the Center. And, this resource becomes even more effective when parents assume the High Support–High Demand stance that most favors the development of their disordered children. We repeatedly find that parents assuming this stance have children who make more significant gains than those characterized by the other stances. Further, parents who are able to shift to the High Support–High Demand from other stances, begin to gain more functioning from their children. For example, one of the two nonverbal children who recently achieved language after age 8 did so only when his mother, after much encouragement, began to use signs with her child at home and to expect him to use them with her.

By reviewing outcomes of the 63 profoundly disordered children who have attended and then left the Center over the past 12 years, we can gain a rough measure of the Center's effectiveness. Of this group 48% (30 children) have returned to their regular public schools able to mainstream in some or all of the classes. Another 32% (20 children), although significantly improved, left the Center because of their age or other reasons and continued at another private school. The remaining 20% (13 children)—usually showing only modest gains—went to residential settings because the pressure they placed on their families became too great.

Management Issues

There are, however, other issues with which parents are concerned. One of the most important concerns the management of the children—particularly when they tantrum, are provocative, and have not yet been toilet trained. Related to this whole issue, of course, is the use of reward and punishment in a program for disordered children. Perhaps we can respond best to these issues by briefly summarizing our views on this matter.

We assume that the major need of the children coming into the Center is to organize their behavior so that they can make meaningful contact with the people and things in their immediate world. To do this they must learn how to communicate with the children and adults in their group. They learn this through highly structured interventions (see Chapter 4), by playing and tussling with each other, and by learning the rules that govern the Center. One such rule is that "No child gets hurt or hurts another." Another rule is that no child may be removed from the group or "timed out" as punishment for inappropriate behavior. Neither may a child be deprived of food because of previous behavior.

Our feeling about removal or time out is that it works against what we are trying to accomplish. If the task is to teach children to communicate with each other, how can the excluded child learn to do this timed out in a separate room? Some staff have argued that a child who has just kicked over a table of paints should be excluded from the group because the entire lesson has been disrupted. Our position is that when this happens, kicking over the table *is* the lesson for these children—one which is far more important than painting. They must learn to cope with overwhelming feelings and to do it in a social context. The angry child who kicked over the table needs to hear how the other children feel and to explain why he or she did it. Finally, the child needs to help clean up the mess.

What is true with verbal children is even more valid with nonverbal children. If, for example, a nonverbal autistic girl were to be excluded for hitting or biting the child next to her, what would that mean to her in the time-out room? Would she relate the bite to her exclusion? And what would it say about encouraging her to try to communicate . . . or about making human contact? It is impossible to let such behavior go by, but we are far more comfortable with the teacher holding the "biter" and with plenty of emotional intensity telling her that such behavior is not acceptable. Following this, the teacher files a report about the incident and may, if the problem is not readily resolved, call a "problem staff."

At this staff meeting we can, with the help of videotape sampling, learn more about the conditions that triggered the biting episode. We are able to do this because all 6 classrooms and 5 therapy/evaluation rooms are equipped with remote-controlled, closed circuit color television cameras. As a result of systematic sampling of that classroom, we may find that the "innocent" child next to the biter has been covertly stepping on her foot and pinching her. Sometimes a simple change in seating arrangement solves the matter.

Tantrums

The next issue concerns tantrums. How one deals with tantrums depends in part how one understands them. We view tantrums as failures of organization that—with nonverbal children—occur when the child cannot connect one space with another or has suffered a loss (see Roy's case, Chapter 4), when the child's systems are inadequate for the task of anticipating what is to happen next, or when a child is unable to get needs met (see Jim's case, Chapter 4). Our method of coping with tantrums depends on the need the child is expressing and the kind of system disorder a child presents. For example, with a child characterized by a closed-system disorder, the tantrum is usually triggered by new circumstances that are too disparate from the child's existing systems (see Jack's case, Chapter 8).

With such a child, the introduction of rituals is often effective. One tantrumming, closed-system child, responded very well to a crayon scribbling ritual in which the teacher placed the crayon in his hand and helped him make repetitive marks. Then, to bring him into emotional contact with her, she began to hand him different colored crayons. Within 2 or 3 minutes the child became calm and could be brought back into the drawing program going on at the time in the classroom. With other closed-system children, large body rituals—rapidly going up, around, and down an elevated board structure a dozen times—often help them organize their functioning.

Tantrums among nonverbal children with system-forming disorders are typically more resistant because the tantrum sources cannot readily be determined and because the children have few systems to draw on. Consequently, such children may require a variety of interventions—compression, calm talking by the care giver, and movement within a familiar setting. The resourceful manner in which Anna's mother, Mrs. J, learned to cope with her daughter's frightening tantrums was described at the beginning of this chapter.

Toilet Training

Getting their disordered child toilet trained is an issue of much concern for parents who frequently have younger children in addition to their disordered child. Toilet training is a fairly complex integrative system with 11 components that the child needs to integrate. They include approaching the toilet, lowering pants, sitting down, defecating and/or urinating, wiping, getting off the toilet, picking up pants, flushing the toilet, washing and drying hands, returning to the classroom. The procedures used for toilet training at the Center are described in Chapter 9, pp. 354–355.

Some Comments on Rewards

Rewards are but one of a variety of important ways to help children establish functional systems. As repeatedly shown in this book, the formation of rituals (systems) from repetitive spheres does not require any externally introduced rewards. Rewards or pleasurable contact with an event not part of the original system become important only when the child begins to experience them as *part* of that system (see discussion of conditioning in Chapter 5, pp. 157–159). Whether or not a particular reward stimulus will help a child learn depends on how it relates to the manner in which the child forms systems. The following incident illustrates this:

> Recently, one of us (AM) was engaged as a consultant to a school under pressure by influential parents who claimed that their child was just as withdrawn now as he had been two years ago. To get some social interaction going, the staff decided to teach the child—a 10-year-old autistic boy—to roll a car back and forth to his teacher at the opposite long end of the table.
>
> To establish this sequence, the worker first helped the boy push the car and then immediately gave him a candy. However, the autistic boy, enjoying the candy, kept turning toward the source of the candy and totally ignored the car. After a while I was asked to intervene.
>
> I first requested that the worker with the candy move away from the table—out of the autistic boy's visual field. Then, I reduced the distance between the boy and me by sitting across the width instead of the length of the table. Finally, I instructed an assistant nearby to help the autistic boy immediately send the car back to me as soon as it reached him and then to keep repeating that assistance until it was no longer necessary. I began sending the car and within 5–6 rapid cycles the assistant was able to withdraw assistance as the boy became fascinated with the back-and-forth movement of the car and began to

push it as soon as it arrived. In addition, I was able to gain brief eye contact by placing the car momentarily in front of my face. After a few more trials I was able to expand the system further by having him send the car the length of the table and to have him play the "back-and-forth game" with others.

The events can be explained as follows: When the worker first introduced the candy, the child rapidly became engaged by and formed a closed-system with the candy. The child did not need rewards to achieve the car-pushing system because he was biologically disposed to form such a system when the object went back and forth at a certain tempo. Having formed the system he could readily expand it to include briefly looking at me and sending the car the length instead of the width of the table and by performing the game with others. For him, getting candy to eat and pushing the car back and forth were two separate systems. The eating-candy system never became part of the car-pushing system—nor did it need to.

In our work, rewards are a natural part of expanding the systems a child is biologically disposed to produce. If a parent or teacher expresses delight when a child cleans the table or overcomes an obstacle, then the child begins to experience the parent's or teacher's delight as an expanded part of those systems in a way that helps invest those tasks with the product of a supportive human presence. Subsequently, when the child next performs this task the system includes the ambience of the teacher's or parent's quality. In short, the importance of the reward is the human quality it adds to an otherwise sterile interaction. When the child—as was the case with Fred in Chapter 3—begins to systematically include the parent and/or teacher within his or her interactions with objects some important progress has been made.

The Nature of Improvement

Sometimes it is difficult for a parent to recognize what actually constitutes improvement. One parent of a nonverbal autistic girl, for example, complained that her previously placid, twiddling, 10-year-old had recently started to be a pest, following her around the house and badgering her for different activities and objects. Such a shift from profoundly autistic behavior to nagging for attention represents a new awareness in that child of her mother's existence. It also implies that she has begun to learn that interchange with people can be gratifying. However, it was only when the mother perceived this shift as a positive step forward that she could meet her child's demands more appropriately.

Other good indications of improvement are the child's ability to follow directions (when he or she couldn't before), the child's ability to take care of bodily needs, to understand and use signs, to begin to understand and use words, to disobey sometimes, to express feelings (when this didn't happen previously), and to no longer confuse fantasy with reality. In short, disordered children are improving when they begin to do those things that are distinctively human. How human these children become, depends at least in part, on the determined support for their human potential by the people who care for them.

SUMMARY

Beginning with a discussion of the concerns that parents of disordered children bring to the Center, the chapter illustrates—through a parent's recollection of her participation in the Umwelt Assessment—how the assessment process may bring needed clarity to a family about the nature of their child's disorder. There is also discussion of how important the Center's "open window" policy is for parents who urgently need information about the nature of the program itself in an unrehearsed manner and who need to see the classroom in which their child would be placed.

Following this, there is a description of the collaborative relationship the parent develops with the C-D systems therapist who works with both child and parent. In the case cited, a parent indicates how her own confusion about her daughter's failure to respond to her, compounded by a professional's incorrect diagnosis contributed to the mother's withdrawal from her autistic child with a consequent worsening in the child's condition. The excerpt also describes this mother's effort to reclaim her disordered child despite the difficulty of coping with the child's screaming tantrums and slow response to interventions.

The next section is designed to help parents of behavior-disordered children deal with them more productively. It is stressed that parents need to review their attitude toward the child and the utility of trying to sense what the reality experience of their child is like. Toward this end, the chapter includes excerpts from autobiographies of two persons who suffered from autism and schizophrenia as children. The reality stance of an autistic child with a system-forming disorder is also inferred.

After this, there is a description of how structuring reality for disordered children helps them organize themselves and make sense of their surroundings. In this context, stress is also placed on the importance of connecting school to home and vice versa, of knowing what the child is learning in school, of communicating in ways that the child is most likely to understand, and in structuring vacations or weekends for the child. In structuring various activities for the child—showering, dressing, chores—there is emphasis on the importance of not doing too much for the child and of periodically interrupting support to see what the child can do alone.

Then there is a discussion of the Center's structure and philosophy. This includes criteria for acceptance to the Center's toddler and school programs, as well as factors that seem to have bearing on a particular child's prognosis. The chapter closes with a discussion of the principles governing child management at the Center. These include no time out or food deprivation. Also offered in this final section are strategies for tantrum management and views on rewards. The chapter ends with a discussion of the nature of improvement.

References

Ainsworth, M. S., Blehar, M. D., Water, E., & Wall, S. (1978). *Patterns of attachment: A psychological study of the Strange Situation*. Hillsdale, NJ: Erlbaum.

Anderson, B. J., Vietze, P., & Dodecki, P. R. (1977). Reciprocity in vocal interactions of mothers and infants. *Child Development, 48,* 1676–1681.

Ayres, J. A. (1979). *Sensory integration and the child*. Los Angeles: Western Psychological Services.

Bates, E., Benigni, L., Bretherton, I., Camaioni, L., & Volterra, V. (1979). *The emergence of symbols: Cognition and communication in infancy*. New York: Academic Press.

Bertalanffy, L. von. (1968). *Organismic psychology and systems theory*. Clark University Press with Barre Publishers.

Blass, E. M., Ganchrow, J. R., & Steiner, J. E. (1984). Classical conditioning in newborn humans 2–48 hours of age. *Infant Behavior & Development, 7,* 223–235.

Bonvillian, J. D., Nelson, K. E., & Rhyne, J. M. (1981). Sign language and autism. *Journal of Autism and Developmental Disorders, 11*(1), 125–137.

Brazelton, T. B., Koslowski, B., & Main, M. (1974). The origins of reciprocity: The early mother-infant interaction. In M. Lewis & L. Rosenblum (Eds.), *The effect of the infant on its caretaker: The origins of behavior* (Vol. 1). New York: Wiley.

Brenner, J., & Mueller, E. (1982). Shared meaning in boy toddlers peer relations. *Child Development, 53,* 380–391.

Brown, M. (1971). *SEIMC's evaluation of the Symbol Accentuation (SA) Program*. Regional Special Education Instructional Material Ctr., State University College at Buffalo.

Brown, R. (1973). *A first language*. Cambridge, MA: Harvard University Press.

Brown, R. (1977). *Why are signed languages easier to learn than spoken language?* Paper presented at the National Symposium of Sign Language Research and Teaching, Chicago.

Bruner, J. S. (1975). The ontogenesis of speech acts. *Journal of Child Language, 2,* 1–19.

Bruner, J. S. (1977). Early social interaction and language acquisition. In N. H. Schaffer (Ed.), *Studies in mother–infant interaction*. New York: Academic Press.

Bühler, C. (1931). *Kindheit und Jugend*. Leipzig: Hirzel.

Bühler, K. (1928). *Abriss der geistigen Entwicklung des Kindes*. Leipzig: Quelle and Meyer.

Caplan, F. (1973). *The first twelve months of life:* New York: Putnam.

Carter, A. (1974). *The development of communication in the sensori-motor period: A case study.* Unpublished doctoral dissertation, University of California, Berkley.

Carter, A. (1975). The transformation of the sensori-motor morphemes into words: A case study of the development of "here" and "there." *Papers and Reports on Child Language Development, 11,* 31–48.

Cassirer, E. (1970). *An essay on man.* Toronto: Bantam Edition.

Coghill, G. E. (1929). *Anatomy and the problem of behavior.* Cambridge: Cambridge University Press.

Condon, W. S. (1975). Multiple response to sound in dysfunctional children. *Journal of Autism and Childhood Schizophrenia, 5,* 37–56.

Condon, W. S., & Sander, L. B. (1974). Neonate movement is synchronized with adult speech. International participation and language acquisition. *Science, 183,* 99–101.

Creedon, M. P. (1973). *Language development in nonverbal autistic children using a simultaneous communication system.* Paper presented at the biennial meeting of the Society for Research in Child Development, Philadelphia.

Curcio, F. (1978). Sensorimotor functioning and communication of mute autistic children. *Journal of Autism and Childhood Schizophrenia, 8,* 281–292.

Decarie, T. G. (1969). A study of the mental and emotional development of the thalidomide child. In B. M. Foss (Ed.), *Determinants of infant behavior* (Vol. IV). London: Methuen.

De Laguna, G. A. (1927). *Speech, its function and development.* New Haven, CT: Yale University Press.

DeMyer, M. K. (1979). *Parents and children in autism.* Washington DC: Victor H. Winston & Sons.

Des Lauriers, A. M., & Carlson, C. F. (1969). *Your child is asleep: Early infantile autism.* Homewood, IL: Dorsey Press.

Dix, W. K. (1911–1923). *Koerperliche und geistige Entwicklung eines Kindes.* Leipzig: Barth.

Dore, J. (1975). Holophrases, speech acts, and language universals. *Journal of Child Language, 2,* 21–40.

Goldstein, K. (1939). *The organism: A holistic approach to biology.* New York: American Book.

Grandin, T., & Scariano, M. M. (1986). *Emergence: Labeled autistic.* Novato, CA: Arena Press.

Halliday, M. (1975). *Learning how to mean: Explorations in the development of language.* London: Edward Arnold.

Head, H. (1926). *Aphasia and kindred disorders of speech.* London: Cambridge University Press.

Huey, E. B. (1968). *The psychology and pedagogy of reading.* Cambridge, MA: MIT Press. (Original work published 1908)

Iwai, K., & Volkelt, H. (1932). Umgang des Kindes mit verschieden geformten Körpern im 9. bis 12. Monat. *Kongr. D. Ges. Psychol. 12.*

Izard, C. E. (1977). *Human emotions*. New York: Plenum.

Jacobson, E. (1931). V. Variation of specific muscles contracting during imagination. *American Journal of Physiology, 96*, 115–121.

Jesperson, O., (1964). *Language: Its nature, development, and origin*. New York: Holt. (Original work published 1922)

Kanner, L. (1943). Autistic disturbances of affective contact. *Nervous Child, 2*, 217–250.

Kanner, L. (1971). Follow-up study of 11 autistic children originally reported in 1943. *Journal of Autism and Childhood Schizophrenia, 1*, 119–145.

Kellogg, R. (1970). *Analyzing children's art*. Palo Alto, CA: Mayfield.

Kolb, L. C. (1954). *The painful phantoms*. Springfield, IL: Thomas.

Konstantareas, M. M. (1984). Sign language as a communication prosthesis with language-impaired children. *Journal of Autism and Developmental Disorders, 14, 1*, 115–131.

Konstantareas, M. M. (1987). Autistic children exposed to simultaneous communication training: A follow up. *Journal of Autism and Developmental Disorders, 17, 1*, 115–131.

Konstantareas, M. M., Oxman, J., & Webster, C. D. (1977). Simultaneous communication with autistic and other severely dysfunctional nonverbal children. *Journal of Communications Disorders, 10*, 267–282.

Kravitz, H., & Goldenberg, D., & Neyhus, A. (1978). Tactual exploration by normal infants. *Developmental Medical Child Neurology, 20*, 720–726.

Lewin, K. (1935). *Dynamic theory of personality*. New York: McGraw-Hill.

Lewin, K. (1936). *Principles of topological psychology*. New York: McGraw-Hill.

Lewis, M. M. (1936). *Infant speech*. New York: Harcourt, Brace.

Lockman, J. (1984). The development of detour during infancy. *Child Development, 55*, 482–491.

Luria, A. R. (1981). *Language and cognition*. New York: Wiley.

Luria, A. R., & Yudovich, F. I. (1959). *Speech and development of mental processes in the child*. England: C. Nicholls. London: Staples Press.

Mahler, M. S., Pine, F., & Bergman, A. (1967). *The psychological birth of the human infant*. New York: Basic Books.

Mandler, G. (1974). The interruption of behavior. In D. Levine (Ed.), *Nebraska Symposium on Motivation: 1964*. Lincoln: University of Nebraska Press.

Mandler, G (1984). *Mind and body:* Psychology of emotion and stress. New York: Norton.

Marko, K. (1968). Symbol Accentuation: Application to classroom instruction of retardates. In *Proceedings of the First International Congress for the Scientific Study of Mental Deficiency*, Montpellier, France (pp. 773–775). Surrey, England: Michael Jackson.

McCarthy, D. (1954). Language and development in children. In L. Carmichael (Ed.), *Manual of Child Psychology* (pp. 452–630). New York: Wiley.

McNeil, D. (1970). *The acquisition of language: The study of developmental psycholinguistics*. New York: Harper & Row.

Messier, L. P. (1970). *Effects of reading instruction by Symbol Accentuation on disadvantaged children.* Unpublished doctoral dissertation, Boston University.

Miller, A. (1959). *An experimental study of the effect of sensorimotor activity in the maintenance of the verbal meanings of action words.* Unpublished doctoral dissertation, Clark University.

Miller, A (1963a). *The intermodal attainment of meaning.* Paper presented in a symposium on *Intermodal Processes* at the meeting of the American Psychological Association, Philadelphia.

Miller, A. (1963b). Verbal satiation and the role of concurrent activity. *Journal of Abnormal Social Psychology, 3,* 206–212.

Miller, A. (1968). Symbol Accentuation: Outgrowth of theory and experiment. In *Proceedings of the First International Congress for the Scientific Study of Mental Deficiency,* Montpellier, France (pp. 766–772). Surrey, England: Michael Jackson.

Miller, A. (1970). *Report on Symbol Accentuation with learning disabled children.* Informal report from the Reading Department of the Wellesley Public Schools.

Miller, A. (1974). *Edge of awareness.* (Documentary film). Produced by Cognitive-Developmental Designs, Inc. Brookline, MA.

Miller, A. (1982). *Ritual to repertoire.* (Documentary film). Produced by Cognitive-Developmental Designs, Inc. Brookline, MA.

Miller, A. (1989a). *Sign and Spoken Language Program.* (Training films videotapes). Produced by Cognitive-Developmental Designs, Inc., Brookline, MA. (Originally distributed 1970)

Miller, A. (1989b). *A small awakening* (Documentary film). Produced by Cognitive-Developmental Designs, Inc., Brookline, MA.

Miller, A. (1989c). *Symbol Accentuation: A new approach to reading* (Teacher's manual, teacher training film, videocassettes, flash cards, and workbooks). Cognitive-Developmental Designs, Brookline, MA. (Original work published 1968)

Miller, A., & Leuthold, B. (1964). *Symbol Accentuation: A perceptual determinant of paired-associate learning.* Paper presented at the meeting of the American Psychological Association, Los Angeles.

Miller, A., & Miller, E. E. (1962). *Symbol accentuation: A method of teaching reading to brain-injured and retarded children.* Paper presented at the meeting of the American Psychological Association, St. Louis.

Miller, A., & Miller, E. E. (1968). Symbol Accentuation: The perceptual transfer of meaning from spoken to written words. *American Journal of Mental Deficiency, 73,* 200–208.

Miller, A., & Miller, E. E. (1971). Symbol Accentuation: Single-track functioning and early reading. *American Journal of Mental Deficiency, 76*(1), 110–117.

Miller, A., & Miller, E. E. (1973). Cognitive-developmental training with elevated boards and sign language. *Journal of Autism and Childhood Schizophrenia, 3,* 65–85.

Miller, A., & Miller, E. E. (1982). *From ritual to repertoire.* Invited presentation to the meeting of the American Speech and Language Association, Toronto.

Miller, A., & Miller, E. E. (1986, July). *Expanding the realities of disordered children.* Presentations at the meeting of the National Society for Children and Adults with Autism, Washington, DC.

Miller, A., & Miller, E. E. (1989). *Miller Umwelt Assessment Scale.* Cognitive-Developmental Designs, Inc. Brookline, MA.

Miller, A., Werner, H., & Wapner, S. (1958). Studies in physiognomic perception: Effect of ascending and descending gliding tones on autokinetic motion. *Journal of Psychology, 46,* 101–105.

Miller, E. E. (1968). Symbol Accentuation: Application to special language problems. In *Proceedings of the First International Congress for the Scientific Study of Mental Deficiency,* Montpellier, France (pp. 776–778). Surrey, England: Michael Jackson.

Miller, E. E. (1970). *The effect of the Symbol Accentuation Reading Program with 10 psychotic children.* Unpublished report to the League School of Boston.

Miller, L. S. (1989). *Plans for elevated boards, playground, and related structures.* Produced by Cognitive-Developmental Designs, Inc., Brookline, MA.

Mitchell, R., & Etches, P. (1977). Rhythmic habit patterns (Stereotypies). *Developmental Medicine and Child Neurology, 19,* 545–550.

Montagu, I. (1964). *Film world.* Harmondsworth, Middlesex; England: Penguin.

Murphy, C. M. (1978). Pointing in the context of a shared activity. *Journal of Child Development, 49,* 371–380.

Nelson, K. (1973). Structure and strategy in learning to talk. *Monographs of the Society for Research in Child Development, 38*(1–2, Serial No. 149).

Nelson, K. (1985). *Making sense: The acquisition of shared meaning.* New York: Academic Press.

Ninio, A., & Bruner, J. S. (1977). The achievements and antecedents of labelling. *Journal of Child Language, 5,* 1–16.

Ornitz, E. M. (1985). Neurophysiology of infantile autism. *Journal of the American Academy of Child Psychiatry, 24,* 251–262.

Ornitz, E. M. (1987). Neurophysiologic studies of infantile autism. In D. J. Cohen & A. M. Donnellan (Eds.), *Handbook of autism and pervasive developmental disorders* (pp. 148–165). New York: Wiley.

Ornitz, E. M., Guthrie, D., & Farley, A. J. (1977). The early development of autistic children. *Journal of Autism and Childhood Schizophrenia, 7,* 207–229.

Pavlov, I. P. (1927). *Conditional reflexes: An investigation of the psychological activity of the cerebral cortex.* Oxford: Oxford University Press.

Pavlov, I. P. (1928). *Lectures on conditioned reflexes* (W. H. Gantt, Trans.). New York: Liveright.

Pavlov, I. P. (1962). *Essays in psychology and psychiatry.* New York: The Citadel Press.

Pavlovitch, M. (1920). *Le langage enfantin.* Paris: Champion.

Piaget, J. (1929). *The child's conception of the world.* New York: Harcourt, Brace.

Piaget, J. (1952a). *The origins of intelligence in children.* New York: International Universities Press.

Piaget, J. (1952b). *The child's conception of number.* New York: Humanities Press.

Piaget, J. (1954). *The construction of reality in the child.* New York: Basic Books.

Piaget, J. (1962). *Play, dreams, and imitation in childhood.* New York: Norton.

Pick, A. (1922). Über Störungen der Orientierung am eigenen Körper, *Psychol. Forschung, 1*, 303–315.

Pillsbury, W. B. (1908). *Attention*. New York: Macmillan.

Preyer, W. (1889). *The mind of the child*. New York: Appleton.

Provence, S. (1978). A clinician's view of affect development in infancy. In M. Lewis & L. A. Rosenblum (Eds.), *The development of affect* (pp. 293–307). New York: Plenum.

Provence, S., & Lipton, R. C. (1962). *Infants in institutions: A comparison of their development with family-reared infants during the first year of life*. New York: International Universities Press.

Rickers-Ovsiankina, M. (1976). The resumption of interrupted activities. In J. de Rivera, *Field theory as human-science* (pp. 49–110). New York: Gardner Press. (Original work published 1928)

Rimland, B. (1964). *Infantile autism*. New York: Appleton-Century-Crofts.

Rosenblatt, B. (1956). *The influence of affective states upon the body image and upon the perceptual organization of external space*. Unpublished doctoral dissertation, Clark University.

Ross, H. S., & Kay, D. A. (1980). The origins of social gains. In K. H. Rubin (Ed.), *Children's play: New Directions for Child Development* (Vol. 9). San Francisco, CA: Josey-Bass.

Rovee, C. K., & Rovee, D. T. (1969). Conjugate reinforcement of infant exploratory behavior. *Journal of Experimental Psychology, 8*, 33–39.

Rovee-Collier, C. K., Morrongiello, B. A., Aron, M., & Kupersmidt, J. (1978). Topographical response differentiation and reversal in 3-month-old infants. *Infant Behavior and Development, 1*, 323–333.

Rubin, E. (1921). *Visuellwahrgenomme Figuren: Studien in Psychologischer Analyse*. Kobenhavn: Gyldendal.

Sacks, O. (1985). *The man who mistook his wife for a hat*. New York: Summit.

Sattler, J. H. (1974). *Assessment of children's intelligence*. Philadelphia: Saunders.

Schilder, P. (1950). *The image and appearance of the human body*. New York: International Universities Press.

Schilder, P. (1951). *Brain and personality*. New York: International Universities Press.

Schopler, E., Mesibov, G. B., Shigley, R. H., & Bashford, A. (1984). Helping autistic children through their parents. In E. Schopler & G. B. Mesibov (Eds.), *The effects of autism on the family*. New York: Plenum.

Schopler, E., & Reichler, R. J. (1971). Parents as cotherapists in the treatment of psychotic children. *Journal of Autism and Childhood Schizophrenia. 1*, 87–102.

Sechehaye, M. (1951). *Autobiography of a schizophrenic girl*. New York: Grune & Stratton.

Senden, M. von. (1960). *Space and sight*. Glencoe, IL: Free Press. (Original work published 1932)

Shaw, W. A. (1940). The relation of muscular action potentials to imaginal weight lifting. *Archives of Psychology, 247*.

Simmel, M. L. (1956). On phantom limbs. *Arch. Neurol. Psychiat., 75*, 637–647.

Sokolov, Y. N. (1963). *Perception and the conditioned reflex.* New York: Macmillan.

Spitz, R. A., & Wolf, K. (1949). Autoerotism: Some empirical findings and hypothesis of its manifestations in the first year of life. *Psychoanalytic study of the child, 314,* 85–120.

Stern, C., & Stern, W. (1928). *Die Kindersprache.* Eine psychologische und untersuchung (4th rev. ed.). Leipzig: Barth.

Stern, D. N., Jaffe, J., Beebe, B., & Bennett, S. L. (1975). Vocalizing in unison and in alternation: Two modes of communication within the mother-infant dyad. *Annals of the New York Academy of Sciences, 263,* 89–100.

Stern, W. (1914). *Psychologie der fruehen Kindheit.* Leipzig: Quelle & Meyer.

Thelen, E. (1981). Rythmical behavior in infancy: An ethological perspective. *Developmental Psychology, 17,* (3), 237–257.

Trevarthen, C., & Hubley, P. (1978). Secondary intersubjectivity: Confidence, confiding, and acts of meaning in the first year of life. In A. Lock (Ed.), *Action, Gesture, and Symbol* (pp. 183–229). London: Academic Press.

Tronick, E., Als, H., Adamson, L., Wise, S., & Brazelton, T. B. (1978). The infant's response to entrapment between contradictory messages in face-to-face interaction. *Journal of the American Academy of Child Psychiatry, 17,* 1–13.

Twitchell, T. E. (1965). The automatic grasping response of infants. *Neuropsychologia, 21,* 247–259.

Uexküll, J. von. (1928). *Theoretische Biologie.* Berlin: Springer.

Uexküll, J. von. (1957). A stroll through the worlds of animals and men. In C. Schiller (Ed.), *Instinctive Behavior* (pp. 5–80). New York: International Universities Press. (Original work published 1934)

Uzgiris, I., & Hunt, J. McV. (1980). *Assessment in infancy: Ordinal scales of psychological development.* Urbana: University of Illinois Press. (Original work published 1975)

Vygotsky, L. S. (1962). *Thought and language.* Cambridge, MA: MIT Press.

Wapner, S., McFarland, J. H., & Werner, H. (1962). Effect of visual spatial context on perception of one's own body. *British Journal of Psychology, 53,* 222–230.

Wapner, S., & Werner, H. (1965). An experimental approach to body perception from the organismic developmental point of view. In S. Wapner and H. Werner (Eds.), *The body percept* (pp. 9–26). New York: Random House.

Wapner, S., Werner, H., & Krus, D. (1957). The effect of success and failure on space localization. *Journal of Personality, 25,* 752–756.

Watson, J. S., & Ramey, C. T. (1972). Reactions to response contingent stimulation in early infancy. *Merrill-Palmer Quarterly, 18,* 219–227.

Watson, M. W., & Fischer, K. W. (1979). A developmental sequence of agent use in late infancy, *Child Development, 48,* 828–836.

Werner, H. (1948). *Comparative psychology of mental development.* Chicago: Follett.

Werner, H., & Kaplan, B. (1963). *Symbol formation: An organismic developmental approach to language and the expression of thought.* New York: Wiley.

Wing, L. (1971). Perceptual and language development in autistic children: A comparative study. In M. Rutter (Ed.), *Infantile autism: Concepts, characteristics and treatment* (pp. 173–197). London: Churchill.

Winnicott, D. W. (1953). Transitional objects and transitional phenomena. *International Journal of Psychoanalysis, 34*(Part II), 89–97.

Wolff, P. H. (1967). The role of biological rhythms in early psychological development. *Bulletin of the Menninger Clinic, 31,* 197–218.

Wolff, P. H. (1968). Stereotypic behavior and development. *Canadian Psychologist, 9,* 474–483.

Wolff, P. H. (1971). Mother-infant relations at birth. In J. G. Howels (Ed.), *Modern perspectives in international child psychiatry.* New York: Brunner/Mazel.

Wolff, P. H. (1987). *Behavioral states and the expression of emotions in early infancy.* Chicago: University of Chicago Press.

Zeigarnik, B. (1927). Ueber das Behalten von erledigten und unerledigten Handlungen. *Psychol. Forsch. 9,* 1–85.

Author Index

Subject Index